MARKETING
RESEARCH

MARKETING RESEARCH

Approaches, Methods and Applications in Europe

Ray Kent

THOMSON

Australia • Canada • Mexico • Singapore • Spain • United Kingdom • United States

THOMSON

Marketing Research: Approaches, Methods and Applications in Europe
Ray Kent

Publishing Director	**Publisher**	**Development Editor**
John Yates	Jennifer Pegg	Rachael Sturgeon
Production Editor	**Manufacturing Manager**	**Senior Marketing Manager**
Sonia Pati	Helen Mason	Leo Stanley
Typesetter	**Production Controller**	**Editorial Assistant**
J&L Composition, Filey	Maeve Healy	James Clark
Text Design	**Printer**	**Cover design**
Design Deluxe, Bath, UK	Rotolito, Italy	Keith Marsh, Fink Creative Partners

Copyright © 2007
Thomson Learning

The Thomson logo is a registered trademark used herein under licence.

For more information, contact
Thomson Learning
High Holborn House
50–51 Bedford Row
London WC1R 4LR

or visit us on the World Wide Web at:
http://www.thomsonlearning.co.uk

ISBN-13: 978-1-84480-327-9
ISBN-10: 1-84480-327-9

This edition published 2007 by
Thomson Learning.

British Library Cataloguing-in-Publication Data
A catalogue record for this book is available from the British Library

Contents

Walk-through tour xi
Accompanying website xiii
Preface xv

Part I Contexts 1

1 Client-based market research 2

Learning objectives 2
Introduction 3
Internet activity 3
What is client-based market research? 4
Why do organizations need market research? 7
Types of client-based marketing research 9
Online marketing research 11
The process of designing research for clients 11

    Diagnosing the problem 12
    Strengths and weaknesses of the company 14
    Decisions and action standards 15
    The information required 15
    The type of research envisaged 16
    The objectives of the research 17
    The research brief 18
    The research proposal 19

Buying and selling research 29

    Buying research – the client perspective 29
    Selling research – the agency perspective 31

The European market research industry 33

    The suppliers of research services 34
    The research buyers 34
    The profession 35
    Trends 36
The changing role of the market researcher 37
Ethical issues 38
Data protection 39
Summary 41
Questions for discussion 41
Case study Flymo 42
Further reading 42

2 Academic research in marketing 43

Learning objectives 43
Introduction 43
Internet activity 44
The nature of academic, scholarly research 44
Philosophical underpinnings 47

    The marketing physicist 51
    The marketing physician 52
    The marketing psychiatrist 53
    So, who is correct? 53

The nature and role of theories and models 55

    Theory 55
    The role of theory 56
    Models 56

Designing academic research 57

    The research background 59
    The literature review 60
    Theories and models 60
    The research objectives 60
    Research methods and techniques 61
    Data analysis 62

Ethical issues 62
Summary 64
Questions for discussion 65
Case study Young people and tobacco marketing 66
Further reading 66

Part II Accessing and constructing good-quality data 67

3 Accessing secondary data 68

Learning objectives 68
Introduction 68

Internet activity 69
What are "data"? 69
Sources of secondary data 72

  Published sources 72
  Commercial sources 74
  Internal data 75

Evaluating secondary data 77
Doing desk research 78
Secondary research and secondary data
  analysis 79
Marketing intelligence 80
Desk research for academic projects 81
Ethical issues 83
Summary 83
Questions for discussion 84
Case study Vodafone 84

Further reading 84

4 **Constructing qualitative data** 85

Learning objectives 85
Introduction 86
Internet activity 86

What are "qualitative data"? 86
Client-based qualitative market research 88
Interviewing groups and individuals 91
Focus groups 91

  Planning focus groups 92

Depth interviews 99

  Planning depth interviews 100

Groups or depths: the choice of method 102
Alternative to interview methods 103

  Observation 103
  Ethnography 107
  Consultation 108

The impact of the internet 110

  Online focus groups 110
  Bulletin boards 111
  Moderated e-mail groups 111

Academic qualitative research 112
Summary 113
Questions for discussion 114
Case study Fox Kids Europe 114

Further reading 115

5 **Constructing quantitative data**
Structuring data and measuring
variables 116

Learning objectives 116
Introduction 117
Internet activity 117

What are "quantitative data"? 117

  Qualitative and quantitative data 118

The structure of data 119

  Cases 119
  Variables 120
  Values 123
  Categorical scales 124
  Metric scales 127

The process of measurement 132

  Direct measurement 133
  Indirect measurement 134
  Derived measurement 134
  Multidimensional measurement 139

Measurement error 141
Ethical issues 146
Summary 146
Questions for discussion 147
Case study The rise of the free daily newspaper 149
Further reading 149

6 **Constructing quantitative data**
Developing the instruments of data
capture 150

Learning objectives 150
Introduction 151
Internet activity 151

Questionnaire design 151

  Specify the information needed 152
  Decide on the method of questionnaire
    administration 153
  Determine the content, format and wording of
    each question 153
  Create a draft of the complete questionnaire 153
  Test the questionnaire 154
  Question formats 155
  Question content 157
  Question wording 161
  Screening 162
  Routing 163
  Sequencing 163
  Questionnaire length 164
  Self-completed and interviewer-completed
    questionnaires 166
  Questionnaire layout 167
  Using computer software 169

Diaries 170

  Diary design 173

Recording devices 175
Ethical issues 178
Summary 178
Questions for discussion 179
Case study eBay 179

Further reading 180

7 Constructing quantitative data
Selecting methods 181

Learning objectives 181
Introduction 182
Internet activity 182
Survey research 182
  Interview surveys 184
  Telephone surveys 189
  Postal surveys 191
  Online surveys 192
  Mixed techniques 194
  Error in survey design and execution 195
Experimental research 203
  Experimental design 204
  Types of experiment 206
  Experimental validity 212
Continuous research 213
  Panel research 214
  Regular interval surveys 219
Client-based and academic quantitative
  research 222
Ethical issues 223
Summary 224
Questions for discussion 224
Case study Levi Strauss 225

Further reading 225

8 Constructing quantitative data
Selecting cases 226

Learning objectives 226
Introduction 226
Internet activity 227
The research population 227
When samples are needed 229
Sample selection 229
Sample design 232
Sample size 236
Sampling in practice 237
Online sampling techniques 240
Sampling errors 241

Systematic error 241
Random error 242
Total survey error 243
Controlling error 244
Ethical issues 245
Summary 246
Questions for discussion 246
Case study Egg plc 247
Further reading 247

9 Mixed research designs 248

Learning objectives 248
Introduction 249
Internet activity 249
Qualitative and quantitative research 249
The nature of research design 251
Mixed methods and mixed designs 253
Types of mixtures 255
  Sequential mixed designs 255
  Concurrent mixed designs 255
  Eclectic designs 256
Research rationales and mixed designs 257
Summary 258
Questions for discussion 258
Case study SMA Nutrition and the
  segmentation of the baby milk market 259
Further reading 259

Part III Data analysis 261

10 Analyzing qualitative data 262

Learning objectives 262
Introduction 262
Internet activity 263
Analyzing qualitative data for clients 263
  Describing 264
  Commenting 265
  Theorizing 266
  Reflecting 266
  Applying 267
Academic approaches 267
  Content analysis 268
  Ethnography 268
  Grounded theory 270
Phenomenology 272
Discourse analysis 273
Semiotics 275

Validity in the analysis of qualitative data 277
Using computer-assisted qualitative data analysis
    software (CAQDAS) 278
Summary 282
Questions for discussion 282
Case study Living 24/7 283
Further reading 283

11 Analyzing quantitative data
Essential descriptive summaries of single variables 284

Learning objectives 284
Introduction 285
Internet activity 285
Preparing data for analysis 286
    Checking 286
    Editing 287
    Coding 288
    Assembly 289
    Data entry 291
Choosing the right data analysis techniques 296
    What does the researcher want to do with the
        data? 296
    On what type of scale are the variables recorded?
        297
    How many variables are to be entered into the
        calculation? 298
Univariate data display: categorical variables 300
    Univariate frequency tables 300
    Simple bar charts and pie charts 304
Univariate data display: metric variables 306
    Univariate frequency tables 306
    Metric tables 306
    Histograms and line graphs 308
Data summaries: categorical variables 309
Data summaries: metric variables 310
    Central tendency 310
    Dispersion 311
    Distribution shape 313
    The normal distribution 314
    Percentile values 315
Data transformations 316
    Upgrading or downgrading scales 316
    Collapsing categories 317
    Class intervals 318
    Computing totals 318
    Multiple response questions 318
    "Don't know" responses and missing values 319

    Open-ended questions 321
    Analyzing summated rating scales 323
Using SPSS 328
    Frequency tables 328
    Graphs and charts 330
    Histograms and line graphs 330
    Data summaries 331
    Using *Recode* 333
    Using *Compute* 334
    Using *Define Variable/Missing Values* 336
    Using *Multiple Response* 336
Summary 337
Questions for discussion 337
SPSS exercises 338
Further reading 338

12 Analyzing relationships between two variables 339

Learning objectives 339
Introduction 340
Internet activity 340
Bivariate data display 340
Bivariate data summaries: categorical
    variables 345
    Coefficients appropriate for binary or nominal
        variables 349
    Coefficients appropriate for ordinal variables 355
    Coefficients appropriate for two ranked
        variables 358
    Coefficients appropriate for mixed
        variables 359
    Selecting the appropriate statistic 359
Bivariate data summaries: metric variables 361
    Correlation and regression compared 363
    Pearson's r and Spearman's rho 364
Using SPSS 366
    Crosstabulation 366
    Measures of association 366
    Correlation and regression 366
Summary 368
Questions for discussion 369
SPSS exercises 369
Further reading 371

13 Making statistical inferences 372

Learning objectives 372
Introduction 373
Internet activity 373

Estimation 374

Estimation for categorical variables 374

Estimation for metric variables 376

Testing hypotheses for statistical significance 377

Testing univariate hypotheses for categorical variables 378

Testing univariate hypotheses for metric variables 380

Testing bivariate hypotheses 383

Testing bivariate hypotheses for categorical variables 383

Testing bivariate hypotheses for metric variables 384

Testing metric differences for categories 385

Statistical inference and bivariate data summaries 388

The significance test controversy 389

Using SPSS 392

Summary 395

Questions for discussion 396

SPSS exercises 396

Further reading 397

14 Multivariate analysis 398

Learning objectives 398

Introduction 399

Internet activity 399

The limitations of bivariate analysis 399

What is multivariate analysis? 402

Looking for patterns 402

Multivariate analysis for categorical variables 404

Three-way and n-way tables 404

Loglinear analysis 405

Multivariate analysis for metric variables: dependence techniques 409

Multiple regression 410

Logistic regression 413

Discriminant analysis 414

Multivariate analysis of variance 417

Multivariate analysis for metric variables: interdependence techniques 420

Factor analysis 420

Cluster analysis 422

Multidimensional scaling 426

Explaining relationships between variables 428

What is an "explanation"? 428

Causal analysis 429

Providing understanding 431

Dialectical analysis 432

Using SPSS 432

Three-way and n-way tabular analysis 432

Loglinear analysis 432

Multiple regression 434

Binary logistic regression 434

Discriminant analysis 435

Multivariate analysis of variance 435

Factor analysis 435

Cluster analysis 435

Summary 436

Questions for discussion 437

SPSS exercises 437

Further reading 437

15 Alternative methods of data analysis 438

Learning objectives 438

Introduction 439

Internet activity 439

The origins of mainstream statistics 440

The limitations of mainstream statistics 442

The focus on variables 442

The focus on covariation 444

Causality and linear relationships 444

Nonlinear variable analysis alternatives 449

Neural network analysis 450

Data mining 453

Bayesian statistics 455

Case-based analysis and combinatorial logic 455

Fuzzy set analysis 459

Using Fuzzy-Set/Qualitative Comparative Analysis (FS/QCA) 461

Holistic approaches to the analysis of data 463

Summary 464

Questions for discussion 464

Case study Fuzzy set analysis of the results of an e-mail survey in Norway 465

Further reading 468

Part IV Applications 469

16 Commercial proprietary techniques 470

Learning objectives 470

Introduction 470

Internet activity 471

Diagnostic techniques 471

Market measurement 472
Media audience measurement 479
Single-source data 491
Usage and attitude studies 496
Customer satisfaction and relationship management
    research 498
Advertising tracking studies 504

Predictive techniques 510

Testing products and product concepts 511
Advertising pretesting 517
Volume and brand share prediction 519

Summary 527
Questions for discussion 527
Further reading 528

17 Cross-national research 529

Learning objectives 529
Introduction 529
Internet activity 530

National and cross-national research 530
The design of cross-national research 532

Identifying market opportunities 533
Building information systems 534
Carrying out primary research 536

Academic cross-national research 543

Ethical issues 543
Summary 544
Questions for discussion 544
Case study Making the Compass Group a preferred
    employer 545
Further reading 546

18 Communicating the results 547

Learning objectives 547
Introduction 548
Internet activity 548

The research report 548

Report content 549

The presentation 552
Research follow-up 554
Reporting cross-national research 554
Academic articles 555

The academic review process 558

Summary 560
Questions for discussion 561
Further reading 561

Glossary 562
Appendix I: The Table Tennis Questionnaire 573
References 577
Index 585

Walk-through tour

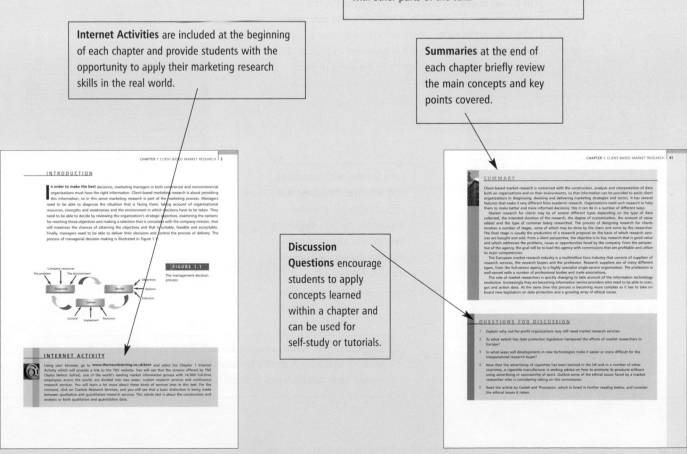

Introductions and **Learning objectives** open each chapter and highlight core concepts covered. These features also allow the student to monitor understanding and progress during the chapter.

Key Points are provided at the end of most major sections in each chapter and assist in identifying the key lessons to be learned from a section. They also suggest limitations, alternative views or links with other parts of the text.

Internet Activities are included at the beginning of each chapter and provide students with the opportunity to apply their marketing research skills in the real world.

Summaries at the end of each chapter briefly review the main concepts and key points covered.

Discussion Questions encourage students to apply concepts learned within a chapter and can be used for self-study or tutorials.

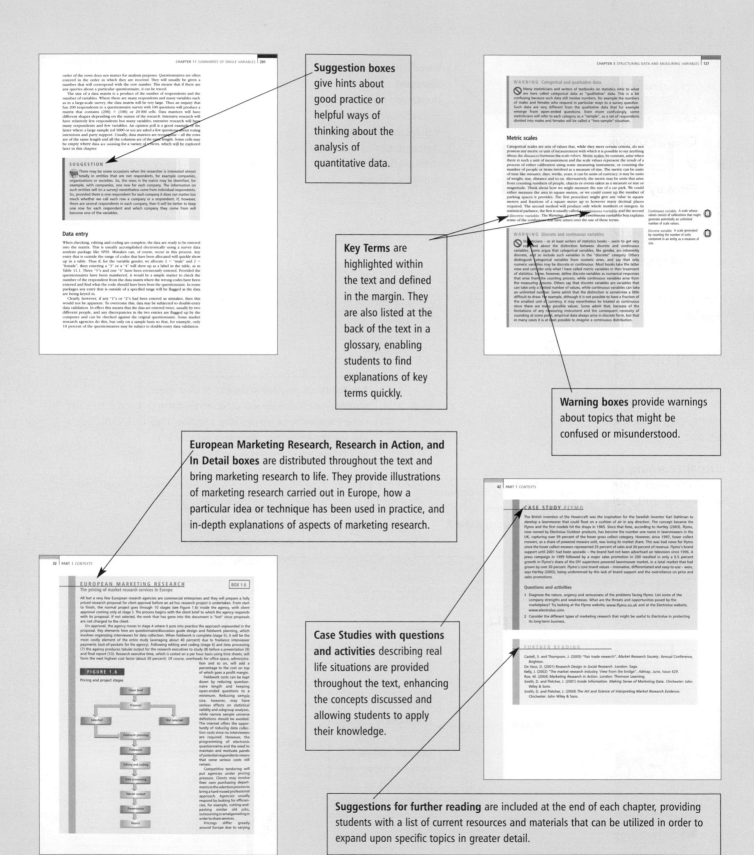

Suggestion boxes give hints about good practice or helpful ways of thinking about the analysis of quantitative data.

Key Terms are highlighted within the text and defined in the margin. They are also listed at the back of the text in a glossary, enabling students to find explanations of key terms quickly.

Warning boxes provide warnings about topics that might be confused or misunderstood.

European Marketing Research, Research in Action, and In Detail boxes are distributed throughout the text and bring marketing research to life. They provide illustrations of marketing research carried out in Europe, how a particular idea or technique has been used in practice, and in-depth explanations of aspects of marketing research.

Case Studies with questions and activities describing real life situations are provided throughout the text, enhancing the concepts discussed and allowing students to apply their knowledge.

Suggestions for further reading are included at the end of each chapter, providing students with a list of current resources and materials that can be utilized in order to expand upon specific topics in greater detail.

Accompanying Website

Visit the accompanying website for *Marketing Research* at **www.thomsonlearning.co.uk/kent** to find further teaching and learning resources including:

For students

- Learning Objectives
- Chapter Overviews
- Multiple Choice Questions for each chapter
- Glossary
- Further Reading
- Software Guidelines
- Additional Datasets

- Self-check Exercises
- Internet Activities
- Links to useful websites

For lecturers

- Instructor's Manual
- PowerPoint Slides

Extra resources will also be added to the lecturers' and students' sides of the site. Please bookmark and check regularly for updates.

Supplementary resources

ExamView®
This testbank and test generator provides a huge amount of different types of questions, allowing lecturers to create online, paper and local area network (LAN) tests. This CD-based product is available only from your Thomson sales representative.

Virtual Learning Environment
All of the web material is available in a format that is compatible with virtual learning environments such as Blackboard and WebCT. This version of the product is available only from your Thomson sales representative.

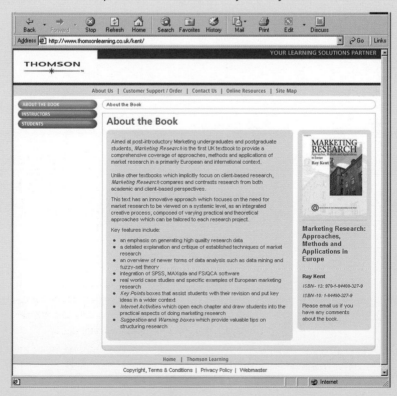

Preface

Marketing research is about constructing, and then analyzing and interpreting data. Marketing managers in both commercial and noncommercial organizations, in order to make the best decisions, must have the right information. The aim of such client-based research is to deliver value to clients and to provide data, information and insights that arc both relevant and actionable. Academics, while still concerned with the construction, analysis and interpretation of data, will undertake research for scholarly purposes rather than on behalf of clients. This text provides a comprehensive yet user-friendly coverage of marketing research approaches, methods and applications in a European context from both the client-based and academic perspectives. It is the first text that takes the advantages of a US style in terms of presentation and format, but is distinctly home-grown for the European market and not adapted from a text that originates in the US.

Special emphasis is placed on the generation of good-quality data when undertaking marketing research, and seeing their analysis in terms of a process of matching client needs or problems, or theoretical issues, on the one hand with data and evidence on the other. The text explains the established techniques and approaches in marketing research, but also points out their strengths and weaknesses. It goes on to consider some of the alternatives to standard approaches, some of which still focus on variables, but in a nonlinear way, for example neural network analysis, some data mining techniques and Bayesian approaches. Other alternatives focus more on the analysis of cases, seeing them as configurations or combinations of characteristics that can be analyzed using combinatorial logic or fuzzy set analysis. Many of these techniques require considerable computing power and therefore, while they may have been around for some time, have only recently become feasible. These approaches give researchers an entirely new way of analyzing data that can find patterns largely or totally missed by more traditional approaches.

Many texts see marketing research as a series of steps, or it is presented as a taxonomy of different types of research design. However, marketing research is not about picking one particular design that is deemed to be appropriate; nor is it about following six stages or ten steps. Each piece of research is a unique combination of methods and techniques that have been designed for a particular issue, problem or theoretical idea. It makes a complete whole, with every element of the research depending for its value on the worth of the other elements and how those elements are combined. Designing research is a creative task that requires many skills, some technical, some inspirational. It is a balance of theory and practice, of ideas and data, of inspiration and perspiration. Whether you see your career as a marketing researcher, as an executive in an advertising agency who needs to evaluate the results of research carried out by others, or whether you want to do a good project or a good dissertation, this text should be your friend.

Audience

This new text is written with intermediate and senior undergraduates in marketing in mind, along with postgraduates who are on taught courses in the subject. Doctoral students, academic researchers and researchers in the commercial world should also find the approach adopted in this book of value. The coverage is comprehensive, yet easy to read. There are numerous diagrams, tables, photos, examples and a range of learning tools that are explained below. The book explains and contrasts marketing research that is designed and carried out for clients (usually, but not necessarily, in a commercial context) with marketing research undertaken for academic, scholarly purposes – largely for publication or to meet the requirements of undergraduate, postgraduate or doctoral qualifications. Students commonly use texts that implicitly are about client-based research. They may even be asked to undertake this kind of research as class projects. However, they are then asked to do a dissertation that is judged by standards very different from client-based research. The result can be considerable confusion. This text begins with separate chapters on each kind of research, carefully explaining the differences between the two. It then points out the implications of the differing approaches, methods and applications in subsequent chapters.

Structure of the text

The book is structured into four parts. Part I, Contexts, contrasts the approaches to research by client-based and academic researchers. Part II focuses on constructing good-quality data. It argues that all data, whether qualitative or quantitative, are the products of human endeavor – they are "constructed" rather than collected as pre-existing objects. The implication is that to judge the quality of data, it is necessary to look at how they were constructed, who constructed them and for what purpose. If rubbish data go into the ensuing analysis, rubbish will come out. Chapter 8 looks at populations and samples, but from a new perspective that sees them both as researcher creations that need to be justified and possibly amended as the research progresses. Chapter 9 reviews a range of strategies for mixing qualitative and quantitative methods.

In Part III data analysis is treated as a kind of "dialogue" between ideas and evidence. Ideas may be vaguer than theories and will include, for example for client-based research, the client problems to be addressed, and for academics perhaps our speculations about the world around us, tentative generalizations based on past experience or understandings, and our explanations – even musings – about how or why things happen. Similarly, evidence is a broader concept than data; evidence is often tentative, incomplete, inconclusive, circumstantial and frequently needs to be assembled or fitted together jigsaw-like with other clues, traces, or everyday details of the entities that are under investigation to create a more complete image, projection or representation of marketing phenomena. Ideas and evidence interact; ideas enable researchers to derive implications from the evidence, and in turn researchers use evidence to extend, revise, support or test ideas. The analysis of qualitative data is treated in considerably more depth than in most texts. The analysis of quantitative data is about making sense of a dataset as a whole, not just performing statistical calculations on numerical variables. The use of formulae is kept to a minimum; instead the statistical package SPSS is used to illustrate the reasoning behind statistical operations and making sense of the results when they come out. Being able to perform the calculations is less essential these days, unless you want to become a statistician, since SPSS will do it for you in a couple of seconds.

The final part, Part IV, looks at applications of market and marketing research. Chapter 16 reviews a range of commercial branded procedures, distinguishing between diagnostic and predictive techniques. Chapter 17 considers cross-national research, particularly in a pan-European context. The final chapter explains the different ways in which the results of client-based and academic research are communicated – to clients or to a wider audience as appropriate.

Integrated software

The use of three pieces of software is incorporated into the text: for quantitative analysis the industry standard, SPSS; for qualitative analysis a text analysis program that is considerably more user-friendly than the more widely-known NUD*IST or NVivo, namely, MAXqda; and for the use of combinatorial and fuzzy logic, a program that is freely downloadable from the internet, Fuzzy-Set/Qualitative Comparative Analysis (FS/QCA).

Learning tools

The text makes full use of a range of pedagogic features. Each chapter begins with an overview that sets the scene in terms of what to expect from the chapter, relating it back to previous chapters or linking forward to chapters yet to come. This is followed by a list of *Learning objectives* that spell out in detail what the reader should learn from the chapter. These will allow readers to monitor their understanding and progress during the chapter. An *Internet activity* is then suggested, which readers can follow to give them a feel for elements of the chapter to come and to introduce them to what is available on the internet.

At the end of most major sections in a chapter is a *Key points* box that not only picks out the key lessons to be learned from the section, but also puts them in a wider context, suggests limitations or alternative views or links with other sections.

There are in each chapter additional boxes that bring marketing research to life following a number of themes. *European marketing research* boxes give illustrations of marketing research that has been carried out in one or more European countries.

Research in action boxes illustrate how a particular idea or technique has been used in practice and may include examples from outside Europe, but the geographical context is not so important.

In detail boxes explain aspects of marketing research in considerably more depth where such explanations might clutter up the text. They can be omitted in a first reading of a chapter, but should prove useful and interesting to follow up later.

In Part III from Chapter 11 onwards there are, in addition, *Suggestion* boxes and *Warning* boxes. These either give hints about good practice or helpful ways of thinking about the analysis of quantitative data, or they give warnings about things that might be confused or misunderstood.

At the end of each chapter is a chapter summary that also links the chapter to other parts of the book. There are questions for discussion, a case study with questions and activities, and suggestions for further reading. The further reading is highly selective. It picks out the most recent and most accessible materials. Wherever possible you should access and read these to follow-up topics in more detail than is possible in this text. The case studies are very much of the "short" variety: they tend to paint a scene, or describe a real-life situation as a context for an activity with out having to read through several pages of detailed scenario.

Full use is made of tables, figures, charts, flow-diagrams and color photographs that bring to life points being made in the text. Important terms are explained in the glossary at the end of the book and are put in **bold** when they first appear and at strategic points where they are used in another context and readers may find it helpful to remind themselves of what they mean.

Supplementary material

A comprehensive supporting website also accompanies the text and can be found at www.thomsonlearning.co.uk/kent.

For students and lecturers (open access)
Chapter support

For each chapter a chapter overview, learning objectives, further reading, internet activities, multiple-choice questions and self-check exercises.

Supporting software programs

Instructions on how to obtain a full demonstration version of SPSS, a download-able demonstration version of MAXqda, and a free download of FS/QCA. There are also guidelines written by the author on how to use each program.

Links to useful websites

Many links to useful websites are provided in the textbook, but additional links are suggested that will help students to flesh out more details on organizations and other resources.

Datasets

Additional datasets on which students can practice data analysis procedures are provided.

For lecturers only (password-protected)
Instructor's manual

This can be download free from the site in PDF format. It includes answers to all the points for discussion at the ends of chapters, teaching notes for the cases and offers hints, suggestions and warnings about teaching the material in the chapter.

PowerPoint slides

These are not just reproductions of tables and figures in the text, but offer key points based on the chapter material that can be adapted by lecturers for their own purposes.

ExamView®

This testbank and test generator CD-Rom provides a range of questions, organized by chapter, for instructors to use to create tests. Tests can be created for use online, on paper, or on a local area network (LAN).

Acknowledgments

Many people have been generous with their time in helping this book come to fruition. The reviewers listed below have provided many constructive criticisms and helpful suggestions. Not all of these have, of course, been incorporated; in some cases they were saying opposite things. However, their comments, if not taken on board, always forced me at least to have a good reason for not doing what they suggested.

Nigel Bradley, University of Westminster

Assistant Professor Niels Nolsøe Grünbaum, University of Southern Denmark

Dr. Sami Kajalo, Helsinki School of Economics

Stavros Kalafatis, Kingston Business School

Dr. Nick Lee, Aston Business School

Geraldine McKay, Keele University

Heather Skinner, University of Glamorgan

Cleopatra Veloutsou, University of Glasgow

Dr. Udo Wagner, University of Vienna

Professor Dr. Martin Wetzels, Maastricht University

I should also like to acknowledge the contribution of those who have either provided or revised my material in the *In action* or *In detail* boxes.

Michael Roe, market research consultant and trainer

Heather Skinner, University of Glamorgan

Jackie Greig, Director, Marketing Science Group, Research International

Richard Bedwell, BMRB

Dominic Twose, Global Head of Knowledge Management, Millward Brown

Georgina Pickford, Consumer Insight Director, TNS Worldpanel

John Stockley, IPSOS

At Thomson Learning, I would like to thank Rachael Sturgeon, Development Editor, for her gentle pressure in keeping me on track and for the care she has taken in attending to all the bits and pieces that need to be done before a text like this can see the light of day. I would also like to thank Jennifer Pegg, Publisher, for championing this text.

Part I Contexts

Research in general is all about constructing, and then analyzing and interpreting data. Data construction, as will be explained in some detail in Part II, involves issues of research design, data capture and data assembly. Data analysis, which is the focus of Part III, entails displaying, summarizing and drawing inferences from the data. Interpretation means going beyond the strict confines of the data to evaluate, or even speculate about, how those data relate to the objectives for which the research was undertaken.

Research in the area of marketing may be undertaken in two rather different contexts: it may be carried out for and on behalf of a client (who may be an individual member or some group or department in the same organization, or in another organization) or it may be undertaken for academic, scholarly purposes – largely for publication or to meet the requirements of undergraduate, postgraduate or doctoral qualifications. Students commonly use textbooks that implicitly are all about client-based research; they may even be asked to undertake this kind of research as class projects. However, they are then often asked to do a dissertation that is judged by standards very different from client-based research. The result can be considerable confusion. Part I of this text contains a separate chapter on each kind of research, carefully explaining the features of and the differences between the two.

Chapter 1 examines the key features of client-based marketing research, and why clients need it. It explains the different types of research undertaken for clients, and the processes of designing, buying and selling research. The nature of the market research industry in Europe is described and the changing role of the market researcher is explored. The chapter concludes by reviewing some of the key ethical issues that arise when client-based marketing research is undertaken and the effects of data protection legislation are considered.

Chapter 2 explains the key features of academic research, how such research is evaluated and the philosophical assumptions that are made by various styles of academic research. The key role played by theory and modeling is emphasized and the format and content of a research proposal for academic research are described. The chapter concludes by considering some of the ethical issues in the conduct of academic research.

1 Client-based market research

LEARNING OBJECTIVES In this chapter you will learn about:

→ the key features of client-based market research,

→ why client organizations need it,

→ the different types of research undertaken for clients,

→ the process of designing the research,

→ buying and selling research,

→ the market research industry in Europe,

→ the changing role of the market researcher,

→ key ethical issues,

→ the effects of data protection legislation.

Client-based marketing research usually involves a contractual arrangement.

© JAIMIE DUPLASS

INTRODUCTION

In order to make the best decisions, marketing managers in both commercial and noncommercial organizations must have the right information. Client-based marketing research is about providing this information, so in this sense marketing research is part of the marketing process. Managers need to be able to diagnose the situation that is facing them, taking account of organizational resources, strengths and weaknesses and the environment in which decisions have to be taken. They need to be able to decide by reviewing the organization's strategic objectives, examining the options for reaching those objectives and making a selection that is consistent with the company mission, that will maximize the chances of attaining the objectives and that is suitable, feasible and acceptable. Finally, managers need to be able to deliver their decisions and control the process of delivery. The process of managerial decision-making is illustrated in Figure 1.1.

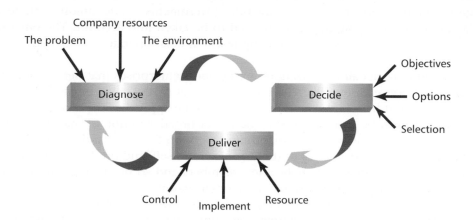

FIGURE 1.1

The management decision process

INTERNET ACTIVITY

Using your browser, go to **www.thomsonlearning.co.uk/kent** and select the Chapter 1 Internet Activity which will provide a link to the TNS website. You will see that the services offered by TNS (Taylor Nelson Sofres), one of the world's leading market information groups with 14,000 full-time employees across the world, are divided into two areas: custom research services and continuous research services. You will learn a lot more about these kinds of services later in this text. For the moment, click on *Custom Research Services*, and you will see that a basic distinction is being made between qualitative and quantitative research services. This whole text is about the construction and analysis or both qualitative and quantitative data.

What is client-based market research?

It is often said that marketing is an approach to business that is based on the idea that the most important person to the company is the customer. The company adopting the marketing concept is, according to marketing wisdom, customer-oriented; it must make what it knows it can sell, not attempt to sell what it knows it can make. If this were true (and if only life were that simple), then client-based marketing research would be largely concerned with collecting data on customer requirements and anticipating their future needs.

As always, reality is not quite so simple. Companies offering goods and services in commercial transactions are constrained to be "customer-oriented" with what they have – with their existing plant, machinery, workforce, location, company reputation, and with their own particular strengths and weaknesses. Furthermore, they must operate in an immediate **microenvironment** which consists not only of customers, but also includes competitors, suppliers, distributors, shareholders and other stakeholders in the company. In the wider general or **macroenvironment** there will be general economic players like financial institutions and factors like trends in the economy, there will be technological factors like the development of e-commerce, social factors that might include values, language and religion, political players that will include governments, trade unions and legal factors that, to varying degrees, all need to be taken into account. The environmental factors within which marketing research must operate are summarized in Figure 1.2.

In addition, not all organizations are business enterprises that need to make a profit to survive. Some, like charities or political parties, may be staffed not by employees but by volunteers. If marketing is to be applied to these organizations as well, it must be concerned with the rather broader notion of matching whatever are the objectives of the organization with, on the one hand, the problems, characteristics and resources of the organization itself, and on the other with the target market, audience, beneficiaries, members and so on, taking into account the various "publics" with a stake in the organization.

If marketing research is to help with this "matching" process, it must be concerned with more than simply collecting data on markets and customers. Certainly, in the early days of marketing research, this was what most researchers did. Even today, there are "field and tab" agencies that restrict their activities to collecting survey data and tabulating the results. Most marketing research, furthermore, still includes, at some stage, data collection and data analysis. However,

Microenvironment The immediate environment of a commercial organization that consists of customers, competitors, suppliers, distributors, shareholders and other stakeholders on the organization.

Macroenvironment The wider environment of a commercial organization that consists of general economic players like financial institutions, trends in the economy, technological factors, social factors, political players including governments, local authorities, trade unions and legal factors.

FIGURE 1.2

The marketing research environment

clients increasingly look for some interpretation of the data, perhaps even going so far as to ask for recommendations for marketing action. Sometimes managers are unclear about the nature of the problem facing them or about the kind of research that is needed. In this situation, market researchers may become involved in diagnosing company problems, analyzing organizational strengths and weaknesses, or identifying threats and opportunities in the environment. Some organizations look for assistance in choosing or evaluating alternative marketing strategies and tactics. Some ask for help in ensuring that such actions are being implemented. In brief, researchers may become involved in helping their clients to formulate their marketing plans and to monitor the progress in their implementation. Some managers seek help with only some of these activities; others may want help with them all, in which case the market researcher may well, in effect, become part of the client's marketing team.

Client-based marketing research, in short, is concerned with the construction, analysis and interpretation of data both on organizations and on their environments, so that information can be provided to assist client organizations in diagnosing, deciding and delivering marketing strategies and tactics. Figure 1.3 illustrates the process. Its aim is to deliver value to clients and to provide data, information and insights that are relevant and actionable. Client-based marketing research is sometimes referred to as "commissioned", "commercial", "market" or "practitioner" research. If the client is another organization, there will almost certainly be a fee involved; in short, it will be a commercial transaction in which the research is undertaken by an agency for a profit, whether the client organization is itself commercial or nonprofit. If, however, the client is internal to the organization it will probably be called **"in-house" research**. In this situation, there may or may not be some kind of internal pricing or budgeting of the work. There is a further category of applied or policy research, which although not commercial is still client-based. Traditionally, such research would be carried out by academics on behalf of government, quasi-government or local authority bodies, although increasingly, professional market research agencies have been used. The range of nonprofit clients has also tended to grow to include, for example, museums and galleries, political parties, educational institutions, the performing arts or even religious institutions. Not all client-based research, then, is commercial.

Client-based research has a number of features that, as will be seen in Chapter 2, contrast strongly with academic, scholarly research. Client-based research is:

- solution-oriented,
- not neutral,
- interventionist,
- client-led,
- contractual,
- confidential,
- pragmatic,
- time and cost constrained,
- report-based.

Client-based marketing research The construction, analysis and interpretation of data both on organizations and their environments so that information can be provided to assist client organizations in diagnosing, deciding and delivering marketing strategies and tactics.

In-house research Research that is carried out for a client who is internal to the organization.

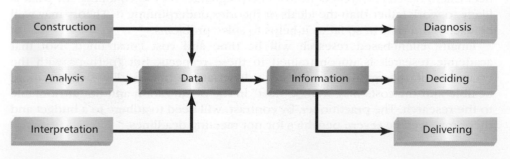

FIGURE 1.3

The client-based marketing research process

Research is undertaken to solve, or help solve, client problems and its quality or value is judged on the basis of its success in doing so, not on the basis of the scientific rigor that was employed. This is not to say that client-based research is not rigorous; only that rigor is a means to an end, not an end in itself. Rigorous research, after all, is more likely to help solve the client's problem; but rigor is a matter of degree – and it costs money. A degree of rigor will be applied only to the extent that it is judged sufficient to achieve the objectives of the research. The solutions are normally brought together in a report that contains a set of recommendations to the client. Academic researchers often also make recommendations, but these are often to the industry at large, not to a specific organization, and they will be secondary to the exploration or testing of theoretical idea and the advance of understanding of marketing phenomena.

The second feature of client-based research is that it is not neutral. It is partisan and it operates on behalf of the client. This is not to say that such research lacks objectivity; it is a kind of "partisan objectivity". The evidence, data, information, interpretation – even speculation – should be uncolored by the researcher's subjective preferences, sensations or emotions. It should set forth what is external, actual and practical; but it will focus on what is valuable to the client.

Most client-based research will be interventionist. Its goal may be to make changes and monitor their effects or to assist the client to bring changes about. The outcome of the research may, of course, be the recommendation that no changes be made – but this is unusual, and it still focuses on the issue of change or no change.

Client-based research is carried out for a third party, so the researcher does not originate or "own" the research problem. It is the client who takes the initiative. The client will approach the researcher in the agency; the client will have a brief in which the client sets out his or her perception of the situation and in varying degrees of detail how the research is envisaged; the client will choose the agency where the research is in a commercial context; the client will be final arbiter where alternative courses of action are being considered.

Unlike a student doing a dissertation or an academic writing a journal article, the market research practitioner must agree with the client exactly what research will be carried out. This will normally be contained in a research proposal and will form the basis of a formal contract between them. The nature of research briefs, research proposals and commercial contracts is discussed in more detail later in this chapter.

While academics undertake research for the express purpose of publishing the results, in client-based research the findings will be confidential. Reports will often contain commercially sensitive information so are unlikely to be available outside the client organization. Furthermore, the results would in any case be of little interest outside the company (except perhaps to competitors!) since the findings will be specific to that company. Quite a lot of client-based research will be repeat business or doing research of a kind that has been undertaken many times before, so there may be few wider implications for marketing theory or practice. Client-based researchers need to be pragmatic; they need an eye for what is likely to work rather than the ideals or theories underpinning it. Theory may well be used – but only in so far as it helps to solve problems.

Finally, client-based research will be time and cost constrained. Not that academic research is unconstrained in these respects, but (perhaps with the exception of undergraduate or master's dissertations) the deadlines will be more flexible and the costs may well be "lost" in the organization and not attributable to the research. The practitioner, by contrast, will need to adhere to a budget and there may well be severe penalties for not meeting deadlines.

The key output of client-based research is usually a report. Reports tend to have a particular style and format which is discussed at some length in Chapter 18, where the report is contrasted with a range of different academic ways of communicating the results. Reports may be hard copy, face-to-face presentations, or, more likely, some combination of the two.

The client-based marketing researcher can be likened to a physician who specializes in diagnosis and treatment. The client is the "patient" whose ailments and symptoms need to be identified before remedies can be sought. The physician cares about what happens – the goal, after all, is to make the patient well again. Marketing research as a form of medical practice is all about finding the means to achieve specified ends. The goal is not to study an organization's problems, but to do something about them. It was Karl Marx (1844: 245) who once said: *"The philosophers have only interpreted the world, in various ways; the point, however, is to change it."* The commitment is not just to study change, but to actually make changes. Marx, of course, was talking about society, but this statement could equally apply to the client-based market researcher.

KEY POINTS

Client-based marketing research is concerned with the construction, analysis and interpretation of data both on organizations and on their environments, so that information can be provided to assist client organizations in diagnosing, deciding and delivering marketing strategies and tactics. Client-based marketing research is oriented to finding solutions to client problems. It is partisan, interventionist and pragmatic; it is contractual and client-led. The output is report-based, confidential and constrained by time and budgets.

Why do organizations need marketing research?

The simplest and best answer to this question is: to help managers make better, more informed decisions. Customers' preferences are always changing, and the micro- and macroenvironment are also constantly developing. Unless managers have at their disposal systematically collected, up-to-date and high-quality data on these changes, then all decisions are likely to be clouded in uncertainty and based on unknown assumptions about what is happening – in short, each decision will be a "shot-in-the dark". Managers can use information derived from marketing research in several different ways:

- to help tackle or resolve "one-off" problems or issues,
- to assist in making plans and setting objectives for the future,
- to monitor changes in the environment as they occur,
- to build up a database or marketing information system that can become a resource for a growing range of analyses or database marketing techniques,
- to use as a common "currency" with which organizations can negotiate with media owners, advertising agencies, distributors, suppliers or other agents whose services they require.

A typical one-off problem may be how to react to a threat from a new product or new technology being introduced by competitors, or to a sudden or persistent decline in sales or in market share. If a competitor introduces a new product, marketing research may be called upon to examine consumer perceptions of the advantages and any limitations of the new product and how it compares with existing products available.

Box 1.1 shows how marketing research was used to tackle a problem of launch failures in French prestige feminine perfumes. Explaining the decline in sales may mean accessing **secondary data** (which are explained in Chapter 3) to collect information on recent trends in the industry and on the structure of the market to show whether the company is unique in its problems or whether competitors are experiencing a similar situation. Various hypotheses about why the decline is taking place can then be tested.

Proactive, marketing-oriented companies will be concerned with making plans for the future. Marketing planning entails diagnosing the current situation, setting objectives, generating potential alternative strategies for achieving them, selecting the best strategies, and undertaking implementation. Marketing research can help with all the various stages of planning, not only by diagnosing the current situation, but also by providing background data for determining what are reasonable or feasible quantitative targets, for example, for market penetration, market development or product development.

Monitoring changes in the environment clearly requires continuous research (this type of research is explained in Chapter 7). This can be used in two different contexts: to generate "advance notice" or "early warning" of changes so that they can be reacted to immediately before they become a major problem, or to keep track of the progress of a strategy that has already been implemented.

While ad hoc research results can be added to a database, it is usual to make regular updates from continuous research. Such a database could be used to show, for example, that although sales of a brand have been fairly steady over the year, there may nevertheless have been considerable changes in the kinds of people purchasing, the quantities they buy and the frequency with which they buy them. This is particularly true for products like toiletries and fragrances. Internal databases are explained in more detail in Chapter 3.

Finally, if a company wishes to persuade a retailer to give shelf-space to its brands, it may need data from retail panels to show that a given increase in such space will generate a particular quantity of extra sales. The selling and buying of advertising time on television or radio depends on having access to audience figures. How these are generated and used is explained in Chapter 16.

Marketing research, then, can be used for a variety of purposes. However, undertaking or commissioning research does not, by itself, guarantee success or that the problem or problems to which it is addressed will be solved. There are many examples of companies ending up in trouble even after extensive research

 Secondary data Data that have already been constructed for another purpose than the research at hand.

EUROPEAN MARKETING RESEARCH

BOX 1.1

Using a global positioning system for French prestige feminine perfumes

Miedzinski and Duquesne (2003) report that the number of new perfumes launched in France has increased significantly (for example 38 were launched in 2000 alone), but their success rate has tended to diminish. A perfume will not sell unless it provokes enthusiasm because there is no objective selling proposition. It has to be positioned within the mind of the consumer. The researchers report the results of an internet survey among 6660 users of French prestige perfumes. The survey covered behavior with respect to perfumes, proximity to brands and personality questions. From the results, the researchers were able to detect core target markets, near competitors, and the values associated with specified brands.

has been carried out; some highly successful companies have never undertaken market research of any kind. There are many other factors apart from the information derived from research activities that determine the success or failure of a company or of its brands. There has, in fact, been little research on the link between marketing research activity and business performance. Hart and Diamantopoulos (1992) suggest that while some research has reported such a link, if the size of the company is taken into account, there is no connection between company performance and the *use* of market research or the type of research used. It depends, suggest the researchers, on the quality of the research and on how effectively it is used.

The value of any marketing research undertaken may, in fact, be limited by a number of factors.

- The problem or problems to be addressed may be poorly defined.
- Client requirements may be inadequately understood.
- Research may have been designed without reference to any decisions that depend on, or at least will be strongly influenced by, the results.
- The research may be poorly designed or carried out.
- The results may be ignored, misused, misunderstood or misinterpreted by managers.
- The results of the research may be inconclusive, giving rise to different opinions about the significance of the findings.

KEY POINTS

Marketing research can be used for a variety of purposes, but it is no substitute for decision-taking. Like any tool, well used it helps managers to do a better job. It helps to reduce the risks in business decisions, but will not make the decision for them. Good marketing requires flair and creativity along with sound judgment and experience. Marketing research is no substitute for these either; but good information can help reduce the area in which hunch, gut feeling or simply good luck have to operate.

Types of client-based marketing research

If you were to ask a research executive in an agency to outline the different kinds of marketing research, you would probably get an answer very different from that found in most of the textbooks on the subject. You could also, to some extent, deduce the underlying dimensions that agencies use to categorize different types or styles of research from the way they are structured. Different departments, teams, or even different subsidiary companies may specialize in a particular type of research. A number of underlying dimensions may, however, be distinguished:

- the kind of data collected,
- the duration of the research,
- the degree of customization,
- the amount of value added,
- the type of customer.

Some market research agencies categorize their activities according to the kind of data collected: qualitative or quantitative. **Qualitative research** is geared

Qualitative research Research that is geared primarily to the construction of qualitative data.

Depth interviews A direct, personal interview, usually with a single respondent, in which unstructured or open-ended questioning techniques are used by the interviewer to uncover motivations, beliefs, attitudes and feelings.

Focus group A discussion amongst a small group of respondents conducted by the researcher or a trained group moderator in a largely unstructured manner.

Quantitative research Research that is focused primarily on the construction of quantitative data.

Ad hoc research A one-off piece of research that has a beginning point and ends with a final report of the results.

Continuous research Measurements taken on a periodic basis with no envisaged end or completion of the research process.

Customized research Research that is tailor-made for a particular client.

Syndicated research Research in which either the research process or the research data are shared between a number of clients.

primarily to the construction of qualitative data, the main features of which are outlined in Chapter 4. Some agencies specialize in this type of research, which consists mainly of **depth interviewing** or **focus groups**. The larger organizations may well have a department, or even a whole subsidiary, devoted to qualitative research. **Quantitative research** is focused primarily on the construction of quantitative data, and will consist of research that uses formal questionnaire techniques at some stage, whether for face-to-face interviews, telephone research or postal research, or it may involve various forms of experimental or quasi-experimental research. Chapters 5–7 explain this kind of research in detail.

Other market research agencies will make a distinction in terms of the duration of the research: whether it is ad hoc or continuous. **Ad hoc research** is a "one-off" piece of research that has a beginning point, and concludes with a final report of the results. It will go through a number of stages from an initial brief or analysis of the problems to be investigated, to data collection, data analysis, and presentation of the findings. **Continuous research**, by contrast, takes measurements on a regular basis in order to monitor changes that are occurring in the marketplace. Such research goes through cycles of data production which, in many respects, resemble a production line that has to meet given deadlines by scheduling its activities, and has to achieve agreed standards of quality control. There is no envisaged "end" to the research process. The data are normally fed into some kind of management or marketing information system where they are added to a database and used as a core asset for a variety of analyses.

Overlapping with the distinction between ad hoc and continuous research is the slightly different distinction between customized and syndicated research. **Customized research** is tailor-made for a particular client to meet the needs of that client. **Syndicated research** means that either the research process or the research data are shared between a number of clients. The word "syndicated" arose when manufacturers got together as a syndicate to supply data that they all required. This function has now largely been taken over by the research agencies, who use the term "syndicated" to mean either that the data are sold to a number of clients, or that several clients share a survey.

There is a tendency for ad hoc research to be customized, and for continuous research to be syndicated, particularly since continuous research requires a lot of investment and other resources, and is usually too expensive for one client to afford. However, some ad hoc research may nevertheless be syndicated, while some continuous research is commissioned by one client and may be thought of as customized. Some research, such as advertising tracking studies, may take place over time, so is continuous, but for a fixed period. Some agencies, however, use the term "ad hoc" to denote any survey carried out for a single client.

Another basis on which some market research agencies structure their activities is by the amount of value that is added. In some cases the client requires only contract research – the agency is contracted only to collect data, or to collect and analyze them, according to specification. At the other extreme, the agency may be involved in a considerable degree of consultancy work before the research even begins. Such consultancy research may:

- assist in the diagnosis of the problem or problems facing a client organization,
- help to draft a research brief,
- make recommendations for actions that need to be taken,
- monitor their implementation.

Such research is, clearly, going to cost the client a lot more, but a recent trend is towards greater involvement of the market research agency in the business of its clients. Some agencies have set up special teams or offer a special service when such involvement is wanted.

There is a growing trend for market research agencies to separate out different kinds of research according to the kind of customer. Some may distinguish broadly between consumer research and business research. **Consumer research** takes the end user – private individuals or households – as the point of data collection. **Business research** takes other organizations who use the client's products or services in the provision of a further product or service as the point of data collection. Again, there may be a separate division or company that specializes in each type of research. Some go further and divide up the markets in a little more detail, for example they may have teams devoted to food and drink, home and personal care, finance, leisure and tourism, medical products, and agriculture.

Consumer research Research that takes the end-user (private individuals or households) as the point of data collection.

Business research Research that takes other organizations as the point of data collection.

> ## KEY POINTS
>
> There are many different types of client-based marketing research, and many will overlap or be combined in practice. Agencies may not use the terms in a consistent fashion. It is probably wise not to get too fussed about the labels being applied; just be clear about the different dimensions involved.

Online marketing research

Computer networks, principally the internet, but also local intranets, can be used for market research purposes in a number of ways, for example:

- gaining access to data that already exist on an electronic database,
- distributing questionnaires online in an internet survey,
- requesting and receiving samples of e-mail addresses online,
- designing questionnaires using online questionnaire design software,
- making data and analyses available online to clients, who can then manipulate the output and undertake their own additional analyses of the data.

Whether these activities amount to a different or additional "type" of research rather than just providing an alternative means of communication is an open question. What is certainly true is that the cost of conducting many types of research has been considerably reduced, while at the same time facilitating more complicated and rigorous study designs (Grossnickle and Raskin 2001: xix). The authors describe this as a "revolution in the research community". Fine (2000: 143) sees the internet as the cause of a major paradigm shift in both marketing and marketing research. However, despite these huge changes, the trend is towards mixed designs and mixed methods, which means that online activities are likely to be one component of many research projects. Online marketing research as a distinct category may eventually cease to exist.

The process of designing research for clients

Authors of textbooks on marketing research tend to have a separate chapter on research design that develops a taxonomy of different types of design. Typically a distinction is drawn between "exploratory designs", "descriptive designs" and "causal designs". The difficulty with these textbook distinctions is that most research in practice will be some combination of exploration, description, investigation of the relationships between variables and causal analysis. Most research projects, however, will have an exploratory phase, will produce descriptive data in the main research stage, and will go on to analyze the nature of relationships between variables. Each stage will shade into the next with exploratory research becoming the basis for description, and description forming the first part of an investigative analysis and so on. Only research that *limits* itself to generating ideas can be legitimately characterized as "exploratory" and only research that *limits* itself to the analysis of variables one at a time is purely "descriptive". The terms "exploratory", "descriptive" and "causal" are, furthermore, probably better seen as objectives for research rather than as designs as such. The topic of research objectives is taken up later in this section.

The topic of research design is taken up in more detail in Chapter 9. At this stage, two key points can be made. First, that any research design is specific to a particular inquiry; it is a unique combination of design elements and will often involve mixing different methods and techniques in the same project. The notion of having fixed categories or types of design is not particularly helpful. Second, design can be seen both as a particular plan in this sense, and as a process by which the plan comes about. The planning of client-based research, for example, will normally include the steps illustrated in Figure 1.4.

The researcher – whether in-house or in a market research agency – will often be involved only in the last stage of drawing up and presenting research proposals. The other stages are often undertaken by the client organization. However, clients increasingly look for help in understanding some or all of the design elements, so the researcher may become involved, for example, in helping the client to produce a research brief, or even right back to helping the client to diagnose company problems.

Diagnosing the problem

Earlier in this chapter it was argued that marketing research may be of limited value unless it is designed in the context of carefully defined problems that particular companies have, or issues or decisions that they face. The first stage in any research design should, then, be a detailed analysis of these problems, issues and

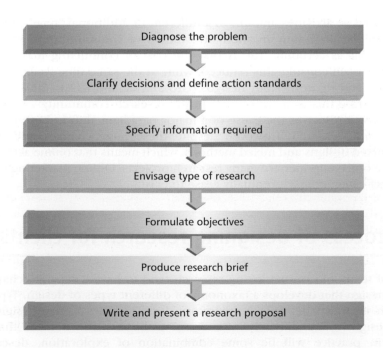

FIGURE 1.4

Steps in designing client-based research

decisions. Problem diagnosis is, unfortunately, often given insufficient attention before research is designed. One reason for this is that it is often the most difficult (and in some cases, depressing) part of the process. Sometimes the person requesting the research has no clear idea about what the key problems of an organization *are* that the research can tackle, or what decisions depend on the results of the research. What particular individuals *see* as "the problem" may well differ from one person to another. One person's "problem" may be another's opportunity. Furthermore, what individuals may be describing are the symptoms rather than the underlying causes.

A problem is a situation that calls for some kind of corrective action, a choice or a change. It may be helpful to think about a number of related issues when diagnosing problems:

- the nature of the discrepancies between actual and desired performance,
- the relationship between problems, and between problems and symptoms,
- the seriousness of the problems,
- the factors that affect or might be affecting the problem.

Problems arise where there is some discrepancy between the actual, current or anticipated future performance of the organization, and the desired performance or outcome. Discrepancies may be of various kinds.

- Historical – for example, the organization is not performing as well as it has in the past; profits are declining or sales stagnating.

- Environmental – for example, the organization is not performing as well as competitors or other similar organizations. What organizations are taken as standards and which measures of performance are used may, however, be crucial in making such comparisons.

- Planned or budgeted – for example, there may be variances between budgeted costs of materials and the actual costs, or between planned growth and actual growth.

- Theoretical or analytical – for example, the organization may be less marketing-oriented than the theory of marketing suggests should be the case, or its planning procedures do not match the principles of marketing planning.

It is helpful to understand what comparisons are being made when the nature of the marketing problems facing an organization are being considered. Making historical comparisons may lead management to view the problem rather differently than if comparisons are being made with selected competitors. There is, furthermore, seldom just one problem facing an organization at any given point of time. Problems are often interrelated and form clusters of related issues, for example, problems in terms of sales, profits and market shares. There is frequently a hierarchy of problems and symptoms; each symptom is the result of a more basic problem. The "problem" may be declining sales; but this may be a symptom of other aspects of an organization. Such deeper problems, like rising costs, may themselves be symptoms of still more fundamental issues, like work practices. Sometimes the relationship between problems is reciprocal rather than hierarchical. For example, advertising expenditure affects sales which, in turn, affect future expenditures on advertising. Sometimes several causes combine to produce a single effect; sometimes a single cause may produce several effects. In Chapter 14 the issues of causal complexity will be addressed directly and in some detail.

Whenever a problem is being described, it is often a good idea to ask, "Why?" Why are sales declining? Why are costs rising? Why are work practices inefficient? There is no ultimate cause, but such probing may help us to dig deeper into the structure and processes of an organization.

Some problems are more serious than others. Some may be urgent, but not important, others may be important, but not urgent, and some may be both. The urgency with which the results are required and the degree of importance attached to the problems to which the research is addressed will clearly have an impact on the kind of research that may be appropriate. Such a diagnosis may be necessary for deciding in which order to tackle problems. Information may be needed to measure exactly *how* serious a problem is. Some of this information may be already available; some may require market research. In any event, it is helpful to spell out exactly what information *is* required for this purpose.

Factors that may affect the problem may be internal or external to the organization. Internal factors may relate to such things as payment or incentive systems, industrial relations, changing technology, depreciation of plant and equipment. External factors will include the immediate microenvironment of trends in market size, changes in market structure or in buyer behavior and attitudes, competitor activity, supplier power, and the role of intermediaries like retailers and wholesalers. The wider macroenvironment will include changes in demographics, the economy, technology, politics, the legal environment, and the social and cultural environment.

Strengths and weaknesses of the company

Any marketing action will need to build upon company strengths or particular capabilities. What these are is not always obvious or easy to diagnose, and may require further analysis or research. It is likely that many of the weaknesses will have surfaced as "problems" at the problem diagnosis stage. However, there may well be other weaknesses that are not connected or obviously related to the problems being diagnosed. Assessment of strengths and weaknesses is often undertaken as part of a "SWOT" analysis – strengths, weaknesses, opportunities, threats – that also looks at the opportunities and threats in the marketplace. Such analyses assume that information is readily available and that accurate assessments can be made of each element. Marketing research often has a key role to play in the more systematic marketing auditing process which is usually comprehensive, periodic and undertaken by a group that is independent of those being audited. The audit will normally have both an internal and an external element. The internal audit will seek to identify:

- those factors that give any company in a market sector or in an industry a strategic advantage,
- the capabilities and incompetences of the company,
- those capabilities that link with the strategic advantage factors.

Marketing research can help assess each of these elements. Where a capability matches a strategic advantage factor, then it is a company strength; where it does not, it may be a weakness. The external audit will take a systematic look at the environment, particularly the immediate environment, and will, for example, seek to discover:

- who are the major competitors,
- what are their objectives and strategies,
- what are their strengths and weaknesses,
- what are their typical reaction patterns.

From this it should be possible to identify the extent of any threat from competitors, the power possessed by customers and suppliers, and the threat of substitute goods and services emerging. What is sometimes called "environmental analysis" will probably involve gathering market intelligence. This might include:

- scanning reports, newspapers and journals,
- speaking to the salesforce, consultants or academics,
- attending meetings or conferences.

The market researcher may be involved in all, some or none of these activities. The topic of marketing intelligence is taken up again in Chapter 3.

Decisions and action standards

It is one thing for the researcher or the client to feel that he or she now fully understands the situation facing the company; it is quite another to be clear about the decision or decisions that need to be taken. It must be remembered that marketing research is not geared exclusively to the taking of marketing decisions. Decisions about pricing or levels of production may have a marketing input, but there will almost certainly also be inputs from accountants or production managers or engineers. Decisions about communications with customers may well be the preserve of the marketing manager, but communications, for example with suppliers, intermediaries, competitors, shareholders and so on, may well involve other kinds of manager. If the company decided, for example, to conduct a survey of opinion among its shareholders, this would probably still be regarded as "marketing research", but decisions to issue additional shares or to merge with another company are unlikely to be for the marketing manager to make.

Decisions may be of many different kinds. They may be operational, tactical or strategic; they may be routine, adaptive or innovative. Furthermore, companies will have very varied ways in which decisions are made, ranging from a formal, fully rational process to rather more informal procedures. The market researcher would be advised to at least be aware of client decision-making processes and of who in the client company are or are likely to be the crucial influencers and final arbiters. These factors may well impact on the kind of research that is undertaken and certainly on the style and more of presentation of the results.

Unless the precise role the results from marketing research activity will play in the making of decisions of whatever kind is defined, the results are likely to be ignored. It is only too easy for managers to argue that research is needed before any decision can be taken, but without first clarifying which decisions in fact depend on further information. The best way to specify the role of research is to define action standards. These are actions or decisions specified in advance of the research that will depend on particular outcomes. Thus a company may specify that it will launch a new product provided at least 40 percent of respondents in a survey say they will either "probably buy" or "definitely buy" the new product. Furthermore, the 40 percent should not be a "finger-in-the-air" approach, but a result of careful diagnosis of the results of past research and how these related to the success or failure of products in that industry or in that company.

The information required

Once the decisions that have to be taken have been clarified, it is necessary to consider:

- exactly what information is required,
- the quality of information needed,
- when it is needed by.

Knowing what information is needed for making a particular decision is often a matter of experience or gut feeling. However, if the decisions to be taken have been clarified then, if, for example, one decision is what size of pack to use for a new product, it should be clear that information is required on the sales of existing pack sizes both for the company and for competitors, on how consumers react to existing packs, and how they would react to new sizes or types of pack. In short, it should be possible to list the key concepts that need to be addressed, and perhaps begin to suggest the key variables that need to be measured.

In some cases the client will already have some of the information. In other situations the researcher may be able to find it from secondary sources or purchase it from other agencies. Accessing secondary data is the focus of Chapter 3. Only when yet more information is still required will thought need to be given to the commissioning of research services.

Considerations about the quality of the data to be generated from conducting primary research will include accuracy, detail and comprehensiveness as well as sample quality where a sample is to be taken. Thus random samples will produce higher quality data than quota samples (sampling is explained in Chapter 8). Bigger samples will be more reliable than smaller ones (but by a declining amount). At the same time, getting high-quality data will be more costly, so a degree of trade-off may be required.

When information is required by will, of course, be governed largely by when the decision needs to be taken, but other considerations, like the time needed to analyze and digest the information, may need to be kept in mind. If the decision has to be taken before any worthwhile research can be carried out, it may be necessary to consider whether the company:

- takes the decision without any research,
- delays taking the decision,
- does a "quick-and-dirty" study.

Each of these has its problems, and in making the choice, very careful consideration has to be taken of the cost (in financial and customer relationship terms) of getting the decision wrong, or making a suboptimal decision. If there *is* time to do the research, then how much time is available will place constraints on the commissioning, phasing and completion of the research.

The type of research envisaged

The different types of research that an agency may offer have been outlined on pp. 9–11. However, these may be combined in various ways in a particular research design. It will need to be decided, for example, how much qualitative and how much quantitative evidence is required. If the amount of each is roughly categorized into high and low, then a cross-classification of the types of research envisaged can be developed, as in Figure 1.5. Large-scale surveys or experiments will produce considerable amounts of quantitative evidence and the results should be generalizable, but the amount of qualitative evidence will be low. This type of research assumes that the key variables are known and can be measured. The process of measurement is taken up in some detail in Chapter 5. Comprehensive qualitative research, by contrast, will be high in qualitative evidence and low on quantitative. It should provide considerable depth of understanding, but there will be limited generalizability. This type of research is considered in more detail in Chapter 4. Some clients may be able to afford only small-scale projects, and these will be relatively low on both qualitative and quantitative evidence. Occasionally, a "dipstick" operation may be all that is required to meet the objectives of the research. Multiphase and multicomponent research may be able to combine the best of both worlds, being high on both qualitative and quantitative evidence – but it will be expensive. Chapter 9 looks at mixed methods.

What type is appropriate for the client's problem may be fairly obvious and straightforward. This can be the case where the problem has occurred previously and the client is asking for a repeat of research that was carried out on that occa-

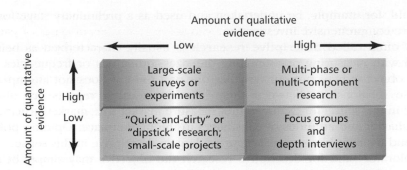

FIGURE 1.5

The kind of research envisaged

sion. The client may, however, ask the researcher for advice, or the client may even be asking for a style of research that the researcher believes is not appropriate to the problem. This may raise ethical issues and these are considered in more detail later in the chapter.

The objectives of the research

Research objectives spell out what the research itself is designed to explore, describe, investigate or explain. Exploratory objectives are aimed at generating information, insight or understanding and might include one or more of the following activities.

- Diagnosing, analyzing and evaluating the real nature, seriousness and urgency of the problem or problems facing an organization.

- Increasing the researcher's familiarity with a topic, with a company, or with a market. Very often the researcher at the outset does not know enough about the situation to be able to design the research or submit a worthwhile research proposal.

- Establishing priorities and objectives of the research. Exploratory work may be needed before it is possible to decide which particular issues require further investigation, and before being able to decide exactly what the research is expected to achieve.

- Providing information on practical problems. It may be necessary, for example, to find out whether certain organizations are willing to co-operate before embarking on a particular style of inquiry. Researchers may need to know certain things about the population before being able to design their sample.

- Generating ideas, gaining insights or suggesting hypotheses that could be tested.

Exploratory research is sometimes identified with particular research methods, particularly qualitative research, but also with observation, consulting experts, accessing secondary data or even buying into an omnibus survey. However, research whose objective is exploratory does not necessarily imply the use of specific methods of data collection (or, indeed, that such methods are limited to exploratory purposes); rather it implies that whatever style of research is used, the *end product* of the research is the generation of information, insight or understanding. Such research, furthermore, needs to be distinguished from the notion that nearly all research has an exploratory *phase*, which is preliminary to the main research and which is used in shaping the direction, design and operation of the main study, or to check that earlier designs will work satisfactorily. Any of the available instruments of data capture (these are explained in Chapter 6) or data collection methods (Chapters 4 and 7), or the special techniques and applications (Chapter 16) may be used for exploratory purposes. A formal, quantitative

Exploratory research Research aimed at generating ideas, insights or hypotheses.

Descriptive research Research that is concerned with measuring or estimating the sizes, quantities or frequencies of characteristics.

Investigative research Research that focuses on the extent of association or correlation between two or more variables.

Causal research Research that analyses the degree of influence of one or more independent variables upon one or more dependent variables.

Research brief A formal document written by a client that is sufficiently detailed for the researcher to be able to write a research proposal.

survey could, for example, be undertaken and used as a preliminary stage for a larger, more comprehensive investigation.

What is often called **descriptive research** is usually characterized as being concerned with measuring or estimating the sizes, quantities or frequencies of things. Its objective is to present variables one at a time; it does not attempt to analyze the relationships between them. Market research reports are often descriptive in this sense; for example, they measure market size, market structure, and the behavior and attitudes of consumers in the marketplace. Opinion polls, censuses and many public sector surveys are largely descriptive in this sense.

For exploratory and for descriptive research the objective may simply be to collect the information that has been specified at the research design stage. **Investigative research** goes beyond simply collecting data to study the relationships between variables. It focuses on the extent of statistical association or correlation between two or more variables, but does not examine the manner in which one or more variables may influence others. What is usually called **causal research**, by contrast, is concerned with establishing cause-and-effect relationships and it examines the degree of influence of one or more independent variables upon one or more dependent variables. Such research is often equated with experimental procedures since, so it is argued, only when some form of experimental control is exerted, can causality be demonstrated. The implication here is that other forms of research, such as survey research, cannot be used to establish causes or offer explanations. However, many different types of research can, with varying degrees of success, attempt to establish the extent to which one or more factors or variables exercise some degree of influence over others.

Causal research is sometimes referred to also as "explanatory" research. However, as will be argued in Chapter 14, causality is only one form of explanation; to establish a cause is not necessarily to explain. As researchers we may be able to demonstrate that one factor causes another, but we may not understand why.

The research brief

The **research brief** is a formal document that is, or should be, sufficiently detailed to enable the researcher to formulate a proposal for marketing research that will produce results that can be used effectively for marketing diagnosis, decision-making and delivery (see Figure 1.1 earlier). Sometimes the company prepares its own brief; sometimes it is prepared with the assistance of a market research agency or business consultant.

The brief will contain a summary of the elements considered so far:

- a diagnosis of the problem,
- an assessment of company capabilities,
- a clarification of the decisions that need to be taken,
- a specification of the information required,
- a statement of the objectives of the research,
- an outline of the kind of research envisaged.

In addition, there should be some indication of the likely budget for the research, a timescale for when a proposal is required and when the research results will be needed, and whether or not the brief is competitive. There may need to be considerable discussion both within the client organization and between client and agency over details of the brief unless the research is very straightforward or it is repeat business. Very often a company's analysis of its own problems may relate more to symptoms than to underlying causes, so the research executive may need to probe by continually asking, "Why?" as symptoms or stated problems are described. Box 1.2 suggests questions that the researcher should ask of clients if the brief lacks clarity.

BOX 1.2

IN DETAIL
Things to ask the client in a briefing session

■ Is the problem or issue to be researched clear? If not, try asking the client:

- What prompted you to commission this project?
- Have you commissioned or undertaken any earlier research?
- What factors, both internal and external to the company, do you think may be affecting the problem/issue/situation?
- How urgent and how important are the issues?

■ Are the decisions that are contingent upon the results of the research clear? If not, try asking the client:

- Why is the research needed?
- What will the research help you to do or to decide?
- Do you think it is a strategic, tactical or operational decision?
- What is the decision-making process?
- Is there a business plan or a planning process?
- Who are the interested parties in this research?

■ Is it clear what sort of information will be required? If not, try asking the client:

- What data or information do you already have?
- Is there information that you could obtain?
- What are the key concepts or variables?
- How accurate, detailed and comprehensive does the information need to be?

■ Does the client have some overall idea about the envisaged or appropriate scope, scale and type of research that may be required? If not, try asking the client:

- What geographical area needs to be covered?
- Is there an overall budget and timescale?
- How important is it to have quantitative information?
- What do you think the research itself should be able to do or show?

Sometimes clients will spell out or tentatively draft what they see as appropriate research objectives. It will then be up to the researcher to evaluate whether these are feasible, whether they relate sufficiently well to the managerial problem as it is understood, or whether they need to be amended or added to. They may well be discussed with the client before they appear in a formal proposal.

An example of a research brief is illustrated in the Box 1.3.

The research proposal

Formal **research proposals** are not always required, particularly for qualitative research. However, if a client is requesting two or three agencies to bid for a quantitative project, then it will be largely on the quality of the proposals received that the client is likely to make a decision about who to commission. Like the research brief, the research proposal is a formal document, but it is drafted by whoever will be conducting the research. Any organization seeking research from a market research agency will base its commission on such a document. From the perspective of the market research executive, the key objective of the proposal will be to obtain the commission from the client, perhaps in the face of stiff competition. The proposal in practice often has to be drafted on the basis of a less than

Research proposal A formal document drafted by the researcher outlining the methods and techniques that will be used to tackle the client's problem.

RESEARCH IN ACTION

BOX 1.3

A research brief

The potential for use of specialized flour in the home

Domestic bread-making has grown in popularity since the electric bread maker has become feasible and affordable. John Ambrose wishes to commission a survey to investigate the use of and attitudes towards the use of specialized flours for home bread-making.

Background

John Ambrose is a medium-sized, family-owned, flour-milling business which has been in existence for over 100 years. It supplies a complete range of flours to the bakery trade to cover every specialized need. Its customers are mostly small to medium-sized family bakers who have been customers for decades. It does not currently supply to the general public. It has no advertising and only limited sales representation.

Sales have been falling steadily in the last few years to a point where the company will need to take corrective action to stay in business. Among the alternatives being considered are to supply the general public the same highly specialized flours currently supplied to the trade. These would be more expensive than standard flours.

Research objectives

In order to investigate the feasibility of offering specialized flour for domestic use, particularly for use in domestic bread-makers, John Ambrose needs information about the stocking and use of flour in the home, the frequency of bread-making and other home-baking activities and current attitudes towards the use of specialized flours.

Methods

The research should consist of a qualitative preliminary to establish the main dimensions of flour usage in the home, attitudes to bread-making, and the possibilities for use of specialized flour. The main study should be a quantitative survey of about 1,200 households to establish the extent of various usages and attitudes.

Qualitative research

Please include a proposal for depth interviews and/or group discussions with individuals, both male and female, of all ages and social classes, and including those who currently do not bake bread at home. The qualitative research should take place in at least two regions. Costing for the qualitative work should be separate from that of the main stage.

Quantitative research

A nationally representative sample of individuals who usually bake bread at home is required. Would you please quote separately for the alternatives of a random or a quota sample design, discussing their relative advantages and limitations, and giving details of how the design would ensure a representative sample.

The qualitative stage will inform decisions on the content of the questionnaire. At this stage we envisage covering the following areas:

■ whether the household currently has flour in stock and what kinds/brands/pack sizes/quantities,
■ how long the flour is usually kept in the house,
■ what types/brands of flour respondents can recall,
■ how often they buy and the price paid,
■ what kinds of baking they do, on what occasions, how often, and what flour they use,
■ whether they have an electric bread-maker,
■ how often they bake bread,

■ what they view as their successes and failures in home bread-making,
■ whether they feel that specialized flours could help with their "failures".

Timetable
We would like to commission the work at the end of July and to receive an interim report on the qualitative stage for execution of the main fieldwork in November. A full written report is required as soon as reasonably possible after that.

Submission of tenders
Please submit two copies of tenders to John Ambrose no later than 15th June. Meetings to discuss the shortlisted tenders will take place on 26th June. If you wish to discuss the research prior to submission of a tender please contact John Ambrose.

adequate brief from the client. The research executive may seek further discussion and clarification from the client before submitting a proposal.

The proposal is a formal statement of the methods and techniques that the researcher feels are required in the circumstances, and should contain the elements outlined in Box 1.4.

IN DETAIL
Format of a research proposal
BOX 1.4

■ A cover/title page that contains:
  – a title for the project,
  – the author or agency who has produced the document,
  – the date submitted.

■ A contents page
■ Section 1 Introduction
  This will include some – not necessarily all – of the following and not necessarily under subheadings or the headings implied by the list:
  – background,
  – the current situation/issues/problems,
  – the decisions that need to be taken,
  – the information required,
  – relevant reports/data/literature,
  – strengths/weaknesses of the organization.

■ Section 2 Objectives
  The research purpose(s)
  This refers to the overall aim of the research, which may be exploratory, descriptive, investigative, causal, or some combination of these. In particular, the overall research aim or purpose may be stated using some of the terms below:
  – explore, investigate, further understand, examine, study, diagnose, evaluate, create,
  – gather, collect data,
  – measure specific variables,

- search for patterns/relationships between variables,
- answer research questions,
- test hypotheses,
- offer causal explanations.

Specific objectives
These will list:

- the concepts, ideas to be explored,
- the variables on which data are to be collected,
- the research questions,
- the hypotheses.

■ Section 3 Research methods

- the overall scope of the research,
- the research approach, design or mix of methods that will be used,
- the rationale for the methods suggested,
- any preliminary stages that will be undertaken, for example a pilot survey,
- the techniques to be used. This will probably be the longest section, normally broken down into subsections that will cover:
  - the target population and any sample that is to be taken,
  - data collection methods,
  - data capture instruments,
  - the approach to or the specific statistical techniques that will be used for data analysis.

■ Section 4 Organization and management
This will cover issues like the personnel to be involved in the research, their relevant experience or CVs, the arrangements for supervision and responsibility, quality control plus a proposed timetable or work schedule.

■ Section 5 The agency
This will attempt to reassure the potential client that the agency has experience of the market/problem area and or techniques being used and will probably include a list of recent clients.

■ Section 6 Fees
This will normally include an overall sum plus the cost of any optional extras. If the proposal contains various stages or different elements, there may be a breakdown of the cost of each element. The conditions or terms of payment should also be specified. It would also be helpful to clarify what "deliverables" are included, for example, interim summary reports, a formal presentation, a written report (plus number of copies), tabulations, further meetings, a helpline and so on.

■ Section 7 Appendices
These might include the terms of contract, further details of any specific procedures used and a list of past clients

In planning the methods and techniques to be used, the basic considerations are whether the research should be ad hoc or continuous, and if ad hoc whether it should be qualitative or quantitative. In selecting from the range of market research techniques available, the research executive will need to bear in mind the resources and the time that will be needed for each technique, along with the appropriateness of each for minimizing the risks among the decisions identified as needing to be taken. A checklist of useful questions to consider would be as follows.

- Will depth interviews with key informants, experts, technicians, colleagues, or suppliers provide sufficient information to take the decision?

- Will focus groups be needed with consumers to explore issues more thoroughly, and if so, what kinds of groups, how many groups, and how are they to be selected?

- Will some form of experimental research be appropriate? If so, should it be in the laboratory or in the field?

- Will some form of survey be required? This is the most expensive, resource-heavy, time-consuming form of research and should be resorted to only when information from other sources is clearly not going to be adequate. Careful thought will need to be given to the size of the sample required, the type of sampling, and the mode of delivery of the questions, for example, face to face, by telephone, by mail or by e-mail.

A company considering commissioning research will normally ask up to three agencies to submit proposals for research in response to a research brief. These would then be evaluated and compared. For large-scale undertakings the agency may be invited to present these proposals in person so that they can be questioned about them. Alternatively, where a client is coming back for repeat business, there may not even be a research proposal – an understanding of what the research is to cover and the cost may be all that needs to be clarified. It would be unreasonable for the client to expect that the agency has done a great deal of work on the problem before the research is commissioned. In particular, it is unlikely that the agency will include a questionnaire even in draft format at this stage. An example of a response to the brief on the use of specialized flour in the home is illustrated in Box 1.5.

KEY POINTS

A research design is a particular – possibly unique – combination of methods and techniques that will enable researchers to obtain data that will address the purpose for which the research is to be undertaken. Design is also a process that involves a number of elements that can also be seen loosely as stages that begin with an analysis of the problem or issue facing a company through to the drafting of a formal research proposal. Implicitly the process is about designing ad hoc rather than continuous research. The design of continuous research will have to wait until Chapter 16.

RESEARCH IN ACTION
A research proposal

BOX 1.5

The Use of Specialized Flour in the Home

June 2006

Prepared for: John Ambrose and Co. Ltd.
Prepared by: Marketing Research in Action, The Research Centre, East Gate, London
Contact: R A Kent

CONTENTS

1   Introduction

2   Objectives

3   Preliminary qualitative research

   3.1   Discussion
   3.2   Sample summary
   3.3   Recruiting and moderating procedures
   3.4   Interview topics and stimulus materials
   3.5   Timing

4   Quantitative research discussion
   4.1   Sampling
   4.2   Sample size
   4.3   Screening
   4.4   Extending the sample

5   Quantitative research method
   5.1   Contact procedure
   5.2   Questionnaire design
   5.3   Quality control
   5.4   Coding
   5.5   Editing
   5.6   Data entry
   5.7   Analysis
   5.8   Reporting

6   Pilot research

7   Interviewer selection

8   Timing

9   Project staffing

10 Fees

1 Introduction

John Ambrose and Co. Ltd is considering the possibility of offering to the general public the same highly specialized flours that it currently supplies to the trade. The Company now wishes to commission research to examine the potential for the use of specialized flours in the home, particularly for bread-making.

Marketing Research in Action has been invited to present proposals for this piece of research. These have been prepared by our Consumer Research Division. They are based on a written brief received in May of this year and subsequent telephone conversations with Mr John Ambrose.

2 Objectives

A combination of qualitative and quantitative research is required to examine the following questions.

■ What proportion of households keep flour of any description in stock?

■ What kinds of flour are usually kept?

- What other kinds of flour may respondents be aware of?
- What is flour currently used for?
- What are the main kinds of home baking?
- How often do they bake bread at home?
- Which groups of people are most likely to make use of specialized flour?
- What quantities are they likely to buy?
- Would they be prepared to pay a slightly higher price?

The research will comprise two elements. The first stage of qualitative research will provide in-depth information on the main dimensions of flour usage in the home, attitudes to home baking and the possibilities for the use of specialized flour for bread-making in particular. This will provide the basis for designing the questionnaire to be used in the second stage among 1,200 respondents.

3 Preliminary qualitative research

3.1 Discussion

We propose to conduct a mixture of group discussions and individual interviews. Group discussions are most appropriate for most individuals because:

- groups often produce a more relaxed and discursive review of a topic, and encourage spontaneous comments and comparisons,
- groups are less expensive "per head",
- differences between consumers are highlighted.

However, depth interviews are often very useful as a "control" for, or supplement to, groups since they enable individual histories and attitudes to be probed more fully. Furthermore, it is sometimes difficult to get a group of older people together. They often need more reassurance and there are frequently mobility and hearing problems.

3.2 Sample summary

The population is all those households in the UK that currently possess an electric bread-maker. We suggest six standard groups of eight men and women aged 18 or more, resident in the UK for at least three years. Groups will be mixed in terms of gender and age but separated by social class. There will be quotas on these variables to keep them in the same proportions as in the UK population. Social class will be measured according to the occupation of the head of the household.

Forty depth interviews are proposed, weighted towards the elderly or immobile.

The sample structure will be as follows:

6 groups
Social class: 3 × BC1 + 3 × C2D
Location: 3 × South + 3 × North or Midlands

20 interviews
Social class: 10 × B or C1 + 10 × C2 or D
Location: 10 × South + 10 × North or Midlands

20 interviews
Age: 65+
Location 10 × South + 10 × North or Midlands

3.3 Recruiting and moderating procedures

Marketing Research in Action uses interviewers specially trained for qualitative recruiting. We are members of IQCS. We will rely mainly on random street or house recruiting, boosted by recruitment in carefully selected public locations appropriate to the particular subgroups or respondents being contacted.

The interviews will be conducted in a domestic setting (a recruiter's home). It may, however, be necessary to hold some interviews in respondent's own homes.

All the groups and interviews will be moderated by a member of the Marketing Research in Action research team. All discussions will be tape recorded, and the transcripts of the groups can be made available if required.

3.4 Interview topics and stimulus materials

A detailed discussion and interview guide will be prepared on commission. Currently we envisage focusing on perceptions of the current range of flours available, attitudes to home baking, and the possibilities for the use of specialized flour. Particular attention will be paid to vocabulary, common assumptions, and areas of possible confusion likely to affect the qualitative study.

3.5 Timing

Following commission a period of three weeks will be required for group and individual interview recruitment. Further recruitment will take place concurrently with the fieldwork. We envisage a period of about eight weeks will be required for the qualitative phase.

All interim reports should be available by the end of September, assuming commission in July. A full written report could then be produced within four weeks and integrated with the quantitative stage once this is complete.

4 Quantitative research discussion

4.1 Sampling
Option 1 *Random sampling*

We suggest a three-stage sampling procedure. First, a set of 100 electoral constituencies will be selected with probability of selection proportional to the size of the electorate. Second, an individual elector will be chosen at random from each constituency. The sampling point will then comprise the electoral ward of which that elector was part. Third, every fiftieth name will be selected from the Electoral Register referring to that ward and these will be given to interviewers. Interviewers will determine whether or not the household possesses an electric bread-maker. Those who have not are screened out. The interviewer continues until all quotas are completed.

Option 2 *Quota sampling*

Stages one and two will be similar to Option 1. However, for stage three, the interviewer will be free to work wherever he or she liked in the defined areas to achieve a quota of interviews. Quotas will vary by region to reproduce the regional profile of individuals by age and social class.

There is the danger that this method will over-represent the "at-home" population. However, quotas could be applied additionally to working status.

For both Option 1 and Option 2 the achieved sample results will be weighted to the population profile in terms of gender, age, social class and working status.

4.2 Sample size

We propose a sample size of 1,200. Results will be grossed up to the population of Great Britain.

5 Quantitative research method

5.1 Contact procedure

For Option 1 the interviewer will continue to call at a selected addresses up to a maximum of four times, varying the time of day and day of the week at each call.

In the case of Option 2, interviewers will be asked to record details of all contacts made and whether there was immediate refusal, noneligible respondents who refused interview, was extra to quota or whether a full interview was achieved.

5.2 Questionnaire design

The questionnaire will be developed in consultation with John Ambrose and Co. Our costings have allowed for a questionnaire that will take on average 40 minutes to administer. Wherever possible we hope to be able to precode questions, drawing on the answers obtained previously in the qualitative research. We have allowed for up to six open-ended questions within each questionnaire. Section 6 describes the procedures for piloting.

5.3 Quality control

All interviewers will be supervised by our regional field directors. Ten percent of interviews will be subjected to back-checks. All interviews meet not only the standards of IQCS, but our own additional training ensures a quality of interviewing that few of our competitors can match.

5.4 Coding

We will prepare code-frames for the open-ended questions based on extractions from 100 questionnaires. These will be submitted to John Ambrose for approval before coding begins.

5.5 Manual editing

The objective is to ensure that information is in the correct format for data entry. It includes checks on the presence of leading zeros in quantity fields and full details of sample point. Our policy is to return any questionnaire that lacks key information to the interviewer concerned.

5.6 Data entry

The computer edit is a comprehensive data validation exercise that ensures the logical consistency of information as well as completeness. Any discrepancies it reveals are checked by a research executive against the original questionnaire.

5.7. Analysis

We have developed costings on the basis that 500 pages of computer tabulations will be required. The specification for the analysis will be discussed with John Ambrose before the analysis is run, including requirements for tests of statistical significance. We will supply two bound copies of laser-printed tabulations.

We will need to discuss with John Ambrose the issue of weighting the data. Using the quota approach, it will be necessary to weight the data to take account of undersampling of working housewives. Weights will also be applied to take account of differential response rates.

5.8 Reporting

In addition to the computer tabulations we have allowed for the preparation of a detailed technical report and an interpretive report. The latter will be structured to meet the needs of John Ambrose. It will be illustrated with charts and diagrams drawn from the computer tabulations. Both reports will be submitted in draft and after approval we will supply four copies of each.

We have not allowed for a presentation of the quantitative research findings, but would be happy to discuss this should one be required.

6 Pilot research

We have indicated the additional cost of pilot research in our section on fees. While it is always desirable to pilot questionnaires, we feel that a pilot survey could be dispensed with in this project given our familiarity with the market. However, should one be required we would recommend that the pilot be conducted in three sample points with 12 interviews in each. The procedure for the pilot would be exactly the same as for the main stage quota option given that the main purpose is to test the questionnaire rather than the sampling method.

Interviewers would attend a personal briefing at Marketing Research in Action at our head office. We would produce a brief report on the pilot, suggesting amendments to the questionnaire or survey design for the main stage. The report would also comment on the implications of any changes for the fee for the main stage.

7 Interviewer selection

Interviewers will receive personal briefings at one of six centers nearest to their home. Our regional managers will attend so that they are completely familiar with the survey. The sessions will be conducted by Marketing Research in Action executives responsible for the survey and will last about two hours. Attendance by relevant personnel from John Ambrose will be warmly encouraged.

The main purpose of the briefing will be to ensure that interviewers and managers are totally familiar with:

- the administration of the questionnaire and any question areas of particular difficulty or complexity,
- the type of respondent they will be likely to interview,
- the type of information that needs to be collected.

There will also be a mock interview to highlight the points made during the session.

Interviewers will, in addition, be given a set of written instructions which reiterate in more detail the points made at the briefing session.

Marketing Research in Action has a national panel of about 950 interviewers. Mostly they are self-employed, but they work to standards and administrative procedures laid down by our operating manual. They are organized under a team of twelve Regional Managers, all of whom are full-time employees of Marketing Research in Action.

We are members of the Interviewer Quality Control Scheme, whose professional standards we either meet or exceed. Normal back-checking and accompaniment procedures would be applied to this survey. This, in summary, requires that:

- interviewers should be accompanied at least once in each six-month period,
- 10 percent of the work will be subject to back-check procedures,
- the back-checking will comprise 10 percent postal checks; the remainder will be face to face or telephone checks.

8 Timing

Our best estimate of how the timing could proceed is as follows:

Weeks 1–7	qualitative research
Week 8	qualitative presentation
Week 11	qualitative report available
Weeks 8–11	quantitative questionnaire development
Week 12	pilot briefing
Week 13	pilot debriefing
Weeks 14–15	questionnaire alterations and printing
Week 16	main stage briefings
Weeks 17–19	main stage fieldwork
Weeks 18–21	codings and data preparation
Week 22	analysis produced
Week 25	draft report available.

This follows the timetable suggested in the brief and we believe it to be realistic, but it could be amended in the light of further discussions with John Ambrose. Thus if there is no pilot survey the project can be shortened by two weeks.

9 Project staffing

The project will be carried out by the Consumer Research Division of Marketing Research in Action, under its director, Kay Brent, who has had many years' experience of consumer survey work. She has specialized in the application of research techniques to the food industry and, before joining the Company in 1982, had spent five years as consultant to the Ministry of Food and Agriculture.

Responsibility for the project would be given to Ken Bray, an Associate Director of the Division. He joined the Company on 1983 and since then has managed a variety of ad hoc projects, several of them in the food sector.

10 Fees

The fees quoted below are exclusive of VAT, and are subject to Marketing Research in Action's standard terms and conditions of contract. The fees are subject to the assumptions contained in these proposals and may have to be amended should any assumptions prove to be incorrect.

Qualitative research	£20,750
Quantitative pilot research	£2,500
Main stage – random sampling	£73,900
Main stage – quota sampling	£53,200

Buying and selling research

Apart from in-house research, most marketing research that is undertaken is as a commercial transaction between buyers and sellers of research services. The client and the agency perspective on these transactions will, of course be very different.

Buying research – the client perspective

From the perspective of the manufacturer or other type of organization wishing to purchase research services, the objective will, of course, be to buy good research, that is, research that is good value and which addresses effectively the problems, issues or opportunities that the company faces. Before approaching any market research agency, however, the client first of all needs to consider:

- whether research is needed at all,
- whether a research brief is needed and if so whether the company is able to produce one in-house,
- whether it can do what research is needed entirely in-house,
- whether it wants to commission a "full" study or just part of the activities required, for example, employing only field and tab assistance, or putting a number of questions into an omnibus survey,
- what companies or agencies to approach for a proposal.

The client company may decide against doing any research if:

- the data or information needed already exist or can be purchased, for example from business publishing houses, from market research agencies or advertising agencies, or by subscribing to continuous research services,
- there is not enough time to conduct research before a decision has to be taken,
- the cost of getting the decision wrong is relatively low so the cost of any worthwhile research would be greater than the likely payoff,
- the situation is too complex with too many factors and variables for research to have a significant impact on the decision that needs to be taken.

In choosing what market research companies to approach for a proposal, some clients will have a "pool" of tried and tested companies that they have a habit of using. Others rely on listings, for example by the UK Market Research Society, or on recommendations from contacts in other organizations. It would be normal to obtain up to three proposals and to advise the market research organizations that it is a competitive proposal, indicating how many have been or will be approached.

The final selection will be based on some combination of:

- evidence that the research executive has fully understood the brief and the problem to be researched,
- the overall approach suggested, including a clear statement of the research objectives, a definition of the population to be studied, the sampling techniques, the fieldwork methods to be used and the data handling and analysis procedures,
- the experience of the researchers assigned to the project,
- the quality of communications with the agency so far,
- the cost, usually a global sum, but it should be clear what that sum includes, for example a written report and a face to face presentation.

The client may need to bear in mind that the "cost" of the research includes not only paying the market research agency, but also the opportunity cost of what is not being done as a result of devoting resources to the research, and the indirect costs of managerial time spent on further contact. However, the client may also need to consider whether the research, besides being used as a basis for taking a decision, may also be a useful input to a marketing or management information system, or may be used as "currency" in negotiating with advertisers, advertising agencies, distributors, retailers and so on. Findings on brand loyalty, inter-purchasing and frequency of purchase may, for example, be used to persuade a retailer to allocate more shelf-space to your brand.

A commissioning letter will be sent to the chosen market research agency accepting the proposal as a formal contract. Thereafter, the client will wish to monitor progress to ensure that deadlines are met, and that the questionnaire, when drafted, meets with its approval. The client may wish some degree of participation in the research, for example, attending one or two group discussions, and may request that it be consulted over the final coding of answers when the questionnaires are received.

Finally, it would be wise to evaluate the market researchers in a systematic manner by giving a series of ratings against a number of selected criteria, for example:

- response to the brief,
- quality of the research,

- client service,
- verbal presentation,
- written report.

Such ratings can then form the basis for making future research commissions.

Selling research – the agency perspective

The major objective of the research executive in a market research agency in designing research and in offering a formal research proposal will be to obtain the commission from the client. He or she will need to bear in mind the strengths and weaknesses of the agency in terms of styles of research, and its current loading of resources already committed to other projects currently underway. If it is a large company, it will be able to offer the full range of research so that if, for example, it looks as though qualitative research is appropriate to the client's problem, then the client can be passed on to the division or subsidiary company in the organization that specializes in that type of research. In smaller specialized agencies, the research executive will, of course, try to show why the company's particular expertise is just what is needed to help the client.

In reviewing briefs received by potential clients and deciding which ones to offer research proposals for, the agency will need to consider:

- the level of detail in the brief and whether further discussions with the client are needed,
- the kind of research envisaged or that the agency thinks is appropriate,
- how the data are to be used (and by whom, when and how),
- any limitations in terms of time and money,
- the scope of the research in terms of geographical area, size of sample, the information required, the input to research design needed from the research executive, and the end product – restricted to data analysis, or to include interpretations and recommendations,
- the kind of report required,
- the competition – how many other agencies are quoting.

If the agency decides to offer a research proposal, it will need to consider all those aspects that will affect the design and cost, for example:

- the availability of past research or published data,
- the size, spread and contactability of the sample,
- the data collection method,
- the need for exploratory research,
- the need for a pilot survey,
- the need for personal briefings,
- the length of the questionnaire,
- the number of open-ended questions,
- the need for evening, weekend or holiday time interviewing,
- the scale and complexity of the data analysis required,
- the type and scale of reporting.

Box 1.6 explains the steps in pricing a research project for the European market. It was written by Michael Roe, a practitioner with over 30 years' experience in marketing research.

EUROPEAN MARKETING RESEARCH

BOX 1.6

The pricing of market research services in Europe

All but a very few European research agencies are commercial enterprises and they will prepare a fully priced research proposal for client approval before an ad hoc research project is undertaken. From start to finish, the normal project goes through 10 stages (see Figure 1.6) inside the agency, with client approval coming only at stage 3. The process begins with the client brief to which the agency responds with its proposal. If not selected, the work that has gone into this document is "lost" since proposals are not charged to the client.

On approval, the agency moves to stage 4 where it puts into practice the approach expounded in the proposal. Key elements here are questionnaire/discussion guide design and fieldwork planning, which involves organizing interviewers for data collection. When fieldwork is complete (stage 5), it will be the most costly element of the entire study (averaging about 40 percent) due to freelance interviewer payments (out-of-pockets for the agency). Following editing and coding (stage 6) and data processing (7) the agency produces tabular output for the research executives to study (8) before a presentation (9) and final report (10). Research executive time, which is costed on a per hour basis using time sheets, will form the next highest cost factor (about 30 percent). Of course, overheads for office space, administration and so on, will add a percentage to the cost on top of which goes a profit margin.

Fieldwork costs can be kept down by reducing questionnaire length and keeping open-ended questions to a minimum. Reducing sample size, however, may have serious effects on statistical validity and subgroup analyses, while narrow sample universe definitions should be avoided. The internet offers the opportunity of reducing data collection costs since no interviewers are required. However, the programming of electronic questionnaires and the need to maintain and motivate panels of potential respondents means that some serious costs still remain.

Competitive tendering will put agencies under pricing pressure. Clients may involve their own purchasing departments in the selection process to bring a hard-nosed professional approach. Agencies usually respond by looking for efficiencies, for example, cutting-and-pasting similar old jobs, outsourcing or amalgamating in order to share services.

Pricings differ greatly around Europe due to varying

FIGURE 1.6

Pricing and project stages

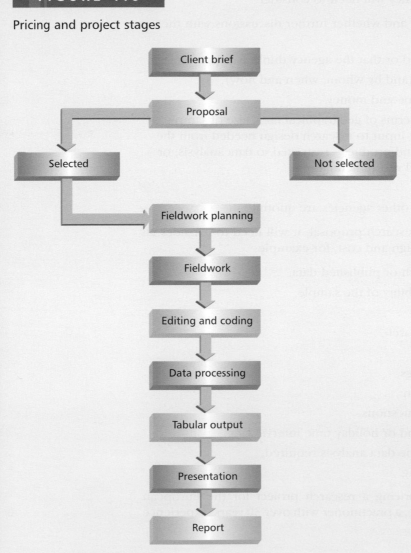

executive salary levels and whether or not interviewers are subject to social security charges. The highest prices, which may be double the lowest ones, will be found in Scandinavia and Switzerland and the lowest in small southern countries. Pricing is often based on many assumptions, such as the complexity of data collection and the amount of executive time likely to be involved throughout, so the risk of getting it wrong is very real.

Michael Roe is a practitioner with over 30 years of experience in marketing research. He has been an international market researcher with Unilever and Research International. He is now a consultant and trainer for multi-nationals such as Shell, BAT, Tetra Pak, Nokia and Friesland Coberco. He has also run training sessions in the universities of Edinburgh, Cranfield, Buckingham and Stirling. He is a faculty member of the Management Centre Europe in Brussels and of the Chartered Institute of Marketing.

KEY POINTS

The bulk of client-based marketing research is undertaken by market research agencies who offer research services as a commercial transaction. The perspectives of those individuals, groups or organizations buying such services will be different from those offering such services for a fee. A key element in the negotiations between buyers and sellers will, of course, be the price.

The European market research industry

Based on information supplied by national market research trade associations, ESOMAR (this organization is described later in this section) has calculated that the total worldwide market for market research in the year 2004 was €16 950 million, of which €7 614 million or 45 percent was based in Europe, a turnover that was greater than that for North America (€6 193 million). The worldwide growth in turnover was 7.5 percent on 2003 (5 percent after adjusting for inflation). The new EU member states and the former Eastern bloc countries showed growth rates of over 10 percent. The old EU member states grew more slowly with the exception of Ireland, which had an adjusted growth rate of 18.7 percent.

These figures exclude work conducted in-house, by advertising agencies, by universities, by government departments and by non-profit-making research institutes. Worldwide, 80 percent of the turnover was accounted for by domestic as opposed to international clients and 80 percent by consumer as opposed to business research. Sixty percent was for ad hoc as opposed to continuous research and 75 percent was quantitative as opposed to qualitative. In Europe, the UK had the largest turnover (€1862) followed closely by Germany and France. No other European country had a turnover greater than €500 million. The spend per head of population, however, was far higher in the UK than anywhere else in the world (at about €30 per head compared with about €20 per head in the USA, Germany and France – and 2 cents in China!).

The European market research industry consists of three main groups of "players":

- the suppliers of research services,
- the research buyers,
- the profession.

The suppliers of research services

Research suppliers can be classified into three broad, but overlapping, categories:

■ full service agencies,

■ specialist suppliers,

■ limited service suppliers.

Full service agencies offer the full range of services in both qualitative and quantitative research, ad hoc and continuous research, and customized and syndicated services. They may specialize to some extent in emphasizing, or at least building a special reputation in, for example, international research or continuous research, but they can supply whatever service the client may need. Full service agencies are often large international organizations (and may baulk at the idea of being described as an "agency"). The largest research suppliers in Europe are listed in Table 1.1. VNU, which is based in the Netherlands and heads the global list, is at the top by virtue of its ownership of ACNeilsen, Neilsen Media Research and a number of other research agencies. The Kantar Group includes the UK companies Research International, Millward Brown and the British Market Research Bureau. These were acquired by the WPP advertising agency and run by Kantar, the research wing of WPP. Most of these agencies will have a client service department, a field department and a data processing department. Executives from client services may well become involved in the client's business and will act for only a limited number of clients – and never for competitors.

Specialist suppliers may focus on a particular research technique like telephone interviewing or e-mail surveys, or they may specialize in a particular market sector, for example the motor trade or pharmaceuticals. Some agencies will offer just qualitative research. Limited service suppliers offer just one or two components of the research process, for example, fieldwork, data processing (or both, usually called "field and tab" agencies) or in statistical analysis. Some provide advice on research or project management.

The research buyers

In the UK the largest buyers of market research are in manufacturing (44 percent, ESOMAR, 2005). Other major buyers are in the media, the public sector and in financial services. Within manufacturing, the food sector is the biggest spender on research, accounting for over £60 million in 2001 followed by non over-the-counter pharmaceuticals (£57 million), health and beauty (£40 million), vehicle

TABLE 1.1	The top European full service agencies	
Agency	**Parent country**	**Turnover (Euros million)**
VNU NV	Netherlands	2 703
Taylor Nelson Sofres	UK	1 355
The Kantar Group	UK	895
GfK Group	Germany	658
Ipsos Group	France	593
Synovate	UK	393
NOP	UK	321
MORI	UK	61

SOURCE: ESOMAR (2005)

manufacturers (£34 million) and retailers (£31 million). The picture changes across Europe, however. For example, in France nearly 60 percent is accounted for by manufacturing and only 5 percent by the media. In Belgium, by contrast, just over 20 percent is accounted for by manufacturing, but utilities, post and telecommunications account for rather more than in the UK (ESOMAR 2005).

Some organizations have a research department that is responsible for purchasing research services, but in others, such a role may be played by a "customer insight" manager or a brand manager. In some organizations in-house services may be available. Here the research executives may well both supply and purchase research services by commissioning out some of the work. Managers internal to the company may be seen as the "clients", for whom the research executives may act as consultants.

The profession

The market research industry in Europe is well served by a number of professional bodies and trade associations that aim to promote high standards in research practice and to represent the industry, for example on government and international bodies. The oldest of the professional bodies is ESOMAR, which was founded in 1948 as the European Society for Opinion and Marketing Research. However, it now sees itself in a worldwide context and calls itself the World Association of Opinion and Marketing Research Professionals. It has over 4000 individual members in 100 countries. It organizes seminars and conferences, it offers training and education through workshops and distance learning, and it makes available a range of professional publications. All its members and all the companies listed in its Directory undertake to comply with the ICC/ESOMAR International Code of Marketing and Social Research Practice, which has been drafted jointly by ESOMAR and the International Chamber of Commerce. The ESOMAR Directory of Research Organizations is an up-to-date, searchable resource of over 1500 organizations worldwide. The code of practice and a selection of guidelines, for example on data protection, on how to commission research, on customer satisfaction studies, may be downloaded from: www.esomar.org.

Other European bodies include the Alliance of International Market Research Institutes (www.aimri.org), which represents over 80 market research agencies in 17 countries and the European Federation of Associations of Market Research Organizations (EFAMRO, www.efamro.org), which is an international federation of market research agency associations within the European Union. It was formed in 1992 to bring together national associations of major countries in Western Europe representing research agencies responsible for between 60 and 70 percent of the total turnover in market research.

In the UK there is the Market Research Society (www.mrs.org.uk), the largest body of its kind in the world. It was founded in 1947, and now has over 8000 members in more than 50 countries, about half of whom are women. The Market Research Society (MRS) seeks to ensure the maintenance of professional standards in the practice of market research of all kinds, to provide its members with an educational, information and social forum, and to represent the interests of the UK market research profession in the world at large. It offers the only UK academic qualification solely covering market research – the Diploma of the Market Research Society. Members of the Society subscribe to a code of conduct that puts a premium on confidentiality, so that the anonymity of respondents is carefully protected.

In 1964 the largest research agencies in the UK formed themselves into a trade association – the Association of Market Survey Organisations (AMSO). Its role was largely as a support group for those running its member companies. However, in 1998 it merged with ABMRC (the Association of British Market Research

Companies), which was an association of smaller research agencies, to form the British Market Research Association (BMRA, www.bmra.org.uk). Its aims are to represent and promote the professional and commercial interests of all its members, to increase the professionalism of the industry and to promote confidence in market research. Members, who are corporate rather than individual and total about 220 companies, must abide either by the MRS or the ICC/ESOMAR code of conduct.

In 1981 the Association for Qualitative Research (the AQR, www.aqr.org.uk) was formed and now comprises over 1200 individual members who work variously in research companies, advertising and major client organizations. It provides a forum for all those interested in the conduct and development of qualitative research. All market research associations in the UK, in Europe and worldwide are listed at market research industry online: www.mrweb.com/assocs/.

Most of the large market research companies are members of the Interviewer Quality Control Scheme (IQCS, www.iqcs.org). This is an offshoot of the original Market Research Society Interviewer Identity Card Scheme. To be a member of the IQCS, a company has to meet specified market research fieldwork standards that cover recruitment, training, supervision and back-checking. Members are audited every year and a report goes to the full Council of the IQCS.

Trends

In the space of 50 years the industry has transformed itself from a cottage industry to one where research suppliers are major organizations on the global stage. Overall growth has been steady rather than dramatic. The major changes have been brought about largely through mergers and acquisitions. The result has been that the top 25 global research organizations between them now account for about two-thirds of the world turnover. Quality standards have improved with the establishment of individual-country accreditation processes. The European Federation of Associations of Market Research Organizations has established a European standard, which may be viewed at www.efamro.org/emrqs.htm. This is being considered by the USA, Japan and others as a possible basis for a worldwide standard (Kelly 2002).

The internet, of course, has had a major impact on the market research industry, particularly in the realm of data collection. It may eventually eclipse all other methods, but at present it accounts for only about 3 percent by volume of data collection (Kelly 2002). While the internet offers new opportunities for, for example, interaction with respondents, it raises its own questions of sampling, privacy and reliability. The emergence of Data Protection legislation in Europe has also had a major impact on the industry.

KEY POINTS

The market research industry in Europe is big business and it is growing at a steady rate. However, it is increasingly being dominated by a few large suppliers and by the explosion of information technologies. All this has had a considerable impact on the role of the market researcher.

The changing role of the market researcher

The practice of research has been greatly affected by developments in information and communications technologies. In many ways it has made the whole process much more efficient. In particular the ability to acquire and to handle ever greater volumes of data and to conduct more sophisticated and complex data analyses has meant that market researchers are increasingly becoming information service providers who have to assemble a jigsaw of imperfect data and evidence. Many researchers will have developed day-to-day practices for data analysis that are currently largely hidden from view – craft skills that as yet have not been articulated and which do not correspond with the research methods detailed in the textbooks.

Researchers nowadays need a new set of information competencies in order to handle the ever-growing, but multisource and variable-quality data. Craft skills need to include the ability to scan, gut and action information (Smith and Fletcher 2001). In particular, say Smith and Fletcher, they need to be able to:

- classify and reduce incoming information very quickly,
- evaluate its likely quality,
- embrace intuition and gut feeling,
- interweave a patchwork of evidence,
- build conceptual models.

When the researcher is dealing with information, he or she needs to:

- check for robustness,
- spot the storyline.

Checking for robustness entails things like reviewing the credibility of the information, its internal consistency, the underlying assumptions being made, the professionalism involved in its construction, the motivation of the information-providers, any likely embellishments or "spin" put on the data, plus corroboration from other sources.

Getting the storyline means:

- understanding the different kinds of summary that may be provided – abstracts, introductions, conclusions, recommendations, action points, sound bites,
- assimilating large volumes of information, for example by using the preview, question, read, reflect, recite and review sequence.

The way in which researchers operate has been affected at all levels by technology. High-quality documents for briefings, proposals, reports and presentations can now be easily produced. Documents can be sent instantly to clients, while face-to-face meetings can now be held using video-conferencing technology. Using the internet it is possible to get access to company information and to census data, for example via the UK Census Dissemination Unit (http://census.ac.uk/cdu). Optical mark readers can scan completed questionnaires or answers can be entered directly onto a database using portable data entry terminals. Computer-aided wireless interviewing (CAWI) means that interviewers can be guided through a questionnaire and the answers transmitted instantly to a database.

Ethical issues

Ethics are moral principles or standards that guide the ways in which individuals treat their fellow human beings in situations where they can cause actual or potential harm, whether economic, physical or mental. Ethics in marketing research are concerned with professional standards of conduct and with the use of techniques in ways that avoid harm to respondents, to clients or to other parties. Ethical standards are important in a research context so that those involved in the research appreciate what is and what is not acceptable behavior.

Market researchers depend for the effective practice of their profession on the goodwill and participation by the public. At the same time members of society are becoming increasingly aware of their rights and sensitive about invasions of their privacy. Any individual, company or agency that violates the implicit trust of participants in a study makes it more difficult and more costly for *all* market researchers to approach and recruit survey respondents or participants to group discussions. Good ethical standards are good business. In consequence, various associations whose members are involved in market research have developed codes of conduct to guide the behavior of their members. ESOMAR has produced a set of European standards which are detailed in Box 1.7.

The main ethical issues that arise in the conduct of client-based marketing research concern:

IN DETAIL

BOX 1.7

The ICC/ESOMAR International Code of Marketing and Social Research Practice

The first ESOMAR code was published in 1948. This was followed by a number of codes that were prepared by national marketing research bodies and by the International Chamber of Commerce (ICC). In 1976, ESOMAR and the ICC decided it would be preferable to have a single international code. A new version was prepared in 1994. This new code states that, in general, marketing research must always:

- be carried out objectively and in accordance with established scientific principles,
- conform to the national and international legislation which applies in those countries involved in a given research project.

Beyond that, the code spells out the rights of respondents, the professional responsibilities of researchers, and the mutual rights and responsibilities of researchers and clients. The rights of respondents include, for example, that their cooperation be entirely voluntary at all stages, they must not be misled when their cooperation is sought, their rights of anonymity must be strictly observed, that they be in no way adversely affected by their participation and they must be told if observation or recording equipment is being used.

The professional responsibilities of researchers include that they must not make false claims about their skills and experience, they must not unjustly criticize other researchers, they should always strive for cost-efficient research designs and they must ensure the security of all records in their possession.

The mutual rights and responsibilities include, for example, the notion that the researcher must inform the client if results are to be shared or syndicated in the same project, they must inform the client if any work is to be subcontracted, and that marketing briefs and marketing data remain the property of the client.

The full code can be checked out on the ESOMAR website: **www.esomar.org**

- privacy,
- confidentiality,
- deception,
- imposition,
- integrity,
- misrepresentation.

If a market researcher telephones a respondent to obtain an interview late on a Sunday evening, or if a researcher observes a customer's behavior in a shop without the customer's knowledge, are these instances of invasion of privacy? It might be argued that since anybody can observe behavior in public places, then the latter example is not unethical, particularly since no harm is involved. In the former case there may be mental harm if the outcome is the annoyance of the householder.

The issue of confidentiality might affect both respondents and, if commissioned research, clients. If respondents are told or reassured that their replies will be treated with confidentiality, then it will be unethical for the researcher to pass this information onto other parties, for example by selling mailing lists. If a client does not wish to be identified to respondents, then it would be unethical for interviewers to pass this information on. If the researcher is working on behalf of a particular client, then confidential information about the business should not be passed on to competitors.

Deception may come in many forms. Misleading a respondent into thinking that an interview will take five minutes when the researcher knows it will take 20 is unethical. Covertly numbering questionnaires that are meant to be "anonymous" so that the researcher can determine who has and who has not returned them could also be seen to be deception.

Respondents' rights to be able to refuse to grant an interview need to be respected and they should not be pressurized. No adverse effects should result from participating in research, like receiving unsolicited sales material or price rises that result from questions about what maximum prices people would accept for a product.

Integrity includes both the technical and administrative integrity of the research so that the results are not "doctored" or "massaged" in any way or tied up in jargon just to baffle the client. Lack of integrity shades into misrepresentation in which research results are presented in a way likely to mislead readers or clients. This might include deliberately withholding information, misusing statistics or ignoring relevant data.

KEY POINTS

It is in the market research industry's own interests to adhere very strictly to clear guidelines that protect respondents, informants, the general public, the business community and clients.

Data protection

The 1995 European Data Protection Directive is concerned with the rights of individuals who are asked for or who provide information about themselves. In particular it seeks to protect their rights to privacy by establishing the core principles of transparency and consent. Transparency means ensuring that individuals have a clear understanding about why the data are being collected or requested and how they will be used. Individuals must, furthermore, give their consent to data collection and be given the opportunity to opt out of any subsequent uses of the data.

ESOMAR gives the advice in Box 1.8.

The implementation of the EU Directive has varied across countries, which causes problems for international research – it causes confusion, it adds to costs and undermines the free flow of research services. In the UK it is enshrined in the 1998 Data Protection Act. The Act requires that all those bodies who collect personal data (the data controllers) notify the Data Protection Commissioner that they intend to hold personal data and they will need to meet fairly stringent conditions. The Market Research Society has attempted to give advice on some of these issues in a document published in October 2002 and updated in January 2004. This is available for download at **www.marketresearch.org.uk/code.htm**. The MRS has agreed a classification of different types of research with the Office of the Information Commissioner. There are five types of "classic" research that, in effect, are bound by the MRS Code of Conduct. Here strict limits have been agreed on the feedback that researchers can give to owners of customer databases where these have been used for sampling purposes, and for sensitive data it has been agreed that "explicit" consent means consent based on a detailed explanation of how the data will be used. A sixth type of data is used for direct marketing and does not fall within the MRS Code of Conduct.

IN DETAIL
How European data protection legislation affects market research

BOX 1.8

Tapes and videos must be regarded as personal data, and you must follow the revised ESOMAR Guideline on this subject relating to respondent permissions. Care must also be taken that even where the data are anonymous there is no element of identifiability. By that it is meant that there is a low probability of an individual being recognized, for example in the way a lottery winner can be identified as being a blue-eyed one-legged Englishman with five cats living in Salerno. Clients will often not be aware of the law and how it affects market research. Care must be taken to give the proper advice. Ignorance or action for a third party is not a defence. The law covers the actions of all companies in the EU and any transfer of data to other countries outside of the EU. Transferring completely anonymous data is OK, but personal data, even a sampling frame, must have the same rules observed by end users as if they were in the EU. The best way to ensure this is through the terms and conditions of your contracts.

Consent

For the collection of most data ahead of their being made anonymous, the agreement to participate in an interview is, as we understand, an adequate consent. However, the Directive introduces a new category of data which is "sensitive" data. This covers such things as ethnicity, religion, trade union membership, medical records, sexual orientation, criminal records and political opinions. For this category of data "explicit" consent is required, but not defined. We are advised that this probably is agreement to participate at the time of interview, but that is a view not shared, it would seem, by all countries. The need to get prior written consent as has been suggested in some places would totally undermine the conduct of legitimate opinion polling, both in terms of accuracy, cost and speed. However, mindful of the current conflict, we need to demonstrate that we are aware of the sensitivities of these areas and that any self-regulation is effective and universal within our own area of control.

SUMMARY

Client-based market research is concerned with the construction, analysis and interpretation of data both on organizations and on their environments, so that information can be provided to assist client organizations in diagnosing, deciding and delivering marketing strategies and tactics. It has several features that make it very different from academic research. Organizations need such research to help them to make better and more informed decisions; this it can do in a number of different ways.

Market research for clients may be of several different types depending on the type of data collected, the intended duration of the research, the degree of customization, the amount of value added and the type of customer being researched. The process of designing research for clients involves a number of stages, some of which may be done by the client and some by the researcher. The final stage is usually the production of a research proposal on the basis of which research services are bought and sold. From a client perspective, the objective is to buy research that is good value and which addresses the problems, issues or opportunities faced by the company. From the perspective of the agency, the goal will be to load the agency with commissions that are profitable and utilize its main competencies.

The European market research industry is a multimillion Euro industry that consists of suppliers of research services, the research buyers and the profession. Research suppliers are of many different types, from the full-service agency to a highly specialist single-service organization. The profession is well-served with a number of professional bodies and trade associations.

The role of market researchers is quickly changing to take account of the information technology revolution. Increasingly they are becoming information service providers who need to be able to scan, gut and action data. At the same time this process is becoming more complex as it has to take on board new legislation on data protection and a growing array of ethical issues.

QUESTIONS FOR DISCUSSION

1   Explain why not-for-profit organizations may still need market research services.

2   To what extent has data protection legislation hampered the efforts of market researchers in Europe?

3   In what ways will developments in new technologies make it easier or more difficult for the inexperienced research buyer?

4   Now that the advertising of cigarettes has been banned in the UK and in a number of other countries, a cigarette manufacturer is seeking advice on how to promote its products without using advertising or sponsorship of sport. Outline some of the ethical issues faced by a market researcher who is considering taking on this commission.

5   Read the article by Castell and Thompson, which is listed in *Further reading* below, and consider the ethical issues it raises.

CASE STUDY FLYMO

The British invention of the Hovercraft was the inspiration for the Swedish inventor Karl Dahlman to develop a lawnmower that could float on a cushion of air in any direction. The concept became the Flymo and the first models hit the shops in 1965. Since that time, according to Hartley (2003), Flymo, now owned by Electrolux Outdoor products, has become the number one name in lawnmowers in the UK, capturing over 99 percent of the hover grass collect category. However, since 1997, hover collect mowers, as a share of powered mowers sold, was losing its market share. This was bad news for Flymo since the hover collect mowers represented 25 percent of sales and 30 percent of revenue. Flymo's brand support until 2001 had been sporadic – the brand had not been advertised on television since 1996. A press campaign in 1999 followed by a major sales promotion in 200 resulted in only a 0.5 percent growth in Flymo's share of the DIY superstore powered lawnmower market, in a total market that had grown by over 30 percent. Flymo's core brand values – innovative, differentiated and easy-to-use – were, says Hartley (2003), being undermined by this lack of brand support and the overreliance on price and sales promotions.

Questions and activities

1 Diagnose the nature, urgency and seriousness of the problems facing Flymo. List some of the company strengths and weaknesses. What are the threats and opportunities posed by the marketplace? Try looking at the Flymo website, **www.flymo.co.uk** and at the Electrolux website, **www.electrolux.com**.

2 Consider the different types of marketing research that might be useful to Electrolux in protecting its long-term business.

FURTHER READING

Castell, S. and Thompson, J. (2005) "Fair trade research", *Market Research Society*, Annual Conference, Brighton.

De Vaus, D. (2001) *Research Design in Social Research*. London: Sage.

Kelly, J. (2002) "The market research industry. View from the bridge", *Admap*, June, Issue 429.

Roe, M. (2004) *Marketing Research in Action*. London: Thomson Learning.

Smith, D. and Fletcher, J. (2001) *Inside Information. Making Sense of Marketing Data*. Chichester: John Wiley & Sons.

Smith, D. and Fletcher, J. (2004) *The Art and Science of Interpreting Market Research Evidence*. Chichester: John Wiley & Sons.

Academic research in marketing

2

Academics usually decide for themselves what research they wish to undertake.

© REBECCA ELLIS

INTRODUCTION

Academic research in marketing is very different from client-based research. It is undertaken for scholarly purposes – largely for publication or to meet the requirements of undergraduate, postgraduate or doctoral qualifications. It is evaluated on a totally different basis from client-based research. Its key aim is to add to our understanding of the way in which marketing phenomena work; it builds upon the work of others who have undertaken research previously and makes its findings as widely available as possible.

INTERNET ACTIVITY

Using your browser, go to **www.thomsonlearning.co.uk/kent** and select the Chapter 2 Internet Activity which will provide a link to the ESRC Society Today website. Select *Funding Opportunities*, then *Postgraduate Training* then *Postgraduate Training Guidelines*. Go to *Framework for research methods training*. In particular look at *Principles of research design*. How does this compare with the elements of research design explained in Chapter 1 in the context of client-based research?

The nature of academic, scholarly research

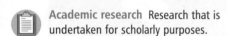

Academic research Research that is undertaken for scholarly purposes.

In Chapter 1 we saw that client-based marketing research is concerned with the construction, analysis and interpretation of data both on organizations and on their environments, so that information can be provided to assist clients in diagnosing, deciding and delivering marketing strategies and tactics. The aim of such research is to deliver value to clients and to provide data, information and insight that are relevant and actionable.

Academic research, while still concerned with the construction, analysis and interpretation of data, is undertaken for scholarly purposes rather than on behalf of clients. The academic decides what he or she wishes to research and for what ends. This might, for example, be for publication in scholarly journals or in trade journals, for books or book chapters, to meet the requirements of a formal academic qualification, or to be in a position to apply for research funding or in pursuit of research that has already obtained funding.

Research that is undertaken by academics in the marketing area has a number of key features that contrast strongly with client-based research. First, unlike client-based research, there is no client and therefore no brief. It is up to the researcher to determine the topic and the approach. How academics come to undertake the research that they do is a complex issue. In some cases this may be a continuation of research begun as part of a master's degree or a doctorate; in others it may be a result of groups of academics within departments who have agreed to cooperate on a particular topic or project. In many cases, however, it is probably pure serendipity – coming across a book or an article that by chance happens to stimulate an academic to pursue a topic in more depth, or a chance meeting with other people, as described in Box 2.1.

RESEARCH IN ACTION
Beginning academic research in marketing

BOX 2.1

I was born in Cardiff, the capital of Wales. At school I took part in St David's Day celebrations wearing traditional Welsh dress. I sang songs in the old language and recited *penillion* verse at Eisteddfodau, our celebrations of traditional Welsh folk culture. Yet being Welsh, to me, was never just about speaking the language. Being Welsh was and still is about having a feeling of belonging to my own nation, a country with its own capital city and unique identity. Being Welsh meant being part of a heritage of music and poetry, of mythology, of the tales of the *Mabinogi*, of stories about fire-breathing dragons, and old tales of Welsh heroes.

I grew up proud to be Welsh and I was completely amazed to find that, when the family went abroad on holiday, few of the non-British people we met even knew where my country was. For most of these people Wales had no point of reference until England was mentioned.

I also grew up with a love of music in Wales, the "land of song". Singing was, and still is, one of my passions. Songs, such as "Myfanwy", sung in four-part harmony by a male voice choir, can still send a shiver down my spine. As a teenager I left behind the old Welsh songs as I was becoming increasingly interested in popular music. But as a teenager in the mid 1970s, the Welsh representatives in mainstream popular music comprised Mary Hopkin, Shakin' Stevens, Bonny Tyler and Tom Jones. Where were my Welsh heroes now, when I needed them most?

In 1998 I was staying at a hotel in North Devon and got talking to a young couple from London. They told me about a new song they had just heard on the radio. It was a song by a Welsh band, and was sung with a strong Welsh accent. The song, "Mulder and Scully", by Catatonia, made no reference to the hills and valleys of Wales, did not have lyrics about mines, daffodils, leeks or dragons but the band was defined as Welsh. The young English couple raved on about this new Welsh band and their new song. The success of the song seemed to prove that a Welsh band had become acceptable to a mainstream popular music audience. This new-found acceptability seemed to be borne out with the successes of other bands such as the Stereophonics and the Manic Street Preachers.

So when I had to choose a topic to research for my master's dissertation I was curious to establish if marketing could provide any answers to this phenomenon. In particular, the focus of my work was to establish whether the successes of these up and coming Welsh bands helped establish a new Welsh branding, and what influence that branding had on mainstream popular music.

I completed my master's dissertation at the University of Glamorgan in December 2000, with the grand title: "An Examination of the Influence of Welsh Branding in Mainstream Popular Music".

Heather Skinner is now Senior Lecturer in Marketing at the University of Glamorgan. She has since published nine academic journal articles and 23 conference papers, 12 of which are on the topic of nation-branding.

Since academic researchers are not operating on behalf of any client, they will usually attempt to be neutral, objective and non-partisan. In practice these are probably more aspiration than accomplishment. Some researchers might even take issue with the very idea of objectivity and argue that this is impossible to achieve. For the most part they will also be noninterventionist. They will often not make or seek to make changes, although there may well be recommendations for change as a result of doing the research and some academic research may be experimental in design and will manipulate variables that are seen to be the independent variables. There is also a form of research called **action research**, which is designed specifically to promote social change. In the marketing area, what is called **social marketing** might involve using marketing principles to change behavior, for example in terms of encouraging people to eat more fruit, to consume less fat, to stop taking drugs or not to smoke tobacco. In action research, it is believed that the best way to test a theory is to make changes and see if it works in practice.

A central goal of all academic research is to add to the stock of publicly available knowledge and understanding of marketing issues and phenomena, so the research is knowledge-led rather than client-led. This also means that the researcher will seek to publish the results. The audience, then, will be largely an academic one, but there will also, hopefully, be a business audience, and students are always being asked to put effort or more effort into providing managerial implications for their dissertations or theses. It is also true that academic researchers may investigate phenomena that can offer insight to commercial organizations. Compared with client-based research, deadlines will tend to be more flexible and costs less important.

Action research Research that is designed to promote social change or improve particular situations.

Social marketing Using marketing principles to change social behavior.

In academic research a key role is played by theory – either the use, illustration or development of existing theory, or the generation of new theory. The nature, role and types of theory and the use of models in academic marketing research are explained later in this chapter.

Academic research will be judged on its scientific rigor rather than by the level of client satisfaction. For student dissertations, whether for undergraduate or postgraduate studies or doctoral theses, key criteria will include:

- how well the topic or issue has been "problematized" so that the research can become, at least in part, the solution,
- a clear statement of the aims and objectives of the research,
- a clear rationale for the design of the research,
- a literature review that demonstrates a sound knowledge of the field and a critical appreciation of the key ideas and their development,
- an explanation of the data construction and data analysis techniques and how these are relevant to the research objectives,
- conclusions that are persuasive and supported by the data,
- the integration of the data with existing theory and evidence,
- the logical and internal consistency of the line of argument,
- originality of thinking.

Articles, books and indeed almost all conference papers will have been subjected to some kind of review process that judges them against scholarly criteria. Articles submitted for publication will be sent by the editor to two or three reviewers or referees for comment and evaluation. The referees, who will be established researchers on the topic of the article, will be asked to evaluate the manuscript, taking into account specified criteria that will include, for example, the significance of the article to marketing learning and management, its originality and innovativeness, the soundness of its methodology, analysis, structure and relevance, and the appropriateness of the author's writing style for an audience of academics in marketing. The review process is explained in more detail in Chapter 18.

Academic research, then, is very different from client-based research. The key contrasts are summarized in Table 2.1. Some academics do undertake client-based research, but in most universities there is a limit to the amount of such research academic staff are allowed to pursue. They tend to be judged on their output of articles accepted for publication by scholarly journals, the presentation of conference papers, the writing of books or contributions to edited books, and the amount of

TABLE 2.1	Some contrasts between client-based research and academic research
Client-based research	**Academic research**
Client brief	No brief
Committed	Neutral
Interventionist	Non-interventionist
Judged on solving the problem	Judged on scientific rigor
Little review of theory	Literature review essential
Goal – to satisfy client	Goal – to add to stock of publicly available knowledge/theory/understanding
Management report the key output	Scholarly publication the key output
Costing very important	Often necessary only to cover expenses
Business/organizational audience	Mostly academic audience
Time-constrained	Timing often open-ended

research monies obtained to pursue academic or policy-oriented research. In the UK, universities and the departments within them are subjected to periodic reviews called a Research Assessment Exercise (RAE) in which the scholarly contributions of each member of the academic staff to outlets of national and international standing are summed and evaluated. The process is described in Box 2.2.

IN DETAIL
The Research Assessment Exercise in the UK

BOX 2.2

The Research Assessment Exercise is carried out on a periodic six-year cycle basis by the four UK higher education funding bodies for England, Wales, Scotland and Northern Ireland. Its purpose is to provide authoritative and comprehensive quality ratings for research in all disciplines carried out in universities and colleges across the UK. These ratings are then used to inform the funding bodies' allocation of grants for research. The review is undertaken by a discipline-based panel of experts. So far, five such exercises have been carried out, the first in 1986. The next one is planned for 2008. Academic staff in departments who are identified as "research active" are asked to identify up to four pieces of work that are submitted for assessment. A key distinction that is made is between publications that are deemed to have "international" significance and those reaching only a "national" level of excellence. Departments or subject areas are awarded an overall rating with 5* at the top, going down to 5, 4, 3, 2 and 1.

KEY POINTS

Academic research is researcher-led rather than client-led. It is neutral and it is noninterventionist (except perhaps in the shape of experimental manipulations or action research). The advancement of theory and its links to previous literature in the field is crucially important. Academic research is judged on its scientific rigor; it is aimed at a largely academic audience and its results are for as wide a dissemination as practicable.

Philosophical underpinnings

All research, whether client-based or academic, makes certain assumptions about the nature of the "reality" that is being studied, about how "knowledge" is produced and about the angle or perspective from which the research is approached. These assumptions are seldom made explicit or are even discussed when the results of research operations are being presented – except perhaps in doctoral theses, where this is normally an expectation. In most books on research methodology in the social sciences – and even occasionally in marketing – there is a chapter on the "philosophy of research", which explains these assumptions in some detail. This branch of philosophy is not something that client-based marketing researchers concern themselves with. They may well not even be aware of its existence. Academic researchers are more likely to have engaged with some of the issues at some point in their careers, particularly if they are more inclined towards undertaking qualitative research, but are nevertheless unlikely to explicitly consider these issues when either planning or reporting the results of research. In many ways, this is a pity, since an explicit attention to alternative assumptions that might be made would enable researchers to see how inquiries could be approached in very different ways.

Ontology A branch of metaphysics that is concerned with the nature of reality.

What follows is an attempt to explain the nature of the various assumptions as simply as possible, even though many of the issues are in fact quite complex. Discussion about the nature of reality is a branch of metaphysics that is called **ontology**. Some researchers, for example, assume that there is a "real", single reality "out there" that can be observed, categorized and measured, and, furthermore, that it exists independently of consciousness or experience and remains unaltered by our attempts to study it. In this respect, social science, which includes marketing, is no different from natural science. Protagonists argue that the social sciences can hope to emulate the natural sciences in their achievements only if they at least act *as if* this assumption were true. Critics contend that such assumptions ignore the ability of individuals to reflect and to act upon those reflections.

An alternative is to assume that "reality" is constructed by individuals who impose meanings on objects and situations. This is particularly true for relationships like "trust", "hostility" or "loyalty"; such relationships are continually defined, redefined, negotiated or renegotiated. Researchers cannot observe "trust", for example, but need to infer it from what people say, what they tell us and what they do. Even physical objects, it can be argued, make no contribution to the generation of meaning. The result may be that there are multiple local and specific realities. Alternatively, there may be a single reality, but one that is shaped by social, economic, ethnic, political, cultural and gender values and which emerges and develops over time. Critics argue that these assumptions are inappropriate for business research since they ignore the clearly real economic, technological and physical dimensions of business.

A compromise is to believe that there *is* a real world to discover, but that it is only imperfectly knowable. Perceptions are not reality, but a *window* on to reality through which a more complete picture of it can be built up. Miles and Huberman (1994) talk about "transcendental realism" – social phenomena exist not only in the mind, but also in the objective world. Patterns of connections between phenomena can be found through observed regularities and sequences. Phenomena like language, decisions, conflicts and hierarchies exist objectively in the world and exert strong influences over human activities because people believe in them and construe them in common ways. Reality is "transcendental" in the sense that it cannot be observed, but can be explained by building theories to account for the real world.

Epistemology An area of philosophy that is concerned with how knowledge is established.

What in the philosophy of research is called **epistemology** relates to researchers' implicit or explicit assumptions about how "knowledge" is established. According to a "positivist" epistemology, the scientist "knows" by following the correct scientific procedure, a procedure based on that of the natural sciences. While there have been many different attempts to outline the key characteristics of positivism and several different varieties have been identified, essentially it means that objectively verifiable knowledge is possible in the social sciences by setting up and then testing hypotheses that relate to identifiable and measurable variables.

An alternative epistemology is to assume that we can only "know" through outcomes – that "the proof is in the pudding". Knowledge consists of ideas that work, and we can often find out what works only by trying things out and making changes to situations. Some proponents of this epistemology argue for methodological anarchy – that anything goes. Anything that might solve the problem is worth a try. While the positivist is detached from the subjects of his or her studies, the "activist" is involved or engaged on their behalf.

According to those who follow what is often referred to as interpretive epistemology, we can only "know" through understanding – through emotional and sympathetic empathy with those whose behavior we wish to explain. Individuals understand and interpret the world around them. They define situations in particular ways and this will guide their behavior. The world is already interpreted before the scientist arrives and it is these interpretations the scientist must understand.

Apart from making different ontological and epistemological assumptions, researchers may approach their inquiries from the **perspective** of the researcher himself or herself, from the perspective of those whose behavior is being researched, or, in the case of commissioned research, from that of a client or in the case of academic research from the perspective of society, the organization or some other social unit.

Perspective From whose viewpoint a piece of research is being conducted, for example the researcher, the client or the research subjects.

Together the ontology, epistemology and perspective adopted by the researcher constitute the philosophical underpinnings of the particular research being proposed or undertaken. They lay the foundations for the theories, methods and techniques used in the research design. Typical research is not, however, a random collection of the various elements that make up the philosophical underpinnings. Many elements tend to be found together. Thus an objectivist ontology tends to be found along with a positivist epistemology and a researcher perspective. These typical patterns may be called **paradigms**. A paradigm is an exemplar – research that is firmly based on a particular style of inquiry that a scientific community acknowledges for a time as supplying the foundation for its further practice (Kuhn 1996). Paradigms act for a time as a common point of reference for all investigations in the area, shaping the discipline's sense of where its problems lie, what its appropriate tools and methods are and the kinds of solutions it might accept as warranted.

Paradigm An exemplar that is firmly based on a particular style of enquiry that a scientific community acknowledges for a time as supplying the foundation for its further practice.

In marketing research, three major paradigms may be distinguished. These paradigms bring together particular positions on ontology, epistemology, perspective, theory, method and technique as summarized in Table 2.2. The three paradigms are certainly not mutually exclusive; indeed the various elements may, in practice, be combined in various ways. Each paradigm represents a different way of "doing science" and *any* topic can be studied using *any* of the paradigms. Different versions of "the truth" can, accordingly, emerge.

Imagine the following scene. On the floor of a hotel room lies, face down, arms and legs spreadeagled, the body of a man. In his right hand there is a gun. Blood is spreading across the carpet from a wound in the head. Beside the body is a piece of paper with a quickly scrawled note that says, "*Jane, I love you*". Four men enter the room; one a uniformed policeman and three casually dressed in somewhat crumpled jacket and trousers. The policeman speaks first: "As clear-cut a case of suicide as I've seen. Very sad. I don't know why they do it . . . but, I understand you three gentlemen are sociologists. How do you explain suicides like this?"

One of the men hunches his shoulders and spreads out his hands in a gesture of mystification. He says:

Suicide is, unfortunately, common to all societies. Curiously, however, while the rate of suicide varies considerably from society to society, it tends to remain remarkably constant from year to year within any one society. For

TABLE 2.2	Paradigms in marketing research					
Paradigm: researcher as	**Ontology**	**Epistemology**	**Perspective**	**Theory**	**Method**	**Technique**
Physicist	Objectivist	Positivist	Researcher	Deductive	Quantitative research	Quantitative analysis
Physician	Realist	Activist	Client	Mixed	Mixed	Mixed
Psychiatrist	Subjectivist	Interpretive	Participant	Inductive	Qualitative research	Qualitative analysis

example, in England and Wales in 2003, 3580 men and 1216 women committed suicide, a total of 4796. That gives an annual suicide rate of 17 per 100 000 for men and 5.4 per 100 000 for women. These rates have varied little from year to year. The suicide rate can thus only be related to social, not individual, factors in society. Sociologists many years ago suggested that lack of social integration, or the breakdown of normal social order, correlates positively with a high rate of suicide in any given community. Statistics indeed show that in a period of rapid economic, social or political change suicide rates increase. Now this poor man may have been prone to suicide by virtue of his psychological make-up, but it will have been social factors that lead people like him to actually carry out the act. Individuals in our society are led to expect happiness, freedom from poverty and a satisfying career. If they are denied access to these they will react by committing crime, becoming mentally ill, getting divorced and so on – and in the extreme, committing suicide. As we begin to learn more about the causes of suicide, we will be able to predict those who are at risk.

"Well, thank you for that detailed explanation" says the policeman, "but do the others agree?" Another of the men has frizzy white hair, a long white beard and wears small round spectacles. He is clenching his right fist and punching the opened palm of his left hand:

It's all very well for my colleague to want to predict suicide rates; surely, the whole point is to DO something about it! It is not social change that is the problem: it is lack of radical change. You can see that this man has the hands of a common labourer; a man who owned nothing and who had only his labour to sell. He did not even own the products of his work. In this society of ours, such workers are exploited by those who own the means of production – the capitalists. Such workers are alienated from their work, they are alienated from society – even from themselves. It is no wonder that some of them are driven to such drastic measures. We must look for the real causes of this man's suicide in the history of the domination of one social class by another – of slaves by master, serfs by lords, and now workers by managers. Only then can we see that he is a victim of the conflict between the proletariat and the bourgeoisie. The only way to stop this form of social injustice is to overthrow the capitalist system. Only then will there be no exploiters and exploited. Philosophers – and too many sociologists – have only studied the world. The whole point is to do something about it. If you are not part of the solution, you are part of the problem.

"Good heavens, now I'm confused" confesses the policemen. "A completely different story – but what about you, sir, which of these gentlemen do you agree with?" "Well neither" says the remaining person, wagging his finger at the other two.

Both my colleagues seem to be utterly indifferent to this man and the personal troubles that have led to his death. I find it interesting that both my colleagues – and indeed the good constable here – have all assumed that this man did commit "suicide" as you call it. How do we know that he intended to take his own life? What evidence and what procedures did the police use to come to their verdict? It's all very well talking about different suicide rates, but these may be just a consequence of different procedures for recording suicide verdicts. What counts as a "suicide" for one person and in one society may not in another. It is we who are labeling this man's death as a "suicide" according to the meaning we attribute to his act. That may not be how he saw the situation. We cannot, of course, ask him now, but we could ask his friends, his family, his neighbors and build up a picture of this man's life and what led him to this act. If we want to understand suicide as a phenomenon then we must study carefully the meanings that people attach to their social lives.

So, here we have three completely different "explanations" of the same situation. One is assuming that suicide is a fact; a reality that exists out there that we can measure and predict. Another is arguing that while suicide clearly exists as a phenomenon, it needs to be understood and interpreted through a particular lens such as dialectical materialism. A third argues that suicide is a label that reflects meanings that are attributed to certain actions. Each is a way of "doing science", just as the nuclear physicist, the physician and the psychiatrist all practice their professions, but in very different ways following different paradigms. It may be helpful to extend this analogy and to develop the idea of the marketing physicist, the marketing physician and the marketing psychiatrist.

The marketing physicist

The marketing physicist sees markets or organizations as *systems* with structures of components that are interrelated, and that can be independently observed, measured, analyzed and predicted. The search is for patterns and regularities that may be explained in terms of theories that apply in a variety of different contexts. The model is very much that of the natural sciences. The validity of the research is judged by asking: were the correct scientific procedures followed? These procedures are based on a set of underlying principles.

- Only phenomena that can be observed can be used to validate knowledge. This rules out all forms of subjective experience.
- Scientific knowledge is arrived at through the accumulation of verified facts derived from systematic observation or record-keeping.
- Scientific theories are used to describe patterns of relationships between these facts and to establish causal connections between them.
- The process is neutral and judgment-free. Observations are uncontaminated by the scientist's own predilections. Thus ethical issues can be included only if they are included as part of the research.

The steps involved in undertaking this kind of research are fairly standard.

1 Begin with the theory that relates to the issue or problem to be studied.
2 Deduce from the theory what you would expect to find in reality.
3 Generate hypotheses that can be tested.
4 Decide how the variables in the hypotheses are to be measured.
5 Decide what other variables need to be controlled.
6 Collect the data.
7 Analyze the data.
8 Report the results.
9 Relate the findings back to the theory.

The objective is to produce scientifically verified knowledge. Personal values are sources of bias and must be eliminated from the process of inquiry. The proper relationship between the marketing physicist and the organizations and individuals that are the object of inquiry is one of emotional, professional and judgmental detachment. The desired state is one of value-neutrality. Ethical and social problems are translated into technical issues. Their resolution is a matter of applying appropriate techniques of observation, measurement and analysis.

The marketing physicist has his or her own rhetoric, which includes reference to dependent and independent variables, hypotheses, correlation, sampling,

Some marketing researchers see themselves as "real" scientists.

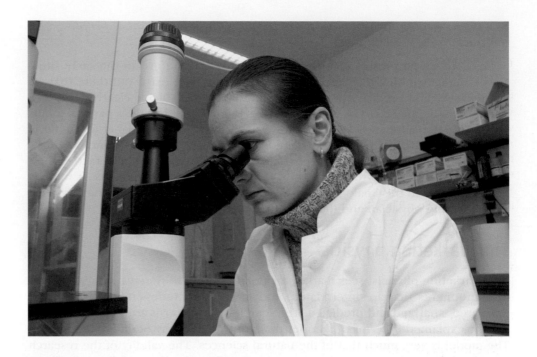

statistical significance, experiment, testing, validity, reliability, causality, generalization and replication. These are the stuff of language to which scientific nostrils are attuned.

The marketing physician

A physician is a specialist in medical diagnosis and treatment. The marketing physician sees organizations, markets or consumers as the "patient" whose ailments and symptoms need to be identified before remedies can be sought. In place of detachment and neutrality is intervention and open partisanship. The physician *cares* about what happens – the aim is to make the patient well again. There is no pretence at being neutral – the physician takes sides – usually the side of the organization which is the focus of the research. The goal is not to *study* social, economic or political problems – it is to *do* something about them – to find solutions or make changes.

Societies, social groups, markets or organizations do not, from this perspective, constitute some kind of balanced and integrated system of mutually interdependent parts, but a vast arena or battlefield where struggles between health and sickness or between competitors takes place. Instead of a medical analogy, a military analogy is sometimes drawn, for example Kotler (1997) suggests that in competitive industries there are strategies for market leaders that include attack, pre-emptive, counteroffensive and mobile defence; there are strategies for market challengers that include frontal attack, encirclement attack and guerrilla attack – and so on. Social science as a form of medical practice or type of military campaign is very much an activist discipline. It is about finding means to achieve ends – what some sociologists would call "functionalist". The concern is as much with what ought to be as with what is. The ultimate goal is not the acquisition of scientifically validated knowledge for its own sake, but the achievement of company growth, profits or other organizational goals. The marketing physician is personally involved in prescribing treatments and monitoring their effects. At the end of the day, it is the results that count and which underpin the validity of an idea or an action.

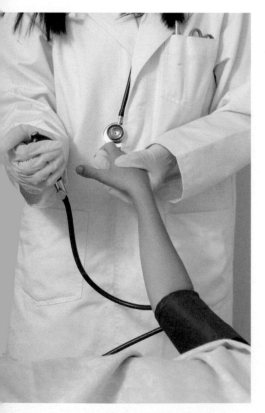

Some marketing researchers see themselves as diagnosing and solving problems.

The marketing psychiatrist

From this perspective, reality is in the mind. It is a subjective, constructed reality – there is no "objective" reality "out there" to be observed and measured. People construct multiple realities so it is necessary to empathize with them if we wish to understand them. Marketing phenomena need to be studied from the perspective of those being researched. To do this the researcher must build up a picture of the realities people construct from the ground up – from specimens of behavior, from careful observation, and above all by asking people about themselves. Markets and organizations are neither an organized system of interrelated parts, nor a battle-field, but an immense gallery of exhibits – of specimens of consumer and organizational behavior. The goal of the marketing psychiatrist is not the accumulation of verified knowledge nor the pursuit of organizational goals, but of understanding. The researcher is neither detached from values nor engaged in them – rather the researcher examines the role values play in the construction of reality. Validity is sought neither in objective analysis nor in the effects of active intervention, but in the views and perspectives of participants in marketing exchanges. The marketer is also, of course, a participant – his or her reflexivity is not just an open admission of values and biases, but rather an awareness of self in the act of studying exchange behavior.

The interpretive perspective comes in a number of subvarieties, some of which have very impressive-sounding names like phenomenology, ethnomethodology, semiotics and ethnography. Some of these are explained in Chapter 10 in the context of analyzing qualitative data. What they have in common, however, is that they focus on how people construct, communicate, negotiate and renegotiate meanings. They are concerned with attitudes, perceptions and interpretations.

There are problems associated with the perspective of the marketing psychiatrist. First, there is the problem of interpretation – how feasible is it to perceive as others perceive? Will not different researchers come up with different interpretations? Second, there is the problem of induction. Concepts, hypotheses, theories, models are all likely to emerge *from* the research rather than be imposed beforehand. While "grounded theory" may have its advantages, the fact that it can never be disproven by the same data that suggested it in the first place means that the data can be consistent with many different interpretations with no "objective" way of distinguishing between them. Lastly, there is the problem of generalization. If each piece of research is being treated holistically, the findings are unique to the particular case or set of cases under observation.

So, who is correct?

The physicist, the physician and the psychiatrist are all scientists, each performing their discipline in an objective manner, that is, in a way that is uncolored by the emotions and feelings of the researcher. They see themselves as engaged in the application of systematic methods of inquiry to the problems and puzzles of managing marketing exchanges. It is just that there are different versions of "science", one empirical-analytic, with the aim of making predictions and controlling the path of future progress; another diagnostic-prescriptive, which aims at success and liberation from ailment; and a third empathetic-interpretive, which aims at complete understanding by seeking to enter the life-world of others and imaginatively experiencing their experiences.

It is often assumed that the various perspectives are mutually exclusive or incompatible, and that the researcher must choose between them. It could be argued, however, that each is appropriate to different kinds of research problem, so the choice becomes a technical or pragmatic consideration based on a thorough diagnosis of the problem.

Some marketing researchers try to understand their customers.

Alternatively, it is possible to consider how the perspectives might be combined, adding the strengths of each together. From the physicist, for example, we get a focus on what, how and how many. From the physician we investigate means and ends, and from the psychiatrist a focus on why and how something is perceived. Any topic or problem may be studied from each of these perspectives. Take brand loyalty. From the perspective of the physicist, the marketing researcher would be concerned to study the factors that are conducive to brand loyalty, to generate then test theories and hypotheses about these factors; he or she would then investigate brand-switching behavior, changes and trends in market structures and market shares in order to be able to predict the outcomes in terms of loyalty of a range of marketing strategies. From the perspective of the physician, the market researcher will seek to make recommendations to a client organization on the most effective ways of enhancing brand loyalty. He or she will look at schemes operated by competitors, find out what constitutes "best practice" and what action to avoid. The advantages and limitations of a range of measures for enhancing brand loyalty will be studied. Finally, from the perspective of the psychiatrist, the market researcher will seek to understand why consumers are loyal or disloyal to brands. He or she will be concerned with how consumers perceive brands, what images they hold of brands and of the companies that make them.

It is tempting to argue that the researcher should, ideally, do all of these to get a complete and richer picture. In practice there will be competing demands and conflicts of interest. Only the physician takes sides, abandoning neutrality and becoming partisan. Finding the "best" course of action for a client may do little to advance theoretical and empirically substantiated knowledge. The physician is bound by confidentiality – the findings of marketing research must not be revealed to competitors. The physicist, by contrast, is interested in publication.

It must be remembered, furthermore, that the suggested paradigms are analytic constructs that are intended to reflect major divisions and overlaps in ideas and in practices. Marketing researchers, of course, do not call themselves "marketing physicists" or "marketing physicians", but use many other names and labels. Nor should these be treated as categories to "put" particular individuals into. Individuals do, after all, change their minds over the course of their careers. What these "ideal-type" perspectives reflect are tendencies to do marketing or marketing research in a particular way. Nor are they pursued in isolation from one another; rather they form the basis for serious debate, even heated controversy, within the discipline. The marketing psychiatrist is likely to argue that the marketing physicists (whom they often actually call "positivists") are blinkered by their arrogance in believing that they have access to privileged knowledge, that they "know better" than those being studied what their "real" problems are and what the future consequences of their actions will be. They will argue that the physicists and the physicians manufacture their data using the same processes of reality construction that everybody else uses, but that they nevertheless continue to behave as if their data reflected some kind of reality external to their own perceptions of it. The creations of marketing academics and marketing consultants are but a pale reflection of the complexity, the sophistication and the wonder of everyday common sense reality and the process of its creation.

On the other hand the marketing physicists and the physicians will retort that subjective impressions are worthless and amount, in effect, to no more than sophisticated journalism. Any study that is based on the subjective impressions of the researcher cannot be "scientific" as that term is commonly understood. Subjectivism is a moral cop-out. To pretend that validity ultimately lay with the social actor or the consumer is a fraud, since the market researcher cannot avoid the responsibility for deciding whom inquiries are to be made about, what they are to focus on, how many people are to be involved and when "enough" information has been gathered. Physicians accuse both the other perspectives of transforming serious organizational issues into technical problems or into semantic debates about definitions. The physicists, in turn, will accuse the physicians of being partial, or working on behalf of organizations without any clear goals for the betterment of society. So the debate goes on.

KEY POINTS

Except for doctoral theses, philosophical underpinnings are seldom discussed in the reports of academic research. However, it is impossible to avoid making assumptions about the nature of the reality that is being researched, about how scientific knowledge is achieved, and about from whose perspective the research is to be or is being undertaken. Marketing researchers tend to follow or at least emphasize one of three main sets of assumptions that have been characterized in this chapter as the marketing physicist, the marketing physician and the marketing psychiatrist. These are by no means mutually exclusive and researchers may in practice combine elements of each. You may well have found this section heavy going; if you did, then try having another look at it at the end of your course.

The nature and role of theories and models

Theory

Believe it or not, we all use theory in our everyday lives, although we probably do not call it "theory", but perhaps a "hunch" or an "idea". We speculate about the world around us, we make generalizations based on past experience, and we use these generalizations to make predictions about what usually happens when certain contingencies arise or to help us to understand and explain things. Theory, in short, consists of ideas that work or may work in more than one context. To marketing academics "theory" is an exposition of abstract principles that are seen to lay behind events or situations like the "product life cycle theory", "consumer behavior theory" or "the theory of the five competitive forces". **Theory** may mean the published results of academic research to date on a topic and may be referred to as a "literature review". To some, the word refers to particular schools of thought like exchange theory, functional theory and so on.

Philosophers have tended to define theories more formally as sets of logically interrelated propositions – or words to that effect. Some writers may add testability as a further criterion. Thus Hunt (1983) suggests that a theory is a "systematically related set of statements, including some law-like generalizations, that is empirically testable". At its simplest a theory is an integrated set of statements about the relationships between variables, for example: "I have a theory that the main factors affecting accurate price recall are the presence of on-pack pricing, frequency of purchase and age of customer."

Theory is often contrasted with practice. Students often complain that a course is "too theoretical" and that it should be "more practical". Such sentiments, while understandable, nevertheless miss the point: that *any* human behavior which is meaningful is underpinned by theory. What varies is the degree of attention we pay to such underpinnings in an attempt to make the theory explicit. Only when it is rendered explicit, however, can we hope to understand the behavior concerned. Even then there are good theories and poor theories. The former correspond with past experience, they enable us to predict with some degree of accuracy, and they help us to understand. *There is, in fact, nothing so practical as a good theory.*

Theory A set of concepts and logically related propositions that work or may work in more than one context.

Theories tend to vary in their breadth of coverage. Thus "grand" theories attempt to explain large categories of phenomena and are most common in the natural sciences, for example, Darwin's theory of evolution. Middle range theories fall between these all-inclusive grand theories and minor working hypotheses of everyday life that are restricted to a particular setting, group, time, population or problem.

The role of theory

The role played by theory in academic marketing research varies considerably. In quantitative research, theory may provide some up-front justification or explanation for the variables being used in the research and for how or why they may be related together in particular ways. In qualitative inquiries it may emerge at the end of a project; it may well be modified as the research proceeds. Alternatively, it may come at the beginning to provide a focus that shapes what is being studied.

Whatever kind of theory we are talking about, it will have a finite existence. It will eventually be replaced or just fall out of fashion or out of usage. In 1988 the American Marketing Association's task force on *Developing, Disseminating and Utilizing Marketing Knowledge* observed that many theories in marketing have a short shelf-life. More recently, Brownlie and Saren (1995) have suggested that, with the increasing "commodification" of marketing knowledge, their shelf-life will continue to shorten, and that academics increasingly trade in FMCGs – fast moving current generalizations – that are marketed and consumed by various groups. However, Hunt (1994) wonders why marketing has produced so few new ideas and made so few original contributions to marketing strategy dialogue. This hardly suggests that the trade in FMCGs is brisk. Elsewhere Kent (1986) has argued that some ideas in marketing – particularly, for example, those relating to the marketing mix and the four Ps – have been around too long and perhaps have had too long a shelf-life.

Models

Model A simplified description of a system or a structure that is devised to assist the process of making calculations concerning the relationships between variables and making predictions.

Reality is inherently complex, and one way of coping with this complexity is deliberately to oversimplify in order to focus on the essentials. **Models** in the everyday sense are *representations* of physical objects on a smaller scale. To the academic, they are simplified descriptions of a system or a structure that are devised to assist the process of making calculations concerning the relationships between key variables and of making predictions.

Simplifications may be achieved in a number of different ways, for example:

- ignoring variables that are of lesser importance and just concentrating on the key variables,

- holding potentially confounding variables constant statistically,

- assuming that the variables other than those in the model do not change,

- making simplifying assumptions that enable the researcher to make deductions or inferences about what would happen if the postulates were true.

Market researchers tend to prefer one or both of the first two. Economists are more likely to use the third and fourth techniques.

Formally we can define a model as a set of variables and specifications about the relationships between them that are deemed to hold amongst a population of cases. As such, models have three main components:

- a set of cases,

- a set of variables,
- one or more interlinked hypotheses that describe a complete system or a structure.

Models are *representations* of a structure or a system, not the structure or the system itself. Thus while I can say, "I have a theory that this is the case . . ." I do not say, "I have a model that this is the case . . .", rather "I have a model *of* a situation . . ." or, "I have a model that represents . . .". Models provide the link between the theory and the data; they are what we *actually* test in terms of specified variables among specified cases. Theories are themselves seldom directly testable.

We can distinguish several different types of model according to a variety of dimensions. Thus on the dimension of specificity we can distinguish between:

- conceptual models,
- graphical models,
- quantitative models.

The least specific are conceptual models; these are models of ideas and will be stated in words. Graphical models, such as the one illustrated in Figure 2.1, are more specific in that they give a visual representation of the relationships between variables. Quantitative models relate variables by way of mathematical formulae. A fully specified model will enable calculations to be made of changes in one or more variables that are a consequence of adjustments to a particular selected variable.

KEY POINTS

The development and testing of theory and the specification of models of various kinds are fundamental activities in academic marketing research

Designing academic research

Chapter 1 outlined the process of designing research for clients which included:

- diagnosing organizational problems or issues,
- assessing organizational strengths and weaknesses,
- clarifying the decisions that need to be taken and defining action standards,

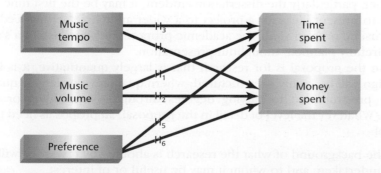

FIGURE 2.1

A graphical model based on Herrington and Capella (1996)

- specifying the information that will be required,
- type of research envisaged,
- formulating the objectives of the research,
- producing a research brief,
- drawing up and presenting a research proposal.

In designing academic research, there is no diagnosis of the client's organizational problems or issues, assessing the client's organizational strengths and weaknesses, or clarifying the decisions that need to be taken. Nor will there be a research brief. The academic research proposal, then, is not a response to a brief, nor is its objective to obtain the commission from the client, perhaps in the face of stiff competition. Research proposals in an academic context, by contrast, are required in two very different contexts: for students to obtain approval to proceed with undergraduate, postgraduate or doctoral research; and as an application for research grants or funding by academic staff to external funding bodies or internal research resources. While there are differences between proposal requirements in these two contexts, there are also similarities. In both cases, for example, the proposal is a pivotal document in which what is being judged is both the viability of the research project and the ability of the student or the academic to carry it out. Viability itself will be judged on two levels: overall viability, and the appropriateness of the research design at a more detailed and technical level. The more general judgments will focus on such issues as:

- Is the proposed research feasible and "doable"?
- What will it contribute to our understanding of marketing processes and issues?
- Will it result in a successful dissertation or thesis?

At a more detailed and technical level, evaluation will be of things like:

- the logical link between the research purpose and the design of the research,
- the likely quality of the data construction process,
- the proposed techniques of data analysis.

Preparing a proposal may entail considerable effort and perhaps some preliminary research on the part of the researcher. The result should be a completed document that can be judged even by peers, colleagues or senior academic staff who may not have discussed the study with the researcher. The proposal for a dissertation or thesis is not a formal contract as with client-based research; it is simply an agreement and the research that is actually carried out may depart in significant ways from the proposal. Such departures may, however, require approval from a supervisor or a research committee. In a research funding context, an approved grant proposal will probably result in a formal contract between the investigator (often the university) and the funding body. For the researcher, particularly the dissertation student, it may be the first time he or she has had to present ideas for a project to a wider audience; getting feedback may be very useful or even vital. The academic proposal, in short, is not a sales pitch: it is a carefully planned, thoughtful presentation.

Where the proposal is for research that is largely quantitative, it is likely that the design will be highly prestructured; where qualitative or largely qualitative it may be prestructured to varying degrees through to unfolding or emergent designs. Whatever the level of detail in the proposal, all proposals need to address issues of:

- the background of what the research is about, why it was (or will be) undertaken, and to whom it may be useful or of interest,

- how it relates to the literature that has already been published in the field,
- the theories or models that are to be used in the research,
- the objectives for which the research is designed,
- the research methods and techniques to be deployed,
- the analysis of the data.

The research background

Any research proposal should explain what is the research area, and the problems, issues or research topics under investigation. There should also be some explanation of *why* the research is being undertaken. It might let you know what, for example, in the past literature, aroused the researcher's interest in the subject matter to begin with. There may be some reference to gaps in the literature, inconsistent or contradictory findings in earlier studies, the possibility of applying existing theories in a new context, a subject made controversial or topical by current events, and so on. The key theoretical and empirical issues should be highlighted along with some comment about why the topic is important, for example because it has wide implications for the way in which marketing may be undertaken or what it might add to the general body of marketing knowledge, and to whom it may be important. Box 2.3 gives an example of a background statement in a proposal for an MSc dissertation.

EUROPEAN MARKETING RESEARCH | BOX 2.3

An evaluation of the EU antismoking campaign 'HELP – for a life without tobacco' in Greece

1 Introduction

1.1 Research area

The research area of the proposed dissertation is social marketing, which, according to Kotler (1997), is a strategy for changing behavior. The study will evaluate the new EU antismoking campaign in Greece six weeks after it has been launched. Aspects to be evaluated include (i) awareness, (ii) recall, (iii) receptiveness, (iv) smoking intentions (to quit or not to start) and (v) successful communication of the dangers of passive smoking.

1.2 The research problem

Smoking is the largest single cause of death and disease in the EU. Over 650 000 Europeans are killed every year because they smoke; one in seven of all deaths across the EU is related to smoking; over 13 million in total suffer from a serious, chronic disease as a result of their smoking. It has been estimated that 100 million will have died because of smoking by 2025. Shocking as these figures are, even more striking is the fact that these deaths could have been avoided.

The EU, having now recognized the importance of this problem, is promoting antismoking publicity campaigns. Between 2002 and 2004, the first campaign "Feel free to say no" achieved more than a billion contacts with its target audience. On 1 June 2005, the second EU campaign "HELP – for a life without tobacco" will be launched. The campaign consists of a roadshow and public relations campaign, an advertising campaign and a website to help people on how to quit smoking. The priorities of the campaign are (i) smoking prevention, (ii) stopping smoking and (ii) awareness of the dangers of passive smoking.

Since the beginning of the campaign coincided with the beginning of research for the dissertation, it seemed an ideal opportunity to evaluate its effectiveness. Furthermore, the Centre for Tobacco Control Research is based at the University of Stirling, from which the research will be conducted.

The research will take place in Greece, which is an interesting example since it is probably the least developed EU country in terms of antitobacco policy. According to the European Opinion Research Group (EEIG), Greece, with the fourth largest group of smokers, and by far the heaviest smokers, measured in cigarettes per day (23.3). According to the European Community Household Panel over 70 percent of males aged 25–34 in Greece are smokers. Furthermore, nonsmoking regulations are not well respected in Greece.

SOURCE: MARIA KARYOTI, MSC MARKETING STUDENT

The literature review

The literature review outlines the kind of literature that might be relevant to the research. It should be fully referenced. The idea is to demonstrate that the dissertation will build on the work of others who have undertaken previous relevant research.

A literature review performs the following functions:

- it informs or shares with the reader the results of earlier work and ideas on the topic,
- it relates the study to the larger, developing literature,
- it provides a framework for identifying the likely significance of the findings,
- it provides a benchmark for comparing the results.

The process of undertaking an academic literature review is explained on pp. 81–82 in Chapter 3.

Theories and models

If the proposed research is quantitative or largely quantitative, then the conceptual framework – the key concepts, the theory, models and hypotheses if appropriate – that is going to be used or developed in the research should be carefully explained. Ideally this should emerge from, or at least be related to, the literature that has been reviewed in the previous section. If the research is qualitative, then one of the objectives of the research may be to explore concepts or to develop theory.

The research objectives

Research objectives should specify exactly what the researchers intend to accomplish as a result of undertaking their research. In published research articles, research objectives are often split into an overall research purpose statement and a series of research questions that the research is designed to answer or a number of hypotheses that the research is designed to test. A research purpose statement will indicate the area of the research, the topic under investigation and the overall approach that this implies, for example "The purpose of this research is to measure the extent to which the application of social marketing techniques can affect fruit and vegetable consumption and physical activity." Herrington and Capella (1996), for example, clearly state that the purpose of their research is to report the findings of a controlled field study examining the effects of background music on shopping behavior in a supermarket environment.

Research questions and hypotheses "unpack" the statement into more specific issues, for example "Is the time spent in a retail environment affected by loud music?", or "Is the amount of money spent in a retail environment affected by loud music?"

If the researcher is undertaking quantitative research and he or she is fairly sure about how variables relate, then hypotheses may be formulated, for example,

H_1: The time shoppers spend in a retail environment will be reduced by loud music.

H_2: The amount of money shoppers spend in a retail environment will be unaffected by loud music.

The nature and types of hypotheses are considered in some detail in Chapter 13. The issue of whether they should be in negative form as a "null" hypothesis as in H_2 above, is also considered in Chapter 13. Box 2.4 illustrates a statement of research objectives from the proposal outlined above.

Research methods and techniques

The purpose of any research design for undertaking academic research in the marketing area is to ensure that the evidence obtained will enable the researcher to address the research objectives, and to answer the research questions or to test the research hypotheses. We saw in Chapter 1 that a design is specific to a particular inquiry; it is a unique combination of elements and will often involve mixing different types of research methods and techniques in the same project. Methods are general approaches to data collection while techniques are rather more specific. Thus survey research is a method, but Likert scaling (which is explained in Chapter 5) is a technique. The methods and techniques that are available to academic researchers are the same as for those undertaking client-based research; however, the manner in which these elements are assembled will reflect the interests and ambitions of the researcher rather than client requirements. Research objectives, furthermore, can often be achieved using very different combinations of methods and techniques; there is seldom one "best" design. Accordingly, in the proposal there should, ideally, be some discussion of the methods and techniques that were considered, plus some justification for those that were finally chosen.

RESEARCH IN ACTION
Research objectives

BOX 2.4

3.1 Research objectives

The overall aim of the study is to evaluate the new EU antismoking campaign in Greece by measuring (i) awareness, (ii) recall, (iii) receptiveness, (iv) smoking intentions (to quit or not to start) and (v) successful communication of the dangers of passive smoking. The findings among different target subgroups can be compared to test whether the campaign is equally successful.

The more specific research questions are as follows.

- To what extent are Greek adults aware of the new campaign?
- Can they recall campaign elements?
- How receptive are they to the campaign?
- To what extent are the objectives of the campaign met in terms of smoking intentions?
- Have the dangers of passive smoking been communicated?
- Is the campaign more effective with some groups than others?

Researchers, or researchers in discussion with clients or with supervisors, need to make a series of decisions, not so much about picking one or more from a selection of particular designs, but about where along a number of key dimensions would be appropriate for the research project. Three key dimensions need to be considered:

- whether or not or the extent to which the research intends to focus on generating quantitative data,
- whether or not or the extent to which the passage of time is taken as an explicit variable in the research,
- whether or not or the extent to which the researcher tries to manipulate or control what are seen as the "causal" variables.

Chapter 3 will explain the different kinds of data that researchers may construct. Broadly we make a distinction between quantitative and qualitative data. Researchers are not "forced" to make a choice between qualitative and quantitative approaches; these can be mixed in a variety of ways that will be explained in some detail in Chapter 9. However, most researchers are, by inclination rather than necessity, predisposed to emphasize one or the other.

If researchers wish to explore, understand the processes of, or measure the extent of change, then they will need to introduce time as a specific variable. The distinction between what is called "ad hoc" or "cross-sectional" research and continuous research will be explained in Chapter 7. The manipulation or control of variables implies some form of experimental design and such designs are considered also in Chapter 7. Box 2.5 illustrates an argument for using ad hoc survey research for the proposal on the antismoking campaign in Greece.

Data analysis

Even at an early stage when the research is being planned, and perhaps even before a formal research proposal is presented, the researcher should have some ideas about how the data that are likely to emerge from the research will be analyzed. This is as true for qualitative as for quantitative data. The whole of Part III of this book, Chapters 10–15, is concerned with the process of data analysis.

> **KEY POINTS**
>
> Academic research proposals are focused around a number of issues that include the background of what the research is about, why it was (or will be) undertaken, and to whom it may be useful or of interest, how it relates to the literature that has already been published in the field, the theories or models that are to be used in the research, the objectives for which the research is designed, the research design itself, and the analysis of the data.

Ethical issues

Academic researchers have the same responsibilities to informants and respondents as commercial and in-house market researchers. Though they are not bound by the ESOMAR or Market Research Society Code of Conduct, they would be wise to follow their guidelines. Academic researchers are just as dependent on public co-operation as are commercial agencies. Furthermore, while there is no

RESEARCH IN ACTION
Design choices

BOX 2.5

In most studies that focus on evaluations of anti-smoking campaigns, the design used is experimental (Wakefiled, Flay, Nichter and Giovino 2003; Sly, Heald and Ray 2001; Pechmann and Reibling 2000). However, the researcher rejected this design because it required resources that could not be obtained. Alternatively, she decided to use a survey design for a number of reasons. To begin with, the aim of the research is to make generalizations from the sample examined to the population, so that inferences can be made about some characteristics, attitudes and behaviors. According to Creswell (2003), the design that responds to this aim is a survey design. Furthermore, given the limitation of time within which the research needs to be conducted, this design offers a rapid turnaround in data collection.

client, there are responsibilities to research grant providers and to qualification-awarding bodies like universities, colleges and professional associations. A key issue here focuses around the honesty with which the results are produced. If an agency began dishonestly manufacturing data, it would quickly lose business since its recommendations would become distrusted. If academics do this, then it is down to the vigilance of supervisors, examiners or grant monitors to detect such behavior.

One form of dishonesty that is of concern to academics is plagiarism. This entails the passing off of somebody else's ideas as your own. Its most detectable form is the "lifting" of text from published sources without acknowledgment of that source. The availability of published work online has made this process only too easy. However, special software has been developed that can detect the copying and pasting of text in this manner. This software is increasingly applied to student dissertations and theses, which are being submitted in electronic form.

Authors of textbooks are usually given guidelines by publishers. Thus Thomson Learning, the publisher of this textbook, advises that authors must seek permission for any tables, charts, illustrations, statistics, quotations or adaptations from any text or material that is not completely the author's own work. The only exceptions to this are quotations that come under a fair dealing category; this includes extracts of fewer than 400 words or a series of extracts totalling fewer than 800 words where no extract is more than 300 words.

SUMMARY

Research that is undertaken for academic purposes is researcher-led rather than client-led. Since there is no client, it is also neutral and it is noninterventionist (except perhaps in the shape of experimental manipulations or action research). The development and testing of theory, the specification of conceptual, graphical or mathematical models and their links to previous literature in the field are crucially important. Academic research is judged on the scientific rigor with which it was conducted rather than on its practical value; it is aimed at a largely academic audience and its results are for as wide a dissemination as practicable.

In undertaking academic marketing research, it is impossible to avoid making certain assumptions about the nature of the reality that is being researched, about how scientific knowledge is achieved, and about from whose perspective the research is to be or is being undertaken. Marketing researchers tend to follow one of three main collections of assumptions that have been characterized in this chapter as the marketing physicist, the marketing physician and the marketing psychiatrist. Any issue in marketing can be studied following each of these paradigms.

Academic research proposals need to be very clear and very specific about the rationale for doing the research at all. (For client-based research it can in effect be because that is what the client wants). This will include a review of the background of the research, the manner in which it relates to previous research and the literature in the field, on the theories and models that are appropriate, and the specific research questions or hypotheses that will be addressed.

The distinction between client-based and academic research is not always clear-cut and sometimes it can be a mixture of the two. Thus research that was originally undertaken for a client may subsequently be published in an academic journal. Sometimes, particularly for policy-based research, the research itself and its reporting, even if for a government or other official funder, need to meet academic standards to be acceptable to the client.

QUESTIONS FOR DISCUSSION

1   Herrington and Capella (1996) examine the relationships between the volume and tempo of music in a retail environment and consumer behavior. Rewrite the "story" of the three sociologists told earlier in this chapter, but from the perspective of three marketing researchers, one a marketing physicist, one a marketing physician and one a marketing psychiatrist who have just been asked by the store manager to explain how they would go about undertaking marketing research on the effects of music in shops.

2   Explain in what ways the process of designing academic research differs from designing client-based research.

3   Compare how client-based and academic research are evaluated in a different manner and according to different criteria.

4   To what extent are you a positivist? On a scale of 5 to 1 from strongly agree to strongly disagree give each of the eight items below a score.

☐   Unless a phenomenon can be quantified, it is not worth investigating.

☐   There is no single "true" picture to discover when it comes to researching consumers' attitudes or behavior.

☐   A good knowledge of statistics is essential to provide the most useful market research.

☐   The researcher, even designing a quantitative survey, has an unavoidable influence on the results.

☐   Whatever the research budget, qualitative research should be used only as exploratory research before the main quantitative research in conducted.

☐   Increasingly, it is better to forgo attempts to quantify and to rely on qualitative insight.

☐   Market researchers must remain objective and independent from the phenomena they are studying.

☐   My personal preference is to put numbers on things wherever possible.

5   Which of the items above indicate a positivist approach if agreed with? If you wanted to construct a total score, how would you go about this?

ITEMS ADAPTED FROM BARKER ET AL. 2001.

CASE STUDY YOUNG PEOPLE TOBACCO MARKETING

MacFadyen et al. (2001) report a cross-sectional, quantitative survey of young people's awareness of and involvement with tobacco advertising and the association of these factors with smoking behavior. Respondents were a stratified random sample of 629 teenagers in North East England aged 15 or 16 who had "opted in" to the research through a postal consent procedure. Results showed that while nearly all were aware of tobacco advertising and point-of-sale marketing, the levels of awareness of other forms of marketing such as sponsorship, merchandising, brand stretching and product placement, and involvement with coupon schemes or receiving direct mail, were significantly associated with being a smoker. Thus 30 percent of smokers had received free gifts through coupons in cigarette packs compared with 11 percent of nonsmokers. The authors concluded that teenagers are aware of and are participating in many forms of tobacco marketing, and both awareness and participation are associated with current smoking status. This suggests that the current voluntary regulations designed to protect young people from smoking are not working and that statutory regulations are required. The research was funded by the Cancer Research Campaign with additional support from the Department of Health.

Questions and activities

1 Was this study client-based research or was it academic research?

2 What ethical issues does this research raise?

3 What was the research paradigm being used or assumed in this research?

FURTHER READING

Creswell, J. (2003) *Research Design. Qualitative, Quantitative and Mixed Methods Approaches*, 2nd edn. Thousand Oaks, California: Sage.

Herrington, J. and Capella, L. (1996) "Effects of music in service environments: a field study", *Journal of Services Marketing*, 10 (2): 26–41.

Punch, K. (2000) *Developing Effective Research Proposals*. London: Sage.

Part II Accessing and constructing good-quality data

Both client-based marketing research and academic research in marketing are about constructing and analyzing data. Part II is all about obtaining good-quality data. There is little point in analyzing data that are not of a standard that is at least acceptable for the purposes for which the research is to be undertaken. If garbage data go into the analysis then garbage analysis will come out. As far as researchers are concerned, to obtain good data they will either have to access data that already exist and have perhaps been collected for another purpose, or they will have to construct their own.

Chapter 3 explains what are "data" and the various types of data that may be used in research. It then shows how data that already exist – usually called "secondary" data – can be accessed and used for a range of marketing research purposes. The remaining chapters in Part II are about how researchers go about constructing data for themselves. The word "construct" is used deliberately because it is argued that data are not "discovered", "captured" or "collected" like so many butterflies in a garden; rather they are built from the activities of individual researchers who, furthermore, operate within an environment of often competing social, political and economic interests.

3 Accessing secondary data

ch v[Jsun-boon

LEARNING OBJECTIVES In this chapter you will learn about:

→ **the nature and types of data,**

→ **the various sources of secondary data – published, commercial and internal,**

→ **the process of doing desk research,**

→ **evaluating the quality of data obtained from secondary sources,**

→ **doing secondary data analysis,**

→ **using marketing intelligence,**

→ **doing desk research for academic projects.**

Some data already exist and can be used by the researcher.

© KAREN GROTZINGER

INTRODUCTION

Accessing and making sensible use of good-quality data that have already been collected for other purposes can save researchers a lot of work – and their clients a lot of time and money. Examination of all the available secondary data is a useful, probably essential, preliminary to the collection of primary data and researchers will be wise to begin their research by seeking out such data. This chapter introduces you to the nature of data; it explains the various sources of secondary data and the process of undertaking secondary research. Undertaking secondary research is useful particularly in the early stages of a project. It can often help in the process of defining problems, issues or opportunities, it can help in the planning of later stages in the research and it can provide a context for the interpretation of data that have been constructed specifically for the project. In the last decade or so, there has been a huge explosion in the sources of secondary data, and these may well provide sufficient information to fulfil the objectives of a particular research project.

INTERNET ACTIVITY

Using your browser, go to **www.thomsonlearning.co.uk/kent** and select the Chapter 3 Internet Activity which will provide a link to the National Statistics website. Click on *Information about National Statistics*. Under *About data* click on *Methodologies and quality assessment*. Click on *Quality* then *Guidelines for measuring statistical quality*. Read Section A.3, What is "quality"?

What are "data"?

Data are often thought of as "the facts" – things that are known to be true. The dictionary tells us that the word is a plural noun (although commonly treated as singular) and derives from the Latin word that translates literally as "things given". Data are thus portrayed as a form of knowledge – sheer, plain, unvarnished, untainted by social values or ideology and, for the most part, unchallengeable. The assumption is that they exist independently of our research activities and that we can simply go out and discover or "collect" them like so many tadpoles in a pond.

In reality, **data** consist of systematic records that have been made by individuals, for example registers of births, marriages and deaths, hospital records, business invoices, completed questionnaires, notes or electronic records of buying and selling activities, or of observations of products or brands on supermarket shelves or of responses from respondents or informants. Data, then, are not collected or discovered, but created, concocted, manufactured – we will use the term "constructed" – by individuals in the process of systematic record-keeping. Data are built up, to continue the construction metaphor, brick-by-brick, but systematically and according to a plan, just like a brick house. Data construction, for the researcher, entails engaging in three main activities:

Data Systematic records made by individuals.

- designing the research that specifies when, where and how the construction process is to take place,
- capturing the data by creating a record,
- assembling the data into their "raw" data format, ready for analysis.

The process of designing client-based research was explained in Chapter 1 and academic research in Chapter 2. These processes of data construction require that the researcher takes a series of decisions, for example about which particular research methods and techniques to use – decisions for which there is usually no scientific template or rule for making the "correct" decision. These decisions will, furthermore, be influenced by researchers' own wishes, prejudices and agendas, and by the circumstances in which they find themselves with careers to foster, deadlines to meet, clients to satisfy or research grants to be obtained. Furthermore, they work within a structure of sometimes competing interests – there are the commitments and ambitions of the researcher's colleagues, the goals of organizational administrators, the objectives and wishes of clients and funding bodies, and the concerns of those to whom the data relate – the participants, respondents or informants.

The recording devices that are used to capture data in marketing research are varied, and will include, for example, tape recorders, video cameras, still cameras, questionnaires, diaries, barcode readers, trip counters and various kinds of meter that are used, for example, to capture who is watching television or listening to a radio at specified times of the day. These devices are explained in more detail in Chapter 6.

Assembling the data ready for analysis might mean physically gathering together tape recordings, questionnaires or diaries, but nowadays is more likely to mean entering data into a computer program ready for analysis. The various programs that may be used for this purpose are explained later in this book.

Data, in short, are not "the facts" or "things given"; rather they are social products that are manufactured, not collected. Data construction, furthermore, is a process that takes place in a social, moral, political, economic and historical context. This is not to say that data are necessarily meaningless artifacts, subject to manipulation, doctoring or media spin (although the British Prime Minister Disraeli did, apparently, once claim in the House of Commons that there are "lies, damned lies and statistics"). The implication is, however, that few data are perfect. Errors will almost certainly be made in the data construction process; data produced by researchers or by nonresearch organizations will vary considerably in terms of quality. There will be "good" data, "poor" data and data that are simply of "acceptable" quality for the purpose for which they will be used. The quality of data, in fact, may be judged in many different ways and on a variety of criteria, for example on their comprehensiveness, on their accuracy, on the speed or timeliness with which they are delivered, or on the manner of their construction. Data may be collected in many different ways, using different data capture instruments and employing different definitions of what is being recorded. Different researchers may produce very different results, apparently from observing the "same" things or events. Even government statistics are often based on questionnaires, and, as we shall see in some detail in Chapter 8, there are many things that can go wrong with this process – see Figure 3.1.

Data may consist of three rather different kinds of record:

- numbers that result from a process of measurement and the imposition of a structure on the data, for example the number of males and females in a specified group, category or organization, or the size of a supermarket in square meters of floorspace,
- words or text, for example in audio tape recordings, interview transcripts, minutes of meetings, reports, historical or literary documents, personnel records, field notes, newspaper clippings,
- images, for example paintings, sketches, drawings, photographic stills, computer-generated images, posters, advertisements.

Quantitative data Systematic records that consist of numbers constructed by researchers utilizing the process of measurement and imposing a structure.

Qualitative data Systematic records that consist of words, phrases, text or images.

Numbers that result from a process of measurement and the imposition of a structure on the data are usually seen as **quantitative data,** while words, phrases, text and visual images (which are often combined, for example in posters) are usually regarded as **qualitative data**. The "structure" that is imposed on quantitative data is explained in detail in Chapter 5, but since this "structuring" is a matter of degree, the distinction may sometimes be a little difficult to draw and researchers may take different views about what kinds of data count as "quantitative" or "qualitative". The details of the processes involved in the construction of both qualitative and quantitative data are explored on Chapters 4 and 5.

The data – or at least some of them – that the researcher requires may already exist; that is to say they have already been constructed by others for other purposes. These are usually called secondary data because the researcher intends to use them for a secondary purpose. The process of accessing secondary data is usually referred to as desk research or secondary research. The process of data construction can be lengthy and costly and it would be wise for any researchers to check out what data already exist and can be accessed before contemplating constructing their own data specifically for the research being undertaken. These are **primary data.** The remainder of this chapter is about accessing secondary data, but bear in mind that such data were originally primary data and were originally constructed using the methods and techniques explained in Chapters 4 and 5.

Primary data Data constructed specifically for the research at hand.

KEY POINTS

Data are systematic records that have been constructed by individuals; they are social products that are created in a social, moral, political, economic and historical context. They are certainly not "the facts", beyond challenge, but rather come in a range of qualities and suitability for different purposes. Many data, as we shall see in Chapter 8, are estimates based on samples that themselves may have many shortcomings.

Quantitative data consist of numbers that result from a process of measurement and the imposition of a structure on the data. Qualitative data consist of words, phrases, text or images. In practice these are often mixed in various ways. Mixed research designs are explained in more detail in Chapter 9.

Primary data are data that have been constructed by the researcher specifically for the project at hand. Secondary data have already been constructed by other individuals for their own purposes and are to be used for a secondary purpose.

FIGURE 3.1

Collecting nice hard facts. Finding out how many people there are

MOLLY! How many kids do we have now?

Sources of secondary data

Some secondary data such as those provided by government departments and statistical offices are often available for free and, furthermore, would be difficult for any researcher with limited resources to construct. Other data may be purchased from commercial suppliers. Some data may be already available within the organization for which the research is being undertaken. It is possible, therefore, to classify secondary sources into three main kinds:

- published sources,
- commercial sources,
- internal sources.

Published sources

Published sources include all those sources that are external to the organization for which the research is being conducted, and which are available in the public domain. National governments, government departments, local authorities and a range of bodies like the European Commission, the United Nations, professional and trade associations, chambers of commerce, newspapers, publishers and periodicals increasingly make data available over the internet. Accessing data from such bodies used to be a tedious undertaking, involving frequent visits to the library to find (or sometimes not find) hard copy, or writing to various organizations for information and waiting for their responses. Finding information nowadays, by contrast, can be very easy, although it may require a degree of trial and error. Basically, there are three main ways of doing this:

- if you know the source organization's website address you can type it into your web browser,
- use a search engine such as Google or as provided by MSN,
- use specialist host sites that list catalogues, directories, guides and databases or act as information gateways.

Figure 3.2 classifies the main providers of secondary data and the following sections give you lots of websites you can go to.

FIGURE 3.2

Sources of secondary data

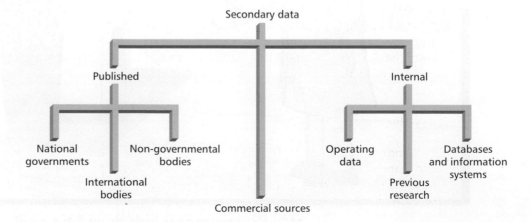

National government sources

All national governments in Europe construct a wide range of social, economic and business data. These will include a decennial census of population (see Box 3.1) and a range of other statistical outputs. Each European country has its own statistics office that either produces lists of the publications available (and the costs involved) or makes the data freely available. The collection and dissemination of government statistics in the UK, for example, is organized by the Office of National Statistics (ONS). This body was created in 1996 from the merger of the former Central Statistical Office (CSO) and the Office of Population Censuses and Surveys (OPCS). Its website can be accessed at **www.statistics.gov.uk**. It provides the data free of charge and it may be downloaded to file or printer for the purposes of research and private study. The use of such data for publication, however, requires a licence and can be quite expensive. If you did the exercise at the beginning of this chapter, you will have some idea of what is available.

A major publication from the ONS is *Social Trends*, which can be downloaded for free from the ONS website. The data are derived from a number of surveys conducted by the ONS including the *General Household Survey*, the *Family Expenditure Survey*, the *National Food Survey*, the *Census of Population* (every 10 years) and the *Census of Production* (every 5 years). The results of these surveys are held in a data archive that is administered by the Economic and Social Research Council (ESRC) and the University of Essex. The archive website (**www.data-archive.ac.uk**) contains full descriptions and documentation of datasets. The results from over 30 different surveys can be reviewed, or downloaded following a registration procedure.

Nongovernmental sources

Nongovernmental sources are many and varied, for example newspapers, journals and magazines, directories, guides, indexes and online databases. Material is also produced by international bodies, trade associations, professional bodies, chambers of commerce, regulatory institutions, and academic and research institutions. The sources can often be tracked down by using information gateway sites such

---

IN DETAIL
The UK Census and marketing

BOX 3.1

The UK Census has been conducted every 10 years since 1801 (with the exception of 1941). The last was in 2001 when 70 000 enumerators delivered Census forms to all households for self-completion and return. Nearly 90 percent of households, representing 21 million forms, returned their forms. The final response rate after follow-up class was 94 percent. Details of the entire process are explained by Leventhal (2003). The main applications of the Census in marketing are, according to Leventhal:

- estimating penetration rates,
- profiling areas,
- setting quotas for areas.

Standard outputs from the Census are freely available on the internet to all users, including all reports and standard area statistics. For the first time, samples of anonymized records (a 1 percent sample of all households) was also made available. These samples of microdata opened up completely new avenues of analysis, allowing the investigation of relationships between variables for subgroups.

as the Social Science Information Gateway (www.sosig.ac.uk). This provides an extensive list to online databases worldwide and covers most subjects relevant to market and social research.

The European Union publishes a lot of data that may be accessed, for example, at the Europa website (http://europa.eu.int/geninfo/info-en.htm). This has gathered together a wide range of sources spanning all the European institutions and agencies. There are also databases located at CORDIS, the Community Research and Development Information Service (www.cordis.lu) and at Euromonitor (www.euromonitor.com), which offers a Marketing Surveys Index. The Statistics Division of the United Nations (http://unstats.un.org/unsd/data bases.htm) provides a wide range of statistical data on a global basis, while the United Nations home page has a wide range of links to online catalogues, bibliographic databases and directories relating to social, economic and market data. In addition, the World Bank (www.worldbank.org), the Organization for Economic Co-operation and Development (www.oecd.org) and the World Economic Forum (www.worldeconomicforum.org) offer further data.

Directories are useful for identifying organizations that collect specific data, for example the *Central and Eastern European Business Directory*. This provides information on businesses and other types of organization in 24 Central and Eastern European countries plus Russia, and may be accessed at www.ceebd.co.uk. It is an interactive site that also gives detailed country profiles. Another example is *Europages,* which classifies 550 000 companies in 35 European countries and may be accessed at www.europages.com. It is available in 24 languages.

> ### KEY POINTS
>
> Published sources include all those sources that are external to the organization for which the research is being conducted, and which are available in the public domain. These sources may be classified into governmental and nongovernmental sources. Many of these data are available online.

Commercial sources

The larger market research agencies collect and sell data designed to serve the information needs shared by a number of clients. These sources are often called "syndicated" sources or services. Box 3.2 describes one such source. In the UK, such sources include BMRB's *Target Group Index, Mintel Market Intelligence Reports, Keynote Publications, Market Research GB* and *Market Research Europe,* and *Retail Business.* Several commercial companies supply data online including Mintel (www.mintel.co.uk), Data Monitor (www.datamonitor.com), and Kompass (www.kompass.com). eMarketer (www.eMarketer.com) specializes in new media research, while the Financial Times Discovery Services (http://ft discovery.ft.com) offers a wide range of information on organizations, industry sectors and countries. Financial analysis reports, business news services or computer access to online databases may be purchased from some agencies. There are also a number of compendiums giving all sorts of useful marketing data, for example, the *Marketing Pocket Book*, published by the Advertising Association.

Subscribing to continuous market measurement services such as consumer panels or retail panels is another possibility. A year's subscription will pay for 12 four-weekly reports on the products or brands you choose, detailing sales by volume and by value on a brand-by-brand basis, classified by a whole series of geographical, demographic and behavioral characteristics. It is also possible to buy into an omnibus survey or to purchase television viewing or radio listening data from the Broadcasters Audience Research Board or from Radio Joint Audience Research. These sources are described in detail in Chapter 16.

Internal data

Companies are now able to capture, store and analyze very large volumes of data for themselves. Three main sources may be distinguished:

- operating data and company accounts,
- previous research,
- data contained in information systems.

Operating data relate to the daily activities and transaction of a business and might include information on the performance of individual products that the firm makes, for example on sales, profits and costs; on the various sections, divisions, factory sites or subsidiaries of the company; on the functions it performs – manufacturing, distribution, marketing, purchasing or research and development. **Company accounts** will supply information on the overall performance of the organization – turnover, costs, revenue, profits, a balance sheet and profit and loss statement. Invoices or records of purchases may be able to supply information on customer addresses, types of purchases, dates and frequencies of purchase, discounts, credits and delivery. From such data it would be possible to analyze:

Operating data Data that relate to the daily activities and transactions of a business or other kind of organization.

Company accounts Information on the overall performance of an organization.

- expenditure and repeat purchase by type of customer,
- combinations of products and product variants that are most popular,
- where customers live or are located,
- how customers pay,
- which customers respond to special offers,
- seasonal or other patterns of purchasing behavior by product and by customer.

Other data may relate to sales-force activity, trade fairs, sponsorship or spend on advertising. Some companies compile comprehensive information about their customers to create a **customer database**. Such data may come from invoices, but also from promotional schemes or loyalty cards.

Previous research may have been carried out both on the company and on the market to which it sells. Reading the reports of such activities may enable researchers to familiarize themselves with the background of the current situation, and perhaps use them as a guide or input to the design of the research to be undertaken. It may even be possible to utilize such research as a benchmark for

Customer database A database constructed by the organization that details customer or member characteristics.

Every company has to provide company accounts including a balance sheet.

© TODD BINGHAM

Data warehouse A very large database in which data are gathered from disparate sources and converted into a consistent format that can be used to support management decision-making and customer relationship management.

measuring change from an earlier period. It makes sense to classify and store such reports in a library and in such a way that they may be easily retrieved on future occasions. Unfortunately it is still common practice for copies of reports to be kept on the shelves of the managers who commissioned them.

Management or marketing information systems combine various data inputs, store them on a computerized database, and usually have the ability to produce integrated reports on a regular basis using an agreed system. They may operate at various levels of sophistication. At a basic level they are simply data storage and retrieval systems that make existing data more readily accessible and presentable. Standard database packages do this very well and they provide the mechanisms for abstracting and indexing information and retrieving it in particular formats. More sophisticated are systems for monitoring and control that check progress and alert management to variations, departures or variances from plans, criteria or budgets.

Internal databases are increasingly used for database marketing, which relies on an extensive database of customer and potential customer profiles in order to be able to target selected market segments. The raw material is derived from transaction processing systems, for example from ATMs, web servers, point-of-sale scanners, call center records, billing systems, registration and application forms – in fact every transaction creates a record. A **data warehouse** is a huge database in which data gathered from disparate sources are converted into a consistent format using a relational database (see Box 3.3) that relates specified elements from each dataset so that it can be used to support management decision-making (DSS) and customer relationship management (CRM) systems.

A well-designed data warehouse should have a number of key characteristics:

- it can store expanding volumes of data without affecting adversely the processing performance,
- it is user-friendly,
- it can be accessed from a number of locations,
- many people can use it at the same time,
- it enables the analysis of data from a variety of viewpoints.

IN DETAIL
Relational databases

BOX 3.3

Data are stored in several small files rather than one big one, as in a traditional "flat-file" database. Each of these small files contains key information that links files together. A customer database might, for example, contain one file that includes customer name, address, telephone, e-mail address and identification number. This information will be updated only occasionally. Purchases made by each customer would go into another file that is updated every time a customer makes a purchase. This will record the product purchased, the price paid, the date of purchase and so on. The two files are linked, however, by the ID number. Personal data are thus stored only once for each customer rather than with every new purchase that is added as it would be in a flat-file. This saves a huge amount of storage space. Any new information can be saved in a new file that is also linked by the ID number. This makes the database flexible, access can be restricted to certain areas of the database, and reports from such databases can be customized.

The *Case Study: Vodafone* at the end of this chapter describes how the company used a relational database technique to create its own data warehouse.

KEY POINTS

Apart from published sources, data may be purchased from market research agencies. However, a lot of data are likely to be available from within the organization itself and will include operating data and company accounts, previous research and data contained in information systems. Many of these data can be brought together in a data warehouse where they can be utilized in a systematic fashion to support management decision-making.

Evaluating secondary data

Secondary data, by definition, have been collected for purposes other than the problem at hand. This means that their usefulness to the current research may be limited, for example in terms of their relevance and timeliness. Because secondary data normally appear in printed or published form, it is often forgotten that they were originally collected as primary data, albeit for some other purpose. Very often the data are estimates based on samples, so it is necessary to bear in mind also all the potential sources of error, which are explained in detail in Chapter 8.

Not all secondary data will be of a quality that is acceptable for the purposes of the current research and it may be wise to ask a number of questions about them.

- Who produced the data?
- Why were the data collected in the first place?
- How were they collected?
- When were they collected?
- Where were they collected?
- What definitions were used?

It is a good idea to bear in mind the agents who were responsible for the original collection, analysis and presentation of the data. We have seen that data are created, not discovered; they are a product of human activity and are manufactured within a structure of competing interests. Irvine et al. (1979) argue that statistical practice is not purely a technical matter of utilizing the "correct" sampling techniques, statistical analyses, probability theory and so on. Data are social products that have been created by individuals, groups or governments with their own economic and social agendas. Data are never totally neutral; they are a selection of the data that could have been collected. There may well be a convenient lack of information on sensitive topics like the real levels of poverty or unemployment, and the data that would have been useful to the researcher are not collected. So, in asking who produced the data, it is as well to recognize that, for example, trade associations exist to further the interests of their members and may well hesitate to publish data that are inimical to those interests.

Answering the question concerning why the data were collected in the first place may well give insights into the value of that information. Thus the original purpose of the Family Expenditure Survey, begun in 1957, was to provide information on spending patterns for the Retail Prices Index, not to measure the levels of poverty.

In terms of how the data were collected, it is important to know the definition of the population that is covered by the data, the size of the sample that was taken and the type of sampling that was used. Chapter 8 takes up issues of populations and samples in more detail. It is also important to know the response rates that were achieved (sometimes this is lower than 20 percent), the data collection procedures and instruments that were used, and the data analysis techniques that were applied. It would also be helpful to know what quality control procedures were used and how missing values were handled. These issues are also taken up again in later chapters. Unfortunately, information on many of these points may well not be given along with the actual data, but it is always open to researchers to contact the source or data publishers to find out.

Quite often, published data will have been collected some time before their publication. This is particularly true of government statistics. The Census, for example, is conducted only every ten years, and although attempts are made to update the figures, they become estimates over a period of time.

Case The entity whose characteristics are being recorded in the process of data construction.

Finally, definitions of the original **case**, for example "household", "small to medium enterprise" or "establishment", or of the original variables and the scales of values used, may not be the ones the researcher would have chosen. The result is that the data are published in a format that is not particularly useful to him or to her, or that, because of changes in definitions, the analysis of trends becomes dubious.

KEY POINTS

Secondary data, where they are available, can be obtained quickly and inexpensively. They can be used in conjunction with primary data or as a preliminary to the conduct of primary research. However, such data need to be evaluated against a number of criteria before the researcher can be reasonably confident of their value.

Doing desk research

Desk research The proactive seeking-out of data, qualitative or quantitative, that already exist and which are to be used for a secondary purpose, and also finding previous reports, studies, newspaper or magazine articles or other literature that might be useful for the purposes of the research at hand.

Desk research entails not only the proactive seeking-out of data, qualitative or quantitative, that already exist and are to be used for a secondary purpose, but also finding previous reports, studies, newspaper or magazine articles or other literature that might be useful for the purposes of the research at hand. There are two key uses of desk research:

- providing background materials for primary research,
- providing an alternative to doing primary research.

In the former application, desk research is usually an exploratory stage in the conduct of a marketing research project. Usually, it will need to be completed before the primary research can be designed, or it may be necessary to check that a similar study has not already been carried out, or that the data required are not already available. It may also be used to explore the background to a problem or issue, to define the problem more closely, to generate research questions or to put issues in a wider context – getting the "big picture". Existing data may, for example, provide an analysis of trends in the industry, or they may be able to profile existing or potential customers and suggest market segments.

However, desk research may also continue while the primary research is in progress, deepening the understanding of the market research executive, keeping him or her abreast of current developments in the marketplace. The results of desk research may be used in the final report to provide an overview of the general economic environment, the size and structure of and trends in the market, and the main competitors before looking at the performance of the client's brand derived from the primary research.

In the second application, desk research may reveal that no further research is required, for example because it has shown that the potential market is just not large enough to support a new product under consideration. Many an annual marketing plan is preceded by a desk research review of the market with no further research input. Sometimes the reanalysis of existing data (that is, secondary analysis, which is explained later in this chapter) provides a sufficient basis for making a marketing decision or pursuing some marketing activity.

Desk research can seldom be fully structured – it is more like a treasure hunt or piece of detection work. What will emerge is often unknown beforehand. It requires skills of methodicalness, persistence and ingenuity. It means knowing where best to begin and how to proceed thereafter. For the research executive in a market research agency, the first step will be to determine from the client what data are accessible in the company itself. There will certainly be accounting and operating data, but there may also be a customer database, and the client may well be subscribing to one or more syndicated sources that provide data on products, brand by brand, and on markets and consumers on a continuous basis. The client may have a library containing past reports or a management information system that can be accessed. Next, the executive may contact the appropriate trade associations to see what data they hold (usually generated from their own members).

A search of the internal sources of data may be adequate. However, if information is required on the wider market or on social trends, then some combination of governmental and nongovernmental sources of external data may be appropriate.

KEY POINTS

Desk research entails the proactive seeking-out of secondary data, qualitative or quantitative, that already exist and which may be useful in the analysis, planning or control of marketing activities. Such data can help researchers to define their research problems, issues or opportunities and to develop their research design, for example by identifying key variables, potential populations and samples and specifying research questions. Such data might also help researchers to interpret primary data in context and with more insight.

Secondary research and secondary data analysis

Some researchers make a distinction between **secondary research** and primary research, but most research is a combination of secondary and primary sources of data. Only if the research is limited to secondary sources could we really call it "secondary research".

Secondary research Research that is limited to the use of secondary data.

Most published statistics are "macro" data, that is, the original cases are no longer identifiable and tables consist of summaries, groupings, averages and so on. Here, although the data can be re-presented in their original or modified form, further analyses are limited because variables in the tables cannot be related

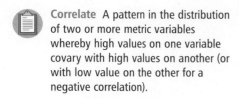

Correlate A pattern in the distribution of two or more metric variables whereby high values on one variable covary with high values on another (or with low value on the other for a negative correlation).

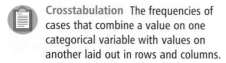

Crosstabulation The frequencies of cases that combine a value on one categorical variable with values on another laid out in rows and columns.

Secondary analysis The extraction of new insights or findings from secondary data.

to variables in other tables on a case-by-case basis. Sometimes, however, the original "micro" data are available, that is, data that relate to individual cases. In this situation it is possible to reanalyze the data, for example by **correlating** or **crosstabulating** them with other variables.

The aim of **secondary analysis** is to extract new insights or findings from the existing data. Some datasets, such as those available in the Data Archive at the University of Essex, have been constructed with the possibilities of reanalysis in mind. It is important that the researcher has available a copy of the original survey questionnaire, a description of the sampling techniques used, the definition of variables, and how the data were coded.

KEY POINTS

Secondary research is research that is limited to secondary sources. Secondary analysis entails the further analysis of an existing dataset using data analysis procedures that were different from those applied to the original dataset.

Marketing intelligence

Marketing intelligence The compilation and evaluation of qualitative and quantitative information on what is happening generally in the marketplace.

Environmental scanning refers to the process of compiling and evaluating qualitative and quantitative information on what is happening generally in the marketplace, particularly the activities of competitors, and in the wider social, political, economic and technological environment. The result is usually referred to as **marketing intelligence**, which is a collection of pieces of information, often incomplete and subjective, but which allows the researcher to keep abreast of events as they unfold. These sources include:

- reading business and financial newspapers like the *Financial Times* or the *Wall Street Journal*, general business magazines like *Business Week* or *The Economist*, trade and technical journals like *Computer Weekly*, and academic periodicals like the *Harvard Business Review* or the *Journal of Management Studies*,

- personal contacts in other organizations,

- feedback from the salesforce,

- watching competitors,

- going to conferences, exhibitions, courses, or meetings.

In many market research agencies, executives are assigned to particular groups of clients and are expected to familiarize themselves with their markets. Most environmental scanning, however, is probably undertaken in-house by company managers. The process of environmental scanning may be very informal with no specific purpose in mind, it may be conditioned to a particular type of information, it may be a proactive but unsystematic search, or there may be formal procedures for finding, storing and retrieving the information. Whatever form the scanning takes, the resulting market intelligence should enable the firm to adapt more easily to a changing environment, it may act as a source of inspiration for innovation, or it may alert management to opportunities or threats.

A problem with market intelligence data lies in the procedures used for their collection. Unless these are systematic the data will be unrepresentative and may be misleading. Managers and salespeople need a straightforward reporting system organized in a way that minimizes the work involved. Perhaps more importantly, however, there needs to be a feeling that such reports are of real value to the organization and that they do actually feed into the decision-making process.

> ### KEY POINTS
>
> Marketing intelligence is a collection of pieces of information, often incomplete and subjective, but which allows the researcher to keep abreast of events as they unfold. Some of this information might not be regarded as "data" by some researchers, but from the point of view of seeing data as researcher constructions, they would be classified as data for the purpose of this book.

Desk research for academic projects

Desk research for client-based research is largely about accessing quantitative data both inside and outside the client organization that can be used for a range of purposes as outlined in the previous sections. A major part of any desk research for academic projects, however, will be a review of the research and the literature that has been published on the topic or the area. Clients are not interested in literature reviews, but dissertation or thesis supervisors or examiners, or reviewers of articles submitted for publication, will expect to see such a review. Strictly speaking, the literature does not constitute secondary data, although the academic researcher may utilize or re-present data that earlier researchers have already published.

A good-quality literature review is more than an annotated bibliography. It performs a number of functions. In the first place it will be used to justify:

- the originality of the project and what it will contribute to our understanding of marketing phenomena,
- the approach to the topic that is being adopted,
- the choice of methods and techniques,
- the hypotheses that are being proposed for testing.

In addition, the review performs a number of other functions. It:

- identifies the key authors and researchers and their particular perspectives on the topic,
- outlines the significant results of earlier research,
- relates the research (whether proposed or completed) to that wider literature,
- provides a benchmark for comparing and evaluating the results of the research.

The literature itself will often be very diverse and the challenge to the reviewer is to create a coherent picture – to "tell the story" of what has been done, or not done, to date. In quantitative studies the literature is usually used as a framework for establishing the research purpose and developing research questions or hypotheses. This means that the review is "up front" both in the sense that the literature is consulted before the data collection begins, and in the sense that in the research article or dissertation it is presented before the methodology and data analysis are explained. Two basic formats are common. One uses the literature to provide a background to the study and to "frame" the research problem. This is frequently done on a chronological basis, beginning with the early literature in the field and tracing its development up to the most recent studies. The other is more integrative – the literature is interwoven with the emergence of the hypotheses or with the dependent and independent variables used in the research.

In qualitative research it is sometimes argued that studying the literature first may direct or pre-empt the questions asked by the researcher. It is not possible, however, to begin a project without any preconceptions and it may be unwise to do so without checking out the literature first. In practice, the literature review itself may be placed in one of three different locations in the final report. This may be in the introduction to the study, it may arise as a separate section or chapter, or it may come at the end. This may be so when the methodology is grounded theory and the objective of the research is to generate theory rather than to test it. Here, the literature is used as a source of further data rather than as background to a particular research design.

Doing the review can be seen as involving a number of stages:

1 searching,

2 accessing sources,

3 reading,

4 summarizing,

5 drafting the review,

6 writing the final review.

Ideally, stages 1–3 should be more or less complete before you collect data. Stages 4–6 can be done later. Searching for and accessing the literature is likely, nowadays, to be done electronically sitting in front of a PC rather than scouring the library. Key databases in marketing will include *Business Elite*, *Emerald*, *Lexis-Nexus*, and the *World Advertising Research Center* (WARC).

Business Elite (available only through your own library subscription) provides full-text coverage from nearly 1100 scholarly business, management and economics journals, including nearly 450 peer-reviewed publications. The full-text coverage dates back as far as 1985. In addition to the full text, this database offers indexing and abstracts for over 1600 journals. Detailed company profiles for the world's 5000 largest companies are also included. Emerald (www.emerald-library.com) is a full-text electronic library that includes 100 journals on marketing, general management, human resources and other management areas. Lexis-Nexus (www.lexis-nexis.com) is a collection of databases containing around 1500 UK and overseas newspapers and magazines, along with company information and financial data. WARC (www.warc.com) provides articles on general advertising, marketing, brands and campaigns, plus brief economic and demographic data.

KEY POINTS

Desk research, which mostly involves checking out what research has been undertaken and what has been published on the topic under study, is a vital component of doing academic research. The role of the literature review is taken up again in Chapter 18 on the communication of results.

Ethical issues

By accessing published sources, purchasing data from a commercial organization or using the academic literature, you are using the data, ideas and findings of other researchers. It is therefore your responsibility to use the work in a way that is responsible, fair and legal. This involves making sure that you acknowledge sources correctly and that you do not infringe copyright. This means avoiding:

- not documenting the source of data that are being used or not acknowledging the authors or organizations whose tables or figures you are using,

- plagiarism – knowingly using another person's work and passing it off as your own,

- falsification – deliberately or unwittingly misrepresenting the work of others,

- fabrication – presenting your own views, opinions or speculations as if they were established facts,

- sloppiness – not providing correct citations.

All this means being scrupulous in your record keeping. Whenever you are reading a source and making notes, make sure you take down all the details you will need for your references.

SUMMARY

Data are commonly treated as "the facts". In reality, they are records that have been systematically constructed by researchers or other individuals. They are social products that have been created in a social, moral, political, economic and historical context. There are different kinds of data. One distinction is between quantitative and qualitative data. The former consist of numbers that result from a process of measurement and the imposition of a structure on the data. The latter arise as words, text or images.

Another distinction is between primary and secondary data. The former consist of data that have been constructed specifically for the project at hand, while the latter consist of data that have already been constructed for other purposes. Some of these data have been constructed by governmental or nongovernmental bodies who have put their data in the public domain. Other data may be available, at a cost, from commercial sources. There may, however, be quite a lot of data that are available within the client organization and will include operating data, company accounts, previous research, and data contained in customer databases, information systems or data warehouses.

Desk research is the act of searching out, accessing, reading and summarizing secondary data. It also means being aware of the advantages and limitations of such data. It may be possible in some cases to reanalyze existing data using some of the statistical techniques explained in Part III of this book. Gathering marketing intelligence, by contrast, is a rather less systematic process of "keeping tabs" on what is happening in the marketplace. Desk research for academic projects is more likely to entail undertaking a literature search and writing a literature review, although secondary data may also be used and incorporated. The key ethical issue that arises in an academic context is avoiding plagiarism.

QUESTIONS FOR DISCUSSION

1 Explain the differences between secondary data, secondary research, secondary analysis and a review of the literature.

2 Go to **www.statistics.gov.uk** and write a one-page summary of the kinds of data that are available from this site.

3 What ethical issues might arise when undertaking desk research for a commercial client?

CASE STUDY VODAFONE

Vodafone made the UK's first mobile telephone call in 1985. Within 15 years the network became the largest company in Europe. Vodafone Group Plc now provides a full range of telecommunications services. Mathur, Tamang and El-Emary (2002) explain that when Vodafone entered the Egyptian market in 1999, it acquired 1.3 million customers within two years. However, the mobile phone market was largely prepaid. This entailed customers subscribing from a retail outlet, providing very little information about themselves. Consequently, Vodafone had inadequate information about their customers regarding their needs, lifestyles and demographics. Vodafone had its own customer database, but it contained only usage and billing information. However, a large-scale conventional segmentation study was carried out, covering demographics, lifestyle, reasons for using a mobile phone, loyalty to service providers and what customers look for in a service provider. The mobile phone numbers were also taken and this enabled the data to be linked to the data held in the data warehouse. Vodafone could now link its own data on subscriber activation date, phone tenure, disconnection date, reasons for disconnection, number and types of calls made, number of text messages sent and so on to all the demographic and lifestyle data.

Questions and activities

1 Check out the Vodafone web site. Go to **www.vodafone.co.uk** and click on *About Vodafone*.

2 Advise Vodafone about what sources of secondary data might be available in the UK and across Europe that might help it to learn more about its customers without having to commission an expensive and large market segmentation study that would need to construct primary data.

FURTHER READING

Creswell, J. (2003) *Research Design. Qualitative, Quantitative and Mixed Methods Approaches*, 2nd edition. London: Sage. Chapter 2, Review of the Literature.

Hart, C. (1998) *Doing a Literature Review*. London: Sage.

Hart, C. (2001) *Doing a Literature Search*. London: Sage.

Irvine, J., Miles, I. and Evans, J. (eds) (1979) *Demystifying Social Statistics*. London: Pluto Press.

Leventhal, B. (2003) "Developments in outputs from the 2001 Census", *International Journal of Market Research*, 45 (1): 3–19.

Constructing qualitative data 4

LEARNING OBJECTIVES In this chapter you will learn about:

→ the nature and construction of qualitative data,

→ the characteristics of client-based qualitative market research,

→ the process of interviewing groups and individuals,

→ the alternatives to interview methods, namely observation, ethnography and consultation,

→ the nature of academic qualitative research.

A lot of qualitative research is undertaken using focus groups.

© ERICSPHOTOGRAPHY

INTRODUCTION

Qualitative marketing research seeks to explore and understand people's attitudes, perceptions, motivations and behaviors by constructing and then analyzing data that are largely qualitative in nature. This chapter explains the nature and types of qualitative data and then focuses on the construction of qualitative data by both client-based and academic researchers. It reviews the more traditional interview-based methods along with observational and ethnographic approaches that, while they have been used for a long while in the social sciences, are becoming increasingly popular in marketing research. The use of consultation is a genuinely recent phenomenon. It is currently used mainly in the public sector, but may become more common in the commercial sector as well. The analysis of qualitative data, including a consideration of their validity and reliability, will be considered later in Chapter 10.

INTERNET ACTIVITY

Using your browser, go to **www.thomsonlearning.co.uk/kent** and select the Chapter 4 Internet Activity which will provide a link to the Association for Qualitative Research website. Click on *Directory*. Read through the *Additional articles*. They are very short, but give you a good feel for what practitioners are writing about qualitative research. There is also a very useful glossary of terms, a collection of short articles, some longer in-depth articles and a downloadable *Industry Facts and Figures* in the *Reference Section*.

What are "qualitative data"?

We saw in the last chapter that qualitative data consist of words, phrases, text or images. Furthermore, like quantitative data, they arise as systematic records that have been constructed by researchers or other individuals. Although it may seem strange to think of qualitative data as being "constructed" when it is quite likely that a direct record has been made of what respondents or participants are saying, or what social actors are doing or saying, the researcher nevertheless constructs the context in which qualitative data are generated. Researchers, furthermore, when they are reporting the results of their research, also construct a "reading" or interpretation of the actors' meanings. The respondent or participant, too, certainly in in-depth interviews and in focus groups, constructs an "account" of his or her behavior, feelings or opinions for the researcher.

Qualitative data of all kinds have the key feature that at the point of data capture no structure has been imposed upon them. The researcher captures the words, phrases, text or images without a predetermined set of categories or codes on which to map responses or observations. Some qualitative data may be captured in naturally occurring, ordinary events in natural settings, giving the researcher a strong handle on what "real life" is like. Such data can provide a source of well-grounded, rich descriptions and explanations of processes in identifiable local contexts. Furthermore, they have the quality of irrefutability; a record of what people have said or done has a concrete, meaningful flavour that is often more convincing to the reader than tables of figures. Other qualitative data may be captured in very artificial settings such as an interview or focus group that has been formally prearranged or in the completion of an open-ended question in a questionnaire.

Researchers construct qualitative data by engaging in the three main activities outlined in Chapter 3, namely:

- designing research that specifies when, where and how the construction process is to take place,
- capturing data by creating a record, for example in audio or videotape recordings, in interview transcripts, field notes, photographic stills, paintings or sketches,
- assembling the data into their "raw" data format, ready for analysis.

The design elements that go into qualitative approaches are likely to involve, to varying degrees, elements that include:

- the degree of personal observation by the researcher,
- the amount of researcher participation,
- the use of interview methods,
- the extent of gathering documents and cultural artifacts.

Researchers, of course, are likely to combine these elements in various ways. The "design choices" amount to the relative emphases placed on each. Varying combinations of observation and participation have, for example, commonly given rise to different designs. An early typology suggested by Gold (1958) has over the years been influential. He distinguished between:

- the complete participant,
- the participant as observer,
- the observer as participant,
- the complete observer.

The complete participant is part of the setting being studied; the researcher takes an "insider" role that involves a covert operation, sometimes described as "disguised" observation. The participant as observer negotiates his or her way into the setting by openly acknowledging his or her exploratory purposes, participating as fully as possible in a range of activities. The agenda of the observer as participant is to observe rather than take part. The complete observer remains hidden from those being observed, using one-way mirrors or static video cameras. In practice these roles are likely to change as the research proceeds.

These roles may also be combined with interview methods like focus groups and depth interviews, with the examination of cultural artifacts like posters, magazine advertisements or even graffiti, and the gathering of secondary data, as explained in Chapter 3.

KEY POINTS

Qualitative data consist of words, phrases, text or images. Like quantitative data, they are constructed into systematic records by individuals who design the research context within which the construction is to take place, capture the data using some kind of recording device and assemble them ready for analysis.

Client-based qualitative market research

Client-based qualitative marketing research seeks to explore and understand customer or supplier attitudes, perceptions, motivations and behaviors on behalf of client organizations. It does so by constructing data that are largely qualitative in nature. Favored methods have been focus groups and depth interviews, but the range of alternative qualitative methods is developing as the profession of qualitative researchers comes of age. Typically such research entails the use of small samples of respondents who are not necessarily representative of a larger population. Also, typically, there will be a direct involvement of the researcher in all the stages of the research rather than subcontracting out components of the project, as often happens with quantitative research.

Commercial qualitative research in Europe generally has evolved in parallel with, but separately from, academic qualitative research, which exists across many disciplines in the social sciences. Relatively few textbooks about the commercial side of this activity have been written (with the exception of Ereaut et al. 2002) – it exists largely as an "oral" or craft tradition. Some of its key characteristics have been summarized by Ereaut et al. as follows:

- researchers have a dual role – they are simultaneously accountable both to research standards and to clients,
- projects are constrained by being commercial contracts,
- projects tend to be clearly defined and relatively narrow in scope,
- it is currently dominated by interview-based methods,
- it is an experienced-based practice,
- it is pragmatic and eclectic – theory is incorporated only as and when it is felt useful.

Qualitative market researchers undertaking client-based research may operate either in a commercial or in a noncommercial context. Commercial practitioners make a professional living by carrying out research projects for a fee on behalf of organizations. In this context they may operate:

- within full-service market research agencies,
- within specialist agencies,
- as researchers working on their own as sole practitioners.

Noncommercial practitioners might include:

- academics who, while probably charging a fee, are not relying on such activity as a professional living,
- students carrying out qualitative projects for clients as part of a course or dissertation.

Until the 1970s, qualitative research was very much the Cinderella of market research, often dismissed as not serious, lacking in scientific rigor, non-replicable, nongeneralizable, and subjective. However, in the past couple of decades, the amount of qualitative research undertaken has undergone an explosive growth. Though accurate statistics on industry size are difficult to find, according to Imms and Ereaut (2002) qualitative market research accounts for some €2–€3 billion of the €17 billion wordwide market research industry. In the UK, commercial qualitative research accounts for 20–25 percent of all market research, and is worth about £156 million per annum. The UK Association for Qualitative Research (AQR: www.aqr.org.uk) has over 1150 members in some 200 different companies.

The industry is characterized by a large number of smaller agencies that will typically consist of a team of 6–10 practitioners, including senior partners, managers and research executives. Analysis of the membership of the AQR suggests that about 50 percent have ten or more years' experience, about 70 percent are female and about 25 percent operate as independent practitioners. Training tends to follow the "journeyman" model with junior researchers working alongside more senior people.

Gordon (1999) picks out two different approaches to commercial qualitative research: descriptive/diagnostic and explanatory/interpretive. The first gives detailed descriptive information on category/brand behavior and attitudes plus diagnostic feedback of consumer responses to new products, pack designs and so on. It tends to be based on a single methodology – usually focus groups or depth interviews – with small samples, a standardized discussion guide and simple, direct research stimuli. The second looks for in-depth explanations and interpretations of the complex relationships people have with brands, services, corporations and so on, using multiple methods, including ethnographic, observational and interactive approaches, larger samples and projective and enabling techniques. Both, however, are eclectic, using whatever strategies, methods, materials or tools that are to hand.

Qualitative research plays a major part in supporting marketing decisions in both commercial and noncommercial organizations. It can perform a number of roles in the organization, for example it can help to explore and clarify the nature of the problems or issues facing organizational members, it can act as a preliminary stage of research to support other modes on inquiry, or it can be a design in its own right. The applications of qualitative research can be grouped loosely into four broad categories, although these will tend to overlap or be combined in one particular project:

- exploratory,
- diagnostic,
- evaluative,
- creative development.

Traditionally, qualitative research has been seen as a "preliminary" to a larger-scale quantitative study and in this sense is being used for exploratory purposes, usually in areas where little research has been done. Qualitative research will tend to be used for exploratory purposes where:

- the researcher does not know enough about a country or a market or some aspect of consumer behavior to be able to design a piece of research, submit a worthwhile research proposal, or decide on the priorities and objectives of the research,
- the researcher wants to generate hypotheses or possible explanations before embarking on the main study,
- the researcher needs to design questionnaires in which the consumer perspective on or images of products and brands need to be tested and are not known in advance, or where the words, phrases or categorizations of markets or products need to be checked before proceeding to quantitative research.

Very often companies are aware that they have a marketing problem, but are unsure whether this is a symptom of a deeper-seated problem or the cause of other problems; they may be unclear how it is related to other problems, whether it is urgent or serious, and what factors may be affecting the problem. Qualitative research may be used to diagnose in detail company or organizational problems. It may be used for diagnostic purpose for consumers as well; for example, the researcher wants to unravel complex decision-making processes, define consumer perceptions of competitive sets and brand substitutes, or the dimensions that differentiate between brands.

In evaluative research, qualitative methods may be used to assess whether or not a particular marketing proposition or marketing mix will satisfy company objectives. Qualitative research, particularly using focus groups, is frequently used to evaluate an advertising or promotional proposition. The procedure can be useful, but only if the criteria for evaluation – the benchmarks of success or failure – are clear. Thus an advertisement can be tested for understanding, link with the brand, memorability, enjoyability and so on. Some commentators (e.g. Sargent 1989: 118) are sceptical about the use of qualitative research for evaluative purposes. If the objective of the research is, for example, to pick a "winner" from a range of ideas or executions, it is, argues Sargent, more sensible to rely on quantitative assessment techniques.

One of the major strengths of qualitative research, particularly interview-based methods, is its potential for creativity and it is frequently used to generate ideas for new products or ideas for modifying products, to identify gaps in the market-place, or to generate advertising themes or ideas for promotional activity. Special techniques, which are explained later in this chapter, may be used for this purpose.

KEY POINTS

Client-based qualitative marketing research entails studying relatively few cases in depth using observation, participation, dialogue, open-ended interview techniques or the study of images or other cultural artifacts as modes of data construction. It is undertaken to help clients explore, diagnose, evaluate and create ideas by helping them to understand people's attitudes, perceptions, motivations and behaviors. Such research tends to have all the features of client-based research outlined in Chapter 1, namely:

- solution-oriented,

- not neutral,

- interventionist,

- client-led,

- contractual,

- confidential,

- pragmatic,

- time and cost constrained,

- report-based.

Interviewing groups and individuals

In client-based market research the main contexts in which qualitative data are constructed are focus groups and depth interviews. Both are interview-based methods. It is tempting to suggest that the key difference between them is that depth interviews are on a one-to-one basis between researcher and respondent, and that groups involve several respondents together with the researcher in the same room at the same time. However, some depth interviews may take place with married couples, families, or even two or three friends together; some focus groups may be in groups as small as five or six respondents. A more crucial difference is that in depth interviews the main lines of communication are between interviewer and respondent; in focus groups, it is the verbal interactions between respondents that assume a major role.

Chrzanowska (2002), who has been a qualitative market researcher for over 30 years, suggests that the skills needed for both group and individual interviews are much the same and she treats them both together. Interviewing groups and individuals is a craft skill that does not explicitly use any particular paradigm or conceptual model. It has often been described as pragmatic and eclectic or as needing the skills of a "bricoleur". Chrzanowska (2002) sees it as a mindset that is nonjudgmental, willing to deal with emotions, aware of their own presence and preparedness to be flexible. The kinds of skills that are needed, she suggests, include:

- being able to elicit information without asking too many direct questions or leading questions,
- good listening,
- sensitivity to nonverbal cues,
- creating trust and empathy,
- keeping people focused.

Qualitative researchers, furthermore, tend to make assumptions, usually unarticulated, that are based on earlier theoretical principles. Thus some may assume, based on earlier psychoanalytic theory, that there is such a thing as the "unconscious" of which individuals may themselves be unaware and it is the purpose of the interviewer to uncover this. The danger here is making unfounded interpretations, so many qualitative researchers instead focus on establishing contexts in which respondents can articulate their emotions, needs and desires for themselves. This means that what people actually say is taken at face value and is not interpreted further as indicators of deeper unconscious feelings or emotions.

There have been longstanding concerns about the nature of interview data. It has been suggested that interviews (whether group or individual) are essentially narratives that afford respondents the opportunity to construct certain self-images rather than providing factual accounts of what they think and how they behave. There are, furthermore, often problems with remembering and describing actions that are processed in the brain in ways that may be hard to recall.

Focus groups

A distinction is sometimes drawn between focus groups and group discussions. The former are seen as American-style groups in which the focus is on getting answers out of participants using structured techniques, while the latter are European-style in which the emphasis is on exploration and understanding in a largely unstructured and free-wheeling discussion. However, the term "focus groups" is increasingly becoming standard to refer to either style of group.

Clients often see focus groups as being little more than a convenient (and relatively cheap) way of gathering the views of more than one person at a time. However, as indicated above, it is the interactions between respondents that are important. Groups take on a life of their own, varying from group to group, and are influenced by a large number of factors including the size of the group, its composition, the personalities of those present, the tasks they are asked to perform, the physical conditions of the meeting place, and the "chemistry" between interviewer and respondents. The group itself has an influence back on the individual, and what is said relates to the total experience of being in the group. The results achieved by group discussions are more than, or at least different from, the sum of what would be obtained by interviewing respondents individually.

Clearly, different views may be taken about the optimum size of group, but the norm that has developed in Europe is that "standard" groups have seven to nine respondents, with eight being the favored number since it facilitates different combinations in terms of the composition of the groups. A standard group discussion will not normally be longer than an hour and a half. Where it is felt that a longer time is needed, for example to perform more complex tasks, then such groups will be referred to as "extended" groups.

Box 4.1 describes how the market research agency Green Light International (www.greenlightresearch.com) conducted a series of focus groups – it calls them discussion groups – in a range of countries. The discussions lasted about two hours.

Planning focus groups

When planning focus groups, the main considerations in terms of setting up and running the groups include:

- the type of group,
- group composition,
- the number of groups,
- recruitment,
- topics to be discussed,
- method of running the group,
- the places, venues and timings.

EUROPEAN MARKETING RESEARCH
What women think, feel and hope for in the 21st century

BOX 4.1

Jack and Burnside (2002) from Green Light International report the results from group discussions held in London, Paris, Munich, Milan, Madrid, Warsaw and Sydney among women in a range of life-stage groups, including pre-family, working mothers, nonworking mothers and post-family. The idea was to gain insights into what makes women of different generations tick, what are their hopes and fears, and how they see their role in society. Respondents were asked to undertake a few tasks before coming to the discussion, for example they were asked to bring along an object that they felt currently represented their life and they were asked to take photos of aspects of their everyday lives.

The researchers looked at the effect of life-stage and found a diversity of attitudes within the groups. The empty nesters, they concluded, were the "new youth", offering untapped opportunities for the marketer and advertiser.

Types of groups

Apart from the standard groups already referred to, the main variations in types of groups include those outlined in Table 4.1. Most groups, however, are standard. The variations may be used where standard groups have not produced fresh information or the kind of information required.

Group composition

Group composition is a difficult decision. There are two main issues.

- Who does the researcher want to talk to?
- Should the groups be homogeneous or heterogeneous in terms of key characteristics?

The first issue means defining the population to be studied and from which the sample of respondents will be chosen. For branded products, a key choice is in terms of product usage. Should the groups consist of:

- brand users only,
- product class users only,
- users and nonusers of the product?

It also needs to be decided whether the usage categories should include both sexes, all ages, all social classes or just some of these.

In terms of the second issue, the choices range from making each group homogeneous in terms of key characteristics to deliberately ensuring a cross-section in each group. Key variables will commonly be product usage, gender and age. If, for example, it has been decided to use four groups with product usage and age as the key variables, the creation of relatively homogeneous groups might be as illustrated in Table 4.2. This facilitates analysis since, apart from perhaps mini-groups, it is not usually possible to identify which individuals have made which

TABLE 4.1	Types of focus groups
Group types	**Characteristics**
Standard groups	7–9 participants for about 90 minutes.
Mini-groups	For 5–6 people. Used for interviewing children, for sensitive, intimate or personal topics, when there is a need to explore individual behavior, or for brief, quick-reaction groups.
Extended groups	Standard size, but last 3–4 hours. Use more complex tasks, a lot of stimulus material or projective techniques. For more in-depth explorations of psychological issues or for studying complex or fragmented markets.
Reconvened groups	Meet on more than one occasion, e.g. two sessions separated by a week. Normally used for trying out a product between meetings.
Sensitivity panels	The same respondents are used on a number of occasions, attending weekly or two-weekly sessions. Respondents are trained using a variety of different techniques. Best for exploration, invention and diagnosis, not evaluation.
Creativity groups	Uses brainstorming or synectics for problem-solving in an innovative manner.

TABLE 4.2	An example of homogeneous groups	
Group	Usage	Age
I	Users	20–35
II	Non-users	36–50
III	Non-users	20–35
IV	Users	36–50

comments. However, if a particular comment comes only from groups I and IV, these are users; if it comes from II and IV, it is the older groups. The drawback is that discussions between users and nonusers is eliminated; so is discussion between younger and older people. If the four groups are all mixed, there is maximum potential for divergent opinions, but relating these opinions to product usage or demographic characteristics will be difficult.

Using more categories, for example four age groups and three usage categories – heavy, medium and light – or more variables, for example sex and region, makes too many combinations for the number of groups required. One possibility is to use other experimental designs like Latin squares (explained later on p. 205) in which not every combination is applied.

Number of groups

Qualitative research is small-scale research, and it would not be normal to run more than about 12 groups. Diminishing marginal returns rapidly set in thereafter and interviewers will find themselves anticipating most responses and learning little new from additional groups. In the 1980s a common design in the UK was to have four groups, two North, two South, two ABC1 and two C2DE. Further multiples of four facilitate other permutations. Goodyear (1990) suggests that for strategic projects or for exploratory research more groups, perhaps up to 30, may be required; tactical projects on the other hand may require only 2–8 groups. Gordon and Langmaid (1988), however, suggest that unless the research is working in a highly segmented market, for example financial services, it becomes unwieldy to conduct a large number of groups. In terms of recruitment, there are two main aspects: sampling and persuading those selected to attend the group discussion. Sampling is usually disproportionate quota sampling. Part-time recruiters, who either work for the agency conducting the research or who operate freelance and who live in the area selected for one or more groups, are asked to recruit the required number of people who meet the quota requirements. Recruiters will receive both telephone and written instructions on the project.

Some groups are very mixed.

Recruitment

Usually there will be a short recruitment questionnaire that screens out those not part of the population to be studied. For those remaining, the recruiter will ascertain the information required for quota controls and, where appropriate, for allocation to a particular group. The quotas will normally be in terms of gender, age, social class and product usage, but not necessarily proportionate to their numbers in the population. Thus the recruiter may be asked to obtain eight users and eight non-users of Brand A, even though, say, only 10 percent of the defined population use Brand A. More recently, life cycle, lifestyle and attitudes may be used as quotas, but this complicates considerably the recruitment questionnaire.

How individuals who meet the quota requirements are located is usually up to the individual recruiter. Normally it will be by door-to-door interviewing, but if, for example, the recruiter is asked to obtain mothers with young children, she may stand outside a number of school gates or health clinics. Care is usually taken to avoid recruiting friends or relatives to the same groups, and to avoid people who have frequently or recently been interviewed for market research purposes. Some difficult-to-find respondents may be obtained through social networks using snowball sampling – using contacts to suggest others who may be in the same category, then using these contacts to suggest further contacts, and so on.

Qualitative research agencies each have their own ways of operating. Some use field managers or supervisors; others may employ direct researcher-to-recruiter contact. There is often a problem of overresearched areas where recruiters happen to live. There has also been talk of "professional groupies" – those who seem to make a habit of appearing in group discussions.

Unlike other areas of market research, respondents in focus groups are usually paid an "incentive" to cover travel expenses, time and inconvenience. Few people, however, attend just for the money. Curiosity is a powerful motivator, but it is usually the skill of the recruiter in establishing rapport on the doorstep that is the deciding factor. Good recruiters plan where and how to recruit, setting daily targets, and try to find the most difficult categories of people first. Sometimes, former respondents are recontacted after a statutory "fallow" period, or members of the respondent's family are co-opted by telephone.

Topics to be discussed

The topics to be discussed in the groups will be those agreed between the client and the agency at the briefing meeting, and may even be formalized in a written research proposal. The interviewers will normally be given guidelines on how the topics are to be introduced and in what order, but it will be up to the interviewer to decide when to move on to the next topic. This may be because time is pressing, or because he or she has decided that the topic has been sufficiently aired or senses that respondents are beginning to dry up or tire of the topic.

Method of running the groups

It is in the method of running groups that there is probably most variation. The three key dimensions here are the role of the group interviewer, the use of stimulus material and the use of projective techniques. The group interviewer is usually referred to as a "moderator". He or she will usually be a research executive from the agency that specializes in qualitative market research and who will have been involved with the initial discussions and briefing with clients and who will write up the results and possibly present them. Where the number of groups is small, the same person will probably do them all, otherwise a small team may be required. Sometimes agencies will subcontract to professional moderators operating on a freelance basis.

The main tasks of the moderator are to:

■ ensure that the conditions of the discussion are correctly set up,

■ get the discussion going,

■ introduce new topics as appropriate,

■ wind up the discussion in a satisfactory manner.

If the venue is a private house, then the moderator will need to check out the seating arrangements. As far as possible, this should be in a circle with all the chairs the same height. This is often difficult with a mixture of sofas, armchairs, stools and dining chairs. Normally, the discussion will be tape recorded, so it is necessary to check that this is correctly placed and in working order. If stimulus materials are to be used, they, too, will need to be checked.

There is no agreed pattern or routine for getting the discussion going. Sometimes respondents are shown into the room where the moderator is as they arrive. The moderator will need to engage them in small talk until all are present, but it does mean that some rapport is set up in advance. Sometimes the respondents gather elsewhere in the house and are shown into the room together. When beginning, the moderator will introduce himself or herself, say on behalf of what agency the research is being conducted, and indicate the topics that are to be covered. Usually there will be reassurances that all responses are confidential, that it is not a "test", so there are no "correct" answers, that the tape recorder is only to help make a note of what people say. Some moderators believe in warm-up or ice-breaking strategies, for example, getting respondents to introduce themselves and say what they do. There is a danger here of establishing a "turn-taking" routine with each communication being directed to the moderator. The moderator needs above all to encourage the respondents to interact and to communicate with each other.

Once a discussion begins, the moderator can follow one of three main roles: take a "back seat" and just observe what is happening with little intervention (although the "fly-on-the-wall" model is no longer accepted); become one of the group; continue to be the focus of attention. Each of these has its strengths and drawbacks. In the end it is probably best for the moderator to play the role that he or she feels most comfortable with or feels is appropriate for that particular group.

There are few general rules or guides as to how the moderator should proceed as he or she introduces the appropriate topics. The sequencing of topics and tasks will have been agreed with the client before the discussions begin. For example, should respondents be shown the new packaging for the product before they discuss the existing brand, or afterwards? The moderator will have a topic guide or perhaps even a full interview guide which explains how respondents are to be asked to take part in all stages of the interview. The moderator will need to understand the processes of group dynamics to ensure a successful outcome. Thus it has been suggested (for example by Tuckman 1986) that all groups go through four key stages: forming, storming, norming and performing. In the forming stage there is a lot of superficial chat. The moderator needs to give respondents easy tasks to do and encourage them to develop a group spirit. As participants begin to size up each other, competitiveness creeps in, and there may be rivalries for attention and control. This is the storming stage, and the moderator will need to help the group to get to the next stage, norming, before it can work together effectively. Acceptable ways of doing things become established and people settle down to the task at hand. In the last stage, performing, the group should be ready to tackle more demanding tasks.

Winding up the discussion in a satisfactory manner is all too frequently neglected. A group that has been operating well together needs a few moments to wind down. Signals that the discussion is nearly over need to be given, for example: "The last thing I'd like you to do is . . .". If the moderator brings the discussion to an abrupt end, people my feel that they have been used and then just dropped, and a sense of dissatisfaction may develop.

In running groups, not only does the moderator have to be aware of group dynamics, but he or she needs to use nonverbal communication – body language such as posture, tone of voice, eye contact, facial expression – to keep the social interaction proceeding smoothly. At the end of the day it is the moderator's responsibility to:

- direct the flow of the discussion over areas that are important to the research,
- recognize important points and encourage groups to explore them and elaborate on them,
- observe all the nonverbal communication between respondents and between respondents and moderator,
- create an atmosphere that allows respondents to relax and lower some of their defences,
- synthesize the understanding gained with the problems and objectives of the research,
- test out hypotheses generated by the information gained as the discussion proceeds.

All this requires training and it takes practice. Gordon and Langmaid (1988: 51) suggest that, in their experience, two years is an absolute minimum from setting out as a novice to attaining a thorough grounding in both group and individual interviewing skills.

The role of the moderator, then, is crucial for how group discussions are run. There are, however, two other key factors that come into play: the use of stimulus materials and the use of projective techniques. Stimulus materials may be shown to respondents to communicate the idea of a new product, pack or advertising, and may be realistic or rough. Real materials include actual products, advertising or promotional materials. Wherever possible, real materials are to be preferred. If the topic for discussion is a particular existing brand of snack or drink then it can become part of the discussion. However, if the products are not yet fully developed, the rough materials might include:

- concept boards,
- storyboards,
- animatics,
- narrative tapes,
- physical mock-ups.

Concept boards are single posters in which the product, pack or advertising for the product is described in words or expressed as drawings. It would be usual to use a set of concept boards for comparative purposes rather than one on its own. Storyboards illustrate key frames from a commercial, drawn consecutively like a comic strip. They may be accompanied by a script written below or by a tape recorder with sound effects. Sometimes the frames are revealed one by one using flip-over boards to stop respondents reading ahead. Animatics are a bit like crude cartoons with a sequence of frames videoed to represent live action and accompanied by a sound track. Variations are photomatics, using photographs to show the story more realistically, or admatics, which use computer-generated images to improve on animatics. Narrative tapes are audiotapes on which the product, the dialogue, the scene and characters are explained. The tapes may be accompanied by key visuals. Physical mock-ups may be of the product itself or of the packaging. The idea is to make the product as "real" as possible.

Projective techniques Unstructured and indirect forms of questioning that encourage respondents to project their underlying motivations, beliefs, attitudes or feelings.

The problem with such rough materials is that they are usually seen as "real" by respondents, who do not "see" the concept board, but a real advertisement. In consequence, many researchers use more indirect means where the stimulus materials are ambiguous. Such **projective techniques** have their roots in psycho-analysis and are based on theories that suggest that as children develop, they deal with those aspects of their behavior and personality that are unwanted by projecting them out onto the environment, or by repressing them, that is, denying their existence. As a consequence, there are aspects of adult personality, feelings and emotions that people are not aware of at a cognitive level. Projective techniques tap these repressed or projected elements by asking individuals to respond to ambiguous stimuli. The result, so advocates of these techniques argue, is that respondents reveal layers of their personality, emotions and feelings that would otherwise remain hidden.

Practitioners tend to have their own preferred techniques, but the most common are procedures for:

- association,
- completion,
- transformation,
- construction.

Association procedures include word association (e.g. "What do you associate with the word . . .?"), collage building (from a wide variety of materials cut out from magazines), or psychodrawing. In word association tests an interviewer reads a word and asks the respondent to mention the first thing that comes to mind. Typically the individual will respond with a parallel idea or an opposite idea. The words are read in quick succession to avoid time for defence mechanisms to come into play.

Completion procedures include sentence completion, story completion or bubble cartoons (asking respondents to fill in thought bubbles of people drawn in simple cartoon style). Transformation procedures involve inviting respondents to imagine transforming brands into people (e.g. "If this brand came to life as a person, what would he or she be like?") or into animals, or to transform them-selves into a brand. Construction procedures ask respondents to construct a role (e.g. acting out a buying situation) or to construct an obituary for a brand, saying what it would be remembered for and so on.

Interpreting responses to these procedures, clearly, requires skill and imagina-tion. It also requires sensitivity to judge when is the most appropriate moment to introduce them. There is also the danger of using such techniques casually and only as a form of substitute stimulus material.

Brainstorming A technique that is used in a focus group setting to generate as many ideas as possible. No judgment or evaluation of the ideas takes place during the brainstorming phase.

Where the aim of the focus group is idea generation, then a technique called **brainstorming** may be used. Thus was developed by Osborn in the late 1930s (see Osborn 1963). A theme for the brainstorm is identified and a group of 8–15 interested participants are invited to amass ideas spontaneously. No judgment or evaluation of the ideas is made. After the brainstorming, the ideas may be grouped into themes and evaluated in a more considered fashion.

The remaining issues concerning the setting up and running of group discussions concern the place, the venue and the timing. It is unreasonable to expect respondents to travel long distances to attend group discussions. In consequence, in the UK, there has been a tendency for groups to be held in the home of the recruiter to which both the moderator from the agency and the respondents come. Respondents are more likely to feel comfortable in a private house, particularly if the discussion is held in the evening. However, there are problems. People's living rooms will vary in many ways and are not always suitable in terms of seating arrangements or space to display a large concept board.

In the USA and in many other countries it is more usual to have specially equipped consumer laboratories or viewing rooms to which respondents are invited. Clients may view one or more of the discussions from behind a one-way mirror to get a feel for how they are conducted and the kinds of things that get said about their products. Viewing facilities in London are now becoming more commonplace, but in the regions they are rare. If a client wishes to see groups in operation he or she will need to join the group in person. However, if clients wish groups to be videoed, then recruiters' sitting rooms may not be suitable. It is frequently argued, however, that central viewing facilities tend to inhibit relaxed discussion and are more likely to induce groups to perform their tasks like committees.

KEY POINTS

In focus groups it is the verbal interactions between participants that are important. There are several different types of group and their planning and running are by no means standard. At the end of the day it is the skill of the moderator that determines the quality of the data that emerge.

Depth interviews

It has already been suggested that the crucial difference between depth interviews and group discussions is that in the former the main lines of communication are between interviewer and respondent (or respondents), rather than between respondents themselves. To distinguish depth interviews from the kind of standard questionnaire-administered face-to-face interviews, it is helpful to remember that qualitative research is based on open-ended interview methods. This means that the interviewer is not constrained by precoded questions or even by a fixed sequence of questions. It is more along the lines of a conversation on an agreed topic, and the data are captured in the form of narrative rather than isolated statements.

A depth interview is more like a conversation with a purpose.

© ANDY BISHOP/ALAMY

Planning depth interviews

When planning depth interviews, the main design considerations are:

- who to talk to,
- the type of interview,
- the degree of "depth" required,
- the degree of structuring,
- the use of stimulus material,
- the location and method of data capture.

Who to talk to

There are three key subissues relating to the first design consideration, who to talk to. First, what kind of person, second, how many people and third, how they are to be selected. "Executive" interviews will be with managers in organizations whether business or nonprofit-making, and will concern either the role, actions or perceptions of that individual in the organization, or information about the way in which the organization (or parts of it) does things. Consumer interviews will be outside the organizational or work context and will treat individuals as private consumers. Since depth interviews are usually one-to-one, they take a considerable amount of time, so 10–15 interviews may be all that is needed to get a feel for the kinds of views being expressed. The selection of potential respondents to approach will, for executive interviews, be based on the position of the individual in the company; the selection of companies or organizations themselves will often be based on business directories or directories of other types of organization. The selection and recruitment of consumers will usually be on the same basis as for group discussions, that is, they are "pre-recruited". This means that they have already agreed to the interview at the recruitment stage.

Type of interview

Who to talk to overlaps with the consideration of the type of interview because, for example, executive and consumer interviews are different types of interview based on the kind of person. Interview type may also be based on the role the interviewee is expected to play, and on the number of people involved in the same interview. Interviewees may act as either (or both) informants or as respondents. As informants, they give information that is not about themselves, but about the organization in which they work or are members. Many executive interviews are of this kind, where the manager is being asked by the researcher for information about the organization and the way it operates. However, consumer interviews may be about information on other members of the family, for example how much television they watch. As respondents, people give personal information – either their role in an organization or their role as consumers. The researcher may, of course, ask the interviewee to act in both these roles.

Not all depth interviews are one-to-one. Some are paired, triangular or family interviews. Executive interviewing will sometimes be with more than one executive together, for example the marketing manager and the public relations officer. Consumer interviews may be with married couples or the whole family at home. Young children can often be more successfully interviewed in a family context than in a peer group environment. Willis (1990: 256) suggests that triangular interviews, consisting of three participants who often know one another, are very useful among teenagers, particularly in sensitive product areas. Such interviews encourage interaction and can even be set up to encourage debate, for example by deliberately recruiting a user, a nonuser and a lapsed user to discuss a product. At this point the depth interview is barely distinguishable from a mini-group discussion, except perhaps in terms of the number of participants. Family interviews may be necessary where it is important to understand the influences of individual family members on the purchase of shared products.

Degree of depth

The term "depth interview" can be a bit of a misnomer for some of the interviews that are included in this category. Depth is a matter of degree, and some may be quite superficial. Some interviews may be journalistic in nature. They accept what people say at face value, they are descriptive and seek basic information from respondents. Genuine depth interviews go beyond the face value, looking for patterns and frameworks, and interpreting the meanings and implications of what was said. Projective techniques may be used to tap "hidden" emotions. "Mini-depth interviews" may be conducted over a short 15–30 minute period, for example to test a specific piece of communication (such as a pack design), or to explore specific research objectives. A "standard" consumer depth interview will last 45 minutes to an hour. "Extended" depths may last for up to two-and-a-half hours and will be used in circumstances similar to extended group discussions.

Structuring

The degree of structuring may be anything from completely open-ended to a semi-structured interview in which there is a detailed interview guide to the topics to be covered.

Stimulus material

The various kinds of stimulus material and the use of projective techniques have already been explained in the context of group discussions, but the choice and design of the stimuli must be appropriate to the one-to-one nature of most interviews. It can be more complex than for group discussions since the respondent is not distracted by the interaction of the group environment.

Location

The location of depth interviews is, in the UK, normally in respondents' own homes, but may be in the recruiters' homes, in a central location with a viewing room, or in a hotel. Factors affecting the decision will include the sensitivity of the topic matter, the status, availability and location of the interviewees, the nature and amount of stimulus material to be used, and the need for the interview to be observed by others. Executive interviews will usually be in the office of the executive or occasionally in one of the company meeting rooms.

Normally, the interview will be tape recorded. In a central location viewing room there will usually be facilities for videoing the interview as well as observing it while remaining unseen. This, however, may be unsettling for the individuals concerned, perhaps more so than for groups, when the feeling of being watched or videoed together may not be so threatening as when being individually "exposed" or "watched".

Groups or depths: the choice of method

Most qualitative research is undertaken using focus groups and it is felt by some writers (e.g. Gordon and Langmaid 1988: 15) that depth interviews are seriously underrated and often misused or misunderstood by buyers of qualitative research. In deciding which of the two methods to use, it is helpful to bear in mind the advantages and limitations of each.

The key advantages of groups are:

- the group environment with "everybody in the same boat" can be less intimidating than individual depth interviews,
- what respondents say in a group often sparks experiences or ideas on the part of others,
- differences between consumers are highlighted, making it possible to understand a range of attitudes in a short space of time,
- it is easier to observe groups,
- social and cultural influences are highlighted,
- groups provide a social context that is a "hothoused" reflection of the real world,
- groups tend to be dynamic and often, though not necessarily, more creative,
- groups are relatively cheaper and faster than depth interviews.

The main disadvantages of groups are:

- group processes may inhibit some people from making a full contribution and may encourage others to play to the audience,
- group processes may stall beyond retrieval by the moderator,
- some groups take on a life of their own, and what is said may have validity only in that context,
- it is not usually possible to identify which group members said what unless it has been videoed.

Turning now to depth interviews, their key strengths are where the group discussion is weak, for example:

- longitudinal information, for example, on decision-making processes, can be gathered one respondent at a time,
- it is possible to identify exactly who said what,
- both majority and minority opinions can be captured irrespective of personalities and group processes,
- intimate and personal material can be more easily discussed,
- respondents are less likely to simply express socially acceptable attitudes and behavior,
- problems of recruitment to a group are avoided.

The main disadvantages of depth interviews are:

- they are time-consuming both to conduct and to analyze; a maximum of three to four a day is often all that is possible and traveling time between interviews can be considerable,
- they are relatively more costly,

- there is a temptation to begin treating depth interviews as if they were a questionnaire survey, thinking in terms of "how many" rather than "how", "why" or "what",

- there is less opportunity for creativity arising from group dynamics.

Which of these advantages and limitations are important depends, clearly, on the objectives of the research, but also, crucially, on a number of other key factors:

- the problems of recruitment,
- the geographical scatter of the sample,
- the nature of the product being researched,
- the amount of information required,
- the constraints of budget and time.

With difficult-to-recruit consumers or with busy executives the only practical solution is to interview individually, irrespective of other advantages and limitations. If the people to be interviewed are widely scattered or very heterogeneous it may be extremely difficult and costly to bring them together for focus groups. Where the subject matter relates to a personal or intimate topic, like sanitary protection, then, again, depth interviews may be called for, as will be the case where the information required means connecting comments with particular individuals, for example on the history of the ownership of consumer durables. Perhaps the main reason, however, for the popularity of focus groups relates to time and budget constraints. This is not the best of reasons for choosing groups, but the alternative may be no research at all if time and money *are* limited.

KEY POINTS

Depth interviews are seen as the main alternative to focus groups. They have a number of advantages and limitations and they may well both be used in a single project. Across Europe, qualitative research accounts for between about 10 and 18 percent of total turnover in the market research industry (ESOMAR 2005). In all countries this is predominantly in the form of focus groups. In-depth interviews tend to account for only 2–3 percent of total turnover.

Alternatives to interview methods

The alternatives to either focus groups or depth interviews include other consumer research designs that rely on direct contact with the consumer, for example:

- observation
- ethnography,
- consultation.

Observation

Personal observation, as opposed to observations taken by mechanical means, can be used whenever it is possible to collect data by watching what consumers do in the process of purchasing goods or services, by checking the quality of

Personal observation Observations made personally by the researcher of consumer or managerial behavior as it occurs, or of the physical characteristics of the marketing environment.

services provided by retail and service outlets, or by noting the availability, quantity and prices of branded goods on shelves in shops or in the home. Observation may be the only realistic option available where to ask people questions may result in misleading information and where there are no mechanical or electronic means of taking systematic records.

Consumer behavior can be watched either in its natural or in an artificial setting. In a natural setting an observer may, for example, note the length of queues at checkouts in a supermarket at specified intervals during the day, the length of time motorists spend in a filling station, or whether or not they are wearing seat belts while driving. In pubs and bars at least one market research company positions "monitors" to watch how people go about ordering drinks. Observation in a natural context is usually disguised, that is, the people being observed are unaware of the fact. This is usually seen to be perfectly acceptable if the behavior is in a public place where it can be watched by anybody. Disguised observation has the added advantage that the behavior being recorded will not be affected by the process of observation.

Undisguised observation in a natural setting is exemplified by what is often called "**accompanied shopping**". An observer from a market research agency accompanies a shopper as he or she goes round a supermarket, noting how she goes about making selection of brands, whether prices are checked and so on. The interview will usually begin in the respondent's own home with a discussion about his or her state of mind concerning the purchase and the influences that may affect the decision. Both respondent and researcher then go to the shop where the respondent will be encouraged to ignore the researcher and carry on looking, choosing and buying as normal. The researcher will observe and record the respondent's progress. The last part of the interview will involve a full discussion of what has taken place, how this matched expectations of the visit and how this differed from recalled behavior. However, there is always the danger that if people are aware of being observed, they may try to act more "rationally" than they would normally do. Box 4.2 shows how accompanied shopping was used in a study of consumer understanding of unit pricing.

Accompanied shopping An observer, usually from a market research agency, who personally accompanies a shopper on her or his shopping trip, noting shopping behavior as it occurs.

Sometimes researchers accompany shoppers on their shopping expeditions.

© DAVID LEVENSON/ALAMY

RESEARCH IN ACTION
Consumer awareness, understanding and usage of unit pricing

BOX 4.2

Mitchell et al. (2003) used accompanied shopping in their study of consumer awareness, understanding and usage of unit pricing along with self-completed questionnaires and simulated tasks. Twenty-one accompanied shopping trips were conducted to capture insights into the nature of consumer problem-solving in a retail setting. In a debriefing session, shoppers were asked, for example, how they worked out – if they did – which alternative brands or packages would work out cheaper. The results were fed into a questionnaire to examine consumer awareness, understanding and usage of unit pricing as well as why they did not use it. Over 1000 shoppers took part in a self-completion questionnaire. The results showed that, for example, 31 percent did not understand how unit pricing was meant to help them to compare products; 35 percent could not be bothered to look at unit prices and 28 percent said that it was too difficult to use.

In an artificial context, focus groups may be viewed by researchers and/or clients behind a one-way mirror, or consumers may be invited to purchase goods in an artificial "store" where their choice behavior is monitored using in-store cameras.

One method for checking the quality of services provided by retail and other service outlets is **mystery shopping** or mystery customer research. This involves visits by specially trained assessors to shops, restaurants, banks or other businesses in which quality of provision is to be evaluated (Morrison et al. 1997). The assessors pose as ordinary customers and check the attainment of predefined service standards that have been drawn up in consultation with the client. Thus, for a bank, was the assessor attended to within two minutes? Was she greeted with a smile? Was the transaction completed efficiently? Was she asked if she wanted any further services? From the results it is possible to compare branches of the bank and see what proportions reach given standards. These performances can then be compared with the performances of competitors. Any failings can be identified and incorporated into a training or retraining program for staff.

Mystery shopping is ideal when the client has certain standards of actual service performance that he or she wants evaluated by a trained customer. There may be some aspects of service that the company deems to be important, so the mystery shopper is trained to look for these things that the ordinary consumer may not notice. One development of mystery shopping is competitor mystery shopping. Instead of getting assessors to pose as shoppers for the organization's own outlets, it does this to competitors. There are ethical issues here, particularly in relation to potentially wasting the time of assistants in competitor outlets.

Mystery customer research, although not without its critics (e.g. Brown 1990), is an industry currently worth an estimated £10 million annually in the UK (Miles 1993) and is growing rapidly. A survey of commercial companies carried out by Dawson and Hillier (1995) found that more than two-thirds had commissioned mystery consumer research in their own companies, on competitor companies or both. Some companies, however, avoid using mystery shopping because of worries about potential problems that might arise in the absence of stringent guidelines to ensure accuracy of evaluations. Despite codes of conduct that have been introduced by ESOMAR and the Market Research Society in the UK, some aspects of the technique are open to interpretation and manipulation. Morrison et al. (1997) comment on potential threats to the reliability and validity of the data collected by such means. Various factors associated with the encoding, storage and retrieval of information by mystery consumer assessors are likely to influence the accuracy of the results. Thus memory may be affected by a range of factors like lighting, physical conditions, time of day, attitudes, social pressures or mood.

Mystery shopping Researchers pose as ordinary customers in a retail or service environment to evaluate the quality or the service provided using predefined service standards.

Furthermore, individual differences between assessors should also be taken into account in designing such research, although such differences may be deliberately planned in to see, for example, if banks or insurance companies treat female or black customers in the same way as male or white.

To note the availability, quantity and prices of branded goods on shelves in shops or in the home, a number of market research agencies, particularly those which offer retail panel services, send observers into selected shops to record systematically, for a specified range of branded goods, whether these products are available on the shelves, in display areas or in the stockroom. The length of facings occupied by a brand may be measured, its price noted and perhaps quantities counted. In a full retail audit such data may be used in combination with records of deliveries to calculate sales. Some agencies restrict themselves to "distribution checks" or offer "shelf-observation" services. It is also possible, of course, to observe what products and what brands people have on the shelves, in cupboards, or in the fridge at home.

Except where observation is being used for exploratory research in order to get the "feel" for some situation, it is usually structured. This means that observations are recorded into predetermined categories so that the frequency of behavioral occurrences, or durations of time, or lengths of shelf-space can be noted. The result is quantitative data, so observation is certainly not an exclusively qualitative method. The key advantage of observation over asking people questions is that no reliance is placed on people's memories, guesses, or honesty. There is little point in asking people if they always wear a seat belt when driving; they will always say "yes". It is better to observe how many in fact do.

Observation, clearly, has its limitations and drawbacks. Often it is just not possible or feasible. It is also labor-intensive – one person can observe the occurrence of only a limited number of phenomena. Observation can be only of behavior – it is not possible to observe attitudes, opinion, or what people think. Box 4.3 explains that observation does not necessarily lead to insight.

The use of mechanical recording devices such as bar scanners to record purchase at a retail outlet, people meters for recording television viewing or recording click-through rates on the internet is sometimes included as "observation". However, these devices are probably best seen as instruments of data capture, and are considered in more detail in Chapter 6.

RESEARCH IN ACTION   BOX 4.3
Observation is not insight

Hall (2003) suggests that a lot of marketing research is obsessed with observation; but observation, even if accompanied by varying degrees of participation in the lives of consumers, does not necessarily result in insight. An insight is something that discerns an underlying truth. For a marketer it is the strongest point of emotional leverage to which companies can connect their products and their brands. Insight does not usually come from flashes of inspiration or even from a group of people having a chat over coffee. It is more likely, argues Hall, to emerge from events dedicated to insight generation. He describes how Research International used a particular process for turning video-clip observation into actionable insights. A team consisting of an ethnographic researcher, an expert in consumer understanding and an innovation manager generated "insight platforms" that could be used to turn insight into marketing ideas for dental health care products for children.

> ## KEY POINTS
>
> Observation in marketing research usually means personal as opposed to mechanical. It is usually treated as a qualitative method although it may well result in the construction of quantitative as well as qualitative data. It is usually mixed with varying degrees of researcher participation, but in some situations observation is used on its own without participation.

Ethnography

Ethnography developed out of anthropology and literally means the writing of a culture. It is therefore based on culture as an organizing concept and involves the idea of researcher immersion in that culture in order to understand it. Ethnographers study the nature, construction and maintenance of commonly held tacit knowledge, beliefs, values and shared systems of meanings in a group, organization, community or society. Culture accounts for a particular way of life and is expressed in social norms, rituals, the use of language and various forms of communication. Early ethnography focused on exotic, often disappearing foreign cultures, but more recently it has been applied to modern societies and to groups and subcultures within them, for example sociologists began studying slums, ghettos and gangs in city areas.

Ethnography involves a combination of the observation of and participation in "real life" in its natural setting by the researcher. Essentially, the researcher becomes immersed in the group, experiencing what participation in that culture is like. He or she tries to uncover the structures of meanings in social settings. This operation may be overt or covert. The aim is to provide a holistic picture of the group in all its aspects, and how these aspects relate together. Ethnography is both a research methodology – a way of constructing data – and a product of that research, that is, a way of analyzing the data. The product is a written description of a culture. Ethnography may combine both qualitative and quantitative elements, but more usually the former. It typically uses a mix of observational techniques, interviewing and the analysis of documents.

These methods are now increasingly used in commercial market research. They are particularly helpful for target audiences that are difficult to reach by conventional methods (e.g. nightclubbers) and product fields where there are strong social pressures to conform or say the right thing (e.g. healthy eating). They can explore the physical and social contexts in which behavior is embedded and look in detail at routine and habitual behavior to which we pay little or no attention and would find difficult to describe (e.g. low-involvement brand choice behavior). Recent studies have included things like consumption experiences of ethnic minorities, professional identities in advertising agencies, brand experiences and loyalty, and cross-cultural communications (Desai 2002). Ethnography, according to Mariampolski (1999), is about as close as the researcher can get to the consumer; it is the "truth serum of research". The categories that call for ethnography tend to be either process-intensive such as doing housework, personal care or food preparation, or interaction-focused such as infant care or game playing. Pettigrew (2000) has reviewed the use of ethnography in consumer research and argues that the social meanings found in material possessions can be viewed as cultural communicators.

Desai (2002) talks about "going wider" and "going deeper" using ethnography. Thus whereas a focus group on beer might concentrate on brand imagery, user imagery, drinking occasions and taste preferences, an ethnographic approach would provide a more detailed explanation of where people consume different

Ethnography An approach to qualitative research in which the researcher immerses himself or herself into a local culture in order to understand it.

brands, who they are with, what they talk about, what music is playing and how beer drinking fits into the context of a "night out". Going wider is like using a wide-angle lens; going deeper is more like a zoom lens, focusing as it does on the minutiae of human behavior. If a researcher wants to understand what people feel when they drive to work, asking them to describe their feeling will produce limited information; but accompanying the driver, the researcher can experience all the frustrations, the nuances, the in-car music and can interact with the driver at various points.

There is always the danger of an "observer effect". People may alter their behavior or act more rationally when they are aware that they are being observed. Desai argues that such effects may not be so relevant to the topic of the research. Thus if the focus is on the *manner* in which people brush their teeth, then doing it more thoroughly than usual may not be so relevant. Furthermore, the observer effect can be integrated into the analysis of the data. Undertaking covert research is, of course, a way around this dilemma – but it produces another. The ESOMAR Code of Conduct says that people must be informed if observational methods are being used, unless the research occurs in a "public place". Supermarkets, town squares and shopping centers are probably fair game, but private pubs, bars, the library or hospital waiting rooms could be more controversial.

KEY POINTS

Ethnography and observation tend to overlap; thus mystery shopping may be called either. In fact Desai (2002) treats them together and makes no distinction. However, ethnography proper involves a sense of researcher "immersion" in a specific culture at a given physical site and usually for extended periods of time. Ethnography has many advantages over interview-based methods, but at a cost, which in a commercial context may just be too much.

Consultation

Consultation A process used largely in the public sector in which consumers are involved in the decision-making process.

Consultation is used mainly in the public sector. While, over the last decade, public sector organizations have considerably increased the amount of research on consumers they carry out, traditional qualitative and quantitative methods do not fully meet their requirements. In particular they are not adapted to engaging and involving consumers in the decision-making process (Desai 2002). New legislative requirements have been placed upon local authorities, health authorities and the police to consult with local people.

Consultation involves more than what is normally understood by market research. Target populations need to be all-inclusive. Public sector providers have a duty to make their services available to everyone. Groups often underrepresented on commercial research – ethnic minorities, the homeless, drug-users, the long-term unemployed and so on – often need to be specifically targeted.

The issues on which views are sought are often complex. Furthermore members of the public often have very little information on them. Accordingly, those consulted need to be given clear, balanced information that they can easily understand plus time to consider the issues. Research in the public sector is often concerned with trade-offs and with balancing conflicting demands. This means using more deliberative methods that give people the opportunity to weigh up the evidence, to consider the options and to discuss with others. Sometimes it is appropriate for panel members to receive training to carry out investigations for themselves.

In many cases the requirements can be met by adapting conventional qualitative methods, for example by using reconvened groups, longer workshops or more creative stimulus materials. In addition, specific consultation methods have been developed. These include panels, area forums and deliberative methods.

Panels

Panels are groups of consumers who have agreed to be approached on a regular basis by public bodies for consultation purposes. While panels have been used for a long time in commercial research, they are usually quantitative, for example consumer panels, retail panels and media panels. These are explained in Chapter 16. Qualitative panels have been used by public sector organizations in a variety of ways. Some aim to recruit a representative cross-section of the general public and tend to be more research-focused with an emphasis on data collection. Others rely more on self-selection among specialist groups and are more consultation-based and focused on involving participants in decision-making and holding policy-makers to account. The main types of qualitative panels include general public panels, user groups and special interest groups. General public panels are commonly used in the health service and may be called "health panels". Typically they will involve 12 members of the general public selected by quota sampling who meet three times a year to discuss topics chosen by the health authority. User groups are often self-selected and will meet with senior management responsible for delivering the service. Special interest groups are attended by people who run community organizations or who provide advice to groups who might otherwise be unrepresented, for example pensioners or ethnic minorities. These people will often have more experience than either the commissioning body or researchers.

Panels Groups of consumers, usually a representative sample, who have agreed to provide specified information or to be involved in a particular form of marketing research at regular intervals.

Area forums

Area forums were developed in the UK in the 1990s as a way of re-engaging local people with their local councils. The existence of these forums is usually advertised locally and people are invited to express an interest. They are subsequently invited to a first meeting, which tries to identify their main concerns using workshop methods. These concerns are then discussed at local meetings with council staff.

Area forums A method of consultation research in which local people are invited to attend an advertised forum in which, using workshop methods, they are invited to identify their concerns with specified aspects of local authority policy.

Deliberative polls

Deliberative polls vary in their operation, but what they all have in common is that they:

- allow people time to consider the issues, often several days,
- provide information and allow people to question professionals and experts,
- put diverse groups of people together,
- aim for some emergent consensus.

Citizens' juries consist of 12–16 members of the public representing a cross-section of the local population who are asked to consider a specific issue and given a briefing session. The jury sits for four days. There are moderators to facilitate discussion, who receive evidence from "witnesses" whom they can question. They discuss in small groups and have plenary sessions. They can request more information. On the final day they draw their conclusions, which are compiled into a report.

Deliberative polls A method of consultation research in which a random sample survey of the local population is conducted on the issue under consideration. A representative subsample of 250–300 is then recruited to constitute a large citizens' jury.

Citizens' juries A method of consultation research in which 12–16 members of the public are invited to act as a 'jury' for four days during which they receive briefings, evidence from witnesses and can ask for more information.

Deliberative polls are similar to citizens' juries, but they attempt to quantify the outcome of the deliberative process. A random sample survey of the local population is conducted on the issue under consideration. This measures views before any deliberation takes place. A representative subsample of 250–300 is recruited and is involved in a very large citizens' jury. After the event, participants complete a questionnaire identical to the one filled in initially to assess how attitudes have changed. Deliberative polls, however, are very expensive to conduct and are beyond the reach of many public sector bodies. Shorter, less expensive, events called "community conferences" have been tried.

Consultation has so far been used mainly by public bodies, but, argues Desai (2002), commercial companies might consider undertaking consultation with their customers. for example by having citizens' juries or deliberative polls.

> ## KEY POINTS
>
> Consultation means engaging and involving consumers in the decision-making process, so it is more than undertaking research into their attitudes and views. A number of different models of consultation are currently widely used by public bodies, but little used by commercial organizations.

The impact of the internet

The use of the internet to conduct online qualitative research has mostly been in the context of online focus groups, although there has been some use of bulletin boards and moderated e-mail groups.

Online focus groups

Online focus group A 'virtual' focus group in which the moderator and participants communicate via the internet.

An **online focus group** is a "virtual" group where the moderator and the participants communicate via the internet. There is no face-to-face contact as with the traditional focus group. Online groups have a number of advantages, for example:

- they are quicker and cheaper than traditional focus groups,
- the moderator can operate from his or her office desk,
- no physical set-up is required,
- participants can be in any geographical location, in any part of the globe,
- participants are in their own homes or offices,
- the text is captured on file without the need for transcription,
- larger numbers can take part, typically 15–20,
- participants may well be more candid,
- shy candidates can express themselves more freely,
- they will tend to compose answers without reading the responses of others first,
- clients can communicate with the moderator while the discussion is in progress.

There are, however, some disadvantages, for example:

- lack of face-to-face interaction can undermine or limit group processes,
- there are few nonverbal means of communication like body language,

- participants cannot physically inspect or taste products,
- they can become distracted by events in their own locations,
- good typing ability has to be assumed,
- participants sometimes get more aggressive than they would in a face-to-face group,
- monitoring written responses on a screen has less impact on the client than being there behind a screen.

Box 4.4 describes how Motorola used online groups to develop its websites. Online groups are particularly suited to situations where participants are geographically dispersed or in business-to-business contexts. Future developments could see the growth of videoconferencing technology, which involves the live video transmission of focus groups directly to client videoconferencing rooms. A related development is videostreaming, which involves the live video transmission of focus groups over the internet. Projects can be viewed right from the client's PC anywhere in the world.

Bulletin boards

Bulletin boards are a web-based technology in which respondents are invited to log onto the board once a day. The moderator posts questions and respondents can post replies at their convenience, as in a news group. Everybody can see everybody else's comments. A new question is posted every morning and the moderator reviews the answers at the end of the day.

Bulletin boards A web-based form of qualitative research in which respondents are invited to log on to the board once a day. Moderators may pose questions and respondents can post their replies at their convenience.

Moderated e-mail groups

Moderated e-mail groups offer the possibility of overcoming some of the problems associated with bulletin boards. They take place over one or two weeks. The moderator e-mails questions to respondents who e-mail their responses back. The moderator then produces a summary of responses, which is then sent to the group for comment along with further questions. In this way the moderator keeps control of the discussion, summarizing and feeding back only the points that the moderator wants other respondents to see (Desai 2002). An example of the use of moderated e-mail groups is given by Adrianssens and Cadman (1999) in a study of online share dealing. They used two groups, one comprising 20 active shareholders who were also internet users and one with 10 passive shareholders. The moderators were able to consult their client and other members of the team on

Moderated e-mail groups Over a period of one or two weeks the moderator e-mails questions to respondents who e-mail their responses back. The moderator then produces a summary.

technical matters in between waves of questions and answers. The method provided well-considered, valuable responses and greater diversity than might have been expected in face-to-face groups. However, the opportunities for probing, seeking clarification and genuine interactions are limited.

Academic qualitative research

Academic researchers tend to take a wider-ranging view of what methods and techniques are encompassed by qualitative research than do client-based researchers. They are more likely, furthermore, to insist that "qualitative research involves an interpretive, naturalistic approach to the world. This means that qualitative researchers study people in their natural settings, attempting to make sense of, or to interpret phenomena in terms of the meanings people bring to them" (Denzin and Lincoln 2000: 3). Client-based researchers, particularly commercial practitioners, are, by contrast, apt to accept or assume that there exists an individual or social reality that can be tapped by way of interview-based techniques. These realities can, apparently, be reported back to clients as "factual" accounts of marketing processes. Academics, on the other hand, are more likely to see multiple realities that are, furthermore, temporary, ongoing accomplishments as individuals interact in their daily lives with organizational representatives and respond to a range of marketing communications. Academic projects are likely to be broader in scope and more loosely defined in terms of objectives than client-based ones. They are more likely to be open-ended in design, and with several stages, a provisional analysis from each stage forming the basis for the next stage.

Academic qualitative research will, furthermore, possess all the features of academic research outlined in Chapter 2. There will be no client and therefore no brief; it will be neutral and noninterventionist; its goal will be to add to publicly available knowledge and understanding of marketing processes; it will be judged on scientific rigor; its timing will often be open-ended and the main audience will be other academics.

In Chapter 2, in turning to academic, scholarly research, we looked at, among other things, the philosophical underpinnings of such research, including matters of ontology, epistemology and perspective. These tend to be combined in typical ways that were referred to as a "paradigm". Three key paradigms were suggested, using the metaphor of the marketing researcher as:

- physicist,
- physician,
- psychiatrist.

The focus for the academic as qualitative researcher is largely on the researcher as a psychiatrist, since this is the paradigm that mostly underlies qualitative research carried out by academics (as opposed to commercial qualitative researchers). The ontology is subjectivist, the epistemology is interpretive and the perspective tends to be that of the participant.

A key feature of contemporary academic qualitative research, however, is its diversity. Tesch (1990), for example, distinguishes no fewer than 27 different varieties depending on the purpose of the research, which may be focused on:

- the characteristics of language,
- the discovery of regularities,
- the understanding of text or social action.

The characteristics of language may include language as communication either as content, for which content analysis may be used, or as process, in which case discourse analysis may be appropriate or language as culture, focusing either on its cognitive basis as in ethnography or on its interactive basis, for which qualitative researchers may use symbolic interactionism or ethnomethodology. The discovery of regularities might include grounded theory or action research, while a focus on text or social action may entail the discovery of themes as in phenomenology or interpretation as in case study life history or hermeneutics. Some of these approaches are explained in Chapter 10 on analyzing qualitative data.

KEY POINTS

 Academic qualitative research tends to be quite different from client-based qualitative research. Client-based qualitative researchers tend to be more positivist in their approach, that is, they assume a reality that can be tapped into by interviewing people or by watching their behavior. Academic researchers are more likely to see reality as much more complex; that reality is an ongoing accomplishment, that is, individuals create their own "realities" as they go about their everyday lives. Such realities will be ephemeral and changing; there will be no single reality that researchers can, with varying degrees of success, uncover.

SUMMARY

Qualitative research comes in many different varieties, but what all these have in common is that they are focused on the construction of largely qualitative data, which consist of words, phrases, text or images. Furthermore, like quantitative data, they arise as systematic records that have been constructed by individuals; they are, like quantitative data, social products that have been created in a social, moral, political, economic and historical context.

Client-based qualitative marketing research entails studying relatively few cases in depth using observation, participation, dialogue, open-ended interview techniques or the study of images or other cultural artifacts as modes of data construction. It is undertaken to help clients explore, diagnose, evaluate and create ideas by helping them to understand people's attitudes, perceptions, motivations and behaviors.

Most client-based qualitative marketing research is based on interview methods that include focus groups and depth interviews. However, increasingly, alternative methods are becoming more popular and these include more use of observation and ethnography, and the development of consultation.

QUESTIONS FOR DISCUSSION

1 Do online focus groups produce results different from traditional focus groups?

2 Log on to **www.focusvision.com** and explain the differences between videoconferencing, videostreaming and video marking.

3 Are *all* data, do you think, "manufactured" in some way, or are there some that we can accept as "given"?

4 A major manufacturer of men's underwear wants to discover the main criteria that purchasers use in selecting the brand and style of underwear. The manufacturer wants a series of group discussions. Advise the company on the kinds of groups and group composition that would be appropriate.

CASE STUDY FOX KIDS EUROPE, TAKING SNAPSHOTS OF CHILDREN ACROSS EUROPE

Fox Kids Europe is a leading pan-European children's entertainment company that produces consumer products, television programs, channels and internet sites in 17 local languages reaching more than 32 million homes in 56 countries. The company operates 12 television channel feeds (Donnenfield and du Crest 2003). The company has to stay in tune with, and ahead of, the dynamic and demanding audience of young children in all the different countries that it broadcasts to. All the offerings of Fox Kids need to stay relevant, inspiring and motivating. A team of researchers at Fox Kids has built an innovative and inexpensive methodology using single-use cameras that minimize interviewer biases, but allow Fox Kids to travel into the minds and lives of its young audience.

A total of 450 single-use camera kits including instructions, a letter to parents, a letter to the children, release forms and a self-completion diary were sent to a sample of children aged 8–11 in nine countries: Denmark, France, Germany, Italy, the Netherlands, Norway, Spain, Sweden and the UK. Recruitment came from a number of sources including recruitment companies, Fox Kids websites, channel databases and subscriber lists. Potential respondents were offered a goody bag, a prize draw for a camera, and a set of their photos. The diaries guided children on what to photograph and contained follow-up questions to capture the motivations and feelings behind the photos taken. They were asked, for example, to take a picture of themselves in their favorite clothes. Follow-up questions revealed that they rated comfort above "coolness" and fashion. They were asked to take a photo of their family and their homes and were asked about the good things and the bad things about living with their families and their homes.

A total of 369 children across the nine counties returned the materials. The data provided were rich, colorful, creative and plentiful. They provided wide range of insights and actionable findings at both local and pan-European levels.

Questions and activities

1 Check out the Fox Kids website, **www.jetixeurope.com**.

2 Suggest other marketing contexts in which qualitative photographic data could be used.

FURTHER READING

Boddy, C. (2005) "Projective techniques in market research: valueless subjectivity or insightful reality?" *International Journal of Market Research*, 47 (3): 239–254.

Carson, D., Gilmore, A., Perry, C. and Gronhaug, K. (2001) *Qualitative Marketing Research*. London: Sage.

Chrzanowska, J. (2002) "Interviewing groups and individuals in qualitative market research", in *Qualitative Market Research: Principle and Practice* (eds Ereaut, G., Imms, M. and Callingham, M.), Volume 2. London: Sage.

Daymon, C. and Holloway, I. (2002) *Qualitative Research Methods in Public Relations and Marketing Communications*. London: Routledge.

Desai, P. (2002), "Methods beyond interviewing in qualitative market research", in *Qualitative Market Research: Principle and Practice* (eds Ereaut, G., Imms, M. and Callingham, M.), Volume 3. London: Sage.

Ereaut, G., Imms, M. and Callingham, M. (eds) (2002) *Qualitative Market Research: Principle and Practice*. London: Sage.

Hall, N. (2003) "Video, ergo agnosco. From observation to insight", *ESOMAR*, April.

Jack, F. and Burnside, G. (2002) "Pandora's box – what women think, feel and hope for in the 21st century", *Market Research Society Conference*, Brighton.

Marks, L. (ed.) (2000) *Qualitative Research in Context*. Henley-on-Thames: Admap/AQR.

Marshall, C. and Rossman, G. (1999) *Designing Qualitative Research*, 3rd edition. Thousand Oaks, CA: Sage.

Constructing quantitative data
Structuring data and measuring variables

5

Measurement involves using some kind of scale.

© PAUL COWAN

INTRODUCTION

Chapter 4 explained that qualitative marketing research seeks to explore and understand people's attitudes, perceptions, motivations and behaviors by constructing and then analyzing data that are largely qualitative in nature. By contrast, quantitative marketing research sets out to measure the extent of, or changes in, marketing phenomena and to test ideas about them in order to make predictions. Quantitative marketing research is based on the construction and analysis of data that are largely quantitative in nature. We saw in Chapter 3 that all data – both qualitative and quantitative – are systematic records that have been constructed by individuals; they are social products that have been created in a social, moral, political, economic and historical context. However, unlike qualitative data that arise as words, phrases, text or images, quantitative data arise as numbers; these result from the imposition of a structure on the data and from the process of measurement. This chapter explains what these structures are and what measurement entails.

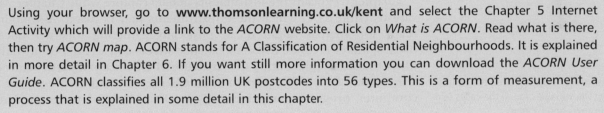

INTERNET ACTIVITY

Using your browser, go to **www.thomsonlearning.co.uk/kent** and select the Chapter 5 Internet Activity which will provide a link to the *ACORN* website. Click on *What is ACORN*. Read what is there, then try *ACORN map*. ACORN stands for A Classification of Residential Neighbourhoods. It is explained in more detail in Chapter 6. If you want still more information you can download the *ACORN User Guide*. ACORN classifies all 1.9 million UK postcodes into 56 types. This is a form of measurement, a process that is explained in some detail in this chapter.

What are "quantitative data"?

Quantitative data are derived from numerical records. Sometimes these numbers refer to magnitudes or calibrations recorded in respect of an individual, a group of individuals, or an organization. Thus a person may be 56 years old, earn €31 000 a year gross and score 7.5 out of 10 on a test of knowledge of unit pricing techniques. Sometimes the numbers are a result of counting the frequency of things, so a company may have 267 employees, own 6 factories and make 37 different products. Sometimes the numbers are just frequencies with which categories occur, for example the number of males and females in a group, or the proportion of respondents to a survey who "strongly agree" with a particular statement. In each situation, the researcher will have recorded a particular value like "27" in respect of a particular characteristic, like age, for a particular entity, like a person or an organization. The researcher, furthermore, will almost certainly have done this for several, perhaps many, characteristics and for several, perhaps a large number of, individuals, groups, organizations or other kinds of entity.

Researchers construct quantitative data by engaging in the same activities as for the construction of qualitative data, namely:

- designing research that specifies when, where and how the construction process is to take place,
- capturing data by creating a record, for example in questionnaires or diaries or by using a range of manual or electronic recording devices,

■ assembling the data into their "raw" data format, ready for analysis.

The process of designing client-based research was explained in Chapter 1 and academic research in Chapter 2. The elements that go into the design process will, for quantitative data, include decisions about:

■ the structure that is to be imposed on the data,

■ the nature of the systems that are to be used to measure marketing phenomena,

■ the instruments that are to be used to capture the data,

■ the methodological context in which those instruments are to be used.

The structure that is to be imposed on the data will have three parts: a definition of the entities about which records are to be made, the characteristics that are to be recorded and the format of the record. The entities whose characteristics are being recorded are usually called cases, the characteristics themselves are the variables, and what are actually recorded are the **values**. The first part of this chapter explains each of these elements in some detail.

In common with all scientists, market researchers must face the problem of how to go about measuring the variables that are at the center of their investigations. There are various ways in which the process of measurement may be undertaken and the second part of this chapter looks at this process.

Chapter 6 explains the instruments of data capture while Chapter 7 looks at the various contexts in which these instruments may be used. Assembling the data ready for analysis might mean physically gathering together questionnaires, diaries, meter records, invoices, balance sheets and so on, but nowadays is more likely to mean representing the structure of the data in a particular format called a **data matrix**, which is explained in Chapter 11, and then entering data into a computer program ready for analysis. The kinds of program that might be appropriate for this purpose are explained in Chapters 10 and 11.

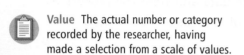

Value The actual number or category recorded by the researcher, having made a selection from a scale of values.

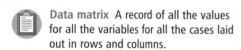

Data matrix A record of all the values for all the variables for all the cases laid out in rows and columns.

Qualitative and quantitative data

At first sight, the distinction between qualitative and quantitative data seems fairly straightforward. It would be too easy, however, just to say that quantitative data arise as numbers and qualitative data do not; the distinction is not always that clear-cut. Data from surveys where questions have been precoded would, for example, probably be accepted as "quantitative" even if the answers like "yes" or "strongly agree" were given in words. Responses to open-ended questions of the opinion or attitude variety and recorded as text would be considered "qualitative" data, even if the answers are subsequently coded and entered into SPSS for statistical analysis. Answers to open-ended questions like occupation, where these are to be coded into standard social grade categories, would no doubt be regarded as "quantitative".

So, the distinction between qualitative and quantitative data is *not* a question of the nature of the actual record made – text or number. The researcher might, for example, in a survey in response to a particular question:

■ circle or enter a number,

■ tick a box,

■ enter a short alphabetical code (like C1),

■ record a word or phrase,

■ write down everything the respondent says,

■ tape record everything the respondent says.

Qualitative data, you may recall from Chapter 4, have the key feature that at the point of data capture no structure has been imposed upon them. The researcher captures the words, phrases, text or images without a predetermined set of categories or codes on which to map responses or observations. To obtain quantitative data, by contrast, a structure must already exist at the point of data capture. The cases, the variables and the values must already have been decided before the data capture takes place. In short, the distinction between qualitative and quantitative data is more a question of whether or not prestructuring has taken place before questionnaires are administered or before interviews have taken place.

KEY POINTS

Quantitative data are numerical records that are constructed by deciding on the cases, the variables and sets of values to be used before the data collection takes place, and then undertaking a process of measurement. These decisions and activities may be seen as part of the research design process.

The structure of data

All numerical data have a structure that consists of cases, variables and values. The values will be selected from a **scale** of values that will have its own format and structure. This section explains each of these terms.

Scale A set of values that met certain formal logical requirements.

Cases

A case is the entity whose characteristics are being recorded in the process of data construction. The case may be an object, a person, a survey respondent, a group of people, an organization, a situation, a geographical area or an event. Quantitative research will always be concerned with a set of cases where the entities that are the focus of the research are of a particular type, for example, "motorists" or "mothers with babies", or "all adults resident in Spain in 2006 aged 16 or over who have their own personal domestic e-mail address". Such a set – the **population** – will always be located in time and space. The time may be a moment of time or a period of time over which change is being researched. The space will be a geographical area that may relate to national or local boundaries or to an area defined by the researcher. In any one particular piece of research there may be more than one type of case; indeed, cases may be nested in hierarchical fashion – individuals within departments, within organizations, within industries, within regions. If there are large numbers of potential cases it may be necessary to take a **sample** and use the sample to make **estimates** for the total set. The topic of populations and samples is considered in detail in Chapter 8.

Population A total set of cases or other units that are the focus of the researcher's attention.

Most quantitative researchers (and indeed many qualitative researchers) see cases as "real" objects that exist independently of any particular research effort. They accept conventionally defined entities, like adults, households, neighborhoods, small to medium enterprises, organizations, firms or cities as cases. Implicit is the idea that cases are sufficiently similar to be identifiable as examples of the "same" general phenomenon, yet sufficiently diverse in terms of characteristics of interest to the researcher to facilitate comparison.

Sample A subset of cases or other units from a total population of cases or units.

Estimates Using the value of a statistic derived from a sample to estimate the value of the corresponding population parameter.

The sets or types of cases deemed to be "relevant" to a particular study will be defined and selected by the researcher; in this sense they are in fact researcher "concoctions" (Ragin 1992). The boundaries between entities defined as cases may, however, sometimes be quite obscure, for example it may be difficult to say or define exactly who is or who is not a "member" of an organization.

Cases are often sets of individuals.

© AARON KOHR

Organizations, or more fluid parts of them like departments, committees or working groups may have holistic, "global", transitory or emergent properties, like "consensus" or "hostility", that are not just the aggregation of individual characteristics. In short, cases can be researcher constructs like "small to medium enterprises" or "bureaucratic organizations" rather than concrete entities. They can also be empirical or legal units (like public limited companies); they can be statistical artifacts (like clusters of cases produced by cluster analysis), or simply individual respondents to a survey. In qualitative research the "relevant" cases may take shape in the course of the research, or the population as stated at the outset of the research is treated as a working hypothesis to be modified as the investigation proceeds. In quantitative research, however, the population of cases needs to be defined up-front, before the data are captured.

Variables

Variable A characteristic of a case that the researcher has chosen to observe or measure and then record. A variable must vary at a minimum between two scale values.

A **variable** is a characteristic of a case that the researcher has chosen to observe or measure and then record. All variables have the feature that they vary – that one out of a set of at least two values may be recorded, for example a person did or did not watch television the previous day. In any one piece of research there will be several – and in some research a hundred or more – variables that are being recorded. These variables will record a variety of types of characteristics and will play different roles in the research.

The characteristics to which variables may relate may be:

- demographic,
- behavioral,
- cognitive.

Demographic variables "Factual" characteristics of cases that are treated as conditions that at least in principle are verifiable.

Demographic variables relate to "factual" characteristics of cases that are treated as conditions that at least in principle are verifiable like a person's age, educational background or occupation, or a company's turnover or number of employees. These conditions may be fixed or relatively fixed (like sex of respondent or type or organization), or slow to change (like age of respondent). Some may be subject to sudden changes interspersed with periods of stability, for example marital status, family size or area of residence. While "demographics" are normally thought of as pertaining to individuals or groups of individuals, organizations, too, can be measured in terms of a range of demographic features like the type of industry, size, age, profitability, growth and so on. See Box 5.1.

Behavioral variables relate to what people actually did in the recent past, to what they usually or currently do, or to what they might do in the future. Typical measures in marketing, for example, relate to the purchase and use of products and brands like purchase/nonpurchase of a product or brand over a specific time period, brand variant purchased, quantity/size of pack, price paid, source of purchase, other brands bought, nature of purchase, and use/consumption of the product. These measures may, in turn, be used to generate calculations of brand loyalty, brand-switching behavior and frequency of purchase. If the research is a product test or product concept test, consumers may be asked about future behavior, for example likelihood of trial of a new product and likely frequency of purchase.

Behavioral variables What people actually did in the recent past, what they currently or usually do, or what they might do in the future.

Cognitive variables relate to mental processes that go on within the individual and include attitudes, opinions, beliefs and images. **Attitudes** are relatively enduring likes or dislikes, preferences or other positive or negative evaluations of objects, persons, organizations, events or situations. Though attitudes do not always correspond directly with behavior, they are, by definition, "predispositions" to act in particular ways, and hence strongly influence behavior. This means that when attitudes of a large number of people are measured or estimated, then predictions about future behavior can usually be made with some degree of accuracy.

Cognitive variables Individual attitudes, opinions, beliefs and images.

Attitudes Relatively enduring likes or dislikes, preferences or other positive or negative evaluations of objects, persons, organizations, events or situations.

Opinions are somewhat different from attitudes. They do not necessarily have a directional quality and may express feelings or views about what other people should or should not do in the world. **Beliefs** refer to what people think they know about social situations, products or communications, but which cannot usually be underscored by factual evidence, while knowledge refers to awareness or memory of such factual knowledge. **Images** are somewhat vaguer than beliefs, being representations in the mind of the character or attributes of a person, object or organization. The measurement of cognitive variables is thus very complex and is considered in more detail later in this chapter.

Opinions Feelings or views about what other people should or should not do in the world.

Beliefs What individuals think they know about social situations, products or communications.

Images Representations in the mind of the characteristics of a person, object, organization or event.

Researchers frequently assume that entities like organizations or groups of individuals can "behave" and "think" like individuals. Companies in particular are often described as doing things like putting up prices or reacting to competitors in particular ways. Companies may be seen to have attitudes and opinions. Companies can now even be sued for "corporate manslaughter". Committees within organizations can, as a result of a vote or some other process, decide to do things or to take a view on an issue.

IN DETAIL   BOX 5.1
The Standard Industrial Classification

In the UK, the main framework for classifying business establishments and analyzing their economic activities is the Standard Industrial Classification (SIC). This was first published in 1948 to encourage uniformity in the preparation of UK official statistics for industry. It has been revised several times since. A revision in 1980 brought it more into line with the European Union's Statistical Office's classification. The most recent update was in 2003. There are 100 primary codes like "45. Construction", which can be further broken down into "451 Site preparation", "452 Building of complete constructions", "453 Building installation" and so on. "451 Site preparation" can be further broken down into "4511 Demolition", "4512 Test drilling and boring".

Cognitive variables relate to mental processes.

In terms of the various roles demographic, behavioral or cognitive variables may play in research, we can distinguish variables being used as:

- descriptors,
- independent variables,
- dependent variables.

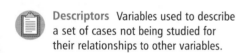

Descriptors Variables used to describe a set of cases not being studied for their relationships to other variables.

Variables used as **descriptors** are not being studied for their relationships to other variables. Demographic variables in particular are often used to provide a framework for defining and describing the key characteristics of the cases that are providing the data in a piece of research, for example, a sample of online shoppers may be described in terms of the numbers of males and females, the age distribution and whether or not they have access to broadband. However, behavioral and cognitive variables may also be used for descriptive purposes. Where, in a piece of research, variables are being used solely in this fashion, then it may be called a "descriptive" study.

Alternatively, variables may be used precisely for the purpose of investigating their relationships to other variables. In some research the purpose of the study may be to explore the extent to which variables covary in some fashion, for example that males are more likely than females to favor a particular brand. Most researchers, however, are interested in examining whether some variables have some influence or impact on other variables, or even whether one variable "causes" another. Variables treated as causes, influences, predictors or factors are known as **independent variables**. Such variables may be seen as, (a) necessary preconditions for some outcome to happen, (b) sufficient by themselves to bring such an outcome about, or (c) just one influence among many, that is, they are neither necessary nor sufficient conditions. Variables treated as the effects, outcomes or simply the characteristics or processes the researcher is interested in trying to explain, understand or predict, are the **dependent variables**.

Independent variable A variable that is treated as a condition, cause or influence.

Dependent variable A variable that is seen as an outcome or effect of an independent variable. A variable that the researcher is trying to predict, understand or explain.

Behavioral, cognitive and some demographic variables may be used in any of the three roles in research (see Figure 5.1). Some demographic variables, however, are difficult to conceive as being used as "dependent" variables, for example trying to "explain" a person's gender or age! Some variables may be used in more than one role in a piece of research. Thus some demographics may be used for both structural and for analytic purposes, for example using age both to describe the sample of respondents and also to see how far it "explains" variation in one or more of the dependent variables. Some variables may be used as both dependent and independent variables in the same piece of research. Thus customer satisfaction may be seen both as a result of a customer's prior expectations about the product or service (it is a dependent variable) and at the same time as causing or influencing repeat purchase behavior (it is also an independent variable).

KEY POINTS

Sets of cases and predefined variables are key elements in any quantitative approach to scientific endeavor. Variables are of different kinds and they may play different, or a combination of, roles in the research. However, few variables are directly observable. While we can "see" a person's gender, or how long they spend in a retail outlet, we cannot "see" their social status, the brands that are in their consideration set or even their age. Researchers may be able to see and count the number of employees in an organization, but cannot directly observe its degree of marketing orientation. The majority of variables, then, are "latent" in the sense that they are idealized constructs of the researcher that are at best only indirectly measurable. The different forms of measurement are considered later in this chapter. Chapter 15 takes up the issue of the "reality" of variables and the limitations of variable-centered data analysis.

Values

Variables, as we have seen above, have the key and obvious characteristic that they vary. At a minimum there must be two possibilities: either a case possesses or does not possess a characteristic, like purchased/did not purchase a particular product. Sometimes, there are many possibilities, for example the age of a person in years. These "possibilities" are called values by researchers. Unfortunately, the word "value" has many meanings in everyday language. It may mean worth, goodness, esteem, price, price in relation to quality, moral principles, or standards. In marketing research, it is what we actually record in the process of record-keeping. A value is selected from a scale of values and it is this value that is recorded as part of the data construction process.

There are, in fact, many different types of scale from which values of the variables may be selected and recorded. A fundamental distinction is between:

- scales that are sets of values that are recorded into categories like "very satisfied", "strongly disagree", "large", "male" or "strawberry flavor", and

- scales that arise from a process of calibration using some kind of metric like money in Euros or age in years, or from a process of counting a

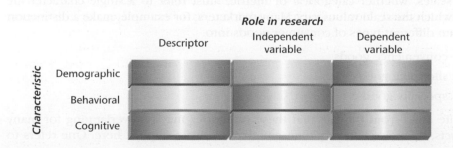

FIGURE 5.1

Vairables can combine different characteristics and role in a piece of research

Categorical scale A scale that consists at a minimum of sets of categories that are exhaustive, mutually exclusive and refers to a single characteristic, but which may, in addition, possess order.

Metric scale A scale that arises from the processes of either calibration or counting.

frequency as a measure of size like the number of employees in an organization.

The first type we will call **categorical scales** and the second type **metric scales**. There are, in fact, several different kinds of categorical scales and two main kinds of metric scales.

Categorical scales

Categorical scales are sets of scale values that at a minimum meet three key criteria:

▪ they are exhaustive of all the possibilities,
▪ they are mutually exclusive, that is, nonoverlapping,
▪ they refer to a single characteristic.

The first criterion means that all the observations that we make must fit somewhere on the scale. To make a set of values exhaustive, it is sometimes necessary to have an "other" category for observations that do not fit into any of the scale values specified, for example, the answers to the question, "For which of the following purposes do you mostly use cooking fat?" may be categorized into:

Deep frying ☐
Shallow frying ☐
Roasting ☐
Pastry making ☐
Other uses ☐
(please specify) . . . .

By adding the "other uses" category, the set of values is now exhaustive of all the possibilities and there is no answer that cannot be put into a category.

The second criterion means that all observations should fit into one and only one category. If age groups are classified, for example, into:

20–30
30–40
40–50
50–60

then somebody aged 30, 40 or 50 will fit into more than one category. These categories would need to be changed to:

20–29
30–39
40–49
50–59

All scales, whether categorical or metric, must refer to a single characteristic along which the scale values vary. Many marketers, for example, make a distinction between different types of consumer goods into:

▪ convenience goods,
▪ shopping goods,
▪ specialty goods.

Quite apart from the fact that these categories may be overlapping for many products, there are two very different characteristics implicit here. One refers to the degree of search behavior involved in selecting a brand (convenience goods versus shopping goods), while the third category, specialty goods, has more to do with brand loyalty. The fact that more than one characteristic or dimension is being referred to is not always obvious.

Once exhaustiveness, mutual exclusivity and single-dimensionality have been established, a number of different subtypes of categorical scale can arise.

Labeling scales

At the most basic level we can assign a unique number, letter or other symbol to each case like registration number, payroll number or hotel room number. Each number is unique: it identifies one particular case and there are as many scale values as there are cases. The set of numbers used will, however, be both exhaustive and mutually exclusive. The scale values, although they often appear as numbers (they may also be a mixture of numbers and letters like car registrations), are being used solely for identification – as labels. So we can call these **labeling scales**. Statistically, we can do very little with them. We cannot add up the values; in fact we cannot summarize them in any way by drawing graphs or creating summary tables. We might be able to group them in some way, like taking student registration numbers and grouping them by year of entry. This transformation of the data would, however, create a different kind of scale.

Labeling scale The assignation of a unique number, letter or symbol to each case.

Binary scales

Some researchers would argue that labeling scales are not really "scales" at all since they do not classify cases in terms of equivalence or non-equivalence. The simplest form of scale that does this is the **binary scale** where there are just two categories, one for cases that possess a characteristic and one for cases that do not. There are many examples of these scales in marketing research – employed/unemployed; married/not married; purchased a particular brand in the last seven days/did not do so; answered yes/no to a question; male/female. To make these proper binary scales we would assign the number 1 to those cases that possess the characteristic and 0 to those that do not. Binary scales (which are sometimes called "dichotomies", but that sounds like a painful Victorian operation!) have interesting statistical properties not possessed by scales that have three or more categories. We can, for example, use them as proportions by taking the proportion possessing a characteristic as opposed to the proportion not possessing it. We can also use the binomial distribution, which is based on the probability of "successes" and "failures" in a specified number of trials.

Binary scale A scale that has two categories, one for cases that possess a characteristic and one for those that do not.

Nominal scales

Where there are three or more categories into which cases are classified, but there is no implied order in the way categories are listed, then we have a **nominal scale**. The main feature of nominal scales (and the illustration of the uses of cooking fat above is a good example) is that the ordering of the listing makes no difference to any statistical operations we might perform on the data.

Nominal scale A set of scale values having three or more categories that are mutually exclusive, exhaustive and refer to a single dimension.

Ordinal scales

Some sets of scale values define the relationships between the scale values not only in terms of equivalence, but also in terms of order. This means we can define the relationships between scale values in terms of greater than and less than, although there is no metric that will indicate by how much. Thus if we classify

Ordinal scale A scale possessing all the characteristics of a nominal scale plus an implied order of the categories.

Ranking scale A set of scale values in which each case has its own rank. There are as many rankings as cases.

Paired comparisons A scaling technique in which respondents are asked to compare objects or images two at a time according to a specified criterion.

product usage into "Heavy", "Medium", "Light" and "Nonuser", then there is an implied order, but no measure of the actual usage involved. These are **ordinal scales**. The various social class, social grading or socioeconomic groups used in various European countries are good examples of such ordinal scales. Box 6.1 in the next chapter explains these schemes.

Ranking scales

In ordinal scales there is usually a limited number of ordinal categories onto which we map a large number of cases. So we might map 200 respondents onto five degrees of customer satisfaction. However, in other situations it may be possible to rank order each respondent. In **ranking** scales each case being measured is given its own ranking. Thus 30 customers may be ranked 1–30 on the basis of their attitude scores to a supplier. We would normally rank order only a fairly limited number of people or objects. To rank order 300 people 1–300 would be rather cumbersome. Alternatively, respondents in a survey may be asked to rank order a number of items, for example customers may be asked to rank seven brands 1–7 in terms of value for money. Respondents may find this tricky, so **paired comparisons** may be used. If, for example, the seven brands of beer are to be ranked, then respondents are asked to say which of two brands they prefer, taking each combination of pairs, of which there will be n(n–1)/2 pairs or 21 combinations. The results can be converted into a rank order by counting the number of times each brand is preferred.

Ranking scales are sometimes called "comparative" scales since the comparisons are relative to one another, not to any absolute criterion. Thus somebody who is not particularly keen on beer may rank or compare them on a "least worst" basis. However, rank order scales do have particular numerical characteristics, which mean that special statistics can be applied to them, for example there is a special statistic for measuring rank order correlation between two ranking scales. This statistic is explained in Chapter 12.

KEY POINTS

Categorical scales may, in short, be labeling, binary, nominal, ordinal or ranking scales. The differences between them are important because the statistics we can apply to them differ, in some cases quite dramatically. What they have in common, however, is that there is no metric that can be used to gauge distances between scale values.

If researchers assign numbers to categories, it must be remembered that the numbers are being used only to identify categories. They may be assigned arbitrarily and it does not matter if we assign 1 = male and 2 = female or 1 = female and 2 = male or even 26 = male and 39 = female. What we certainly cannot do, for example, is, if we take 1 = male and 2 = female and we have 60 males and 40 females, calculate the "average sex" as 1.4! As we will see later, any self-respecting computer will happily perform this calculation for you: the trick is to realize that the result is total nonsense. At the ordinal level, again we can assign the numbers arbitrarily, but they must preserve the order. So, we can assign the numbers 1–5 to represent the degrees of satisfaction, or 5–1, or 1, 3, 5, 7, 9, but to put 1, 5, 3, 9, 7 would be "out of order".

Categorical scales are sometimes seen as resulting in "qualitative" data. This can be confusing. Read the *Warning: categorical and qualitative data* box.

Metric scales

Categorical scales are sets of values that, while they meet certain criteria, do not possess any metric or unit of measurement with which it is possible to say anything about the distances between the scale values. Metric scales, by contrast, arise when there *is* such a unit of measurement and the scale values represent the result of a process of either calibration using some measuring instrument, or counting the number of people or items involved as a measure of size. The metric can be units of time like minutes, days, weeks, years; it can be units of currency; it may be units of weight, size, distance and so on. Alternatively, the metric may be units that arise from counting numbers of people, objects or events taken as a measure or size or magnitude. Think about how we might measure the size of a car park. We could either measure the area in square meters, or we could count up the number of parking spaces it provides. The first procedure might give any value in square meters and fractions of a square meter up to however many decimal places required. The second method will produce only whole numbers or integers. In statistical parlance, the first is usually called a **continuous variable** and the second a **discrete variable**. The *Warning: discrete and continuous variables* box explains some of the confusions that have arisen over the use of these terms.

Continuous variable A scale whose values consist of calibrations that might generate potentially an unlimited number of scale values.

Discrete variable A scale generated by counting the number of units contained in an entity as a measure of size.

Yet others will see the process of rounding off, or grouping into sets of values, like taking ages 20–29, 30–39 and so on to create a limited number of values, as creating discrete data. Many statisticians talk about discrete and continuous probability distributions. Among the former are included the binomial distribution and the Poisson distribution. Continuous probability distributions include the normal distribution, the t-distribution and the F-distribution. Oddly, while the binomial distribution relates to binary variables, they are still often regarded as appropriate for "discrete" data, even though, apparently, only "numeric" variables (as opposed to categorical ones) can be discrete or continuous.

There are two sources of confusion here. The first is whether we are really saying that the important point is whether the scale values are necessarily integers (whole numbers) or whether the number of scale values being used is very small. In practice, *both* these ideas really need to be combined so that the distinction becomes important only when the scale values *in principle* can only be whole numbers (like number of employees) and, furthermore, are few in number (for example, number of children in a household). If we create whole numbers for continuous variables by rounding off, that does not make them discrete. If the number of discrete scale values is small, then calculating an average size (for example 2.47 children) may not be appropriate or meaningful. If the number of discrete values is large, then the distinction is not important.

The second source of confusion is the failure to distinguish between scale values and frequencies. The distinction between discrete and continuous applies only to features of the set of scale values – that they are limited in number and can in principle only be integers. To define discrete in terms of the process of counting confuses situations where, on the one hand, we count the number of instances as a numerical measure of size, and, on the other, where we count the number of times a categorical scale value occurs, for example numbers of males and females in a group. In the latter case, the scale value recorded will be either "male" or "female" and the number refers to a frequency; in the former case the scale value recorded will be the number of employees in an organization.

If you are now very confused over these terms, do not worry: you are in good company. However, even if you avoided reading the warning box, do have a look at Box 5.2, which gives examples of each type of scale.

RESEARCH IN ACTION

BOX 5.2

Some examples of the different types of scales

Whatever type of scale is being used, the recorded values of variables will normally be laid out as a table, so they are illustrated here as tables, even though we have to look in more detail at tables and table construction in Chapter 11. Labeling scales will appear as lists of numbers against each case, as in Table 5.1. Table 5.2 shows what a simple table of binary data would look like, while Table 5.3 illustrates nominal data.

Notice that with all of these tables we could put the categories in any order and it would not change the sense of the table. We need, however, to arrange the categories in some way, even if it is arbitrary or random. Thus Table 5.1 lists the students in alphabetical order and this makes sense, while Table 5.3 puts the categories in order of the frequencies involved with the biggest at the top. However, changing

TABLE 5.1	Labeling scale: students by ID number
Student	**ID number**
Able	985672
Brown	975539
Chapman	985798

TABLE 5.2	Binary scale: respondents by gender	
	Frequency	**%**
Male	138	44.5
Female	172	55.5
Total	310	

TABLE 5.3	Nominal scale: company by type	
Company type	**Frequency**	**%**
Manufacturing	356	42
Construction	284	33
Retailing	173	20
Service	39	5
Total	852	

the order to, say, alphabetical, will not affect the interpretation, only its appearance. We shall see later that this means that any statistics we calculate on the data are unaffected by the order in which they are laid out.

Table 5.4 shows ordinal data – the categories are arranged in order of degrees of agreement with a statement. This is a natural ordering inherent in the meaning of the categories. Statistics appropriate for ordinal scales will be affected by the ordering of the categories. Table 5.5 shows six students who have been ranked according to their performance in two examinations in Mathematics and English. You can see that the rankings are very similar, and we could calculate a special statistic – Spearman's rho, which is explained in Chapter 12 – to show how strongly the rankings agree.

TABLE 5.4	Ordinal scale: agreement with the statement "This is a first class service"	
	Frequency	**%**
Strongly agree	23	10.7
Agree	56	26.2
Neither	45	21.0
Disagree	78	36.4
Strongly disagree	12	5.6
Total	214	

TABLE 5.5	Ranking scale: performance in maths and English	
Student	Rank, maths	Rank, English
A	1	1
B	2	3
C	3	2
D	4	5
E	5	4
F	6	6

Table 5.6 illustrates discrete metric data whereby size of household is measured by the number of individuals in it. Finally, Table 5.7 shows continuous metric data in which the ages of respondents have been grouped into class intervals of ten years. Remember that what characterizes all metric data and distinguishes them from categorical is that we can add up the quantities involved. Thus we can add up amounts of money to get a total, or we can add up the number of employees in different factories to obtain a total of corporation size. We can also add up the ages of a group of people to obtain a total, although this does not make much sense unless we also divide by the number of people to obtain an average age. For Table 5.7 it would be necessary to assume, for example, that all 46 people in the 20–29 category were at the midpoint of that category, namely 24.5. This would make it an estimate rather than an actual figure, but provided the 46 individuals were evenly spread between 20 and 29 then not much error would arise.

TABLE 5.6	Discrete metric scale: household size
Household size	Frequency
One person	45
Two people	68
Three people	74
Four or more	51

TABLE 5.7	Continuous metric scale: age or survey respondents
Age	Frequency
20–29	46
30–39	58
40–49	69
50–59	44
60–69	31
70+	15

If you have already read material in other books on what is often described as "measurement theory", you will have come across the categories nominal, ordinal, interval and ratio scales. This classification has been accepted somewhat uncritically over the years, but there are problems with it. First, binary scales are usually treated as just a form of nominal scale, but, statistically, binary scales have very different properties from scales having three or more categories. Thus it is impossible to put two scale values "out of order" so the issue of ordinality does not arise. Also, the "distance" between two categories cannot be compared with other distances. A consequence of this is that binary scales can be used in circumstances where nominal scales cannot. As will be explained in Chapter 14 on multivariate analysis, researchers sometimes create what they term "dummy variables", by regrouping a nominal scale as a set of binary scales in order to use them in a statistical technique that requires metric variables. Second, the standard categories do not distinguish between ordered categories and sets of rankings. Statistical operations that may be performed on the latter are, however, totally different from those that are applied to the former.

The third problem with the standard classification is that the distinction between interval and ratio scales is not particularly useful or helpful. While interval scales possess a unit of measurement, they have an arbitrary zero. For example, zero degrees centigrade is an arbitrary point on a scale and we cannot have "no temperature". In consequence we cannot say that 20°C is "twice" as hot as 10°C. There are, however, few examples of genuine interval scales. Once a unit of measurement exists, it is nearly always possible to conceive of "zero" units. The measurement of temperature is usually the only example of an interval scale that is ever suggested, although it is possible to add calendar time, index numbers and some measures of attitudes that utilize rating scales. In the event, statistically, there are few implications of the difference between interval and ratio scales, and sometimes you will see these grouped together anyway as "interval/ratio" scales. In this text they are called metric scales, which may be either discrete or continuous.

WARNING Data, variables and scales

Researchers sometimes distinguish different types of data on the basis of the kind of characteristic being recorded, so they might, for example, refer to "demographic" data, "behavioral" data or "attitudinal" data. They might refer to different kinds of data depending on the kind of scale used, so there may be references to "nominal" data or "metric" data. Finally, they might distinguish data based on the role they play in research, so there might be "descriptive" data, and "analytic" data. Bear in mind that the words "data", "variable" and "scale" are often used interchangeably, so some researchers might refer to nominal data, nominal variables or nominal scales. Notice, however, that we "record" a scale value, we "measure" a variable, but "construct" data.

KEY POINTS

All scales must at a minimum be sets of exhaustive and mutually exclusive values that represent a single dimension. Sets of values that do *not* represent a metric and where there is, furthermore, no sense of order may be labeling scales, binary scales or nominal scales. Those scales that have no metric, but where there is an implied order may be ordered categories or ranking scales. Metric scales may be discrete or continuous. Figure 5.2 summarizes the various scale types. These may themselves be seen as an ordinal scale that goes from the most basic labeling scale up to the most sophisticated, continuous metric. Some researchers will describe these as "levels of measurement", although we will be using the term "measurement" in a different and more specific sense. Sometimes the distinctions between the different kinds of scale are by no means clear-cut and in Chapter 11 we will see how, when we are analyzing data, we may wish to transform them in such a way that may upgrade (or downgrade) these scales before we undertake any statistical analyses.

The process of measurement

In common with all scientists, market researchers must face the problem of how to go about measuring the variables that are at the center of their investigations, whether they are demographic, behavioral or cognitive, or whether they are to act as descriptors, independent or dependent variables. However, unlike natural scientists, social scientists need in addition to contend with the fact that the subjects of interest are human beings, and that many of the variables that are the focus of their research have to do with the ways in which they perceive and define their own behavior and with the ways in which they think. Furthermore, individuals do not always make willing subjects and may (and often do) refuse to answer questions put by the researcher. There is always some nonresponse in any survey and its implications for measurement are, as we shall see, far from clear or obvious.

Measurement is a process by which researchers develop their "yardsticks" for the concepts that are the focus of their attention. The characteristics of cases that are to be used as variables for a given concept must be spelled out. The steps in the process are summarized in Figure 5.3. The researcher first needs to define the concept involved. Some concepts like age, although they have no physical or observable referent, are nevertheless fairly easy to define because people probably understand the concept in more or less the same way. For example, if we said that age is "the number of calendar years since birth rounded off to the last birthday", then most people would probably agree. If, however, we use a term like "brand loyalty" we may need to spell out what we mean by it and what are its boundaries. We would need a constitutive definition that specifies our idea in terms of other concepts, the meaning of which is assumed to be more familiar to the reader. So, we might define brand loyalty as "the preferential attitudinal and behavioral

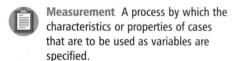

Measurement A process by which the characteristics or properties of cases that are to be used as variables are specified.

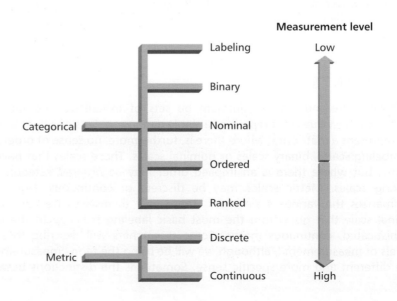

FIGURE 5.2

Summary of scale types

response towards one or more brands in a product category expressed over a period of time by a consumer (or buyer)" (Engel and Blackwell 1982). Such definitions are a bit like dictionary definitions that aim to capture the essence or key idea of a concept and distinguish it from other similar but distinct concepts.

Even when we are clear about a concept, however, there will nearly always be several ways in which it can be measured. Take what appears to be the relatively simple concept of the size of a firm. We could measure size in terms of sales volume, sales value, number of employees (and how do we handle part-time employees?); or perhaps we should look at the value of the firm's assets, which could be gross, net, and maybe could include intangibles like brand equity. We could even measure age in several ways: we could ask people their age in years, or in years and months, or in age groupings like 25–29. We could ask them their date of birth and make our own calculation, or get them to show us their birth certificates!

A statement of precisely what observable characteristics will be used to measure the concept is usually called the **operational definition**. Operational definitions can be approached in one of four main ways:

Operational definition A statement of precisely what observable characteristics are to be used to measure a concept.

- directly,
- indirectly,
- derivation from a number of measures,
- treated as multidimensional.

Direct measurement

Direct measurement is possible when one of two circumstances holds. First, a "true" value, which is unambiguous (or relatively unambiguous), may be held to exist independently of the researcher's attempts to measure it and which is approximated by the value of the variable recorded. This may arise either because the characteristic may be observed, as in color of packaging, or because some record exists that verifies the recorded value such as a birth certificate. Second, where individual cognition or interpretations of behavior are involved, the researcher may want a direct record of what these are and may ask respondents directly. In a survey the researcher might ask: "How satisfied are you with the quality of the food in this café; very satisfied, somewhat satisfied or dissatisfied?" The implication here is that we have defined satisfaction in terms of self-reported levels of satisfaction. We are assuming a literal one-to-one (or "isomorphic") correspondence between the concept and the recorded scale value. The concept is *defined* by the way we choose to measure it. We take what individuals say at face value and accept their answer as a "true" record of their feelings. If a respondent says he is "very satisfied", then this is the "correct" scale value.

Direct measurement A one-to-one correspondence between the concept and the variable used to measure.

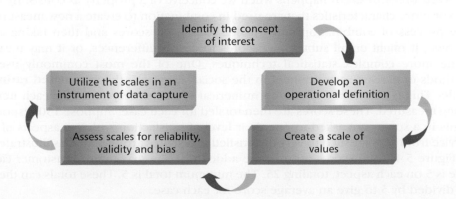

FIGURE 5.3

The process of measurement

This is fine if, as researchers, what we wish to measure is perceived satisfaction, or perceived loyalty or self-defined social class. But different individuals will define satisfaction in different ways and what one person means by "very satisfied" may not be the same as another person giving apparently the "same" answer. Furthermore, for various reasons, the respondent may give a "wrong" answer, for example because he or she has incorrect recall, has misinformation, is exaggerating or fabricating. The respondent's answers are also likely to be affected by mood, situational factors, willingness or reluctance to impart feelings or information, the wording of the question, the way it was addressed, or the understanding of the question.

In these circumstances, researchers may seek a more "objective" measure – one that tries to take measures that are comparable across respondents. There are two possibilities: first, the researcher may take some kind of indirect indicator of the concept he or she is trying to measure or, second, the researcher may derive a measure from the combination of two or more items.

Indirect measurement

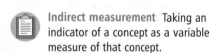

Indirect measurement Taking an indicator of a concept as a variable measure of that concept.

Indirect measurement entails taking an indicator of the concept rather than the concept itself. Thus the number of defective products returned or the number of complaints received are commonly taken as indicators of customer satisfaction. When the bus company Stagecoach won the franchise to run South West Trains in 1996, its chairman, Brian Souter, paid a visit to his new business. He was amazed to discover that SWT received 40 000 letters of complaint a year from passengers. Stagecoach, apparently, received no such letters. Souter summarized his approach somewhat pithily: "We judge customer satisfaction by the number of bricks we get through the window." Occupation is commonly taken as an indicator of social class and repeat purchase is taken as an indicator of brand loyalty.

Indirect measurement assumes that there is a degree of correspondence between the concept and the indicator deployed, but recognizes that the indicator is not the concept itself, but only a reflection of it. Such measurement depends on the presumed relationships between observations and the concept of interest. It has been described as "measurement by fiat" (Torgerson 1958) because the choice of indicator is usually arbitrary.

With concepts as complex as customer satisfaction, social class, or brand loyalty, asking just one question of respondents or taking just one measure may be insufficient. Such concepts will have several if not many aspects or facets. It may be necessary in respect of many cognitive variables to ask several questions, each relating to a slightly different aspect of the item or items being evaluated. If this is the case, then we might need to think about using derived measurement.

Derived measurement

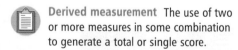

Derived measurement The use of two or more measures in some combination to generate a total or single score.

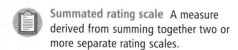

Summated rating scale A measure derived from summing together two or more separate rating scales.

Derived measurement happens when we conceive of a property as consisting of two or more characteristics that are used in combination to create a new measure. The process of combination may involve adding up scores and then taking an average, it might entail subtracting scores to derive differences, or it may mean using more complex statistical techniques. One of the most commonly used methods of derived measurement in the social sciences is the **summated rating scale**. This is created by allocating numerical scores to responses for each item being measured. These scores are then totaled for each case. Suppose 150 respondents in a survey are asked to rate their level of satisfaction with five aspects of a service from very satisfied to very dissatisfied and scores are allocated as illustrated in Figure 5.4. Total scores can now be added up. The maximum a customer can give is 5 on each aspect, totaling 25. The minimum total is 5. These totals can then be divided by 5 to give an average score for each case.

How satisfied were you with the performance of our staff on each aspect of service when you last telephoned us?

	Very satisfied	Fairly satisfied	Neither	Fairly dissatisfied	Very dissatisfied
Speed of getting through	5	4	3	2	1
Getting the right person	5	4	3	2	1
Politeness	5	4	3	2	1
Staff knowledge of products	5	4	3	2	1
Efficiency	5	4	3	2	1

FIGURE 5.4

A summated rating scale – customer satisfaction with service provided

A particular version of a summated rating scale to measure attitudes was developed by Likert in 1932. **Likert scales** are based on getting respondents to indicate their degree of agreement or disagreement with a series of statements about the object or focus of the attitude. Usually, these are on 5-point ratings from "strongly agree", through "agree", "neither agree nor disagree", "disagree" to "strongly disagree". Likert's main concern was with single-dimensionality, that is, making sure that all the items would measure the same thing. Accordingly, he recommended a series of steps.

Likert scale A summated rating scale derived from the summation of 5 or 7-point ratings of agreement or disagreement with a number of statements relating to an attitude object.

1 A large list of attitude statements, both positive and negative, concerning the object of the attitude is generated, usually based on the results of qualitative research.

2 The response categories are assigned scores, usually 1–5, but some researchers prefer −2, −1, 0, +1, +2. These may need to be reversed for negative statements.

3 The list is tested on a screening sample of 100–200 respondents representative of the larger group to be studied and a total score is derived for each respondent.

4 Statements that do not discriminate (that is, everybody gives the same or similar answers) or that do not correlate with the overall total score, are discarded. This is a procedure Likert called **item analysis** and it avoids cluttering up the final scale with items that are either irrelevant or inconsistent with the other items. Correlation is considered later in Chapter 12.

Item analysis A process used in Likert scaling whereby items that do not correlate with the total score are discarded.

5 The remaining statements, such as the ones in Figure 5.5, are then administered to the main sample of respondents, usually as part of a wider questionnaire survey. Usually the statements will be ordered randomly to mix positive and negative ones. The items in Figure 5.5 were generated by "converting" the items in Figure 5.4 into a set of Likert items.

6 Totals are derived for each respondent.

There are a number of fairly fundamental problems with Likert, and indeed all summated rating scales.

■ The totals for each respondent may be derived from very different combinations of responses. Thus a score of 15 may be derived either by neither agreeing nor disagreeing with all the items or by strongly agreeing with some and strongly disagreeing with others. Consequently, it is often a good idea also to analyze the patterns of each response on an item-by-item basis. The analysis of data from summated rating scales is considered in some detail in Chapter 12.

FIGURE 5.5

A Likert measurement

Below is a series of statements that people have made about the ABC Club. Please indicate to what extent you agree or disagree with each statement by putting a circle around the appropriate number

	Strongly agree	Agree	Neither	Disagree	Strongly disagree
I get through very quickly	5	4	3	2	1
I always get the right person	5	4	3	2	1
The staff are not very polite	1	2	3	4	5
Staff know their products well	5	4	3	2	1
The staff are not very efficient	1	2	3	4	5

- The derived total scores are not in any sense absolute, so that a respondent scoring 20 is not "twice" as favorable as another scoring 10. All we can really say is that a score of 20 is "higher" than a score of 10 or 15 or whatever.

- The screening sample and subsequent item analysis are often omitted by researchers who simply generate the statements, probably derived from or based on previous tests, and go straight to the main sample. This is in many ways a pity, since leaving out scale refinement and purification will result in more ambiguous, less valid and less reliable instruments.

- The process of summating the ratings is potentially imposing a number system that forces scale characteristics (see scaling below) onto concepts that may not inherently possess these characteristics.

- Such scales assume that individuals lie along a dimension from positive to negative when he or she responds to a 5 or 7-point rating scale.

In addition to these problems, the current standard format of Likert scales has been recently criticized by Albaum (1997), who argues that the standard 5-point scale confuses two characteristics: the direction (positive or negative) and the strength of the attitude held. Thus a person may like or dislike particular changes in society, but may hold this attitude with varying degrees of intensity or conviction. The responses agree/disagree show direction, but when "strongly" is added to these it implies intensity. Albaum suggests a two-stage process in which respondents are asked first whether they agree, disagree, neither agree nor disagree or have no opinion, and second whether they hold their opinion very strongly or not very strongly. The traditional one-stage format is likely to underreport extreme positions since they represent the "ends" of a scale; this may lead to clustering around the midpoint. The two-stage format, argues Albaum, is a better predictor of preferences and results in higher-quality data. A major drawback to this procedure, of course, is that it will considerably lengthen any questionnaire.

Despite these limitations, summated rating scales, and Likert scales in particular, are very popular among both client-based and academic marketing researchers. A search in the *Business Elite* database for "Likert scale" produced 1600 articles. There is little doubt, say Lee and Hooley (2005), that the development of such scales has immeasurably enriched marketing science as a discipline, but perhaps in part because of the availability of computer software like SPSS, they have often been used without proper understanding of the mathematical and conceptual underpinnings of derived measures and multiitem scales.

In designing summated rating scales, there are three key decisions:

- the content and wording of each item,
- the number of items that are to be summed,
- the format of the response categories.

The statements that are to be used for each item and with which respondents are to be invited to agree or disagree cannot just be dreamed up while taking a leisurely bath. They may be based on statements made by respondents in focus groups or depth interviews carried out at an earlier stage in the research. They may be based on earlier research so that the items have at least been pretested, or they may be derived from standard scales that can be accessed from handbooks of marketing scales such as that by Bearden and Netemeyer (1999).

There are no guidelines for the number of items required. They may be grouped so that subsets of items are designed to pick up different dimensions of the concept. More than 30 or so items may begin to be off-putting to respondents. Box 5.3 illustrates the development of a multiitem scale for measuring the market orientation of commercial organizations.

RESEARCH IN ACTION
Developing a scale of market orientation

BOX 5.3

Narver and Slater (1990) have argued that market orientation consists of three key behavioral components: customer orientation, competitor orientation, and interfunctional coordination. Each was measured by asking top managers in 140 strategic business units of a major corporation to say to what extent a number of activities happened in their unit on a 7-point scale ranging from "not at all" to "to a very great extent". Thus customer orientation included:

- customer commitment,
- creating customer values,
- understanding customer needs,
- driven by customer satisfaction,
- measure customer satisfaction,
- provision of after-sales service.

Competitor orientation included:

- sales people share competitor information,
- respond rapidly to competitors' actions,
- top managers discuss competitors' strategies,
- target opportunities for competitive advantage.

Interfunctional coordination included:

- information share among functions,
- functional integration in strategy,
- all functions contribute to customer value,
- share resources with other business units.

"Not at all" was given a scale value of 1 and "to a great extent" a scale value of 7. The scores for each item like *Customer commitment* were totaled across all 371 managers who responded and then averaged. Also, for each respondent the total scores for all six items under customer orientation were calculated and averaged across all respondents. The same was done for the other two behavioral components. Finally, overall market orientation was taken as the average of the three components.

The format of the response categories (often referred to as "items") for derived measurements (often called "multiitem" scales) can vary in terms of:

- the number of scale categories used,
- the provision of a no opinion category,
- the balance of the scale,
- the degree of verbal description for each category,
- the layout of the scale.

The more scale categories used, the finer can be the discrimination between responses; but respondents find it increasingly difficult. Most scales are 5- or 7-point, giving a middle category with equal balancing either side. A Likert scale is a balanced rating scale with an odd number of categories and a neutral position. Some researchers, however, may want to force respondents to make a choice and will provide an equal number of responses with no neutral position. The extent to which each category is labeled will vary and this may have some considerable effect on the results. Some of the possibilities are illustrated in Figure 5.6. Stronger anchors like "very fast" will produce fewer extreme responses than weaker anchors like "fast".

The results from summated rating scales are, strictly speaking, ordinal. The numerical scores derived indicate only relative positions, so that a score of 15 is "higher" than a score of 12, but by how much is unclear because there are no "units" of measurement. There is no metric for measuring people's attitudes. In practice, however, researchers commonly treat the results, particularly of Likert scales, as metric; they will calculate average scores, and use the results in statistical procedures that require metric data. Such a practice is making the assumption of equivalence of distance between scale values, so that the difference, for example, between "strongly agree" and "agree" is the same as the distance between "agree" and "neither" and between "disagree" and "strongly disagree". This may be a reasonable assumption for the standard Likert scale and little error may result from acting as if the resulting scale is metric, but for some scales that measure degrees of customer satisfaction the assumption may be unwarranted. The various ways in which data from Likert and other kinds of summated rating scale may be analyzed are explained in Chapter 11.

Flynn and Piercy (2001) analyzed 24 articles derived from a range of databases that described new multiitem scales where the authors cited the seminal article by Churchill (1979) as a source of scale construction and which contained sufficient information about the methodology. They found four common "subtle sins" in scale development, including insufficient scale development sample sizes, insuffi-

---

FIGURE 5.6

Some rating scale formats

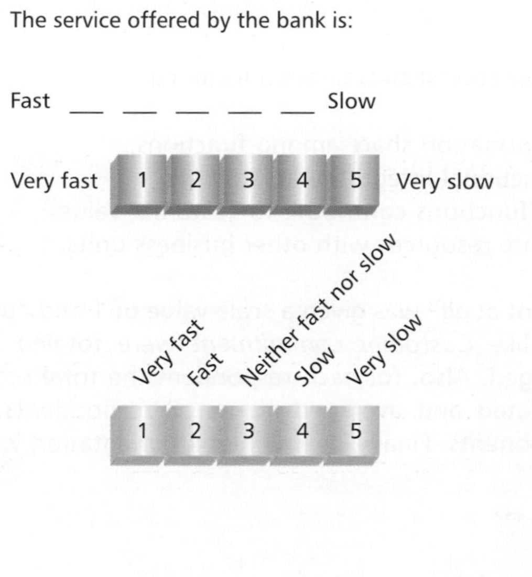

The service offered by the bank is:

Fast ___ ___ ___ ___ ___ Slow

Very fast | 1 | 2 | 3 | 4 | 5 | Very slow

Very fast / Fast / Neither fast nor slow / Slow / Very slow

| 1 | 2 | 3 | 4 | 5 |

cient replications, inconsistent use of exploratory factor analysis (which is explained in Chapter 14), and confusion between scales designed for applied purposes and those destined to test theories.

Multidimensional measurement

Derived measurement creates a single total or mathematically generated score; it is a single-dimensional measure. Multidimensional models, by contrast, allow for the possibility not only that there is more than one characteristic underlying a set of observations, but also that these cannot be summed or transposed into a derived score. Sometimes these characteristics need first to be identified and some statistical techniques like factor analysis are geared to this end (factor analysis is explained on pp. 420–422). Once they have been identified, there are two main possibilities. One recognizes that each characteristic is independent and cannot be added together or transposed into a single score. Rather, a profile of each dimension is described separately in order to present a more complete picture. The other approach sees the respondents as being represented by a single point, but in three-dimensional or multidimensional space.

It would be possible to use Likert-type items for profiling by calculating an average across cases separately for each item, so that, for Figure 5.5 for example, there would be an average score for *I get through very quickly* and another for *I always get the right person,* and so on. There would be no attempt to add up scores for the five items. A more common way of obtaining a profile is to use a **semantic differential**. These measures were developed by Osgood et al. (1957) and were designed originally to investigate the underlying structure of words, but have subsequently been adapted to measure images of stores, companies or brands and attitudes. They present characteristics as a series of opposites, which may be either bipolar, like "sweet . . . sour", or monopolar, like "sweet . . . not sweet". Respondents may be asked to indicate, usually on a 7-point rating where between the two extremes their views lie, as illustrated in Figure 5.7. In most semantic differentials there are three groups of adjective pairs:

- an evaluation dimension such as "good . . . bad" or "sweet . . . bitter".
- a potency dimension such as "strong . . . weak", or "deep . . . shallow",
- an activity dimension such as "fast . . . slow", or "noisy . . . quiet".

Unlike Likert items, which may be classified into positive and negative statements, semantic differentials may not be classifiable in this way, for example "bitter . . . sweet" – which is the "positive" one? For this reason there may be no attempt to add the items together, but to present them as a "snake" diagram as in Figure 5.8. The seven positions on the rating will be scored 1–7 (or−3 to +3) and an average taken separately for each item across the respondents. It is then possible to compare profiles of two or more brands, stores or companies.

Semantic differential scale A multidimensional scale that represents a profile of characteristics expressed as bipolar opposites like "sweet-sour" that constitutes a 7-point rating scale.

Please put an X at a point between the two extremes which indicates your view about the services you received from the Club

Fast to get through : ___ : ___ : ___ : ___ : ___ : ___ : ___ : Slow to get through

Get the right person : ___ : ___ : ___ : ___ : ___ : ___ : ___ : Get the wrong person

Staff are polite : ___ : ___ : ___ : ___ : ___ : ___ : ___ : Staff are impolite

Staff know products : ___ : ___ : ___ : ___ : ___ : ___ : ___ : Staff do not know products

Staff are efficient : ___ : ___ : ___ : ___ : ___ : ___ : ___ : Staff are inefficient

FIGURE 5.7

A semantic differential

FIGURE 5.8

A snake diagram

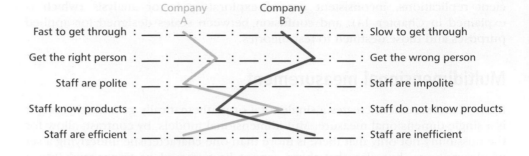

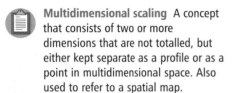

Multidimensional scaling A concept that consists of two or more dimensions that are not totalled, but either kept separate as a profile or as a point in multidimensional space. Also used to refer to a spatial map.

If the items *are* to be added up, they must be clearly classifiable into positive and negative and subject to an item analysis procedure on a screening sample as for Likert procedures. In practice this is often not done, which, again, is a pity because the potential for error is considerable.

An alternative to profiling is to locate each respondent as a single point in multidimensional space. What is known as **multidimensional scaling** (often referred to as MDS for short or as perceptual mapping) refers in fact to a series of techniques that help the researcher to identify key characteristics underlying respondents' evaluations. They attempt to deduce the underlying dimensions from a series of similarity or preference judgments of objects, products, services, organizations and so on made by respondents. The results are then presented as a two-dimensional map, which takes account of the multidimensional distances between cases. The technique is explained in more detail in Chapter 14.

KEY POINTS

Measurement entails either the assignment of cases to categories on the basis of observed or recorded characteristics, or the assignment of numerical values to cases that are intended to reflect the extent to which each case possesses a defined characteristic. This assignment may be on the basis of a single measurement that either directly or indirectly reflects the characteristic the research wishes or intends to measure. These may be called single-item scales. Alternatively, multiitem scales may be developed that either combine several items into a single overall derived measure, or treat the scale as a profile or as multidimensional.

Concepts can usually be measured in a number of different ways. The particular manner in which a measurement is taken is its operational definition. Thus a researcher may say something like: "Customer satisfaction was measured using a 13-item, 5-point Likert scale." Unpacked, this means that there were 13 statements with which respondents were asked to indicate their degree of agreement or disagreement with five response categories running from strongly agree to strongly disagree. The scores were then totaled and then averaged across the 13 items.

WARNING Measurement and scaling

The terms "measurement" and "scaling" are sometimes used interchangeably, but sometimes to distinguish different aspects of the measurement process, for example that measurement relates to the process of developing yardsticks and deciding what variables to use as measures, while scaling is the assignment of cases to different kinds of scale. Unfortunately, the scales used are usually called "levels of measurement", which confuses the issue, while "scaling" is often used to mean the process of developing multiitem scales such as Likert scales, semantic differentials or "multidimensional scaling". The development of yardsticks and the mapping of cases onto scales are clearly interrelated, so it is probably safer just to use the term "measurement". This chapter has not used the word "scaling", to avoid confusion.

Measurement error

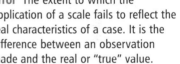

When researchers measure, they either assign cases to categories on the basis of observed or recorded characteristics of those cases, for example, assigning respondents to "high", "medium" or "low" usage of the internet on the basis of observed frequency of use, or they assign numerical values to cases that are intended to reflect the extent to which each case possesses a defined characteristic, for example giving respondents a total score from a set of attitude statements. Measurements, in short, are reflections of characteristics. To the extent that these reflections are inappropriate or wrong, then a degree of **error** is involved. Technically, error could be defined as the difference between the observation made and the real or "true" value. Unfortunately, this definition is not very helpful since the real or true value is usually unknown – and if it were known then there would be no need for the measurement in the first place.

In practice, error can only be estimated on the basis of various pieces of evidence, usually discussed under the headings of scale **reliability** and **validity**. A scale is said to be reliable to the extent that it produces consistent results if repeat measures are taken. A scale is valid to the extent that it measures what it is intended to measure. A valid measure must, clearly, be reliable, but a reliable measure may not be valid. Thus a poorly adjusted pair of scales will give consistently wrong results; but they will still be useful for recording any change.

Researchers, furthermore, usually take measures for a large number of cases, so there is the further issue of **bias** – a tendency for measures to be in a particular direction. A valid measure will be both reliable and unbiased over a number of measurements. However, a reliable measure may be invalid if it is biased over a number of measures; and, alternatively, an unreliable measure may be valid if the measures are unbiased and errors cancel out over a number of repeats or when measures are taken for a large number of cases.

If measurement is direct, the variable being used to measure a concept either is defined *as* the concept, or can be checked against an independent record or observation – so there is, by definition, no measurement error. This is not to say, of course, that no error is involved – there can still be survey design and execution errors or sampling errors. If the measurement is indirect then measurement error may arise because the "wrong" variable is being used as an indicator. Occupation may, for example, be a poor indicator of income.

Where measurement is derived from a multiitem scale, other sources of measurement error potentially emerge:

- repeated measures do not produce similar results,
- equivalent measures do not produce similar results,
- the items in the scale are not internally consistent,
- the items in the scale do not adequately sample the domain of features that should be included,
- the scale fails to predict what it was designed to predict,

Error The extent to which the application of a scale fails to reflect the real characteristics of a case. It is the difference between an observation made and the real or "true" value.

Reliability The extent to which the application of a scale produces consistent results if repeated measures are taken.

Validity The extent to which the application of a scale that measures what it is intended to measure.

Bias A form of error that tends to be in a particular direction.

■■ the scale does not relate to other constructs to which it is theoretically related.

The first three sources of error relate to scale reliability and the last three to various forms of scale validity. Repeat measures, where these are taken, give an indication of scale stability over time and depend on one or more retests at a later date. There are, however, some important problems with this measure:

■■ how long to wait between tests,

■■ what differences between measures count as "significant",

■■ to what extent differences discovered reflect scale instability as opposed to genuine changes in the characteristics being measured.

The length of time between tests will affect all of these. Wait too long and the probability of changing characteristics like attitudes is quite high; too quick and there will be test bias – people may remember how they responded the first time and be more "consistent" in their responses than is warranted by their attitudes. The recommended time interval has been put at two weeks (see Nunnally 1978).

Scale equivalence measures how two equivalent indexes given at virtually the same time are in agreement. This is sometimes called the "split-half" technique. The total set of items in divided into two equivalent halves. This may be done on a random or systematic basis. The total scores of the two halves are then correlated. There are two key problems with this approach:

■■ what degree of correlation indicates reliability,

■■ the split between the scales may be carried out in many different ways, each way producing different results.

Narver and Slater (1990), for example (see Box 5.3), randomly split their data into two samples before assessing reliability. Reliability analyses were carried out on the first sample and then replicated in the second.

Internal consistency is a matter of the extent to which the items used to measure a concept "hang" together. Ideally, all the items used in the scale should reflect some single underlying dimension; statistically that means that they should correlate one with another. An increasingly popular measure for establishing internal consistency is a coefficient developed in 1952 by Cronbach that he called "alpha". **Cronbach's coefficient alpha** takes the average correlation among items in a summated rating scale and adjusts for the number of items. This measure is in fact the equivalent of taking every possible split-half combination and is often taken as a measure of scale reliability. Reliable scales are ones with high average correlation and a relatively large number of items. The coefficient varies between zero for no reliability to unity for maximum reliability.

Alpha has effectively become *the* measure of choice for establishing the reliability of multiitem scales. According to the Social Sciences Citation Index it has been referenced in over 2200 articles in 278 different journals in the past 20 years (Peterson 1994). Its availability at the click of a mouse button in survey analysis programs like SPSS has almost certainly meant that it is commonly reported by researchers, but often with little understanding of what it means and what its limitations are. There is a background discussion on the interpretation of the coefficient in Box 5.4.

Cronbach's coefficient alpha A measure of scale reliability. It takes the average correlation among items in a summated rating scale and adjusts for the number of items.

IN DETAIL
Cronbach's coefficient alpha

BOX 5.4

Cronbach's alpha is a measure of internal reliability for multiitem summated rating scales. It takes the average correlation among items in a scale and adjusts for the number of items. Reliable scales are ones with high average correlation and a relatively large number of items. The coefficient varies between zero for no reliability to unity for maximum reliability. The formula subtracts from unity the sum of the variance for each item (σ_i^2) divided by the variance of the scale (σ_s^2) and multiplies by the number of items divided by the number of items minus 1.

$$a = \left(1 - \Sigma \frac{\sigma_i^2}{\sigma_s^2}\right)\left(\frac{k}{k-1}\right)$$

The latter value, of course, approaches unity as the number of items increases. If the variance for each item is identical, or the variances are converted to Z scores, the formula reduces to the interitem correlation, r, multiplied by the number of items, k, divided by 1 plus the interitem correlation multiplied by the number of items minus 1.

$$\frac{kr}{1 + r(k-1)}$$

Strictly speaking, *Cronbach's* alpha is the first of these procedures; the "standardized" alpha may give a slightly different result (Cortina 1993).

Despite its wide use, there is little guidance in the literature (and none from Cronbach himself) as to what constitutes an "acceptable" or "sufficient" value for alpha to achieve. Most users of the statistic cite Nunnally's (1978) recommendation that a value of 0.7 should be achieved. It is assumed that if alpha for any scale is greater than 0.7 then it's OK. However, all those authors making recommendations about acceptable levels of alpha, including Nunnally, indicate that the desired degree of reliability is a function of the purpose of the research, for example whether it is exploratory or applied. Nunnally himself in 1978 suggested that for preliminary research "reliabilities of 0.70 or higher will suffice". For "basic" research, he suggests that "increasing reliabilities much beyond 0.80 is often wasteful of time and funds" (Nunnally 1978: 245). In contrast, for applied research, 0.80 "is not nearly high enough". Where important decisions depend on the outcome of the measurement process, a reliability of 0.90 "is the minimum that should be tolerated".

None of Nunnally's recommendations, however, have an empirical basis, a theoretical justification, or an analytical rationale. Rather they seem to reflect either experience or intuition. Interestingly, Nunnally had changed his own recommendations from his 1967 edition of *Psychometric Theory*, which recommended that the minimally acceptable reliability for preliminary research should be in the range of 0.5 to 0.6.

Peterson (1994) reports the results of a study to ascertain the values of alpha actually obtained in articles and papers based on empirical work. From a sample of over 800 marketing- and psychology-related journals, conference proceedings and some unpublished manuscripts, he reviewed all alpha coefficients found in each study, resulting in 4286 coefficients covering a 33-year period. Reported coefficients ranged from 0.6 to 0.99 with a mean of 0.77. About 75 percent were 0.7 or greater and 50 percent were 0.8 or greater. Peterson found that reported alphas were not greatly affected by research design characteristics, such as sample size, type of sample, number of scale categories, type of scale, mode of administration, or type of research. One exception to this is that during scale development, items are often eliminated if their presence restricts the value of alpha. Not surprisingly, the alpha coefficients reported were significantly related to the number of items eliminated.

It is important to remember that alpha measures only internal consistency; if error factors associated with the passage of time are of concern to the researcher, then it will not be the most appropriate statistic. However, since alpha approximates the mean of all possible split-half reliabilities, it can be seen as a superior measure of scale equivalence. It is not, however, as is commonly supposed, an indication of unidimensionality. Alpha can, in fact, be quite high despite the presence of several different dimensions (Cortina 1993).

When interpreting alpha coefficients, it is often forgotten, furthermore, that the values achieved are in part a function of the number of items. Thus for a three-item scale with alpha = 0.80, the average interitem correlation is 0.57. For a ten-item scale with alpha = 0.80 it is only 0.28. What needs to be kept in mind is that in evaluating, say, a 40-item scale, alpha will be relatively large simply because of the number of items, and the number of items is not exactly a great measure of scale quality. When many items are pooled, internal consistency estimates are inevitably large and invariant, and therefore of limited value.

Alpha, in short, should be used with some caution. It is appropriate only when the researcher requires a measure of internal consistency, and is helpful only then if the number of items used is fairly limited. The value of alpha to be taken as "acceptable" must be related to the purpose of the research, and even then only used as an indication rather than a "test" to be passed with a fixed value. Furthermore, if researchers are concerned about dimensionality, then procedures like factor analysis are probably more appropriate. For a more recent review of Cronbach's alpha see Lee and Hooley (2005).

Narver and Slater (1990) calculated Cronbach's alpha for each of the three components of market orientation (see Box 5.3). The six items for customer orientation produced an alpha of 0.86, the four items for competitor orientation 0.72 and the items for interfunctional coordination 0.71. They concluded that the three scales exceeded the threshold suggested by Nunnally for exploratory research.

In terms of validity, what is commonly referred to as **content validity** focuses on the adequacy with which the domain of the characteristic is adequately sampled by the measure. Thus measuring customer satisfaction with a new car by asking a series of questions about speed and acceleration would not adequately sample the domain of characteristics or features that determine customer satisfaction. It would, in other words, lack content validity. Content validity is sometimes known as "face" validity because the measure is reviewed on the basis of whether or not it seems to be reasonable "on the face of it". The key to content validity lies in the procedures that we use to develop the instrument. Such a procedure would begin with a clear definition of the concept, perhaps relating this to how the concept has been defined in the past. The next step is to formulate a large number of items that broadly represent the concept as defined. In the last stage the items will be pruned and refined so that items that do not discriminate between respondents or cases are excluded, and any items that overlap to too great an extent with other items are avoided.

To establish face validity for their measure of market orientation, Narver and Slater (1990) developed a large number of items that potentially might characterize the components of market orientation. These were submitted to a panel of three academics who were recognized authorities on strategic marketing. They rated each item for its consistency with market orientation and recommended other items for inclusion in the scale. Items that received a high rating (or were suggested by the panelist) were submitted to a second panel of three academics. Items that the second panel considered to have a high consistency were included in the final questionnaire.

The usefulness of the measuring instrument as a predictor of some other characteristic or behavior is usually referred to as **criterion validity**, but also sometimes called "pragmatic" or "predictive" validity. If, for example, a particular measure of customer satisfaction enables us to predict with some accuracy whether or not a consumer will repeat purchase then we could say that it has criterion validity. The focus is purely on the size of the correlation between the measure and what it is predicting. It does not really address the issue of what in fact is being measured.

Content validity The extent to which the domain of a characteristic is adequately sampled by the measure.

Criterion validity The extent to which a measure successfully predicts some other characteristic to which it is related.

Scales ideally should relate to other concepts to which they are meant to be related. Some authors refer to this as **construct validity** or "convergent" validity. Thus a good measure of social class would relate to characteristics like lifestyle, leisure pursuits, holidaymaking, purchasing behavior and so on. At the same time scales should not correlate with other measures from which they are meant to be theoretically different. This is often called **discriminant validity**.

To assess discriminant validity in their scale of market orientation, Narver and Slater (1990) included in their questionnaire a scale for measuring human resource management policy. This and interfunctional coordination are both "people management" policies. However, to affirm that customer orientation, competitor orientation, and interfunctional coordination are measuring market orientation instead of some general effect describing "good management", it was hypothesized that the correlation between human resource management policy and interfunctional coordination should be substantially less than the correlation between interfunctional coordination and either customer orientation or competitor orientation. The results showed that this hypothesis was upheld.

Kalafatis, Sarpong and Sharif (2005) point out that a lot of marketing research employs scales borrowed from other studies but with little questioning of their contextual suitability or testing of their stability. There are in fact whole books of ready-made scales that researchers can use, such as by Bearden and Netemeyer (1999). The authors warn, however, that using different scales can produce very different results when looking at the structural relationships between latent variables.

Construct validity The extent to which a measure relates to other measures to which it should be related.

Discriminant validity The extent to which a measure does not correlate with other measures from which they are meant to be different.

KEY POINTS

Measurement error is a difficult concept. Overall we can say that measurement errors give rise to inaccuracies in the data; but these inaccuracies are of different kinds. The concepts of reliability and validity have not served the topic of measurement error particularly well and are in any case usually applied only to multiitem scales. Single-item scales also need to be accurate, which in turn means that in terms of reliability, repeat measures should produce similar results, and in terms of validity, while internal consistency cannot be assessed on a single item, it should still have "face" or "content" validity in the sense that if the measure is indirect then it should still be a good reflection of the intended characteristic. It should also have predictive and construct validity.

Multiitem scales should, in addition, also be internally consistent and should adequately sample the domain of characteristics that are deemed to be relevant to the research. The issue of measurement bias is not really addressed by the concepts of reliability and validity, since these concepts are usually applied to the measurement of a single case when normally there will be many cases whose characteristics are being measured in a piece of research. Any tendency for the measurement of many cases to err in a particular direction can happen for both single and multiitem scales.

One final point; validity can sometimes be approached by taking measurements of a concept in more than one way and then seeing if they produce consistent results. This is a process that is sometimes referred to as triangulation. This concept is explained further in Chapter 9.

A scale that is deemed to be valid is, furthermore, not necessarily error free. Measurement error is only one of many kinds of error. The different potential sources of error that can occur, for example in the design and execution of market research surveys, are explained in Chapter 7.

Ethical issues

It is only too easy to frame the descriptors of a scale in such a way as to manipulate the results. Thus a customer satisfaction survey could give respondents more "satisfied" categories than dissatisfied ones, thereby biasing results in a positive direction. If the positive end of a semantic differential is simply "good", but the negative end is "extremely poor" rather than just "poor", then the result again will come out towards the higher scores.

Ideally, multiitem scales should be developed through a process of systematic generation of a large number of items that are then "purified". Thus item analysis should be a central part of developing Likert scales. Purification should ensure that the items finally used do capture the underlying construct as fully as possible, but without redundancy. Cronbach's coefficient alpha may be used for this purpose, but as explained in Box 5.4, the unthinking application of this measure as some kind of "test" can be misleading. Alternatively, some researchers will use exploratory factor analysis. This statistic is explained in Chapter 14. However, Lee and Hooley (2005) suggest that this procedure, too, has its shortcomings.

In any event, proper scale development is a lengthy and expensive process that should involve several attempts at scale refinement. Some research agencies have indeed developed proprietary scales that are protected by copyright. However, most probably do not have the time or the resources to refine scales in this way. Many scales will not be tested for reliability and validity and this can present an ethical dilemma if researchers, for example, find evidence of problems, but do nothing to resolve them.

SUMMARY

Quantitative data are numerical records that are prestructured at the point of data capture. They are constructed by deciding on the cases, the variables and sets of values to be used before the data collection takes place, and then undertaking a process of measurement. Cases are the entities whose characteristics are being recorded in the process of data construction. They may be objects, people, survey respondents, groups of people, organizations, situations, geographical areas or events.

Variables are characteristics of cases that the researcher has chosen to observe or measure and then record. They may relate to demographic, behavioral or cognitive characteristics, and they may play different, or a combination of, roles in the research. The majority of variables are "latent" in the sense that they are idealized constructs of the researcher that are at best only indirectly measurable.

A value is selected from a scale of values and it is this value that is recorded as part of the data construction process. Scales may be categorical or metric. Categorical scales may, in turn, be labeling, binary, nominal, ordinal or ranking scales. The differences between them are important because the statistics we can apply to them differ, in some cases quite dramatically. What they have in common, however, is that there is no metric that can be used to gauge distances between scale values. Metric scales arise when there is a unit of measurement and the scale values represent the result of a process of either calibration using some measuring instrument, resulting in continuous metric scales, or counting the number of people or items involved as a measure of size, which result in discrete metric scales. All scales, however, must at a minimum be sets of exhaustive and mutually exclusive values that represent a single underlying characteristic.

Measurement is concerned with spelling out which characteristics of cases are to be used as variables for a given concept. It entails either the assignment of cases to categories on the basis of observed or recorded characteristics, or the assignment of numerical values to cases that are intended to reflect the extent to which each case possesses a defined characteristic. This assignment may be on the basis of a single measurement that either directly or indirectly reflects the characteristic the research wishes or intends to measure. These may be called single-item scales. Alternatively, multi-item scales may be developed that either combine several items into a single overall derived measure, or treat the scale as a multidimensional profile or as a point in multidimensional space.

Except where measurement is direct, there is likely to be a degree of error in the measurement process. This can seldom be assessed with any accuracy, so evidence is collected on the likely reliability and validity of the measures taken. Single-item scales need to be accurate, which in turn means that in terms of reliability, repeat measures should produce similar results, and in terms of validity, while internal consistency cannot be assessed on a single item, it should still have "face" or "content" validity in the sense that if the measure is indirect then it should still be a good reflection of the intended characteristic. It should also have predictive and construct validity. Multiitem scales should, in addition, also be internally consistent and should adequately sample the domain of characteristics that are deemed to be relevant to the research. The issue of measurement bias, however, is not addressed by the concepts of reliability and validity, since these concepts are usually applied to the measurement of a single case when normally there will be many cases whose characteristics are being measured in a piece of research. Any tendency for the measurement of many cases to err in a particular direction can happen for both single and multiitem scales.

QUESTIONS FOR DISCUSSION

1   Think of the concept "degree of religiousness". How could this be measured in a way that is (a) direct, (b) indirect, (c) derived, and (d) multidimensional?

2   Table 5.8 shows some summary results from the study of table tennis in Northern Ireland.

  ■   How many respondents are there?
  ■   What are the variables to which the data refer?
  ■   Which ones are demographic, which ones are behavioral and which are cognitive?
  ■   What kind of scale is being used for each variable?

3   If all data are in one way or another "manufactured", are there any data that we *could* accept as "the facts", as "things given"?

4   Is the distinction between discrete and continuous metric scales any more (or less) useful than the distinction between interval and ratio scales?

5   Is direct measurement any more (or less) "scientific" than indirect or derived measurement?

6   The single-dimensionality of scales is commonly assumed rather than demonstrated. Why do you think this may be so?

7   How would you measure – and on what sort of a scale – each of the following?

  ■   how many times somebody reads a newspaper in a week,
  ■   customer satisfaction with a restaurant,
  ■   attitudes to Radio 1,
  ■   brand loyalty to Nescafé Gold Blend over the course of a year,

TABLE 5.8	A survey of table tennis players in Northern Ireland		
		Count	Col %
In which league do you compete?	Bangor and District	46	38.3
	Belfast	37	30.8
	Greystone	30	25.0
	Antrim	7	5.8
Total		120	100.0
In which division do you compete?	first	38	31.7
	second	41	34.2
	third	36	30.0
	fourth	5	4.2
Total		120	100.0
What sex are you?	male	103	85.8
	female	17	14.2
Total		120	100.0
How many times do you play per week?	once	43	35.8
	twice	52	43.3
	three times	18	15.0
	four or more times	7	5.8
Total		120	100.0
Social benefits	unimportant	11	9.2
	fairly unimportant	18	15.0
	neither unimportant or important	41	34.2
	fairly important	37	30.8
	very important	13	10.8
Total		120	100.0

8   What sort of scale will consumer responses to the following questions generate?

■ Have you purchased a magazine in the past few days?
■ Would you say you were satisfied, fairly satisfied or dissatisfied with the video you have just hired?
■ On a scale of 1–10 how would you rate the university course you have just completed?
■ Would you please put these six brands in order of your preference?
■ How many brothers and sisters do you have?
■ What size of pack did you last purchase – 0.5 kg, 1.0 kg or 1.5 kg?
■ Where did you go on holiday last year?

9   Why are Likert scales so popular?

CASE STUDY THE RISE OF THE FREE DAILY NEWSPAPER

Bakker (2005) reports that the global growth in free daily newspapers since the turn of the century has been spectacular. Between 2000 and 2005 total circulation doubled from 8 million to 19 million and by May 2005 there were 81 titles in 29 countries. The most spectacular growth has been in Canada and the southern part of Europe. In Spain, free dailies account for 42 percent of total circulation. Europe has more than 50 free newspapers. All this has been happening when newspaper circulation has been steadily declining over the years, particularly among younger people. Free dailies are proving to be an easy way to reach young readers; today's paid newspapers do not appear to be delivering the kind of readers that advertisers most desire. Only in Japan and Germany has the idea of free daily newspapers been unsuccessful.

Questions and activities

1 Suggest what kinds of factors Spanish paid newspapers would need to research among their readers if they are to reverse the trend towards free dailies.

2 Explain how you would measure each of these factors and what kind of scale would be used.

FURTHER READING

Flynn, L. and Pearcy, D. (2001) "Four subtle sins in scale development: some suggestions for strengthening the current paradigm", *International Journal of Market Research*, 43 (4): 409–423.

Kent, R. (2001) *Data Construction and Data Analysis for Survey Research*. Houndmills, Hants: Palgrave.

Lee, N. and Hooley, G. (2005) "The evolution of 'classical mythology' within marketing measure development", *European Journal of Marketing*, 39 (3/4): 365–385.

Spector, P. (1992) *Summated Rating Scale Construction. An Introduction*. London: Sage.

6

Constructing quantitative data
Developing the instruments of data capture

LEARNING OBJECTIVES In this chapter you will learn about:

→ the process of designing questionnaires,

→ the different types of questionnaires,

→ the different types of questions that may be used,

→ the different features that go into questionnaire design and layout,

→ using computer software to help produce questionnaires,

→ the use of diaries and diary design,

→ capturing data using manual or electronic recording devices.

Some instruments of data capture use electronic devices.

© FERRUCCIO/ALAMY

INTRODUCTION

I n Chapter 5 I explained that quantitative data need to have a structure of cases, variables and values imposed upon them, and that to obtain the variables it is necessary to operationalize them by deciding on the processes of measurement that are to be used. Once this has been decided, the data need themselves to be captured through the creation of systematic records. This chapter focuses on the ways in which such records can be created by using a range of different data capture instruments. The focus is on the instruments themselves, not on the manner and context of their use – that is the focus of Chapter 7. Most quantitative data in marketing will be captured using some form of questionnaire, although diaries and mechanical or electronic recording devices may also be used.

INTERNET ACTIVITY

Using your browser, go to **www.thomsonlearning.co.uk/kent** and select the Chapter 6 Internet Activity which will provide a link to the National Statistics website. Follow the pathway *About National Statistics/About data/classifications/Other standards/Harmonized concepts and questions/Secondary set of harmonized concepts and questions/income for analysis and income as a variable*. You will see from the resulting document that measuring household income is a very complex matter. Have a look at some of the other standardized questions under *Primary set of harmonized concepts and questions*.

Questionnaire design

Asking people questions and systematically noting their responses has been a method of conducting social research since the 1790s (see Kent 1981 for a historical account of social research in Britain). **Questionnaires** in marketing, certainly in the textbook literature, tend to be associated exclusively with survey research, but in practice they may be used in a number of different data collection contexts, as we shall see in the next chapter. Some market researchers, furthermore, refer rather loosely to any documents used for the purpose of data collection as "questionnaires", although we will be distinguishing questionnaires from diaries, manual recording sheets and interview guides, which are also used "in the field".

A questionnaire may be defined as any document that is used as an instrument with which to capture data generated by asking people questions and which, furthermore:

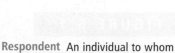

Questionnaire Any document that is used as an instrument with which to capture data generated by asking people questions.

- lists all the questions a researcher wishes to address to each **respondent**,
- provides space or some mechanism for recording the responses,
- puts questions in a logical sequence,
- draws accurate information from respondents,

Respondent An individual to whom questions have been successfully addressed or who has completed specified information-giving tasks.

■ standardizes the format of the questions,

■ facilitates data processing.

Questionnaires, in short, systematize the data collection process so that the data obtained are consistent and can be analyzed in a coherent manner. Designing questionnaires, however, is always difficult. There are no scientific principles that can ensure an "optimal" questionnaire. It is a skill that cannot be learned from books, but has to be acquired and honed through experience (although reading this chapter should make these experiences more productive). The first draft of a questionnaire is invariably a far cry from what is needed; usually, several redrafts are needed. Although different researchers will have their own ways of approaching questionnaire design, it is probably helpful to think of the design of questionnaires as going through several stages, as depicted in Figure 6.1.

Specify the information needed

In most client-based research, the information required will already have been discussed and spelled out in the research brief – it is part of the research design process. The researcher will need to review this very carefully before proceeding to the next stage. Furthermore, the researcher may well need to bear in mind that the particular demographics that will be useful for data analysis purposes may not have been specified, and these will need to be included. The researcher would also be wise to review the stated research objectives to ensure that the information to be obtained will be adequate to address them.

The researcher will also need to be clear what quality of data is necessary and when the data are needed by. Considerations of quality include accuracy, detail and comprehensiveness as well as sample quality where a sample is to be taken. Thus random, probability samples will produce higher-quality data than non-probability samples like quota samples (sampling is explained in Chapter 8). Bigger samples will be more reliable than smaller ones (but by a declining amount). At the same time, getting high-quality data will be more costly, so a degree of trade-off may be required. When data are required will, of course, be governed largely by when the client needs to take the decisions that will be based on the research results. The time available to the researcher may well, in turn, influence the remaining stages of the questionnaire design process, particularly the method of questionnaire administration.

For the academic researcher, what data are needed may be less clear-cut. There may be a detailed research proposal to which the questionnaire designer can refer, but this may or may not spell out the data requirements. The quality of the data will be evaluated more by the manner in which they are collected than by the extent to which the results help managers to make good decisions. The questionnaire designer will need to bear this in mind. For academic research the

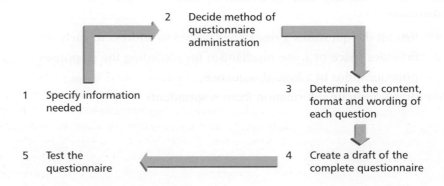

FIGURE 6.1

Steps in questionnaire design

1 Specify information needed

2 Decide method of questionnaire administration

3 Determine the content, format and wording of each question

4 Create a draft of the complete questionnaire

5 Test the questionnaire

questionnaire designer will normally be the researcher, whereas for client-based research it may be handed to a team of design specialists.

Decide on the method of questionnaire administration

Questionnaires may be administered face-to-face or over the telephone by an interviewer, or they may be postal or electronic questionnaires. In the first two situations, the questionnaire will be completed by the interviewer on the respondents' behalf, whereas in the last two situations, they will be self-completed by the respondent. These circumstances, which are explained in detail in Chapter 7, will have a considerable impact on questionnaire design. In personal interviews, for example, respondents are not usually shown the questionnaire, so where response categories are fixed (see fixed choice questions, later in this chapter) the respondents need to be told or shown what are the categories from which they are to choose. Furthermore, because the interviewer is present to guide, prompt and encourage, questions can be more complex and varied. With telephone interviews respondents cannot be shown anything; furthermore, the lack of face-to-face contact means that sustaining a lengthy telephone call can be very difficult. This limits the number of questions and ideally the questions will be fairly short and simple. For self-completed questionnaires, detailed instructions for filling in questions must be provided. Since the respondents can see all the questions, they do not, however, need to be told or shown response categories.

Determine the content, format and wording of each question

This stage can be really tricky. It means thinking about whether the measurements are to be direct, indirect, derived or treated as multidimensional. It means thinking about the wording, the response formats and layout of each question. Later in this chapter you will find lots of examples of different formats and layouts.

You will also need to think about how the data will be processed. If you are using a survey analysis package like SPSS, you will need to be clear which variables you intend or wish to be metric and which ones may be categorical. If the technique of analysis that you intend to use presupposes metric data (e.g. factor analysis) then you will need to design your questionnaire in ways that will generate such data. That means, for example, asking people for their actual ages and not in broad groups. It means that, if you are using derived measurement, you need to design your categories so that as far as possible they can be assumed to have equal intervals between the categories. If you wish to use questionnaire design packages like Snap or SPSS Data Entry (these are explained later in this chapter), then you need to be aware of the design possibilities and limitations of the software.

Create a draft of the complete questionnaire

This means deciding on the sequencing of the questions and making sure that the respondent (or the interviewer) knows what is the next relevant question to answer. This is called **routing**, a topic that is considered in some detail with examples later in this chapter. Generally, it is best to begin a questionnaire with a few easy-to-answer questions that relate clearly to the topic that the respondent has been led to believe the research is about. Once the draft is complete, the client will normally be given the opportunity to comment and agree that all the important issues have been covered. Clients may not appreciate all the technical details

Routing Guiding whoever is completing a questionnaire to answer questions that are appropriate when these depend on responses to earlier questions.

of questionnaire design, but they will be concerned that the objectives of the research are being addressed.

Test the questionnaire

When the draft is complete, and approved by the client, it needs to be tested on a "pilot" group of respondents similar to those who will be used in the main study. The questionnaire is likely to go through further drafts before reaching its final form. There will inevitably be questions that:

- do not mean what the researcher intended,
- have been missed out completely,
- people do not understand or find too difficult,
- everybody gives the same answer to, that is, do not discriminate,
- give response categories that do not allow some respondents to answer in ways that are relevant to them,
- do not provide sets of categories that are exhaustive, mutually exclusive, and refer to a single dimension (key requirements for nominal scales),
- have routings that leave the respondent "stranded" in the middle of the questionnaire or lead them into inappropriate sections of the questionnaire.

The piloting of questionnaires is frequently shortchanged by market researchers and by students and academics undertaking research in marketing. It is, however, critical for successful research. Once the questionnaire has been taken forward into the main data collection phase it is too late to make any changes. There are three main kinds of pilot study:

- qualitative research among the target population to check language and the range of likely opinions,
- pretesting the questionnaire to see how it works,
- a small-scale pilot survey to obtain approximate results.

Pretesting is essential for a successful survey – it is often surprising how many errors of design are uncovered at this stage, particularly if it has not been preceded by qualitative research or based on question-naires that have already been tried. Small-scale pilot surveys are often regarded as a luxury except for large projects.

Questionnaires should be tried out before they are used in the main study.

© SHARON DOMINICK

KEY POINTS

Questionnaire design is a complex process that involves a number of stages that include:

1 specifying the data required,
2 deciding on the method of questionnaire administration,
3 determining the format, content and wording of each question,
4 drafting the complete questionnaire,
5 questionnaire testing.

Stage 2 is explained at length in Chapter 7. The following sections explain stages 3 and 4 in more detail.

Question formats

Two main formats may be distinguished: **fixed choice** and **open-ended** questions. Fixed-choice questions give respondents a list of possible answers from which to choose. Some of these questions allow the respondent to pick only a **single response** from a list. The simplest result in a binary scale, for example, a yes/no answer to a question like "Do you have access to a microwave in this household?" However, many questions of this kind also require "don't know", "no response" or "cannot recall" categories, so they result in a nominal scale. Some questions ask respondents to pick a category that applies to them where the categories themselves are in some kind of order, as illustrated in Figure 6.2. The result is, of course, an ordinal scale. The summated rating scales and semantic differential scales that were considered in Chapter 5 have ordered single-response categories of this kind. Notice also that a number is written against each response category. This is called **precoding**. Each response is given a unique number that can then be entered into a survey analysis package like SPSS. Each question will have its own set of numbers, each normally beginning with 1. If the coding is not done at this stage, it will need to be done after the questionnaires are in. This will mean either spending a lot of time writing in the numbers or using a template for checking appropriate numbers as data are entered.

For metric variables, the scale values will need to be grouped as in Figure 6.3 if the researcher wishes to create a fixed-choice question. The alternative is to get the respondent to write in the appropriate value, like the actual age in years. Which of these is advisable depends on how the researcher wishes to use the data. If the researcher wishes to use the data to be able to calculate a product moment correlation coefficient (Pearson's r – to be explained in Chapter 12) with another metric variable, for example income, then he or she will need the actual age for each respondent. Such variables can always be grouped later if the researcher wants to crosstabulate them with categorical variables. The downside of asking for actual age (or for income for that matter) is that people may be reluctant to reveal this information, so broad categories may be better provided the researcher is not likely to need the full metric scale.

Fixed choice question A question that gives respondents a list of possible answers from which to choose.

Open-ended question A question that allows respondents to reply in their own words.

Single-response question A fixed-response question that allows respondents to select only one of the response categories.

Precoding Assigning a numerical code to each response category at the questionnaire design stage.

How important is it to you that the leisure centre has up-to-date equipment?

Very important	1
Fairly important	2
Not important	3

FIGURE 6.2

A single-answer question (ordinal scale)

In which of the following age groups are you?

<20	1
20–39	2
40–59	3
60+	4

FIGURE 6.3

A grouped metric scale

Multiple-response question A fixed-choice question that allows a respondent to pick more than one response category.

Some questions, however, allow respondents to pick more than one category as a response, as illustrated in Figure 6.4. In such **multiple-response** questions the total number of responses will usually be greater than the total number of respondents, since many respondents will have ticked more than one category. This means that it is possible either to report the proportion of respondents who tick a particular response category, or the proportion of the total number of responses accounted for by each category. Such questions may pose problems at the analysis stage because some computer programs (like spreadsheets and some statistical packages like Minitab) cannot handle multiple-response questions. Programs like SPSS, which is explained in Chapter 11 and which can handle such questions, require that each response category be treated as a separate binary variable – either it is ticked or not ticked.

One of the mistakes frequently made in questionnaire design is not to make it clear to the respondent whether the question allows for more than one response category. It is usually a good idea to add an appropriate instruction like, "Tick one box only" or "Tick as many responses as apply to you". Fixed-choice questions, whether single-response or multiple-response, are relatively easy to analyze since all that is required is a simple frequency count of each answer category. However, they do tend to force respondents into answering in ways that may not correspond with their true feelings, or respondents may be tempted to just pick responses without a great deal of (or indeed any!) thought.

Open-ended questions leave respondents free to formulate replies in their own words. The interviewer (or the respondent in a self-completed questionnaire) writes in the answer, usually word for word. Normally there will be one or more blank lines for this purpose. Open-ended questions tend to be used in the following situations:

- The researcher is unsure about what the responses might be, for example, "Why did you decide to select Brand X?"
- The possible responses are too many to list, for example, "How old are you?" or, "What is the name of the shop where you last purchased toothpaste?"
- The researcher wants to introduce a topic by getting the respondents to formulate their thoughts in their own words, or to focus the respondent's attention on the subject.

FIGURE 6.4

A multiple-response question

In which of the following countries have you been on holiday in the past five years? (Please tick as many as apply to you)

UK		1
France		2
Spain		3
Greece		4
Turkey		5
Italy		6
Other		7

■ The researcher wants to avoid prejudging responses with set-choice answers.

■ The researcher wants to "mop up" any views that may not have been elicited from fixed-choice questions.

■ The researcher wants to be able to enliven the final report with quotes from respondents.

Some open-ended questions ask for factual information like: "Which brand of toothpaste did you last purchase?" or "How many employees are there in your company?" The responses to such questions will probably be categorized and coded or put into groups and coded at a later stage by the researcher.

Some questions may be a combination of fixed and open elements, for example giving respondents a list of responses including "Other (please specify)" with a space or line to treat as open-ended. Some questions may be grouped together into tables, grids or checklists where the response categories are the same for each question, as for summated rating scales that were illustrated in the last chapter in Figures 5.4 and 5.5.

Most questionnaires will contain some open-ended questions, although relatively few will consist entirely of such questions. The particular combination of open-ended and fixed-choice questions in a questionnaire is often referred to as its degree of "structuring". Highly structured questionnaires consist largely of fixed-choice questions; unstructured questionnaires are mostly composed of open-ended questions, while semi-structured questionnaires contain more of a balance between the two. Except for those questions eliciting a factual response, open-ended questions can often be difficult and time-consuming to analyze. They produce qualitative data that need to be interpreted, evaluated, or content-analyzed (Chapter 10 will review the analysis of qualitative data). In consequence, the number of open-ended questions is normally kept to a minimum. Even factual open-ended questions still require that the responses be classified and numbered later on back in the office (a process called "post-coding") so that the frequency of types of response can be counted.

> ### KEY POINTS
>
> Questions may be fixed-choice or open-ended. Fixed-choice questions may be single- or multiple-response while open-ended questions may seek qualitative or factual information. Questionnaires are generally some mixture of these different types.

Question content

Questions may be designed to measure demographic, behavioral or cognitive variables. These types of variables were explained in Chapter 5, pp. 120–121. The most commonly used demographic variables for consumer surveys relate to:

■ gender,

■ age (either age in years at last birthday or in class intervals),

■ socioeconomic classification or social grade,

■ marital status (single, married, widowed, divorced, separated),

■ occupational status (employed full-time, employed part-time, unemployed),

- income (usually in broad bands),
- household size and composition,
- household status (head of household, housewife, other adult),
- level of education age,
- type of accommodation (owner occupied, rented privately, local authority housing),
- area of residence (these may, for example, be television regions or local authority areas).

Some of these demographics can be difficult to measure, particularly social grade. Box 6.1 shows some of the differing approaches. Measuring levels of income can also be quite complex. Try the Internet Activity at the beginning of this chapter if you have not already done do.

EUROPEAN MARKETING RESEARCH BOX 6.1
Social classification systems across Europe

In most parts of the world, socioeconomic classification schemes have been developed so that populations can be segmented into categories that define the status of the individuals within them. Most systems are hierarchical, giving ordinal categories of status. They are usually based on asking a variety of questions, for example about occupation, the highest level of education or income. In Columbia, socioeconomic status is based purely on the types of residence or area where a respondent lives; in Mexico, the number of showers is a strong influence on status (Wicken, van Staveren and Dinning 2005).

In the UK, social grading is based mainly on a series of questions about the occupation of the chief income earner in the household. The system was initially developed for the UK National Readership Survey (which is explained in detail in Chapter 16). There are six grades A–E with grade C split into C1 and C2, as shown in Table 6.1. Research practitioners in the UK use a publication called *Occupation Groupings: A Job Dictionary* published by the Market Research Society (5th edition, 2003) to determine the social grade (A–E) of respondents to a survey. It covers most job titles current at the time of print and is based on the Census data.

TABLE 6.1	National Readership Survey social class groupings	
Social	**Social status**	**Head of household's occupation**
A	Upper middle class	Higher managerial, administrative or professional
B	Middle class	Intermediate managerial, administrative or professional
C1	Lower middle class	Supervisory or clerical, and junior administrative or professional
C2	Skilled working class	Skilled manual workers
D	Working class	Semi and unskilled workers
E	Those at lowest level of subsistence	State pensioners or widows (no other earner), casual or lowest-grade workers

The UK government's Office of National Statistics always had its own system for socioeconomic classification. In the 2001 Census, the ONS introduced a new system that it called National Statistics Socio Economic Classification (NS-SEC). This, too, uses occupations, but the manner in which they are grouped is different. For an explanation of this system go to: **www.statistics.gov.uk/methods_quality/ns_sec/default.asp.**

Spain uses a classification system similar to that of the UK, but the system in France is less hierarchical and includes, for example, "Agriculteurs", "Petits patrons", "Affaires et cadres". In Germany it is based on annual family income groups. ESOMAR has suggested a European Social Grade Variable, which is constructed from the occupation of the main income earner in the household, the age at which the main income earner finished formal education and, in the case of "nonactive main income earners", the economic status of the household based on the ownership of ten selected consumer durables. The result is six ESOMAR Social Grades that are lettered the same as the UK National Readership categories.

Other more complex demographics may be used, for example life-stages or geodemographics. **Life-stages** are usually defined into a number of stages that families typically undergo. Thus respondents may be classified according to whether they are:

Life-stages A demographic in which individuals are classified by the stage of family life they are currently at, for example, "young parent".

- young, free and single,
- young parents,
- older parents,
- empty nesters,
- retired.

The theory is that individuals tend to have different aspirations, opinions and needs as they go through the various stages, exhibiting changing patterns of consumer behavior in the process. Different market research agencies will have their own particular classifications and may combine these stages with other demographic characteristics. The applicability of such stages has, however, been brought into question, for example by O'Donoghue and Steele (2004). Changes in European society mean that classes are now seldom linear, but a labyrinth with groups of consumers who fall between the gaps of the model. O'Donoghue and Steele (2004) suggest that instead of life-stages there are four groupings in terms of the way people respond to brands and these cut across life stages. "Self-seekers" want to feel young and the brands they choose are nonapologetic and noncompromising. "Adapters" have a pragmatic approach to change and tend to be very loyal to brands. "Wanderers" are always wanting to reinvent themselves. They seek comfort and security from brands. Finally, "worth-seekers" search for the greater meaning of life and are keen to know how a brand fits into the "bigger picture".

What are known as **geodemographics** are based on the demographic composition or structure of a small local area or neighborhood. All households and all individuals in a neighborhood are given the "average" characteristics for that area. These characteristics may be used as a basis for drawing samples, for market segmentation, targeting, the planning of store locations, or, more recently, for database marketing. CACI Limited, an international firm of management consultants, was the first agency to develop a classification of residential neighborhoods in a system it called ACORN (A Classification of Residential Neighborhoods). This is based on the principle that knowing where people live enables them to be defined as living in a certain type of area, and hence they are likely to have certain social characteristics, lifestyles, or buying habits that are of interest to marketers. CACI has developed 56 neighborhood types, for example "wealthy achievers" subdivided into "affluent mature professional, large houses", and "villages with

Geodemographics The grouping of consumers on the basis of characteristics of the neighborhoods in which they live.

wealthy commuters" and so on. All 1.9 million postcodes in the UK are assigned to one of these types. Try the Internet Activity at the beginning of Chapter 5. This will give you a lot more information on ACORN.

For many of the commonly asked demographic questions, many market research agencies have a standard format so that they do not need to be designed from new for each questionnaire. This not only makes questionnaire preparation much easier and the questions more effective because they are tried and tested, but also responses can be compared across surveys or even fused together. A committee of the Market Research Society attempted in 1971 and again in 1984 to generate a more universal set of standard questions (reported by Wolfe 1984). However, many agencies have continued to approach the design of classification sections in accordance with their own inclinations or "house styles".

The UK has a wide range of government surveys that provide sources of social and economic information. The Census of Population is the largest and best known, but there are many others, covering topics such as economic activity, income, expenditure, food, health, education, housing and transport. Most of these are continuous household surveys. Others, covering topics such as crime, dental health and house condition, are repeated regularly. The government also commissions single surveys from time to time on subjects of national importance, such as the prevalence of disability and mental ill health. These surveys were designed at different times, to meet different needs, and have been commissioned by a range of departments. Consequently, the surveys were developed mostly in isolation from each other.

This resulted in a lack of cohesion. Differences arose in concepts, definitions, design, fieldwork and processing practices, or "inputs", and also in the ways results are released, or "outputs". This lack of cohesion was a source of frustration for many users. A cross-governmental program of work is currently looking into standardizing both inputs and outputs, a process that it calls harmonization. If you did the Internet Activity at the beginning of this chapter then you will have some idea of the progress that has been made.

In terms of behavioral and cognitive variables there is little standardization of question content. Some market research agencies, however, have developed or adopted their own proprietary approaches to the analysis of lifestyles that relate to the activities, interests, attitudes and opinions of respondents. Activities might include hobbies, entertainment, club membership and sports. Interests may concern the home and family, the community, fashions, or the media, while opinions may be about themselves, social issues, politics, education and so on. Statistical analysis like factor analysis and cluster analysis (explained in Chapter 14) are then used to identify groups or categories of people who tend to have similar characteristics. The typologies generated, however, tend to be specific to particular classes of product. Attempts to develop more generalized classifications have not been widely accepted. Thus Baker and Fletcher (1989) generated six clusters using data from the British Market Research Bureau's Target Group Index, which includes nearly 200 lifestyle statements on a regular basis. The system, which the authors called "Outlook", defines the groups as:

- trendies – people "into" current fads, demographically upmarket, affluent and concentrated in the 25–44 age group,
- pleasure-seekers – people who want things now. They are against long-term planning and have a low sense of responsibility,
- the indifferent, who do not react in any particular way,
- working-class puritans who are "antifun", parochial and traditional,
- social spenders who like to go out and enjoy themselves, be lavish and sociable,
- moralists who are against everything that it enjoyable.

This system, the authors claim, maintains its validity across subsamples and over time, is a powerful discriminator and is independent of the social class components of attitude and behavior patterns. Ward (1987) argues, however, that such systems are single-dimensional and cannot compete with interlaced demographics for discrimination and predictive ability. Product- or market-specific studies are usually more helpful than generalized systems. Furthermore, attitude-based systems are difficult to apply in the field and are thus not easy to utilize for structural purposes, for example to apply quota controls. Finally, they provide too simple a view of humanity – people may change category depending on their mood or on the social context; they may be "trendy" about some things and "moralists" about others.

KEY POINTS

Questions may seek to capture data on demographic, behavioral or cognitive characteristics of individuals. Various attempts have been made to standardize or harmonize question content, but as yet there are no widely accepted standard questions. Whether or not organizations or other groups may be been to possess behavioral or cognitive characteristics is an open question. Strictly speaking, only individuals behave and think, but organizations are sometimes treated as if they are organisms with ability to act and to reflect.

Question wording

Designing an effective series of questions is never easy. Getting the wording right can be even trickier because changing just one word in a question can make a difference to how participants respond to a question. Some words have a great potential to create problems. Respondents may, for example, be in general agreement with an idea or a proposition, but hesitate to accept the extreme of "all", "always", "every", or "never". The difference between asking "Do you always observe speed limits when driving?" and "Do you nearly always observe speed limits when driving?" will result in very different responses. Words like "any" or "anybody" can mean one only or some. "Country" can mean a nation or a rural area.

Three conditions need to be satisfied to maximize the possibility of obtaining valid responses:

- respondents must *understand* the questions (and understand them in the same way as other respondents),
- respondents must be *able* to provide the answers,
- respondents must be *willing* to provide the information.

The first of these is largely a function of question wording, the second a function of routing, and the third has more to do with sequencing and overall length. For respondents to understand a question, it must be clear, specific, brief, unambiguous and cover a single issue. In general, this means avoiding:

- long words that people may not be familiar with,
- leading questions,
- complex sentences,
- ambiguous questions,
- vague questions.

Using words like "unilateral", "devolution", or "proximity", or jargon like "marital status" or "retail outlets" will cause misunderstanding of questions. Never present the respondent with just one of the answer categories – that amounts to a leading question, for example "Do you agree that dogs should be banned from public parks?" Always present both or all the alternative responses equally, so instead of "Do you like Brand X?", ask "Do you like or dislike Brand X?" or "Do you agree or disagree that . . .?"

Complex sentences often arise because the researcher wishes to qualify statements or define terms. Where such qualifications or definitions *are* necessary, then it is better that they be part of a separate sentence, for example, "Do you have full central heating in this house? By 'full' I mean outlets in living rooms and most bedrooms." Beware of the double question like "Do you know or are you known personally by the shop assistants?"

Avoiding ambiguity is notoriously difficult. A question like "How many children are there in your family?" may refer to brothers and sisters for somebody who is unmarried, and to offspring for those married with their own children. "Where did you buy this packet of soap?" may mean "In what shop?" or "In what geographical location?" Words like "frequent", "good" or "recently" may be interpreted in various ways.

Vagueness and ambiguity tend to go together, but, as a general rule, be as specific as possible, for example by defining timings and frequencies of purchases. Thus, "Have you personally bought shampoo in the last seven days?" is better than "Have you personally bought shampoo recently?"

Hypothetical questions, for example "What would you do if . . .", or questions that relate to future behavior, need to be avoided as far as possible. However, they sometimes are required to establish purchase intentions, for example "Would you buy this product for your personal use?" or "How likely are you to purchase this product, very likely, fairly likely or unlikely?"

Eliciting motivations or reasons for doing or not doing things can be particularly difficult. This may be approached by asking the respondents what they do and then asking "Why do you do that?" It is tempting for the researcher to try to list most of the possible responses in advance and then get the interviewer to tick the appropriate categories. This can only be done, however, if there has been considerable pretesting or exploratory research in advance. If this has not been done, then it is probably better to leave the question open-ended and to classify answers at the analysis stage.

KEY POINTS

Respondents are often very sensitive to changes in the wording of questions, so the choice of words is very important. At the same time, avoiding ambiguity and vagueness is not always easy.

Screening

In many surveys it is necessary to determine the eligibility of individuals to take part. Thus if a survey is of motorists, it may be necessary to ask as a first question: "Do you have a current driving licence for a car?" perhaps followed up by: "Is there a car in your household that is available for you to drive?" or even: "Have you driven a car in the past 6 months?" A "No" answer to any of these questions may result in an interviewer closing the interview or the respondent being directed to another part of the questionnaire to obtain a few demographic details. Thus in a study of brand purchasers' reactions to the brand, those who have never purchased the brand or not purchased it within a specified period of time may be asked about their age, education, work status and so on to be able to make some comparisons between purchasers and nonpurchasers of the brand.

Routing

For respondents to be able to provide information it is essential that they be asked only those questions that they are likely to be able to answer with some accuracy. This may mean establishing that the respondent has some experience of the situation or products that they are to be asked about, and not asking them to perform unreasonable feats of memory about past events. This is achieved through the use of "filter" questions that sort respondents into categories so that follow-up questions can be asked only where appropriate. If the respondent does not fit in with that category (e.g. does not smoke), then the next few questions that relate to people who do, need to be skipped. This is routing the respondent through the questionnaire. Sometimes there is a special "Skip to" column that indicates the next relevant question for response categories for which the following question is *not* the relevant one. Some responses may have "Go to Q . . ." written against them. Examples of routing can be seen in Figure 6.5.

Sequencing

As a general rule the questionnaire should begin with simple questions that relate clearly to the topic the respondent has been led to believe the survey is about. Topics need to flow logically, rather than jump about, although this may be difficult in omnibus surveys (which are explained in Chapter 7) where respondents can be asked about anything from dog food to airline travel in the same questionnaire. If this happens, it is useful to indicate that a change of topic is taking place, for example "I would now like to turn to the topic of holidays" or "May I now ask you a few questions about motoring?" It is usually better to put general questions before more specific ones. This may mean, for example, introducing the topic of leisure activities, then clothing used, then type of footwear, and finally use of a particular brand of trackshoe. This procedure is often referred to as "funneling".

    Demographic questions are usually asked at the end of any questionnaire as "rounding-off" questions – they may be a little too personal to begin with. However, any demographics that are used for quota controls need to be asked at the outset. An example of a demographic section of a questionnaire is illustrated in Figure 6.6. Notice that the information required in the right-hand column is for identification rather than classification purposes, that is, it identifies one particular interview. It will be completed by the interviewer once the interview is finished. The information is required in case any check-back is needed, either to ensure that the interview took place, or if questions are missed out or completed incorrectly. The respondent may need to be reassured that his or her name and address are required only in case queries arise concerning any of the answers.

Funneling The sequencing of questions in such a way that it begins with general questions followed by progressively specific questions. The aim is to prevent specific questions biasing general questions.

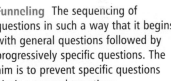

KEY POINTS

Screening, routing and sequencing are all about getting the right people to answer the right questions.

A questionnaire with routing instructions

SHOPPING AND TRAVEL

Would you help us by spending a few minutes answering the questions below.
Please put a tick in the box that corresponds to your answer

Q1 About how often do you buy groceries for regular major shopping?

Every day	1
4–5 days a week	2
2–3 days a week	3
Once a week	4
Less often	5
Never	6 Go To Q5

Q2 Are there any particular days you buy most of your major regular shopping?

Yes	1
No	2 Go To Q4

Q3 Which days are they?
PLEASE SELECT NO MORE THAN TWO DAYS

Monday	1
Tuesday	2
Wednesday	3
Thursday	4
Friday	5
Saturday	6
Sunday	7

Q4 When you make your regular major grocery purchases, what form of transport do you usually use?

Car	1
Bus	2
Train	3
Bicycle	4
Motorcycle	5
Walk	6

Q5 During a normal week, how many hours would you spend travelling using each form of transport, for whatever purpose, not just travelling.
PLEASE TICK THE APPROPRIATE BOX IN EACH COLUMN

	Car	Bus	Train	Bicycle	Walk
None	1	1	1	1	1
<1 hour	2	2	2	2	2
1–2 hours	3	3	3	3	3
3–4 hours	4	4	4	4	4
5–8 hours	5	5	5	5	5
8 hours or more	6	6	6	6	6

Questionnaire length

When drafting questionnaires there is always a tendency to put in all questions that might seem relevant or just interesting. This often happens when the objectives of the research have not been clearly defined and questions are added "just in case". The result can be very long questionnaires that may have an impact on the respondent's willingness to finish. Interviews carried out in the street may

FIGURE 6.6

A demographic page

Q1	Sex of respondent	Male ☐ 1		Q7	SAMPLING POINT NUMBER ☐☐☐☐☐☐☐☐☐☐
		Female ☐ 2			

Q2 In which of these age categories are you?
SHOW CARD 1

- 15–24 ☐ 1
- 25–34 ☐ 2
- 35–44 ☐ 3
- 45–54 ☐ 4
- 55–64 ☐ 5
- 65+ ☐ 6

Q3 How many adults (aged 16 or more) live here including yourself?

WRITE IN NUMBER _____

Q4 How many children aged 15 or less live here?

WRITE IN NUMBER _____

Q5 What is the occupation of the head of household or chief wage earner?

JOB TITLE _____

WHAT HE/SHE DOES _____

_____

TYPE OF BUSINESS _____

_____

Q6 INDICATE SOCIAL CLASS

- A ☐ 1
- B ☐ 2
- C1 ☐ 3
- C2 ☐ 4
- D ☐ 5
- E ☐ 6

Q7 SAMPLING POINT NUMBER ☐☐☐☐☐☐☐☐☐☐

Q8 INFORMANT'S NAME AND ADDRESS. PLEASE USE BLOCK CAPITALS

NAME _____

ADDRESS _____

_____

_____

POSTCODE _____

Q9 DATE OF INTERVIEW _____

Q10 LENGTH OF INTERVIEW

- Up to 15 minutes ☐ 1
- 15–29 ☐ 2
- 30–45 ☐ 3
- Over 45 minutes ☐ 4

I certify that this interview has been personally carried out by me with the respondent at his/her address. He/she is not a friend or relative

SIGNATURE _____

DATE _____

NAME _____

need to be very short, perhaps taking no more than ten minutes or so. To keep the questionnaire within reasonable limits:

- make sure every question is actually needed to fulfil the objectives of the research,
- restrict the number of demographic questions to what is needed for sample validation and analysis. A page of classification questions can take ten minutes to fill in, perhaps more when detailed occupational data are required,
- use checklists or grids wherever possible to condense the material.

It is difficult to be prescriptive about the optimum or maximum lengths of questionnaires. Certainly questionnaires intended for in-home use in face-to-face interviews can usually be longer than those intended for use in telephone surveys or in the street, but anything that takes over an hour to complete could be considered as "overly long". Anything that takes over 30 minutes for a telephone interview or a street survey could also be considered in the same manner. For self-completed questionnaires there may well be differences in opinion about how long they can be. A questionnaire for self-completion used by the British Market Research Bureau for its Target Group Index runs to over 100 pages. The Target Group Index in explained in detail in Chapter 16.

Self-completed and interviewer-completed questionnaires

Questionnaires may either be completed by the respondent without an interviewer being present, or they may be filled in by an interviewer who asks the questions and completes the questionnaire on behalf of the respondent. **Self-completed questionnaires** may be sent and returned through the post, they may be personally delivered, to be returned by post or to be personally collected at a later date, or they may be delivered online. The main implications for questionnaire design for self-completed questionnaires arise from the fact that:

Self-completed questionnaires
Questionnaires that are completed by the respondent without an interviewer present.

- there is no interviewer,
- the respondent can see all the response categories before putting in a response,
- the respondent can read through the questionnaire before answering.

The absence of an interviewer means that it must be clear to the respondent how replies are to be indicated. This will usually mean ticking boxes, putting circles around appropriate code numbers, or deleting responses as appropriate (but do not mix all three in a questionnaire – stick to one format). Respondents will be able to see all the suggested response categories without having to show them on a separate card or reading them out; however, the use of the "funneling" technique may be inappropriate since the respondent may spot the "correct" answer by looking at later questions.

Self-completion surveys are one of the most cost-effective ways of collecting data, mainly because no interviewers are involved. They can be administered in a variety of ways and even included as part of a personal interview to collect data on sensitive issues. They are an effective way of reaching people who would not otherwise take part in an interview survey. They are also free of interviewer bias or error. Where respondents need time to give considered responses or to consult others, then self-completion techniques are an obvious choice.

Self-completion techniques, of course, do have their disadvantages. Response rates tend to be lower, and in some cases much lower, than for interview surveys. Response rates may be as low as 15 percent – 30 percent would be doing well. By contrast, response rates of 70 percent would be common for interview surveys. Compared with an interview survey there is less control over the data capture process in a self-completed questionnaire, for example:

- respondents can consult with others before answering the questions – this may not be what the researcher wants,
- respondents may not answer all the questions they are supposed to or in the way required,
- there may be little detail on open-ended questions,
- there is no opportunity to probe or seek clarification,
- there is no opportunity to observe, for example, the home of respondents or the body language or tone of voice.

Without the presence and encouragement of an interviewer, self-completed questionnaires that take more than about 10–15 minutes may not get finished. If a long and/or complex questionnaire is required, then face-to-face techniques should be used.

Many of the characteristics special to **interviewer-completed questionnaires**, which may be administered face-to-face or over the telephone, arise from the fact that respondents cannot see the questionnaire. While, on the one hand, this makes it possible to use the funneling technique because the respondents cannot see questions yet to come, on the other, it means that if the researcher is looking for choices from preset categories then, because the respondent cannot see the responses, it is necessary to do one of three things:

Interviewer-completed questionnaires Questionnaires that are completed by the interviewer, who asks the questions and fills in the answers on the respondent's behalf.

- incorporate all the possible responses into the question, for example "Do you personally eat bananas less than once a week, between one and three times a week, or four times or more?",
- get the interviewers to read out the categories to the respondent,
- list the categories on a separate card that can be shown to the respondent.

The interviewer will need an instruction as to whether he or she is to read out the responses or show a card, as illustrated in Figure 6.7. Where a large number of cards are needed they should ideally be clipped or bound together in order of use to help the interviewer. Incorporating responses into the question is, clearly, possible only when there are no more than three or four categories. Open-ended questions may instruct the interviewer to "probe" (for example by asking "Why did you say that?", or "Is there anything else?")

Questionnaire layout

Space is at a premium in a questionnaire, but if it is too cramped it will be difficult to read and to write down answers. If space is wasted the questionnaire will look very long, it will be cumbersome to handle, and it will be expensive to print. It is helpful to remember that the questionnaire may need to be used in places where the lighting is not very good, so the print needs to be clear and probably at least 12-point in font size.

It is nearly always preferable for response categories to be listed vertically rather than across the page. This is easier for both the person completing the questionnaire and for the researcher who can glance down the answer code column for data entry purposes. This, in turn, often implies that the page as a whole is better in two-column format to avoid wasting a lot of space, for example Figure 6.6. Boxes for ticking may be placed to the left or to the right of the response categories – to the right is usually preferable. It is also a good idea if the boxes are numbered, since this facilitates data entry. It is also usually helpful to

Which of the phrases on this card best describe how you feel about this product?

SHOW CARD C

CARD C	
I certainly would try this product	1
I might try this product	2
I'm not sure that I will try it	3
I don't think I will try it	4
I certainly will not try it	5

FIGURE 6.7

A show card instruction

number all the questions. This is useful for routing purposes, for example "If yes, skip to Q12". Sometimes questions are grouped into topics or related issues, for example Q6a, Q6b Q6c, Q7a, Q7b and so on.

Instructions for completing the questionnaire need to be distinguishable from the questions themselves and from the precoded answers. The convention – by no means universally followed – is to use capitals underlined for instructions, capitals for the responses, and lower case for the questions themselves.

There will normally be an introduction to the questionnaire which is vital in winning the cooperation and interest of the respondent. For self-completed questionnaires there may be a separate covering letter, such as the one illustrated in Figure 6.8, or it may be an introduction printed at the top of the first page. For interviewer-completed questionnaires the interviewer makes the introduction, but he or she will need to be told what to say. It is probably best for it to be written out at the top of each questionnaire. The introduction does a number of things. It:

- explains what company or organization is undertaking the survey,
- describes briefly what the survey is about,
- checks that the respondent fits any criteria used for screening or for quota controls,
- provides assurances that the survey is for market research only and that replies will be confidential,
- asks the respondent for help by answering a few questions,
- indicates how long it is likely to take.

KEY POINTS

If questionnaires need to be long, or if a lot of material needs to be shown to the respondent, then it is best if they are interviewer-completed, preferably face-to-face. The design and layout of interviewer-completed questionnaires might be quite different from self-completed ones. Having said that, in some surveys these elements may be mixed. Thus there may be self-completed components (like a set of Likert items) that an interviewer hands over during the course of an interview. Some questionnaires, particularly when questionnaires may be left by interviewers for self-completion and collection later, may be designed so that they can be suitable for both modes of completion.

Good questionnaire design is vital if good-quality data are to be constructed. The questionnaire plays a key role in helping the researcher to capture data accurately and effectively. It has to be a workable, useable-friendly tool for the interviewer, for the respondent and for the data analyst. Put the other way round, a poorly designed questionnaire can result in many different kinds of error. These errors are explained in more detail in Chapter 7. Apart from causing error, a poorly designed questionnaire can lead to an unpleasant experience for the respondent and a poor perception of research and the market research industry. The questionnaire is the "front line" of the research industry – it is what the general public sees and responds to. With declining response rates, the onus is more than ever on the researcher to design questionnaires that are easy to understand, easy to administer and interesting to the respondent.

At the same time, well-trained interviewers can be equally important. If good interviewers are not available, then it may be possible to use computer packages in which respondents read questions on a laptop screen, enter answers and are guided through the questionnaire. The next section explains the use of computer packages in more detail.

FIGURE 6.8

A covering letter

ABC Research
11 Eastgate
London

Dear Mr Brown

I am writing to a carefully selected sample of people throughout the UK.
Your name has been selected as someone who could answer a few
questions on gardening, and I would greatly appreciate your help.
It will only take a few minutes of your time.

The survey is designed to provide information on the way in which
gardeners use the products and services that are available from garden
centres. The results will be used to improve the range of products that
such centres can offer to people like yourself.

Your reply is very important to us and it will be treated as totally
confidential. It will be analyzed along with other responses and none of
your views will be tied to your name. Please take my personal assurance
that you will not be pestered by any salesmen as a result of helping me.

All you need to do is read through the questions and put a tick in the box
which corresponds to your answer. Please remember that there are no
"correct" answers – it is your opinion that I am interested in.

When you have finished, please send the questionnaire back to me in the
stamped, addressed envelope that I have provided. It would be very helpful
if you could do this by the end of the month.

To show my appreciation of your efforts I will send you a mystery gift when
I have received your reply.

I look forward to hearing from you

Yours sincerely

James Auld
Marketing Manager
ABC Research

Using computer software

Word-processing packages are commonly used for producing questionnaires, but
software like Microsoft Word was not really designed for this purpose. Such software
has a number of limitations:

■ getting all the tick boxes in all the right places is tedious,

■ moving questions and response categories around the page is not
possible,

■ any alternations to the questionnaire may upset tab stops, resulting in
line breaks where they are not wanted,

■ putting in or taking out questions will mean all the questions have to be
renumbered,

■ all the variables' names and all the response categories will need to be retyped into whatever survey analysis package is being used.

Desktop publishing packages can provide some extra graphical functionality – in particular text can be moved around the page – but there is a range of software designed specifically for producing questionnaires to use either in hard copy or as online surveys. Snap Survey Software, developed and published by Mercator, a privately owned company, has been around for more than 20 years. It provides fully integrated software for questionnaire design, printing, data collection and analysis. It consists of a core product with specialist add-ons for web and e-mail surveys, for portable fieldwork data collection, for telephone interviewing and for scanning in data electronically from paper questionnaires. The core module provides questionnaire templates, a question library and a survey constructor wizard. There are four different data entry modes and a range of statistical procedures for analyzing the data and providing charts and graphs. For more information go to **www.snapsurveys.com** where you can download an evaluation copy of the software for the current version, Snap 8.

A comparable product is Keypoint, developed by Cambridge Software Publishing, which is part of Logotron Ltd, an educational software publisher. For more details visit **www.camsp.com**, where you can also download a demonstration version of Keypoint 4. A more sophisticated questionnaire design package is offered by SPSS called SPSS Data Entry. It is more sophisticated than either Snap or Keypoint, but is less user-friendly. It has the main advantage, however, that, being an SPSS product, it creates an SPSS file automatically as data are entered, so is immediately ready for analysis by SPSS. For more details visit **http://www.spss.com/Data_Entry/**, where you can download a demo version of SPSS Data Entry.

There are limitations with all these packages, however, in the ability to customize forms and data collection in the way the researcher wants. They all include the possibility of producing questions as grids, which is fine for Likert and other types of summated rating scale, but producing semantic differentials may be either impossible or clumsy.

KEY POINTS

Software can help considerably with the design and layout of questionnaires. Packages like Snap and Keypoint can handle question numbering, sequencing and routing and can serve as a basis for entering data. Usually this is by way of clicking with the mouse on the answer given in each questionnaire. A data worksheet is then created which is ready for data analysis. These packages can be used for interviewer-completed, self-completed or online questionnaires.

Diaries

Diary A contemporaneous record made by the consumer of their purchases or other forms of consumer behavior between specific dates or at specified periods during the day.

Though questionnaire design is a topic that is treated at some length in all texts on marketing research, diary design is rarely mentioned. It is possible to treat diaries as just another form of questionnaire, but they are sufficiently distinct to benefit from separate treatment. **Diaries** are distinguished by the fact that they are designed to record consumer behavior on or between specific dates, perhaps even at specified time periods during the day. Furthermore, they require the respondent to complete an entry every time that behavior occurs over the time period to which the diary refers – often a week, but maybe two weeks or longer.

Diaries thus record behavior that is normally repeated at fairly frequent intervals, and which it would be difficult for a respondent to recall all at the one time in a questionnaire. Normally, attitudes are not measured in a diary, since such an activity may well influence the consumer behavior being recorded. Thus if a respondent indicates certain negative views concerning a brand, then he or she may well be tempted to swap brands at the next purchase in order to be more "consistent".

Diaries are often used in continuous research either for panels or in regular interval surveys (see Chapter 7), but may also be employed in ad hoc survey research, experimental research of various kinds, and perhaps even to record observations made by the researcher. Normally, however, diaries will be self-completed; some may be placed personally by the interviewer, or sent by post, and may be collected personally or returned by post. Diaries may relate to individual consumers or to household activity. In the latter case, one person is usually made responsible for diary completion for the whole family.

There are three rather distinct kinds of diary:

- product diaries,
- media use diaries,
- contact diaries.

Product diaries record consumer purchasing and in some cases product use. They normally arrange entries on a product-by-product basis, usually covering a whole week's purchases. An example of a page from such a diary is illustrated in Figure 6.9. Such an arrangement makes it easier to obtain the specific details required for different brands, for example to determine the flavor of yoghurt, or the kind of toothpaste dispenser. A diary also acts as a "reminder" to the respondents, and this improves the completeness of reporting. Depending on the size of the product field, the level of detail required, and the frequency of purchasing, the diary format may be either structured, that is, all the answers are precoded, or semi-structured, where respondents write in the brand, brand variant, shop, price, type of offer and so on. Many are a mixture of the two. Precoded diaries are better from the data entry and data analysis point of view, but may require very long code lists, and may need to be changed frequently as new brands are added or existing ones withdrawn. Semi-structured diaries, on the other hand, require less space, but need to be supported by sophisticated data entry systems that can allocate the appropriate codes at the data entry stage. Some product diaries are more time-based, for example, asking people to record what they ate by "meal occasion" – breakfast, lunch, evening meal and snacks between meals.

Product diary A contemporaneous record made by consumers of their purchases between specific dates or at specified periods during the day.

FIGURE 6.9

A product diary

Coffee	Brand name	Type (please tick one)				(please tick) Decaffeinated		Weight or size on pack	No. of packs bought	Price paid per pack		Shop name	Offer on pack
		Instant		Ground									
		Powder	Freeze	Fine	Med	Yes	No			£	p		
Ground instant, freeze-dried													

Media use diary A contemporaneous record made by consumers of their use of the broadcast media, usually on a time segment basis.

Media use diaries record the use of broadcast media and tend to arrange entries by time segment on a daily basis. Radio listening diaries, for example, typically give 15-minute or 30-minute periods down the left-hand side of the page, and particular radio stations across the top, as illustrated in Figure 6.10. The respondent may be asked to tick every box against any station listened to for each time segment, or to draw vertical lines through all the time segments where listening took place.

Diaries are often used in continuous research rather for panels or in regular annual surveys (see Chapter 7), but may also be employed in ad hoc surveys; experimental research or diaries, fields, and perhaps even to record observations. As the examples usually has more questions will be helpful.

FIGURE 6.10

A media diary: radio listening

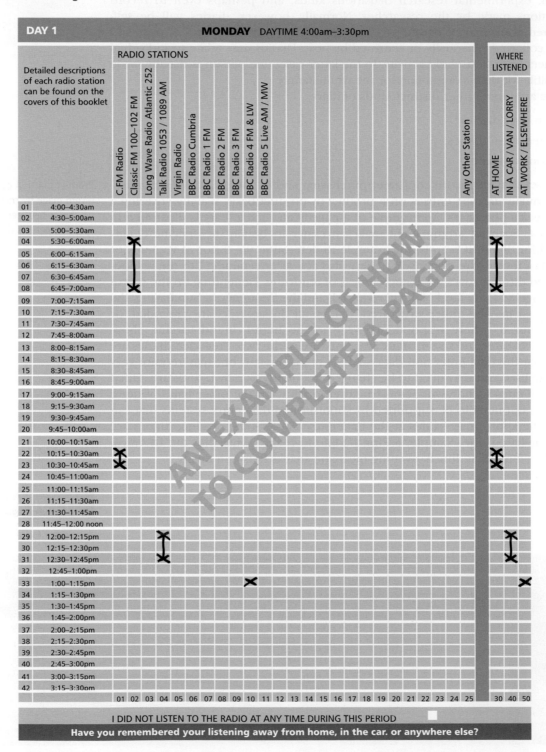

Contact diaries ask respondents to list, check or tick each contact made with another member of a communication network. Communication networks consist of individuals who are interconnected by patterned flows of information and who create and share information with one another in order to reach mutual understandings. Communication network analysis is a series of techniques for identifying the communication structures in a system and is based on the techniques of the much earlier idea of sociometry. The contacts made may be face-to-face, postal or telephone and the diary may well record contacts made on a daily basis, as in Figure 6.11. The results may be fed into a communication network analysis program that measures, for example, the degree to which individuals have networks that overlap, the number of links in the shortest path joining two individuals, or the extent to which participants have like patterns of links and nonlinks.

Contact diary A contemporaneous record made by consumers of their contacts with other people in order to establish social networks.

Diary design

A key problem with the design of all diaries is the need to keep them up to date. Thus for structured product diaries new brands or brand variants may need to be added and others deleted where a manufacturer has dropped them from their range. Even semi-structured product diaries need to take into account the introduction of new product categories. For media diaries, the stations that radio listeners or television watchers can receive need to be continually updated, while program diaries are notoriously difficult since last-minute changes may be made to the published programs. Furthermore, there may need to be several versions of such diaries to take account of the different ranges of program that may be received in different parts of the country.

In considering the overall layout and design of diaries it is necessary to bear in mind the potential sources of error in diary-keeping.

- The diary-keeper forgets to enter purchases, listening, viewing or contacts in the diary. This will often be because instead of making entries as they go along, many respondents will try to remember after a couple of days or even at the end of the week before sending the diary off.

- The record-keeper makes an entry, but makes a mistake on the details through faulty memory or erroneous recording.

- The diary is deliberately falsified either by omission of purchases, media use or contacts, or by the inclusion of imaginary purchases, uses or contacts.

FIGURE 6.11

A contact diary

MONDAY		Contacts made by you							Contacts received by you						
Name	Organization														

■ The diary-keeper is unaware of purchases or contacts made by other members of the household, or of their listening or viewing of broadcasts.

All of these sources of error may be affected by a number of factors, for example:

■ the type of product or program,

■ the frequency of the activity,

■ the position of the page in the diary,

■ the position and prominence of the entry on the page,

■ the complexity of the entry,

■ the overall length and workload involved,

■ the method of contact between researcher and respondent.

Thus grocery items are more likely to be remembered by whoever does the main household shopping than personal care products, which are more often purchased by other household members. The more frequent the activity, the more likely it is to be remembered. Items at the beginning of the diary and on the tops of pages are more likely to be remembered then those in the middle and at the end of the diary, and those lower down the page. Some users of diaries, for example for radio audience measurement, rotate the order of the radio stations listed in the diary for different samples of respondents. Deliberate falsification is likely to increase with the complexity of the entry and with the overall length and workload involved.

In designing the layout of a diary, those products that are most likely to be forgotten should be put at the beginning or at the tops of pages. The effects of small diary changes can be measured by introducing changes in only a subsample of the total and noting differences in response. From the results of experiments in the USA, Sudman and Ferber (1979: 74) report that adding or deleting a check box or changing the wording does not measurably affect the level of recording, but changing product headings, moving the position of a product listing in the diary, and putting in special reminders may alter, temporarily or more permanently, the level of product recording. In short, diaries are probably more sensitive than questionnaires to overall presentation and layout, but less sensitive to wording.

Though it has been reported (for example by Sudman and Ferber 1979: 77) that for consumer purchasing there is some evidence to suggest that survey recall data from questionnaires tend to overstate purchases compared with diaries and that the difference is greatest for well-known brands and for perishables, for media use it has been found that diaries produce more listening or watching than questionnaire recall methods (Menneer 1989).

A recent development in diaries is the use of electronic diaries. Box 6.2 explains how e-diaries can be used for radio audience measurement.

KEY POINTS

Diaries are an underutilized mechanism for capturing data, particularly where frequent and repeat behavior is concerned. They are less useful, however, for measuring attitudes.

Appel (2001) explains that in the Netherlands, radio audience measurement is normally carried out by means of paper diaries with preprinted radio stations. However, response rates have been declining over the years, particularly among young people, and by 1999 had fallen below 50 percent. Qualitative research showed that this group hardly ever needed to go to the post, so it was suggested that the diaries should be made available over the internet. In 2000 an e-diary was designed which could be completed directly in the browser program and which was comparable with the paper version. This eliminated the need to drop the diary into the mailbox and the need for respondents to post them back. It also meant that completion could be tracked continuously, e-mail reminders sent and processing the listening behavior is much quicker. However, the research agency Intomart found that the e-diaries were less flexible in the sense that the respondent was tied to a physical location with a computer and required basic browser experience. The result was not the success hoped for.

Recording devices

Questionnaires and diaries are mechanisms for capturing data that have been elicited by addressing listed questions to individuals. However, where a researcher observes products on a shelf, how consumers behave, some event taking place like the purchase of a product or the watching of a television program, or where a discussion without listed questions is being pursued, then some form of device, manual or electronic, needs to be employed to capture such data.

Manual recording devices are commonplace in business. Invoices, credit notes, stock lists, delivery notes, receipts, ledgers and accounts are often filled in by hand. The market researcher may, for example, use invoices to check how many customers, what they purchased, how frequently, what they paid and where they come from. Delivery notes may be used for retail panel operations as an input to making an estimate of sales once changes in stock levels have been checked.

When engaging in primary data collection, the researcher may use manual record-sheets of various kinds to record observations. Thus interviewers from a market research company conducting a shop audit may use a manual audit form for writing in quantities of branded products observed on the shelves, on the counter and in the stockroom, and for recording the deliveries made after inspecting delivery notes. Structured observation may entail the researcher as observer noting on a record-sheet the number of times a particular piece of behavior occurs, and the amount of time taken to do or perform it. The difference between a manual record-sheet and an unstructured questionnaire is that the latter depends on addressing questions to people and writing in their answers, while record-sheets are used mainly to record observations made personally by the researcher.

Electronic recording devices are becoming increasingly popular, particularly among the large market research organizations, who can afford the cost of the capital equipment involved. Electronic data capture may be put into four main groupings of technology:

- electronic point of sale data capture using scanning technology,
- electronic questionnaires and diaries,

- television set-meters and "people" meters,
- audio and video recording devices.

One innovation that is changing the focus of instruments of data capture away from paper questionnaires and paper diaries more than any other is the introduction of barcoding on products and the utilization of laser scanners at the point of sale (sometimes called "electronic point of sale" or EPOS technology) to capture the details of each purchase made. Barcodes give unique identification of products down to country of origin, manufacturer, brand, size, flavor and offer. In Europe, a 13-digit code is used. The first two digits identify the country of origin, the next five are allocated by the Article Numbering Association to identify the manufacturer, the next five are allocated by the manufacturer to identify products and the last is a check digit allocated by a computer. When a laser is run over the barcode the price and other details are looked up from a central file held on a computer in the store, and are then printed out at the checkout cashdesk.

Retailers have used such technology to improve the efficiency of stock control and the speed of checkout operations. Each time a sale is made, the stock inventory is automatically amended, and details of products at the checkout are entered much faster. The customer also receives a detailed receipt giving a printout of each item, right down to the flavor of a brand of cat food.

Customer-based information can now be linked with each purchase by using "smart" cards. These are similar to credit cards, and are presented at the checkout. Details of household demographics derived from the card application form and perhaps from the geodemographic characteristics of the postcode address are linked through the identification number to the purchases made on any shopping trip. Such systems do, however, require not only cooperation from the customer, but for manufacturers to benefit from such information the retailer has to pass it on, either directly or to a market research agency. It also requires that a substantial number of retailers have scanning equipment. Purchase data from such electronic recording devices can be linked with in-store customer behavior and in-store pricing, layout and ranges of products to test the effectiveness of "below-the-line" activity.

Scanning technology is now also being used in the home. The two largest consumer panels in Europe are equipped with electronic scanners able to read barcodes. This means that details of purchases can be recorded by the panelist simply by running the scanner over every item as the shopping is unpacked. Computer terminals may be used to enable panelists to key in prices and the names of the shops where the goods were bought. All this information is then transferred to a central computer, enabling rapid analyses of purchasing patterns to be produced. These procedures are explained in more detail in Chapter 16.

Electronic questionnaires are increasingly used in three main contexts:

- computer assisted telephone interviewing (CATI),
- computer assisted personal interviewing (CAPI),
- computer assisted web-based interviewing (CAWI).

With CATI the questionnaire is programed into a central computer before interviewing begins. It is then displayed question by question on a number of visual display units in a central location. An interviewer sits in front of each screen and telephones the selected number. The replies are immediately entered via the keyboard. The advantages of this system are:

- no paper questionnaires are required,
- last-minute changes can be made to the questionnaire,

A lot of data are captured at the checkout.

- routing is automatic, with the interviewer being passed straight to the next relevant question,

- results can be assessed at any time during the survey,

- tables can be run as soon as interviewing is completed,

- range checks and logical checks can be applied automatically.

With CAPI the interviewer has a market research terminal that is in effect a small portable computer with a screen that displays the questions as for CATI. Either the interviewer can key in the answers, or, in some cases, the respondent is handed the terminal to key in his or her own. The data can then be sent down the telephone at the press of a button (using portable telephone technology). Using CAPI has slashed the time it takes to produce comprehensive research results, but, of course, it is very much more expensive.

A more recent development still is interviewing over the internet, or Computer Assisted Web Interviewing (CAWI). It is easy to attach a questionnaire to a World Wide Web site, but it is difficult to control who responds to it. Those who do may be very unrepresentative of the population of interest.

Meters have been used for measuring the use of television since the 1940s in the USA. Early meters simply recorded the total time the television was tuned on, and were used as a check against gross error in diary completion among a representative sample of panel households. More recent "set meters" recorded the channel to which the set was tuned on a continuous basis, but were still used in conjunction with diaries to record who was watching. Diaries could be abandoned only with the introduction in 1984 of AGB's "peoplemeter". This uses a remote control handset associated with each television for members of the panel household to indicate their presence in the room where a television is switched on by pressing a button with a number to which they have been allocated. They press the number again when they leave the room. Such "push-button" or "active" meter systems have had to become more sophisticated to cope with the use of VCRs to time-shift viewing, viewing on prerecorded video tapes, viewing and recording at the same time, multiset households, the use of television for teletext, home computers, and the introduction of cable and satellite television. At present, the peoplemeter system can cope with guest viewing by allocating button numbers to additional guests, but viewing of household members outside the home is still a problem. Systems for measuring television audiences are explained in detail in Chapter 16.

Further developments may well take the form of linking some of the various technologies together. Thus technically it is possible to link the purchases made by homes that have scanning equipment or "smart" cards with those that have television meters installed. This means that television viewing may be directly linked with purchasing behavior and with below-the-line activity in the shop. The direct effect of television advertising can thus be monitored on a continuous basis.

KEY POINTS

Recording devices, both manual and electronic, are used extensively in marketing research, both for quantitative and for qualitative research. In a sense, questionnaires and diaries can also be seen as recording devices – they are, after all, instruments of data capture. However, the use of devices where data have not been generated by addressing listed questions to individuals in questionnaires and diaries is best seen as a separate category of data capture.

Ethical issues

Researchers, when designing questionnaires, need to keep in mind the fact that the administration of a questionnaire represents, to a greater or lesser extent, an intrusion into the lives of respondents. In particular, excessively long questionnaires can be a burden on the respondent and may adversely affect the quality of the responses given. Questions that are confusing or that exceed the ability of respondents to answer them may upset respondents. Some questions are, by their nature, sensitive. Respondents may be reluctant to answer questions about their income or their savings and may feel embarrassed about questions on sexually transmitted diseases, drug use or feminine hygiene products. If such questions are to be asked, it is vital that it be made clear at the beginning of the interview that respondents are not obliged to answer any question that makes them uncomfortable.

SUMMARY

Quantitative data may be captured using one or more of three key instruments: questionnaires, diaries or recording devices, which may be manual or electronic. Questionnaires may be structured to varying degrees and may be self-completed or interviewer-completed. Formal, structured questionnaires tend to have a predominance of set-choice, precoded questions which may be used to collect data on demographic, behavioral or cognitive variables. Questionnaire wording needs to ensure, as far as possible, that respondents understand the questions, have the information to be able to provide answers, and are willing to provide the answers. Questionnaire layout and presentation are particularly important for self-completed questionnaires, but must not be overlooked where part-time paid interviewers are being used. Layout needs to bear in mind not only the respondent's convenience, but also the needs of the interviewer and the data analyst. Questionnaires that are not pretested in some way are unlikely to meet the needs of the researcher and his or her client.

Diaries may be distinguished from questionnaires on the basis that they are time-based, and refer exclusively to repeated behavior rather than to attitudes or possessions. Product diaries tend to be laid out on a product-by-product basis while media diaries are likely to utilize time segments. Diary design needs to bear in mind the potential sources of error in diary-keeping and the various factors that affect them. The issue of whether diaries or questionnaire recall methods result in the recording of higher or lower levels of activity is one on which the evidence so far is, at best, inconclusive.

Recording devices may be manual or electronic, but it is the latter that have seen the major development in recent times. These devices include point-of-sale scanning equipment, electronic questionnaires and diaries, television meters, and audio and video recording equipment. Further developments in technology are likely to see these devices being used in conjunction with one another to provide quantities of data which, on present data analysis expertise and facilities, may be difficult to handle. Though the use of electronic equipment often obviates the need for sampling and making estimates, they tend to be expensive and, in their more sophisticated versions, the preserve of the larger market research organizations.

QUESTIONS FOR DISCUSSION

1   A manufacturer of hairdryers wants to find out:

    ■   what proportion of households own a hairdryer,
    ■   what proportions and types of individual in households with hairdryers use it on every occasion after hair-washing,
    ■   the major product features respondents are looking for.

    Design a questionnaire for use in face-to-face interviews that will obtain this information from a sample of households.

2   Specify the changes that will be needed if the questionnaire in the previous exercise is to be used as a postal questionnaire.

3   British Telecom wants to discover the age profile and telephone use behavior of different age groups. Discuss the strengths and weaknesses of using a diary compared with a questionnaire to capture such data

CASE STUDY EBAY

eBay is The World's Online Marketplace®, with a global customer base of 181 million. Founded in 1995, eBay has created a powerful marketplace for the sale of goods and services by individuals and small businesses. eBay now has a global presence in 33 markets worldwide. On any given day, millions of items are listed on eBay across thousands of diverse categories, including antiques, toys, books, computers, sports, photography and electronics, among many others. Launched in October 1999, eBay.co.uk is the UK's largest online market place and is now the UK's number one e-commerce site (Nielsen Net Ratings, May 2003). eBay.co.uk has also achieved the three million live listings landmark, meaning there are three million items for sale on the site at any given time.

According to Manning (2003), loyalty is the secret of eBay's success. Half of eBay users are recruited by word of mouth by current users. The ability to maintain this level of loyalty depends on the company's responsiveness to customers and ability to resolve problems that could damage the cohesiveness of the community of eBay users. To do this, eBay uses a number of feedback mechanisms. There are customer ratings whereby, as customers trade, they give each other a feedback rating. There are customer support systems, chat-boards and data mining is used on the enormous amounts of data about what is selling through the site. Finally, there is customer e-mail research including a customer satisfaction and feedback survey.

Questions and activities

1   Check out the eBay website, www.ebay.co.uk. Click on *About eBay* and *company overview*.

2   Design a customer satisfaction questionnaire for eBay that uses Likert scaling techniques to measure customers' attitudes towards the company, rating scales for satisfaction with previous transactions on eBay and collects essential demographics.

Data mining A range of techniques for extracting actionable information from large databases, usually stored in a data warehouse, and applying it to business models.

FURTHER READING

Alaszewski, A. (2005) *Using Diaries for Social Research*. London: Sage.

Brace, I. (2004) *Questionnaire Design. How to plan, structure and write survey material for effective market research*. London: Kogan Page.

Hague, P. (1993) *Questionnaire Design*. London: Kogan Page.

Evans, N. (1995) *Using Questionnaires and Surveys to Boost Your Business*. London: Pitman.

Manning, J. (2003) "Dirty data and customer feedback applications", *Market Research Society Conference*, London.

O'Donoghue, D. and Steele, L. (2004) "Is lifestage losing its meaning?", *Admap*, September, Issue 453.

Wicken, G., van Staveren, M. and Dinning, A. (2005) "Global socio-economic levels. Development of a global non-occupational classification system", *International Journal of Market Research*, 47 (6): 597–614.

Constructing quantitative data
Selecting methods

research, but they can also be used for personal observation and for the various forms of qualitative research that were described in Chapter 5.

LEARNING OBJECTIVES In this chapter you will learn about:

→ the nature and different types of marketing research surveys,

→ the kinds of errors that can arise in survey design and execution,

→ the nature and types of experimental research in marketing,

→ panels and regular interval surveys as forms of continuous research,

→ the contrasts between client-based and academic quantitative research in marketing.

Questionnaires can be administered in many different ways.

© DETAIL NOTTINGHAM/ALAMY

INTRODUCTION

The instruments of data capture that were considered in Chapter 6 may be used in a variety of contexts. Thus questionnaires and diaries may be used not only for undertaking survey research of various kinds, but also for obtaining reactions of participants in experimental research and for continuous research. All these types of research are detailed in this chapter. Recording devices may also be used as data capture instruments for undertaking quantitative research, but they can also be used for personal observation and for the various forms of qualitative research that were described in Chapter 4.

INTERNET ACTIVITY

Using your browser, go to **www.thomsonlearning.co.uk/kent** and select the Chapter 7 Internet Activity which will provide a link to the Survey.Net website. Try out one or two of the surveys. What do you think of the survey design?

Survey research

Survey The capture of data based on addressing questions to respondents in a formal manner and taking a systematic record of their responses.

There are three main ways of obtaining quantitative data in marketing research: surveys, observation and experiments. Of these, surveys are by far the most widely used, certainly in client-based marketing research. Surveys allow the collection of substantial amounts of data in an economical and efficient manner and they allow for large sample sizes. An advantage of surveys is that respondents react to identically worded questions that are normally presented in the same order and with the same response options for each question. This ensures that, as far as possible, answers across the population or sample surveyed are comparable.

A **survey** entails the capture of data based on addressing questions to respondents in a formal manner and taking a systematic record of their responses. The recording instrument will normally be a questionnaire, but may be a diary or direct data capture using electronic means. This section addresses itself to the design and conduct of ad hoc surveys, which are one-off pieces of research, and are usually custom-designed for a particular purpose or client. They also tend to be cross-sectional, that is, they treat the period over which the research is conducted as one unit of time. Continuous research is described in a later section.

Ad hoc surveys, whether client-based or academic, tend to go through a number of stages such as those outlined in Figure 7.1. The researcher begins by analyzing the problems, issues or objectives that the research is to address before designing the most appropriate kind of survey to conduct. However, before data are collected it may be wise, if not essential, to undertake some exploratory research, as a consequence of which some redesign of the survey may be advisable or necessary – hence the double arrow in Figure 7.1. It may then be possible to proceed directly to data capture without further exploratory research. Once the data have been assembled they need to be analyzed and interpreted, and a report, conference paper or journal article written of the results. The report, paper or article should, in turn, address the original purposes of the research to complete the loop in the survey research process.

Stage 1, analyze the problem, for client-based research was considered in Chapter 1, while Chapter 2 introduced the equivalent for academic research in terms of a rationale for the research and more specific research objectives. This section is concerned with stage 2, survey design and stage 4, data capture. Chapter 1 explained that exploratory research (stage 3) is defined by its objective, namely to generate insights and understanding of marketing phenomena. In the context of survey design, however, exploratory research means an exploratory phase where the researcher does not have enough information or understanding to proceed with the research project. Data analysis and interpretation are the subject of Part II of this book, while Chapter 18 looks at the process of writing reports.

In looking at the various types of ad hoc survey, we can make distinctions along a number of dimensions, for example:

- by topic,
- by type of researcher,
- by method of questionnaire administration.

A basic distinction in terms of topic is between consumer surveys, which study individuals or private households as final consumers of products and services, and business surveys, which address questions to individuals in business organizations concerning those organizations, not their private purchasing or consumption behavior.

Surveys distinguished by type of researcher include the following.

- In-house surveys, which are carried out by the company itself using its own market research department.

- Market research agency surveys, which are commissioned by a client organization. These may be custom-designed for a particular client, or syndicated in some way, for example companies may share either the organization of a survey or the data that emerge.

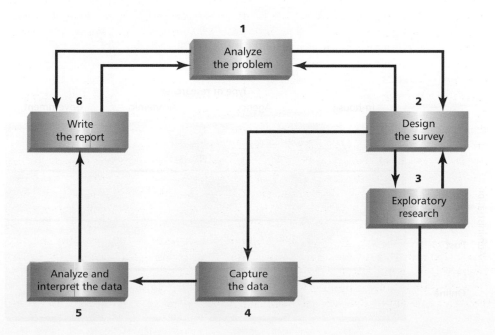

FIGURE 7.1

The stages of ad hoc survey research

■ Academic surveys. These may be done on a consultancy basis, or for the purposes of scholarly research.

■ Governmental surveys such as those carried out by the Office of National Statistics.

Surveys distinguished by method of questionnaire administration include:

■ interview surveys,

■ telephone surveys,

■ postal surveys,

■ online surveys.

These classifications of types of survey can be combined, for example each of the types of survey by researcher may be undertaken by each of the types of administration, giving 16 possibilities, as in Figure 7.2. However, in terms of survey design issues, it is the method of questionnaire administration that is most important and has become the standard basis for distinguishing different types of survey.

Interview surveys

Interview survey A survey that involves face-to-face, personal contact with respondents.

Interview surveys involve face-to-face, personal contact with respondents. Normally the interviewer asks the questions, which are read out from the questionnaire or interview schedule, and records the responses by ticking appropriate boxes or noting down answers in spaces provided in the questionnaire. Figures produced by the British Market Research Association (**www.bmra.org.uk**) suggest that, in terms of commercial marketing research, over 40 percent of overall agency revenue comes from such interviews.

The prevalence of this method of questionnaire administration is explained largely by the key advantages of this form of social encounter:

■ the interviewer can check and ensure respondent eligibility before the interview is started,

■ personally administered questionnaires ensure that all questions are asked in the required order, and that all applicable questions are asked,

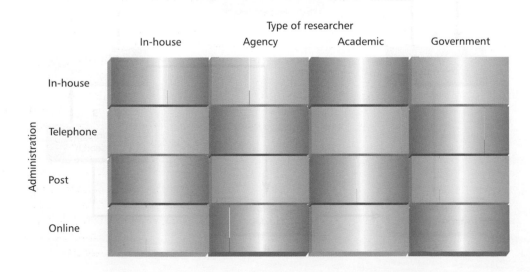

FIGURE 7.2

Types of surveys

- the interviewer can encourage respondents to answer as fully as possible and check, as appropriate, that the question is correctly understood,

- materials that need to be shown to the respondents can be properly presented,

- response rates are consistently higher than for other methods of questionnaire administration,

- where quotas are applied, the interviewer can ensure that the target number of interviews is achieved,

- interviewers can usually persuade respondents to complete the interview.

These advantages together mean that the quality of the data derived from interview surveys is generally superior to that obtained by other methods.

Types of interview

Interview surveys can be grouped into five styles according to the type of location in which they occur:

- the street,
- the home,
- a hall,
- a shop,
- a business organization.

Street surveys are usually conducted in busy town centers, particularly in shopping malls or precincts. In the USA researchers call them "mall intercept" interviews. The interviewer tends to stay in one position, approaching potential respondents as soon as a previous interview is completed. This eliminates travel time between interviews and makes recruitment fairly speedy. However, street interviews need to be brief, since respondents are unlikely to stop for more than about ten minutes, and the use of materials to show also needs to be controlled. Furthermore, enclosed shopping malls are considered to be private property and the permission of the center manager will be required to carry out the interviewing. Some centers have a no-interviewing policy; others may charge for the facility on a pre-booked basis.

Street survey A survey conducted in busy town centers or shopping malls, usually combined with quota sampling.

In-home surveys entail approaching potential respondents in their own homes – or on their doorsteps. Interviewers may be given lists of names and addresses or they may be limited to a prescribed number of streets, or to an area (a sampling point). In addition, they may have instructions about how to proceed, for example, calling at every n^{th} house, or missing out a certain number of houses after every successful interview. Whereas street interviews are always "cold", in-home interviews may be pre-recruited by telephone. Door-to-door recruitment can be time-consuming and it relies on people being at home. Although longer interviews are usually possible, interruptions are always a hazard, whether from other members of the household (including pets) or from the television or the telephone.

In-home survey A survey in which potential respondents are approached in their own homes.

Interviews carried out in a pre-booked location are usually referred to as **hall tests**, even though it may not be in a hall, but in a public room in a hotel. Furthermore, it may not be a "test" in the sense of the kind of hall tests conducted and described later as a form of experimental research. Recruitment is usually from a street nearby and respondents are invited to "answer a few questions" about a particular product or whatever is the topic of the survey. Respondents can be given refreshments while being interviewed and this facilitates completion of more complex tasks. Interviews conducted indoors, furthermore, can use a much greater array of materials, including videos or elaborate displays. A team of interviewers may work from the same hall where they can be supervised and monitored.

Hall test A survey, often accompanied by an experimental design, in which respondents are invited to a prebooked, local venue to answer questions or respond to specified stimuli.

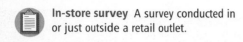

In-store survey A survey conducted in or just outside a retail outlet.

Business survey A survey that takes place on a business premises.

In-store surveys may take place in a shop or just outside. The researcher or the market research agency will, clearly, need to obtain permission from the store, and in many cases also the co-operation of the store personnel. Recruitment may be on the basis of people entering or leaving the store – whatever is appropriate will be determined by the subject matter or objectives of the research. Thus a study of shopping intentions will require the former. As with interviews taking place in halls being called "hall tests", so interviews taking place either outside or inside the shop are usually called "store tests", even though they are not, strictly speaking, tests using any form of experimental design.

Business surveys will normally take place in the interviewee's office or in one of the company meeting rooms and will probably have been prearranged. There is always the danger, however, that some "crisis" has occurred and the interview is cancelled, postponed or truncated.

The interviewing process

How many interviews the interviewer is able to conduct in a day or in a week depends on a number of factors, for example the location, the recruitment time, the interviewing time and the travel time. It may be possible to conduct 20–30 interviews a day using street quotas; an interviewer will be lucky to do 10 in-home, or perhaps 2 business interviews.

Wherever the interview is carried out, the interviewer has a number of key tasks. These include:

- preparation,
- locating the respondents,
- obtaining the agreement to conduct the interview,
- asking the questions and noting down answers,
- completing records of interview assignments and returning completed questionnaires.

Interviewers' jobs begin when their instructions from the marketing research agency arrive. The interviewers will need to go through the pack carefully, making sure that all the materials and information needed have been provided. If there are any problems, he or she will need to contact the supervisor or the office. The interviewer may need to prepare a strategy for recruitment, since there may be considerable freedom as to when the interviews are carried out and where recruitment takes place. Strategies may, in fact, be similar to those adopted for recruitment to group discussions. Finally, the interviewer must be thoroughly familiar with the questionnaire. He or she is then ready to face the public.

With **random sampling** techniques, interviewers are given lists of names and addresses. In the UK these will usually be taken either from the Electoral Registers or the Postcode Address File. Sampling techniques and sampling frames are considered in more detail in the next chapter. Having found the address, the interviewer needs to locate the named person drawn as part of the sample. If the person concerned is not at home, there is usually an instruction to make at least three callbacks at different times of the day. No substitutes are allowed. In **random location** and **random route** sampling, the interviewer will have instructions about the selection of houses and the streets in which such selections are to be made. With **quota sampling**, there may be no instruction about how, within a specified sampling point, the interviewer obtains her quotas, but whether the interviews are to take place in-home or in the street *is* usually specified.

Interviewers are normally trained on the best ways of obtaining the agreement of the named or selected person to participate. The response rate for experienced

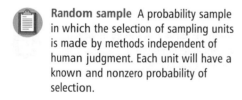

Random sample A probability sample in which the selection of sampling units is made by methods independent of human judgment. Each unit will have a known and nonzero probability of selection.

Random location sampling Interviewers are assigned to randomly-chosen sampling points and then asked to undertake quota sampling.

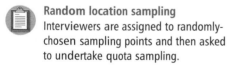

Random route sampling A nonprobability sample in which interviewers are instructed to begin interviewing at specified points that are randomly chosen and to call on households at set intervals.

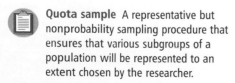

Quota sample A representative but nonprobability sampling procedure that ensures that various subgroups of a population will be represented to an extent chosen by the researcher.

interviewers is generally consistently higher than for novices. The interviewer will have an identity card which shows that the person named on the card is registered as a bona fide interviewer. This is usually presented while the interviewer explains that they are conducting market research on a given topic (usually the agency will be identified, but not the client), and would like to ask a few questions seeking their opinion. Assurances of confidentiality and that personal details will not be used for selling purposes are usually given.

When asking the questions, apart from conversational pleasantries, the interviewer is normally instructed to follow exactly the wording in the questionnaire. Some questions may have "probe" written against them, indicating that the interviewer has discretion over whether to pursue a more detailed answer than the one the respondent has just offered. When recording the answers, for fixed-choice questions, the interviewer just has to tick boxes or put circles round numbered responses. For open-ended questions the interviewer may be instructed to write down exactly what the respondent says, or to paraphrase.

An interviewer will normally be given an assignment of perhaps 15–20 interviews to do in a week if in-home, or rather more if based on street interviews. A record of all contacts and non-contacts will be kept and this will be returned to the agency at the end of the week along with the completed questionnaires. In some cases, interviewers have hand-held market research terminals. The terminal will have a screen that displays each question in turn and the responses. The selected response is entered as the respondent gives it. The terminal then prompts with the next relevant question, which may depend on which response has been entered. The data are stored on a disc which is then returned to the agency where the data are read directly into the computer.

Interviewing is a skilled activity. The interview itself is a process of social interaction that is highly artificial and its outcome, including answers to questions, will often depend on the gender, age, social class, dress, accent and personality of both interviewer and respondent. It is quite easy to obtain systematic differences between interviewers that need, as far as possible, to be controlled. The interviewer is, on the one hand, trying to be "standard" in all his or her approaches to respondents, but, on the other hand, may need to react to individual circumstances for the successful completion of the interview – in short, the interviewer needs to act like a robot with all the appearance of a human being.

Interviewer bias may present a problem and may occur in one or more of several ways. At the recruitment stage an interviewer given an assignment with quotas may, consciously or unconsciously, select (or avoid) people of a particular type. The way the interviewer handles the initial approach will affect the response rates and probably differentially by type of respondent; the way she or he asks the questions may affect the responses given, so might the way he or she reacts verbally or nonverbally. Probing or prompting may be approached in different ways. Market research agencies recognize these problems and try to minimize their impact in a number of ways. These include:

- training,
- briefing,
- quality control,

Some interviews take place on the doorstep, although they are usually called "in-home" interviews.

© PHOTOFUSION PICTURE LIBRARY/ALAMY

- fieldwork management,
- industry guidelines.

All interviewers are put through some kind of training program, which should have two components: teaching the interviewers the skills they will need to carry out good interviews, and integrating them into the industry. The skills required include the techniques for finding the right respondents, persuading them to take part, and sustaining their level of interest. Interviewers frequently need to be able to classify respondents very quickly into **social grade** categories; they need to be aware of the importance of asking questions and reading out instructions exactly as they appear on the questionnaire. They need to be clear about the extent of probing allowed or required and the manner in which such probing is to be done. They need to know how to use any data collection equipment and how to complete all paperwork accurately.

Social grade An ordinal classification of occupational status.

Interviewer integration into the industry means that the interviewer needs to be able to understand what marketing and marketing research are about, they need to know about issues of confidentiality and the implications of the Data Protection Act and they need to be aware of what happens to the data once they have collected and passed them on. Training programs usually involve an in-house session (of, typically, 1–3 days) entailing lectures, exercises and simulations. Normally, there will be a manual for the interviewer to study and for future reference. In-field training will usually be under the supervision of a field supervisor. As each new topic of work is assigned, the interviewer may be accompanied by a senior interviewer or the supervisor.

Before each new assignment, there will usually be briefing sessions. These may be formal personal briefings where area field staff are gathered together and the researcher explains all the aspects of the survey. Supervisors may be briefed first and they, in turn, brief the interviewers. Some briefings may be over the telephone. There will usually also be detailed written instructions, sometimes standing on their own, sometimes supporting other briefing methods. Any of these methods may, of course, be combined together.

The methods used for quality control are various. The accuracy of the data collected and the legitimacy of respondent recruitment may be subjected to "back-checks". Supervisors recall on respondents and readminister part of the questionnaire. Some 5–10 percent of respondents may be re-contacted in this way. It may be done over the telephone, by post or by personal visit. Some agencies have a policy of accompanying interviewers in the field on a regular basis. Any bad habits can then be picked up and rectified. Central monitoring may be used to identify interviewers who regularly make mistakes or submit incomplete work; feedback from field supervisors on how well the questionnaire is performing may be used to alert other supervisors of potential difficulties.

The overall management of the field-force is an important factor in maintaining standards of interviewing. There will typically be a head office team led by a senior manager. A number of regional supervisors will be working from home, controlling local teams of interviewers. These people may be salaried or they may work freelance. They all try to assure a high standard of selection and training in their area and they will try to get each interviewer to work across the entire range of types of respondent so that any biases will be equally distributed.

Across Europe, industry guidelines are given by ESOMAR, which provides a Code of Conduct for research, parts of which apply directly to interviewers. In the UK, the Market Research Society (MRS) also publishes more general guidelines for interviewers, which can be viewed at its website **www.mrs.org.uk**. The MRS has also introduced a uniform interviewer identity card that seeks to reassure the public as to the legitimacy of the interview, and to stop the practice of **sugging** – selling under the guise of doing market research. There is also an Interviewer Quality Control Scheme (IQCS), which is a voluntary scheme set up in 1978 to

Sugging Selling under the guise of doing marketing research.

address the differences in quality buyers experienced when purchasing fieldwork. The IQCS is an independent legal entity that is managed by a Council of Management elected by its members who consist of over 60 of the largest market research agencies in the UK. It offers clients the assurance that interviews will be adequately trained and supervised and their work validated in accordance with minimum standards specified by the scheme. For details see www.iqcs.org.

The skills of professional interviewers have allowed data collection methodologies to become more complex and sophisticated; but they are costly and time-consuming, particularly where geographically dispersed sampling is required, or where quota requirements make respondents hard to find. Though interview surveys are still the dominant mode of data collection, that dominance is being challenged, particularly with the growth in telephone research and online surveys.

Telephone surveys

In the 1970s, telephone interviewing became well-established as a method used by industrial or business market researchers to obtain information and opinions from managers and professional people. Business premises were usually on the telephone and managers were accustomed to using them. By the end of the 1980s, however, most private households throughout Europe had a telephone and the number of agencies offering telephone research grew rapidly.

Employing interviewers and supervisors to telephone from their own homes was, however, not practicable and most agencies offering telephone interviewing services now have central location telephoning. This concentrated interviewing in a small number of closely supervised locations. In addition, most of these centers have taken advantage of computer assisted telephone interviewing (CATI), which has greatly increased the advantages of central location interviewing. The questionnaire is programed into the computer prior to the commencement of the interviewing, and is displayed question-by-question on a visual display unit in front of each interviewer. The reply is immediately input into the computer via the keyboard.

Telephone interviewing is usually done from a call center.

© DAVID PARTINGTON

Telephone interviewing has a number of advantages over face-to-face interviewing:

- it produces faster results,
- it is convenient and relatively inexpensive,
- it offers anonymity,
- it is easily controlled and supervised,
- it is not necessary to cluster the interviewing in sampling points, thereby reducing sampling error.

There are also a number of drawbacks:

- they are limited to verbal exchanges – it is not possible to show people lists, cards or other visual materials (unless they are posted in advance),
- there are no observational data; in particular, it is not possible to watch the facial expression and body language of respondents,
- telephone interviews have to be very short and factual, which does limit their use,
- the rise of telesales – selling over the telephone – has made many people suspicious of calls from strangers,
- answerphones and call-screening equipment has made telephone interviewing more difficult,
- drawing samples of individuals or households from telephone directories can be problematic.

In the UK, unlisted telephone numbers are estimated to be up to 40 percent of the total number of landlines either because people are ex-directory, or because of removals or new installations since the last print of directories. There is, furthermore, no directory of mobile telephone numbers, and when people begin to abandon their landlines to rely on their mobiles, there will be growing problems with this mode of questionnaire administration. These problems have been approached in a number of ways.

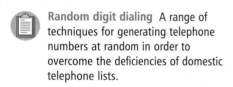

Random digit dialing A range of techniques for generating telephone numbers at random in order to overcome the deficiencies of domestic telephone lists.

The problem of unlisted numbers can be partly overcome by using **random digit dialing**. This is a two-stage process in which area and local code combinations are drawn at random from a list of all known combinations. A random four-digit number is then added to create a complete telephone number. These numbers are dialed and if they prove to be working lines then further numbers are created by randomizing the last two digits. This method will generate unlisted numbers in appropriate proportions. However, telephone subscribers who have paid to be ex-directory may well be irritated at being contacted in this way. Where this has been tried, the response rate is not good. Furthermore, it does nothing to solve the problem created by the explosive growth of mobile telephones.

Other alternatives to random digit dialing are to impose quotas on the recruitment of respondents so that groups who would otherwise be under-represented are correctly represented, or weight the data afterwards to correct for over- and under-representations. These may help to some extent, but the procedure assumes that the telephone-listed section of the population who are in the under-represented groups are themselves representative of those who are unlisted. For business research, the ex-directory number problem does not exist, so using various lists of business numbers as a sampling frame should pose few problems.

In telephone surveys, a key to a high response rate is the skill of the interviewer, who has to be able to deal with reluctance, resistance or even hostility and still elicit co-operation as well as conduct a survey in the appropriate manner (Brennan, Benson and Kearns 2005). Box 7.1 explains that the way a survey is introduced is crucial and describes some useful suggestions for improving responses.

Postal surveys

While postal research accounts for only about 8 percent of turnover of commissioned research, some 25 percent of all interviews are conducted using this method. Postal surveys are, in fact, extremely cost-effective, requiring neither interviewers nor telephone systems. They are perhaps one-third of the cost of telephone surveys and one-eighth of interview surveys. The growth of direct marketing has in recent years, furthermore, given an impetus to postal surveys since recipients of postal questionnaires are likely to be customers of the company and therefore more likely to respond. Other advantages of postal surveys are:

- central control of the survey is facilitated,
- unclustered sampling is possible without cost penalties,
- more time can be devoted to the completion of questionnaires by respondents,
- respondents can fill them in when it is convenient to them,
- respondents can confer with other members of the household before filling in answers,
- there is no interviewer bias.

It is often argued that the main disadvantage of postal questionnaires is the low response rate. While response rates for some postal questionnaires are, indeed, very low, perhaps as low as 30 percent or even lower, if they are used in appropriate situations and properly executed with good covering letters, reminders, incentives and so on, the response rates can be equal to that of telephone surveys and may, on occasions, approach that of interview surveys. The use of mail surveys varies across countries in Europe, however, and Box 7.2 explains that their use is very low in Spain, perhaps undeservedly so.

and misinterpretation of the instructions. Diaz de Rada had already shown in an earlier piece of research (Diaz de Rada 2000) that the reluctance to use mail surveys is unfounded. In the current research, the author reports a study carried out in Nevarra that obtained a response rate of over 80 percent. Quality of responses was measured using four criteria;

- the number of non-responses to a question,
- the cases where a double response is made when only one was requested,
- the proper reading of the instructions,
- the presence of contamination between questions.

The rate of nonresponse and double response was very low and the results hardly changed when multi-item questions were answered. There was little evidence of contamination.

There are, however, a number of other disadvantages of postal surveys:

- there is no assistance or encouragement from an interviewer,
- respondents can read all the questionnaire in advance, so "unfolding" or "funneling" techniques cannot be used,
- there are usually delays in getting completed questionnaires back,
- the person filling in the questionnaire may not be the one selected in the sample,
- answers have to be accepted as they are written without further probing.

Evidence suggests that a good covering letter is crucial to the response rate, other things being equal. The letter must "sell" the value of the survey to the respondent and encourage him or her to respond. An example of a covering letter was given in Figure 6.8 in the previous chapter. It may, in addition, help to emphasize why it is important for people to participate, how the survey will help others in the future, and that they will receive a mystery gift or token of appreciation if they return the questionnaire by a certain date. Enclosing the incentive (for example, a pen) with the original letter is, so it is sometimes argued, more effective. It is normal to include a stamped, addressed envelope. If it is intended to send reminders after 2–3 weeks, questionnaires will need to be numbered to identify those who have not responded. The letter may need to explain that the number will be used only for this purpose.

Online surveys

Online survey A survey that is administered using computer networks such as the internet or local intranets.

Online surveys are administered using computer networks such as the internet or local intranets and may be either e-mail surveys or web-based surveys. E-mail surveys themselves can be of two kinds. At its simplest, the researcher can simply e-mail text questions or fixed-choice questions contained in the body of the e-mail. Respondents hit the "Reply" button on their mailer, fill in the answers to the questions and hit "Send". Respondents can indicate their answer to fixed-choice questions by putting an "X" against the answer or by deleting response categories that do not apply. There are, however, limitations to the format of the questions. The mail editor is not as sophisticated as a full word-processing package, and no graphics can be included, although Likert-type scales, for example, could be constructed for respondents to reply to. These, however, will be clumsy since even boxes for respondents to tick or lines to form a grid cannot be drawn. For the researcher, the reply is equivalent to receiving a paper questionnaire. The responses must be entered into a survey analysis package by hand.

A more sophisticated questionnaire with graphics, lines and boxes can be sent as an attachment. The respondent can then either print this off and return by post or save as a Word file, complete and return as an attachment. This can be fairly straightforward with Windows-based systems, but some respondents will be using other platforms like UNIX which may limit accessibility. Again, however, responses need to be entered into an analysis package by hand.

Web-based surveys use hypertext markup language (HTML) to post the questionnaire on a website. Respondents will normally be contacted by e-mail and asked to go to the website by clicking on the web address. Alternatively, people browsing the web can be intercepted on the website using banners or pop-ups. It is possible in HTML to construct buttons, checkboxes and data entry fields that prevent respondents from selecting more than one response where only one is required and skip patterns can be programmed and performed automatically. The responses can be collected on an adjoining database. While web-based surveys require more skill than e-mail surveys, most survey analysis packages that include a questionnaire design function such as Snap, Keypoint or SPSS Data Entry have the facility to formulate the questionnaire automatically into e-mail and internet formats, and will include, for example, the possibility of having drop-down menus. Box 7.3 illustrates the use of an online questionnaire in Belfast.

There are considerable advantages to online surveys.

Speed. The instant transmission of the questionnaire and its return will save considerable time compared with a postal survey. Data entry is automatic for web-based surveys and does not need to be keyed in. Miller (2000) reports that a study carried out by Burke Interactive found that respondents complete a web-based survey more quickly than a comparable telephone survey.

Coverage. International boundaries have no significance on the internet, so an online survey can be global just as easily as a local survey.

Cost. E-mail surveys can be undertaken at virtually no cost except for the time setting up the questionnaire. Once a package like Snap has been purchased, there are no further costs.

Anonymity. People are more inclined to respond to sensitive issues, admit embarrassing circumstances or failures in the privacy of their own homes and not facing a group of other respondents or even an interviewer. They can answer thoughtfully and at leisure and without distraction or interruption.

24/7 convenience. Respondents can reply at any time of the day on any day of the week.

EUROPEAN MARKETING RESEARCH — BOX 7.3
Using e-mail for audience research

When Belfast Children's Festival (BCF) launched its own dedicated computerized box office and online sales system in May 2005, it was able to access a range of details and accurate information about its customers (Hadley 2005). This also opened up the potential for gathering even more information using an e-mail survey. BCF wanted to measure new attenders' awareness of new branding, its advertising campaign and its print materials. BCF worked together with Audiences Northern Ireland to compile a questionnaire that would be available online on the BCF website. Every patron with an e-mail address (about 400 people) was sent an e-mail with a hyperlink to the questionnaire. Completion was incentivised with a £25 Marks and Spencer voucher. The response rate was 27 percent. The responses were then matched up with data from application forms. Responses showed that BCF had a committed family audience who were willing and eager to engage in an ongoing dialogue with the organization.

Control. Large-scale surveys are relatively easy to set up and manage. Response rates can be monitored. Researchers can check the website for current tabulations whenever they like.

There are, however, disadvantages.

Sampling frames. There are no publicly available lists of e-mail addresses. Those lists that may be obtained will include many redundant addresses. This may not be a problem for some companies, however, who may well have the e-mail addresses of all their customers. The problems of internet sampling are considered in Chapter 8.

Response rates. These can be very low for e-mail and web-based surveys. The explosion of spam and the application of filters on unknown senders means that many potential respondents will either not receive the e-mail or will delete it as soon as they receive it.

Access to the web is not universal and many groups will not be represented. Unless a reasonable proportion of the survey population can be expected to be online, then traditional methods should be used. The study reported by Miller (2000) found that any research on the web is really done among a subsample of skilled web users.

Inappropriate topics. Some topics may be inappropriate for online surveys, for example a survey on why people do not participate in online surveys, or research into the effect of retirement on shopping patterns.

Online surveys also suffer from all the drawbacks associated with all self-completion techniques. These were explained on pp. 166–167. Some of these limitations have been approached by using online panels. A pool of people is recruited (using traditional techniques or online) who are willing to take part in research over a specified period of time. This is a good way of achieving a sample that represents a specific population, for example users of online banking facilities. The panel can be balanced demographically and maintained by replacing drop-outs by others with similar demographics.

Mixed techniques

Interview, telephone and postal surveys may, of course, be used in combination. For example, pre-recruiting by telephone can avoid a lot of wasted leg-work. After an initial personal interview, a self-completed questionnaire can be left with the respondent to complete in order to collect additional information, perhaps from other members of the household. If the survey requires an interview and follow-up, the call-back may be conducted by telephone, or a postal questionnaire may be sent. Using combinations of techniques in this way can increase the flexibility of research design. In a study that compared responses to a web survey and a telephone survey, Miller (2000) reports that in customer satisfaction studies carried out by Burke Interactive, findings were the same whether conducted over the web or over the phone. This opens up the possibility that studies could be changed from phone-based to web-based or that some combination could be used with little or no impact on the integrity of the data.

KEY POINTS

Survey design is geared mainly to the method of questionnaire administration, namely in person by the interviewer either face-to-face or over the telephone, or by post or online, in which case the questionnaire will be self-completed. Figures produced by the British Market Research

Association (**www.bmra.org.uk**) suggest that among commercial researchers, face-to-face interviews generate about 40 percent of agency revenue, but account for only 20 percent in terms of volume. Over the three years between 1998 and 2001, the volume of face-to-face interviews dropped by 27 percent while the number of online questionnaires rose by 4000 percent. In volume terms, postal questionnaires still account for over 40 percent, although this has been in decline over the years.

Error in survey design and execution

Anything that can go wrong with a survey is a potential source of error. While it would be a futile venture to attempt to discuss every possible pitfall, the discussion here selects some of the more common factors that can result in data being of a quality that is lower than can reasonably be expected. Aspects of survey design that often cause trouble include:

- the specification of the population of cases to be studied,
- the frame used for the selection of respondents,
- the design of the questionnaire.

Aspects of survey execution that sometimes give rise to problems include:

- nonresponse,
- inaccurate, inappropriate or incorrect responses,
- interviewer error.

Population specification error

What is often referred to as the "target population" is the set of cases that the researcher would, ideally, like to study. This should be defined carefully and should include:

- a specification of the type of case that is the focus of the research,
- the geographical extent or location of the study,
- the time frame involved.

An example might be a study of "all private motorists in England and Wales who have driven their own, a rented or a borrowed car in the past four weeks". Any element in this specification that is left out will result in an incomplete definition of the population to be studied, yet it is surprising how many researchers do not specify their population very carefully, and in some published research there is no specification at all. Ideally, too, there should be some statement or estimate of the numbers of cases involved.

Researchers sometimes choose an inappropriate set of cases from which to collect data. Thus the relative ease of contacting married women who are not in full-time employment and who are looking after the children at home has resulted in perhaps too much reliance on responses from this quarter. A lot of published academic research involves taking students as cases for further study, presumably because they are at hand and are more easily persuaded to complete questionnaires or take part in group discussions, experiments or depth interviews. This is fine if the focus of the research is one that relates specifically to students, but all too often students are taken as a "sample" of the general public. If the limitations inherent in doing so are explained by the researcher and the possible effects on the results are seriously considered this may be acceptable. What is certainly less acceptable is where the population specification fails to justify the exclusion of certain types of cases where these might reasonably be included, for example restricting a study to adults defined as 18 or over when the views of younger teenagers may well be very important. Sometimes a specification of the population is entirely absent from the report of research findings and the researcher just refers to his or her "sample" without saying what it is a sample of.

Frame error

Even if the survey population is adequately specified, the total set of cases will, for most research, still need to be identified. This may entail using one or more lists. Suppose the researcher wanted to study males who are currently in paid employment in Scotland who suffer from osteoporosis. How could such a population be identified? Since no lists currently exist, or will not be accessible to the researcher, a total list – a "frame" – will need to be constructed. Candidates for frames might include lists of businesses in Scotland, lists of General Practitioners, lists of hospitals, the telephone directories or the Electoral Registers depending on whether the researcher tries to identify cases at work, through medical centers, through hospitals, by telephoning individuals at home. Some of these procedures may be combined. The frame or frames chosen will, clearly, affect the quality of the survey results. Some of the frames will include large numbers of people who are not of interest to the researcher and will need to be screened out; some lists may miss out members of the survey population.

The frame plays a fundamental role when cases in the population are to be sampled (Chapter 8 takes up the issue of sampling). The sampling frame may not be identical to the target population, for reasons explained later, but will, nevertheless, constitute the set of cases about which inferences are made from the sample. Some writers have called this the "inferential" population. To make life even more complicated, the researcher may make inferences about various subgroups in the population, so there may be several inferential populations.

Ideally, the nature of the target population should determine the type of frame. In practice it may be the other way round. Thus a researcher wishing to study *people* who have been discharged from hospital over a period of time in a specified area, will find that hospital lists are of discharges, and people may have been discharged more than once or discharged in a different area or in a different hospital. So, the frame forces the researcher to study discharges rather than unique individuals who have been discharged within the time frame.

Constructing a frame may be one of the most difficult tasks the survey designer faces. The cost in terms of time and money in constructing the frame must be weighed against the gains in the efficiency and accuracy of the survey results. Deficiencies in the frame can introduce error where the frame is to be used for a census and may cause bias in survey estimates when the frame is to be used for sampling. **Frame errors** may be grouped into six main categories:

Frame errors Errors arising from the use of lists of the population to be studied that have various shortcomings.

- ▪ missing population cases,
- ▪ inclusion of nonpopulation cases,
- ▪ duplication,
- ▪ failure to account for clustering,
- ▪ incorrect auxiliary information,
- ▪ incorrect accessing information.

Failure to include some members of the population of cases is probably the most serious type of frame error since it can be extensive, difficult to detect and difficult to measure. It is often referred to as "undercoverage", "noncoverage" or "incomplete coverage". Frames may, alternatively, contain cases that are not part of the target population, sometimes called "overcoverage". This is usually not too serious since nonpopulation cases (and nonexistent cases like empty houses or deceased persons) can normally be recognized. In some surveys undercoverage and overcoverage will tend to cancel each other out. Thus, in a population census, a person erroneously omitted from one enumeration distract may be erroneously included in another. The end result is a "net coverage error".

Duplication of cases in a frame, such as will occur in the *Yellow Pages*, will, clearly, produce frame error for censuses and for samples will undermine probability of inclusion calculations. Clustering – the selection of cases within small geographical areas – may cause errors where frame elements include clusters of target population cases. This often happens where the researcher samples households, but households may contain more than one population target case. For censuses this may not be a problem, but as a sampling frame may well result in bias.

Incorrect auxiliary information is a problem only if such information is to be used for special sampling techniques, but incorrect accessing information will have the same effect as undercoverage since the result may be a noncontact. Thus a university wishing to survey its alumni may well have a full and correct list of names, but addresses may well be out of date or unknown.

It is often necessary to use imperfect frames for a survey. This may be a conscious decision in view of the time or expense of building a better frame. One way of dealing with the problem is to redefine the target population – the target population is simply considered to be that population that can be accessed by the frame. In terms of simplicity and cost it has a lot to recommend it – and it is not always a poor technique. Sometimes the result still enables the survey to obtain its objectives. An alternative that is sometimes possible is to use a technique that will identify missing population cases, for example using random digit dialing, which was explained earlier in this chapter. Finally, it may be possible to integrate more than one frame to create a master frame that is more correct than any of the constituent frames. Failing these techniques, the researcher will just have to live with the frame limitations, warning the reader of some of the inadequacies.

Questionnaire design error

There are many things that can go wrong both in the design of individual questions and in the overall design of the questionnaire. Some of these problems arise because the researcher has not followed the guidelines for good questionnaire design explained in the previous chapter, in particular the stages for questionnaire construction, for question wording, routing and sequencing. Any of these problems will result in errors of various kinds and their extent is unlikely to be known. It has been shown many times over that the responses people give to questions is notoriously sensitive to question wording. However, answers are also affected by the response alternatives they are given in fixed-choice questions, by whether or not there is a middle category in a rating scale, by whether or not there is a "don't know" filter, or by the ordering of the questions, the ordering of the responses, or their position on the page. All the researcher can do is to minimize the likelihood of errors arising from poor questionnaire design through design improvements.

Questions on sensitive or embarrassing topics need to be handled with care. Subjects that tend to be sensitive to most people and in most cultures include money, voting, religion, sexual activity, criminal behavior, and the use of alcohol and drugs. Questions that deal with being well-informed or cultured, fulfilling moral and social responsibilities or being a good citizen are likely to suffer from what is sometimes called social desirability bias and may well result in over-reporting of what is seen as socially desirable behavior. There may, on the other hand, be under-reporting of behavior that may be seen as socially undesirable. Social desirability bias is more likely in a face-to-face interview and in these circumstances a self-completed questionnaire may be preferable. If they are to be used in an interview it is important that low prestige answers are as easy to give as higher prestige ones. So, instead of asking, for example: "Did you vote in the last general election?" it may be preferable to phrase it so that an admission of nonvoting is made easier: "We have found that many people did not manage to vote in the last election. How about you – did you manage to vote in the last election?"

Nonresponse error

A source of error in virtually all survey research is nonresponse. It is seldom that all individuals who are selected as potential respondents are successfully contacted, and it is seldom that all those contacted agree to co-operate. In coping with nonresponse error it is difficult to appreciate all the many things that can go wrong with an attempt to contact a designated individual. Figure 7.3, for example, illustrates a variety of outcomes of an attempted telephone contact.

Noncontacts are unlikely to be representative of the total population of cases. Married women with young children, for example, are more likely to be at home during the day on weekdays than are men, married women without children or single women. The probability of finding somebody at home is also greater for low income families and for rural families. Call-backs during the evening or at weekends may minimize this source of bias, but it will never be eliminated.

The **contact rate** takes the number of eligible cases contacted as a proportion of the total number of eligible cases approached. Interviewers may be compared or monitored in terms of their contact rates. Those with low rates may be required to undergo further training if, on investigation, it appears not to be the result of working in a difficult area. Attempts have been made to adjust for noncontact bias by **weighting** answers against the probability of respondents being at home. The weightings are derived by asking respondents on how many days they were at home during the five preceding days. The answers of those who were less likely to be at home are given more weight than those who are at home most days on the basis that these are the ones likely to be missed out.

Contact rate The number of eligible respondents successfully contacted as a proportion of the total number of eligible respondents approached.

Weighting The application of a multiplying factor to some of the responses given in a survey in order to eliminate or reduce the impact of bias caused by under- or overrepresentation of respondents with particular characteristics.

FIGURE 7.3

Telephone survey contact outcomes

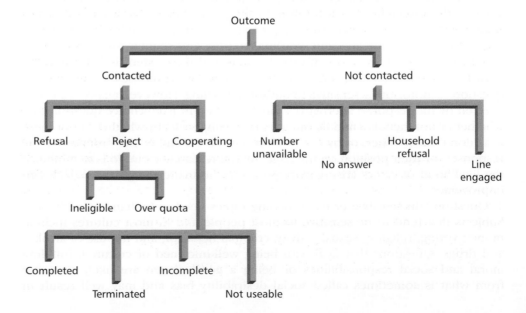

Potential respondents who have been contacted may still refuse co-operation for a whole variety of reasons including inconvenience, the subject matter, fear of a sales pitch, or negative reaction to the interviewer. The **refusal rate** generally takes the number of refusals as a proportion of the number of eligible cases contacted. Once again, refusals are unlikely to be representative. Refusals are more likely among women, nonwhites, the less educated, the less well off and the elderly (De Maio 1980). The detection of refusal bias usually relies on checking differences between those who agreed to the initial contact and those who agreed only after later follow-ups on the assumption that these are likely to be more representative of refusals.

Refusal rate The number of refusals in a survey as a proportion of the number of eligible respondents contacted.

Most researchers report a **response rate** for their study and this will normally combine the ideas of a contact rate and a refusal rate. However, in terms of its actual calculation a bewildering array of alternatives is possible. At a minimum it is:

Response rate The number of completed questionnaires as a proportion of the total number of respondents approached.

$$\text{response rate} = \frac{\text{Number of completed questionnaires}}{\text{Number of cases approached}}$$

Some researchers will argue, however, that it is misleading to include those approached but found to be ineligible for the study as a "nonresponse" so,

$$\text{response rate} = \frac{\text{Number of completed questionnaires}}{\substack{\text{Number of cases successfully contacted and} \\ \text{deemed to be eligible} + \text{noncontacts}}}$$

Yet others will argue that the same applies to noncontacts, terminations and rejects. The result will be dramatically different calculations of the response rate. Whichever of these is reported, however, what is important as far as error in measurement is concerned is the extent to which those not responding – for whatever reason – are in any way systematically different from those who successfully completed. Whether or not this is likely to be the case will depend substantially on whether or not there were call-backs and at what times of the day and days of the week individuals are approached.

The UK, as in most countries, has experienced a decline in response rates over the years. Meier (1991) reports that the 30-year trend between 1960 and 1990, as experienced by the National Readership Survey (which is explained in Chapter 16), shows a drop in response rates from 77 percent to 62.6 percent. Most of this is accounted for by an increase in refusals, which now account for 50 percent of the nonresponses. This is despite an increase in the number of call-backs made by interviewers from an average of 2.4 in 1983 to 3.4 by 1989. The NRS is generally regarded as a "model" of sampling and survey analysis and its response rate is somewhat higher than many interview surveys. Thus even the Government's National Food Survey manages only just over 50 percent. For mail surveys, the response rate is often under 30 percent.

Apart from total nonresponse there will, in addition, usually be item nonresponse where individuals agree to participate in the survey, but refuse to answer certain items. A refusal to answer is not always easy to distinguish from a "don't know", but both need to be distinguished from items that are not responded to because they have been routed out as inappropriate for that respondent. All, however, are instances of "missing values", which is a topic taken up in Chapter 11.

Researchers faced with nonresponse have a number of options:

- simply report the response rate as part of the findings,
- try to reduce the number of nonrespondents,
- allow substitution,

■ assess the impact of nonresponse,

■ compensate for the problem.

Many researchers choose to report survey results based only on data derived from those responding and simply report the response rate as part of the results. This shows that the researcher is unaware of the implications of nonresponse, believes them to be negligible, or has chosen to ignore them. Nonresponse may not itself be a problem unless the researcher ends up with too few cases to analyze. What is important is whether those not responding are in any significant ways different from those who do. In postal surveys typical response rates are 20–30 percent and it is unlikely that there will be no or even little nonresponse error.

The number of nonrespondents can usually be reduced through improvements in the data collection strategy. This might entail increasing the number of callbacks, using more skilled interviewers, or offering some incentive to potential respondents. The effort to increase the rate of return becomes more difficult, however, as the rate of return improves and costs will rise considerably. Allowing substitution can sometimes be a sensible strategy in a sample survey, provided the substitutes are selected in the same way as the original sample. This will not reduce bias from nonresponse, but it is a useful means for maintaining the intended or needed sample size. For censuses, substitution is, of course, not an option.

Assessing the impact of nonresponse calls for an analysis of response rates, contact rates and so on, plus an investigation of potential differences between respondents and nonrespondents, and some model of how these relate to total survey error. There are various ways of checking for nonresponse bias. Researchers sometimes take late returns in a postal survey as an indication of the kinds of people who are nonresponders. These are then checked against earlier returns. In an interview survey, supervisors may be sent to refusers to try to obtain some basic information. Interviewers can also be sent to nonresponders in a postal survey. Another technique is to compare the demographic characteristics of the sample (age, gender, social class and so on) with those of the population. If this is known, the comparison is relatively straightforward, although deciding on how "similar" they should be to be acceptable is not clear-cut. If the demographic of the population from which the sample was drawn is unknown, then census or other data thought to characterize the population may be used.

If differences are discovered then, again, this can simply be reported along with suitable caveats applied to the results. Alternatively, the researcher may try to compensate for the problem by using a weighted adjustment of responses. A weight is a multiplying factor applied to some or all of the responses given in a survey in order to eliminate or reduce the impact of bias caused by types of case that are over or under represented in the sample. Thus if there are too few women aged 20–24 in a sample survey compared with the proportions in this age group known to exist in the set of cases such that only 50 out of a required 60 are in the achieved sample, the number who, for example, purchased brand X in a measurement period of, say, four weeks, will be multiplied by a weighting which is calculated by taking:

$$\frac{\text{target sample number}}{\text{actual sample number}} = \frac{60}{50} = 1.2$$

This means that if, for example, this group are heavy purchasers of brand X, then estimates of sales of brand X will not be underestimated because that group is underrepresented in the sample from which the estimate is to be made. A worked example of weighting is given in Box 7.4

IN DETAIL
A worked example of weighting

BOX 7.4

A random sample of 100 adults produces 40 men and 60 women; but it is known that in the population from which the sample was drawn there are 48 percent men and 52 percent women. The weighting for the men would be 48/40 = 1.2 and for the women, 52/60 = 0.87. Table 7.1 shows the unweighted results from the sample, who were asked if they had drunk beer in the past four weeks. From this it can be said that 30/40 or 0.75 of the men had done so, whereas this was true for only 25/60 or 0.42 of the women. A projection to the population based on the unweighted results will suggest that 55 percent of the population (55 people out of the 100) had drunk beer in the past four weeks.

TABLE 7.1	Unweighted sample results		
	Drank beer	Did not drink beer	Total
Male	30	10	40
Female	25	35	60
Total	55	45	100

Table 7.2 shows the weighted results after the responses of the men have been weighted by 1.2 and the responses of the women by 0.87. This shows that the proportions of men and women is now correct at 48 percent and 52 percent. The new estimate will be based on the 57.7 percent having drunk beer in the past four weeks.

TABLE 7.2	Weighted sample results		
	Drank beer	Did not drink beer	Total
Male	36.0	12.0	48
Female	21.7	30.3	52
Total	57.7	42.3	100

Taylor (2000) argues that online surveys in particular suffer from substantial under-representation of some groups. This makes weighting even more crucial. The Harris Poll, explains Taylor, has developed what it calls "propensity weighting". Some 500 weighting criteria have been chosen to reflect the different propensities of individuals to respond to online surveys and include attitudinal and behavioral variables as well as the usual demographic ones. Included, for example, are measures of health status, political party identification and number of telephone lines.

Response errors

Response error deals with differences between respondents' reported answers and actual or true values of a survey item. Actual values can be obtained only by external validation such as checking shelves in the household for items that have been reported as having been purchased or through access to confirmatory sources like sales records, savings account balances, telephone bills and so on. Lacking any actual or true value, response errors arising through dishonesty, forgetfulness, faulty memories, unwillingness or misunderstanding of the questions being asked are notoriously difficult to measure. Research on response error, furthermore, is limited due to the difficulty on obtaining external validation.

Response error is affected by a large number of factors that will include:

- demographic characteristics of the respondent,
- perceptions, attitudes, expectations or motives of respondent,
- temporary situational circumstances,
- interviewer characteristics,
- interviewer–respondent interaction.

Both interviewer and respondent bring certain background characteristics and psychological predispositions to their interaction. The face-to-face interview and the telephone interview are interactive processes, each participant perceiving and reacting to the specific behaviors of the other. Evidence suggests that for face-to-face interviews, better co-operation and more information is obtained when backgrounds are similar and, furthermore, that interviewers' opinions, perceptions, expectations and attitudes all affect the responses they receive.

At the end of the day, individuals do as they please, and attempts to isolate variables that change behavior in a consistent manner are fraught with difficulties. The so-called "Hawthorne effects", where it was found that any changes made to experimental conditions increased productivity largely on account of the extra attention given to participants, are evidence of such problems.

Interviewer errors

In interview surveys, whether face-to-face or by telephone, interviewers may themselves misunderstand questions or the instructions for filling them in, they may be dishonest, inaccurate, make mistakes or ask questions in a nonstandard fashion. Interviewer training, along with field supervision and control can, to a large extent, remove the likelihood of such errors, but they will never be entirely eliminated, and there is always the potential for systematic differences between the results obtained by different interviewers.

KEY POINTS

There are many potential sources of error in the design and execution of surveys. Design issues include the inappropriate specification of the population of cases to be studied, shortcomings in the frame used for the listing or selection of respondents, and the design of the questionnaire itself. Potential problems in the execution of surveys include nonresponse, response error, and interviewer error. Errors in design and execution are sometimes described as "nonsampling" errors. This reminds us that in addition to these potential sources of error, there may well be errors that result from the sampling process. These errors are considered in the following chapter. The sum of sampling and nonsampling error is sometimes called "total survey error", which is also considered in Chapter 8.

Experimental research

Instead of relying on answers to questions addressed to individuals in a survey, in an **experiment** the market researcher tries out some marketing action on a small scale, carefully observing and measuring the results and controlling, as far as possible, for the effects of factors other than the marketing action being taken. Experiments have three main characteristics:

- the manipulation of one or more variables that the researcher wishes to test the effects of,
- a comparison of at least two measures of a dependent variable,
- the control of extraneous factors that may affect the results.

The factors that are manipulated by the researcher in an experiment are the independent variables, although they may be referred to as "treatments" or "interventions". An experiment is thus by definition interventionist; furthermore the intervention is up-front. It takes place first and the effects are observed afterwards. The dependent variables are the outcomes in which the researcher is interested. **Extraneous variables** are all variables other than the independent variables that may affect the test results. These are the variables that need to be controlled.

Groups or geographical areas to be subjected to a test are usually matched in such a way as to control for selected demographic characteristics that may affect the outcome of the research, for example, gender, age, social class, marital status or neighborhood type of those participating. In some cases, recruitment to tests may be restricted to certain kinds of people, for example users of a particular brand. Other factors that are *not* subject to control may, of course, also affect the results of the experiment. These might include unanticipated events during the course of the experiment, maturation or fatigue of those taking part, measurement inadequacies or errors, bias in the selection of respondents, or loss of participants during the experiment.

The main components of an experiment are summarized in Figure 7.4. The experimental group is affected by both the independent variables and the extraneous variables, but the control group should be affected only by the latter.

The key advantage of experimentation is that researchers choose which factors or variables they are going to try out. This in turn facilitates the drawing of conclusions in respect of causal relationships between variables. Indeed, some textbooks on market research, having made the distinction between exploratory, descriptive and causal research, proceed to equate causal research with experimental procedures. This is not totally justified, since it is possible to draw causal inferences from other types of research, although the analysis is "ex post facto", that is, after the event. In other words the investigation of relationships between variables and of the robustness of those relationships when other variables are controlled, is done *after* the data have been collected. Controls are established by performing

Experiment A research design in which one or more independent variables are manipulated by the researcher to examine their effects on one or more dependent variables, while controlling for extraneous variables.

Extraneous variable A variable whose effect is controlled, minimized or excluded in the design of an experiment.

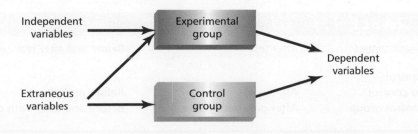

FIGURE 7.4

The components of an experimental design

analyses on subgroups of the sample instead of assigning categories of people to experimental situations.

Experiments tend to get used where new or revised elements or combinations of marketing mix variables would be difficult or expensive to try out on the entire market; hence the emphasis on "small-scale" tests in the definition of experimentation. Changing marketing mix variables for the total market is, in any case, not really "experimentation", but taking the decision itself.

Experimental design

Experiments may be designed in many different ways. There are, however, two main dimensions along which most can be identified:

- whether or not there is an attempt to make observations or take measurements *before* as well as after the test or manipulation has taken place,
- whether or not there are control groups of people who are similar in terms of the control variables to the test group, but are not subjected to the test condition.

Table 7.3 combines these two factors in a cross-classification, giving four different types of experimental design. **After-only designs** are not truly experimental, and amount only to a "try-it-and-see" approach on a small scale. Thus attitudes towards a product may be measured only after an advertising campaign. The problem is that there may be no measurement of what those attitudes were before the campaign began, so the amount of change is unknown. Furthermore, there is no control over extraneous variables that could have affected the results. Such designs cannot justifiably be used to test hypotheses, but can be useful where a "quick-and-dirty" analysis is adequate for the kinds of decisions to be taken.

After-only with control designs add a control group to the after-only design in order to take account of extraneous sources of bias. Participants are normally randomly assigned to the treatment and control groups, and in addition may be matched on a set of demographic variables. The difference between the experimental group and the control group is taken to be a result of the test conditions. However, there is no guarantee that both the control and experimental groups were not affected by extraneous factors and may have changed since before the test was conducted.

Before and after designs allow for some calculation to be made of the amount of change in a dependent variable before and after the test. There is, however, the danger that the process of making observations or taking measurements before the test may itself affect the behavior or attitudes of those participating. In some cases, of course, measurements of, say, sales, already exist before the test and may readily be compared with sales after it.

Before and after with control designs add a control group to the before and after design. This is the "full" experimental design. The difference between the

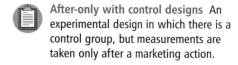 **After-only designs** An experimental design in which there is no control and a measurement taken only after a marketing action.

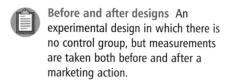 **After-only with control designs** An experimental design in which there is a control group, but measurements are taken only after a marketing action.

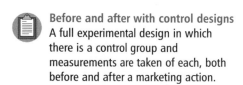 **Before and after designs** An experimental design in which there is no control group, but measurements are taken both before and after a marketing action.

Before and after with control designs A full experimental design in which there is a control group and measurements are taken of each, both before and after a marketing action.

TABLE 7.3	Types of experimental design	
Measurement	**After test**	**Before and after test**
Control		
No control	After only	Before and after
Control group	After only with control	Before and after with control

control group and experimental group before the test is compared with the difference between them after the test has been applied to only one group. The aim is to discount both extraneous variables and the impact of the first measurement on the second.

In practice, control groups are often not used in marketing experiments. More often there will be two or more matched experimental groups each given a different product formulation, pack design, or advertisements to try out or react to. A large number of experimental groups may be set up in different parts of the country to detect any regional differences. This may be done systematically by, in effect, "stratifying" by region using a **randomized block** design. Suppose there are three product formulations, A, B and C, to test; the market is limited to England, which is divided into three regions, North, Midlands and South. Within each region the three formulations could be tried separately in each of three branches of a retailer that has agreed to have the experiment staged in some of its branches. The design would look like Table 7.4. The assignment of the product formulations (and the selection of branch) could be by random processes. Analysis of variance (which is explained in Chapter 13) may be used to test the statistical significance of differences between product formulations, and to isolate this from between-region sources of error.

Sometimes a factor like region may be only one of two or three crucial factors. To take every combination, for example every product formulation in every region in every type of outlet, would produce a very large number. A more economical design is the **Latin square**. This could, for example, take every product formulation A, B and C and test it in each type of outlet (multiple, cooperative or independent) and in each region, but not in each type of outlet in each region. The design might look like that in Table 7.5. Here, there are two extraneous variables, region and outlet type. These form the rows and the columns of the table. Product formulations A, B and C are then assigned randomly to cells in the table, but subject to the restriction that each appears only once in each row and once in each column. A randomized block design with every combination would have required $3 \times 3 \times 3$ or 27 test sites. The Latin square reduces this to nine sites, but it is still possible to estimate error due to the two sources of error, again using analysis of variance. There is the assumption, however, that there is no relationship between type of region and type of outlet.

Randomized block experimental design An experimental design in which test units are grouped on the basis of one or more extraneous variables to ensure that each combination of characteristics is tested.

Latin square An experimental design that allows for the control or two noninteracting extraneous variables in addition to the manipulation of the independent variable.

TABLE 7.4	A randomized block design		
Region	**Type of product formulation**		
North	A	B	C
Midlands	A	B	C
South	A	B	C

TABLE 7.5	A Latin square design		
Region	**Type of outlet**		
North	A	B	C
Midlands	C	A	B
South	B	C	A

Factorial design An experimental design that allows for the effects of interactions between independent variables.

If it is necessary to take account of the effects of two or more factors at the same time, a **factorial design** may be more appropriate. Unlike the randomized block design and the Latin square, factorial designs allow for the effects of interactions between variables. This design is frequently used for product testing. Suppose a new biscuit can have different levels of salt content (high, medium and low), and different levels of sweetness (high, medium and low). Each combination may then be tested. These combinations are shown in Table 7.6. This would require nine matched groups of testers. This may well be feasible, but if there were, for example, also a crucial decision about making the biscuit with either butter or margarine, then 18 matched groups may be too many. Again, some kind of Latin square may be designed so that the butter and margarine biscuits are tested separately at each level of sugar content and at each level of salt content, but not in each combination.

Types of experiment

Experiments in marketing are of many different kinds, but a broad distinction can be made between:

- laboratory experiments,
- field experiments.

Laboratory experiments take place in an artificial environment in which the experimenter has direct control over most, if not all, the crucial factors that might affect the experimental outcome. They are often used for product testing, package testing, and in advertising effectiveness studies. Sometimes their purpose is to optimize the marketing mix *before* a product or service is exposed to the open market; such tests may be referred to as "pretests". However, laboratory experiments may also be used on existing or previously launched products and may be referred to as "post-tests". For either type of experiment, a key dilemma is that while elements of the marketing mix such as formulation, packaging, pricing and so on are likely to be the subject of separate experiments to help assess the contribution made by each to the overall performance, perceptions of overall performance will be influenced by the interaction and impact of all these elements together. Ideally, some attempt to assess the interaction effects needs to be included in the design of experiments.

 Laboratory experiment An experiment that takes place in an artificial environment set up by the researcher.

There are three main research environments in which laboratory type experiments may be conducted:

- hall tests,
- van tests,
- test centers.

In hall tests, people are recruited off the street or shopping precinct in the vicinity of the hall that has been hired by the research agency. The purpose is to show products, packages or advertisements to people selected by quota sampling in order to measure their reaction. Selection is often restricted to users of the

TABLE 7.6	A factorial design				
Sugar content			**Salt content**		
1	1A		1B	1C	
2	2A		2B	2C	
3	3A		3B	3C	

product being tested. Where hall tests are used for product testing, the products are generally new or modified, and the aim is to obtain a measure of acceptance, preference, or attitude. The tests are often blind and comparative. Not all products, of course, are suitable for hall tests. Thus toiletries would be more suited to home placement tests. However, hall tests are popular for food and drink. Samples tend to be quite large (maybe 500 or so) and spread over several venues and probably in different parts of the country. They may be subject to various forms of experimental design like randomized block or Latin square.

Van tests are similar to hall tests, but recruitment is to a mobile van that can be taken to many different venues. Van tests have the advantage that all the equipment needed for testing does not need to be set up in every location. However, space may be too restricted for some types of test.

Test centers may be used in preference to vans or halls where the product for testing is too large, expensive or complicated to be taken to the consumer. An example is the **car clinic**, which is a product test on vehicles held in a test center. Respondents are invited to evaluate one or more individual aspects of car design such as exterior styling, roominess, or interior layout. For a description of the procedures used in such clinics, see Wimbush (1990).

What actually takes place in a hall, van or test center is often really only a survey in which respondents are asked questions and their responses noted. Although they are usually called "hall tests" or "van tests" they are experiments only if there are before and after measures and, ideally, if there are control groups. This is frequently not the case.

Field experiments are conducted in a realistic research environment in which the products are exposed to the open marketplace and tested in situations where they will be bought, used or consumed in circumstances similar to those where these activities will normally happen. The degree of control exercised by the researcher is considerably less than for a laboratory experiment, but, being less artificial, may be a better guide to future behavior. Field experiments are used mainly for trying out products or marketing mix variables in the marketplace in either the home or factory, or in a selected test area. Inevitably this makes them more expensive than laboratory experiments since the products need to be made, packaged, priced, possibly even promoted, in their final form. Exposure, furthermore, means that competitors become aware of what the company is about, and may copy the idea and perhaps even launch it first.

Many factors make field experiments more difficult to control than laboratory experiments, for example uncharacteristic competitor activity during the course of the test. At the same time, however, there are important elements in the marketing mix that do not lend themselves to laboratory tests, for example experiments relating to distribution, trade incentives or merchandising. Relying on the results of experiments in an artificial laboratory may be an unsound basis on which to make serious estimates of what will happen in a national launch of a new product.

The principles of experimental design explained earlier apply as much to field experiments as to those in the laboratory, so decisions have to be made about the use of data or taking observations before as well as after the test and whether or not there will be control groups or control areas. The main types of field experiments that may be distinguished include:

- in-home placement tests,
- store tests,
- test marketing,
- social intervention,
- action research.

In-home placement tests give selected consumers the product to try at home and to report back. Several large companies make regular use of products placed

Van test A survey or experiment that takes place in a mobile van.

Test center A survey or experiment that takes place in a fixed center.

Car clinic A form of experiment in which cars are evaluated in a test center.

Field experiment An experiment conducted in a realistic research environment.

In-home placement test Gives selected consumer a product to try at home and to report back.

Product testing panel A panel of consumers who have agreed to try out or test products on a regular basis.

with panels of consumers, which are sometimes referred to as **product testing panels**. Demographic and product-use characteristics of panel members are recorded, and experimental and control groups with the required characteristics for the particular tests are then selected. Test products are distributed by hand or through the post to panel members who complete questionnaires on the reactions to the products received. There is the danger, of course, that panel members learn from their testing experience and cease to be typical consumers. However, if the panel is sufficiently large it is possible to avoid overexposure of panel members to a particular type of product. On the other hand, if panel members receive products too infrequently, their level of interest tends to drop and the questionnaire response rate drops.

Store test The testing of a range of price and package formulations in a number of selected retail outlets.

Some of the elements of the marketing mix such as packaging and point of sale promotions lend themselves to **store tests**, although some manufacturers are tempted to try out new products or price adjustments in selected stores. The design of some experiments amounts to no more than "let's try it in a few shops and see if it sells" strategy. However, the more thoughtful designs of store test will take account of:

- the need to include a cross-section of types of retail outlet,
- the need to allow for regional differences,
- the need for "control" stores matched against those trying the test product,
- the completeness, accuracy and validity of the data that will be used to measure the results of the test.

Obtaining the co-operation of stores to participate in the tests is often a problem. Such co-operation, furthermore, needs to extend to allowing the researchers to control the conduct, layout or positioning of the test product. For most in-store tests the effect of the test is measured by changes in sales, but for consumer promotions may in addition be measured in interviews with matched groups of consumers.

Test marketing A controlled experiment carried out in a limited, but carefully selected test market.

Test marketing is a controlled experiment carried out in one or more limited, but carefully selected, parts of a market area. Test marketing uses a range of experimental designs to predict and explore the consequences of one or more marketing actions for new or modified product introductions, or to estimate the payoffs and costs of changes in the marketing mix for existing products.

The "consequences" (the dependent variables) that test marketing seeks to predict might include:

- sales by volume and by value,
- market shares,
- profitability and return on investment,
- consumer behavior, e.g. trial and repeat purchase, and attitudes concerning products,
- the reactions of retailers and distributors to the product,
- the effects of different marketing strategies in different test areas.

The conduct of test marketing includes a number of key stages:

- planning,
- pretests,
- main test,
- post-test,
- evaluation.

Planning includes defining clearly the problem or problems to which the test marketing is addressed and the measures that will be used to evaluate the outcome. It also means deciding where the test is to be conducted. In selecting test areas it will be necessary to pay attention to:

- the demographic structure of the area, which should be representative of the total market,
- the industrial and occupational structure,
- the structure of retailing and distribution,
- the availability and use of media, especially local newspapers that could be used for advertising.

Once the test areas have been selected, it is necessary to pretest measurements of the variables to be used to evaluate outcomes – it is changes in these as a result of the test that will be recorded. Sometimes sufficient base data may already be available; sometimes it may be necessary to conduct primary research. More often, manufacturers will purchase into retail panels so that they can monitor the effects of the test over a period of time. Pretests may also be carried out in areas that are to be used as "controls", that is, not subject to the experimental stimulus.

The main test might involve the launch of a new or modified product along with associated marketing communications, or the change in the marketing mix itself, for example a new pricing policy. The duration of the test has to be long enough to allow the situation to stabilize after the new experimental conditions have been imposed. In the post-test, measurements are repeated of the key dependent variables and compared with measures derived from the pretest.

In the last stage of evaluation, account needs to be taken of the factors that may have influenced the results, and some prediction made of what is likely to happen in a national launch. This is not a simple matter of extrapolation of the results in the test area to the whole country – that would be dangerous. It means taking account of any special circumstances in the test area, including actions of competitors, that may not hold for the country as a whole.

Test marketing has not been so fashionable in recent years, largely because there are a number of problems with it. Thus test marketing may not be the best way of predicting sales or market shares when:

- surprise is vital to the success of the product,
- lead times are too short to protect the advantage of being first into the market,
- competitors can easily sabotage the tests, for example, by running a competitive advertising campaign in the test area,
- competitors are already doing tests that you can capitalize upon,
- the costs and risks of launch are low,
- the product is subject to rapidly changing fashion,
- the product life cycle is very short.

Quite apart form the circumstances in which test marketing is inappropriate, it can also be very expensive. Thus the direct costs include:

- equipment or plant needed to make the new or modified product,
- the advertising and employment of advertising agencies to support the test product,
- the research data needed for the pretest and the post-test; this may mean purchasing syndicated data from consumer panels or retail panels,
- sales promotions at the point of sale,
- dealer discounts and incentives for participating in the test.

In addition, there will be indirect costs that include:

■ the opportunity cost of what the company could be doing instead of the test market,

■ the management time taken up with the tests,

■ the diversion of salesforce activity on the new product,

■ the impact of the test product on the sales of other products in the range,

■ the cost of letting the competition know what you are up to.

Perhaps the key problem of test marketing, however, is that of projecting the results in the test area to the total market. Test results may be unrealistic because:

■ there is experimenter effect, for example salesmen have been trying harder to make the new product a success,

■ special inducements may have been used, for example to get traders to accept the product,

■ competitors may deliberately (or unwittingly) confound your results,

■ many retail chains will not allow companies to sell products in only part of the country.

Attempts have been made by market research companies to minimize the effects of some of these drawbacks by developing:

■ mini-test marketing,

■ simulated test market modeling.

Mini-test marketing A simulation of test marketing conditions without exposing the product to the open market and without incurring the cost of a full test market.

Mini-test marketing is designed to simulate test marketing conditions without exposing the products to the open market and without incurring the costs of a full test market. Its purpose is to estimate or predict potential sales volume or market share for new products. Research International ran a Mini Test Market for over 20 years. This consisted of a panel of 1000 households who were visited weekly by a mobile grocery van fitted out like a supermarket, but which was operated by the company itself. All products in the van were barcoded, and the panel member had a shopping card with an identification number. The actual purchases made by panel members, including quantity, brand, size, price and any special offers were recorded electronically at the checkout using EPOS equipment. Panelists were given a magazine that contained high-quality advertisements for selected products including the one being tested. The procedure enabled measures to be taken of the cumulative market penetration achieved by the new product, the repeat purchases made, and the average purchase quantity.

There are a number of advantages of using mini-test markets:

■ they avoid exposing the test product in the open market until its repeat purchase potential is known,

■ they require only small quantities of the test product,

■ they need advertising only in embryo form,

■ they obtain results more quickly than in the open market because awareness of the test product is rapidly obtained through the magazine,

■ new products are tested in a real-life market situation alongside competing products, and may be supported by advertising, promotions and merchandising,

■ the agency can control the range of competitive products on sale and the competitive pricing, promotion and so on,

■ different versions of the product can be tried out in different parts of the country.

Research International finally had to abandon its Mini Test Market, however, because of mounting overheads. Furthermore, since it was a real shop on wheels, it had to be run every day, whether or not there was a client, while competition from the superstores meant that people could not be bothered with the van, and it still took 16–20 weeks to complete a study.

Simulated test market modeling uses sophisticated modeling techniques to estimate trial and repeat purchase for new, modified or relaunched products. Trial and repeat purchases are, in turn, used to make predictions of sales volume and brand shares that will be achieved. These models are described in detail in Chapter 16. They are not really "field" experiments since most are based on some kind of hall test in which a product or product concept test takes place.

Social interventions are often undertaken by governments, governmental bodies, local authorities or large charities using social marketing to change people's behavior, for example not to drink and drive, smoke or take drugs or to eat more fruit and vegetables, consume less fat or take more exercise. The intervention may take the form of a media campaign, educational activities, taste tests, changes in school food, family or community involvement, motivational interviewing, leafleting or some combination, indeed all of these together. The bodies responsible for these campaigns need feedback on how effective their campaigns were, and recommendations on how to enhance their efforts. Specific geographical areas or certain social groups are selected at which the social marketing campaign is aimed, while a comparable area or group is taken as a control. Usually the design is a before and after with control. The change before and after the campaign in the experimental group is then compared with any changes that may have occurred anyway in the control group. Box 7.5 describes one such intervention.

The problem with evaluating such social interventions is that the campaigns are invariably complex and multifaceted. This makes it difficult to single out the impact of any particular campaign element. It has been argued, for example by McKinlay (1993), that traditional experimental designs may not be appropriate, particularly where the objectives of the intervention may be unclear, where the boundaries of the intervention are "fuzzy", where the nature of the intervention continually changes, and where there is uncertainty about the causes and effects of such interventions.

Action research is distinguished by being not only interventionist, but also iterative. Essentially it involves a group of people, including the researcher, who work together to improve their work processes by going through a cycle of activities that include planning, acting, observing and reflecting (Carson et al. 2001). The term was first coined by Lewin some 60 years ago (Lewin 1946). His concern was to make use of scientific knowledge to make social improvements. In a contemporary marketing context a small team or workforce may, for example, be set up to reduce the company's time in getting a new product to market. It would apply what is currently known about the processes of new product development to

Simulated test market modeling The use of sophisticated modeling techniques to estimate trial and repeat purchase rates for new, modified or relaunched products.

Social intervention The introduction of one or more marketing techniques in order to observe its effects on social behavior.

RESEARCH IN ACTION
A social intervention campaign

BOX 7.5

Birnbaum et al. (2002) report the results of a multicomponent school-based intervention aimed at raising the consumption of fruit and vegetables using a before-and-after design with exposure to different levels of intervention plus a control group where there was no intervention. The fruit and vegetable intake was measured for 3500 students from 20 schools in Minnesota. It concluded that while school-environment interventions were ineffective on their own, when combined with classroom intervention and influence from peer groups they resulted in improved fruit and vegetable intake.

improve the current situation. In turn the goals of science and the development of theory may also be followed. It involves collaboration and participation by both researcher and client; it is ongoing, iterative and a learning process.

Action research is a process that often occurs in management anyway even though it may not be called "action research" and may not explicitly follow its procedures. As an approach to research it runs counter to the one-way mirror of the marketing physicist – the positivist approach. It is closer to the marketing physician – it is activist, goal-oriented and interventionist. The account of action research by Carson et al. (2001) is in their book on qualitative marketing research, but is included here under the experimental framework in a chapter on quantitative research methods. In reality an action research project is likely to use some combination of qualitative and experimental elements. There will be elements of thought, discussion and reflection that may be captured as narrative and there will be attempts to try out new ways of doing things and observing the results. The researcher may play different roles in the research: technical consultant, facilitator, member of the team or some combination.

Analytic induction A method of qualitative data analysis that provides a logic for generating and testing theory in an interactive process in the same study.

Action research has been both acclaimed and criticized. It is seen by some as nonscientific and anecdotal and difficult to publish (Jonsson 1991). In an attempt to counter such criticism, Wilson (2004) reports an action research study aimed at improving how decision support systems (DSS) can be used in strategic marketing planning. This involved the iterative development of a prototype DSS for the task, the trial of various versions of the DSS in live marketing planning exercises in a range of 11 organizations, and the evaluation of the results with a view to informing further development of the DSS. To underline the validity of the study, Wilson uses a method of qualitative data analysis called **analytic induction** which provides a logic for generating and testing theory iteratively in the same study. Analytic induction is explained in more detail in Chapter 10. Action research, he claims, is a valuable addition to the methodological armory, catering for cases where interventions need to be made and evaluated in an iterative, theory-building way.

Perry and Gummeson (2004) suggest that action research is rare in marketing for a number of reasons. First, it is focused on internal employee resolution of problems rather than on markets and external forces. Second, there is an emphasis in business schools on positivist survey methodology and third, marketing researchers are either ignorant of action research or see it as a high-risk strategy in terms of their academic careers.

Experimental validity

Contamination The impact of factors or changes that are external to an experiment.

Maturation An extraneous variable in an experiment that is attributable to changes in the test units over time.

Drop-out The tendency in an experimental design for test units to become unavailable for repeat measurements.

Experimental designs are difficult to use in the real world and it is not always possible to isolate or account for the complexity of variables. Furthermore, care needs to be taken in interpreting the results and using them as a basis for marketing actions. Ideally, experiments should have both internal and external validity. Internal validity refers to the extent to which the manipulation or intervention alone accounts for the changes occurring. If external factors are at work and are not controlled by the design of the experiment, the internal validity is compromised. External validity refers to the extent to which findings can be applied in the real world. Laboratory experiments are more likely to have internal validity whereas field experiments are more likely to have external validity. Both, however, tend to suffer from **contamination**, **maturation** and **drop-out**. Particularly when the time interval between before and after measurement is lengthy, events may occur that will contaminate the results, for example there may have been an economic downturn that affected sales. The evaluation of social interventions may have been compromised where media campaigns aimed at the experimental group or area have also influenced the control groups or areas at which they were not directed. Individuals between the before and after measurements have changed their circumstances, become bored or more experienced or may, for a number of different reasons, have dropped out or become unavailable for the follow-up.

KEY POINTS

In an experiment the market researcher tries out some marketing action on a small scale, carefully observing and measuring the results and controlling, as far as possible, for the effects of factors other than the marketing action being taken. There are several types of experimental design, but a "full" or "proper" experiment involves a before and after design with control groups. The other designs are sometimes called "quasi-experimental". Experiments may be carried out in the laboratory or in the marketplace and there are several versions of each. However, the distinction between laboratory and field experiments sometimes gets a little blurred. Thus Research International's Mini Test Market was really part van test and part test marketing. Furthermore, different procedures may be used in combination. Thus participants in a hall test, say for a new brand of whisky, may be given a bottle to take home and try. They are subsequently telephoned or sent questionnaires to record their reaction.

It must be remembered that, since experiments are, by definition, small-scale and based on samples, they are subject to sampling error. This means that, although compared with surveys there are many more controls over extraneous variables, there will be random sampling fluctuations so that discovered differences between treatments may not, in fact, represent real differences in the population from which the sample was drawn. Alternatively, the failure to discover differences may also be a result of random errors.

Continuous research

In Chapter 1 continuous research was distinguished from ad hoc research. The latter is "one-off" research, usually geared to specific issues or problems and custom-designed for a particular company or client. As a "piece" of research, it has a beginning point and comes to a conclusion, going through a number of stages from an initial brief or analysis of the problem to be investigated to data collection, data analysis and the presentation of a final report. Continuous research, by contrast, takes measurements on a regular basis in order to monitor changes that are taking place, often in the consumer market, but maybe in the business market or even within the client organization itself. There is no envisaged end to the research process, and it is not normally custom-designed for a specific client. Because of the expense of setting up and maintaining a system for the continuous or regular collection and production of data, continuous research is typically syndicated, that is, the research process or the data or both are shared between a number of clients. Usually this means either that a large market research agency collects the data and sells them to a number of clients on a regular basis, or that several clients buy into a continuous survey conducted by the agency.

Some continuous research really *is* continuous in the sense that interviews are conducted every day of the year, even though aggregation of the results may take place weekly, two-weekly or four-weekly. Other research, which some purists might argue is, strictly speaking, not continuous, is conducted at regular intervals with a gap between periods of data collection. The continuity of data collection, whether periodic or not, may be achieved in one of two ways:

- obtaining data from the *same* individuals, households or organizations on a continuous or regular basis,
- picking a *fresh* sample of respondents every day or every measurement period.

Panel research uses the first procedure and regular interval surveys the second.

Panel research

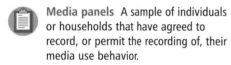

Market measurement panels A sample of individuals, households or organizations that have agreed to record, or permit the recording of, their activities or opinions in respect of an agreed range of products or services.

In panel research the same data are collected at regular intervals from a representative sample of a defined survey population. A panel is a sample of individuals, households or organizations that have agreed to record, or permit the recording of, their activities or opinions in respect of an agreed range of products or services on a continuous or regular basis. Panels are used mostly either to provide quantified estimates of market characteristics (**market measurement panels**) or of the use of the media (**media panels**). For the most part they measure behavior rather than attitudes, since there are problems in asking respondents for their attitudes towards products on a repeated basis. However, for the purpose of evaluating audience reaction to television or radio programs, television opinion panels or listeners' panels may be asked their opinions of the programs they have watched or heard.

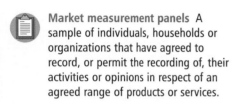

Media panels A sample of individuals or households that have agreed to record, or permit the recording of, their media use behavior.

Market measurement panels are themselves of two main kinds:

- consumer panels,
- retail panels.

Consumer panels

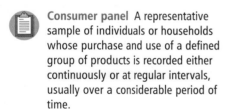

Consumer panel A representative sample of individuals or households whose purchase and use of a defined group of products is recorded either continuously or at regular intervals, usually over a considerable period of time.

Consumer panels are representative samples of individuals or households whose purchase and use of a defined group of products is recorded either continuously or at regular intervals, usually over a considerable period of time. The first commercial panel in the UK was launched in 1948. Since then the number of panel services available has grown steadily, and the defined groups of products concerned have extended from panels concerned with groceries and fresh foods to panels recording the acquisition of consumer durables and electrical goods, motorists' panels, household (nonfood) panels, and panels recording the purchase of toiletries and cosmetics, or baby products.

Unlike regular interval surveys whose respondents are approached for information only on one occasion (or twice if there is some kind of follow-up), panelists are asked to provide information or to perform data collection tasks on a regular basis, often without any specified time limit. Consequently, besides the problem of making the initial selection of panelists in such a way that they are representative of the population being studied, there is the additional problem of maintaining the representativeness of the panel over time. Furthermore, panels can provide consistent trend data over time only if, once they have been set up, there are no changes in panel methodology. Consequently, the initial design needs to be as accurate as possible, and capable of being sustained at a consistent quality over time.

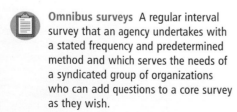

Omnibus surveys A regular interval survey that an agency undertakes with a stated frequency and predetermined method and which serves the needs of a syndicated group of organizations who can add questions to a core survey as they wish.

Recruitment to panels tends to be a little more difficult than for ad hoc surveys, since respondents are being asked to do rather more. Some recruitment may be on the back of another large-scale survey operation that the market research agency or one of its subsidiaries or sister companies is already conducting. Respondents to an **omnibus survey**, for example, who have the required demographic characteristics may be screened for willingness to participate in the panel at the time of the interview. Recruiters may then subsequently approach such respondents to explain the tasks involved, the incentives offered, and to give any training needed.

Once the panel has been recruited it needs to be maintained at a consistent quality of representativeness; furthermore, its members need to be encouraged to report regularly for as long as is desirable. Each year the panel is, of course, getting a year older and would, if no other changes took place in membership, rapidly become unrepresentative. It is, therefore, necessary to recruit younger members and to retire some of the older ones just to keep the age profile correctly balanced. However, for a variety of reasons, people leave the panel, or their circumstances change, for example they get married, set up separate households, have children and so on. In consequence there is the constant need to "balance" or "control" the panel by replacing those who leave with respondents whose demographic characteristics are underrepresented. It must be remembered, furthermore, that the population that the panel is meant to represent is itself changing all the time, and panel composition must reflect these changes.

To locate individuals or households required for panel balancing it is normal to use a database of screened respondents from a regular interval survey that the agency undertakes anyway. To keep panelists reporting, there is usually a system of newsletters, prizes, competitions, mystery gifts or points accumulated for catalogue gifts – it is not normal to pay them directly. The newsletter can be important for making the panelist feel a member of a team and to keep them informed of developments or reminders to complete certain tasks. If panelists repeatedly fail to report or to perform the agreed tasks then they may be dropped.

The capture of data from panelists is undertaken using one or some combination of the three main instruments of data capture: diaries, questionnaires or electronic recording devices. Until recently, diaries have been the most common. Diary design was considered in detail in Chapter 6. Diaries are designed either for the individual or for the household; in the latter case details will normally be entered by the housewife. The details collected will normally include:

- brand name,
- size of pack,
- flavor, color, type of dispenser, or other brand variant,
- price paid,
- quantity bought,
- any special offers,
- name of shop,
- type of shop.

Questionnaires have been used to a lesser extent, largely in an interviewer-based home audit procedure. Interviewers visit panel members on a regular weekly basis, they carry out a visual inspection of stocks of groceries and other household items by checking cupboards, pantries, fridges and so on, and enter on a questionnaire all items purchased since the previous week. Items consumed during the week are recorded from packaging or labels that are retained. The costs of undertaking home audits are, clearly, very high, and in practice they are seldom used.

New technology has transformed consumer panel data collection techniques, and Taylor Nelson Sofres's electronic panel, Worldpanel, is described in detail in Chapter 16. Essentially, it involves equipping each panel household with computer terminals and laser scanners for reading the barcodes on packs following each shopping trip.

Panels provide a wealth of data that, if not translated into succinct information that can be absorbed and acted upon, can readily become indigestible. Most panel operators offer both standard and special analyses. Standard trend analyses are produced usually at monthly or four-weekly intervals, and they show the progress of the market and its major brands since the previous period. Clients usually subscribe on an annual basis to receive these reports over the year. The reports are tables of figures that give results by product field grossed up to the national population, or to a particular region. Such tables typically show for the current month, the previous month and the same month in the previous year:

- sales volume for the total market, for each brand and each brand variant,
- consumer expenditure at current retail prices for the total market, for each brand and each brand variant,
- market shares for each brand,
- market penetration,
- special offers,
- average prices.

Special analyses tend to be fairly standard "optional extras". Thus a "source of purchase" analysis will show volume, value and prices paid by type of outlet, including breakdowns by key accounts like Tesco, Sainsbury or Asda. A "cumulative penetration" analysis will measure the rate of increase in the number of new buyers over time, and can be used to show the effect of promotional support. A "frequency of purchase" analysis shows the percentage of buyers purchasing each brand at least once, twice, three times and so on. This will show the extent to which a brand is dependent on a small number of regular buyers rather than a larger number of infrequent buyers. There will, in addition, be a variety of demographic analyses, describing the buyer profile of the market and its major brands in terms of age of purchaser, social class, household size, ACORN classification, presence of children and so on. Because panel data are longitudinal and can track individuals through time, it is possible to look at interpurchasing between brands, brand loyalty, repeat buying, and gains from and losses to competitors. These, in turn, can be used as inputs to making volume and brand share predictions (see Chapter 16).

Because panels are samples, they are subject to both sampling and non-sampling error. Although panels are balanced to keep them representative as far as possible, this is not always, if ever, totally achieved. In consequence, the results from panels are weighted to make finer adjustments for over and under representation of subgroups. In addition, they suffer from problems of coverage and pickup. Lack of coverage means that consumer panels often produce lower estimates of total sales than are reflected in either ex-factory shipments or trade estimates. Consumer purchase panels measure only purchases made by private households, not purchases by offices, forces bases, old people's homes, student accommodation, exports, purchase by other organizations or items lost, damaged or pilfered in transit. Some market research companies may apply "field weights" to their data to make adjustments for lack of coverage so that market estimates eventually reflect actual total market volumes and values.

Pickup errors result from tendencies of panelists to overlook some of their purchases, or not to know about the purchases made by other members of the household. Occasionally, deliberate falsification may be provoked by the complexity of the tasks respondents have to perform, or they may be suffering from lack of motivation and commitment to the panel. The level of pickup tends to vary from product to product, and may be anything from 50 percent to 200 percent of independent market estimates. However, provided this level is fairly constant then "product field" or "market size" weights may be applied before estimates are grossed up to the population.

Retail panels

Retail panels are representative samples (or, in some cases, the complete universe) of retail outlets whose acquisition, pricing, stocking and display of a defined group of products are recorded either continuously or at regular intervals. Such panels were first set up by the A. C. Nielsen Company in the USA in the 1930s. Nielsen began retail tracking operations in the UK in 1939. In the 1950s and 1960s demand tended to exceed supply and the key problem for any manufacturer to solve was efficient distribution to ensure product availability. In this situation, information on distribution was crucial. Nielsen rapidly expanded its operations and a number of companies set up competing retail panel services. The current Nielsen Retail Measurement Services are described in detail in Chapter 16.

Retail panels are used largely to provide estimates of over-the-counter sales of products, brand-by-brand and brand variant. This information is sometimes available directly from the use of electronic data capture techniques using barcode-scanning equipment. It is otherwise necessary to undertake a **retail audit**. This involves physically counting the stocks in the panel shops at the beginning and at the end of the audit period (usually four weeks or a month). By subtracting stocks for each brand and brand variant at the end of the audit period from deliveries and those stocks held at the beginning, sales can be deduced. Even where electronic data are available, it may still be necessary to undertake retail audits in order to determine the prices charged, the shelf-space allocated to brands, the quantities held in the "reserve" areas, and any in-store promotions. Auditors from the market research agency offering panel services visit the panel shops on a regular basis. They may spend two or three days in the shop, counting stocks and entering their observations into a portable data entry terminal. These may then be placed in a modem for transmission of the data to a central computer via the telephone.

Where universe data are not available, it is necessary to take a sample of shops from which to make estimates. The key problem with sampling retail outlets is that stores vary enormously in terms of turnover. Over- or underrepresenting stores of different sizes will seriously affect the estimates made. Consequently, it is necessary to stratify the selection of shops by turnover range as well as by type of shop (e.g. multiple, cooperative or independent) and by region. Unfortunately, in order to do this it is necessary to know:

- how many shops of a given type fall into a particular turnover range in that area,
- the annual turnover of the sampled shops,
- annual turnover of the universe.

Acquiring this information is a major undertaking. For most of the major multiples and for the co-operatives this information may be provided by the multiple chain, or by the Co-operative Wholesale Society in the case of co-operatives. For independents and smaller multiples Nielsen, for example, carries out an extensive enumeration followed by a survey of a sample of enumerated shops.

Once shops have been selected and have agreed to co-operate, data collection is likely to be some combination of:

- visual inspection of products on shelves and their location in the store,
- checking delivery notes,
- getting retailers to complete questionnaires or other records specially for the agency,
- obtaining data that have been captured electronically or that have been entered on a computerized database.

Retail panel A representative sample (or in some cases the complete universe of) retail outlets whose acquisition, pricing, stocking and display of a defined group of products is recorded either continuously or at regular intervals.

Retail audit The physical counting of stocks in a panel retail outlet both at the beginning and at the end of the audit period, plus a record of deliveries, to obtain sales for each band and brand variant of a defined group of products.

All operators of retail panels produce tables that give distribution and price data along with estimates of sales volumes and values on a brand-by-brand and brand variant basis. Since the major multiples normally supply data on deliveries to their outlets and allow access to their barcoded data only on the understanding that the tables do not identify particular named groups, the tables aggregate data for these groups. It is not possible, therefore, for example, to compare what is happening in Tesco with Sainsbury or Asda.

Consumer panels and retail panels compared

Both consumer panels and retail panels generate estimates of sales volumes, values and market shares on a brand-by-brand and brand variant basis every four weeks or every month. Such information helps companies to:

- evaluate company strengths and weaknesses in the marketplace,
- diagnose market opportunities and competitor threats,
- set realistic long-term objectives,
- develop plans to achieve them,
- monitor the impact of trends in the market.

Beyond this, consumer panels and retail panels are suited to different purposes. Consumer panels are able to track consumer behavior, for example in terms of purchase frequency and brand loyalty; retail panels can track what happens in the distribution system up to the point where the consumer makes a purchase. The manufacturer can, for example, tell how many shops who usually handle his stock were out of stock in the last period, what competitor brands are set alongside his own brands and in what kinds of shops, what the price differentials are, what levels of stock are held where in the shop, and how these have changed since the last measurement period.

Operators of both types of panel will make claims to the superior accuracy of their service for the data produced in common. Consumer panel operators will point out that by asking consumers about where they purchased their products, *all* the outlets selling the particular brand will be covered. Retail panels cover only those outlets included in the particular sample of shops. Because their data are derived from consumers, consumer panels are able to produce named group data, that is, data broken down by named account. Retail panels are restricted by their agreement with the major multiples, as explained above, *not* to produce such data. Retail panel operators will claim, on the other hand, that retail panels do not rely on the memories of consumers, but systematically record actual sales in the sample shops. Some of the data, furthermore, are not estimates based on samples, but universal data. They will argue, too, that in highly fragmented markets, consumer panels will pick up only small quantities of a particular brand. Retail panels, by contrast, will record all the sales of every brand in the sample shops. Since the services are, in many ways, complementary, the trend has been for the larger agencies to offer both types of panel.

Other types of panel

Media panels are used mostly for television audience measurement and for estimating audience appreciation of television and radio programs. These panels are described in detail in Chapter 16. Some panels are "single source", that is, they collect data both on product purchasing and on media usage. TNS, for example, has installed television set meters in a subset of 3000 of the 15 000 Worldpanel homes. These are called the tvSPAN panel, which itself is representative of the population.

Regular interval surveys

Regular interval surveys are surveys of respondents carried out at regular intervals using independent samples for each measurement period. Like panels, they are used for market measurement and for media usage, but, in addition, they are used by the Office for National Statistics and other government bodies for collecting various forms of government statistics.

Market measurement regular interval surveys include:

- omnibus surveys,
- market tracking surveys.

Omnibus surveys

Omnibus surveys are surveys that market research agencies undertake to run with a stated frequency and with a predetermined method. Clients buy space in the questionnaire by adding and paying for questions of their own according to number and type of question. The agency draws a fresh sample of respondents each time, administers the questionnaire, processes the data and reports the results. This means that the costs of setting up the survey, administration, collection of demographic data and analysis are shared between several clients. Over the past decade omnibus research has become more popular, varied and competitive, giving clients the opportunity to buy inexpensive research as and when required. More than 30 companies in the UK now run such surveys; other companies "offer" the service on a consultancy basis, buying their fieldwork from those organizations actually running an omnibus. Omnimas, the biggest, is described in detail in Chapter 16. There are, however, different types of omnibus depending on:

- the general or specific nature of the population being sampled,
- the type of sampling method,
- the method of questionnaire administration.

General consumer omnibuses sample a general cross-section of the adult population, while special omnibuses are dedicated to specific groups in the population, for example motorists, mothers with babies, doctors, businessmen, architects, travel agents or farmers. Random omnibuses use random sampling techniques to select respondents, while quota omnibuses use random location or straight quota samples. The next chapter explains these forms of sampling. Random omnibuses tend to be a little more expensive, but the accuracy of the sampling is, on the whole, superior. They are worthwhile if good estimates are required of population values. Some omnibuses are personal, using face-to-face interviewing, while others use telephone research. The latter are quicker, but may work out a little more expensive; furthermore, no visual material can be shown to respondents. They tend to use a random selection methodology for selecting the telephone numbers, and then to impose quotas on age, sex and social class.

Consumer omnibuses tend to be run on a weekly basis while the more specialized ones may be monthly. Sample sizes vary from 1000 up to 3000. Telephone omnibuses are mostly 1000; face-to-face consumer omnibuses are typically between 1500 and 2000.

Most agencies have a master questionnaire with a classification section containing the demographic questions that are asked each time. These are usually completed at the end of the interview. The main part of the questionnaire is often divided into two sections: continuous and ad hoc. The continuous section includes questions that are inserted for clients on every survey. They will usually be in the same order and in the same place every time to avoid the effect on answers of changing positions. This will also mean that the questionnaire always

Regular interval surveys Surveys of respondents carried out at regular intervals using independent samples for each measurement period.

begins in the same way, which helps the interviewers to begin their interviewing. The ad hoc questions are usually inserted on a first-come-first-served basis, but the agency will try to put them together in a sensible way. Question sets for competing fields cannot be allowed in the same survey.

Agencies tend to place few restrictions on the topics covered. However, questions on security, for example "Do you have a burglar alarm in your home?" may not be allowed. Some agencies place restrictions on the number of questions that may be included from any one client (or on the amount of time they take) plus an overall limitation on the size of the survey. The average number of questions per client is 6–10; omnibus surveys cease to be cost-effective if many questions are to be included. The questions themselves may be pre-coded or open-ended. Some agencies place restrictions on the number of code positions allowed, or may charge extra. Open-ended questions may cost up to double the cost of pre-coded ones. Sensitive probing of answers is not usually feasible – interviewers already have a tough time handling a questionnaire that is really a series of questionnaires going from topic to topic.

Some clients will submit their questions already worded in the way they want them; others require the help of the market research agency in framing them. Such help is normally included in the price of the question. Most companies will do split runs, that is, testing two or three versions of a question or question-set among different respondents. However, these can seriously complicate the organization of the survey. The use of show cards is fairly common; these might give definitions, lists of products or brands, photographs, copies of advertisements, telepics or pack fronts. Sometimes these may all be made into a specially produced booklet.

All suppliers of omnibus services make a charge per question, currently ranging from £200 per question to over £500. However, it would be misleading to buy into an omnibus on that basis alone. The analyses and services that are included as part of the price vary considerably. Some agencies charge extra for questions with many pre-codes, for prompt cards, show cards or other materials, and for open-ended questions. Some give discounts for more than a certain number of questions or for inserting them on a regular basis. Some give discounts when only part of the sample is being used. Some charge a joining fee that may vary from £100 to £500 or more. Sometimes this fee is waived when more than a certain amount of business is commissioned. Agencies have different approaches to deciding what counts as one question. A question with four sub-sections may be treated as one or as four questions.

Basic analyses of the pre-coded questions are usually available within a few days of fieldwork completion. Open-ended questions are usually post-coded (in cooperation with the client) and these will take a little longer. Results may be accumulated over a period of time to produce monthly, quarterly or even annual reports. Most agencies include standard breakdowns by key demographic questions within the price of the question. Optional extras include the production of charts, writing mini-reports, market or brand mapping, cluster analysis or analysis by one of the geodemographic systems like ACORN. The tables themselves will normally refer to volumes, frequencies or sterling values that have been grossed up to the population, usually after weighting.

Omnibus surveys may be used for continuous or for ad hoc purposes – or some mixture of the two. The range of uses to which clients put omnibuses includes:

- market measurement, for example the volume and value of sales, brand shares, frequency of purchase, brand loyalty, brand switching,
- assessing the effectiveness of an advertising campaign, for example by tracking brand or advertising awareness,
- media measurement, for example the readership of certain magazines,
- tracking the impact of or forecasting sales of new product launches,

- tracking brand image or corporate image,
- new product concept tests and product tests,
- test market assessment,
- product usage and attitude,
- testing questions using split run techniques,
- building up samples of minority groups.

The main advantages of omnibus surveys are:

- the questions are custom-designed and the results are confidential to the client,
- they are quick and relatively inexpensive where the information can be gathered with a few questions,
- they are there when needed and can be used at short notice,
- they are, on the whole, well-conducted and well-respected in the industry,
- they can obtain samples of a reasonable size for minority groups over a period of time,
- they can be used for recruitment purposes for other surveys.

Omnibuses are unsuitable, however, for detailed probing or where lengthy question-sets are required. Telephone omnibuses have the additional disadvantage that they cannot be supported by showcards or other visual materials. Sample designs are fixed by the market research organization and cannot be modified to suit client needs. Clients can, of course, shop around for an omnibus that is more suitable in terms of sample design.

Market tracking surveys

Market tracking surveys are carried out at regular intervals, but the agency designs the whole questionnaire, and the data collected are sold to as many clients as possible. Most tracking services are of advertising, brands, or campaigns. An example is Millward Brown's Awareness Index, which is explained in Chapter 16. The Target Group index offered by the British Market Research Bureau (BMRB) combines product usage with media exposure. The TGI is explained in detail in Chapter 16.

Market tracking surveys use a wide range of sampling techniques, although few go to the expense of random probability sampling. A key advantage of market tracking surveys is that it is possible to base analyses on large numbers of individuals, offering the ability to do lots of breakdowns. Clients can buy from the agency just those data that they require for their purposes. However, the results are not confidential and data are available to groups of competing manufacturers.

Market tracking survey A regular interval survey in which the agency designs the entire questionnaire and the data collected are sold to as many clients as possible.

Panels and regular interval surveys compared

The main advantages of panels over regular interval surveys include:

- sampling errors tend to be less since there is statistical association between successive measurements,
- memory errors will tend to be less because regular interval surveys depend on recall of purchases while panels either record purchases in a diary or they are recorded electronically,
- it is possible to follow through an individual's purchasing behavior over time, making it possible to analyze brand switching, brand loyalty, and repeat purchasing behavior.

The main advantages of regular interval surveys over panels include:

- over a period of time large numbers of respondents are interviewed, making it possible to build up samples of minority groups,

- it is possible to include attitude questions because there are no fears about respondent conditioning over time,

- they are cheaper to operate, largely because there is no panel maintenance to be undertaken,

- the real response rate tends to be higher because individuals are being asked to do less,

- they will pick up a higher proportion of purchases for products that are bought infrequently or only by minority groups,

- they are more flexible, for example it is easier to change the questions being asked without upsetting other clients,

- they can be used for questionnaires that take longer to complete.

These advantages and limitations need to be kept in mind when considering what kind of research is appropriate for resolving or analyzing the problems faced by a particular company.

KEY POINTS

Continuous research takes measurements of market characteristics on a regular basis in order to monitor changes that are taking place. There is no envisaged "end" to the research process, and the research is usually syndicated. The two main forms are panels and regular interval surveys. The former obtain data from the *same* individuals, households or organizations on a continuous or regular basis, while the latter pick a *fresh* sample of respondents every day or every measurement period. Panels are normally either market measurement panels or media panels. The former may be consumer panels or retail panels. Regular interval surveys for market measurement include omnibus surveys and market tracking surveys. Such panels are also used for media research.

The main advantage of continuous research is that it can track changes and trends, but it is expensive and clients normally need to subscribe to continuous services for minimum periods of time.

Client-based and academic quantitative research

Both client-based researchers and academic researchers use survey research, which is certainly the most popular in both camps. Over two-thirds of agency revenue comes from survey research. Comparable figures are not available for academic research, but a glance at papers for the European Marketing Academy Conferences over the years will quickly show the predominance of survey methodologies. The setting up and running of continuous research, however, is almost totally the preserve of the larger agencies, while academics are unlikely to run hall tests, van tests, or test markets. Social intervention research is more likely to be undertaken by academics, while action research is probably more common in a commercial context.

It would be too simplistic to say that client-based quantitative marketing research adopts the paradigm of the marketing physician and that academic research tends towards that of the marketing physicist. Client-based research will be solution-oriented, partisan and interventionist, but may well be objectivist in its ontology (a reality exists "out there" that is independent of the researcher's attempts to measure it) and positivist in its epistemology (it will utilize "scientific" methods, for example to generate and then test mathematically specified models). At the same time academics are constantly being urged to look at the practical and policy implications of their research. Academic research may also be interventionist in the sense that the manipulation of variables in an experiment are interventions; so are the changes that are brought about in social intervention research and action research.

When it comes to reporting the results of quantitative research and utilizing them, however, client-based researchers and academic researchers live on different planets. In the 1950s and 1960s some of the most enthusiastic contributors to scholarly marketing journals were practitioners – market researchers in industry, other organizations and in the market research agencies. Nowadays this is rare and the output, even for journals that claim practitioners among their target readership, is dominated by academic researchers. Although marketing activity in business and nonprofit organizations is essentially the laboratory for the academic researcher, the benefit to co-operating firms depends on communication of the results. However, a survey – albeit a small one – of marketing managers carried out by McKenzie et al. (2002) showed that none read any of the academic journals, although some read marketing magazines like *Marketing Week* on a regular basis. The authors concluded that academics are writing for each other even if that was not their intention. At the same time academics are being pressurized to publish only in refereed journals and this is only adding to the problem of communication.

Ethical issues

The market researcher has a duty to protect the identity of respondents, not revealing them to clients or to outside bodies. Completed questionnaires must be handled securely and any material that can identify questionnaires with respondents must be either destroyed or locked away. Experimental research raises further ethical issues. For the success of an experiment, it may be necessary to disguise the purpose of the research from participants. One way around this is to warn participants in advance that in experiments of the kind they are about to take part in often need to have their purpose disguised. They should, at this stage, also be told about the general nature of the experiment and what they will be asked to do. They need to be reassured that they can leave the experiment at any time and upon conclusion of the research they can be told the real purpose of the study.

SUMMARY

Quantitative research methods include survey research, experimental research and continuous research. Each of these comes in a number of different varieties, each with its own strengths and limitations. Survey research, whether ad hoc or continuous, can construct a lot of data from many respondents relatively quickly and produce results that should be generalizable to a wider population. Such research is particularly good for finding patterns of relationships between variables. How this is done is the focus of Chapter 12. Ad hoc surveys are geared to one-off problems and issues and are not particularly good for measuring change, which is the major strength of continuous research. All forms of survey research, however, are prone to inaccuracies and errors arising from their design and execution.

An experiment gives the market researcher much more control. The researcher controls the timing of the experimental treatment and the timing of the measurements of the effects. There is also more opportunity to control the impact of confounding variables to some extent. This makes it more effective for measuring and testing cause and effect relationships. Causal analysis is possible from the results of survey research, but it is rather less conclusive and open to different interpretations. There are several types of experimental design, but a "full" or "proper" experiment involves a before and after design with control groups. Experiments may be in the laboratory or in the field. The former allow for more control and are more likely to generate internal validity. Field experiments, however, are more realistic and will normally be better for external validity. Both, however, suffer from contamination, maturation and drop-out. Experiments are not always possible, and they can be very expensive and difficult to administer.

QUESTIONS FOR DISCUSSION

1   A manufacturer of office furniture wants to find out the key characteristics of desk users and on the sizes and uses of desks. The managing director has asked for a survey of medium to large companies in the UK. Would you recommend an interview, telephone, postal or an online survey? Give your reasons.

2   A large producer of confectionery wants to find the best combination of levels of raisins, nuts and honey in a chocolate bar. Each may be high, medium or low in content. Explain to the manufacturer the various ways of designing an experiment to find this out. Which would you recommend?

3   To what extent are retail panels and consumer panels in direct competition for the continuous monitoring of consumer markets?

4   Design 6–10 questions for inclusion in an omnibus survey that would enable a travel company to analyze the relationship between type, destination and duration of holidays taken in 2005 by UK nationals.

CASE STUDY LEVI STRAUSS

Thygesen and McGowan (2002) report that from 1985 through to the mid-1990s, Levi Strauss & Co. enjoyed unprecedented growth year after year, stimulated by the Original Jeans advertising campaign. Increasingly, the Levi's® brand name became synonymous with the 501 jeans. "Consumer insight" was the exclusive domain of a handful of designers while product innovation meant finding new ways of communicating 501 jeans. The role of research, say the authors, "became that of principal cheerleader". In focus groups, consumers always spoke in glowing terms about the brand. The research tools were focused largely on advertising. Tracking meant interviewing consumers who had bought jeans in the past six months.

By 1997, however, the jeans market was in free fall as consumers found other garments than jeans to wear. The company lost over 50 percent of its consumption among young consumers between 1997 and 2000. An internal turnaround team was formed to work with its market research agency, Added Value, to come up with a new brand vision. The team wanted answers to the following questions:

- In what market does Levi® compete?
- Who are the core consumer targets and what are their key needs?
- What defines the enduring distinction of the Levi® brand?
- What product line will most effectively deliver the brand for the target?

Questions and activities

1 Check out the Levi Strauss website, **www.levistrauss.com**.

2 What kind of research would you recommend that Levi Strauss should undertake to answer the questions?

FURTHER READING

Brennan, M., Benson, S. and Kearns, Z. (2005) "The effect of introductions on telephone survey participation rates", *International Journal of Market Research* 47 (1): 65–74.

Diaz de Rada, V. (2005) "Response effects in a survey about consumer behavior", *International Journal of Market Research*, 47 (1): 45–64.

Duffy, B., Smith, K., Terhanian, G. and Bremer, J. (2005) "Comparing data from online and face-to-face surveys", *International Journal of Market Research*, 47 (6): 615–639.

Evans, N. (1995), *Using Questionnaires and Surveys to Boost Your Business*. London: Pitman.

Punch, K. (2003) *Survey Research. The Basics*. London: Sage.

Turley, S. (1999) "A case of response rate success", *Journal of the Market Research Society*, 41 (3): 301–309.

8 Constructing quantitative data
Selecting cases

All good chefs regularly take samples of what they are cooking.

© SERGEY KASHKIN

INTRODUCTION

Whatever the research method being used – ad hoc survey, experimental or continuous research – the researcher needs to think through what sorts of case will be appropriate for achieving the research objectives. If, for example, a client wants research into the effectiveness of the use of humor in advertising on repeat-purchase rates for brands of soup, the researcher will need to consider whether the appropriate type of case is the household or the individual. Soups may be stocked in the household for individual or family consumption and they may be purchased separately by individuals for consumption at work. The researcher will have to be clear, furthermore, about how a "household" is defined, about what geographical area is included and over what period of time purchases are to be either recorded or recalled. Alternatively, individuals do purchase soups for their own consumption, but not necessarily of all ages, and are people who never purchase soup, or have not made a purchase in the past month, two months, six months or whatever, to be included?

Once the type of case has been decided, the researcher needs to think about the total number of cases involved and whether some form of sampling may be necessary. This chapter looks at the nature of the researcher choice between attempting to survey or observe the whole population of cases by taking a census or taking some kind of sample. Sampling is a complex issue and this chapter reviews the various processes of sample selection, sample design, sample size, sampling in practice and sampling error.

INTERNET ACTIVITY

Using your browser, go to **www.thomsonlearning.co.uk/kent** and select the Chapter 8 Internet Activity which will provide a link to the Survey Sampling International website. See what is offered by way of internet and telephone sampling.

The research population

In Chapter 5 we introduced the notion of cases, which are entities whose characteristics are being recorded by the researcher. Cases can be empirical or legal units, theoretical constructs, statistical artifacts or simply the objects, persons, survey respondents, groups of people, organizations, situations or events that are the focus of the researcher's attention. Quantitative research is never concerned with just one or a few cases, but with a set of cases, possibly a very large number, that the researcher would like to study. This is the population, which in research terminology has a broader meaning than its common usage to refer to the total number of inhabitants, including children, in a particular country or geographical area. It is the total set of cases that are the focus of the research and is sometimes referred to as the "universe" or "target population". Populations need to be defined very carefully; any ambiguities will result in ambiguities in the results of the research. Populations should always be located in time and space, and their definition should involve a specification of the type of case that is the focus of the research which is as precise as possible. This is not always easy. If, for example, a researcher says that the population is "all retired people currently resident in France", there will be considerable ambiguity about what counts as "retired". Does it refer to all individuals who are at or over the age at which a state pension may be drawn? Does it include those who have retired early from their jobs? Does it include individuals who are entitled to state pensions but who are casually employed or self-employed? Does it include those who have taken formal retirement but who are reemployed on a part-time basis? What does "resident in France" mean? Does it include people who spend only part of the year in France?

Population specification was listed in Chapter 7 as one potential source of error in the design and execution of surveys. Very often researchers fail to specify their population at all, as illustrated in Box 8.1.

The way the population is defined should reflect the issues that the research proposes to address. If, for example, the researcher is interested in the spending habits or purchasing power of retired people, then it may be sensible to exclude those in residential care or nursing homes. These issues need to be clarified and decided before any data can be captured.

Research populations need to be carefully specified.

© LAWRENCE SAWYER

 Census An attempt by a researcher to contact or to study every case or unit in the population.

If the number of cases in the population is relatively small, it may be possible for the researcher to study all of them – or at least attempt to study all of them. This is usually described as taking a **census**. If, for example, there are only 350 companies that offer a particular service that the researcher wants to study, he or she may send a postal questionnaire to all of them. It is quite likely, of course, that not all companies will respond and the census will be incomplete. The response rate will be the number of responses as a proportion of the population of cases. It would be quite wrong in these circumstances, however, to treat those who did respond as a "sample" of the population – but that is precisely what some researchers do.

RESEARCH IN ACTION
Defining the population

BOX 8.1

Herrington and Capella (1996) report the findings of a controlled field study examining the effects of background music on shopping behavior in a supermarket environment. However, there is no explicit definition of the population being sampled. We are told that the surveyed sample "represents a diverse group of 140 adults from a metropolitan area in Southeastern USA". So, is the sample of 140 individuals intended to be a sample of:

- ■ all shoppers in the USA,
- ■ all shoppers at supermarkets in the USA,
- ■ all shoppers/supermarket shoppers in Southeastern USA,
- ■ all shoppers/supermarket shoppers in metropolitan areas in the USA/Southeastern USA?

Technically, it is none of these. From evidence in the article we can reconstruct the population actually being sampled as "all adult shoppers aged 18 or over who shop on Mondays to Thursdays between 13.00 and 20.00 at one supermarket somewhere in the Southeast of the USA". Any generalization of the results beyond this group is suspect. Thus weekend shoppers are omitted, as are morning shoppers and shoppers at any other supermarket in the USA. Furthermore, there is no indication of the total number of shoppers that the sample of 140 is meant to represent.

CHAPTER 8 SELECTING CASES | **229**

If the population of cases is fewer than 100 or so, or if the response rate is such that fewer than 100 questionnaires, diaries or manual or electronic records are returned, than there may be insufficient numbers to be able to perform a reasonable quantitative analysis on the data. In these circumstances, the researcher should consider undertaking – or recommending to the client – qualitative research. Chapter 15, however, does look at some alternative methods of data analysis that, for example, uses combinatorial logic to analyze smaller numbers of cases.

In some situations, even if the population of cases is very large, it may still be possible – and indeed sensible – to undertake a census. Thus where retail outlets have barcode readers, it is possible to record the sales of every product, every brand and every brand variant in every store without having to take a sample of stores from which to make estimates.

When samples are needed

In some circumstances, taking samples is the only feasible course of action. A chef is unlikely to eat the whole dish to try it. A car manufacturer is unlikely to test all its cars for crash characteristics by driving them into a wall at 80 kph. For the conduct of survey research, while it may be theoretically feasible to contact every case in a population consisting of millions of cases (this *is* done across Europe on a regular basis in official censuses of the residential population of a nation, for example every ten years in the UK), for most market researchers, taking a sample is the only option with limited resources and limited time. A sample is a subset of cases that is selected and then studied by the researcher for the purpose of being able to draw conclusions about the entire population of cases. Researching a small sample carefully may, in fact, result in greater accuracy than either a very large sample or attempting a complete census, since the problems associated with handling a large number of interviewers and a large number of questionnaires may create errors of a greater magnitude than those arising from the sampling process.

Sample selection

A lot of confusion about sampling arises because, while any piece of quantitative research necessarily involves a population of cases, what the researcher actually samples may not be those cases at all, but some other kind of entity. Thus a researcher may sample primary schools, but in order to interview the teachers in each school; or businesses making a particular product, but in order to telephone the marketing managers. Households are often sampled, but in order to contact individuals within them. The entities being sampled are usually referred to as **sampling units**. Sampling units may correspond with cases where the units being sampled are the same as the cases of interest to the researcher, for example sampling households in order to determine household characteristics. Where survey research is being used, it is always individuals who are being asked questions; but these questions may be about themselves, or they may be asked about the organization for which they work or the household in which they live. It is possible, then, for example, to sample schools in order to ask teachers about the children. The sampling unit is the school, the case is the child and the teacher is the respondent or informant. This introduces the intriguing notion that there are three populations: the population of schools, the population of children and the population of teachers. Add to this the possibility that the researcher, besides being interested in the children, is also interested in the characteristics of

Sampling unit Whatever entity is being sampled.

classrooms and maybe the schools themselves, and we can see that in a single piece of research there may be several "populations" involved. Alternatively, where individuals are sampled in order to ask those individuals about themselves, the sampling units, cases and respondents are all the same entity.

There are two rather different bases on which researchers may make their selection of sampling units:

- purposive,
- representative.

Purposive sample A nonprobability sample in which the selection of sampling units is made by the researcher using his or her own judgment or experience.

Purposive samples are generated when the selection of units is made by the researcher using his or her own judgment about what cases are important to the research or can be used for the research. The selection may be made, for example, on the basis of contacting those units that are easiest to access, those that are deemed to be the most important, those that reflect a variety of extremes, or those that are typical. A researcher may select those organizations in which he or she already has contacts, or those that are within traveling distance. If the study is of retailers and electronic data are not available, then a sample of retailers may need to be taken; but some have much higher turnovers than others. So, the researcher may deliberately choose all the major multiples, and then make a purposive selection of the remainder based on turnover, type of shop and location. The researcher may choose units on the basis that each one is an example of every type of entity that the researcher wishes to cover. Sometimes the researcher may pick extreme units, for example all the most marketing-oriented companies may be selected in order to look at the extent to which or the manner in which they use marketing planning procedures. Finally, units may be chosen because they are "typical". Thus particular towns, cities or areas may be chosen because they have typical or average populations, or industrial, institutional and social structures.

Purposive samples are used, quite legitimately, for exploratory research, for qualitative research and for some experimental research where the focus is on understanding situations, generating ideas or evaluating social situations, products, ideas for products, advertising or ideas for advertising. Purposive sampling, however, is not normally appropriate for survey or experimental research, since the purpose of such research is normally to use the results from them to generalize about the population of units or cases from which the sample was drawn.

Organizations like schools may be sampled, but in order to interview teachers or pupils.

© BONNIE JACOBS

Representative samples, by contrast, are chosen in such a way that they attempt to reproduce the structure and features of the population of units from which the sample was drawn; ideally, they are a microcosm of the entire set of units. They are used primarily for quantitative analysis, either to make estimates of the size or frequency of a population characteristic, or to measure and test the extent to which the characteristics of units or cases are related together in the population. Ideally, the results obtained from the sample should be broadly the same as those that would have been obtained had the whole population of units been studied.

The selection of units to create a representative sample is usually made using one of two main approaches:

- probability,
- nonprobability.

Probability samples (also commonly called random samples) are ones in which members of the population (the cases) have a known chance of being selected into the sample. "Known" can be a bit misleading here, however, since a calculation of an exact probability requires that the exact size of the population be known – and commonly it is not, for example the number of readers of a particular magazine. This will change from week to week and in any case can only be estimated from sales over a given period of time. "Known" in this context means, then, that given that a particular technique of selection has been deployed, if the exact size of the population were known at the moment the sample took place, the probability could be calculated.

The techniques in question involve **randomization**, using a method that is independent of human judgment to select from a complete list of the population of units that is to be sampled (the "sampling frame"). Sampling techniques entail using some form of lottery, like taking names out of a hat, using tables of random numbers to select numbered units, or relying on computerized random procedures. An alternative to using randomized techniques is systematic selection from a list. **Systematic selection** creates a rule that determines the selection of the units, thereby removing, or largely removing, human judgment. This may mean taking every nth name from a list at N/n intervals where N is the population size and n is the sample size. If, for example, the researcher wants a sample of 100 from a list of 1000 names he or she can pick every 10th name. In principle the starting name should be a name between the first and the ninth name picked at random. Suppose, using a pack of cards, we just pull out a card at random and it is a six (of whatever suit). The names selected will then be the 6th, 16th, 26th and so on. This gives each name in the list at the outset an equal probability of being selected at random and is independent of the judgment of the researcher, who might otherwise tend to pick out certain types of case. Another form of systematic sampling is to take every nth house along a street and follow some rule about the selection of streets.

Because the chances of selection are at least in principle calculable, it is possible to apply the laws of chance (probability theory) to undertake a statistical evaluation of sampling error, enabling the researcher to assess how likely the sample is to be unrepresentative and by how much.

Nonprobability samples (also commonly known as nonrandom samples) are ones in which the chances of selecting a case from the population of cases (even if this is known) is not calculable since the selection is subjective. The subjectivity involved is commonly that of the interviewer. Interviewer selection may be used for sampling individuals as respondents and clearly this will involve human judgment, but this judgment will, normally, be limited in a number of ways, often in combination, by restricting:

- the numbers of types of people to be chosen, that is, interviewers are given quotas, for example of so many men and women, so many of different age groups,

Representative sample The selection of sampling units in such a way that they attempt to reproduce the structure and features of a population of units.

Probability sample A sample in which the selection of sampling units is made by methods independent of human judgment. Each unit will have a known and nonzero probability of selection.

Randomization The selection of sampling units by chance.

Systematic selection The selection of sampling units using a rules that remove human judgment from the selection process.

Nonprobability sample A sample in which the chances of selecting a case from the population of cases is not calculable since the selection is made on a subjective basis.

- the time of day at which interviews may take place, for example allowing no interviews of males before 5 p.m. to get a cross-section of men in employment, or observing customers in pubs and bars at specific times of the day,

- the area in which the interviewer may make his or her selection, for example to particular streets or other locations.

KEY POINTS

There is always a population of cases in which the researcher is interested for the purpose of the research. It may or may not be necessary or advisable to take a sample from this population, using the sample to make precise and accurate statements about it. The process of sampling, however, can be quite complex and the entities that are being sampled (the sampling units), may not be the same as those that are the focus of the research (the cases), or indeed as those who provide the information (the respondents or informants). For quantitative research, samples need to be representative rather than purposive and this means using a mode of sample selection that is, as far as possible, independent of human judgment.

Sample design

Sample design The particular mix of procedures used for the selection of sampling units in a particular piece of research.

Simple random sample Each sampling unit has an equal chance of being selected from a list.

Most textbooks on marketing research make a very clear-cut distinction between probability and nonprobability samples and will continue to list a range of different types of each. Different types of probability sample will typically include simple random samples, stratified samples, cluster samples, multistage samples and multiphase samples. Nonprobability samples will include quota samples, convenience samples, snowball sampling and asking for volunteers. However, as with research design, each **sample design** will tend to be unique and will commonly be a combination of probability and nonprobability elements. Furthermore there are varying degrees of "independence" from human judgment, while neither practitioners nor theorists tend to agree among themselves as to which particular sample selection procedures count as "random".

What statisticians do tend to agree, if not insist, upon is that the "theory" of statistical inference, which is based on probability theory and which is explained in Chapter 13, is based on the assumption that the sample drawn is a particular kind of probability sample called a **simple random sample**. Such samples use either randomized or systematic selection techniques (and some statisticians would argue that systematic procedures are not strictly "random", but only an approximation) from a complete list of the population of units, giving all units to be sampled an *equal* chance of being selected. Thus if we select a sample of 300 names from a list of 3000 students at a university, then each student has a one in ten chance of being selected.

However, in practice, simple random samples are seldom used because:

- they require a sampling frame for the total population of units to be sampled – this could mean taking random selections from lists containing maybe 40 million people, perhaps on a regular basis,

- if face-to-face interviewing is to be carried out (or even questionnaires or diaries left personally for respondent completion), the interviews would be scattered throughout the length and breadth of the geographical area to be sampled, and interviewers would have a considerable amount of traveling to do,

■ the resulting samples may still not accurately reflect the structure of the population of units in respect of a number of variables whose incidence or size is already known – in other words, simple random samples do not utilize data that are already available on the population structure.

Departures from simple random sampling are a result of the application of one or more of four main procedures that are used in the design of samples:

■ stratification,

■ clustering,

■ imposing quotas,

■ staging.

Stratification is a procedure that utilizes information already contained in sampling frames to construct a sample that is guaranteed to be representative in respect of that information. Thus if a list of individuals contains information on the gender of each person, then the proportion of males to females is known. Suppose it is a list of members of a golf club, and 60 percent are male. We can then ensure that 60 percent of our sample is male. Thus if we wanted a sample of 100 members, we could select 60 men at random and 40 women at random. If the list also contained data on age, and we knew that 30 percent of members are aged 16–30, we could select 30 individuals from this age group (again at random) and the appropriate numbers from other age groups. If we stratified by gender *and* age together, then our 30 individuals aged 16–30 could be selected on the basis of 60 percent (that is 18) men and 40 percent (12) women. Provided the proportions in the sample are the same as the proportions in the population (usually called **proportional stratification**) then the resulting sample is likely to be *more* accurate and representative than the simple random sample because some of the sources of variation have been eliminated. However, it does require an accurate sampling frame and one that contains information on the factors we want to use for stratification.

> **Stratification** A random sampling technique in which simple random subsamples are drawn from separate groups or strata.

Sometimes the stratification is disproportionate. Suppose our golf club contained only 10 percent women and we wanted to be able to compare the views of the women with those of the men on the facilities provided to members. A proportionately stratified sample of 100 would give only 10 women – not enough on which to base an analysis of responses to a questionnaire, so we might select 50 women and 50 men, that is, deliberately over-sample the women. This would enable us to make our comparisons, but if we wanted to estimate the extent of certain views or characteristics overall, then the answers of the men would have to be upweighted and the answers of the women downweighted to their original proportions.

> **Proportional stratification** The stratification of a sample in such a way that the strata are in direct proportion to those in the population of cases.

Clustering is used where interviewing is to be face-to-face. It makes sense for each interviewer's respondents or potential respondents to be geographically concentrated in order to minimize travel time. Accordingly, it is normal to cluster interviewing in limited geographical areas. This is normally achieved by selecting (usually at random) a fixed number of **sampling points** and allocating one interviewer to each. These will usually be political constituencies or areas, or postcode sectors. The sampling points are usually carefully chosen in such a way that they are a representative cross-section of types of areas. Normally, the selection of sampling points will be stratified by a number of variables. This is possible because, while there may be no lists if individual respondents that contain data on variables that can be used for stratification, there *will* usually be lists of areas to be used as sampling points, and there will usually be plenty of information about each.

> **Clustering** The random selection of cases or units in geographically concentrated areas.

> **Sampling point** A designated geographical area within which an interviewer conducts his or her selection of cases or units.

Face-to-face interviewers need to concentrate their efforts on sampling points.

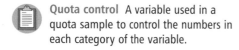

Quota control A variable used in a quota sample to control the numbers in each category of the variable.

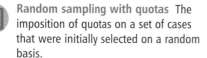

Random sampling with quotas The imposition of quotas on a set of cases that were initially selected on a random basis.

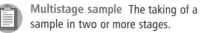

Multistage sample The taking of a sample in two or more stages.

FIGURE 8.1

Interlaced quota controls

While the effect of stratification is to reduce errors arising from the sampling process, the effect of clustering is to increase it. How much it will do so depends on how "tight" clustering is. For small-area clusters the error will be greater than for larger areas. In practice, the reduction in error due to stratification is very limited since it is usually only the selection of sampling points that is stratified, not the selection of individuals or households within them. Accordingly, the departure from simple random sampling brought about by the stratified selection of clusters has the effect, overall, of increasing the sampling error.

Imposing **quota controls** can take a number of forms. In some situations, respondents are selected from a list at random, but interviewers are then asked to fill quotas from these lists. Such a procedure might be called **random sampling with quotas**, but the imposition of quotas will increase the sampling error since substitutes are, in effect, being allowed. The main context, however, in which quotas are imposed is for quota samples in which the interviewer decides who to approach in the street.

Quota sampling is generally regarded by statisticians and textbooks on market and social research as nonprobability sampling. This is mainly because the final selection of respondents is made by the interviewer, so human judgment enters into the selection process. The interviewer, instead of being issued with a preselected list of names and addresses, is given an assignment in the form of a quota. This might, for example, require the interviewer to find, usually at a fixed sampling point, 20 adults aged 16 and over:

- 10 of them female,
- 10 aged 45 or over and 10 aged 16–45,
- 8 in social grade ABC1,
- 12 in social grade C2DE.

In this case, gender, age and social grade would be described as quota controls. These controls may be interlaced, as in Figure 8.1, so that individuals who combine these characteristics need to be located and persuaded to participate in the survey. Though this ensures that, for example, not all 10 under-45s are in social class ABC1, the interlacing can get quite complicated, and independent quotas are often applied. The selection of which variables to use as quota controls depends on which variables the researcher thinks are most strongly associated with the variables being estimated or tested. The usual quotas are on gender, age and social grade, because these are associated with many other characteristics, behaviors and attitudes. However, for some products, like double-glazing, type of property or tenancy may be more relevant.

Samples may be drawn in two or more phases or stages. **Multistage samples** take samples within samples, for example selecting electoral areas at random and

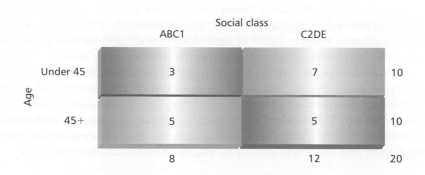

then selecting electoral districts within the areas selected. Such a procedure is useful where populations are widely dispersed and can be used as a way of achieving clustering. If, at the final stage, all the units within an area are included in the sample, then it is cluster sampling. If the final stage is itself another sample, then it is multistage sampling. Stratification may also be applied at each stage. In **multiphase sampling**, the same type of sampling unit is used at each phase, but some units are asked to give more information than others. Thus some of the sample may be asked only some of the questions, but a subsample is asked more detailed questions.

Samples that use one or more of these departures from simple random sampling are generally considered to be either the equivalent of random probability samples or at least approximations of them. However, where simple quotas are used on their own without any attempt at randomization, for example by asking interviewers to attempt to approach every tenth person coming out of a cinema, then the approximation may be very rough. Just asking interviewers to find 60 men and 60 women without any further restriction is more like a **convenience sample**. Here, interviewers are approaching people who happen to be conveniently around in the right place at the right time. University lecturers using their students or church members using fellow churchgoers would also come into this category. **Volunteer samples** may be obtained in various ways. Customer satisfaction surveys may be undertaken by leaving questionnaires for customers to complete if they wish. There may be tear-out forms or cards in newspapers or magazines. Website users may be invited to access and complete an online questionnaire. **Snowball samples** may be used for difficult-to-locate respondents. Those who are located may be asked to suggest others who fit the population specification.

Multiphase sample A multistage sample in which some sampling units are asked for more information than others.

Convenience sample A sampling technique in which interviewers are asked to find respondents who happen to be conveniently accessible.

Volunteer sample A sampling technique in which potential respondents are asked to complete a survey by way of general invitation rather than being approached individually.

Snowball sample A nonrandom sampling technique used to locate difficult-to-find respondents. Those who are located are asked to suggest others who may fit the population specification.

KEY POINTS

Sample design is an integral part of the overall research design. The quality of the sample has a significant impact on the overall quality of the research, but designing an appropriate sample is seldom easy, partly because many factors need to be taken into account and partly because, particularly for country-wide samples, the design may need to be both complex and sophisticated.

Like research designs, sample designs for any one particular piece of research tend to be a unique combination of elements. It is, accordingly, often quite difficult and not always sensible to try to classify any particular design into a specific type of sample. The apparently clear-cut distinction between probability and nonprobability samples is, furthermore, illusory. Many samples have random and nonrandom components. What counts as "random" is, in any case, open to dispute. According to the "theory" of sampling, which is explained in detail in Chapter 13, only samples where the selection of cases or sampling units is made from a list using a randomized technique that is independent of human judgment count as random samples. The fact that these are commonly referred to as "probability" samples is an indication that probability theory should be applied only to such samples. In practice, researchers tend to apply statistical inference to samples that at best are only an approximation of probability sampling and it may be argued that this is inappropriate. The argument is taken up in detail in Chapter 13.

One final point is that, as explained above, the sampling units and the research cases may be different entities. If, for example, households have been sampled in order to ask individuals within them about themselves, is it appropriate to make generalizations about a population of individuals when it was a population of households that was sampled? Again, this point is taken up in Chapter 13.

Sample size

Determining the size of sample that is needed for a particular piece of research is a complex issue that needs to take into account a large number of factors. Textbooks tend to take a statistical approach that calculates the size of sample needed in order to achieve a specified degree of sampling error and a minimum level of accuracy. The problem with such calculations is that they assume that the researcher is able to specify an acceptable level of sampling error in advance of undertaking the research. This is usually impossible, particularly since errors will vary from variable to variable. Such calculations also fail to take into account very practical issues such as the fact that larger samples will cost more and will take more time to complete. There may well be a limit to the size of sample that can be afforded or is practicable. Furthermore, how large a sample is needed also depends on the variability of the population characteristics and on the purpose of the research. The more variable the characteristics the larger the sample will need to be. Furthermore if the purpose of the research is accurate assessment of quantitative variables then larger samples will again be required. If the purpose is to generate ideas for new products then a small sample of product category users may well be sufficient.

Sample sizes are sometimes based on a kind of rule-of-thumb. Clients may specify in their requests for a proposal that they want a sample of a particular size. This may be based on no more than past research and experience. If the researcher feels that the client has asked for a size of sample that is too small or too large for the purpose then he or she has a responsibility to present an argument about why the sample should be some other size.

In any sample size determination, consideration has to be given to the anticipated number of subgroups that will be analyzed. If a study needs to compare the television channel switching behavior of heavy, medium and light television viewers, then there will be three subgroups and there will need to be adequate numbers in each. It has been suggested, for example by McGoldrick et al. (2001), that a sample should provide at least 100 respondents for each major subgroup and at least 50 for less important subgroups. This means that a sample of at least 300 would be required for the study of television channel switching behavior.

It could also be argued that for any kind of quantitative analysis, a minimum sample size of 100 or so is needed even to be able to calculate simple percentages for each variable. Most market research agencies will need to do a series of subgroup analyses (or "breakdowns") for clients and will tend to take samples of at least 1000. Few samples for ad hoc research will be much above 3000, but where the research is continuous and based on separate samples in each period it may be possible to accumulate samples of 30 000 or more over the course of a year.

In thinking about sample size it is helpful to draw a distinction between:

- the size of sample attempted or drawn from a list,
- the number of questionnaires returned,
- the number of usable returns.

A researcher may draw a sample of, say, 300 from a list, but only 150 are returned, of which 120 are useable. It is the number of useable returns that is entered into the data matrix and which will form the basis for any analysis. In these circumstances it would be sensible and normal to draw a sample that is larger than is required to allow for anticipated nonresponse. Where quota samples are used, however, the researcher can just continue until the required numbers are reached.

It often happens that the population of cases from which a sample is to be taken is not very large, for example there may be 1000 companies in which the researcher is interested and intends to sample 500 of them. A "small" population is not any fixed total size but is usually defined as one in which the sample exceeds 5 percent of the total population. Statistically, in this situation, a smaller sample size is needed to obtain the same level of accuracy. In the example above, a sample of 355 would be just as accurate as one of 500 from a large population. What is called a **finite multiplier** is used, which is an adjustment factor that is equal to the square root of that proportion of the population not included in the sample, in this case the square root of 0.5.

Finite multiplier An adjustment that is made to the variance of a population statistic to correct for overestimation of the variance when the sample represents more than 5 percent of the population.

Sampling in practice

The kind of sampling used in practice will depend, in the first instance, on whether respondents are to be approached via the telephone, through the post, face-to-face or online. For telephone interviews, clustering is not required and there seems little point in using other than systematic random sampling from the names listed in the telephone directories, or random digit dialing may be used if unlisted numbers are required. The only decision is whether there should be prior stratification, for example by region and whether there should be any imposition of quotas as the telephoning proceeds. This would amount to random sampling with quotas. For postal surveys in the UK, the Post Office Postcode Address File would be a more appropriate sampling frame. These sampling frames are described below. Again, clustering is not required and the imposition of quotas is not possible since this requires information on the quota variables at the point of initial contact.

It is for face-to-face interviewing that a real choice needs to be made between random sampling and quota sampling. In both cases there is likely to be clustering into sampling points to minimize interviewer traveling time. Random sampling in practice means that interviewers are given lists of names and addresses and they have to make systematic efforts to obtain interviews with the individuals listed and to take no substitutes. The main advantage of random sampling is its accuracy. Compared with sampling techniques that are not strictly random, random samples:

- minimize bias in the selection procedure,
- minimize the variability between samples,
- will, with a measurable degree of error, reproduce *all* the characteristics of the population from which the sample was drawn, not just those selected as quota controls,
- will, where samples are drawn at regular intervals, reflect any changes that are taking place in the population,
- allow probability theory to be applied to calculate the chances that the sample result was not a random sampling fluctuation.

There are, however, disadvantages to random samples:

- they are slower and more expensive than nonrandom techniques,
- they need a sampling frame,
- the sample achieved will almost certainly be smaller than the sample drawn.

Surveys using quota samples can often complete fieldwork in two to three days: for random samples it is likely to be two to three weeks. This can be important when quick results are needed. Random samples are, furthermore, an expensive process in terms of administration and interviewer costs. The sample drawing procedures can be quite complex, while interviewers may be instructed to make at least three callbacks in the evenings or at weekends before recording a "noncontact". This all adds to the cost. Random samples can in fact easily be twice the cost of quota samples of the same size. However, some statisticians argue that, because such samples are more accurate, it is more cost-effective (in terms of accuracy per £1 spent on fieldwork) to design a smaller, high-quality random sample than a larger quota sample.

 Sampling frame A complete list of the population of units or cases from which a sample is to be taken.

Random samples need a **sampling frame**, that is, a complete list of the population that is to be sampled (normally within selected sampling points). In Box 8.2, two such frames are explained.

Other kinds of sampling frame include:

- membership lists of clubs, associations, societies or other kinds of organization,
- registers of various kinds, for example the Kompass Directory of companies,
- frames that have been constructed from market intelligence or from surveys that have been carried out on a regular basis.

One "solution" to an inadequate sampling frame is to redefine the population of cases being studied. Thus it is known that certain kinds of people are missing from the UK Registers of Electors. If the problem is ignored, then the survey population is being redefined as only those addresses appearing in the Registers. A sample that uses the telephone directories can define its population as all telephone subscribers.

Perhaps the most serious drawback of random samples, however, arises from the fact that there is always a degree of nonresponse. There will always *be* non-response whatever method of selection is used, and at least the response rate is known for random samples. However, it does mean that the sample that is drawn (the target sample) is seldom the sample that is achieved. For ad hoc surveys the response rate will typically be 60–70 percent of the sample drawn. Provided those

IN DETAIL
Sampling frames in the UK

BOX 8.2

Two frames commonly used to obtain names and addresses of potential respondents in the UK are:

- the Registers of Electors,
- the Post Office Postcode Address File.

The Registers of Electors have been the standard sampling frame for decades, but there are problems with them. They are completed every October and published the following February, so are already four months out of date. They contain the names and addresses of all British subjects aged 18 and over who are entitled to vote and are registered. No information about age and gender of the person is available (other than first names). Any study that takes "adults" to mean 16 and over will require special procedures to obtain a sample of 16–18-year-olds. Also, many of the 18-year-olds will be missing from the lists; so will people who are not entitled to vote (e.g. not British subjects), or who are not registered. While the Registers are readily accessible, their validity is constantly affected by deaths and population movements. Up to 12 percent of electors are no longer at their registered address by the time the Registers come up for renewal.

The Postcode Address File covers some 26 million addresses in 1.7 million postcodes within 8900 sectors within 2700 districts within 120 postcode areas. The file tends to be more complete and more up-to-date than the Registers of Electors, and is good for sampling households in several stages. However, for sampling individuals it is necessary to have some procedure for selecting individuals within a household. The postcodes are often used in association with geodemographics (these were explained on p. 159).

not responding are not significantly different in key respects from those who do, the size of the achieved sample may simply have to be lived with, and the response rate reported as part of the results.

By contrast with random sampling, the key feature of quota sampling in practice is that it is the interviewer who makes the final selection in the street or in the shopping centre. Unlike stratified samples where a random selection is made in advance of the data collection process according to defined proportions within strata, in quota sampling the characteristics to be used for quotas are not known in advance and the interviewer needs to establish these. A typical approach will be to address a person who looks likely to meet quota requirements as follows: "Good morning, my name is [name of interviewer] from [name of research agency]. We are looking for men aged 30–49 who have a driving licence to answer a few questions about motoring. Do you fit into that category?"

The key advantages of quota samples are that they:

- are quicker, cheaper and relatively simpler to administer than random samples,
- they do not require a sampling frame,
- the sample size and sample composition in terms of the quota controls is always achieved.

The speed of quota sampling is derived from two sources. First, if in-home quotas are used, no callbacks are required, and if street quotas, there is no traveling time between interviews. Second, the procedures for drawing the samples are very simple and there is no need to give interviewers lists of names and addresses. In terms of cost per interview, quota samples thus work out a lot cheaper. Furthermore, no sampling frame is required – however, data on the structure of the population being sampled are needed in order to be able to set the size of the quotas. Since each interviewer continues until his or her quotas of sexes, ages and social classes are filled, the exact size and basic structure of the sample can be determined in advance.

There are, however, a number of disadvantages:

- there is considerable potential for bias,
- there is more variability between samples,
- the application of probability theory to such samples is questionable,
- they impose a structure on the sample.

Bias arises from two main sources: the interviewer and the high (and generally unrecorded) level of nonresponse. It is normally left to the interviewer how he or she goes about finding respondents who meet quota requirements in the sampling point. This leaves open the possibility of the interviewer avoiding certain types of locations or types of people, and for there to be systematic differences between one interviewer and another. Thus one interviewer may consciously or unconsciously avoid approaching people in groups, while another may avoid people who look like they are in a hurry.

It is, furthermore, often forgotten that there is considerable nonresponse when either street or in-home quotas are used. On the surface, there is no problem of nonresponse since all quotas are filled, or mostly filled. However, this is only because the nonresponse is undeclared and, effectively, substitution is being allowed. People who cannot be contacted or who refuse at the first attempt are excluded. The effective nonresponse rate in quota sampling is unknown, but certainly very large. The average random sample survey achieves a response rate of only about 25 percent at first calls. This is boosted by subsequent callbacks to 60–80 percent. So quota samples, at best, probably have an effective response rate of 25–30 percent.

Design factor A multiplier used to convert standard errors calculated by methods appropriate to simple random sampling into standard errors appropriate to more complex sample designs.

Work on actual surveys suggests that even good-quality quota samples produce at least twice as much variability from one sample to another as do random samples. The implication, according to some researchers, is that estimates made or inferences deduced from quota samples need to be adjusted to take this extra variability into account. Such adjustments, in the form of a **design factor**, are explained in Chapter 13. Others will argue that, because quota sampling is nonrandom, then the application of statistical inference to such samples is not legitimate, since the probability of inclusion in the sample for any one case is unknown. In practice, researchers often treat quota samples as an *approximation* of random samples and will apply such techniques, frequently without making any adjustment in recognition of the fact that the sample is not a simple random one.

The structure imposed on the sample by the quotas will have been derived from data that reflect the population of cases as a whole. This, in turn, means that these quotas will not reflect the different composition of the sampling points, nor any changes that have taken place since the original data were collected. Thus social grades A and B may be overrepresented in a sampling point in a depressed mining village, and underrepresented in expensive, fashionable areas. It can even be difficult to fill some quotas in some of the sampling points.

KEY POINTS

There are many practical considerations when samples are being designed. Whether or not a suitable sampling frame is available is certainly an important consideration, but the advantages and limitations of quota sampling need also to be carefully considered. At the end of the day there is no one "best" sample design and the researcher will need to make a series of decisions for which there is no template or even expert advice.

Online sampling techniques

Random online intercept sampling The random selection of website visitors.

Sampling for internet surveys poses special challenges. It is almost impossible, for example, to select an internet-based sample that is representative of the general population of adults resident in a given geographical area since many people as yet do not have access to the internet. This may not matter if the research itself is concerned with the characteristics of internet users. Even then, obtaining a representative sample of internet users has its own challenges. To date internet research has been based overwhelmingly on the use of volunteer participants. Placing announcements on websites or to user-groups advertising the study and providing instructions on how to take part is in effect asking for volunteers. The result is a distinctly nonprobabilistic sample that may be open to all kinds of biases. An alternative is to obtain lists of e-mail addresses from commercial agencies. The main problems here are that many addresses will be redundant and, being unsolicited and counting as spam, will in some countries be illegal or will be filtered out before they are received.

There are, however, some procedures that have been developed in an attempt to minimize the impact of these problems. **Random online intercept sampling** depends on a random selection of website visitors. Provided the population is redefined as website visitors, then this amounts to a simple random sample of those visitors within the time frame imposed. The actual selection can be randomized or systematic. However, if the population is other than website visitors and the website is used because there are many visitors, then this is equivalent to convenience sampling, or quota sampling if quotas are imposed.

Invitation online sampling involves alerting potential respondents that they may fill in a questionnaire that is hosted on a specific website. To avoid unsolicited e-mails (spam), however, researchers must have established a relationship with potential respondents who may expect to receive an e-mail, for example existing customers on a customer database who have given their permission to receive e-mails, or the invitation needs to be through some other means, for example including an invitation with till receipts in a retail outlet.

Online panel sampling means sampling from online panels that have been set up by agencies for the purpose of conducting online surveys with representative samples. Compared with ad hoc recruitment, this procedure reduces costs associated with locating appropriate respondents, it ensures their immediate availability, it facilitates the specification of sample parameters, for example in terms of income, education family characteristics and so on. Response rates, furthermore, tend to be high, of good quality and with shorter turnaround times. On the basis of previously collected data, answers can be cross-referenced and questions can be limited to relevant items so that panelists do not need to answer the same questions again (Goritz 2004).

Invitation online sampling Alerting potential respondents to an online survey that they may fill in a questionnaire that is hosted on a specific website.

Online panel A pool of people who have been recruited who are willing to participate in online surveys on a regular or occasional basis.

Sampling errors

Chapter 7 explained the different kinds of error that can occur in the design and execution of surveys. Such errors can happen whether or not a sample has been taken and may be thought of as **nonsampling errors**. When samples are taken, then besides these potential errors in survey design and execution, there are additional **sampling errors** that might arise from the sampling process. Such errors will arise whatever kind of sample is taken and whatever the sample size. The extent of such error may be defined as the difference between a sample result, and the result that would have been achieved by undertaking a complete census using identical procedures. Such errors arise because particular types of sampling units or cases are under-represented or over-represented in the sample compared with the population as a whole. If, for example, there is under- or over-representation of the genders, ages or social grades of individuals, it will affect the measurements (and, more importantly, the estimates made from them) of a large number of variables. Lack of representation in the appropriate quantities may be a product of two factors:

Nonsampling errors Survey errors that are not a result of the sampling process.

Sampling error Error that arises from the sampling process. It may be defined more precisely as the difference between the result of a sample and the result that would have been obtained from a census using identical procedures.

- systematic error (or bias),
- random error (or variance).

Systematic error

Systematic error when the sampling procedures used bring about over- or under-representation of particular types of unit in the sample that is mostly in the same direction. This may happen because:

- the selection procedures are not random,
- nonrespondents are not a cross-section of the population,
- the selection is made from a list that does not cover the population, or uses a procedure that excludes certain groups.

Systematic error Error arising from sampling procedures that result in the over- or underrepresentation of particular kinds of sampling unit mostly in the same direction.

If the selection procedures are not random then it means that human judgment has entered into the selection process. For example, interviewers may be asked to choose respondents at some geographical location or to select households in specified streets. The result is likely to be that certain kinds of people or households or organizations are excluded from the sample. Thus choosing respondents in a shopping center will miss out people who seldom or never go shopping; the selection of households by an interviewer may result in the omission of flats at the tops of stairs.

Nonresponse was considered in Chapter 7 and is a problem for both censuses and samples. For censuses nonresponse means that the enumeration will be incomplete. If large numbers are missing, it would, furthermore, be inappropriate to treat those successfully contacted as a representative "sample". For samples, it means that estimates made from the sample will be biased if nonrespondents are not themselves representative of the population. If they are representative, then nonresponse is not so much of a problem; but it may still mean that analyses are made on the basis of too small a sample.

Frame error was also considered in Chapter 7. Again, it will be a problem both for censuses and for situations where the list of the population is used as a sampling frame, so there may be missing population cases, the inclusion of non-population cases, and duplication,

Whatever the reason for the systematic error, the effect will be that all samples that could be drawn from a population will tend to result in the same direction of over- or under-representation. The average of all these samples will then not be the same as the real population average or proportion. Thus if we took lots of samples using a procedure that tended to omit working mothers with young children, then all the samples will manifest such under-representation rather than some over-representing them and some under-representing them so that the average of all samples was very close to the real population proportion.

Systematic errors cannot be reduced simply by increasing the sample size. If certain kinds of people are not being selected, cannot be contacted or are not responding, it will not be "solved" by taking a bigger sample. Indeed, some kinds of errors will increase with more interviewers, more questionnaires and greater data processing requirements. All the researcher can do is minimize the likelihood of bias by using appropriate sample designs. Biases for some variables can be checked, for example against Census data or data from other sources. Sometimes attempts are made to discover the characteristics of nonresponders, as was explained in Chapter 7.

Random error

Random error Error arising from a random sampling procedure in which there will be chance fluctuations.

If we took a number of random, unbiased samples from the same population, there will almost certainly be a degree of fluctuation from one sample to another. Over a large number of samples such **random errors** will tend to cancel out, so that the average of such samples will be close to the real population value. However, we usually take only one sample, and even a sample that has used unbiased selection procedures will seldom be exactly representative of the population from which it was drawn. Each sample will, in short, exhibit a degree of error.

> **WARNING**
>
> 🚫 Such error is often called "sampling error", but it would be clearer to think of it as "random error" to distinguish it from bias (which some statisticians and some textbooks, confusingly, categorize as "nonsampling" error).

Unlike bias, which affects the general sample composition and relates to each variable being measured in unknown ways, random error will differ from variable to variable. The reason for this is that the extent of such error will depend on two factors:

- the size of the sample – the bigger the sample, the less the random sampling error (but by a declining amount),
- the variability in the population for that particular variable – a sample used to estimate a variable that varies widely in the population will show more random sampling error than for a variable that does not.

These two factors are used as a basis for calculating the likely degree of variability in a sample of a given size for a particular variable. This, in turn, is used as an input for establishing with a specified probability the range of accuracy of sample estimates, or the probability that sample findings are only random sampling fluctuations. These calculations are explained in Chapter 13.

Total survey error

Any research that is based on addressing questions to people and recording their answers risks error resulting from measurement (see Chapter 5), from survey design and execution (see Chapter 7) and from any inadequacies of sampling. **Total survey error** is the addition of all these sources of error, both sampling and nonsampling. It is difficult to estimate what the total survey error is in any one survey, and it will tend to vary from question to question. What is certainly true is that the error that results from random sampling fluctuations – which is the only kind of error that is taken into account when statistical inference is being used – accounts for only a very small proportion of the total survey error. Assael and Keon (1982), for example, estimate that it is perhaps only about 5 percent. For a full discussion see Kish (1965) or Churchill and Iacobucci (2002, Chapter 12).

Errors of various kinds can always be reduced by spending more money, for example, on more interviewer training and supervision, on random sampling techniques, on pilot testing or on getting a higher response rate. However, the reduction in error has to be traded off against the extra cost involved. Furthermore, errors are often interrelated so that attempts to reduce one kind of error may actually increase another, for example minimizing the nonresponse errors by persuading more reluctant respondents may well increase response error. Nonsampling errors tend to be pervasive, not well-behaved and do not decrease – indeed may increase – with the size of the sample. It is sometimes even difficult to see whether they cause under- or overestimation of population characteristics. There is, in addition, the paradox that the more efficient the sample design is in controlling random sampling fluctuations, the more important in proportion become bias and nonsampling errors.

While errors arising from sampling may be clearly classified into random or systematic, nonsampling errors may well be some combination of randomness and bias. Thus mistakes made by interviewers *may* tend to cancel out, but may, alternatively, result in systematic error. Not only does this mean that the magnitude of such errors is often unknown, but also it is often hard to see whether they cause under- or overrepresentation of the population values.

As yet there is no comprehensive theory for assessing the impact of error other than for random sampling error. This is hardly surprising given the complex nature of surveys and the multiple opportunities for error. What has become known as "total survey design" is the attempt to control total error, bearing in mind all sources of error. This involves assessing the level of error associated with different procedures and choosing that combination that will minimize total error of estimates made within the resources of the survey. The procedure, however, assumes that total error and total cost models are available and that good information to put in them can be obtained. Contact rates, refusal rates, response rates, missing data, edit failure rates, consistency checks, and re-interviewing are just some of the methods used to detect errors. Setting up the parameters of total error models would involve introducing experimental procedures into the survey

Total survey error The sum of all sources of error, both those arising from the sampling process plus non-sampling errors.

process that allow for the determination of the size of the impact of a particular error source on total error estimates. Unfortunately, all this takes considerable time and additional expense which many, if not most, researchers are unwilling to face. The temptation must be to fall back on the familiar practice of utilizing probability theory to measure the likely impact of random sampling error. Readers and users of survey findings are interested in the substantive results, not in technical qualifications, warnings and limitations.

There is a considerable literature on ways of calculating errors of various kinds (see Lessler and Kalsbeek 1992 for a review). However, the calculations can get quite complex and most formulae assume metric data, taking the "mean square error" as the key dependent variable that is explained by a range of sources of bias plus random error. In practice, researchers are more likely to focus on ways of minimizing the likelihood of error arising in the first place by adopting strategies and procedures to control its occurrence.

Controlling error

Survey researchers should make all reasonable attempts, within the limits imposed by cost and time constraints, to minimize, or at least measure the impact or make some estimate of, nonsampling errors and of bias in the sampling procedure. To minimize response errors researchers would be well advised to:

- pilot-test questionnaires in order to check for misunderstandings of questions,
- analyze tendencies to over-claim or under-claim for certain kinds of individual behavior, for example the tendency to under-claim the consumption of alcohol, or to over-claim television watching,
- use "aided-recall" techniques (prompted lists) to help respondents remember products that they may have purchased and forgotten about, or radio programs that they forgot they had listened to,
- use questioning techniques that minimize the effort respondents need to make.

To minimize interviewer error, researchers should:

- set rigorous training standards for interviewers,
- monitor the process of interviewing by doing "back-checks" – calling or telephoning respondents who have already been interviewed to check that the interview was carried out properly, or sending supervisors to accompany interviewers on a regular sample basis,
- make statistical analyses of questionnaire errors to identify interviewers who may need retraining or reminding of particular points.

To minimize errors resulting from nonresponse, several procedures need to be considered:

- for interview surveys interviewers may be asked to make a specified number of call-backs if the respondent was not at home on the first call. Three or four such call-backs may be made, ideally at different times and days of the week,
- interviewers may make an appointment by telephone with the respondent,
- self-completed questionnaires may be left where no contact has been made,
- monetary incentives or gifts may sometimes help to improve the response rate,

- interviewers may get a "foot-in-the-door" by having respondents comply with some small request before presenting them with the larger survey,

- nonrespondents to a postal survey may be sent interviewers to persuade respondents to complete the questionnaire, or they may be sent further reminders.

Processing errors will be minimized by careful editing and checking of the questionnaires in addition to the use of data entry validation procedures (see Chapter 11). Sampling bias will be minimized by using carefully constructed sample designs that use random procedures wherever possible, or by imposing restrictions on interviewer choices where it is not. These sample designs were described earlier. Biases will still remain, however, and sometimes these are known. Thus it may be known that there are too many women in the sample, or too few men aged 20–24, compared with known population proportions. It is possible to make corrections to the data to adjust for these biases by weighting them. Weighting was explained in Chapter 7.

One form of error that cannot be controlled (although it may be influenced by adjusting the size of the sample) is random error. However, it is possible, for such error, to calculate, using probability theory, what are the chances that the error will be of a certain magnitude. Such calculations come under the general title of statistical inference and Chapter 13 takes up this topic.

KEY POINTS

There are many sources of error that can arise from the sampling process. These may be loosely categorized into systematic and random error, although in some situations these may be mixed. Sampling error is, however, only one source of errors. Others arise from measurement and the design and execution of surveys. Random sampling error is, certainly for survey research, whether ad hoc or continuous, only a small part of total survey error. Errors that may arise, for example from nonresponse or incorrect responses, may swamp any errors from random fluctuations from sample to sample.

Ethical issues

Researchers have a responsibility to clients to develop a sample design that minimizes both sampling and nonsampling errors. They need to decide on a sample size that is adequate for the purpose and not unnecessarily large. When nonprobability sampling is being used, the researchers should make clear to clients the limitations of this technique. It is unethical to treat nonprobability samples as if they were probability ones by applying statistical inference to the results and presenting them as "findings".

Researchers need to be sensitive to preserving the anonymity of respondents when conducting business-to-business research with small populations. The sampling details should not be too revealing, for example when undertaking employee research.

SUMMARY

Where it is not feasible, economic or practical to study every unit or case for the purpose of undertaking any particular piece of research, a selection will have to be made. This may be done on a purposive or on a representative basis. Purposive samples are selections made by the researcher and are used mainly for exploratory or for qualitative research; representative samples are chosen by randomized or systematic techniques, or by an interviewer following certain rules, and are used for quantitative research where the objective is either to estimate the size or frequency of characteristics or the relationships between them in the population of units or cases from which the sample was drawn.

In designing samples, the researcher will almost certainly want to make use of procedures for stratification, clustering, imposing quotas and staging. Clustering is needed only where face-to-face interviews are to be conducted. The selection of clusters to use as sampling points is nearly always on a random basis, but is usually combined with stratification. The final selection of respondents may be random or quota, and both procedures have their strengths and limitations. For telephone, postal and online surveys no clustering is required and there is no need to use interviewer selection, but where the sampling frame used to get telephone numbers or postal addresses is felt to be inadequate, quotas may be imposed, even if the selection from the list was random. Whether this procedure counts as a "random" sample is an issue that will either be hotly debated – or send people to sleep!

The errors that arise when taking samples are a combination of those errors that might happen irrespective of the procedures used for selecting cases and will occur even when census studies are made, and those errors that arise from the over- or underrepresentation of types of case when sample selections are made. Sampling errors include both bias (systematic error) and variance (random error). Statistical measures based on probability theory that are used to estimate "sampling error" in fact refer only to variance, and, strictly speaking, only to those samples where random selection of the final cases is made. Variance, furthermore, accounts for only a very small proportion of total survey error.

QUESTIONS FOR DISCUSSION

1   Given the kinds of error that can arise when taking samples, is it better to go for census operations wherever possible?

2   Are purposive samples really "samples" at all?

3   Why are quota samples so popular when they clearly produce more error?

4   Carefully define the relevant population for the following projects. Decide whether sampling is necessary and if so suggest an appropriate sample design:

   ■   A manufacturer of domestic lawnmowers in Scotland wants to know the proportion of households that own various types of lawnmower.
   ■   A hospital administrator wants to find out if the single parents working in the hospital have a higher rate of absenteeism than parents who are not single.
   ■   A company is about to launch a new product, which is a vibrating massage cushion for use by motorists. The manufacturer wants to know what kinds of motorists are likely to consider purchasing the product.

CASE STUDY EGG PLC

Egg was founded in 1988 as a telephone and online bank by Prudential plc, one of the UK's biggest and most well-established finance and insurance companies. In its short history, say Pearson and Macer (2001), the company has moved away from telephone and postal services to a situation where it deals almost exclusively with its 1.6 million customers over the internet. Market research and customer feedback is the responsibility of Egg's Consumer Intelligence team, which consists of just three members of staff. Customer feedback is particularly vital given the lack of traditional "personal" contact with its customers. At any one point in time, there will be numerous internet surveys either live, in preparation or being analyzed. A fast turnaround time is important on these projects. Egg keeps a sample database of respondents already identified as willing to participate in research.

Questions and activities

1 Check out the Egg website, **www.egg.com**. Click on *Company info* and then *About Egg*.

2 What size of sample would it be appropriate for Egg to take of its customers?

3 Consider a range of different probability samples that might be appropriate and say which one you would choose.

FURTHER READING

Assael, H. and Keon, J. (1982) "Non-sampling versus sampling errors in survey research", *Journal of Marketing*, 46, Spring: 114–123.

Herrington, J. and Capella, L. (1996) "Effects of music in service environments: a field study", *Journal of Services Marketing*, 10(2): 26–41.

Kish, L. (1965) *Survey Sampling*. New York: John Wiley.

Lenth, R. (2001) "Some practical guidelines for effective sample size determination", *American Statistician*, August: 187–193.

McGoldrick, T., Hyatt, D. and Laffin, L. (2001) "How big is big enough?", *American Statistician*, August: 54–58.

Pearson, M. and Macer, T. (2001) "Joined up research on the eHighway", *ESOMAR*.

9 Mixed research designs

In this chapter you will learn about:

→ the differences, similarities, strengths and weakness of quantitative and qualitative research,

→ the nature of research design,

→ the distinction between mixed methods and mixed designs,

→ the different ways in which data, research methods and research paradigms may be mixed,

→ the relationship between the rationales for conducing research and the use of mixed designs.

Research can be mixed in many different ways.

© ROUSLAN GILMANSHIN

INTRODUCTION

Chapter 1 explained the process of designing research for clients, while Chapter 2 looked at the design of academic research. This chapter brings together a number of design issues, including a review of what is normally included when the term "research design" is used, and looks at how the various approaches to research can be mixed in various ways. As pointed out in Chapter 1, textbook writers tend to develop taxonomies of different types of designs; typically a distinction is made between "exploratory designs", "descriptive designs" and "causal designs". The implication is that researchers normally pick or select a particular prespecified design that they feel matches the problems at hand. Attempts to put any particular design into a category of "type" of design are, however, unlikely to be helpful. Problems and issues that companies, clients and researchers face tend to be unique and each piece of research will have its own unique design constructed from the research tools available. "Exploratory", "descriptive" and "causal" in fact do not really refer to designs at all, but to potential research objectives. In a sense all designs are mixed, since each piece of research has its own design which is a combination of subdesigns, for example survey design, experimental design, sample design and so on. Each of these in turn will be a mixture of elements. This chapter focuses on the nature and types of such mixtures.

INTERNET ACTIVITY

Using your browser, go to **www.thomsonlearning.co.uk/kent** and select the Chapter 9 Internet Activity which will provide a link to a website containing Statnotes by G. David Garson. Go to *Research Designs*. Note that Garson makes a key distinction between experimental and non-experimental designs. Have a look at the different types of each. In this chapter, we will be treating design as a unique combination of elements that might include both experimental and nonexperimental components. It might also, as is also explained in this chapter, include elements of both quantitative and qualitative research.

Qualitative and quantitative research

Researchers are not "forced" to make a choice between qualitative and quantitative approaches to their research; they can be mixed in a variety of ways, as explained later in this chapter. However, researchers are, by inclination rather than necessity, predisposed to favor or emphasize one or the other. There will usually be no one "correct" or "best" way to research a problem; a valid case can probably be made for a whole range of different approaches.

As far as published academic research in marketing is concerned, researchers seldom attempt to justify why they have adopted a particular research design. Box 9.1 explains how two researchers just assumed that self-completed questionnaires were the best way of proceeding.

RESEARCH IN ACTION
The effects of music on buyer behavior in the retail environment

BOX 9.1

In the Herrington and Capella (1996) study, which was introduced on pp. 60–61, there is no discussion of the type or different types of research that might be appropriate to testing their hypotheses. It is just assumed that self-completed questionnaires are the best way of proceeding. It could be argued, however, that the topic could well have been studied, at least in its early stages, using qualitative methodologies to explore customers' own perceptions of the service environment.

When thinking about the appropriateness of qualitative or quantitative research for a particular project, it is useful to bear in mind the key differences between and strengths and weakness of qualitative and quantitative approaches. In terms of differences, quantitative research is variable-centered. Variables are constructed by researchers by engaging in the processes of measurement and scaling. The resulting data are entered into a data matrix; statistical patterns are then sought in which variation in one or more of the variables is "accounted for" by variation in one or more other variables. In some analyses some variables are seen to "do" things to other variables. The number of cases – whether samples or populations – on which analyses are performed needs to be sufficiently large for statistical purposes, which means, in practical terms, that with fewer than 150 or so it begins to create problems.

Qualitative approaches, by contrast, are case-centered. They will offer detailed and, hopefully, "insightful" analyses of each case and perhaps how they relate to one another and to the wider environment. Such research is sensitive to process, context, lived experience and local groundedness. In short, it is holistic. The number of cases may be quite small: in the extreme just one case in a case study.

The design of quantitative research is very much "up-front". Researchers need to have planned very carefully their questionnaire, how it is to be administered, how respondents are to be chosen and even how the data are to be analyzed. Entering data into SPSS and getting out tables, graphs, even multivariate analyses, is quick and relatively straightforward, as you will see in Chapters 11–14. By contrast it is very easy to begin qualitative research, even in a quite tentative way. Procedures can be refined as the researcher goes along. The difficult bit comes

Studying the effects of music in a retail environment does not have to use a particular research method.

© MAARTJE VAN CASPEL

later in the analysis. Writing up the results can be quite a challenge, particularly if it is to go beyond mere "reportage" to generate more analytic and abstract accounts.

The strengths of quantitative research are that it is systemic, it is replicable and its findings may be compared. Hypotheses can be tested and the results may be generalizable, at least to the population on which the research is based, and perhaps to other similar populations. It may also be used as a basis for prediction. The downside is that such research can be simplistic – it loses the context, the identity and the narrative associated with individual cases; reality is being fragmented at several stages. The complex world is fragmented into entities that researchers have created, concocted or just accepted as "real" and which they call "cases"; variables are then constructed from observed or measured traces of these entities; the "patterns" in the data sought are driven by the statistical procedures used, which means that in traditional data analysis, the search is for "covariation".

Qualitative approaches are more flexible; they can be used in a wider range of situations and can be modified as the research progresses. The "validity" of such research inheres in its grounding in local realities and contexts and in focusing on participants' perspectives. It is more able than quantitative research to handle complexity.

Both approaches, then, have their strengths and weaknesses. Furthermore, the distinctions between them can be overdone. Both can be a mixture of induction and deduction, both can be used for exploration as well as for testing ideas. Neither is "superior" to the other and both are needed in marketing research. The important point is that research approaches are linked to research questions. The spelling out of research objectives may imply quantitative research, qualitative research, both, or some mixture of the two. How previous researchers have approached the topic may also be a relevant consideration. There may also be very practical considerations like resources, access to organizations or particular individuals. There has been some reference in the literature to the "quantitative/ qualitative debate"; the danger of even thinking in these terms is that the methods become fixed first and then the research questions adapted to them.

The nature of research design

The term "research design" gets used in a variety of ways by researchers and textbook writers. It can be used to refer to a blueprint, plan or framework for conducting a marketing research project that has not yet begun; it is often used by researchers to refer back to the particular assemblage and sequence of research methodologies and techniques that were deployed in a study now completed; it can also be used to refer to the processes and tasks involved in planning and executing a piece of research.

In the first sense, a research design materializes in the form of a research proposal. For client-based research the proposal will typically include all the elements outlined in Chapter 1. In other words it will include all the issues involved in planning and executing a research project, from identifying the research problem through to the anticipated approaches to data analysis and the practical arrangements for managing the project. The academic research proposal will include some of the same elements, but there will be no brief to respond to and there will be more emphasis on the relevant literature and the development of theory.

The extent to which each of these elements of design is detailed and pre-specified in the proposal before the process of data construction actually begins varies considerably between different styles of research. Punch (1998), for example, distinguishes between "prespecified" and "unfolding" designs; Miles and Huberman (1994) talk about "tight" and "loose" designs. Quantitative research will tend to have prespecified designs; qualitative research, however, varies considerably in terms of tightness and looseness.

Writing the research proposal itself, however, is only one stage in the process of designing research. For client-based research, the process was seen in Chapter 1 as a series of steps that were illustrated in Figure 1.4. Here, presenting the proposal is the final step. An equivalent set of steps for academic research might look like Figure 9.1. Activities carried out after the design has been submitted or presented might be seen as activities in pursuit of execution or implementation, but some authors will see the collection of the data, their analysis and writing up the report as part of the overall "design".

Market researchers, whether they are conducting client-based or academic research, will, in writing up the results of their research in management reports or in an academic article, have a section on the research methodology used and so will be talking about design issues even if they do not actually use the term "design". They may, for example, say that "the research was carried out in two stages", or "a quasi-experimental design was used to show that". It would not be normal for researchers to discuss the different research approaches that were used and rejected, but they do often outline why a particular approach was adopted.

The purpose of any design is to ensure that the evidence to be obtained will enable the researcher to address the objectives for which the research is to be undertaken. Usually, however, there will be a number of ways in which this can be achieved; there is seldom any one "best" design. A number of trade-offs may be needed. No design is perfect and there are many actual and potential sources of error, as was explained in Chapters 7 and 8. Errors of various kinds can always be reduced by spending more money, for example on more interviewer training and supervision, on random sampling techniques, on pilot testing or on getting a higher response rate. However, the reduction in error may have to be traded off against the extra cost involved. Furthermore, errors are often interrelated so that attempts to reduce one kind of error may actually increase another, for example, minimizing the nonresponse errors by persuading more reluctant respondents may well increase response error. The information generated needs, ideally, to be accurate, up-to-date, complete, timely and relevant, but accuracy may, for example, have to be traded off against completeness or timeliness.

In formulating a design, the client-based researcher may have to balance the needs and perspectives of the client with his or her own experience and expertise.

FIGURE 9.1

The process of designing academic research

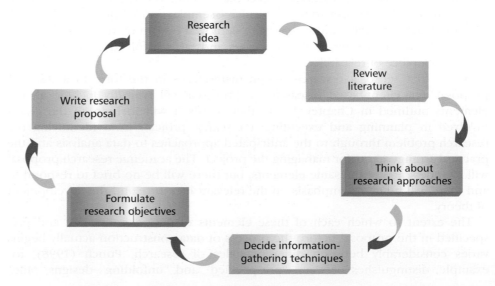

If what the client is asking for is not in the view of the researcher the best way of proceeding, then the researcher faces a dilemma. Its resolution may involve a degree of persuasion, compromise or trade-off.

KEY POINTS

A research design is a unique combination of research elements that may be seen either as a blueprint for a piece of research yet to be undertaken, or as an historical description of how a particular study was carried out. Design is also a process that may be seen as entailing a series of stages, or as an iterative, even cyclical process, but in any event is likely to involve the researcher in making a number of compromises and trade-offs. Developing taxonomies of different types of designs is not particularly helpful, particularly since most designs are combinations of many different elements.

Mixed methods and mixed designs

Academic researchers in the social sciences have mixed different styles of inquiry for many years. They have long recognized that all methods have their strengths and their limitations and that the limitations of one approach can to some extent be compensated for by mixing it with another or even several others. What is relatively recent is a small but growing literature that is devoted specifically to what has become known as "mixed methods". Several authors have, for example, made attempts to create taxonomies of mixed methods designs including Greene et al. (1989), Morse (1991), Tashakkori and Teddlie (1998, 2003) and Creswell (2003). The literature is, however, largely about mixing traditional quantitative with traditional qualitative procedures.

Tashakkori and Teddlie (2003), for example, explain that the methodology of social and behavioral research has undergone dramatic changes over the past 30 or so years. During most of the twentieth century, such research was dominated by quantitative methods with its positivist paradigm. However, in the 1980s and 1990s, qualitative methodology emerged with a different perspective. This was seen as a reaction against the dominant paradigm and became popular among those who were dissatisfied or disillusioned with the established methodological order. It also suited a new trend towards culturally sensitive research and a greater emphasis on applied research. Despite the obvious merits of each, proponents of the favored paradigm have tended to criticize what they saw as an opposing world view. The result was a series of "paradigm wars" (Gage 1989). Even as late as 1994 in the second edition of their *Handbook of Qualitative Research*, Denzin and Lincoln were still talking about qualitative *versus* quantitative methods and how a "qualitative revolution" has overtaken the social sciences.

Unfortunately, the literature is also becoming confused because not only are there many different ways of achieving mixtures, but the mixtures themselves may take place at several different levels. At the most basic level is the construction of both qualitative and quantitative data in the same piece of research, for example including both open-ended and set-choice questions in the same questionnaire. At this level, probably most research is mixed anyway. What varies may be the relative weight given to these two types of data. Data mixing might also take the form of data transformation or data fusion. The transformation of one type of data into another, for example converting qualitative data into quantitative, may be undertaken using content analysis or the coding procedures explained in Chapter 10.

Data fusion The merging of the results from two or more separate surveys with different samples into a single database.

The conversion can also be in the other direction, for example using factor analysis to create qualitative categories.

Data fusion combines data from two or more surveys or databases so that they can be analyzed as if they came from one complete sample. A single "virtual" source is created by attaching respondents from a "donor" survey to respondents from a "recipient" survey by matching them on variables common to both surveys. In effect, virtual respondents have been created who have given answers to questions from both surveys. The techniques of data fusion are explained in more detail in Chapter 15. Another form of fusion is to create fuzzy sets that are qualitative and quantitative at the same time. Fuzzy-set analysis is also explained in Chapter 15.

At a deeper level is the mixing of research methods. Thus qualitative research methods including depth interviews, group discussions, consultation and ethnography may be mixed with ad hoc and continuous surveys and experiments.

At the deepest level is the mixture of paradigms. Most of the discussion in the literature has been about combining positivist with interpretivist paradigms (these were explained in Chapter 2). There has been much discussion of "paradigm wars" in which the inherent superiority of positivist versus interpretivist assumptions about the nature of reality and the manner in which knowledge is produced are hotly debated. While some commentators have seen the two paradigms as incompatible, others have adopted a more pragmatic position. Each, according to this approach, has its strengths and weaknesses; each adds something to the analysis of social or market phenomena; each may be better suited to some kinds of problems and issues than others. In terms of the paradigms explained in Chapter 2, however, it may mean combining the approaches of the marketing physicist, the marketing physician and the marketing psychiatrist.

Tashakkori and Teddlie (2003) have argued that mixed methods have emerged as a third methodological movement with its own worldview (pragmatism), vocabulary and techniques. Mixed approaches, they argue, are often more complex and sophisticated than simple combinations of traditional qualitative and quantitative methods. Pragmatism rejects the incompatibility thesis and supports the use of both qualitative and quantitative research methods in the same research study. More important than either the methods used or the paradigm that underlies them is the research question and how it is addressed.

This chapter has been called "mixed research designs" rather than "mixed methods" to emphasize that the mixing of methods is only one level at which the mixing may take place. The mix may, indeed, take place at all levels. The mixture may, furthermore, be of more than qualitative and quantitative procedures, but of different types of each.

KEY POINTS

Mixed designs include not only the mixing of methods, but of data and even of research paradigms. Mixed designs include not only the mixing of qualitative and quantitative research, but the mixing of the several different types of each, for example mixing survey research with experimental research, or combining depth interviews, observation and focus groups. Whatever is being mixed, however, may be mixed in various ways, as the next section explains.

Types of mixtures

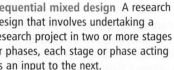

Whether the mixing is of data, methods, paradigms or all of these, whether the mixing is of qualitative and quantitative approaches or of types of each, the mixing itself can take several forms. First, **sequential mixing** involves undertaking a research project in two or more stages or phases, each stage acting as an input or preparation for the next. **Concurrent mixing**, by contrast, entails undertaking two or more styles of research at the same or overlapping times, or even at separate times, but as independent enterprises and considered as a single phase of research. There might even be different groups of researchers involved in the different components of the research. Finally, **eclectic designs** might mix not only both sequential and current elements, but any approach or method that might help to resolve a client problem.

Whether the mixing is sequential or concurrent, however, there can also be variation in the weight or priority given to the various elements. These may be equal or weighted towards one or the other. Morse (2003) distinguishes between situations where one procedure is used to supplement another "base" method, and situations where different methods are used in projects that themselves are relatively complete, but as part of a wider research program. The latter she calls "multimethod" as opposed to "mixed method" designs. In multimethod approaches, it is the *results* of each method that inform the emerging analysis or interpretation. Data are not usually combined in within projects as they may be in mixed method designs (Morse 2003).

Sequential mixed design A research design that involves undertaking a research project in two or more stages or phases, each stage or phase acting as an input to the next.

Concurrent mixed design A research design that entails undertaking two or more styles of research at the same or overlapping times, or even at separate times, but as independent enterprises and considered as a single phase of research.

Eclectic designs A research design that mixes in different ways any approach or methods that might help to solve a problem.

Sequential mixed designs

In sequential mixed designs, the research is conducted in two or more phases, one phase contributing to the next. Two-phase designs are in fact quite common, particularly where there is an initial phase of exploratory research followed by the main inquiry (see the *Case Study: Segmentation of the baby milk market* at the end of this chapter). Sequential mixed designs may, of course, entail several stages. Furthermore, the stages may be linear, each stage leading on to the next, or iterative – a cyclical moving backwards and forwards between different stages.

The stages may consist of two or more different types of qualitative research, for example focus groups followed by setting up consultation panels, two or more different types of quantitative research, for example a survey followed by an experiment, or a sequence of qualitative followed by quantitative stages or vice versa.

Probably the most common form of mixed sequential design is the use of a qualitative method used as an input to quantitative research. Depth interviews or focus groups may be used, for example to generate typologies that will form either the basis for the measurement of quantitative variables or the basis for forming groups, clusters or segments of cases. An alternative two-phase design might entail beginning with an analysis of quantitative data to find outliers or extreme cases that can then be followed up with depth interviews.

Concurrent mixed designs

Concurrent mixed designs entail undertaking two or more styles of research at the same or overlapping times, or even at separate times, but as independent enterprises and considered as a single phase of research. This type of mixing may be undertaken for a number of purposes including triangulation, comparison or expansion.

Triangulation is the use of two or more approaches to research to see if they come to similar conclusions. Such an approach is generally considered to have

Triangulation The use of two or more approaches to research to see if they come to similar conclusions.

emerged from the work of Campbell and Fiske (1959) who used several quantitative methods to measure a psychological trait. They called their method the "multimethod-multitrait matrix", although the term "triangulation", coined by Denzin (1978), has now become standard. Denzin, in fact, described four different methods of triangulation: data triangulation, investigator triangulation, theory triangulation and methodological triangulation.

Comparison might involve looking for differences, paradoxes or contradictions rather than convergence. Thus a qualitative study of whisky drinkers using focus groups may be used to see if there is any discrepancy between the stated amounts consumed and the amounts coming from a questionnaire survey.

Expansion might involve supplementation or incorporation. Data, methods or paradigms are sometimes mixed concurrently in order to add breadth, depth and scope to a project. Thus a separate project involving depth interviews may be carried out to explore audience reaction to a theater performance to add to a questionnaire survey aimed at analysing market segments of theater-goers.

Comparison A form of mixed research design that concurrently looks for differences, paradoxes or contradictions in different forms of research.

Expansion A form of mixed research design that concurrently seeks to add breadth, depth and scope to a research project.

Eclectic designs

Barker, Nancarrow and Spackman (2001) suggest that the new paradigm for the twenty-first century is not quantitative, not qualitative nor even a hybrid, but a new approach that they called "informed eclecticism", in which market research is itself positioned within a wider knowledge mix. It requires that researchers be informed about the range of approaches that are possible. It is about looking beyond research, drawing on disciplines and worlds outside research. Until recently, market research has been too internally focused. Briefs have focused on the research needs and on the technicalities rather than on business or organizational objectives. Data tend to be presented with reference to other data in the dataset, without referring to any other knowledge, other datasets, or theories or models outside their own boundaries.

Being eclectic means utilizing and combining any approaches that might be useful. Also mentioned in this contect is the idea of *bricolage*. A *bricoleur* is a maker of quilts, an assembler of images, a "Jack-of-all-trades" deploying and adapting whatever strategies, methods or empirical materials that are at hand. Barker, Nancarrow and Spackman (2001) suggest that eclecticism refers to approach and *bricoleur* to methods, but it is difficult to maintain this distinction. Both imply an "anything goes" paradigm. Gordon (1999) talks about "prosearch" rather than research. This focuses on the marketing possibilities of the future; a pluralistic vision rather than an analysis of historical records and their simplistic projection into the future. It is looking at the "big picture" and anticipating future scenarios. Uncertainty and ambiguity are celebrated rather than avoided.

KEY POINTS

With sequential mixed designs the research program is divided into two or more phases, each phase feeding into the next. Normally there is a "base" method into which previous phases contribute and which subsequent phases might supplement. With concurrent designs, each component is a relatively complete project and the mixing is likely to occur only at the interpretation stage of the overall research program. This interpretation may involve triangulation, comparison, supplementation or incorporation. Eclectic designs take the idea of mixture a stage further by mixing anything that might be useful, including incorporating ideas, theories, models or other data from outside the research itself.

Research rationales and mixed designs

The underlying rationale for a research study consists of the *reasons* for doing it. A rationale is a reasoned account of some action, structure or enterprise. It offers some justification based on rational principles as to why that action, structure or enterprise was undertaken. These reasons will in turn relate to the intended outcomes of the research and to their implications for clients in the case of client-based research or for the addition to knowledge, understanding and generalizable theory for academics. The research rationale is the researcher's or the client's "bottom-line". There will, of course, normally be more than one reason; there may well be hidden agendas or game-plans which may even change as the study unfolds. The research rationale may be written in the final report as the "purpose", "aim", "justification", "importance" or "contribution" of the study. Researchers may, alternatively use words like "purpose" or "aim", but in effect refer to standard research objectives like testing hypotheses. Although the rationale usually initiates the research study, it may be revealed or become evident only at the conclusion of a research report when the results are being interpreted. Researchers may not in fact reveal or discuss the research rationale at all. An academic researcher is unlikely to admit that a key aim in undertaking the research is to obtain one or more publications in top refereed journals; but this will, nevertheless, still be an important influence on the research designs used. An agency researcher is unlikely to admit that a key purpose is to win a contract with a client, although this will clearly underlie the research design proposed. However, because these things go unreported does not mean that they should not be seriously considered.

Newman et al. (2003) argue that research purposes are more intimately related to the choice of appropriate methodologies than are research questions. However, in developing their typology, the authors in effect develop a typology of research objectives like "predict", "add to the knowledge base", "measure change", "test new ideas" and so on. These are indeed intimately linked to appropriate methodologies, but the reasons why researchers undertake research lie deeper than this. They may have more to do with issues like liberation, emancipation, empowerment, progress, improvement, saving the planet or career opportunities. For the client in a commercial organization, the "bottom-line" has a more specific reference, namely profit, usually in the medium to longer term, since this links to survival. While there is no one-to-one link between any of these agendas and particular research methodologies, researchers will, consciously or unconsciously, take them into account. Thus an academic researcher who wants to persuade a government or local authority to introduce more restrictions on smoking in public places may conclude that traditional quantitative methods will be more in tune with the scientific nostrils of officials and civil servants. An agency-based researcher may feel that focus groups are more likely to persuade his or her client to change a branding policy.

Any one piece of research may serve several rationales or purposes; this is only another way is saying that different individuals will have different expectations from the research. Thus a study of recycling behavior in an organization may be undertaken, but to one person this is in order to encourage and enhance recycling behavior and to another to reduce costs. These differing rationales may imply or suggest different types of data, methods and perspectives; this in turn may be suggestive of the need for more complex mixed designs to accommodate the various agendas of stakeholders in the research. In this process the researcher is a dynamic element with his or her own experiences, intentions, lifestyles, ambitions and so on. Studies need to be initiated with a clear, singular lens that will focus the research.

Research is a puzzle-solving process. It is not linear but iterative, cyclical and multidimensional. Researchers come to an understanding piece by piece. This may mean that even the notion of an individual "project" becomes clouded as researchers decide they need to add another component to their studies, or they need a follow-up or another way of constructing or analyzing the data. They may see their activities as part of a more extensive program of research aimed at addressing one overall topic, or as a series of complementary or related projects. Over time new interconnections are made, discrepancies may be resolved and comprehension becomes deeper.

KEY POINTS

The real reasons for undertaking a research project – its rationale – probably go deeper than most researchers would care to admit or at least to report in the findings of their inquiries. For any one particular research program there will usually be a number of stakeholders, each with his or her own rationale or agenda. There is undoubtedly a link between rationales and the research methods proposed or deployed, but it is probably inexplicit, indirect and undiscussed. This is in many ways a pity, since rendering explicit the real reasons for doing research would probably lend considerable weight to the need for not only mixed methods, but mixed designs.

SUMMARY

The design for a piece of research is a unique combination of research elements whose purpose is to ensure that the evidence to be obtained will enable the researcher to address the objectives for which the research is to be undertaken. Designs may be seen as proposals for research, as accounts of how a particular study was carried out, or as a process that may entail several stages and may involve the researcher in making a number of compromises and trade-offs.

Mixed designs include not only the mixing of qualitative and quantitative research, but also the mixing of the several different types of each, and at the levels of data, methods and paradigms. Mixed designs may, furthermore, be sequential in which the research program is divided into two or more phases, or concurrent where each component is a relatively complete project. Mixed designs are also linked to the underlying reasons for undertaking research, but in ways that are seldom made explicit.

QUESTIONS FOR DISCUSSION

1   A facilities manager in a commercial organization has discovered from feedback from cleaners that employees are still putting waste paper into their normal waste bins rather than using the special desk-top trays provided for recycling paper. Suggest a sequential mixed research design that would analyze what sorts of employees are not using the trays provided and their reasons for not doing so.

2   The manager of a restaurant feels that the results from a customer satisfaction questionnaire handed to customers at the conclusion of their meal do not give a realistic view of those who have used the restaurant. Suggest a concurrent mixed design that would reassure the manager that valid results will be obtained from a new program of research.

CASE STUDY SMA NUTRITION AND THE SEGMENTATION OF THE BABY MILK MARKET

Hindmarch, Wells and Price (2005) of Leapfrog Research and Planning, and SMA Nutrition, explain that the SMA baby milk was first introduced in the UK in 1956 when the birth rate was almost one-third higher than it is today. SMA wanted to know how attitudes to infant feeding changed during the first year of a baby's life, what factors impacted on brand choice of baby milk, and what were the different market segments with different needs. This information would be used to inform product and packaging development, guide their customer relationship management program and enhance the support that can be given via healthcare professionals. In the first, qualitative phase of the research that was conducted, 38 paired depth interviews across eight different geographic locations in the UK were conducted among mothers of babies ranging from newborn to 12 months and also among pregnant women. The pairs were pairs of friends.

The quantitative phase consisted of telephone interviews with mothers who had 12-month-old babies. The main challenge, say the researchers, in designing the questionnaire was to ensure that the differences in approach to baby feeding highlighted in the qualitative phase were similarly identified in the telephone interviews. This was achieved by having teams of both qualitative and quantitative specialists from the agency working together throughout the fieldwork and analysis. From a battery of attitudinal statements and using a combination of factor analysis and cluster analysis the researchers identified eight segments like "the modern capable mum" and "lonesome mums".

Questions and activities

1   Check out the SMA website **www.smanutrition.co.uk**.

2   Using the content of this chapter, what other mixed designs would have been possible for this research?

FURTHER READING

Barker, A., Nancarrow, C. and Spackman, N. (2001) "Informed eclecticism: a research paradigm for the twenty-first century", *International Journal of Market Research*, 43 (1): 3–27.

Creswell, J. (2003) *Research Design. Qualitative, Quantitative, and Mixed Methods Approaches*. London: Sage.

Punch, K. (1998) *Introduction to Social Research. Quantitative and Qualitative Approaches*. London: Sage.

Tashakkori, A. and Teddlie, C. (eds) (2003) *Mixed Methods in Social and Behavioural Research*. Thousand Oaks, CA: Sage.

Part III Data analysis

Data analysis is the process whereby researchers create information from the raw data they have constructed: information that addresses the objectives for which the research was undertaken. The raw data are of little value until they have been structured in some way, summarized and a range of conclusions drawn from them. This is true whether the data are qualitative or quantitative. Data analysis, then, is not just about performing statistical calculations on numerical variables; it is also about procedures for analyzing text, about making sense of a dataset as a whole, and, as will become clear from Chapter 15, about a range of alternative ways of analyzing data.

Chapter 10 looks at commercial and academic approaches to the analysis of qualitative data and reviews some of the software that may be used. Chapters 11 to 14 explain the analysis of quantitative data using currently accepted statistical techniques. These include the essential descriptive measures that are applied to single variables, analyzing relationships between variables two at a time, the process of making statistical inferences from samples of cases to the populations from which the sample were drawn, and multivariate techniques that include, for example, multiple regression, cluster analysis and factor analysis. Chapter 15 is very nontraditional and considers some of the alternatives to statistical analysis including the use of combinatorial and fuzzy logic, data fusion, data mining techniques and holistic approaches.

10 Analyzing qualitative data

LEARNING OBJECTIVES In this chapter you will learn about:

→ the craft skills that have been developed by qualitative market researchers for the analysis of qualitative data for clients,

→ academic approaches to the analysis of qualitative data, including content analysis, ethnography, phenomenology and hermeneutics, discourse analysis, semiotics and grounded theory,

→ the validity of analyses arising from the use of qualitative procedures,

→ using computer-assisted qualitative data analysis software (CAQDAS).

INTRODUCTION

Qualitative data, as was explained in Chapter 4, consist of words, phrases, text or images. They arise as systematic records that have been made by researchers in a context – a research design – that has been constructed by the researcher or other individuals in a social, moral, political, economic and historical environment. They possess the feature that at the point of data capture no structure has been imposed upon them. The researcher captures the words, phrases, text or images without a predetermined set of categories or codes on which to map responses or observations. This means that the analysis of qualitative data can be undertaken in a number of different ways. There are few commonly agreed techniques and not many clearly defined procedures. The analysis, furthermore, is not usually a discrete phase undertaken after the fieldwork is completed, but begins as soon as data are being captured. The products of these early, tentative analyses may indeed influence the manner in which further fieldwork is conducted.

Market researchers will be looking for patterns, themes and relationships, but they will often have their own ways of achieving this. Very often they do not explain or write down how such data were analyzed, and if they do it is usually anecdotal or a personal reflection. This is particularly true for commercial qualitative market research, and the first part of this chapter describes one of the few attempts to codify the day-to-day practices and craft skills of client-based qualitative researchers. Academic approaches to the analysis of qualitative data tend to be based around certain assumptions about the nature of reality, about how this reality may be accessed and about the appropriateness of specific research procedures. These approaches have been grouped, classified and explained in many different ways by commentators on qualitative research procedures in the social sciences (see Tesch 1990), but the second part of this chapter picks out six different – although in many respects overlapping – approaches that are likely to be used in marketing research.

INTERNET ACTIVITY

Using your browser, go to **www.thomsonlearning.co.uk/kent** and select the Chapter 10 Internet Activity which will provide a link to the CAQDAS Networking Project at the University of Surrey. Read the brief section on what this Project is about and then click on *Choosing a CAQDAS Software Package*. Read the first four pages, which explain the different types of software and the basic functions that they provide.

Analyzing qualitative data for clients

In the commercial, client-based qualitative market research industry, the analysis and interpretation of data are activities often hidden from view. They tend to be carried out in private in the researcher's office or home, using notepad, colored pencils, the brain or, rather less than might be expected in a multimillion pound industry, the computer. There are two key reasons for this situation according to Ereaut (2002). First, qualitative market researchers find it difficult to explain exactly *what* they do in carrying out analyses of data and reaching conclusions. Interpretation in particular is often portrayed as a mystical or magical process, a "black box" in the mind that is intuitive, creative, inspirational, imaginative, freewheeling, casual, unbounded, aesthetically satisfying, idealistic and often impassioned. Commercial researchers who have tried to describe how they analyze their data talk about ideas "swimming about in the head", "mulling them over", "looking for the space between the lines" or those "Eureka moments". Yet they have certainly developed a set of day-to-day practices or craft skills that they either cannot or have not as yet attempted to articulate. One attempt to do exactly that, however, is by Ereaut (2002).

The second reason why the craft skills of the qualitative researcher have remained hidden is that clients are just not interested in or concerned about this part of the research process (Ereaut 2002). The details of these activities are rarely discussed between researcher and client, and it is unusual for clients to judge the quality of a research proposal on the intended analysis.

There have been some dissenting voices that suggest that the analysis of qualitative data can be approached in a systematic, fully articulated, manner. Miles and Huberman (1994), for example, see qualitative data analysis as a process parallel to quantitative analysis, and include data reduction, data display and drawing conclusions. This more "mechanical" approach, however, is one that appeals more to academics than to commercial qualitative researchers. The reasons why this is so are discussed later.

According to Ereaut (2002), "analysis" and "interpretation" are distinct, but interrelated, aspects of the data analysis process. Analysis involves the physical or functional operations of sifting, comparing, sorting, ordering, summarizing and coding the data. Interpretation has more to do with the cerebral, cognitive parts of the process – thinking, asking questions, finding solutions, creating meanings. These may be seen by some researchers as "alternative" ways of approaching qualitative data. However, Ereaut argues that both tasks are or should be undertaken together and cumulatively throughout the project. In a commercial context, furthermore, both must be firmly related to client needs and to organizational objectives. The distinction between analysis and interpretation is, as Ereaut herself admits, difficult to draw because some activities can be seen as fitting into either category, for example deciding on which codes to apply to the text, or may be seen as a bit of both, for example comparing and contrasting subgroups, like different age groups, among the cases being studied.

Following Ereaut (2002), the overall process of analysis can be seen as involving the stages illustrated in Figure 10.1.

Describing

Describing involves reviewing the data on a case-by-case basis. It represents the more mechanical part of the process. It is a combination of different activities, for example it involves bringing together all the various types of data to be analyzed ready for revisiting. These data may include:

- interview records, which might be audio or video recordings of focus groups or depth interviews that may have been transcribed,
- respondent-produced materials, for example enabling and projective techniques may have been used that result in drawings, lists, stories, collages,
- field notes and observation records that might include notes made by observers during focus group discussions, during tours of the organization, impressions of respondents,
- client-produced materials, for example reports, documents, notes made or offered during briefings.

Interview records are not always transcribed – researchers may just listen to or watch the tapes and write up their analysis as they go along. Commercial qualitative researchers are under severe time pressure and may not in any case feel that there is time for transcription. Where transcription is undertaken, it may be by hand or directly into a word processor. Some researchers insist on doing this themselves, or, at least, claim a preference for doing so. The argument is that the person who has to report the results needs to pick up the cues on not just *what* was said, but *how* it was said. If it is a video recording, then other cues are picked up from who said it and the accompanying body language. However, some qualitative researchers do not have the time or the inclination for what, after all,

FIGURE 10.1

Analyzing qualitative data for clients

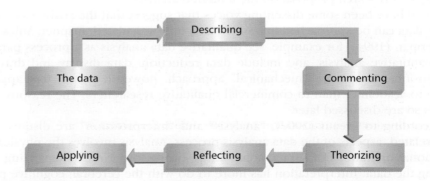

is a tedious activity and will hand the tapes over to secretaries to transcribe. Transcription may, of course, be literal, including all the "ums" and "ers" and false starts; others may be a paraphrase into grammatically correct English, or may even be just notes and summaries of what was said. For depth interviews the transcript will be on a respondent-by-respondent basis; for group discussions on a group-by-group basis.

Once the data have been assembled, they need to be revisited. This may entail relistening to tapes, rereading transcripts or looking again at videos of interviews or focus groups. It may be necessary to make several "passes" at the data at various points in the analysis. Next, the researcher needs to focus his or her attention on particular issues in the data by asking key questions like:

- What are the data about?
- What is happening?
- Who are the actors?
- How do they differ?

Researchers then need to pick out text segments, respondent materials, notes or documents that are relevant and clearly reflect the research objectives agreed with the client. It is then necessary to sort and classify what people said into categories with a view to bringing together comments that are on the same topic. This may mean generating, modifying, developing and refining a framework of categories as the analysis proceeds. Several attempts or "passes" at the transcripts may be needed before a set of categories is satisfactory. As far as possible the categories should be exhaustive and mutually exclusive, and they should not be too many in number. More than six or so will make the next stages all the more difficult. The categories at the outset will be tentative, provisional and probably overlapping. The category sets may be revised many times.

The categories are next given a code, which means selecting a particular word or phrase that "stands for" what is in the text or image and indicating what text this applies to. Manually this may be limited to using different color highlighters to indicate different categories, for example, "brand associations" or "company image". Electronically, using CAQDAS (see the Internet Activity at the beginning of the chapter), the number of codes is limitless and may be used in hierarchical fashion, that is categories within categories.

Following **coding**, researchers will look for similarities and differences between subgroups of cases, for example are male respondents saying the same or different things from female respondents? Finally, there will be a search for combinations of codes that seem to occur together, for example when one idea is mentioned, it tends to be mentioned along with another idea.

Coding The transformation of edited questionnaires into machine-readable form.

If the researcher stops at this stage, the analysis of the data will remain at a journalistic level. Researchers will simply report back to clients what respondents have said. This may, indeed, be all that the client wants.

Commenting

This part of the analysis sticks with the case-by-case review of the materials, but goes beyond description to delve into meanings, narratives, explanations, contexts and processes. Commenting on meanings entails trying to go beyond the actual words used to discover what the respondent probably meant beneath the surface. To analyze meanings, the researcher might ask the following questions:

- How does the respondent or group define the situation?
- What is the respondent's experience really like from the inside?
- Can it be described and conceptualized from the outside?

- Of what is this an example?
- What does this contradiction/anomaly mean?
- How else could this be looked at?
- How does this compare with the client perspective?

Respondents will often describe their situations as a kind of story – a sequence of events that can be analyzed as a narrative. This would mean paying attention to characteristics of the narrative – its "unfolding" of ideas, its assumptions or implications about causes and consequences, the language being used to refer to "players" or "actors" and so on. Respondents will often suggest their own explanations of events, and these could be focused upon again to see what assumptions are implicitly being made.

Meanings, narratives and explanations will need to be seen in terms of the context or contexts in which they occur. Qualitative data are always captured in a particular cultural, social, political, even technical environment. On process, the researcher might ask:

- Why this, now?
- What is *not* being said?
- What is the respondent's purpose in making this comment?
- Can the words be believed?
- What kinds of group effects are going on?

Theorizing

To academic researchers, the development of theory may be seen as the end product of the research. In client-based research, theory will be either down-played or seen simply as a vehicle for not reinventing the wheel next time around. This is in some ways perhaps unfortunate. After all, there is nothing as practical as a good theory. Theories are, by definition, sets of ideas, propositions, hypotheses, frameworks or models that can be used in a range of different contexts. In general terms, however, developing theory entails attending to the concepts and the dimensions that lie behind what respondents are actually saying, for example degrees of skepticism about the effectiveness of brand placement in television programs. There may be patterns and clusters of characteristics, ideas, events or behaviors that might, for example, indicate hostility or support for extending opportunities for gambling. There may be indications of change or underlying dynamics, systems, logics or structures.

Reflecting

So, how good is all that theorizing? To what extent are researchers getting to the "truth"? The researcher needs to reflect on issues of validity, robustness, and believability.

What clients value are experienced researchers who have a kind of validity-checking ability that comes about through repeated exposure to respondents and the qualitative research process. There is also a kind of commercial pragmatism – it is valid if it helps to solve the client's problem or is what the client wants. Reflecting on preconceptions and sources of bias certainly helps, while triangulation – getting a better "fix" on an idea by approaching it from several angles – may enhance the believability of findings. If, for example, the results of both depth interviews and focus groups result in similar conclusions, then more confidence can be placed on the findings.

Applying

In the context of client-based research, this means applying everything back to the client. Researchers can ask the following questions:

- How does what they have done in terms of describing, commenting, theorizing and reflecting fit with the objectives of the research or the research questions that were asked?
- What is the significance of all this for the client?
- What recommendations should be made to the client?
- What future research might be needed or how should the study be extended? (Always a good gambit for getting more business!)

KEY POINTS

The analysis of qualitative data by commercial market researchers tends to be more of a craft skill than a set of analytic procedures. From the data, it tends to involve the activities of describing, commenting, theorizing, reflecting and applying. However, not all these elements will necessarily be included in any given project. A researcher may go straight from the data to commenting without going through description. The researcher may then skip theorizing and reflecting and go straight to applying. In more extreme cases the researcher may go directly from the data to applications.

Clients are less interested in how these craft skills are applied than in the results and implications of the findings for the organization. The word that increasingly emerges to describe the qualitative market research is *bricoleur* – a maker of quilts, an assembler of images, a "Jack-of-all-trades" deploying and adapting whatever strategies, methods or empirical materials are at hand.

Academic approaches

While the commercial qualitative market researcher may be seen as a *bricoleur*, the academic may see many different kinds of *bricoleur* (Denzin and Lincoln 2000). Techniques for conducting qualitative research and for analyzing the data have been drawn from many different disciplines within the social sciences. A key feature of contemporary academic qualitative research is its diversity and it comes in many different varieties. Tesch (1990), for example, distinguishes no fewer than 27 different varieties depending largely on the purpose of the research, which may, for example, focus on the characteristics of language, the discovery of regularities, or the understanding of text or social action.

Unlike quantitative research, there is no unified set of principles agreed by networked groups of scholars. Qualitative approaches are complex, changing and often contested with frequent tensions, contradictions and hesitations. Debate on methodological issues has continued vigorously. There are huge handbooks on qualitative research such as by Denzin and Lincoln (2000) which is over 1000 pages. Sage Publications has 90 volumes in its Qualitative Research Methods series. There are new journals, newsletters, annual forums, conferences and special interest groups.

The approaches most likely to be used by academic market researchers include:

- content analysis,
- ethnography,
- grounded theory,
- phenomenology and hermeneutics,
- discourse analysis,
- semiotics.

These approaches are sometimes seen as methodologies – ways of "doing" qualitative research – and will include both the construction and the analysis of qualitative data. Alternatively, they can be seen as essentially ways of analyzing text and other qualitative data that may have been constructed in ways that were explained in Chapter 4. In reality, the methodology and the analysis of the data are closely interlinked, more so in some approaches than in others. It is convenient, however, to focus in this chapter on data analysis, but not to the exclusion of overall methodologies.

Content analysis

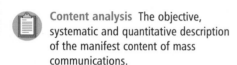

Content analysis The objective, systematic and quantitative description of the manifest content of mass communications.

Although **content analysis** is sometimes used, somewhat loosely, as synonymous with coding and retrieving the content of any textual or visual materials, including transcripts arising from interview methods, it is more appropriately used to refer to the objective, systematic and quantitative description of the manifest content of mass communications. The technique was initiated by communication, sociology, and journalism scholars some 50 years ago and has gained validity as a research tool in thousands of studies examining messages ranging from television beer commercials to gender issues in advertising. It will typically involve counting up the use of words, phrases, characters, themes, topics or space and duration measures in a sample of advertisements. Content analysis in effect creates quantitative data from qualitative materials.

Many examinations of advertising content have analyzed features of the medium itself, for example the characteristics of headlines, graphics, print advertisements and copy. Others have focused on the content of the message such as the subject of the advertisement or the approach to the subject (e.g. use of humor, fear, puffery, celebrity endorsement, message complexity). Some studies have been quite comprehensive; Stewart and Furse (1986), for example, developed a 151-item content analysis scheme for television commercials, which they related to measures of recall, comprehension and persuasiveness for 1059 spots. They found both recall and persuasion to be influenced by brand performance characteristics (e.g. a brand-differentiated message, convenience of product use) and attention and memory factors (e.g. humor, mnemonic devices, front-end impact, brand sign-offs). More recently, Naccarato and Neuendorf (1997) have argued for the application of content analysis to advertising as a method of predicting advertising effectiveness.

Content analysis can be used for analyzing the content of magazines.

© ELLY GODFROY/ALANY

Ethnography

Ethnography, which was explained as a method of data construction in Chapter 4, can also be seen as a way of analyzing data arising from the ethnographic mix of observational techniques, participation, interviewing and the analysis of documents. One of the key characteristics of ethnographic reports is what is often referred to as "thick" description – a dense and detailed account of everyday life, the habits and routines of informants and their experiences and social relationships. It may be written in a manner that aspires to objectivity and neutrality, in the third person and with the ethnographer being excluded from the text. Alternatively, personal language, often in the first person, may be used to describe in detail the strategies and techniques used by the ethnographer in the field. It will include a "natural history" of how the research proceeded, a demonstration of what the ethnographer has done to demonstrate how the knowledge was gained and a degree of reflexivity. The researcher is seen to be no more detached from the objects of study than are the informants. Researchers have their own understandings, their own convictions and prejudices. They, too, are – or become – part of the culture being studied and so are able to reflect directly upon it to some extent. The researcher can also reflect on his or her role and preconceptions, actions, feelings and conflicts. Reflexivity also requires the researcher to take stock of his or her relationships with participants. Experiences of surprise, shock, amusement or mistakes made may also be part of the account.

A feature of thick description is that it defies summary and analysis. There will be no selecting, categorizing and coding. It is the detail that counts. This means that such accounts tend to be long and not suitable for publication in this form for journal articles. Interpretation, furthermore, may be creative, imaginative, impressionistic and with a strong and lively storyline. In this format it may be judged by some as "unscientific" or lacking on rigor. The *Case Study: Living 24/7* at the end of this chapter describes a piece of ethnographic research carried out in Brazil.

The use of ethnography within marketing is becoming fairly widespread. Other examples of ethnographic work in marketing include Stebbins (1997), who illustrates the potential of such research for the study of lifestyles, Arnould and Wallendorf (1994) who discuss the relevance of market-oriented ethnography to developing marketing strategy, Hill's (1991) study of homeless women and the meaning of possessions, and Ritson and Elliott's (1999) analysis of adolescents and their use of advertisements, which was based on extended encounters with groups of teenagers.

Ethnographic research is not easy to do. Researchers need to immerse themselves in the field over a long period of time and at the same time try to be an impartial observer. Such research impacts on researchers' emotions, on their personal lives and maybe on their ethical frameworks. However, it can provide data on small groups that cannot be gathered in any other way. There is a closeness to the reality of the processes under investigation.

Ethnography has attracted some criticism on ethical grounds, particularly when the researcher is not known to be a researcher by those studied, and if this is known how much the participants understand about the research. The participation of the researcher may sometimes result in situations that are upsetting or even harmful to the groups studied. Brownlie (1997) has argued that ethnography as pure description is just not possible, and that where the researcher is known to be a researcher, then members of the group may put on performances for the benefit of the researcher. Meaning is never neutral nor finally fixed, but becomes embedded in what Brownlie calls "writerly accounts" and as far as academic research is concerned in academic prose and scholarly rhetoric that is designed to enhance to probability of publication in scholarly journals.

Grounded theory

Grounded theory A method of generating theory inductively from the data.

If ethnographers consciously avoid categorization and coding, those who follow the grounded theory approach positively embrace these activities. **Grounded theory** is a method of generating theory inductively from or grounded in the data. It is useful when little is known about a topic, or when a new approach to a familiar setting is required. It has a particular set of techniques that were developed in the 1960s by two medical sociologists, Glaser and Strauss (1967).

The key steps involved in a grounded theory are illustrated in Figure 10.2. Finding conceptual categories in the data is a process grounded theorists call "open coding". This refers to the notion of "breaking open" the data into more abstract conceptual categories. The key question is always, "What is this piece of text an example of?" Open coding is thus more than just putting labels or codes onto pieces of data. It entails looking at the dimensions that lie behind them. There is no *a priori* coding scheme that is imposed: the codes emerge from, are generated by, the data. They are provisional and any piece of text may be coded in several different ways at the same time. Each piece of text, ideally, indicates a more abstract idea and the researcher will go through all the text line by line. Thus a study of television commercial break behavior might suggest, from an analysis of what people say they do when the commercial break comes on, a series of categories like "the zapper", "the channel-hopper", "the program loyalist" and the "commercial avoider".

Finding relationships between the categories is called "axial" or "theoretical" coding by grounded theorists. "Axial" denotes the idea of putting an axis through the data to form the connections. There are many ways in which these relationships can occur, but they tend to parallel those for quantitative variables, for example looking for causal relationships or conditions, intervening factors and reciprocal relationships. Text segments are continuously compared for similarities and differences. The output is a series of propositions. Thus television commercial break behavior may appear to be related to weight of television viewing, the presence of other watchers, age and gender.

Accounting for the relationships at a higher level of abstraction is "selective" coding in which "core" categories are selected. These are the central phenomena

---

FIGURE 10.2

Key steps in doing grounded theory

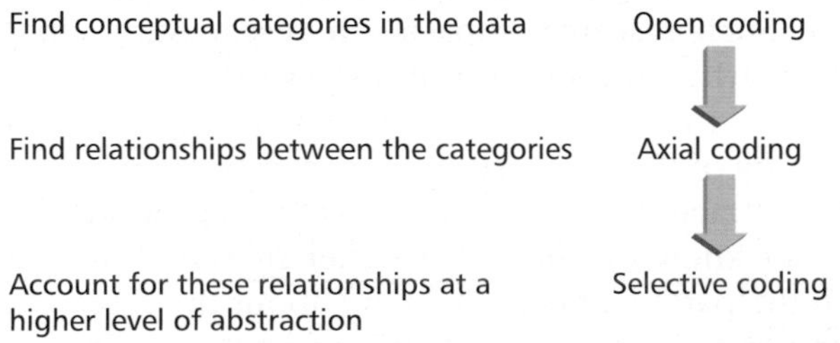

Find conceptual categories in the data	Open coding
Find relationships between the categories	Axial coding
Account for these relationships at a higher level of abstraction	Selective coding

about which the categories are integrated. Thus television commercial break behavior may itself be an instance of a wider phenomenon of reactions to advertising and their relationship to involvement with the media.

A key process in grounded theory is **memoing**. Researchers continuously write memos to themselves about their own observations, thoughts and ideas. There should be comments on the categories and codes being developed. When collected together, these memos should form the basis for the third stage of selective coding and the development of the theory.

A feature of grounded theory is that data collection and data analysis alternate – a process that continues until new data are no longer showing any new theoretical elements. This is a point called "theoretical saturation" and the process itself is usually referred to as "theoretical sampling". The researcher works both inductively and deductively. Early hunches may subsequently be checked against further data. Box 10.1 shows the key role played by memoing.

Other applications of grounded theory in marketing include Belk et al. (1989) who used aspects of grounded theory in their analysis of the sacred and the profane in consumer behavior, Hirschman and Thompson's (1997) analysis of advertising and the mass media, Burchill and Fine's (1997) study of product concept development, De la Cuesta (1994) on marketing and health visiting and Goulding (1999, 2000) on consumer experiences at heritage sites and museums.

Grounded theory has its critics, who point out that the theory generated is by definition context-specific; taking the theory and "testing" it in other contexts would be against the spirit of the approach. Others have argued that its rhetoric can be misleading and it fails to acknowledge the implicit theories that guide the early analysis. The main problems with grounded theory according to Goulding (2005) appear to stem largely from its misuse and abuse. Studies are commonly labeled as "grounded theory", but have not followed its principles. Grounded theory can of course be used alongside other approaches. Pettigrew (2000), for example, discusses the "marriage" of grounded theory with ethnography to gain deeper insight into consumer experiences. A significant deterrent to the use of grounded theory is that it takes a long time and it is very difficult to give an accurate timescale for the research. This may be acceptable for academic research, but will cause problems for client-based research.

Memoing The writing up of ideas, observations and thoughts as they strike the analyst in the analysis of qualitative data and which become the basis of an emerging theory.

EUROPEAN MARKETING RESEARCH

Surfing the web in Belgium

BOX 10.1

Muylle et al. (1999) studied the behaviors and underlying motivations of Belgian consumers and business people surfing the web. They observed and videoed people navigating the web and then interviewed them, confronting them with video images of their own navigation behaviors. In analyzing the transcripts, the authors, in engaging in open coding, noted (in a memo) the concept of "waiting", but this appeared to have two dimensions, namely, "duration" (short/long) and "degree of continuity" (continuous/intermittent). When engaging in axial coding, the authors noted (in a separate memo) that "waiting" was related to "purposiveness of information search". Those who had low search purposiveness were less willing to wait for information.

Phenomenology

Though in both ethnography and in grounded theory there is an attempt by the researcher to understand consumers or business managers from their own perspective, it is the interpretation of the researchers that takes precedence. The literature may, furthermore, provide informative contributions to that interpretation. However, to prepare an interpretation "is itself to construct a reading of these meanings; it is to offer the enquirer's construction of the constructions of the actors one studies" (Schwandt 1994). In phenomenological research, by contrast, primacy is given to the subjective experience of the participant. The words of informants or the texts they produce are seen as the only valid sources of data; the participant's view is taken at face value as "fact". Respondents, furthermore, are selected only if they have "lived" the experience under study. Sampling is therefore purposive and samples tend to be very small – perhaps no more than ten or so.

Phenomenology has its roots in the European philosophy of Husserl (1859–1938). He suggested that each of us exists in a unique "life-world" that is each person's subjective experience of their everyday life and is made up of objects, people, actions and institutions. This life-world is each person's social reality and it determines the meanings that people attach to their actions and to the actions of others. Husserl wanted to understand how life-worlds were constructed through a process of sense-making in everyday life. Phenomenology has since developed into a number of strands including social phenomenology, which focuses on social acts and group experiences, transcendental phenomenology, which emphasizes individual experiences, and hermeneutic phenomenology, in which texts (including transcripts of interviews) are interpreted according to the context in which phenomena occur.

The aim is to look at phenomena in a fresh way. This means that researchers have to state their own assumptions regarding the phenomena being studied and then put them aside – or to "bracket" them as phenomenologists would say. This means that preconceptions should not get in the way of understanding the experiences of others. They then immerse themselves in the taped or transcribed interviews with respondents, trying to empathize with their experience of the phenomenon under investigation. Deeper analysis follows, involving both common-sense and theoretical interpretations of each transcript or tape. The goal is to present an exhaustive, analytic description of the phenomenon under study.

Action is behavior endowed with meaning. These meanings do not have an objective existence independent of the social actor; rather they are ongoing accomplishments each time an action is performed. Phenomenologists often work with interview transcripts, but they are careful, even dubious, about condensing their material. They do not, for example, use coding, but attempt to reach the "life-world" of the respondent through "thick" description and a practical understanding of meanings and actions. As with ethnography, reflexivity on the part of the researcher plays a key role. Phenomenology helps researchers to empathize with, to "get into the shoes of", other people and to understand how they experience everyday life. Box 10.2 illustrates how one set of phenomenological interviews were carried out.

Phenomenology A method of research in which primacy is given to understanding the subjective experiences of the participant in the research.

A phenomenological interview can be very intensive.

© TOM DE BRUYNE

RESEARCH IN ACTION
A phenomenology of shopping

BOX 10.2

Thompson et al. (1990) report the results of ten "phenomenological interviews" with married women aged from 27 to 42 who had children and who were not currently engaged in full-time employment. In a phenomenological interview the course of the dialogue is set by the participant rather than being guided by prespecified questions. The interviewer seeks to provide a setting that is conducive to a descriptively focused, nonjudgmental dialogue. Each interview began with the question, "Can you think of a product that you have bought that you would like to talk about?" All other questions emerged spontaneously from the ensuing dialogue. Interviews lasted from one to two hours and once they were under way the opening question exerted little influence on the overall course of the conversation.

Thompson et al. then describe in great detail a conversation with one respondent showing how the themes of "completeness" and "incompleteness" of a shopping experience were crucial to how she felt about that experience. Other themes included a sense of being organized or disorganized and of purchases being perfect or imperfect. This was her "lived experience" of shopping. The authors then investigated the sense in which these experiential meanings are shared in other conversations. They suggest that a phenomenological theme is like a melody. Our experience of it does not depend on any specific set of notes; what is crucial is the organization of the notes relative to each other. Thompson et al. then provide a detailed analytic description of participants' feelings and perspectives contained in these themes. Finally, they did a "member check" in which they showed their findings to participants to check that the description validated their original experiences.

Phenomenological analysis is in many ways similar to grounded theory, but the aim is not so much to generate abstract theory as to present the experience in a holistic way and to contextualize it with the "life-world" settings of participants, for example in Box 10.2, the demands of shopping. While grounded theory is very much a one-way inductive process, moving from the data to generate hypotheses and theory, phenomenological analysis uses both induction and deduction in a circular process that moves backwards and forwards between data and theoretical ideas. Researchers using this approach talk about the "hermeneutic circle", in which researchers study "parts in relation to the whole and the whole in relation to the parts" (Kincheloe and McLaren 2000: 286). When this process of "double-fitting" becomes stable then the hermeneutic circle is said to be closed.

Other work by Thompson explores gendered consumption and lifestyle (Thompson 1996) while Thompson and Haykto (1997) deconstruct the meaning of fashion discourses and the link to identity. Other consumer studies that have adopted a phenomenological position include Mick and Demoss's (1990) exploration of self-gift giving and O'Guinn and Faber's (1989) work on compulsive shopping.

More recently, Woodruff-Burton et al. (2002) have studied gender and addictive consumption, while Goulding et al. (2002) have analyzed dance culture and its link to identity fragmentation and the emergence of neocommunities.

Undertaking a phenomenological study means understanding the philosophy underpinning the approach. It is not an easy form of analysis to do. Finding people who have experienced the phenomenon you wish to investigate and who are willing to spend time in extended discussion about it may be difficult.

Discourse analysis

Discourse analysis focuses on language, both as talk and as text, and recognizes that language is not simply a device for producing and transmitting meaning – it

Discourse analysis A method of qualitative data analysis that focuses on language, both as talk and as text.

is a strategy that people use to try to create a particular effect. Advertisers in particular use language in ways that try to create particular brand images or associations. Of special importance is the cultural and political context in which discourse occurs and the way language is used to construct different versions of events or activities.

Interviews are approached as "conversational encounters" in which the focus is on how communication is constructed and what it achieves rather than on what people believe. This means trying to generate informal conversational exchanges rather than question-and-answer sessions.

In the analysis of the data the focus is on whole chunks of language rather than on key words or themes. Patterns of rhetoric are sometimes called "interpretive repertoires" that may then be given labels like "corporate view", "managerial imperative", or "knowledge of the client". The assumption behind much discourse analysis is that reality is manufactured through such discourse.

Discourse embraces all aspects of communication – its content, who says it, its audience, its authority, its objective. It encompasses ideas, statements, knowledge, questions and a range of forms of nonverbal communication. It is not, however, a unified body of theory, method and practice, but includes several different types of work, for example focusing on the speech used, on the strategies used for turn-taking during discourse or on looking at how social behavior itself consists largely of discourse.

For all these, however, discourse both reflects human experience and at the same time constitutes important parts of that experience. Social realities are to some extent created or manufactured through discourse. To the extent that it does this, however, it is overlooking preexisting material, social objects or mechanisms that exist independently of language. Discourse analysis is not easy to undertake and it is a time-consuming method of analysis involving the critical reading of talk and texts. Box 10.3 shows how a discourse analysis revealed that a management was "running silent" on exercising any corporate authority.

RESEARCH IN ACTION
Advertising agency interpretive repertoires

BOX 10.3

In 1998, Hackley (2000) spent a number of days in a top UK advertising agency interviewing account managers, creatives and planners to come out with 35 000 audio recorded words from conversational interviews. His focus was on the discourse itself rather than the objects of the discourse. After painstakingly typing and rereading the transcripts for the best part of a year, Hackley realized that in the agency, organizational members had to assimilate discourses (expressed through interpretive repertoires) that were ever present, but nameless. These were used to construct a credible professional identity through momentary authoritative expressions of them. He finally generated eight main categories of interpretive repertoires that he called "corporate way", "strategic imperative", "managerial imperative", "intellectual contingency", "power of rationality", "knowledge of the client", "knowledge of the consumer", and the "power of creativity". Management appeared to be "running silent" in the sense that explicit, overt, bureaucratic, sanction-backed directive corporate authority was not evident; but power, authority and professional identity were discursively reproduced in the service of corporate goals.

Semiotics

While most qualitative methods involve direct contact with the consumer, Desai (2002) explains that semioticians aim to interrogate the *products* of consumer culture directly. The consumer is viewed not as an independent, self-determining agent making his or her own choices, but as a product of culture. Consumer needs, wants and desires are not the result of freely made choices, but rather reflect surrounding cultural discourses. Meanings are constructed within popular culture and consumers are influenced by this cultural context. Lawes (2002) puts it as follows: whereas traditional interviews and focus groups are geared to getting psychological phenomena such as perceptions, attitudes and beliefs out of people's heads, semioticians ask how these things got into people's heads in the first place. The answer is that they come from the surrounding culture that includes the ways in which people communicate with one another. Semiotics is, accordingly, "tailor-made for understanding packaging, advertising, all kinds of marketing literature and even spaces such as retail environments" (Lawes 2002). If, for example, most people associate gold on packaging with luxury goods, then this amounts to a sign or cultural code that underpins the communication. Signs, however, change over time and it is important to avoid lapsed or outdated signs and to use the latest or emergent ones.

Semiotics has its origins in structural linguistics. This is based on the theories of a nineteenth-century Swiss linguist, de Saussure. He argued that words have no intrinsic meaning – they acquire meaning only through context. Language itself is a system of signs. A sign is an image or symbol that by convention stands for something else. There are many different sign systems – music, mathematics, codes of various kinds, street signs and, of course, language can be seen as a symbolic sign system. Saussure argued that rather than language reflecting reality, it is the case that language constructs the way we see our world.

Modern semiotics is, in fact, concerned with everything that can be taken as a sign, for example fashion, car advertising, packaging, architecture. These can be analyzed as sign systems with conventions about the connection between the arbitrarily chosen sounds used to bring to mind a particular concept and the idea itself. Signs derive their meaning from underlying structures, and semioticians strive to identify the mechanisms by which meaning is produced. They have suggested a range of techniques for doing this (see Feldman 1995).

According to Lawes (2002), although semiotics has been around for a long time and most market research suppliers and probably many clients know of its existence, it is seldom used. Not many agencies offer it and few clients request it, although one or two agencies like Semiotic Solutions (**www.semioticsolutions. com**) do specialize in it. This is possibly because semiotics is seen as something of a "black box". Analytic material goes in at one end and some conclusions come out at the other. What happens in between is something of a mystery. Laws suggests a semiotic "toolkit" that tries to explain what goes on in the black box. The kit includes, she suggests, looking for visual, linguistic and aural signs, at the implied communication situation, the textual structure, the information structure, the visual emphasis, the contrasts and the communication codes. Semiotic analysis is complex and it is often not easy to convince clients that the analysis is more than "just" opinion, and that there is corroboration and a certain dignity and status attached to opinion in any case. Semiotics, in fact, works really well when combined with other forms of qualitative research. Box 10.4 explains the hidden messages in many of the things that market researchers write or what they call their agencies.

Semiotics A method of analyzing qualitative data in which the focus is on the products of consumer culture and the signs that they give off.

RESEARCH IN ACTION
The semiotics of market researchers

BOX 10.4

Valentine (2002) reports the results of a semiotic analysis of the language and imagery that market researchers use to communicate who they are, what they do and how they might contribute to the modern world of strategic planning. There has been concern for a number of years about the way the market research industry markets itself. Valentine concludes that market research communication is based on a set of taken-for-granted assumptions and cultural beliefs that encoded the old imagery of researcher as backroom technician rather than strategic planner and boardroom action-maker. A close scan of the Market Research News weekly website, literature produced by the Market Research Society, advertisements by agencies, websites, agency names and logos and so on suggests that the industry is inward-looking, concerned with its own systems and economics. Its discourse is fixed firmly in the language of company organization and industry economics. The existing code emphasizes technical expertise, knowledge, information, stability, predictability, control, rational quantitative analysis, minimization of risk and so on. Customers, on the other hand, are emphasizing change, flexibility, vision and values, imagination and creativity. To relaunch market research as a brand would involve using entirely different language. This is beginning to happen, with agencies calling themselves "Leapfrog", "Vision" or "Talking Shop" rather than the staid "Infoseek", "Diagnostics", or "Scientific Service".

KEY POINTS

Content analysis, ethnography, grounded theory, phenomenology, discourse analysis and semiotics are all ways of approaching the analysis of qualitative data. They tend to be associated with academic qualitative research, although some client-based studies are undertaken using one or more of these approaches. Most client-based research and probably much academic research, however, uses none of these approaches. Researchers rely on summarizing what respondents or participants have said, using quotes or text as illustrations or evidence of the points being made and perhaps moving towards generating more abstract ideas or categories that represent a layer of researcher interpretation. This procedure, almost standard, has no name, but could be called something like "analytic description". Clients want to know what their customers are saying and what the implications are for the issues and problems that face them. Students doing dissertations are likely to find doing grounded theory, phenomenology, discourse analysis or semiotics too challenging, while spending extended periods of time in the field to do an ethnography is just not an option.

Most of the procedures for analyzing qualitative data are based on data generated using one or more of the mechanisms for constructing qualitative data explained in Chapter 4. Only phenomenology prescribes or at least heavily influences the manner in which qualitative data are generated. The phenomenological interview has particular characteristics that were explained earlier. Ethnography will rely less on formal interviews or focus groups and more on informal conversations, observation, participation and the discovery of or access to a range of cultural artifacts. Content analysis and semiotic analysis, however, will focus on the artifacts themselves, including the products of marketing communications like newspaper or magazine ads.

None of the procedures are mutually exclusive and they may be used in combination. It is perfectly feasible, for example, to undertake a grounded theory approach on data that have been the result of an ethnographic undertaking, or imposing a discourse analysis on data derived from what was intended as a phenomenological interview. To combine them all, however, besides amounting to a lifetime's work, may well result in findings that are confusing and maybe contradictory. As to which of the approaches is "best", it is a matter of "horses for courses"; it depends on the nature of the problem and probably also on the personal inclinations of the researcher.

Validity in the analysis of qualitative data

It would be tempting to argue that clients are not interested in issues of validity and that such concerns are largely the preserve of academics. However, analyses that are invalid will be of limited practical value to clients. What clients may be less interested in are the procedures and techniques that can be or have been used to establish validity.

The terms "validity" and "reliability" were introduced in Chapter 5 in the context of the reliability and validity or measurement operations to construct quantitative data. However, these concepts have sometimes been applied to evaluate the quality of qualitative research. Hammersley (1998) and Silverman (2001) are, for example, among those who promote these as benchmarks for qualitative research to follow.

Some researchers have argued, however, that the concepts of validity and reliability are derived from quantitative, positivist approaches to research and are not appropriate to qualitative data; that concepts like "believability" or "robustness" may be more useful. Carson et al. (2001: 67) talk of the "trustworthiness" of qualitative findings that may be derived from the three separate dimensions of credibility, dependability and conformability. Other terms that get used in his context include the ideas of corroboration, triangulation, longitudinal rigor and authenticity. Hammersley (1998) mentions the criterion of "relevance", while Ereaut (2002) talks of "commercial pragmatism" – it is valid if it helps to solve the client's problem or is what the client wants.

Daymon and Holloway (2002: 89) suggest that internal validity can be checked by showing findings to participants and asking for their comments (this is sometimes called "member checking"); reliability may be achieved by creating an audit trail of decisions made during the project. According to Sykes (1990), in qualitative research "validity" may refer to:

- the "goodness" of the data – the kind, accuracy, relevance, richness, colorfulness of the data derived from individual sample units, be they single individuals or groups,
- the "status" of the qualitative findings – their hardness, generalizability, truth, or the extent to which they are "scientific".

Which of these is appropriate depends on the research objectives. If the purpose is to generate ideas for new products, then the number and quality of ideas is important; the question of "truth" in any absolute sense is certainly not. It is in this sense of validity that qualitative research has a particular advantage over other types of research. Topics and ideas can be pursued from a variety of angles and perspectives; it is the flexible and responsive interaction that sparks ideas and gets respondents to think creatively.

If the purpose of the research is for evaluation, or to pick the "best" idea for an advertising theme, then the status or truth of the data is crucial. It is this question that concerns the confidence with which inferences can be made from the data.

Some researchers have argued simply that *no* inferences can be made – because samples are too small and purposively selected, and because the inductive approach does not allow hypothesis-testing. The smallness of the samples has been shown by some studies not to be a great impediment to the kinds of conclusions arrived at, and that qualitative samples can and do satisfy the theoretical requirements for making generalizations, a point argued by Griggs (1987).

KEY POINTS

In quantitative research, "validity" refers to the extent to which measurements accurately reflect "reality" or "the truth". For qualitative research, the term can really be applied – if it is applied at all – only to the validity of the analyses and interpretations performed by the researcher on the data; but as we have seen, these analyses and interpretations may be performed in a number of different ways, focusing on different aspects of the data. There is no one "correct" way of performing qualitative analysis; accordingly, there is no agreed way of assessing validity.

Using computer-assisted qualitative data analysis software (CAQDAS)

Qualitative research can generate huge amounts of unstructured data that can easily result in data overload. While no computer program can perform the analysis for the researcher, there are programs that can help with the more mechanical parts of the process. Word-processors, although not developed with the needs of qualitative researchers in mind, are tools designed for the production and revision of text. They are thus used extensively to assemble qualitative data. Tape recordings of interviews or focus groups can be transcribed; field notes of observations and memos of researcher thoughts can be written and edited. For the purpose of data analysis, however, word-processors have their limitations. Although text can be shifted around using electronic cut and paste or can be copied to other parts of the document, and the "find" facility can be used for limited searches for words and phrases, it is not possible to code and retrieve text segments.

Some of the earlier computer packages that were designed for the analysis of text allowed researchers to perform simple code-and-retrieve operations. They could find and count all instances of words, phrases and combinations of these in one or several files. They could thus be used for content analysis of text (but not for advertisements). Some packages could do various things with the text they found, for example marking them or sorting them into new files. More sophisticated text base managers organized the text more systematically for search and retrieval not only of words and phrases, but also of coded text segments, memos and other materials. Such systems usually organized the text into "records" and "fields" and were more or less a mechanization of the cut-and-paste and colored pens used by most qualitative researchers operating manually. The problem with these storage and retrieval systems was that the record structure needed to be defined *in advance* of entering the data. This made it difficult to change the coding system during the process of analysis.

More recent nonformatted textual database systems (sometimes referred to as "theory-building" packages) keep the original textual data unchanged during the process of coding. Text segments can be coded in several different ways at the same time, while the coding system itself can be changed at any point. These systems enable the researcher to build theory by going beyond simply looking at connections between codes and text to looking at relationships between codes, and links between text segments to develop higher-order categories. They may also have graphic and mapping capabilities, enabling researchers to formulate propositions and test them against the text.

All these systems allow the qualitative researcher to do a number of things:

- the assembly of word-processed files (and in some packages other materials as well) into a single project,

- the attachment of codes to any text segments. Some systems limit the definition of text segments to lines or paragraphs. Others allow the researcher to simply highlight any text for coding. Codes may be free-standing or part of a hierarchical system of codes within codes. The codes are used to signify text rather than to indicate some fact contained in the text. The codes (called "indexes" or "categories" in some systems) are usually words or phrases that indicate an abstract concept rather than codes as combinations of letters and numbers that "stand for" something else,

- the retrieval of all segments from a defined set of documents to which the same code has been attached. These collected segments can then be printed off. The original text remains unaltered, so the retrieved segments are copies of the text. Some programs allow the researcher to retrieve the context of segments by including a specified amount of text either side of the coded segment,

- facilities for recording (and retrieving) memos that can be linked to codes or text segments or both,

- features for defining linkages between codes, both "free" codes and hierarchical codes,

- the use of hypertext systems that allow for direct connections between text segments without using codes,

- the use of variables that can be attached to documents allowing for selective retrievals, e.g. respondents in a certain age group,

- algorithms for searching for co-occurring codes. Some packages allow the use of Boolean operators like "AND". "OR", "NOT" and so on,

- the retrieval of quantitative attributes of the database. Such data can then usually be put into quantitative packages like Excel or SPSS.

Some packages allow direct entry of text into the system while others will operate only with imported files. Some allow external files incorporating video and other material to be indexed. The program that became something of an industry standard was developed in 1981. It was called NUD*IST (which stands for Non-numerical Unstructured Data Indexing, Searching and Theory-building) and was distributed by QSR International in 1995. QSR now calls it "N6". This has, however, become very sophisticated, and accordingly takes considerable investment of time and effort to learn how to use. It is now geared towards handling large-scale projects in a team environment. It is less useful for free-wheeling analyses such as in discourse analysis, grounded theory and phenomenology. QSR accordingly has developed NVivo, launched in 1999, to facilitate more intuitive and graphical approaches. In 2004, QSR launched XSight, which is specifically designed for use in a market research context and on short-term projects. Free demonstration versions of these programs can be downloaded from **www.qsr international.com**.

For those doing "one-off" projects or who have little time to learn how to use software, one of the most user-friendly is MAXqda published by VERBI Software in Germany (**www.maxqda.com**) from where a free demonstration program is available. Using MAXqda (the second version called MAXqda2 was launched in 2005) is explained in Box 10.5. Like much computer-assisted qualitative data analysis software, MAXqda is suited ideally to a grounded theory approach to data analysis, but it can also be used for more straightforward analytic description. Even if you do not have access to this program or have no intention of using it, the description of what it does will give you some idea of how software like this can help.

IN DETAIL
Using MAXqda

BOX 10.5

MAXqda can be used for straightforward code-and-retrieve operations on text files as well as for the more sophisticated approaches like grounded theory. It lets researchers work with both qualitative and quantitative data simultaneously, using one to make better sense of the other. All operations are performed on-screen. There are separate windows for listing the documents that are to form the basis for the analysis, the text being analyzed, the codes being developed and the display of retrieved text segments. These segments can be retrieved in a number of ways including by the use of Boolean logic. Codes, which can be free-standing or hierarchical, can be developed and amended as the researcher goes along. All four screens or any combination may be on display at any one time. This feature makes it highly suitable to the demonstration of text operations.

Typical steps in a MAXqda analysis are as follows.

1 All the texts to be analyzed (transcripts, field notes, memos, letters or other documents) need to be created as rich text files (RTF). This can be done directly in MAXqda or imported from Word (the files need to be saved as RTF files first). If there are a number of interviews or groups, it is better to create a separate text file for each. In MAXqda, all the files that belong together are called a *Project*. The texts in a *Project* can be organized into *Text Groups*. These will be listed on the *Document System* screen (see Figure 10.3). They act as organizing containers for the data.

2 The researcher then selects a file with which to begin analysis. This will then appear in the *Text Browser*. The researcher will read the text, perhaps several times, and begin to think about content and how it could or should be categorized. Figure 10.3, for example, shows part of a transcribed interview with Godfrey concerning neighborhood values. Godfrey, when asked how he feels about the community in which he lives, has launched into a list of the facilities available in the area – schools, churches, parks, housing and so on. Is this how he "defines" how he feels about different areas? A code system can be developed that lists facilities as in Figure 10.3. Text can then be high-lighted and assigned to a code. The remaining documents will need to be coded in the same way. The researcher may now begin to ask, What facilities are important? What aspect of those facilities appeal? Will others mention not facilities, but other aspects of or feelings about the community? All these thoughts can go down in a memo that attaches to this text segment.

3 The next stage is to retrieve all text segments with a particular code, so that all mentions of schools, for example, can be brought together in the retrieved segments screen. These can be copied and pasted to another application or simply printed off. Boolean logic can be used to select various code combinations, for example mentioning schools and churches in the same text segment.

4 In a final stage the researcher may think of ideas at a higher order of abstraction, for example, mention of "facilities" may be seen as an example of an "instrumental" approach to neighborhood evaluation that may be contrasted with a more "expressive" or "emotional" approach. MAXqda allows the researcher to create an amended coding hierarchy and move or copy the codings to the new taxonomy. The objective is to build theories out of text segments, codes and memos.

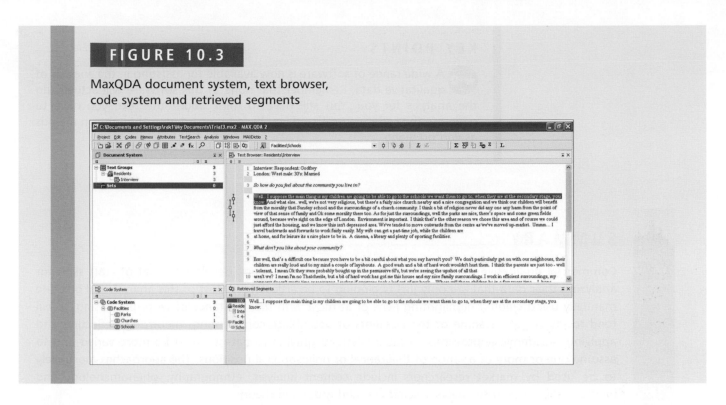

FIGURE 10.3

MaxQDA document system, text browser, code system and retrieved segments

While many academics, particularly in the social sciences, have embraced CAQDAS, commercial qualitative market researchers have been either reluctant to use it or remain ignorant of it. General antipathy to the use of computers in qualitative analysis is evident in the writing by experienced practitioners. Many wish to distance themselves from what they see as a mechanistic and superficial approach that is incompatible with creativity and interpretation. It has been argued that to use CAQDAS for group-discussion material is of limited value and may even hinder the analysis by focusing on code-and-retrieve operations, ignoring the group processes that may have taken place. Critics fear alienation from the data, with the package defining what "analysis" means through the logic of the software program. The programs tend to overemphasize coding, and in so doing neglect other forms of textual analysis such as the fine-grained analysis used in discourse analysis. Computers require exact and precisely stated rules that are context-free and contain no ambiguities. To use them in the domain of human understanding, text and talk is, in some views, therefore wholly absurd.

For large-scale interview-based projects, however, CAQDAS can make the handling of data much simpler and much more systematic. It would also make the analytic processes used more explicit and open up the possibility of building up cumulative research data over several projects. Modern CAQDAS programs allow vast amounts of data to be handled, while coding and retrieving can now be accomplished with amazing speed and efficiency. Researchers can categorize, sub-categorize and re-categorize data as they go along. Categories can be revised and integrated with ease. Data can be retrieved that meets a whole range of conditions, making possible more and better comparisons between text segments. It can be argued that CAQDAS programs lend rigor and transparency to the process of data analysis and that they will enable researchers to use the computer to create entirely new methods, for example links can be established in terms of chronology, causality, explanation, contradiction and so on. This means that researchers may be able to analyze data in ways that were not previously practicable.

KEY POINTS

A wide range of software is now available for assisting in the analysis of qualitative data. Remember that none of this software will actually do the analysis for you. You still have to think about the text, you have to generate the codes yourself and you have to record your thoughts in memos as you go along.

SUMMARY

Commercial qualitative market researchers have, over the years, developed a set of craft skills for analyzing their data that are only just beginning to be articulated. Most of this analysis will be done manually using colored highlighting pens or at most with the assistance of word-processing. It will tend to involve all or some of the elements of describing, commenting, theorizing, reflecting and applying. Academic approaches to the analysis of qualitative data tend to be more varied and to assume one or more of a range of theoretical or philosophical positions. The approaches most likely to be used by market researchers include content analysis, ethnography, phenomenology and hermeneutics, discourse analysis, semiotics, and grounded theory.

The validity of the analyses produced by qualitative researchers has been a matter of much debate. There is no one "correct" way of performing qualitative analysis; accordingly, there is no agreed way of assessing validity. Other terms like "believability" or "robustness" may be more appropriate.

A wide range of software is now available for assisting in the analysis of qualitative data, but none of it will actually do the analysis for the researcher. Its advantages for very small projects where there are only a few interviews or recorded focus group discussions are quite limited. The analysis may as well be done by hand. However, for larger projects the use of software like MAXqda, or the better-known NUD*IST and Nvivo programs, can help researchers handle quite large quantities of data.

QUESTIONS FOR DISCUSSION

1   In what ways does the analysis of qualitative data differ between commercial and academic researchers?

2   To what extent do you think the traditional concepts of reliability and validity can or should be applied to the results of qualitative research?

3   To what extent does the use of computer-assisted data analysis software constrain the ways in which qualitative data are analyzed?

CASE STUDY LIVING 24/7

In 2002, two large companies in Brazil (Proctor and Gamble and Sadia) joined forces to conduct ethnographic research (Mariano et al. 2003). They called the study "Living 24/7" and it consisted of researchers from an agency living seven days, 24 hours a day in 25 low-income households. They participated in the family's everyday life, focusing mainly on the housewife. They studied the life stories of household residents, they took photographs of all objects, products and rooms in the house and how products and brands related individually with each person. Data were collected in a "guided notebook" that featured more than 200 items that should be observed. They kept a field diary and audio-recorded interviews. The purpose was to understand more deeply the family's lives, habits, activities and aspirations. The companies' aim was to target this low-income segment. In Brazil this corresponds to over 75 percent of the Brazilian population. They found that low-income consumers do not purchase exclusively on price, but rather looked for the "smart purchase". They will take advantage of reduced prices; they will experiment; they prefer small local stores and door-to-door sales. All this meant that the companies needed to adapt their product, communications and distribution strategies to reach low-income consumers.

Questions and activities

1 To what extent do you think this was a "valid" piece of research?
2 What other forms of qualitative research than ethnography could have been used?

FURTHER READING

Daymon, C. and Holloway, I. (2002) *Qualitative Research Methods in Public Relations and Marketing Communications*. London: Routledge. Chapters 8, 9, 10.

Elliot, R. and Jankel-Elliot, N. (2003) "Using ethnography in strategic consumer research", *Qualitative Marketing Research*, 6 (4): 215–223.

Ereaut, G. (2002) *Analysis and Interpretation in Qualitative Market Research*. Volume 4 in Ereaut, G., Imms, M. and Callingham, M. (eds), (2002) *Qualitative Market Research: Principle and Practice*. London: Sage.

Goulding, C. (1998) "Grounded theory: the missing methodology on the interpretivist agenda", *Qualitative Market Research: An International Journal*, 1 (1): 50–57.

Kozinets, R. (2002) "The field behind the screen: using netography for marketing research in online communities", *Journal of Marketing Research*, 39 (1): 61–72.

Lawes, R. (2002) "Demystifying semiotics: some key questions answered", *International Journal of Market Research*, 44 (3): 251–264.

Miles, M. and Huberman, M. (1994) *Qualitative Data Analysis*, 2nd edn. Thousand Oaks, CA: Sage.

Riffe, D., Lacy, S. and Fico, F. (1998) *Analyzing Media Messages: Using Quantitative Content Analysis in Research*. London: Lawrence Erlbaum.

Thompson, C., Locander, W. and Pollio, H. (1990) "The lived meaning of free choice: an existential-phenomenological description of everyday consumer experiences of contemporary married women", *Journal of Consumer Research*, 17 (December): 346–361.

11

Analyzing quantitative data
Essential descriptive summaries of single variables

→ the process of preparing data ready for analysis, including checking, editing, coding, and assembly in a data matrix,

→ the key factors affecting the choice of data analysis technique,

→ the display of categorical and metric variables in tables and charts,

→ the statistics used to summarize categorical and metric variables,

→ the data transformations that may be necessary before further analysis is carried out,

→ how to use SPSS to do the calculations for you.

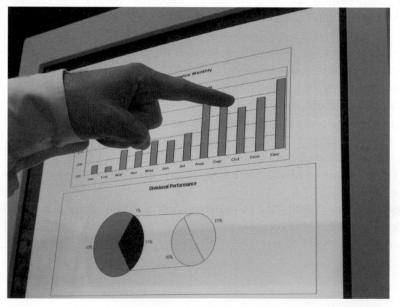

Quantitative data can be presented visually.

© ROB FRIEDMAN

INTRODUCTION

In **Chapter 5 it was explained** that quantitative data are constructed by designing research that specifies when, where and how the construction process is to take place, capturing the data and then assembling them together ready for analysis. So, data assembly was presented as part of the data construction process. However, it is appropriate to consider data assembly here at the outset of data analysis (as it was in the previous chapter on analyzing qualitative data). Chapter 5 also explained that all quantitative data have a structure that consists of three parts: the entities whose characteristics are being recorded (the cases), the characteristics themselves (the variables) and the values that have actually been recorded. This chapter explains how these components are normally laid out in the form of a data matrix ready for analysis. However, before data are entered into this matrix they need to be "cleaned" and prepared in various ways.

Data analysis is not just about performing statistical calculations on numerical variables; it is also about making sense of a dataset as a whole, and thinking about a range of alternative ways of approaching the analysis of the dataset. This chapter and Chapters 12 to 14 explain the analysis of quantitative data using currently accepted statistical techniques. These include the essential descriptive statistical summaries that are applied to single variables, which are the focus of this chapter. Chapter 12 turns to analyzing relationships between two variables, while Chapter 13 considers the process of making statistical inferences from samples of cases to populations. Chapter 14 explains multivariate techniques that analyze the relationships simultaneously between three or more variables often combined with statistical inference. Finally, Chapter 15 considers some of the alternatives to "mainstream" statistical approaches. A summary of the steps involved in conducting quantitative research is illustrated in Figure 11.1.

Though it is not necessary for marketers, or even market researchers, to become experts in statistical analysis, and though computers and their software will actually perform any calculations that researchers need to make, it is nevertheless true that they will encounter data summarized in statistical terms during the course of their careers, and they may well need to use or instruct others how to use data analysis software. So it is important to have a conceptual understanding of the commonly used statistical procedures, to know when each measure may be appropriately used, to be able to interpret and utilize the results of statistical analysis, and to be aware of the assumptions made by and limitations of such procedures.

INTERNET ACTIVITY

Using your browser, go to **www.thomsonlearning.co.uk/kent** and select the Chapter 11 Internet Activity which will provide a link to the Royal Statistical Society website. Take a look at careers in statistics.

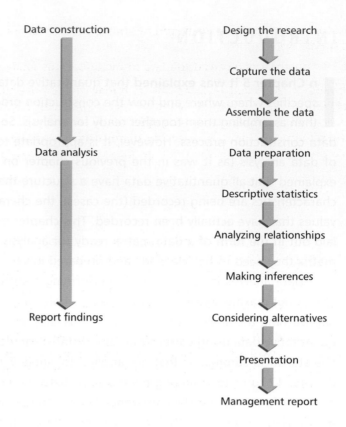

FIGURE 11.1

Steps in conducting
quantitative research

Preparing data for analysis

Handled with care, data preparation can substantially enhance the quality of data analysis. Paying inadequate attention to it can seriously compromise the validity of the results. The key steps involved are shown in Figure 11.2.

Checking

Most quantitative data will have been captured using some form of questionnaire, whether paper or electronic, so the first step involves checking all the questionnaires for useability. Questionnaires returned by interviewers, by post or over the internet may be unuseable for a number of reasons:

- a number of the questions that are appropriate for a given respondent have not been answered,

- the pattern of responses is such that it indicates that the respondent either did not understand or follow instructions,

- one or more pages is physically missing,

FIGURE 11.2

The data preparation process

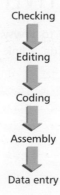

■ the questionnaire has been answered by somebody who is not a member of the survey population,

■ the questionnaire was received too late to include in the analysis.

If questionnaires are checked as they come in, it may still be possible to remedy fieldwork deficiencies before they turn into a major problem. If problems are traced to particular interviewers, for example, then they can be replaced or undergo further training. It may be possible to re-contact respondents to seek clarification or completion before the last date they can be entered into the data matrix.

Editing

Questionnaires (either respondent-completed or interviewer-completed) are returned to the researcher for every respondent successfully contacted. **Editing** is the process of scrutinizing completed data collection forms and taking whatever corrective action is required to ensure that the data are of high quality. It is a kind of quality control check on the raw data to ensure that they are complete, accurate and consistent.

Editing The scrutiny of returned questionnaires to ensure that as far as possible they are complete, accurate and consistent.

A preliminary or field edit is a quick examination of completed data collection forms. Its purpose is twofold: to ensure that proper procedures are being followed in selecting respondents, interviewing them and recording their responses, and to remedy fieldwork deficiencies before they turn into a major problem. Speed is crucial and it needs to be done while the fieldwork is still in progress. Typical problems that are discovered in field edits include:

■ inappropriate respondents,

■ incomplete questionnaires,

■ illegible or unclear responses.

When any of these arise, the errors will be traced back to the interviewers concerned, who will be advised of the problems and, if necessary, undergo further training.

A second stage of editing, a final or office edit, is undertaken after all the field-edited questionnaires are received. It involves verifying response consistency and accuracy, making necessary corrections, and deciding whether some or all parts of a questionnaire should be discarded. Some of these checks include:

■ logical checks, for example the 17-year-old claiming to have a PhD or the male claiming to have had an epidural at the birth of his last child,

■ range checks, for example a code of "8" is entered when there are only six response categories for that question,

■ response set checks, for example somebody has "strongly agreed" with all the items on a Likert scale.

Where a question fails a logical check, then the pattern of responses in the rest of the questionnaire may be scrutinized to see what is the most likely explanation for the apparent inconsistency. Range check failures may be referred back to the original respondent. Response set checks may indicate that the respondent is simply being frivolous and the questionnaire may be discarded.

The useable questionnaires are then normally edited. This may involve screening the questions themselves for legibility, completeness and consistency. Obvious inconsistencies can easily be detected, for example a respondent may have answered a series of questions about his or her usage of a particular product, but other responses indicate that they do not possess one or have never used one. In some cases, questions that require a single response may have been given two or more responses. There may still be time to return questionnaires with such unsatisfactory responses to the field department so that interviewers can re-contact respondents. If this is not feasible, the researcher can assign missing values, that is, treat the questions involved as unanswered. This may be suitable if the unsatisfactory responses are not key variables and the number of questions involved is quite small. If this is not the case the questionnaire may be discarded and treated as unuseable. If the number if unuseable questionnaires is small or if the sample size is large, this may not be a problem. If the number of discards is quite large, the researcher will need to check whether they are in any obvious way different from those that are useable. Either way the number of discards should be declared in the report of the research.

Coding

The tasks involved in transforming edited questionnaires into machine-readable form are generally referred to as coding. Most survey analysis packages will accept responses or other data that are in various forms. A key distinction is normally between numeric and alphanumeric or "string" variables (which are strings of letters). This corresponds to the distinction between quantitative and qualitative variables. All quantitative variables should, ideally, be entered into the data matrix in numeric form – there is little point in typing in "male" or "female" if you can type in "1" or "2". Thus binary variables should be coded into 1 or 2 and the categories for nominal and ordinal variables numbered 1, 2, 3, 4, etc. Answers to open-ended questions will either need to be classified and coded, or left as strings, in which case the original comments will simply be listed. Metric data already have numerical scale values that can be entered directly, for example a person's age as "59".

Some, if not all, of the categorical responses will usually be precoded, that is, they are numbered on the questionnaire. If not, they need to be coded afterwards by the researcher. Qualitative responses to open-ended questions may be classified into categories, and the categories then numbered. The procedures for doing this were considered in Chapter 10.

If a question is unanswered, the researcher, when entering data into a survey analysis program, can leave blank the cell in the data matrix (this is explained later in this chapter) and the system will record a missing value. Alternatively, the researcher may, for example, enter a zero to indicate missing values or may wish to distinguish different reasons for the missing value, for example:

90 = not applicable,

91 = refused to answer,

92 = don't know,

93 = forgot to answer.

Coding for the purpose of quantitative analysis (as opposed to the kind of coding that was described in the previous chapter for qualitative data) means assigning a number to each possible answer to each question, usually beginning with 1. It is this numerical code that is then entered into the data matrix. In most questionnaires the majority of questions will have been precoded. However, there will usually be a few open-ended questions that require the researcher to read through them, develop categories of answer and then allocate a code to each category. The set of categories developed should meet the minimum requirements for a nominal scale, namely they should be exhaustive, mutually exclusive and refer to a single dimension. If, however, most of the spaces left for text in the questionnaire have been left empty, it may not be worthwhile doing this. Some pre-coded questions may have an "Other, please specify" category, in which case some further coding may be worthwhile. If fixed-choice questions have not been precoded, then the researcher will need to generate a template that shows what codes are to be allocated as the data are entered. Some survey analysis packages, however, allow the research to enter data by clicking the answer given on an electronic version of a paper questionnaire. This avoids the need to enter codes since the tables generated by the software will reproduce the response categories. For multiple response questions, each response category will need to be treated as a separate variable, coded as 1 if the category is ticked and zero if not. The analysis of open-ended and multiple response questions is considered in more detail later in this chapter.

In large-scale projects, and particularly when the data entry is to be performed by a number of people or by subcontractors, the researchers use a **codebook**, which lists all the variable names (which are short, one-word identifiers), the variable labels (which are more extended descriptions of the variables and which appear as table or chart headings), the response categories used and the code numbers assigned. This means that any researcher can work on the dataset irrespective of whether or not they were involved in the project in its formative stages.

Codebook A list of all the variable names, variable labels, the response categories and the codes assigned for a complete dataset.

Assembly

A record of all the values for all the variables for all the cases in a "piece" of research is normally referred to as a **dataset**. The assembly of all these values is normally in the form of a data matrix, which records all the values for all the variables for all the cases. A data matrix interlaces each case with each variable to produce a "cell" containing the appropriate value, as illustrated in Figure 11.3, which shows the gender, age, social grade and nationality of the first three respondents of a set of n respondents, so the first respondent is male, aged 26, is in social grade C2 (social grades were explained on pp. 158–159) and is British. To be able to analyze the data using computer software like SPSS, which is introduced in the next section of this chapter, all the values that appear as words or letters, like "female", "C1" or "French" need to be given a code number, as illustrated in Figure 11.4.

Dataset A record of all the values for all the variables for all the cases in a research project.

	Gender	Age	Social grade	Nationality
1	Male	26	C2	British
2	Female	32	C1	French
3	Male	19	B	Spanish
•	•	•	•	•
n	Female	33	C1	British

Respondents (vertical axis) — *Variables* (horizontal axis)

FIGURE 11.3

A survey data matrix

Cases	Gender	Age	Social grade	Nationality
1	1	26	4	1
2	2	32	3	2
3	1	19	2	3
•	•	•	•	•
n	2	33	3	1

Respondents (vertical axis) — *Variables* (horizontal axis)

FIGURE 11.4

A survey data matrix

The columns in a data matrix are identified with the variables that are being measured and coded, one column for each variable. Each value down a column will have come from a different respondent, and in an interview survey, for example, different interviewers are likely to have contributed to each column. For the most part, each variable will correspond with a particular question on the questionnaire: the responses will each be coded (see Figure 11.5) and the code that corresponds to the response given will be entered into the data matrix. In some situations, however, one question may give rise to several variables. This will be so, for example, for all multiple-response questions, as illustrated in Figure 11.6, where respondents can pick more than one response category or, indeed, as many categories as apply to them. Each category will be ticked or not ticked, so each gives rise to a separate binary variable. It would have been possible, of course, to have precoded the questionnaire in such a way that [0:1] is placed against each box, but this can be confusing for the respondent, so it would be more usual the leave the numbers 1–7 or whatever against the response categories, even though they will be coded differently when the data are entered into the data matrix.

The order in which the variables are placed in the matrix will tend to follow the sequence in which they occur in the questionnaire. The order is unimportant for analysis purposes, but such a sequence usually makes sense for data entry, otherwise it will be necessary to move about the questionnaire to find each variable.

The rows in the data matrix are identified with the cases, one row for each case, which usually means one row per questionnaire in a market research survey. A row consists of a series of values that have been entered for each respondent. In an interview survey, each row will be the work of a single interviewer. Again the

FIGURE 11.5

A coded single-answer question

How important is it to you that the leisure center has up-to-date equipment?

Very important		1
Fairly important		2
Not important		3

FIGURE 11.6

A multiple-response question

In which of the following countries have you been on holiday in the past five years? (Please tick as many as apply to you)

UK		1
France		2
Spain		3
Greece		4
Turkey		5
Italy		6
Other		7

order of the rows does not matter for analysis purposes. Questionnaires are often entered in the order in which they are received. They will usually be given a number that will correspond with the row number. This means that if there are any queries about a particular questionnaire, it can be traced.

The size of a data matrix is a product of the number of respondents and the number of variables. Where there are many respondents and many variables such as in a large-scale survey, the data matrix will be very large. Thus an inquiry that has 200 respondents to a questionnaire survey with 100 questions will produce a matrix that contains (200) $\times$ (100) or 20 000 cells. Data matrices will have different shapes depending on the nature of the research. Intensive research will have relatively few respondents but many variables; extensive research will have many respondents and few variables. An opinion poll is a good example of the latter where a large sample (of 1000 or so) are asked a few questions about voting intentions and party support. Usually, data matrices are rectangular – all the rows are of the same length and all the columns are of the same length. Some cells may be empty where data are missing for a variety of reasons, which will be explored later in this chapter.

SUGGESTION

There may be some occasions when the researcher is interested almost totally in entities that are not respondents, for example companies, organizations or societies. So, the rows in the matrix may be identified, for example, with companies, one row for each company. The information on such entities will (in a survey) nevertheless come from individual respondents. So, provided there is one respondent for each company it does not matter too much whether we call each row a company or a respondent. If, however, there are several respondents in each company, then it will be better to keep one row for each respondent and which company they come from will become one of the variables.

Data entry

When checking, editing and coding are complete, the data are ready to be entered into the matrix. This is usually accomplished electronically using a survey data analysis package like SPSS. Mistakes can, of course, occur in this process. Any entry that is outside the range of codes that have been allocated will quickly show up in a table. Thus if, for the variable gender, we allocate 1 = "male" and 2 = "female", then entering a "3" or a "4" will show up as a label in the table, as in Table 11.1. Three "3"s and one "4" have been erroneously entered. Provided the questionnaires have been numbered, it would be a simple matter to check the number of the respondent from the data matrix where the wrong codes have been entered and find what the code should have been from the questionnaire. In some packages any entry that is outside of a specified range will be flagged as the data are being keyed in.

Clearly, however, if any "1"s or "2"s had been entered as mistakes, then this would not be apparent. To overcome this, data may be subjected to double-entry data validation. In effect this means that the data are entered twice, usually by two different people, and any discrepancies in the two entries are flagged up by the computer and can be checked against the original questionnaire. Some market research agencies do this, but only on a sample basis so that, for example, only 10 percent of the questionnaires may be subject to double-entry data validation.

TABLE 11.1	Errors in data entry		
	Gender of respondent		
		Frequency	Percent
Valid	Male	10	41.7
	Female	10	41.7
	3	3	12.5
	4	1	4.2
	Total	24	100.0

It is normal nowadays to enter data directly from the questionnaires. For some programs like SPSS, which is explained in Box 11.1, this means entering the appropriate values row-by-row, that is, questionnaire-by-questionnaire, directly into the data matrix. Some packages like Snap or Keypoint (referred to in Chapter 6) allow the researcher to enter the data by clicking the appropriate box with a mouse on an electronic version of the questionnaire. A worksheet is then created that functions like a data matrix and can be saved in a format that can be transferred to other packages. With online surveys, the data matrix is built as respondents submit their completed online questionnaires. The codes are programmed into the HTML questionnaire, but they do not appear as code numbers such as those normally placed on a paper-and-pencil questionnaire. This means that the codebook may be vital since it is the only way to match the numbers in the data file with the answers to the questions on the questionnaire.

The number of cases entered into the data matrix will usually be the number of useable returns. Missing values will either be left blank or a special code will be entered. For non-missing values, what is entered for each variable is a number. If the scale is continuous metric, each scale value may be a unique number, each having a frequency of one and perhaps measured to several decimal places. We could, however, round off, round down or round up each scale value, for example to the nearest whole number, in which case a scale value may happen more than once. Thus in a group of 130 people, there may be 6 persons recorded as aged 23 (age in years rounded down to age last birthday). The number of times a scale value happens is the **frequency** – in this example the frequency of people aged 23 is 6. If the scale is discrete metric, the scale values will be whole numbers anyway and we could record the number of times each value occurs. The result, however, may still be a very large number of scale values. For observed price of Brand X, for example, there may be many different prices observed on the shelves in shops. One way of reducing the number of scale values, but keeping an overall view of the distribution, is to group values together. The number of shops selling Brand X at various prices may be grouped into under 40p, 41–45p, and over 50p. The researcher can then produce a frequency for each grouping.

For categorical scales there will usually be a limited number of categories used as scale values, so it makes sense to report the frequency with which each occurs. The results will often be laid out as a table, the scale values forming the rows, and the frequencies (and perhaps relative frequencies) the columns. Frequency tables are considered in detail later in this chapter.

If respondents are allowed only one response category for a question (a single-answer question), then, by definition, the total number of recorded answers plus the total number of missing values should for each variable always equal the number of useable returns. If it does not, then values have either been omitted or duplicated. For multiple response questions where respondents can tick as many boxes as apply to them, then clearly, the total number of recorded answers may

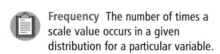

Frequency The number of times a scale value occurs in a given distribution for a particular variable.

considerably exceed sample size. How such questions are analyzed is considered at the end of this chapter.

If the data have been captured online, using computer-assisted telephone or personal interviewing or using optical mark reading equipment, then it may not be necessary to key in the data.

IN DETAIL
Entering data on SPSS

BOX 11.1

In 1968 three young men from disparate professional backgrounds developed a software system based on the idea of using statistics to turn raw data into information essential to decision-making. These three innovators were pioneers in their field, visionaries who recognized that data and how you analyze them are the driving force behind sound decision-making. This revolutionary statistical software system was called SPSS, which stood for the Statistical Package for the Social Sciences. This package, offered by SPSS Inc. and called "SPSS for Windows", is now one of the most widely used survey analysis computer programs. It has gone through many versions, the latest being SPSS 14.0. For more information and a free download of a demo version visit **www.spss.com/spss**.

You can almost certainly obtain access to SPSS by logging onto your own university or college network applications. The first SPSS window you will see is the *Data Editor* window (Figure 11.7). The window is a data matrix whose rows represent cases (no row should contain data on more than one case) and whose columns will contain the values of the variables for each case. No cell can contain more than one value.

Imagine now that you have done a very short customer satisfaction survey in which 20 respondents have filled in a brief questionnaire that records gender, age in years, and their response to a 5-point

FIGURE 11.7

The SPSS *Data Editor* window

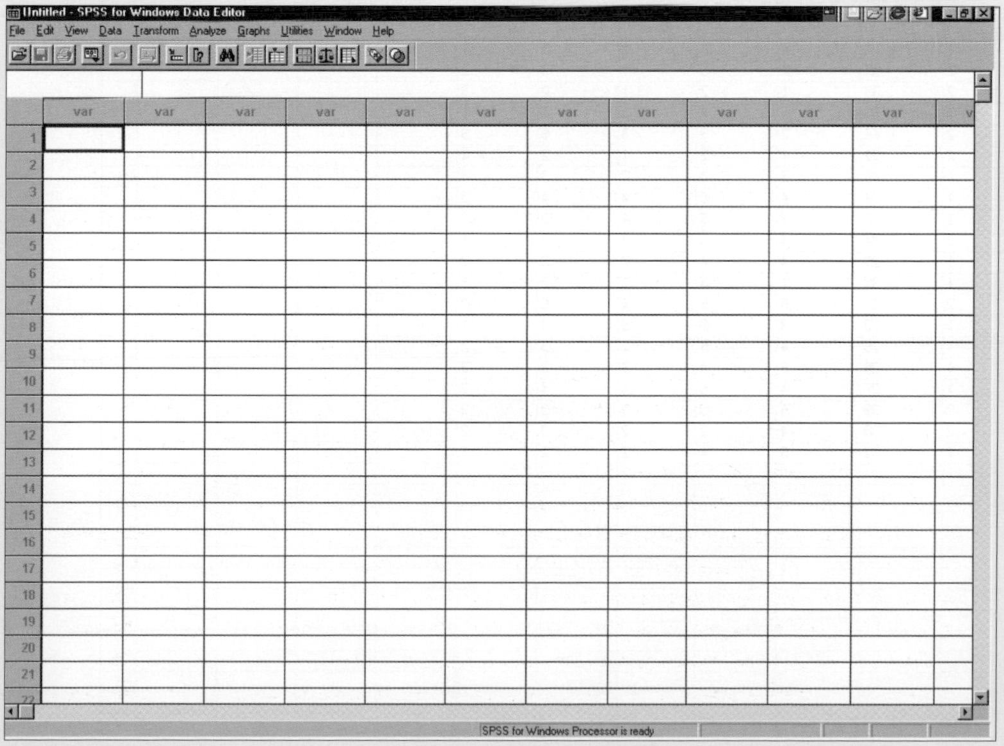

rating of satisfaction on each of 5 dimensions as illustrated in Figure 11.8. Before entering any data, it is advisable first to name the variables (if you don't, you will be supplied with exciting names like *var00001* and *var00002*!). These names must not exceed eight characters, they must begin with a letter and must not end with a full stop. There must be no spaces and the names chosen should not be one of the key words that SPSS uses as special computing terms, for example AND, NOT, EQ, BY, ALL. So, we can name the first variable *gender* and the second variable *age*. For the others we need to think of names that are short and that remind us which variable it refers to. For "speed of getting through" we might just call this *speed*, "getting the right person" we might call *person*; the others we can call *polite*, *know* and *efficy*.

To enter variable names, click on the *Variable View* tab at the bottom left of the *Data Editor* window. Each variable now occupies a row rather than a column as in the *Data Editor* window. Enter the name of the first variable in the top left box. As soon as you hit *Enter* or down arrow or right arrow, the remaining boxes will be filled with default settings, except for *Label*. It is always better to enter labels, since these are what are printed out in your tables and graphs. For categorical variables, you will also need to put in *Values* and *Value Labels*. Click on the appropriate cell under *Values* and click again on the little grey box to the right of the cell. This will produce the *Value Labels* dialog box. Enter an appropriate value, e.g. 1 and *Value Label*, e.g. Male, and click on *Add*. Repeat for each value. The completed *Variable View* screen is shown in Figure 11.9.

The default under *Decimals* is usually 2. If all the variables are integers, then it is worthwhile changing this to zero. Simply click on the cell and use the little down arrow to reduce to zero. Under *Measure*, you can put in the correct level of measurement – nominal, ordinal or scale (i.e. metric). SPSS does not

FIGURE 11.8

The completed data matrix

	gender	age	speed	person	polite	know	efficy	var	var	var	var
1	1	23	4	5	2	3	1				
2	2	27	2	3	1	3	2				
3	2	33	1	2	1	2	3				
4	1	56	5	4	3	4	3				
5	2	46	2	3	3	5	3				
6	2	22	1	2	1	2	4				
7	1	48	3	3	2	3	4				
8	1	34	4	5	4	4	3				
9	2	37	3	5	4	3	2				
10	2	34	4	3	3	3	1				
11	1	25	4	4	2	3	2				
12	1	34	1	3	1	3	3				
13	2	23	5	5	4	5	2				
14	1	22	3	3	3	3	1				
15	1	25	4	5	2	3	2				
16	1	36	5	4	3	3	3				
17	1	27	4	5	4	4	2				
18	2	39	5	3	3	3	3				
19	2	38	4	2	2	2	2				
20	2	32	5	4	2	2	1				
21											
22											
23											
24											
25											
26											
27											
28											
29											
30											
31											
32											
33											

FIGURE 11.9

Completed *Variable View*

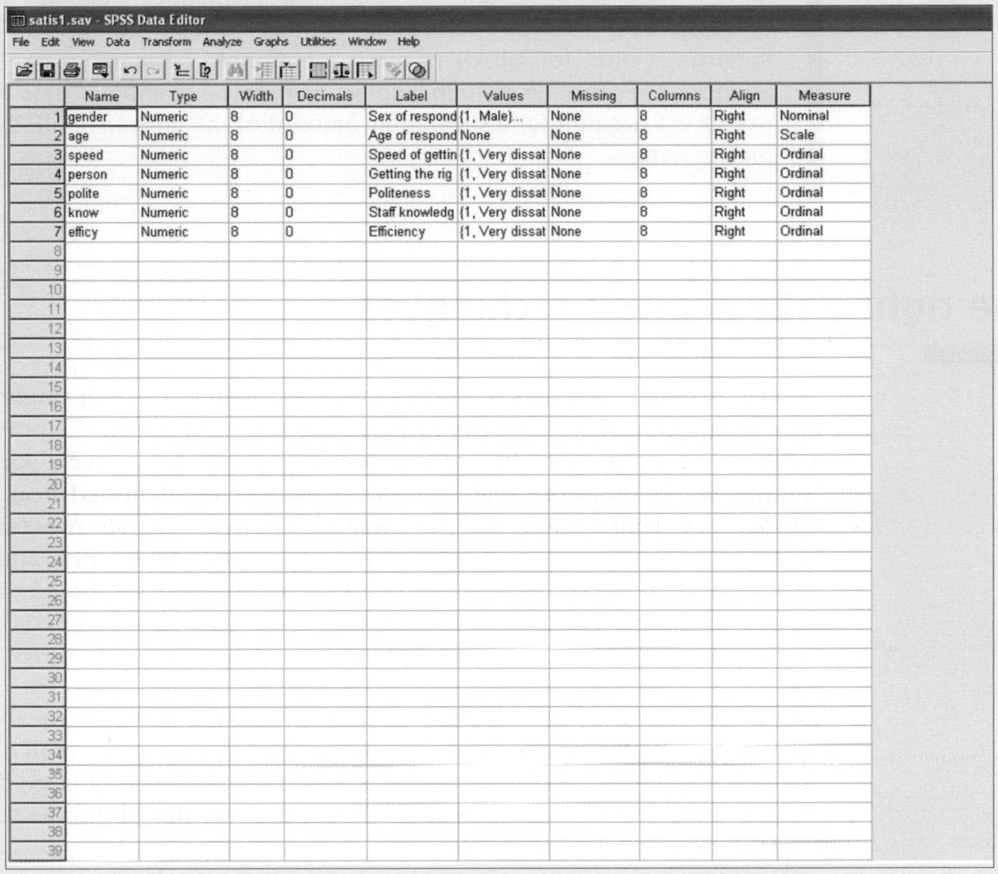

	Name	Type	Width	Decimals	Label	Values	Missing	Columns	Align	Measure
1	gender	Numeric	8	0	Sex of respond	{1, Male}...	None	8	Right	Nominal
2	age	Numeric	8	0	Age of respond	None	None	8	Right	Scale
3	speed	Numeric	8	0	Speed of gettin	{1, Very dissat	None	8	Right	Ordinal
4	person	Numeric	8	0	Getting the rig	{1, Very dissat	None	8	Right	Ordinal
5	polite	Numeric	8	0	Politeness	{1, Very dissat	None	8	Right	Ordinal
6	know	Numeric	8	0	Staff knowledg	{1, Very dissat	None	8	Right	Ordinal
7	efficy	Numeric	8	0	Efficiency	{1, Very dissat	None	8	Right	Ordinal
8										
9										
10										
11										
12										
13										
14										
15										
16										
17										
18										
19										
20										
21										
22										
23										
24										
25										
26										
27										
28										
29										
30										
31										
32										
33										
34										
35										
36										
37										
38										
39										

distinguish between binary and ranking categorical scales, nor between discrete and continuous metric scales. The default setting is *Scale*. Changing the *Measure* to nominal or ordinal in fact makes very little difference to SPSS operations, but it is worthwhile making the changes, even if only to force you to think about what kind of scale is attained by each variable.

To copy any variable information to another variable, like value labels, just use *Edit/Copy* and *Paste*. A list of the codings used on any SPSS file is easy to obtain. Use the *Utilities/Variables* command to produce variable information on each variable.

SPSS does not have an automatic timed backup facility. You need to save your work regularly as you go along. Use the *File/Save* sequence as usual for Windows applications. The first time you go to save you will be given the *Save As* dialog box. Make sure this indicates the drive you want. Drive a: for your floppy disk, Drive c: for your hard disk or Drive h: if you are on a networked system. *File/Exit* will get you out of SPSS and back to the *Program Manager* or Windows desktop. Unlike most other applications, SPSS does not allow you to have several files open at once. You will need to save everything you wish to save before moving to another file or opening a new one.

Choosing the right data analysis techniques

In data assembly the focus is on the entry of a single value for a single respondent on a single variable. The focus of data analysis, by contrast, is upon data in the aggregate, and the individual respondent along with his or her associated values "disappear" in the sense that they can no longer be identified from the results. Though data construction and data analysis are thus separate processes, they are nevertheless interdependent. Both the design of the data matrix and its analysis must reflect the objectives of the research as outlined by the researcher or as agreed between researcher and client. The particular analysis procedures deployed must reflect a clear understanding of how the data were constructed, and in particular the measurement and scaling procedures used. The fact that data construction and data analysis are separate processes, however, means that good-quality data can be used for a number of purposes using a variety of different data analysis techniques. Secondary analysis and the emergence of large data archives (which were considered in Chapter 3) depend on this ability to separate data construction and data analysis.

 Data analysis The process whereby researchers take the raw data that have been entered into a data matrix to create information that can be used to tackle the objectives for which the research was undertaken.

Data analysis is the process whereby researchers take the raw data that have been entered into the data matrix and create information that can be used to tackle the objectives for which the research was undertaken. The raw data are of little value in themselves until they have been structured and summarized and a range of conclusions drawn from them. Such conclusions, furthermore, need to be relevant to the objectives of the research.

Data will have been entered into the data matrix row-by-row; analysis proceeds by performing a range of operations on the columns. Survey knowledge is produced by entering the responses as a row of values that profile a single respondent and then interpreting these entries in columns across respondents to produce distributions. However, before any researcher can decide what analysis techniques to deploy, three key questions need to be answered:

- What does the researcher want to do with the data?
- On what type of scale are the variables recorded?
- How many variables are to be entered into the calculation?

What does the researcher want to do with the data?

The researcher may wish to do one or more of three main things with the data in the data matrix:

- display,

■ summarize,

■ draw conclusions.

Data display takes the raw data and presents them in tables, charts or graphs so that it is possible for readers to "eyeball" the total distribution on a single variable or to observe the pattern of relationships between two or more variables. **Data summary** uses statistical methods like calculating an average on a single variable, or measures of association or correlation on two or more variables to reduce the data to a few key summary measures. Data display and data summaries are components of what is commonly referred to as **descriptive statistics**.

Drawing conclusions may involve one or more of three main activities:

■ statistical inference,

■ evaluating hypotheses against the data,

■ explaining discovered relationships between variables.

Sometimes the data in the data matrix relate to a set of respondents who are part of a sample that was chosen using probability (random) methods. The issues of when survey researchers take samples, sample design and the errors that may arise from the sampling process were considered in Chapter 8. The researcher who has taken a sample may wish to make estimates based on the sample of total, proportional or average values for the population of cases from which the sample was drawn. Alternatively, the researcher may wish to test statements or hypotheses made about the population of cases against the probability that survey research findings were, in fact, a result of random sampling fluctuations. Chapter 13 explains how researchers make inferences both for categorical and for metric variables. These procedures are known usually as "inferential" statistics or "statistical inference". Making estimates is, unsurprisingly, generally referred to as "estimation". The second procedure is commonly called "hypothesis-testing", which in many ways is unfortunate, because testing the statistical significance of a statement is only one of several ways in which hypotheses may be evaluated.

In evaluating hypotheses, the researcher is more concerned about the extent to which the data in the data matrix "fit" or support his or her initial ideas, hunches or formally stated hypotheses. Hypotheses come in many different forms; they may be stated formally before the data analysis begins, or they may emerge during or even after the analysis. All these different circumstances, not surprisingly, affect the ways in which they may be appropriately evaluated.

Once hypotheses have been evaluated, it might still be necessary to explain why the research findings appear to be as they are. What counts as an "explanation", however, can vary enormously from causal analysis to providing understanding to an audience or discovering a dialectic. The last part of Chapter 14 looks at these issues.

On what type of scale are the variables recorded?

Chapter 5 introduced you to different types of scale. It made a basic distinction between categorical and metric scales with the former subdivided into binary, nominal, ordinal and ranked, and the latter subdivided into discrete and continuous. The type of scale crucially affects the kind of statistical operations that may be performed on the data, so after clarifying what they want to do with the data, researchers must be very clear about the nature of the scale for *each* variable being mapped into the matrix.

 Data display The presentation of data in tables, charts or graphs.

 Data summary Reducing the data in a distribution of a single variable or the relationship between variables to a single statistic that acts as a summary.

 Descriptive statistics The display and summary or variables in a dataset.

How many variables are to be entered into the calculation?

Univariate analysis The display, summary or drawing of conclusions from a single variable or set of variables treated one at a time.

When approaching a data matrix, the first thing a researcher needs to do is to look at the distribution of each variable, one at a time. This is usually called **univariate analysis**. So, the researcher might use data display, data summary or statistical inference separately on each variable. What particular techniques are used depends on the scale involved. For categorical variables it would be usual to get SPSS to create univariate (or "one-way") tables, bar charts or pie charts. How this is done is explained later in this chapter. For metric variables it is also possible to create one-way tables for discrete variables, but for continuous variables it would normally be necessary to group the values into class intervals like age grouped into 20–29, 30–39 and so on before this can be done. What summary measures and what procedures for statistical inference can be used on variables one at a time similarly depend on the scale involved.

Bivariate analysis The display, summary or drawing of conclusions from the way in which two variables are related together.

Univariate analysis, however, tells the researcher nothing about the relationships between the variables. **Bivariate analysis** takes variables two at a time to see whether there is any pattern in the way the two values jointly occur, for example do older people have more loyalty to brands than younger people? If the two variables are categorical, it is possible to display the relationship between them in a crosstabulation and to calculate summary measures of the degree of association. If both are metric, then the relationship may be graphed in a **scattergram** and summarized by using **correlation** and **regression**. Similarly, it is possible to undertake statistical inference for bivariate relationships, for example calculating the probability that the degree of association found between two variables could have come about as a result of random sampling fluctuations.

Scattergram A graphical display of the relationship between two metric variables in which each case is represented by a dot that reflects the position of two combined measurements.

Correlate/correlation A pattern in the distribution of two or more metric variables whereby high values on one variable covary with high values on another (or with low value on the other for a negative correlation).

Bivariate analysis is limited to looking at the relationships between variables two at a time; **multivariate analysis** techniques allow the analysis of three or more variables simultaneously. It has a number of advantages over univariate and bivariate procedures, namely:

- it permits conclusions to be drawn about the nature of causal connections between variables (establishing causality is discussed in Chapter 14),

Regression The use of a formula describing a straight line that represents the "best fit" in a scattergram to predict the values of one metric variable from another.

- it facilitates the grouping together of variables that are interrelated, or cases that are similar in terms of their characteristics,

- it provides the ability to predict dependent variables from two or more independent variables and hence improve on predictions made on the basis of only one variable.

Multivariate analysis The display, summary or drawing of conclusions from variables taken three or more at a time.

Where all the variables to be used in multivariate analysis are categorical, then it is possible to "layer" or "control" the relationship between two variables by a third, fourth, fifth variable and so on in the process of crosstabulation. How this is done is explained in Chapter 14. Where all the variables are metric, then much more sophisticated techniques like multiple regression, factor analysis, and cluster analysis are possible. Where variables to be used in multivariate analysis are a mixture of categorical and metric, then other techniques like analysis of variance may be used. This is explained in Chapter 13.

KEY POINTS

Data analysis is not a "one-off" enterprise that a researcher undertakes on one single occasion. Rather it is an iterative process in which the researcher moves backwards and forwards between the objectives of the research and a number of "sessions" of analyzing data from the matrix. For each session, the researcher needs to answer the three questions posed at the beginning of this section:

■ What do I want to do with the data – display, summarize or draw conclusions?

■ Onto what type of scale are the variables recorded – categorical or metric?

■ How many variables do I want to enter into a single calculation – one, two or more than two?

Thus a researcher in one session may wish to display the relationship between two categorical variables and in another may wish to summarize a single metric variable. The various factors that will affect the researcher's choice of technique are illustrated in Figure 11.10, which can be seen as a kind of "map" of the rest of Part III of this book. Notice that, for the sake of completeness, there is a fourth element in Figure 11.10, namely respondents. If these constitute a probability sample then it is possible to deploy statistical inference. If the sample is a nonprobability sample or is a census or an attempt at a census, then such techniques are not appropriate.

FIGURE 11.10

Factors influencing choice of technique

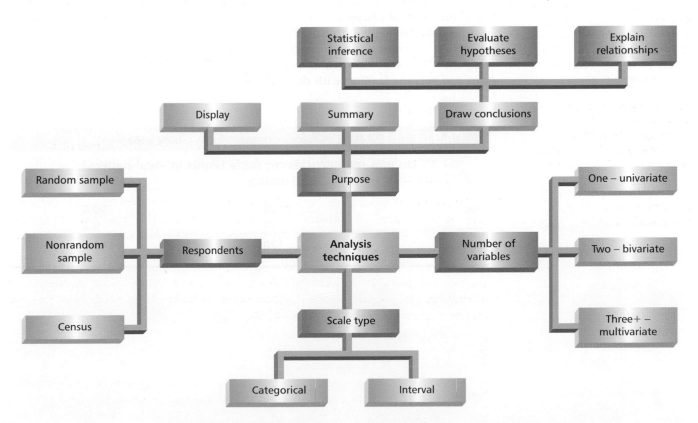

Univariate data display: categorical variables

The statistical techniques that are available for the display of variables one at a time depend in the first instance on whether the variables are categorical or metric. For categorical variables the main techniques will include:

- univariate frequency tables,
- simple bar charts,
- pie charts.

Univariate frequency tables

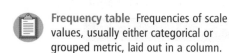

Frequency table Frequencies of scale values, usually either categorical or grouped metric, laid out in a column.

Categorical variables, you should recall from Chapter 5, are mapped onto sets of values that represent categories that are exhaustive, mutually exclusive and refer to a single dimension, but which possess no metric with which to measure distances between scale values. They may, furthermore, be subdivided into binary, nominal, ordinal or ranked scales. A first stage in analyzing any data scaled in this way is to display them in the form of tables or charts. In the first instance, this display will be univariate – treating variables one at a time.

A table is any layout of two or more values in rows, in columns, or in rows and columns combined. For categorical data, we can display the frequencies or relative frequencies (percentages) of the various categories. Tables for univariate analysis are often called "one-way" or "single-variable" **frequency tables**. Clearly, for binary variables there will be only two categories giving, for example, the number of people saying "yes" and the number saying "no" to a question in a survey, as illustrated in Table 11.2, which was produced by SPSS and is taken from a survey of table tennis players in Northern Ireland. This survey, which will be used throughout Chapters 11–14 to illustrate a large number of procedures and outputs from SPSS, is introduced in Box 11.2. Note that the layout of Table 11.2 is rather different from the tables in Chapter 5, which are in the standard publisher's format. Most tables from now on will be reproduced from SPSS so that you can become familiar with their layout.

TABLE 11.2	A frequency table for a binary variable	
Do you read articles on table tennis in local papers?		
	Frequency	Percent
Yes	109	90.8
No	11	9.2
Total	120	100.0

RESEARCH IN ACTION

BOX 11.2

Introduction to the table tennis survey

Table tennis in Northern Ireland has been in decline for several years. The number of people playing the game is getting smaller while the adult male is dominating the sport. The standard of club and league table tennis playing is well behind most other countries. Table tennis desperately needs more younger players, but attempts to recruit new players have so far been largely unsuccessful. The purpose of the research was to produce data that would help promoters to target the sport to a wider audience. More specifically, the research objectives were to:

- identify who plays table tennis and why,
- determine when and where the sport is first played,
- establish the perceptions of nonplayers and their level of awareness of the sport,
- examine the extent to which table tennis is played in primary schools.

The data, which are available from the Thomson website (**www.thomsonlearning.co.uk/kent**), relate to the first two of these objectives. Other stages of the research looked at nonplayers and at primary schools. The questionnaire to players, which is reproduced in Appendix 1, was generated following preliminary qualitative interviews with a cross-section of those who have a direct role in the game as a competitive sport. The population being studied is all members of table tennis clubs in Northern Ireland. A representative random sample of 150 such members was drawn from membership lists after stratifying by the major leagues in Northern Ireland and then by the four divisions within each league to represent all standards of player. Self-completed questionnaires were mailed and 120 useable returns were received. Such a size of sample is the absolute bare minimum that will allow for quantitative analysis. The topic of sample size was covered in Chapter 8, although some of the implications of sample size – in particular the limitations imposed by having a sample as small as 120 – will emerge during the chapters that follow.

The questionnaire consists of 19 questions, but some of these produced more than one variable, giving 30 variables in total. Once you have accessed the data you should obtain a screen similar to Figure 11.11.

Now have a look at some of the data.

- If you position the pointer over the grey area that contains the variable name but without clicking, SPSS will show you to what question the variable relates.
- Go to the *Variable View* and in the *Values* column check out the categories that are used for the variables.
- Notice that *agebegan* is a metric variable, so there are no value labels.
- Notice that *agenow* is grouped into intervals of 10 years.

FIGURE 11.11

The table tennis data

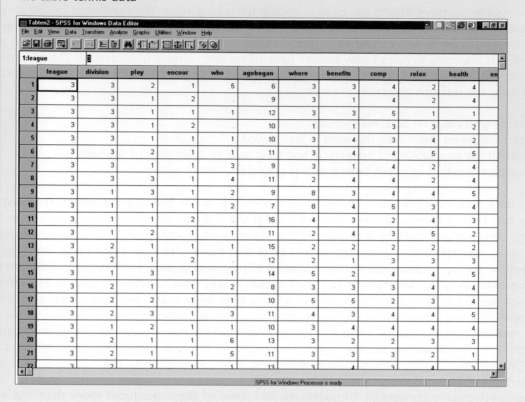

When reporting the findings from binary variables in the text that accompanies a table, it is really only necessary to state one of the two percentages (or proportions). If, for example, 90.8 percent said "yes" to a question then, by definition, 9.2 percent must have said "no" since they must total 100. For such binary data it could be argued that it is not really necessary to tabulate the results at all.

For nominal data there will be three or more categories. Precisely because the scale is nominal it does not matter in what order the categories are placed. However, if the number of categories is large it may make sense to list or group them in a particular way, for example alphabetically or by frequency. For ordinal data the scale values should be in the intended order of magnitude, usually with the highest, largest, fastest and so on at the top. Table 11.3, for example, shows the level of importance respondents give to the social benefits arising from playing table tennis.

Table 11.3 illustrates a number of points about table layout:

- the response categories, the frequencies and the percentages are usually in columns,

- the columns are labeled at the top so that we know to what variable the categories refer and whether the figures represent frequencies, percentages or proportions,

- totals are given at the bottom of the columns,

- there is a table number and a title, which is usually at the top of the table,

- there may be a source of the data at the bottom of the table if these data were derived from other than the results of the research being reported.

TABLE 11.3	A frequency table for an ordinal variable	
Social benefits		
	Frequency	**Percent**
Unimportant	11	9.2
Fairly unimportant	18	15.0
Neither unimportant or important	41	34.2
Fairly important	37	30.8
Very important	13	10.8
Total	120	100.0

Some tables may contain two or more adjacent univariate distributions, as in Table 11.4. Such **multivariable tables** do not relate or interlace the variables. Thus we do not know from Table 11.4 which males are in which social classes or in which age groups.

Looking at one-way tables enables the researcher to do two main things. First, the researcher can see whether any variables fail to discriminate between respondents. If all, or most, respondents give the same answer, then, while it may be an "interesting" finding, such a variable will be of limited value for further analysis. The findings in Table 11.2, for example, are no great surprise and may really just confirm what the researcher would have anticipated anyway – that table tennis players will normally read (or say they read) articles on table tennis in local papers. However, since only 11 respondents said they do not read articles on table tennis in local papers, then these 11 cannot sensibly be compared with the other 109 against another variable.

Second, and this is clearly related to the first point, if any categories are empty or very low in frequency, then the researcher will need to consider whether the variable can be sensibly collapsed into a smaller number of categories. Thus in Table 11.3 we may want to add together the "unimportant" and "fairly unimportant" categories, and add together the "fairly important" and "important" categories to generate Table 11.5. How to do this on SPSS is explained at the end of this chapter.

Multivariable table A table displaying the distributions or two or more variables that are not interlaced.

TABLE 11.4	A multivariable frequency table: respondents by gender, social class and age		
		Frequency	**Percent**
Gender	Male	104	52
	Female	96	48
Social class	AB	30	15
	C1	50	25
	C2	70	35
	DE	50	25
Age	20–29	10	5
	30–39	30	15
	40–49	64	32
	50–59	56	28
	60+	40	20

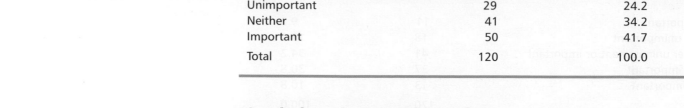

TABLE 11.5	Table 11.3 regrouped	
	Frequency	Percent
Unimportant	29	24.2
Neither	41	34.2
Important	50	41.7
Total	120	100.0

Simple bar charts and pie charts

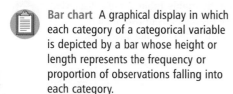

Chart/graph Any form of graphical display of numerical information.

Bar chart A graphical display in which each category of a categorical variable is depicted by a bar whose height or length represents the frequency or proportion of observations falling into each category.

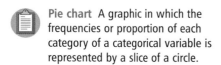

Pie chart A graphic in which the frequencies or proportion of each category of a categorical variable is represented by a slice of a circle.

Chart and **graph** are terms that are often used interchangeably to refer to any form of graphical display. Charts for categorical variables are limited largely to bar charts and pie charts. In **bar charts** each category is depicted by a bar, the length of which represents the frequency or percentage of observations fitting into each category. All bars should have the same width, and a scale of frequencies or percentages should be provided. What each bar represents should be clearly labeled or given a legend. A simple bar chart is illustrated in Figure 11.12, which shows the distribution of table tennis players between division played in.

Notice that while for tables the title is, as we have seen, usually at the top, for figures it is often at the bottom. The bars will sometimes be constructed horizontally rather than vertically for categorical data and the actual figures for each bar may be written at the end of the bar or within the bar, as illustrated in Figure 11.13.

In a **pie chart** the relative frequencies are represented in proportion to the size of each category by a slice of the circle, as is illustrated in Figure 11.14, which shows the proportions of those who are in the various table tennis leagues. The bar chart is normally preferred to the pie chart because the human eye can more

FIGURE 11.12

Bar chart: the division in which players play

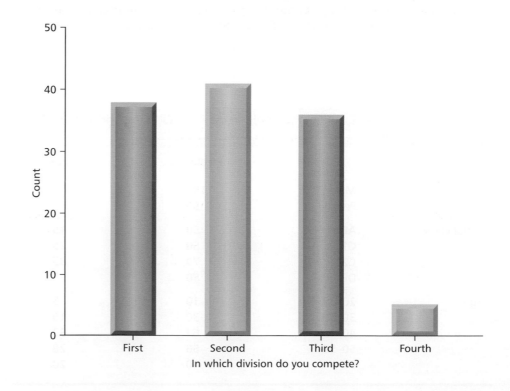

In which division do you compete?

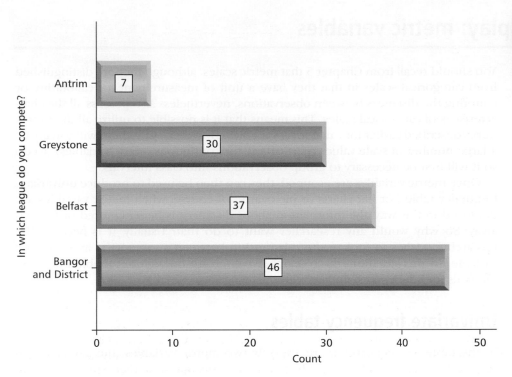

FIGURE 11.13

A horizontal bar chart: the league in which players compete

accurately judge length comparisons against a fixed scale than angular measures. However, pie charts are nicer to look at and they clearly show that the total for all slices adds up to 100 percent.

Neither bar charts nor pie charts, however, are particularly useful for binary data. For nominal data they can certainly help to display the data where there are between about 4 and 12 or so categories. Bar charts in particular can preserve the order of the categories for ordinal data, but the sense of ordering may be lost in pie charts.

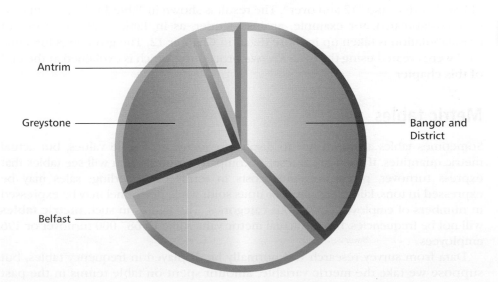

FIGURE 11.14

A pie chart

Univariate data display: metric variables

You should recall from Chapter 5 that metric scales, although they are distinguished from categorical scales in that they have a unit of measurement for calibrating or counting the distances between observations, nevertheless also possess all the characteristics of categorical scales. This means that it is possible to utilize all the procedures described earlier for categorical variables. However, since there will usually be a large number of scale values (particularly for continuous metric variables), to do so it will first be necessary to group observations into class intervals.

Once metric variables are grouped, they can then be used to produce univariate, frequency tables, or bar charts or pie charts. Of course, when metric variables are deployed in this way, the information about distances is being ignored or thrown away. So why would any researcher want to do that? Usually, it is because the researcher wishes to look at the relationship between a categorical and a metric variable. In this situation, the researcher will group the metric variable into class intervals and then crosstabulate with the categorical variable.

Univariate frequency tables

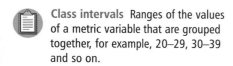

Class intervals Ranges of the values of a metric variable that are grouped together, for example, 20–29, 30–39 and so on.

In the table tennis survey there are only two metric variables: the age at which respondents began playing table tennis and the amount they spent on table tennis in the past six months. If we did a straight frequency count on these the result would look like Table 11.6, which illustrates a frequency table for *agebegan*. While most began playing between the ages of 8 and 14, there are many ages with a frequency of only one. There are in fact 21 different ages and if we tried, for example, to crosstabulate this with sex of respondent we would have a 21 by 2 table with 42 cells. That would be impossible to interpret and would be fairly useless for any kind of statistical analysis. The solution is to group the ages into what are often called **class intervals**. These might be classes of equal size, for example, 6–10, 11–15,16–20, 21–25, but there would still be four people outside this range so we would need a "26 and over" category. That still leaves five groupings, which for a sample of 120 will still be too many if we want to use it for crosstabulation.

The *Cumulative Percent* column shows that just under half (45 percent) began at the age of 11 or earlier and the rest began at the age of 12 or later. So, if we wanted to split them into two roughly equal halves, we could have two categories, "11 and under" and "12 and over". The result is shown in Table 11.7. This can now be crosstabulated, for example, against gender, as in Table 11.8. The topic of crosstabulation is taken up in more detail in Chapter 12. The groupings for Table 11.7 were created using the SPSS *Recode* procedure, which is explained at the end of this chapter.

Metric tables

Metric table A table used to display metric quantities.

Sometimes tables are used not to display frequencies of scale values, but actual metric quantities. If you look at a set of company accounts, you will see tables that express turnover, profits, revenue, costs in terms of £ sterling; sales may be expressed in tons, kilograms, liters or units sold; while personnel may be expressed in numbers of employees in various categories. The figures in such **metric tables** will not be frequencies, but the actual metric values like £5 687 000 turnover or 496 employees.

Data from survey research will normally be displayed in frequency tables, but suppose we take the metric variable, amount spent on table tennis in the past 6 months, and calculate a grand total. This comes to £6 208.80, averaging at

TABLE 11.6	A frequency table for age began playing table tennis		
Agebegan	Frequency	Percent	Cumulative Percent
6	1	.8	.8
7	2	1.7	2.5
8	12	10.0	12.5
9	7	5.8	18.3
10	20	16.7	35.0
11	12	10.0	45.0
12	16	13.3	58.3
13	11	9.2	67.5
14	12	10.0	77.5
15	8	6.7	84.2
16	5	4.2	88.3
17	2	1.7	90.0
18	4	3.3	93.3
19	1	.8	94.2
21	1	.8	95.0
22	1	.8	95.8
24	1	.8	96.7
27	1	.8	97.5
28	1	.8	98.3
32	1	.8	99.2
43	1	.8	100.0
Total	120	100.0	

TABLE 11.7	Table 11.6 regrouped into two categories	
Began table tennis	Frequency	Percent
11 and under	54	45.0
12 and over	66	55.0
Total	120	100.0

TABLE 11.8	Age began by gender of respondent		
	Gender		
Began table tennis	Male	Female	Total
11 and under	44	10	54
12 and over	59	7	66
Total	103	17	120

£51.74 per person. We could break this down by gender and say that the average expenditure of the males was £53.05 and for the females £43.82. There could be further breakdowns by age, what league they compete in and so on. The point is that the figures in the table would relate to £ sterling, not frequencies.

Histograms and line graphs

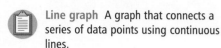

Histogram A graphical display for metric variables in which the width of the bars represents class intervals and the length or height represents the frequency or proportion with which each interval occurs.

Line graph A graph that connects a series of data points using continuous lines.

If a metric scale has been grouped into class intervals, it is perfectly feasible to produce a bar chart; but this is throwing away information. The class intervals themselves have a certain width and in a **histogram** the width of the bars represents the size of the class intervals. Figure 11.15 shows the age at which players say they began playing table tennis. Notice that SPSS has scaled the horizontal axis into major blocks of 10 years, each subdivided into four bars each representing 2.5 years. These are the automatic default options picked by SPSS, but they can be changed using the *Chart Editor*, which is explained at the end of the chapter.

A **line graph** can be used to represent the frequencies or percentages of metric variables as in Figure 11.16, but they are not particularly helpful when used in this way, since it does not give much feel for the shape of the distribution. They are of more use as time graphs where the X-axis is used for elapsed time or for dates and the Y-axis for the quantities of a variable that are changing over time.

FIGURE 11.15

A histogram for continuous metric data

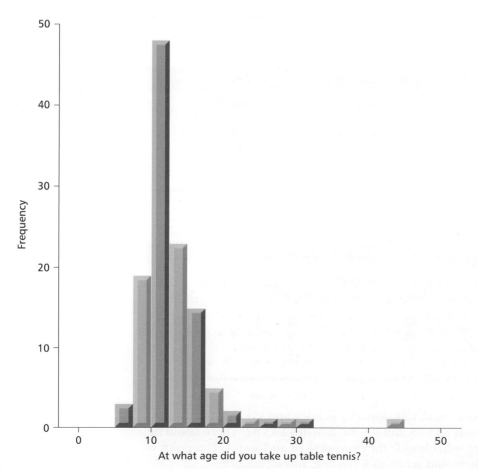

Mean = 12.8
Std. Dev. = 5.002
N = 120

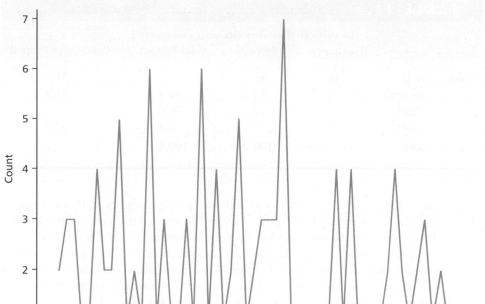

FIGURE 11.16

A line graph

Approximately how much have you spent on table tennis in the past 6 months?

KEY POINTS

When a researcher is looking at a dataset that is ready for analysis, the first thing he or she will do is get SPSS, or an equivalent statistical or survey data analysis package, to produce tables of frequencies for each variable. This should give the researcher a feel for the distribution of each variable. From this it will become clear whether any transformations of the variables in ways that are explained later in this chapter need to be applied. Researchers will commonly use univariate tables, graphs and charts to describe the key features of the survey population or sample when they are presenting the results of their analysis in a report or to an audience.

Data summaries: categorical variables

The calculation of univariate summary measures for categorical variables is fairly limited. The SPSS *Frequencies* procedure offers three measures: percent, valid percent and cumulative percent, as illustrated in Table 11.9 for the variable *division*, which is scaled at the ordinal level. Thus 31.7 percent of respondents compete in the first division, 34.2 percent in the second, and so on. Valid percent excludes missing cases, which are explained later in this chapter. Where there are no missing cases, as in Table 11.9, then percent and valid percent are identical. Cumulative percent accumulates the valid percent so a total of 65.8 percent compete in the first or second division and most (95.8 percent) in one of the first three divisions.

The only other univariate summary statistic that might be appropriate for categorical data is the mode. This is the most commonly occurring value. You can get

TABLE 11.9	Summary measures for categorical variables			
In which division do you compete?				
	Frequency	Percent	Valid Percent	Cumulative Percent
Valid First	38	31.7	31.7	31.7
Second	41	34.2	34.2	65.8
Third	36	30.0	30.0	95.8
Fourth	5	4.2	4.2	100.0
Total	120	100.0	100.0	

SPSS to give this to you, but all it will tell you is the category with the highest frequency, which, for example for Table 11.9, is the second division, which has the highest frequency. For nominal scales the very notion of "central tendency" does not meaningfully apply. You can hardly have a "central point" about which values cluster if they cannot be put into any order. For ordinal scales the idea of a central point does make some sense, but if there are very few categories, as for the variable *division*, it does not help very much to say that the second division has the largest number of players when, in this case, numbers are fairly evenly split between the first three divisions. The mode makes more sense with metric data.

Data summaries: metric variables

For metric variables there is a large assortment of statistics for calculating univariate summary measures. These statistical techniques may be put into four main groups:

- central tendency,
- dispersion,
- distribution shape,
- percentile values.

Central tendency

Central tendency focuses on the extent to which the metric values in a dataset are concentrated about a central figure. They can be used to describe the "typical" respondent or "typical" response. SPSS offers three measures of central tendency:

- the mean,
- the median,
- the mode.

Mean A measure of central tendency for metric variables calculated by totalling all the scale values in a distribution and dividing by the number of observations made.

The **mean** is commonly what we understand by "average". It is calculated by adding all the values together and dividing by the number of values included. Table 11.10 illustrates an SPSS output for the mean, median and the mode. It also gives the sum, which is the total of all the values. For the variable *agebegan* in our table tennis data the sum of all 120 ages is 1536. There are 120 values recorded, so 1536/120 = 12.8, which is the mean value. The mean takes account of every value in the distribution. While this is normally seen as an advantage, it may be unduly affected by extreme values. Thus one person began playing table tennis at the age of 43. If we exclude him from the analysis then the mean goes down to 12.55.

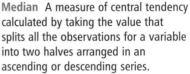

TABLE 11.10	Measures of central tendency for *agebegan*
At what age did you take up table tennis?	
N Valid	120
Missing	0
Mean	12.80
Median	12.00
Mode	10
Sum	1 536

Another tricky feature of the mean arises when the scale is discrete rather than continuous. Being discrete, all the scale values will be integers, but the mean may be a fraction, like the average family having 2.4 children. Remember that the mean is appropriate only for metric data, but SPSS is very obliging and will, for example, happily take the variable *division*, which is ordinal, and calculate an average of 2.07. This is nonsense, of course, but you cannot expect SPSS to know this.

The **median** is the middle value in an ascending or descending series of values. It is that value that splits the observations into two halves. For the variable *agebegan* the median is 12. You would have to imagine putting respondents in a row in order of the age at which they say they began playing and a line dividing the 60th and the 61st respondent would lie between two people who had given the answer 12. If there had been 121 respondents, then the median would have been the value of the 61st person. One advantage of the median is that it is un-affected by extreme values, so if the person who began playing table tennis at 43 had been 73 instead, this would leave the median value unaffected, but, of course, would have put up the mean age considerably!

It is commonly argued that to calculate the median you must have at least ordinal data. Strictly speaking, that is true, but calculating the median on such data is not usually very insightful. If the scale is fully ranked, then the median value is always the middle rank (wow!). If we have 300 respondents put into three categories of high, medium and low satisfaction, then surprise, surprise, the median value will probably be "medium". Only on metric data can the median be used for its main advantage: excluding outliers, or extreme values.

The **mode** is the most commonly occurring value. For categorical scales it is that scale value (or category) that has the largest frequency. For metric variables, certainly if they are continuous, each scale value may occur only once. If the values are grouped, then there will be a modal class interval, but that may change with different intervals being used. The modal age for *agebegan* is 10. This is because age 10 was reported most often as the age at which they began playing table tennis compared with other ages. It is often claimed that the mode is the appropriate measure of central tendency for categorical data, but the notion of "centrality" is very weak, particularly since the categories may be arranged in any order and the category with the highest number is not in any sense in the "middle" of a distribution.

Dispersion

Dispersion measures variability or the amount of spread in the data. These meas-ures describe how similar or dissimilar respondents or responses are from the typical or average respondent. The measures offered by SPSS are shown in Table 11.11 for the variable *agebegan*. From Table 11.12 you can see that the maximum age at which respondents began playing table tennis was 43 and the minimum 6, giving a **range** of 37 (i.e. 43–6). The problem with the range, however, is that it

Median A measure of central tendency calculated by taking the value that splits all the observations for a variable into two halves arranged in an ascending or descending series.

Mode A measure of central tendency established by taking the most commonly occurring value in a distribution.

Range The difference between the minimum and maximum value in a distribution of a metric variable.

Standard deviation An average of deviations of values about the mean for a given statistic.

does not tell us how far on average the individual values are spread out either side of the mean. This is what the standard deviation measures and it tells you the extent to which the set of values tend to be fairly close to the mean of the set or are considerably spread out.

The **standard deviation** is the average of deviations about the mean. Its calculation involves taking the mean and working out how far each value is above or below the mean. These distances are then squared and added up. Finally this sum is divided by the number of cases and the square root is taken. For the variable *agebegan*, we have seen that the mean age is 12.8. If you look at Table 11.12 you will see that one person began at the age of 6, that is 6.8 years (6 − 12.8) below the mean. The square of this is 46.24. There are two respondents who began at

TABLE 11.11	Measures of dispersion for *agebegan*
At what age did you take up table tennis?	
N Valid	120
Missing	0
Std. Error of Mean	.46
Std. Deviation	5.00
Variance	25.02
Range	37
Minimum	6
Maximum	43

TABLE 11.12	The frequency distribution for *agebegan*
At what age did you take up table tennis?	**Frequency**

Valid		
	6	1
	7	2
	8	12
	9	7
	10	20
	11	12
	12	16
	13	11
	14	12
	15	8
	16	5
	17	2
	18	4
	19	1
	21	1
	22	1
	24	1
	27	1
	28	1
	32	1
	43	1
	Total	120

the age of 7, so they are both 5.8 below the mean. The square of this is 33.64 and we need to take account of the fact that there are two of them. We do this for all 120 cases and add up the grand total. That comes to 3002.4. Divide by 120 and take the square root and you get a standard deviation of 5, as seen in Table 11.11. It is actually quite a lot of calculation if you are doing it by hand. Fortunately, SPSS will do it for you in less than a second. The **variance** is the sum before we have taken the square root. It is this figure that tends to get used in further calculations rather than the standard deviation. The remaining statistic in Table 11.11 is the standard error of the mean. We will be returning to this statistic when we come to deal with statistical inference for metric variables in Chapter 13.

Variance The mean squared deviation of all the values in the distribution of a metric variable.

So, the standard deviation of *agebegan* is 5. So what? To answer this question more fully it will be necessary to wait until we have considered statistical inference. For the moment, we will have to content ourselves with saying that the average of deviations about the mean age of 12.8 years is 5 years. Provided the distribution of values has a central concentration, most of the values will be within two standard deviations of the mean, in this case between 2.8 and 28.8. In fact there is nobody who began playing under 3 years old and only two who began after the tender age of 28 (see Table 11.12).

Distribution shape

You can get a good idea of the actual distribution of a metric variable by getting SPSS to draw you a histogram, as in Figure 11.15 for the variable *agebegan*. This distribution would be regarded as skewed to the right or positively skewed. If a distribution is completely symmetrical, then the values of the mean, the median and the mode will be the same. However, if the distribution is skewed, they will not. If positively skewed, the mean will be higher than the median and the median will be higher than the mode. The reverse will be true if the distribution is skewed to the left. This gives a basis for a measure of the extent of **skewness**. This uses simply the difference between the mean and the median and is a measure of the asymmetry of the distribution. It will have a value of zero if the median and the mean are the same. A measure of skewness that is less than 1 (or minus 1) is generally taken as an indicator that the distribution is approximately normal in shape. The value calculated by SPSS for *agebegan* is 2.869 (Table 11.13), which shows that the distribution cannot be regarded as normal in shape.

Skewness A measure of distribution shape based on the difference between the mean and median values in a distribution.

The other measure of the distribution shape given by SPSS is **kurtosis**. This is a measure of the extent to which the values cluster about the mean more or less than would a normal distribution. It will have a value of zero for a normal distribution, a positive value for high clustering and a negative value for low clustering. For *agebegan* it has a high positive value so the clustering is high with a long tail, which you can see from the histogram.

Kurtosis A measure of the distribution shape based on the extent to which values cluster about the mean compared with a normal distribution.

TABLE 11.13	Measures of distribution shape	
At what age did you take up table tennis?		
N	Valid	120
	Missing	0
Skewness		2.869
Std. Error of Skewness		.221
Kurtosis		12.575
Std. Error of Kurtosis		.438

The normal distribution

Reference has been made in several places earlier to something called a "normal" distribution. This is a special kind of distribution that has a number of crucial properties. It has a bell-shaped curve that can be described by a mathematical equation and has a zero measure for skewness and kurtosis. It is symmetrical in shape and its tails never quite touch the base. The last feature means that, in principle, the range is infinite, but in practice nearly all observations will lie within three standard deviations above and below the mean (that is, a range of six standard deviations). The mean and the standard deviation together allow statisticians to distinguish one particular normal curve from another. Each time we specify a particular combination of mean and standard deviation a different distribution will be generated. Figure 11.17 shows three different distributions. Distributions A and B have the same mean but different standard deviations. Distributions A and C have the same standard deviation but different means. Distributions B and C depict two distributions that differ in respect of both.

Because the normal curve has a standard shape, it is possible to treat the area under the curve as representing total certainty that any observation will be encompassed by it. We can say, furthermore, that 50 percent of the area is above the mean for that variable, and 50 percent below. In other words there is a 50 percent chance that any observation will be above (or below) the mean. This argument can be taken further so that we can calculate the area under the curve between the mean and one standard deviation. The area is, in fact, 34.1 percent (see Figure 11.18). Thus just over two-thirds or 68.2 percent of the area is between plus one standard deviation and minus one standard deviation from the mean. Thus if the mean score of a set of cases is 20 with a standard deviation of 6, then just over two-thirds of the area (and, by implication, of the observations) would be within 20 ± 6 or between 14 and 26. Figure 11.18 also shows that all but 4.6 percent of the area lies between plus and minus two standard deviations. There are, in fact, tables of areas under the normal curve, so that if we wished to know how many standard deviations encompassed exactly 95 percent of the area, we could look it up and discover that 1.96 standard deviations either side of the mean do so. This characteristic becomes very important when we move on to consider statistical inference.

FIGURE 11.17

Three normal distributions with differing parameters

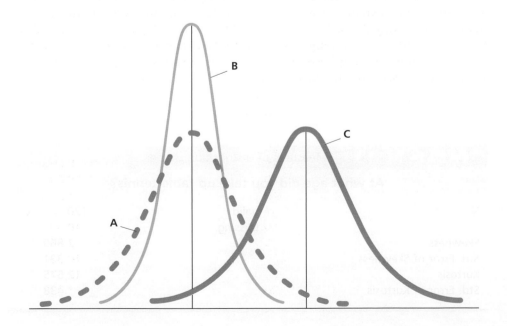

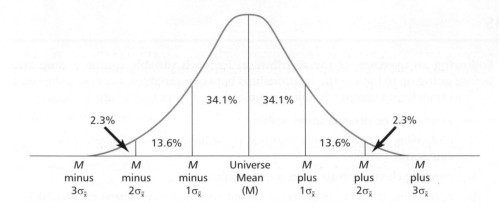

FIGURE 11.18

Areas under the normal distribution

Percentile values

Percentiles are values of a metric variable that divide the ordered data into groups so that a certain percentage is above and another percentage is below. The median, described above, is, in fact, the 50th percentile. Quartiles (the 25th, 50th, and 75th percentiles) divide the observations into four groups of equal size. Table 11.14 shows the percentile values in 10 equal groups plus the 25th, 50th and 75th percentiles. The middle 50 percent (i.e. between the 25th and 75th percentile) is often called the **interquartile range**, which in this case lies between the ages of 10 and 14, so half of the respondents lie between these ages.

Percentile Values of a metric variable that divide the ordered data into groups so that a certain percentage is above or below that value.

Interquartile range The range of a distribution that encompasses the middle 50 percent of the observations (between the 25th and 75th percentile).

KEY POINTS

The statistical techniques used to produce data summaries for metric variables are fairly standard procedures that are covered in all texts on statistics or data analysis. The arithmetic mean and the standard deviation are perhaps the most commonly used of these. They can, however, be calculated only for metric variables, for variables derived from summating ordinal measures and assumed to be metric, or from single 5- or 7-point scales whose intervals are assumed to be equal and may be assumed to approximate a metric variable.

TABLE 11.14	Percentile values for *agebegan*	
At what age did you take up table tennis?		
N	Valid	120
	Missing	0
Percentiles	10	8.00
	20	10.00
	25	10.00
	30	10.00
	40	11.00
	50	12.00
	60	13.00
	70	14.00
	75	14.00
	80	15.00
	90	17.90

Data transformations

Following an overview of the distribution for each variable one at a time and before going on to look at the relationships between variables, the researcher may wish to transform current variables in a number of ways that might include:

- upgrading or downgrading scales,
- collapsing categories on a nominal or ordinal scale to create fewer categories,
- creating class intervals from metric scales,
- computing totals or other scores from combinations of several variables,
- treating groups of variables as a multiple response question,
- handling missing values and "don't know" responses,
- coding open-ended questions,
- analyzing the results of Likert and other summated rating scales.

Some of these can be accomplished by using SPSS procedures, which are explained in the final section of this chapter.

Upgrading or downgrading scales

Researchers sometimes upgrade the scale achieved by some of their scales in order to apply the more sophisticated statistical techniques that thereby become available. The most usual transformation is for sets of ordered categories to be upgraded to metric scales. There are two main ways in which this may be accomplished. The researcher may allocate numerical scores to ordinal categories, and then treat the scores as if they referred to metric quantities. Thus the level of interest in a television program may be recorded on a 5-point scale:

	Allocate score
Extremely interesting	5
Very interesting	4
Fairly interesting	3
Not very interesting	2
Not at all interesting	1

A score is allocated to each individual response, as above, and the total for all respondents can be added up and divided by the number of respondents to give an average score. This process, however, assumes that the "distances" between each point on the scale are equal so that, for example, the distance between "very interesting" and "fairly interesting" is the "same" as the distance between "fairly interesting" and "not very interesting". Such an assumption may seem reasonable in this example. It also tends to be reasonable for Likert items (see Chapter 5) where respondents are being asked about their degree of agreement or disagreement with a number of statements. However, for levels of satisfaction, where a set of categories like "very satisfied", "fairly satisfied" and "dissatisfied" have been used, this assumption is suspect, since the "distance" between "dissatisfied" and "fairly satisfied" is probably much greater than the "distance" between "fairly satisfied" and "very satisfied". In any event, it would be unwise to treat total scores in any absolute sense. However, for measuring change, for example from one week to the next, then changes in the average scores *are* likely to reflect real changes in people's level of interest. Error, provided it is constant, does not affect measures of change.

The other way to create metric scales is to define categories of an ordinal scale in numerical terms. Thus a distinction between "small", "medium" and "large" organizations is only an ordinal distinction. However, if the researcher defined "small" organizations as having fewer than 50 employees, "medium" as having between 50 and 200 employees, and "large" as having over 200 employees then a discrete metric scale has been created, the "metric" in this case being size measured by the number of employees. With a larger number of categories, more precisely defined, with upper and lower limits, it becomes possible to calculate an average size. This procedure is fine provided there is accurate information, for example in the situation earlier, on the number of employees in each organization of interest.

By creating (or assuming the creation of) metric scales, the researcher can now, for example, add up and then calculate average scores, calculate standard deviations, and use the variables in ways that will be explained in Chapters 12 to 14.

There are some circumstances when a researcher may downgrade a scale and treat it as if it were at a lower level. Thus a metric scale may be treated as a ranked scale by ignoring the distances between categories. A class test out of 100 may be used to create ranks of first, second, third and so on. This may be undertaken by the researcher either because he or she feels that the assumptions of the original metric are unwarranted, or because the variable is to be correlated with another ranked scale and the researcher wants to apply Spearman's rho, which requires two ranked scales. Metric scales can be ranked in SPSS using *Transform/Rank Cases*.

Another example of downgrading is when a researcher wishes to crosstabulate a nominal with an ordinal scale. An appropriate measure of association may be chosen that treats both variables as nominal, thereby ignoring the ordering of the categories in one of the variables. A more extreme example is when a researcher takes a continuous metric scale like age and groups respondents into a binary scale of "old" and "young" or into an ordinal scale of "old", "middle-aged" and "young". This may be undertaken if the researcher wishes to crosstabulate age with another binary, nominal or ordinal variable, for example "purchased" and "did not purchase" Brand B in the past seven days. The age split would normally be done in a way that creates two (or three or more as required) roughly equal groups. The SPSS procedure *Transform/Compute* can be used to create a new variable grouped in this way. This procedure is explained at the end of this chapter.

Collapsing categories

Where there are more than three categories of a nominal or ordinal scale, particularly if the number of cases in the data matrix is fewer than 300 or so, or if the frequencies in some of the categories are very small, it may make sense to add together the frequencies in adjacent categories if the scale is ordinal or in a way that "makes sense" if the scale is nominal. Table 11.5, for example, was created from Table 11.3 by collapsing together the "unimportant" and "fairly unimportant" categories, and the "fairly important" and "important" categories. This makes sense because only 20 percent of respondents went for either of the extreme categories. The result, furthermore, in Table 11.5 is fairly balanced between the three new categories.

Class intervals

Class intervals are used to group together ranges of values on metric variables to enable the researcher to "eyeball" the distribution. The intervals must be non-overlapping and as far as possible of the same width. If the number of metric values is fairly limited, as in Table 11.6, it may be unnecessary to group; the distribution can be seen from this table. If, however, the number of values is large, then groups may be essential to view the distribution.

Grouping into class intervals may also be required if the variable is to be cross-tabulated with another categorical variable. In this case it will probably be necessary to create a limited number of wide intervals, the most extreme version being to create two categories, as in Table 11.7. The number, width and placing of the intervals is a matter for researcher judgment and may be subject to trial and error, with the researcher trying out different groupings to see to what extent this may affect the results. To view a distribution a useful rule of thumb is to create between about 5 and 15 intervals. If there are **outliers** – values that are substantially different from the general body of values – then there may need to be open-ended classes at either or both ends of the table. This is quite a common way of dealing with one or two, or even a few, extreme values.

Outliers Values that are substantially different from the general body of values.

Computing totals

Chapter 5 explained summated rating sales such as Likert scales. Totals are created by adding together the scores on each item in the scale. This is fine provided the items are adding up aspects of the same dimension. The most common way to test this is by looking at the intercorrelations between the items. The technique of Cronbach's coefficient alpha was explained in Chapter 5 as providing evidence that items could be sensibly added together.

Multiple response questions

There are often questions in a survey that allow respondents to pick more than one answer. Question 19 on the table tennis questionnaire, for example, asks respondents to tick whether or not they play one or more of four other sports. In principle a respondent could tick all of them (although how he or she could fit them all in is another matter!). For the purpose of analysis, each sport will need to be treated as a separate variable, each one of which is ticked or not ticked. In other words each is binary. SPSS, as is explained later in this chapter, can then be instructed to treat the set of sports as one question. The result is shown in Table 11.15. This shows that in total there were 140 ticks over the four items in the question, and that 58.6 percent of these responses indicated football, 20.7 percent tennis and so on. There are 111 "valid" cases in the table and 9 are missing. This means, in effect, that there were 9 respondents who did not play any of the four sports indicated, and so are excluded from the table. Of the 111 valid cases, 73.9 percent indicated football, 26.1 percent tennis and so on. It would, however, probably have been more useful to have these percentages relating to all 120 cases. If we had another item on the question for "None of these" and included this in the multiple response set, then all 120 cases would have been covered.

In this situation, the percentage of cases would give the same result as a frequency table for each item, but put into the same table, while the percentage of responses takes the four items together.

TABLE 11.15	A multiple-response question			
Group $SPORT Play other sport (Value tabulated = 1)				
Dichotomy label	Name	Count	Pct of Responses	Pct of Cases
Play badminton	BADMIN	12	8.6	10.8
Play football	FOOT	82	58.6	73.9
Play squash	SQUASH	17	12.1	15.3
Play tennis	TENNIS	29	20.7	26.1
Total responses		140	100.00	126.1
9 missing cases; 111 valid cases				

"Don't know" responses and missing values

"Don't know" answers are one type of noncommittal reply that a respondent may give along with undecided, no opinion or neutral responses in a balanced rating scales with a middle point. These responses may be built into the design of the questionnaire with explicit options for a noncommittal response. With explicit don't know options available, the proportion of such responses may be anything up to 90 percent and rates of over 10 percent are common (Durand and Lambert 1988). Even without such options on the questionnaire, up to 60 percent of respondents in some studies have still given "don't know" replies. An understanding of the pattern of such replies is thus important for:

- formulating research methodology, particularly questionnaire design, item phrasing or sampling plan,
- interpreting the results when there are many "don't know" responses.

Noncommittal replies have been very differently interpreted by researchers. These interpretations fit into two broad patterns:

- "don't know" responses are a valid indicator of the absence of attitudes, beliefs, opinions or knowledge,
- "don't know" replies are inaccurate reflections of existing cognitive states.

The first interpretation provides a rationale for including explicit noncommittal response categories in the questionnaire. It also implies that such responses should be excluded from the analysis, even if this means that the number of cases on which the analysis is based is thereby reduced. If there are a lot of respondents in this category, then it is possible that the question to which people are being asked to respond is not well thought through and there may well be an argument for excluding the question from the analysis altogether.

The second interpretation has been used to set in motion various efforts to minimize don't know responses on the basis that only committed responses will reflect a respondent's true mental state. Such efforts will include providing scales that have no middle position or noncommittal option, or have interviewers probe each noncommittal reply until a committal response has been obtained.

If there are relatively few "don't knows" then leaving them out of the analysis may well be the best course of action to take, particularly if the number of remaining cases is still adequate for the statistical analyses being proposed. There will certainly usually be a case for including the "don't knows" in the preliminary univariate analysis. A decision can then be taken about whether they are to be excluded from subsequent bivariate and multivariate analyses. If they are to be excluded, then the researcher, in SPSS, can define such a category as a user-defined missing value.

Survey research findings are certainly not invariant to decisions about what to do with noncommittal responses. Treating such responses as randomly distributed missing data points when in fact some responses are a genuine result of ambivalence or uncertainty may introduce bias into the data. The same would be true if responses are included as neutral positions when they are in fact an indicator of no opinion or refusal to answer. A first step in any analysis would be to investigate the extent to which noncommittal responses are a function of demographic, behavioral or other cognitive variables. Some studies, for example, have reported an inverse relation between education and don't know responses (the better educated are less prone to give them), but it has to be said that other research has found exactly the reverse. Durand and Lambert (1988) found that don't know responses vary systematically with sociodemographic characteristics and with involvement with the topic area.

In any survey, not all respondents will answer all the questions. This is less likely to be the result of individual refusal to answer some of the questions (although this does happen) or people accidentally omitting to consider some of the questions, than a result of questionnaire design whereby not all the questions are relevant to all the respondents. Approaches to the treatment of missing values vary. At one extreme is what is sometimes called listwise deletion. *All* questionnaires that contain missing values for reasons other than nonapplicability are excluded from the analysis – in fact the data from such questionnaires will not even be entered into the data matrix. This means that each questionnaire included is fully complete. This procedure is fine and appropriate where there are relatively few exclusions as a result, and where the number of questionnaires returned is large enough for the analyses that will be performed. Where the number of resulting exclusions is considerable, however, or the number of cases is critical, then listwise deletion may not be a wise course of action.

A little less extreme is to enter all the questionnaires into the data matrix, but to exclude from the particular calculation or table involved cases for which values are missing, for whatever reason. This is fine when the number of cases entered into the data matrix is large or at least sufficient for the kinds of analyses that are required. However, there is always the danger that this approach may reduce the number of cases used in a particular analysis to such an extent that meaningful analysis is not possible.

Where values are missing because the question item does not apply to a particular respondent, there is little the researcher can do except maybe increase the size of the sample or impose quotas that will ensure a minimum number of applicable responses. Where a question *would* be appropriate to a given respondent, but an answer is not recorded, then such missing values may be referred to as "item nonresponse". Most researchers are inclined to just accept that there will be some item nonresponse for some or even many of the variables and will simply exclude them from the analysis. There is, however, a bewildering array of techniques that have been suggested in the literature for other ways of dealing with item nonresponse. Most of these involve filling the gaps caused by missing values by finding an actual replacement value. The process is sometimes called "explicit imputation" and the idea is to select a replacement value that is as similar as possible to the missing value.

Where variables are metric, one remedial technique, for example, is to substitute the mean value for the missing value. More sophisticated approaches involve regression analysis or factor analysis. For categorical variables one technique that is sometimes used is to give the questionnaire with the missing value the same value as the questionnaire immediately preceding it.

Most of the techniques assume, however, that question items not responded to are not responded to at random. This can be quite difficult to determine. Furthermore, when the amount of item nonresponse is small – less than about 5 percent – then applying any of the methods is unlikely to make any significant difference to the interpretation of the data. Ideally, of course, researchers should, in reporting their findings, communicate the nature and amount of item nonresponse in the dataset and describe the procedures used to remedy or cope with it.

SPSS makes a distinction between two kinds of missing value: *system missing values* and *user defined missing values*. The former result when the person entering the data has no value to enter for a particular variable (for whatever reason) for a particular case. In this situation the person will just skip the cell and SPSS will enter a period in that cell to indicate that no value has been recorded. For univariate output, SPSS will produce a *Statistics* table that gives you the number of valid and the number of missing cases, and a *Frequencies* table that lists the valid (nonmissing) values and the system missing values (see Table 11.16). Percentages are then calculated both for the total number of cases entered into the data matrix and for the total of non missing or valid cases – what it calls the *valid percent*. The treatment of missing values on *Graphs* varies from graph to graph. A *Bar Chart*, for example, has a default of including a bar for missing values, but this can be omitted by selecting the *Options* button on the *Define Bar* dialog box.

User-defined missing values are ones that have been entered into the data matrix, but the researcher decides to exclude them from the analysis. The same procedure might be applied to those respondents giving a "Don't know" reply. This is achieved in SPSS by using the *Define Variable/Missing Values* procedure, which is explained at the end of the chapter. All values defined in this way will be excluded from all the analyses.

It would be a sensible policy to reserve system missing values in effect for questions that are not applicable to the respondent in question and to give another code for those where responses are missing for other reasons, so we might enter a code of zero for item nonresponse. The combination of system-defined and user-defined missing values can mean that, for some tables or calculations, the number of cases used is considerably less than the number of cases entered into the data matrix. Furthermore, it will mean that the number of cases included will vary from table to table or statistical analysis. If the number of cases in the data matrix is quite small to begin with, this can have serious implications for the analysis.

Open-ended questions

Coding is the process of converting verbatim answers into numerical code. The process might be called "post-coding" or may even be referred to as "content

TABLE 11.16	SPSS *System Missing* values			
	Who encouraged you?			
		Frequency	Percent	Valid Percent	Cumulative Percent
Valid	Friend	33	27.5	38.8	38.8
	Parent	30	25.0	35.3	74.1
	Other relative	4	3.3	4.7	78.8
	Teacher	2	1.7	2.4	81.2
	Club leader	15	12.5	17.6	98.8
	Other	1	.8	1.2	100.0
	Total	85	70.8	100.0	
Missing	System	35	29.2		
Total		120	100.0		

analysis", although, as explained in Chapter 10, the latter term tends to be restricted to the processes that are used to analyze the content of printed or broadcast communication, particularly advertising copy.

The approach to coding can be split into two situations. In the first situation, the open-ended question is being used to capture factual information, since listing all the options for responses in a closed question would take up too much space. Where respondents can give their answer in numerical form, for example putting in their age, then no additional coding is necessary. The actual age can simply be put into the data matrix. This might be called "empirical coding" in which the numerical value of the code corresponds with the specific magnitude of the quantity being measured. Where responses are in words, then coding will involve creating a list of the answers given, assigning number codes to the list, and recording codes for each respondent's answers. It may be necessary to develop coding rules that specify codes to be allocated when the answer does not fit any of the obvious categories. For example, if respondents are asked, "Not counting yourself, how many other people were you with?", then most will give a clear number, but some may say "30–40" or "a lot". In this situation, one rule might be to give the midpoint of a range of values, so the answer "30–40" will be coded as 35.

Where open-ended questions are being used not to capture factual information, but to record respondent opinions, attitudes, views, knowledge and so on, then creating a sensible code frame is the most important part of the analysis. By definition this is likely to get quite complex – if it were easy then the question could no doubt be precoded! The aim is to formulate a set of categories that accurately represents the answers and where each category includes an appreciable number of responses. Ideally, the set of categories should be exhaustive, mutually exclusive and minimize the loss of information. Furthermore, the categories should be meaningful, consistent and relatively straightforward to apply. There may also need to be codes for "no response", "not applicable" and "don't know". Where the information is very detailed there may need to be many codes and two- or even three-digit codes may be developed.

Developing a frame may require several "passes" over the data. It is probably a good idea to have all the comments collected and typed out, but this may not be possible. A method of constant comparison is probably best. Begin by looking at a few of the comments and see whether they should be put into separate categories. Then look at a few more and see if some can be put into the same category or whether more categories will need to be developed. When too many categories begin to emerge, look for similarities so that some categories can be brought together. If there are a large number of responses then it may not be sensible to look through all of them to develop the frame, but take a sample. Thus if there are 500 cases, a sample of 50–100 should enable the frame to be finalized. It also helps if more than one person develops a code frame separately; they should then work together on a final code. This maximizes the objectivity, validity and reliability of the process.

Question 13 in the table tennis data is open-ended. This asks respondents what they think could be done to encourage people to take up table tennis on a regular basis. The responses were coded into the categories shown in Table 11.17, which also shows the results of the analysis.

It helps if the researcher sets up the objectives for which the code frame is to be used before beginning the process. Thus if the objective is to look for positive and negative statements about a situation or a product, then answers will be coded along this dimension, perhaps with categories of very positive, vaguely positive, mixed, vaguely negative and very negative. Sometimes answers to open-ended questions can be coded in several ways according to different dimensions. Thus a study of injuries following an earthquake could look at the way injuries occurred, the parts of the body affected, where the injury occurred, what the

TABLE 11.17	Analysis of an open-ended question		
How to encourage people to take up T.T.?			
		Frequency	Percent
Valid	Facilities/beginner-orientated clubs	23	19.2
	Coaching	17	14.2
	School/youth club involvement	24	20.0
	Advertising/promotion/exhibitions	21	17.5
	TV/media/publicity	28	23.3
	Improved image	6	5.0
	Money in the sport	1	.8
	Total	120	100.0

person was doing at the time and so on. Each of these aspects may need to be recorded separately in a different variable.

At one time researchers had to code all open-ended questions before data entry could begin. With modern survey analysis packages like SPSS, however, this may be done after all the precoded questions have been entered. This is a big advantage because researchers are not always sure how responses to open-ended questions should be coded until they have started analysis of the data. In short, it is sometimes better to delay coding of open-ended responses until they are needed for analysis.

Analyzing summated rating scales

In the table tennis survey, respondents were asked how satisfied they were with various elements of table tennis in Northern Ireland. These included practice facilities, competition facilities, administration, coaching opportunities and competitions. Answers were recorded into a 5-point rating scale from unsatisfied to very satisfied. The first stage in any analysis will be to review the raw frequencies (SPSS calls these the "count") and the relative frequencies or percentages for each level of satisfaction for each of the five variables. Table 11.18 shows an output from SPSS using the *Analyze/Custom Tables/Basic Tables* procedure. The *Basic Tables* dialog box is explained at the end of the chapter. Table 11.18 gives an overall picture of the numbers and proportions responding in each of the categories. There is a lot of data here to take in, so each variable could be summarized by calculating the average score for each of the items, as in Table 11.19. From this we can see that the overall satisfaction with the competitions is quite high compared with the other elements, while satisfaction with coaching opportunities is relatively low. This was not evident from Table 11.18.

Table 11.19, however, does not give an overall evaluation of all the elements added together. This is what a summated rating scale will do. Using the *Transform/Compute* facility on SPSS to create a new variable, *totalsat*, Table 11.20 shows the overall average satisfaction score, and that score broken down by sex of player using the *Analyze/Compare Means* procedure. You can see that the overall score for the men is a little higher than that for the women. It would then even be possible to do an independent samples t-test on the difference to show, for example, that the difference is not statistically significant.

Given that *totalsat* is being treated as a metric variable, it would be possible to draw a scattergram of the relationship between this and both *agebegan* and *spend*. These are shown in Figures 11.19 and 11.20. As you can see, there is little point in getting SPSS to calculate a measure of correlation – there clearly *is* no pattern. Overall satisfaction does not appear to be related to either the age at which people

TABLE 11.18	Satisfaction with various elements of playing table tennis		
		Count	Col %
Practice facilities	unsatisfied	23	19.2
	fairly unsatisfied	27	22.5
	neither unsatisfied nor satisfied	43	35.8
	fairly satisfied	21	17.5
	very satisfied	6	5.0
Group Total		120	100.0
Competition facilities	unsatisfied	7	5.8
	fairly unsatisfied	26	21.7
	neither unsatisfied nor satisfied	53	44.2
	fairly satisfied	29	24.2
	very satisfied	5	4.2
Group Total		120	100.0
Administration	unsatisfied	17	14.2
	fairly unsatisfied	27	22.5
	neither unsatisfied nor satisfied	54	45.0
	fairly satisfied	18	15.0
	very satisfied	4	3.3
Group Total		120	100.0
Coaching opportunities	unsatisfied	26	21.7
	fairly unsatisfied	34	28.3
	neither unsatisfied nor satisfied	43	35.8
	fairly satisfied	15	12.5
	very satisfied	2	1.7
Group Total		120	100.0
Competitions	unsatisfied	9	7.5
	fairly unsatisfied	16	13.3
	neither unsatisfied nor satisfied	40	33.3
	fairly satisfied	37	30.8
	very satisfied	18	15.0
Group Total		120	100.0

TABLE 11.19	Mean satisfaction score for elements of playing table tennis
	Mean
Practice facilities	2.67
Competition facilities	2.99
Administration	2.71
Coaching opportunities	2.44
Competitions	3.33

began or how much they spent on the game in the past six months. Remember, however, that negative findings like these are as useful as positive ones.

It would, of course, be possible to compare the mean satisfaction scores for any subgroup in the sample. However, this may hide patterns in the ways the different

TABLE 11.20	Total satisfaction (TOTALSAT) scores by sex of player	
What sex are you?	Mean	N
Male	2.8447	103
Female	2.7176	17
Total	2.8267	120

levels of satisfaction vary with some other variable. It would, instead, be possible to crosstabulate each of the items making up the overall scale separately against, for example, whether there is anybody else in the household who plays the game. Table 11.21 shows this for *Practice facilities*. The table is a little difficult to interpret because there are too many categories and too small frequencies in the cells. If we use the *Recode* facility to regroup the satisfaction categories into satisfied, neither and unsatisfied, we obtain Table 11.22. It begins to look as though those players who have somebody else in the household who plays are less likely to be satisfied with practice facilities. However, the pattern is very small (Cramer's V is only 0.087) and the result is not statistically significant ($p = 0.632$) These terms are explained in the next chapter. The remaining elements can be checked out in this way.

Notice from Table 11.18 that over a third of all respondents for each of the five elements gave a "neither unsatisfied nor satisfied" rating. On the argument that

FIGURE 11.19

A scattergram of *agebegan* by total satisfaction score

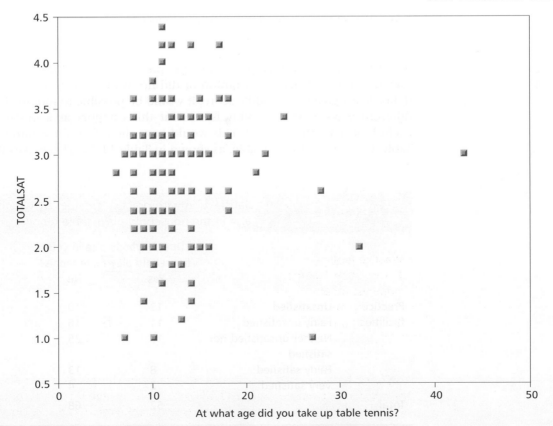

FIGURE 11.20

A scattergram of *spend* by total
satisfaction score

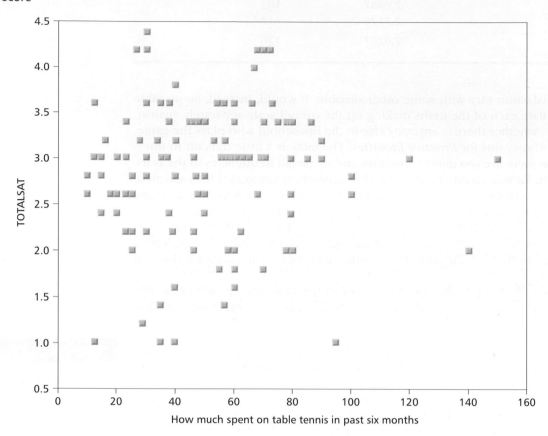

this category may well contain many people who checked this category because
they did not really have an opinion or did not want to think about it rather than
deliberately giving it a middle score, it would be possible to modify the analysis in
different ways. One possibility is to treat this category as a missing value and
exclude it from the analysis. This would have the effect, for example, of making
Table 11.22 a two-by-two table, as shown in Table 11.23. This makes the pattern a

TABLE 11.21		Satisfaction with practice facilities by whether anybody else in the household plays table tennis		
		Does anybody else in your household play table tennis?		
		Yes	No	Total
Practice facilities	Unsatisfied	13	10	23
	Fairly unsatisfied	11	16	27
	Neither unsatisfied nor satisfied	18	25	43
	Fairly satisfied	8	13	21
	Very satisfied	2	4	6
Total		52	68	120

TABLE 11.22	Satisfaction with practice facilities by whether anybody else in the household plays table tennis			
		Does anybody in your household play T.T.?		
		Yes	No	Total
Satisfaction with practice facilities	Unsatisfied	24	26	50
	Neither	18	25	43
	Satisfied	10	17	27
Total		52	68	120
		Value	Approx. Sig.	
Cramer's V		.087	.632	

little clearer and the value of Cramer's V has risen, although not by enough to make it statistically significant. This, however, is partly because the number of valid cases has now dropped to 77.

Reducing the number of cases deployed in an analysis in this way does, then, have its drawbacks. Another possibility would be to add the "neither" category into either the satisfied or the unsatisfied categories. However, in this situation, there is no clear rationale for performing either of these modifications. Both actions would have the effect of creating one category much larger than the other and, furthermore, creating categories that do not make a lot of sense, like "satisfied and no opinion" versus "unsatisfied" (or "satisfied" versus "unsatisfied and no opinion").

What does seem fairly clear from the analyses performed so far is that the data are fairly robust, and no matter how we modify them, we obtain largely the same result. That should give us cause for some degree of confidence in the results. The moral of the story, then, is to take your data and analyze them in a number of ways and see if the conclusions are broadly the same. If they are not, then it will be clear that the conclusions are to some degree at least dependent on the method of analysis and will need to be treated with caution.

TABLE 11.23	Satisfaction with practice facilities by whether anybody else in the household plays, excluding "neither" category			
		Does anybody in your household play T.T.?		
		Yes	No	Total
Satisfaction with practice facilities	Unsatisfied	24	26	50
	Satisfied	10	17	27
Total		34	43	77
		Value	Approx. Sig.	
Cramer's V		.105	.355	
N of valid cases		77		

One technique that is frequently applied to the analysis of summated ratings is factor analysis. This technique is considered in Chapter 14. It may be used where a large number of attitude statements are recorded on rating scales that can reasonably be assumed to have achieved the metric level. The results may enable the researcher to detect underlying dimensions that were not apparent from looking at a series of bivariate or even multivariate correlations.

> ### KEY POINTS
>
> Before further analysis can take place, for example to examine the relationships between variables, a number of data transformations may be necessary or advisable. Such transformations might include upgrading or downgrading scales, collapsing categories on a nominal or ordinal scale to create fewer categories, creating class intervals from metric scales, computing totals or other scores from combinations of several variables, treating groups of variables as a multiple-response question, handling missing values and "don't know" responses, coding open-ended questions and analyzing summated rating scale data in a number of different ways.

Using SPSS

Frequency tables

To obtain one-way descriptive summaries for categorical variables, you will need the SPSS *Frequencies* procedure. This is in the *Analyze/Descriptive Statistics* drop-down menu from the menu bar at the top. So, access the table tennis data, click on *Analyze*, then move the pointer to *Descriptive Statistics* and then to *Frequencies* and click. The *Frequencies* dialog box will appear (see Figure 11.21). All variables are listed in the left box. To obtain a frequency count for any variable simply transfer it to the *Variables* box by highlighting it, then clicking on the direction button in the middle. If you hold down the left mouse button while dragging the mouse you can highlight adjacent variables in one move. Click on OK and you obtain a frequency count for each variable. Table 11.16 illustrates the default table, which gives you *Frequency*, *Percent*, *Valid Percent* and *Cumulative Percent*. Notice that there are 35 *Missing* and a total of 85 *Valid* cases in this table. That means that 35 people did not answer this question. So the 33 valid cases who said they were encouraged by a friend represent 27.5 percent of the total sample of 120, but 38.8 percent of the 85 valid cases – this is the *Valid Percent*. The *Cumulative Percent* accumulates the *Valid Percents* so that, for example, a total of 74.1 percent were encouraged either by a friend or by a parent. Since the scale here is nominal, the order is not important and reflects the order in which the value labels were entered.

Where there are no missing cases the *Percent* and *Valid Percent* are the same. You can edit the table to remove these columns if you wish. Just double-click on the table. Click on *Valid Percent* and hit *Delete*. Then highlight the figures in the column and hit *Delete* and the column will disappear and the table will close up. You can do the same with the *Cumulative Percent* column. To get out of *Edit* mode just left-click outside the table area. With the table highlighted (there will be a frame around it and a red arrow to the left) you can select *Edit* and *Copy* and then *Paste* it into any other application like Word or PowerPoint.

The *Frequencies* procedure will produce a separate table for each variable entered into the *Variables* box. To produce a multivariable table you will need the SPSS *Basic Tables* or *Tables of Frequencies* procedures. The *Basic Tables* proce-

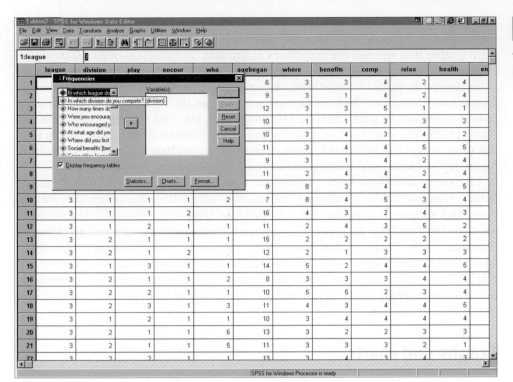

FIGURE 11.21

The SPSS *Frequencies* dialog box

dure is for listing selected variables in a single table where the response categories are varied. Select *Analyze/ Tables/Basic Tables*. Put the first three or four variables in the table tennis data into the *Subgroups/Down:* box and change the radio button to *Each separately (stacked)*. Click on the *Statistics* button and bring *Count* and *Col %* across to the *Cell Statistics* box. Click on *Continue*. If you want totals, click on *Totals* and check the box *Totals over each group variable*. Click on *Continue* then *OK*. The result should look like Table 11.24. Try some of the other functions on the *Basic Tables* box, e.g. *Layout, Format and Titles*.

TABLE 11.24	**SPSS basic tables**		
		Count	Col %
In which	Bangor and District	46	38.3
league do you	Belfast	37	30.8
compete?	Greystone	30	25.0
	Antrim	7	5.8
Group Total		120	100.0
In which	First	38	31.7
division do you	Second	41	34.2
compete?	Third	36	30.0
	Fourth	5	4.2
Group Total		120	100.0
How many	Once	43	35.8
times do you	Twice	52	43.3
play per week?	Three times	18	15.0
	Four or more times	7	5.8
Group Total		120	100.0

Basic Tables is fine for separate variables where the categories are different for each variable. Suppose, however, the response categories are all the same and you want a table that sets out the responses as a matrix. For this you need the *Tables of Frequencies* function. Select *Analyze/ Tables/ Tables of Frequencies*. Put the variables *Social Benefits, Competition, Relaxation, Health* and *Enjoyment* into the *Frequencies for:* box. Click on *Layout* and change the radio button for *Variable Labels* to *Down the side*. Click on *Continue*, then *OK*. The result should look like Table 11.25. You may need to adjust some of the column widths. Double-click on the table to get the *Edit* mode then drag the column bars to increase the width. Again, try out some of the function buttons in the *Tables of Frequencies* box.

The other functions under *Tables* are *General Tables* and *Multiple Response Tables*. *General Tables* produces publication-quality tables displaying crosstabulations and subgroup statistics. You can produce tables showing different statistics for different variables, multiple-response variables, mixed nesting and stacking, or complex totals. *Multiple Response Tables* produces basic frequency and crosstabulation tables in which one or more of the variables is a multiple-response set. You are not required to have a multiple-response set defined to use this procedure, but you may obtain better results with *Basic Tables* if you do not need to use a multiple-response set.

Graphs and charts

If you click on *Charts* in the *Frequencies* dialog box you obtain the *Frequencies:Charts* dialog box. Simply click on *Bar Chart* or *Pie Chart* as appropriate and indicate whether you want the axis label to display frequencies or percentages, click on *Continue* and then *OK*. This will give you a basic bar chart or pie chart in addition to the frequencies table.

Once you have obtained your chart you can edit it by double-clicking in the chart area. This will give you the *SPSS Chart Editor*. You can transpose the chart to make the bars horizontal and edit in a number of ways including changing the colors, titles, labeling and so on. Close the *Editor* when you have finished. If you single-click on the chart area you highlight it. If you now select *Edit/Copy* you can copy the chart into other applications.

Histograms and line graphs

These procedures are contained in the *Graphs* drop-down menu. Click on *Graphs*, then *Histogram*. The *Histogram* dialog box will allow you to enter only one variable. This should be a metric variable, so try putting in *agebegan*. You have the option of being able to superimpose a normal curve on the result, so try it. Notice that the distribution is not a very close approximation to a normal distribution.

TABLE 11.25	SPSS *Tables of Frequencies*				
	Unimportant	Fairly unimportant	Neither	Fairly important	Very important
	Count	Count	Count	Count	Count
Social benefits	11	18	41	37	13
Competition	3	10	35	45	27
Relaxation	9	18	37	41	15
Health and fitness	7	14	24	44	31
Enjoyment	8	2	6	33	71

The *Graphs/Line* procedure will give you the *Line Charts* dialog box. From this you can choose from three types of chart – *Simple*, *Multiple* and *Drop-line*. The *Simple* chart plots your chosen variable along the X-axis. Enter it into the *Category Axis*. It will plot the number of cases or the percentage of cases against each scale value. A line graph for *agebegan* is shown in Figure 11.22. The multiple line chart enables you to plot the frequencies of one variable against the categories of another, as in Figure 11.23. This shows the frequencies of the various ages at which people took up table tennis separated out by sex of respondent.

Data summaries

There are two ways of obtaining univariate statistics for metric variables in SPSS. One is to use the *Statistics* button in the *Frequencies* dialog box. So, access the *tabten.sav* file, select *Analyze/Descriptive Statistics/Frequencies*. Put *agebegan* and *spend* in the *Variable(s)* box and then click on the *Statistics* button. You should obtain the *Frequencies:Statistics* dialog box as illustrated in Figure 11.24. Just put a tick in the box against the statistics you want by clicking with the left mouse button. By clicking with the right mouse button you will get a quick explanation of each statistic. The SPSS output is shown in Table 11.26.

The other procedure is found under *Analyze/Descriptive Statistics/Descriptives* and gives a quick summary of each variable that includes the minimum and maximum scores and the mean and standard deviation. This is a more useful layout if there are many variables since they are listed by column rather than across the page.

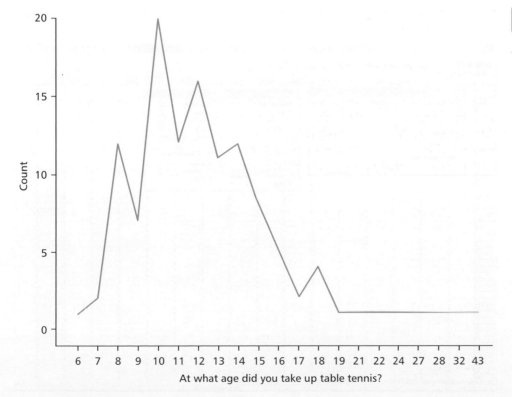

FIGURE 11.22

A line graph of *agebegan*

FIGURE 11.23

Agebegan plotted by sex of respondent

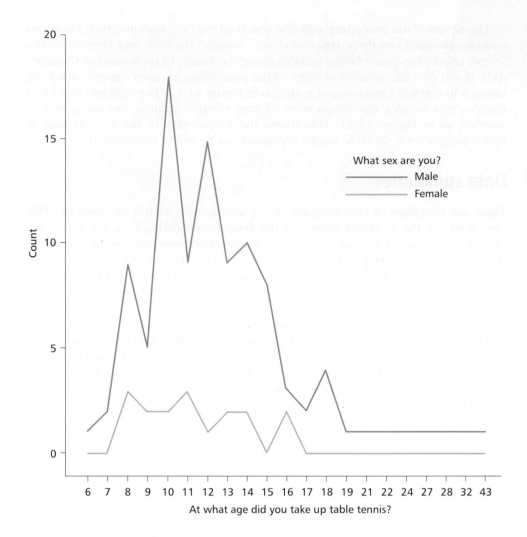

FIGURE 11.24

SPSS *Frequencies:Statistics*

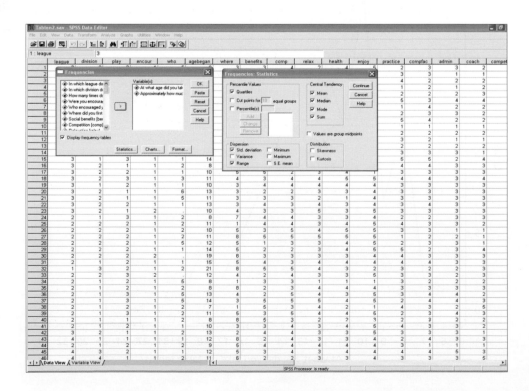

TABLE 11.26		SPSS frequencies/statistics output	
		At what age did you take up table tennis?	Approximately how much have you spent on table tennis in the past 6 months?
N	Valid	120	120
	Missing	0	0
Mean		12.80	51.74
Median		12.00	50.00
Mode		10	60
Std. Deviation		5.002	26.341
Range		37	140
Sum		1536	6209
Percentiles	25	10.00	30.00
	50	12.00	50.00
	75	14.00	68.00

Using *Recode*

If you need to transform a variable by regrouping categories, then it is the SPSS *Recode* procedure that you need. Select *Transform/Recode/Into Different Variables*. To create Table 11.5 from Table 11.3 it was necessary to add together "unimportant" and "fairly unimportant" into a new category, and to add together "fairly important" and "very important" into another category. To do this, select *Social benefits* and put into the *Input Variable* –> *Output Variable* box (see Figure 11.25). Now click on *Old and New Values*. We need codes 1 and 2 to become code 1 so in the *Old Value* dialog area on the left click on the first *Range* radio button and enter 1 through 2. In the *New Value* dialog area on the right enter 1 in the *Value* box and click on *Add*. See Figure 11.26. This instruction will now be entered into the *Old* – –> *New* box. Code 3 we want to change to 2 so click on the *Value* radio button under *Old Value* and enter 3 and 2 under *New Value* and click on *Add*. We now want codes 4 and 5 to be code 3. Click on the Range radio button and enter 4 through 5. Under *New Value* enter 3 and click on *Add*. Click on *Continue*. Give the *Output Variable* a name in the *Name* box, for example, "socben3" and click on *Change* then *OK*. The new variable will appear as the last column (see Figure 11.27). To add value labels for the new variable, double click on the variable name and on *Labels*. Under *Value Labels* enter 1 in *Value* and "Unimportant" under *Value Label* and click on *Add*. Now enter 2 in *Value* and "Neither" under *Value Label* and click on *Add*. Finally, enter 3 in *Value* and "Important" under *Value Label* and click on *Add*. Now click on *Continue* and *OK*. You can now check this out using the *Analyze/Descriptive Statistics/ Frequencies* procedure.

SUGGESTION

The *Recode* procedure can also be used to group continuous metric variables into grouped categories. You could, for example, put the variable *agebegan* into groups of 10 years, for example under 10, 10–19, 20–29, 30–39 and so on by using *Range* in the *Old Value* box.

FIGURE 11.25

The *Recode into Different Variables* dialog box

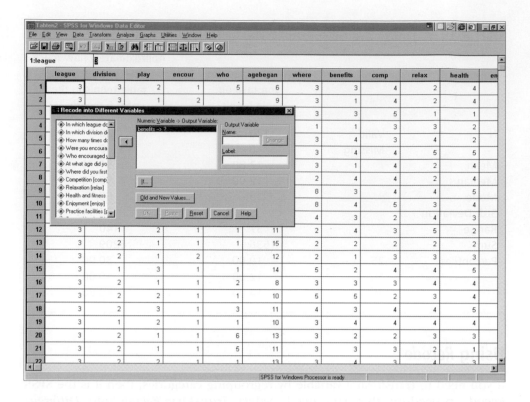

FIGURE 11.26

Old and New Values

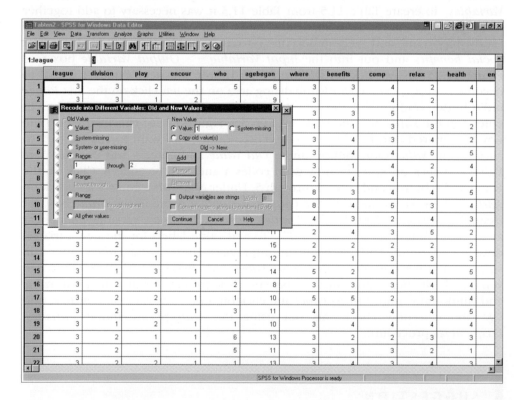

Using *Compute*

Imagine that you want to create a total satisfaction score from the five items in Question 9 in the *tabten* data. This means we need *for each case* to add up all the scores to give a total, which will have a maximum of 25 and a minimum of 5. It will be a new variable – let's call it *totalsat*. Select *Transform*, then *Compute*. You

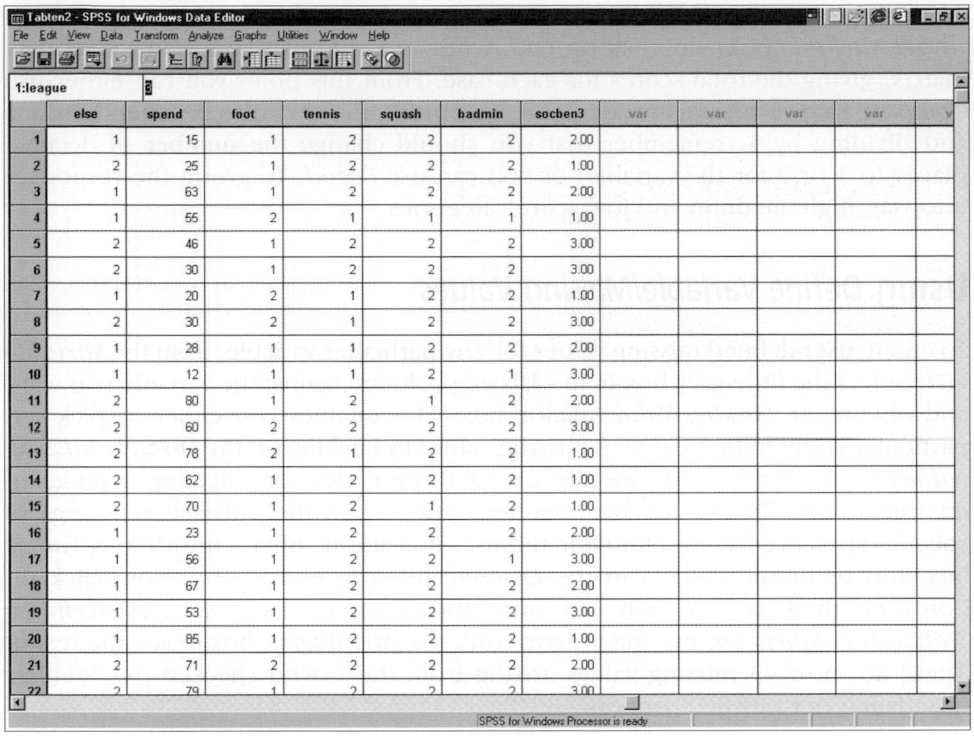

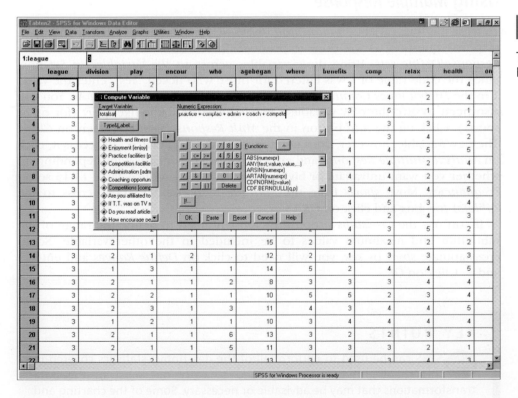

FIGURE 11.27

The new recoded variable

FIGURE 11.28

The *Compute Variable* dialog box

will obtain the *Compute Variable* dialog box (Figure 11.28). Notice that there are lots of functions that we could perform on the variables – but all we want to do is add the five variables together, so highlight *practice* and put into the *Numeric Expression* box by clicking on >. Now click on the + button and bring over the variable *compfac*, then on + again and so on until you have the five variables added together as in Figure 11.28. Enter the new variable name *totalsat* in the *Target Variable* box and click on *OK*. A new variable will appear on your data matrix, giving the total scores for each case. From this point you can either use *Compute* to give you an average score by putting the variables between brackets and dividing by 5 (remember that you should change the number of decimal places to 1 or 2 for the variable) or you can use *Recode* to group the responses into, say, high, medium and low score categories.

Using *Define Variable/Missing Values*

To create user-defined missing values for any particular variable, from the *Variable View* select the little grey box in the *Missing* column against the variable you want and obtain the *Missing Values* dialog box. This enables you either to pick out particular codes to be treated as missing values by clicking on the *Discrete missing values* radio button and entering up to three codes, or selecting a range of missing values. To exclude the "neither" category in the satisfaction ratings of specified practice facilities for table tennis, for example, obtain the *Missing Values* box and enter the code 3 in the *Discrete missing values* box. Now click on *Continue* then on *OK*. You can now, for example, use *Analyze/Descriptive Statistics/Frequencies,* putting *practice* into the *Variable(s):* box to see the result. There are now 43 missing values arising from those who checked the "neither unsatisfied nor satisfied" option.

Using *Multiple Response*

To treat the four variables *badminton, football, squash* and *tennis* as a multiple-response question, as was done to produce Table 11.15, select *Analyze/Multiple Response/Define sets*. Bring these variables across to *the Variables in Set* box. Since the code value of 1 was entered for those who ticked "Yes", enter the value 1 in the *Dichotomies Counted value:* box under *Variables Are Coded As*. You will also need to give the new variable a name. Give it a name like *sport* (for other sports). Click on the *Add* button in the *Mult Response Sets:* box, then on *Close*. The new variable, however, does not appear in the data matrix. To access it, click on *Analyze/Multiple Response* and either *Frequencies* or *Crosstabs* depending on whether you want univariate or bivariate analysis. To produce Table 11.15 select *Frequencies*. Move *sports* from the *Multiple Response Sets:* box across to the *Table(s) for:* box and click on *OK*.

If you use the *Crosstabs* procedure, you will need to define the range of the minimum and maximum values to be included in the other variable. So to crosstabulate *sport* by *sex*, you will need to click on *Define Ranges* and enter 1 and 2. Click on *OK*.

KEY POINTS

SPSS can be used to perform all of the descriptive statistics covered in this chapter. It can also be used to carry out most of the data transformations that may be advisable or necessary. Some of the charting and graphical procedures on SPSS are perhaps not as sophisticated as in some other packages, for example Excel, but the data can always be saved as an Excel file and the graphs produced using this package.

SUMMARY

Before a dataset can be analyzed, the data need to be prepared by checking questionnaires, or other instruments of data capture used, for useability, editing responses for legibility, completeness and consistency, coding any responses that are not precoded, and assembling the data together by entering all the values for all the variables for all the cases in a data matrix. Data entry into the survey analysis package SPSS was explained in some detail. The careful preparation of data ready for analysis should never be neglected. If poor-quality data are entered into the analysis, then no matter how sophisticated the statistical techniques applied, a poor or untrustworthy analysis will result.

Data analysis is the process whereby researchers take the raw data that have been entered into the data matrix to create information that can be used to tackle the objectives for which the research was undertaken. It is not just about performing statistical calculations on numerical variables; it is also about making sense of a dataset as a whole, and thinking about a range of alternative ways of approaching its analysis. The raw data are of little value in themselves until the distributions of each variable have been examined and summarized, relationships between variables have been explored and a range of conclusions drawn. These conclusions will entail evaluating ideas or more specific hypotheses against the data, testing them for statistical significance where a random sample has been drawn, and explaining the results.

What particular statistical techniques are appropriate for data display, summary and the drawing of conclusions depends crucially on the kind of scale onto which variables have been mapped (for example, binary, nominal, ordinal, ranked or metric) and the number of variables that are to be included in any particular calculation. Researchers will commonly begin with the univariate display of categorical and metric variables, using tables, charts and graphs to examine the distribution of each variable. They will then proceed to summarize these variables using measures of central tendency, dispersion, distribution shape, and percentile values for metric variables. Summary statistics for categorical variables are limited.

Before the relationships between variables can be examined, which is the focus of the following chapter, a number of data transformations may be necessary or advisable. Such transformations might include upgrading or downgrading scales, collapsing categories on a nominal or ordinal scale to create fewer categories, creating class intervals from metric scales, computing totals or other scores from combinations of several variables, treating groups of variables as a multiple-response question, handling missing values and "don't know" responses, coding open-ended questions and performing a number of operations on summated rating scales. Finally, using SPSS to produce most of the descriptive statistics covered in this chapter and performing many of the data transformation operations was explained.

QUESTIONS FOR DISCUSSION

1   Is there a danger that the procedures used to analyze a dataset become largely a function of the procedures that happen to be available on a particular computer package like SPSS?

2   Do pie charts have any advantages over bar charts?

3   You can get SPSS to produce any kind of nonsense. The trick is to know what counts as "nonsense". Suggest some of the main ways in which the researcher might produce nonsensical tables and charts.

SPSS EXERCISES

ITEMS ADAPTED FROM BARKER ET AL, 2001

1 Get SPSS to create a bar chart comparing the mean satisfaction scores of the various elements of playing table tennis in Northern Ireland (Question 9). Try changing the output to a pie chart.

2 Get SPSS to draw a histogram of the variable *agebegan*. Use the Chart Editor to change/improve its appearance.

3 Try plotting a scattergram of the perceived importance of the social benefits of playing table tennis against the importance of health and fitness.

FURTHER READING

Argyrous, G. (2005) *Statistics for Research with a guide to SPSS*. London: Sage.

Bryman, A. and Cramer, D. (2004) *Quantitative Data Analysis with SPSS 12 and 13*. Hove, UK: Routledge.

Coolidge, F. (2000) *Statistics. A Gentle Introduction*. London: Sage.

Pallant, J. (2005) *SPSS Survival Manual*, 2nd edition. Maidenhead: Open University Press (McGraw-Hill Education).

Salkind, N. (2005) *Statistics for People Who (Think They) Hate Statistics*. London: Sage.

Smith, D. and Fletcher, J. (2004) *The Art and Science of Interpreting Market Research Evidence*. Chichester: John Wiley & Sons

Analyzing relationships between two variables

12

LEARNING OBJECTIVES In this chapter you will learn about:

→ bivariate data display, including clustered and stacked bar charts and crosstabulation,

→ bivariate data summaries for both categorical and metric variables, including a range of measures of association for two categorical variables, and correlation and regression analysis for two metric variables,

→ how to use SPSS for bivariate data analysis.

Women are likely to be charged more for a new car than men.

© STOCK CONNECTION/ALAMY

INTRODUCTION

The essential descriptive measures explained in Chapter 11 focused on displaying and summarizing the distribution of variables one at a time. This chapter turns to how researchers explore or demonstrate how the distributions of two variables may be related in some way. Thus a manager may well be interested to know how many and what proportions of his or her customers say they are "very satisfied", "fairly satisfied", "dissatisfied" or "very dissatisfied" with the services offered by the company. However, that would only be a first stage in the analysis. The next stage would be to see what factors might be related to expressed satisfaction. Are males more (or less) satisfied on the whole than females? Are there differences in age groups? In social classes? In lifestyles or leisure pursuits? Bivariate analysis is the process of examining the extent to which there are patterns in the way two variables are related together. Such analysis may be used in one or both of two main contexts. The researchers may want to explore what factors are related to one or even several dependent variables or even to explore whether or not there are any patterns between any of the variables. Alternatively, the researcher may have ideas, hunches or even very specific hypotheses about what variables are in fact related and may use bivariate statistics to establish the extent to which these hunches or hypotheses are supported by the data.

This chapter explains a range of statistical measures that may be used for bivariate analysis, first for the purpose of displaying graphically the relationships involved and second for providing summaries of the extent of association or correlation between variables. As for univariate procedures, the actual techniques that may be deployed will depend on whether the variables are categorical or metric. The chapter then turns to situations where the scales are mixed and finally to how all the measures may be performed using SPSS.

INTERNET ACTIVITY

Using your browser, go to **www.thomsonlearning.co.uk/kent** and select the Chapter 12 Internet Activity which will provide a link to a website containing Statnotes by G. David Garson. Under *Additional Topics*, check out *Association*, *Dichotomous Measures*, *Nominal Measures* and *Ordinal Measures*. We will be looking at the lot of these measures in this chapter. You might find that it is a good idea to go back to Garson when you have read this chapter.

Bivariate data display

Clustered bar chart A chart that shows the frequency or percentage of the categories of one variable separated out by the categories of another and placed side by side.

Stacked bar chart A chart that shows the frequency or percentage of the categories of one variable separated out by the categories of another and placed one on top of the other.

The relationship between two categorical variables can to some extent be displayed graphically by using a more sophisticated form of bar chart than was presented in Chapter 11 for univariate analysis. Figure 12.1 illustrates a **clustered bar chart**, which shows the frequency (or percent) of the categories of one variable separated out or clustered by the categories of another. Figure 12.1 was generated from the table tennis data and shows that only in Greystone is there a relatively higher number of households where somebody else also plays table tennis. An alternative is a **stacked bar chart**, as in Figure 12.2. This shows the division in which players compete, stacked by gender of player. It looks as though females are more highly represented in the third division. In both types of graph, however, the clustering or stacking variables should not have more than three or four categories, otherwise the chart, while colorful, is difficult to interpret.

As well as providing displays for groups of cases, as above, a bar chart can be used as a summary for separate variables, as in Figure 12.3. This shows the average (mean) of each of the five aspects of playing table tennis for which

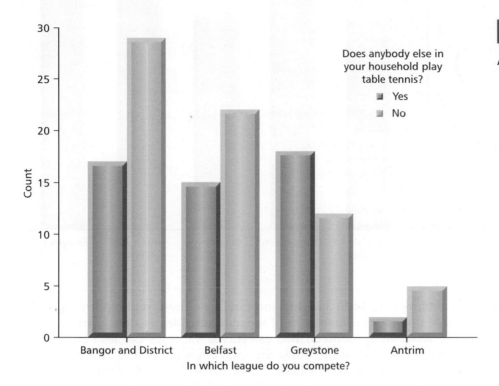

FIGURE 12.1

A clustered bar chart

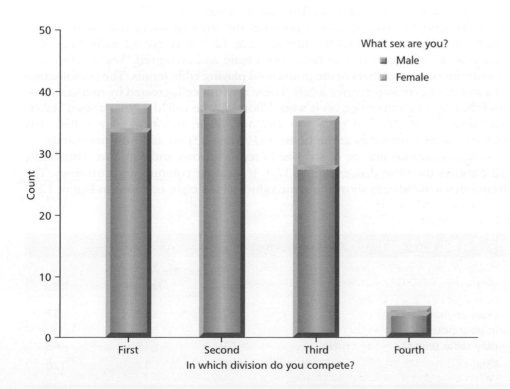

FIGURE 12.2

A stacked bar chart

CHAPTER 12 …

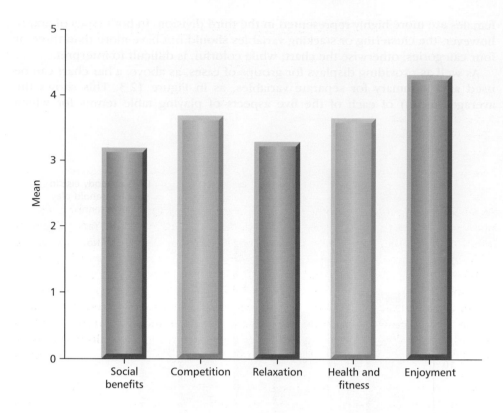

FIGURE 12.3

Summaries of separate variables

respondents have been asked to indicate their perceived importance. It is also possible to illustrate summaries of separate variables as a pie chart.

The relationship between two categorical variables can also be shown as a **bivariate crosstabulation**. These are sometimes referred to as "contingency" or "two-way" tables. A crosstabulation is a particular kind of table in which the frequencies or proportions of cases that combine a value on one categorical variable with a value on another are laid out in combinations of rows and columns. In other words a crosstabulation presents the frequencies of two variables the values of which are interlaced. Thus in Table 12.1 there are 42 individuals who combine the characteristics of being both male and answered "Yes" to the question about other members of the household playing table tennis. The combination of a row and a column creates a **cell**. There are four cells created by two variables, each having two categories, so it would normally be called a "two-by-two" table. The totals at the end of each row (52 and 68 in this table) are called **row marginals**, and the totals at the bottom (103 and 17) are **column marginals**.

Crosstabulations may be of any size in terms of rows and columns. Thus Table 12.2 shows the same data as Figure 12.1. It has four columns and two rows. The frequencies in the cells show the same values as the eight columns in Figure 12.1.

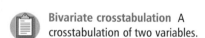

Bivariate crosstabulation A crosstabulation of two variables.

Cell The combination of a row and a column in a crosstabulation.

Row marginal The totals at the end of each row in a crosstabulation.

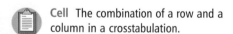

Column marginal The totals at the foot of each column in a crosstabulation.

TABLE 12.1	A bivariate crosstabulation			
		What sex are you?		
		Male	Female	Total
Does anybody else in your household play table tennis?	Yes	42	10	52
	No	61	7	68
Total		103	17	120

TABLE 12.2		League by other household players				
		In which league do you compete?				
		Bangor and District	**Belfast**	**Greystone**	**Antrim**	**Total**
Does anybody else in your household play table tennis?	Yes	17	15	18	2	52
	No	29	22	12	5	68
Total		46	37	30	7	120

As tables get larger they become increasingly difficult to interpret and they require many more cases to avoid having very small numbers in most of the cells. The only solutions are either to increase the number of cases or to reduce the size of the table by, for example, using the SPSS *Recode* procedure explained in Chapter 11.

Where the totals at the end of the rows or the foot of the columns (the marginals) are unequal (as they are in Table 12.1), direct comparison of cell frequencies is difficult to make. If, however, we standardize the frequencies to a common denominator, patterns of association become more apparent. The best solution is to calculate percentages, either down the columns or along the rows. Which of these is appropriate depends on how the researcher wishes to interpret the data.

Suppose we hypothesize that males are more likely than females to have somebody else at home who plays table tennis. Since there are many more males it is difficult to compare the frequencies in the table. What we need to do is compare the percentage of the males who answer "Yes" with the percentage of females who answer "Yes". This means calculating percentages down the columns as in Table 12.3. This shows that, contrary to expectation, a higher percentage of females (58.8 percent compared with 40.8 percent for males) have somebody else in the household who plays table tennis (but remember that this is based on very few females).

Notice here that we have percentaged downwards in the direction of the "independent" variable, gender. It is independent in the sense that it is not the variable we are trying to investigate or explain, which is table-tennis playing. It is not that we are necessarily saying that the gender of the player determines or has some effect on whether or not there are other players in the household. It could just as easily be the case that the existence of other players in the household is more likely to encourage females. The normal assumption that "independent" means cause and "dependent" means effect does not necessarily hold. It is a convention (not universally followed, but useful nevertheless) that the independent variable forms the columns of the table, and the dependent variable the rows. So, as a

TABLE 12.3		Table 12.1 as column percentages		
Percentage within What sex are you?				
		What sex are you?		
		Male	**Female**	**Total**
Does anybody else in your household play table tennis?	Yes	40.8	58.8	43.3
	No	59.2	41.2	56.7
Total		100.0	100.0	100.0

general rule, put the independent variable at the top and percentage downwards. Notice also that the comparison was made across the direction of percentaging.

The relationships between two metric variables can be illustrated using a scattergram. The horizontal axis is used to represent the values of one of the metric variables and the vertical axis to represent the other. The combination of two scales values is then plotted for each case, as in Figure 12.4. There are 120 points, one for each respondent. It shows that there is a tendency for those who took up table tennis at a later age to have spent more on it in the past six months. It shows, furthermore, that the relationship is approximately linear. We will see later in this chapter how this property can be used to calculate a measure of correlation. Note that if one of the variables is considered to be independent (like age began playing table tennis) then it is plotted along the horizontal or X-axis. The dependent variable (*spend*) is put on the vertical Y-axis.

KEY POINTS

Bivariate data display will be used by researchers in two main contexts. First, it will be used in a preliminary diagnostic context in which the researcher runs a number of key crosstabulations to get a feel for the nature of relationships between variables two at a time or plots scattergrams to check whether relationships between metric variables are roughly linear and whether there are any outliers. Second, in a presentational context, the researcher may use clustered or stacked bar charts, crosstabulations or scattergrams to illustrate key findings in a report.

FIGURE 12.4

A scattergram of *spend* by *agebegan*

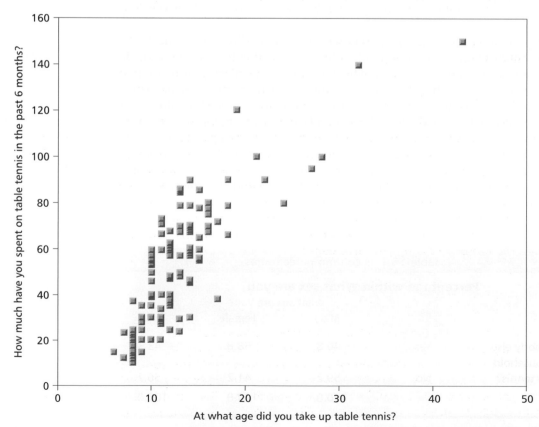

Bivariate data summaries: categorical variables

Data displays enable researchers to eyeball the data distributions, whether they are univariate or bivariate. However, they also want to be able to condense bivariate relationships to a single summary figure just as the average condenses a single univariate distribution to a single figure. To do this we can think either about differences or about associations. Differences refer to comparisons that are being made between two or more numbers, proportions or percentages for two or more groups. Thus the researcher may want to compare the number or proportion of males and females who have somebody else in the household who plays table tennis. As can be seen from Table 12.3, there is an 18 percent difference (58.8–40.8) between the males and the females. The percentage difference will range from zero percent when the proportions are the same to 100 percent when there is the maximum difference possible. The percent difference, however, only works in this way when both variables are binary, otherwise there are lots of differences. It is therefore of limited value; fortunately, there are alternatives that work much better.

Statisticians have, in fact, developed a bewildering array of measures of association for crosstabulated variables. Each statistic, however, will give a different answer. Each will have its own strengths and weaknesses, and there will be circumstances in which its calculation is misleading or inadvisable. Many of these measures are just not considered in standard textbooks on statistics. Many textbooks consider none of them; some mention just a selection, but will take a different view as to their strengths and weaknesses. The student looking for a comprehensive guide will be disappointed. Such a guide, if developed, would necessarily be long and complex. The solution adopted here is to take the measures offered by SPSS and to explain in some detail the collection of statistics proposed in its *Crosstabs* procedure. Although the SPSS manual docs, of course, refer to the statistics selected, the description is very brief, and there is no evaluation or comparison.

All the measures of association explained below have been developed on one of three rather distinct bases:

- departure from independence,
- proportional reduction in error,
- pair-by-pair comparisons.

Departure from independence involves imagining what the data would look like if there were no association, and then saying that association is present to the extent that the observed data depart from this. Thus if 120 respondents consisted of 60 males and 60 females responding "yes" or "no" to a question, and equal numbers of each said "yes" and "no", the marginals would look like Table 12.4: 60 out of 120 are male, that is, half. Therefore if there were no association, we would expect half of the 60 yeses to be male. The expected frequency for any cell can always be found by multiplying the row and column marginal for that cell, and dividing by n, the number of cases. In this example:

$$\frac{(60)(60)}{120} = 30$$

The expected frequencies for each cell are illustrated in Table 12.5. This shows that just as many men as women are likely to say "yes" (or "no"). Suppose, however, that all the men said "yes" and all the women said "no". The result is shown in Table 12.6. The difference between the observed and expected frequencies for each cell is now either +30 or −30 (the maximum difference that is possible in this table). Simply adding these up will, of course, produce zero. If,

Departure from independence The extent to which observed data depart from what the data would look like if there were no association.

however, we square the difference and take that as a proportion of our expectations for each cell, then we take account of whether the absolute difference is based on a large or small expectation. We can now add these up for each cell.

If fo = observed frequency and fe = expected frequency, then the calculations are as in Table 12.7. The maximum value that the sum of the squared differences as a proportion of expected values can take in 120. This is a statistic called *Chi-square*, usually symbolized as χ^2. **Chi-square** will be zero if there are no differences between observed and expected frequencies. The maximum value it can take depends on the number of cases and the number of cells. For a two-by-two table the maximum value for Chi-square is always the number of cases, n. While it is difficult to use Chi-square itself as a measure of association, various adjustments to it have been proposed that result in more acceptable measures. These measures make no assumptions about the order in which the categories are placed – in fact, their calculation is unaffected if we list them in different ways. Accordingly, they are particularly appropriate for tables where both variables are scaled at the binary or nominal levels. They are all based on calculating Chi-square in the first instance and are described below. One feature of this basis for measuring association is that it does not require us to select one variable as dependent, hence all measures based on Chi-square are symmetric measures.

Proportional reduction in error involves arguing that if two variables are associated then it should be possible to use knowledge of the values of one variable to predict the values of the other for each case. Thus if, in a survey, all the men say "Yes" they would purchase Brand X and all the women say "No", then, for each person, if we know their gender, we can perfectly predict their answer to the question. In practice, of course, prediction is seldom perfect, but what we can do

Chi-square A statistic that measures the overall departure of a set of observations from some theoretical proposition.

Proportional reduction in error The extent to which it is possible to predict the values of one categorical variable from the values of another categorical variable with which it might be associated.

TABLE 12.4	Responses by gender		
Answer	Male	Female	Total
Yes	–	–	60
No	–	–	60
Total	60	60	120

TABLE 12.5	Responses by gender: expected frequencies		
Answer	Male	Female	Total
Yes	30	30	60
No	30	30	60
Total	60	60	120

TABLE 12.6	Responses by gender: actual frequencies		
Answer	Male	Female	Total
Yes	60	–	60
No	–	60	60
Total	60	60	120

TABLE 12.7	Calculating Chi-square		
fo	fe	(fo − fe)	$\dfrac{(fo - fe)^2}{e}$
60	30	+30	30
0	30	−30	30
0	30	−30	30
60	30	+30	30
			120

is to measure the extent to which knowledge of the value on one variable reduces the number of errors in predicting the other.

To generate a measure of association we imagine that we are called upon to predict, for each case, which value of a dependent variable each is likely to exhibit. We do this first without any knowledge of the value of an independent variable for each case, and then see whether such knowledge enables us to improve our predictions. The proportion of errors that we can eliminate in this process is called the proportionate reduction in error. There are many statistics that use this notion, and they may be referred to as "PRE" statistics. Like those measures based on departure from independence, these measures are unaffected by the order of the categories and hence are also described in the section later on coefficients appropriate to two nominal scales. Unlike departure from independence, however, all PRE measures require that we select one of the variables as dependent; choosing the other variable as the dependent one will produce a different result. In other words, all PRE measures are asymmetric.

Making **pair-by-pair comparisons** relies on assessing the tendency for all possible combinations of pairs of cases to show similar orderings on both variables. Recall that the essential property of ordinal measurement is the ability to determine which of two observations is the larger. We can then consider a pair of cases and note whether or not the case that is larger on variable A is also larger on variable B. If there is a general tendency for this to happen, then there is a positive association. Relatively high values on one variable are associated with relatively high values on the other. Negative association means a tendency for relatively high values on one variable to be associated with relatively low values on the other.

> **Pair-by-pair comparisons** A measure of association based on the tendency for all possible combinations of pairs of cases to show similar orderings on both ordinal variables.

Look at Table 12.8. The case in cell *a* is higher than case *d* on both variables (this is called a "concordant" pair). If there is a predominance of pairs of this type in a table then there is a positive association. If there are predominantly more pairs like *b* and *c* (a "discordant" pair) there will be negative association. Various measures of association have been developed that assess the relative predominance of concordance over discordance or vice versa.

The idea of pair-by-pair comparisons can be generalized to tables of any size. Measures of association based on these comparisons differ largely in the way they

TABLE 12.8	Pair-by-pair comparisons	
Variable A Variable B	High	Low
High	a	b
Low	c	d

treat the pairs that show no association. However, these statistics all depend on the way in which the categories are ordered and changing the order will alter the statistic. They are therefore appropriate for crosstabulations where both scales are ordinal. They cannot sensibly be used where both or one of the variables is nominal, but since a binary variable cannot be "out of order", if one is binary and the other ordinal or both are binary, then these statistics can be applied. Pair-by-pair comparisons do not depend on selecting one of the variables as dependent, so they are therefore symmetric measures, but, given that there is a sense of order in the categories, these measures do introduce the notion of negative association, that is, high values on one variable being associated with low values on the other.

Whatever measure of association is used, it needs, ideally, to meet certain criteria to be useful for the purpose of making reliable analyses of the data. The basic criteria are:

- it must be applicable to all sizes of table,
- it must vary between zero to represent no association and unity or minus 1 to represent perfect association,
- it must be possible to interpret the results,
- it must be robust.

Some measures of association are restricted to two-by-two tables, or to tables where either rows or columns have only two categories. Measures that apply to only certain sizes of table are of limited value since the researcher is likely to have a variety of tables of different sizes. It is, of course, possible to reduce all the tables to the appropriate size, but information may well be lost in the process and there may not be a sensible way of collapsing categories together. Since different statistics produce different results, the researcher cannot simply apply different statistics according to table size. If, however, the sample (or the population) is very small, it may be necessary to reduce the size of the tables anyway. Either way, the same statistic *must* be used if the degree of association between tables is to be compared.

Measures of association are usually designed so that they vary either between zero (no association) and plus 1 (a perfect association), or between minus 1 (a perfect negative association) and plus 1. The results of calculating such measures are usually described as **coefficients**. Some coefficients, however, may take values greater than 1, or have maximum values less than 1. The problem here is that if, say, the maximum value a statistic can take is 0.707, then what does a coefficient of 0.51 mean? If the two scales are nominal, the statistic should vary between zero and plus 1 – the notion of "negative" association is nonsensical unless there is some kind of order between categories. If the two scales are ordinal, then the statistic should be negative if higher order values on one variable are associated with lower order values on the other. It is not that applying a statistic that cannot take negative values to two ordinal scales is necessarily "wrong" – it is just that the statistic will not reveal whether the association is positive or negative. This may be no big deal, however, since this is usually obvious just by looking at the table.

PRE measures are probably best for allowing the researcher to interpret the numerical result. Thus if the result is, say, 0.52, then it is possible to interpret this as showing that 52 percent of the errors in predicting the dependent variable have been eliminated by using knowledge of the dependent variable. Measures based on pair-by-pair comparisons can be given a "PRE" interpretation, but it is a little stretched. Thus we could say that if any pair of cases is drawn at random from a crosstabulation and we try to predict whether the same or reverse order occurs, our chances of being correct depend on the relative preponderance of either concordant or discordant pairs. However, a result of, say, +0.8 can really only be interpreted as saying that, of all the pairs considered, 80 percent are concordant. Chi-square based measures are probably the most difficult to interpret, because

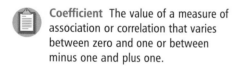

Coefficient The value of a measure of association or correlation that varies between zero and one or between minus one and plus one.

the result is only a measure of a general tendency for the table to depart from what would be expected if there were no association.

As far as possible, statistics should be robust, that is, they can be applied in a wide range of circumstances and do not produce nonsensical results if particular conditions hold. Some statistics, for example, are overly sensitive to marginal distributions that are highly skewed and may, for example, revert to zero even if there is clearly some association in the table. Some statistics revert to unity if any of the cells in the table are empty, even if the association is clearly not perfect. Such statistics will have a tendency to exaggerate the degree of association if the frequencies in some of the cells are very low. A surprising number of statistics are affected if the tables are nonsquare, that is, do not have the same number of rows and columns. Ideally measures of association should not be affected by the marginal distributions, by empty or low frequency cells, or by the table being rectangular.

> ### SUGGESTION
>
> If the researcher constructs large tables with many cells when the number of cases is small – 100 or fewer – then there will be many empty cells or very small numbers in the cells. In these circumstances *all* statistics loose their cool! If you have a small sample, it is wiser to collapse the tables to two-by-two or two-by-three before calculating your measures of association. Also, bear in mind that few measures meet all the criteria for a good statistic, so what counts as the "best" statistic to use in any particular situation is not always evident.

Coefficients appropriate for binary or nominal variables

The coefficients offered by SPSS for Windows are shown in Figure 12.5. Notice that they are conveniently grouped into measures appropriate for nominal data, measures appropriate for ordinal data, and one for nominal by interval (metric) combinations. Binary variables are normally included as nominal, but, as explained earlier, binary variables can be treated at any level. The value of Chi-square may be obtained separately by clicking the appropriate box. The contingency coefficient, Phi and Cramer's V are all measures of association based on Chi-square and require the calculation of this statistic first. They are thus measures based on the notion of departure from independence, and they are symmetric. Phi is, as we shall see, identical to Cramer's V for two-by-two tables, and for tables where either rows or columns are binary (having two categories). This is why they are put together. The statistics Lambda and the uncertainty coefficient are both based on the proportional reduction in error in measuring association.

The **contingency coefficient**. The problem with Chi-square itself is that while it reflects the extent to which the observed values in a table depart from what would be expected if there were no association, it does not vary between zero and one. Certainly the minimum value is zero, but the maximum value depends on the number of cases. For a two-by-two table this maximum value is the number of cases itself, as we saw earlier. For larger tables the maximum value can exceed the number of cases. Various measures have been proposed that adjust for sample (or population) size. One of the earliest measures was proposed by Pearson. This divides Chi-square by the number of cases added to the value of Chi-square itself and takes the square root. The formula is:

Contingency coefficient A measure of association calculated by taking Chi-square and dividing by the number of cases added to the value of Chi-square and taking the square root.

$$C = \sqrt{\frac{\chi^2}{\chi^2 + N}}$$

FIGURE 12.5

SPSS *Crosstabs/Statistics*

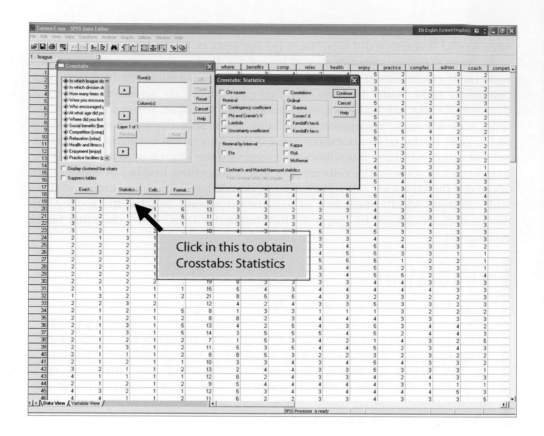

To calculate the statistic, follow the procedures below.

1 Calculate the statistic Chi-square. Use the formula:

$$\chi^2 = \sum \frac{(fo - fe)^2}{fe}$$

where fo is the observed frequency for any given cell and fe is the expected frequency. Calculate fe by multiplying the column and row totals for that cell and dividing by N.

2 Enter Chi-square in the formula for C above.

Table 12.9 records whether or not 85 women and 120 men in a survey accurately recalled the price of Brand X. The expected frequency for women with accurate recall is (115)(85)/205 = 47.7. If 85 out of 205 respondents are women, we would expect 85/205 of the 115 who have accurate recall to be women, i.e. 85/205 (115) = 47.7. In other words, if gender and price recall are independent then the expected frequency, fe, is 47.7. In fact there are 75 women who have accurate recall. The remaining expected frequencies can either be calculated in the same way, or subtracted from the marginals. The full calculation is set out in Table 12.10.

The key features of the statistic are that C becomes zero when the variables are independent, that is, for each cell there is no difference between what would be expected if there were no association and what is, in fact, observed. The upper limit of C, however, depends on the number of rows and columns. For a two-by-two table, for example, it is 0.707. Although this upper limit increases as the number of rows and columns increases, this upper limit is always less than 1. For this reason, C is more difficult to interpret than other measures. Thus it is not easy to interpret a result of 0.48 when the maximum value is 0.707. A further complication is that two contingency coefficients are not comparable unless they are derived from tables of the same size.

TABLE 12.9	Price recall by gender		
Price recall	**Women**	**Men**	**Total**
Accurate recall	75	40	115
Inaccurate recall	10	80	90
Total	85	120	205

TABLE 12.10	The calculation of the contingency coefficient for Table 12.9			
	fo	fe	(fo − fe)	$\dfrac{(fo - fe)^2}{fe}$
a	75	47.7	+27.3	15.6
b	40	67.3	−27.3	11.1
c	10	37.3	−27.3	20.0
d	80	52.7	+27.3	14.1
				60.8

$$C = \sqrt{\frac{60.8}{60.8 + 205}} = 0.48$$

The contingency coefficient may legitimately be used on a table of any size when both variables are scaled at the binary or nominal level and where no distinction is being made between the dependent and the independent variable. However, given the very serious nature of its limitations, there are few contexts in which it is preferable to other statistics that do not suffer from the same drawbacks. C is the oldest of the contingency measures and therefore has been used quite widely, but better measures are available.

Phi and **Cramer's V.** It has already been noted that Chi-square is directly proportional to N for a given size of table. If we simply divide Chi-square by N and take the square root, we obtain a measure called Phi. This has a minimum value of zero when the two variables are independent. For two-by-two tables and for tables where either rows or columns are binary, it also has an upper maximum of unity when the relationship between the two variables is perfect. For tables of this size, then, Phi is a good measure. However, for larger tables, it can attain a value considerably larger than unity. An adjustment to the formula was suggested by Cramer, and is known as Cramer's V. This divides Chi-square by N multiplied by a value that is either rows minus 1 or columns minus 1, whichever is the minimum. The formula is:

Phi A measure of association calculated by taking Chi-square and dividing by the number of cases and taking the square root.

Cramer's V A statistical measure of association for two categorical variables that have been crosstabulated and based on the notion of departure from independence.

$$V = \sqrt{\frac{\chi^2}{N Min(r-1)(c-1)}}$$

Notice that the value of Min(r−1)(c−1) for a two-by-two table or any table where either variable is binary is 1, so V is identical to Phi. Whether we choose to call the resulting measure Phi or V is perhaps not important.

Table 12.11 crosstabulates how many times per week respondents play table tennis with whether or not anybody else in the household plays. Clearly, if there are other people in the household who play, then respondents are likely to play more often. It does indeed seem that where there is somebody else, then respondents are more likely to play two or three times a week. But how strong is this tendency?

The SPSS output showing Chi-square, which SPSS calls *Pearson Chi-Square*, and Cramer's V is illustrated in Table 12.12. The achieved value of V is, then, 0.196. The contingency coefficient for the same data is 0.192. Both statistics thus show that there is a small degree of association between the two variables. It is difficult to give the result a more precise statistical interpretation. However, if, for example, we crosstabulated the number of times respondents reported playing table tennis with another variable, like gender, we could calculate V and then compare the result. We could then conclude whether the presence of others in the household playing table tennis, or gender, was more strongly associated with frequency of playing.

Cramer's V is, then, a good statistic. It can be used on any size of table. It can be used for binary, nominal or ordinal scales, or any combination like one binary and one ordinal. It is a fairly robust measure in that it can be applied in a wide range of circumstances and does not produce nonsensical results under certain conditions. For example, unlike some other statistics, it does not revert to zero simply because one or more cells are empty. It also makes no assumptions about the shape of the population distribution of the variables from which it is computed and requires only categorical measurement.

However, Cramer's V is not perfect and it has its limitations. First, although V is always zero when there is a complete lack of association between the two variables, when it is unity there may not be a "perfect" association. If the table is square (for example, a two by two, a three by three, a four by four and so on) then V = 1 does indeed indicate that the variables are perfectly associated. However, if the table is nonsquare (for example, a three-by-five) then V can reach unity even when there is clearly not a perfect association.

TABLE 12.11	Play frequency by whether anybody else in the household plays		
		Does anybody else in your household play table tennis?		
		Yes	No	Total
How many times do you play per week?	Once	15	28	43
	Twice	22	30	52
	Three times	10	8	18
	Four or more times	5	2	7
Total		52	68	120

TABLE 12.12	Chi-square, Cramer's V and the contingency coefficient for Table 12.11

	Value
Pearson Chi-square	4.618
Cramer's V	.196
Contingency Coefficient	.192
N of Valid Cases	120

A second limitation is that since V depends on calculating Chi-square it must be amenable to the use of that statistic. This statistic assumes that the expected values are large. A rule of thumb that is commonly applied is that the statistic should be calculated only if fewer than about 20 percent of all the cells have expected frequencies of less than 5 and no cell has an expected frequency of less than 1. (As we shall see, SPSS will warn you if this is the case.) Also, it has to be said that Chi-square tends to give greater weight to those columns or rows having the smallest marginals rather than to those with the largest marginals. It is therefore sensitive to marginal distributions.

A third limitation is that the magnitude of achieved values of V has no direct interpretation, and, furthermore, it is not directly comparable with any other measure of association, except in the case of the two-by-two table, when it is identical to Pearson's r statistic, which will be explained in the next section.

Finally, the statistic is designed for use with binary and nominal scales. When it is being used for ordinal scales it does not violate any statistical assumptions and its use is legitimate, but it may be less informative than measures that are specifically for ordinal data. Thus V does not indicate a direction of association. This is fine for nominal scales where the notion of a "negative" association does not apply. However, for ordinal scales it could happen that high values on one variable are associated with *low* values on the other. This would indicate a negative association, but Cramer's V cannot be negative. Furthermore, the statistic is insensitive to the ordering of categories. Putting the scale values in a different order on either variable will not change the value of V. This again is fine for nominal scales, but for ordinal scales it ignores information that could be derived from the ordering of categories.

Despite these limitations, Cramer's V is an extremely useful coefficient because of its wide applicability. It does not make any distinction between dependent and independent variables. This may be seen as an advantage if the researcher does not wish to make such a distinction, but where he or she does, then other measures of association may be better.

Lambda. If two variables are associated, then, as explained earlier, it is possible to use knowledge of the value of one variable to predict the value of the other for each case. Thus if all men say "yes" and all women say "no", then for each person, if we know their gender, we can safely predict the answer to the question. In practice, prediction is seldom perfect, so what we can do is measure the extent to which knowledge of the value on one variable reduces the number of errors in predicting the other.

Take the case where nearly all men say "yes" and most of the women say "no", as in Table 12.13. To generate our measure of association, we need to calculate how many errors predicting the answer to the question we would make *not* knowing a person's gender. If we know the marginal totals of yeses and nos, but not each individual case, then the "best" guess we could make for each person is to predict that all answers are "yes" (since there are more of these), and be wrong for 90 out of the 200 cases.

Lambda A measure of association for two categorical variables based on the proportional reduction in error.

TABLE 12.13	Responses by gender		
Answer	Male	Female	Total
Yes	90	20	110
No	10	80	90
Total	100	100	200

Suppose, now, we know a person's gender, then knowing that a person is male and that 90 out of 100 males say "yes", clearly, it is sensible to predict "yes" for all males and make only 10 errors. If, on the other hand, we predict "no" for all 100 women, we make only 20 errors. That totals 10 + 20 = 30 errors in all. This may be compared with the original 90 errors. This is a 66 percent reduction, or 0.66. Clearly, if we eliminate all errors, we will end up with a measure of unity. If we eliminate none, we will end up with a value of zero.

It is difficult to generate a formula for Lambda that you can use just to plug in selected values. Most formulae that have been generated are rather complex. It is probably best to be clear that Lambda is based on the following calculation:

$$\frac{\text{number of errors eliminated}}{\text{number of original errors}}$$

In the above example, this is:

$$= \frac{90-30}{90} = 0.66.$$

The SPSS output for Lambda is shown in Table 12.14. It calculates an asymmetric Lambda for each of the variables. Thus predicting whether or not anybody else plays in the house from play frequency reduces errors by just under 10 percent, but making the prediction in the other direction results in no reduction at all. In addition, a kind of average of the two is calculated, giving a symmetrical version that makes no assumption about which variable is independent; it measures the overall improvement when the prediction is done in both directions.

The main features of Lambda are:

- it varies between zero and plus 1; it cannot be negative,

- it can be used on *any* size of table. The errors remaining after taking the "best guess", not knowing, then knowing the value of the other variable, need to be added up,

- it is an asymmetric measure, that is, the prediction is one-way. It makes sense to predict the dependent variable from the independent variable. If the independent variable is at the top, then it is the categories forming the rows that should be predicted. If the prediction is made in the other direction, then a different value for Lambda will be derived.

Lambda has an advantage over Chi-square based measures in that its interpretation is much clearer. Thus a result of 0.60 means that 60 percent of errors can be eliminated by using knowledge of categories of the independent variable to predict categories of the dependent variable. The main drawback of Lambda is

TABLE 12.14	SPSS output for Lambda		
			Value
Nominal by Nominal	Lambda	Symmetric	.042
		How many times do you play per week? Dependent	.000
		Does anybody else in your household play table tennis? Dependent	.096

that it will take on a numerical value of zero in instances where all the other measures will not be zero and where we would not wish to refer to the variables as being statistically independent. This may occur where one of the row marginals is much larger than the rest, so no matter what the category of the independent variable, the prediction of the dependent variable category will be the same. In large tables, even if a single marginal total does not dominate, it is likely that some of the less numerous categories will not enter into the computation of Lambda at all.

> ## SUGGESTION
>
> Where an asymmetric measure for two nominal variables is required, Lambda is to be preferred over Cramer's V, partly because it takes account of which variable is independent, and partly because its interpretation is much clearer. However, where the marginals of the dependent variable are very unevenly distributed the statistic will revert to zero and another measure may be required.

The uncertainty coefficient. This measures the proportion by which uncertainty in the dependent variable is reduced by knowledge of the independent variable. The concept of uncertainty comes from information theory and has to do with the ambiguity of data distributions. Whereas Lambda takes the modal category as the "best guess" for a set of categories, the concept of uncertainty recognizes the probability that any one particular case may be in one of the nonmodal categories. Hence the entire distribution, not just the mode, is considered. It uses a logarithmic function to calculate the average uncertainty in the marginal distribution of the dependent variable, and then calculates what proportion of uncertainty may be eliminated by looking at the categories in the independent variable.

The maximum value for the uncertainty coefficient is 1.0, which denotes the complete elimination of uncertainty. The minimum value is zero when no improvement occurs. As with Lambda, SPSS calculates both asymmetric versions and a combined symmetrical version. Though this measure clearly eliminates one of the main failings of Lambda by taking into account the distribution in the marginals of the dependent variable, its calculation is a "black box" to all but a fully fledged mathematician. The statistic is so unknown that the only reference to it is in the manual for the mainframe version of SPSS. It was, apparently, originally developed by Theil (1967).

Uncertainty coefficient A measure of association for two categorical variables based on the proportion by which uncertainty in the dependent variable is reduced by knowledge of the independent variable.

Coefficients appropriate for ordinal variables

SPSS lists four statistics as appropriate for ordinal data, but, fortunately, they are all based on the principle of pair-by-pair comparisons that was explained earlier. The key difference between them is in the way they treat "tied" pairs.

Gamma. This statistic was developed by Goodman and Kruskal. It calculates the number of pairs in a crosstabulation having the *same* rank order of inequality on both variables (concordant pairs) and compares this with the number of pairs having the *reverse* rank order of inequality on both variables (discordant pairs). Gamma is the simplest of the pair-by-pair measures because it ignores all other combinations in the table. Gamma takes the difference between concordance and discordance and divides this by the total number of both concordant and discordant pairs. Its formula is:

Gamma A measure of association for two ordinal variables based on calculating the number of pairs in a crosstabulation having the same rank order of inequality on both variable compared with the number of pairs having the reverse order of inequality.

$$G = \frac{C - D}{C + D}$$

The calculation of the statistic is demonstrated in Table 12.15, which is a three-by-two crosstabulation of product usage by product satisfaction. To obtain the number of concordant pairs, take each cell and multiply its frequency by the sum of the frequencies of all the cells below and to the right. Add together the results for each cell. Begin in the top left-hand cell. Only two cells are below and to the right. The next cell along has only one cell below and to the right. No other cells have others both below and to the right, so the calculation is:

$$C = 10(8 + 10) + 8(10) = 180 + 80 = 260$$

To calculate the number of discordant pairs the procedure is the same, except that we take cells below and to the left. So, begin in the top *right-hand* cell. The calculation is:

$$D = 4(4 + 8) + 8(4) = 48 + 32 = 80$$

$$G = \frac{C - D}{C + D} = \frac{260 - 80}{260 + 80} = \frac{180}{340} = 0.52$$

Gamma varies between minus 1 and plus 1. Zero indicates no association – the number of concordant pairs equals the number of discordant pairs. A result of 0.52 indicates a 52 percent predominance of concordance over discordance, so there is a moderate degree of association between the two variables. Remember that G is a symmetric statistic – we do not need to distinguish between dependent and independent variables. Notice also that it is "margin-free" – its value does not depend on the row or column marginals. Gamma can be applied to any size of table, but the variables must be in categories that can be ordered. It has the drawback, however, that it is overly sensitive to empty cells. This is because no matter how many cases in a cell, if multiplied by zero in an empty cell, the result will be zero.

For two-by-two tables Gamma is identical to a statistic that is commonly used on such tables, namely Yule's Q. This is calculated from the formula:

$$Q = \frac{ad - bc}{ad + bc}$$

a–d refer to the cells as labeled in Table 12.8. Notice that ad = C, the number of concordant pairs and bc = D, the number of discordant pairs.

Gamma can be used on any size of table provided both scales are ordinal. It is simple to calculate and easy to understand. However, it is insensitive to other than concordance and discordance. This is why the other measures calculated by SPSS may be more appropriate.

Somers' d. This statistic is similar to Gamma except that it takes account of those pairs that are tied on one variable but not on the other. Accordingly, it is an asymmetric measure since there will be two results depending on which variable is taken. The numerator of the equation is the same as Gamma, but the denomi-

Somers'd A measure of association for two ordinal variables that is similar to Gamma except that it takes account of those pairs that are tied on one variable but not on the other.

TABLE 12.15	Customer satisfaction by product usage		
Product usage satisfaction	High	Medium	Low
High	10	8	4
Low	4	8	10

nator adds a value, T, which measures the number of ties on Variable A, but not on Variable B, or vice versa for the other result. The general formula is:

$$d = \frac{C - D}{C + D + T}$$

To calculate T take each cell in turn, beginning in the upper left-hand cell, multiply the frequency in that cell by all the cases falling to the right of the cell in the same row. The calculation for Table 12.15 is:

$$T = 10(8 + 4) + 8(4) + 4(8 + 10) + 8(10) = 120 + 32 + 72 + 80 = 304$$

$$\text{So } d = \frac{260 - 80}{260 + 80 + 304} = 0.28$$

The alternative d will perform the same operation, but on the columns. d will always give a result substantially below G, since in all cases we are dividing by a value to which T has been added.

Kendall's tau-b. This is a still more stringent measure of association. It includes ties in both directions, so it is similar to Somer's d, but includes both versions of T, Tx and Ty. The formula is:

$$\tau_\beta = \frac{C - D}{\sqrt{(C + D + Tx)(C + D + Ty)}}$$

Kendall's tau-b A measure of association for two ordinal variables that is similar to Gamma except that it takes account of those pairs that are tied in both directions.

This is now a symmetrical measure. However, it varies between minus 1 and plus 1 only when the table is square, that is, the number of rows equals the number of columns. It is appropriate where the researcher is concerned with the strict ordering of the variables.

Kendall's tau-c. Tau-b can be used only when the number of rows and columns in a table is the same. Otherwise it is better to use Tau-c. This uses the following formula:

$$\tau_c = \frac{2m(C - D)}{N^2(m - 1)}$$

Kendall's tau-c A measure of association for two ordinal variable based on pair-by-pair comparisons, but only when the number of rows and columns is the same.

m is the smaller of rows or columns. For Table 12.15 this is calculated as follows:

$$t_c = \frac{(2)(2)(260 - 80)}{44^2} = \frac{720}{1936} = 0.37$$

In the case of square tables where R = C, tau-c will generally be smaller than tau-b, though it may be greater than tau-b in rectangular tables.

SUGGESTION

Gamma is a somewhat loose interpretation of association that looks only at the general tendency for either concordance or discordance to predominate. It is always larger than tau-b, tau-c or Somers' d. This is not necessarily a disadvantage if Gamma is being used to compare degrees of association in a number of tables. Tau-b, tau-c and Somers' d probably give a better assessment of the actual degree of association since they take into account tied pairs. Tau-b is best for square tables, tau-c for rectangular tables and Somers' d where the researcher wishes an asymmetric measure. Different textbooks give different advice on the advisability of various statistics. At the end of the day it is up to the researcher to make up his or her own mind.

Coefficients appropriate for two ranked variables

Spearman's rho A measure of correlation between two fully ranked scales.

There is only one statistic on SPSS appropriate for two ranked variables: **Spearman's rho**. Recall that in a ranked scale each observation is assigned a number from 1 to n to reflect its standing relative to other observations. There are as many ranks as cases to be ranked. Consider five types of ground coffee ranked 1 to 5 in terms of taste and aroma by five people, as in Table 12.16. Spearman's coefficient is calculated from the formula:

$$\text{rho } (r_s) = 1 - \frac{6\sum d^2}{n(n^2 - 1)}$$

where n is the number of paired observations and d is the difference between ranks for each pair of observations. Where the ranks are identical then d = 0 and rho = 1. The calculation for Table 12.16 is set out in Table 12.17. Rho varies between +1 and −1. Zero indicates no association. To use rho on metric data it is necessary to convert the metric values into ranks. This has the advantage that, by doing so, it is unaffected by extreme values.

TABLE 12.16	Coffee ranked by taste and aroma	
Respondent	**Taste**	**Aroma**
A	5	3
B	3	4
C	1	1
D	2	2
E	4	5

TABLE 12.17	Calculation of Rho			
Respondent	**Taste**	**Aroma**	**d**	**d²**
A	5	3	2	4
B	3	4	1	1
C	1	1	0	0
D	2	2	0	0
E	4	5	1	1
Total				6

$$\text{Rho} = 1 - \frac{6(6)}{5(25 - 1)} = 0.7$$

Coefficients appropriate for mixed variables

SPSS suggests only one statistic for situations where the independent variable is binary or nominal and the dependent variable is metric (or interval in SPSS), namely **Eta**. Eta squared is sometimes known as the **correlation ratio** and can be interpreted as the proportion of the total variability in the dependent variable that can be accounted for by knowing the categories of the independent variable. The statistic takes the variance (the square root of the standard deviation) of the dependent variable as an index of error in using the mean of the variable to make a prediction for each case. This is then compared with the variance in each subgroup of the independent variable. If the variables are associated, the variance within each subgroup will be less than the overall variance. The correlation ratio is then:

Eta A statistical measure of association where the independent variable is binary or nominal and the dependent variable is metric.

Correlation ratio A measure of association for situations where the independent variable is binary or nominal and the dependent variable is metric. It measures the proportion of the total variability in the dependent variable that can be accounted for by knowing the categories of the independent variable.

$$n^2 = \frac{\text{original variance} - \text{within-group variance}}{\text{original variance}}$$

The correlation ratio (Eta squared) is always positive and ranges from zero to 1. It is an asymmetric measure and is an index of the degree to which scores on an interval scale can be predicted from categories on a nominal scale. To use it in SPSS the nominal variable must be coded numerically.

For other combinations of scales there are other statistics. Thus for one nominal and one ordinal scale there is a measure called the coefficient of differentiation developed by Wilcoxon which is an extension of Wilcoxon's signed-ranks test. For describing association between one ordinal and one metric scale there is Jaspen's coefficient of multiserial correlation. Neither of these statistics is calculated by SPSS and will not be covered here. For further details see Freeman (1965). If you do have these combinations of scales, it would be more usual to treat the higher-order scale as at a lower level of measurement. So, for an ordinal by nominal combination, treat them as two nominal scales. For an ordinal by metric combination, treat them as two ordinal scales. Treating a metric by nominal combination as two nominal scales will mean throwing away a lot of information with a much less sensitive measure, but for this situation, SPSS does give us Eta, which we can square to give us the correlation ratio.

Selecting the appropriate statistic

In deciding what statistics are appropriate for your crosstabulations, it is first essential to be clear about the scales used for measurement purposes. This will enable you to use the appropriate grouping of statistics – nominal, ordinal or nominal by metric. If either or both variables are nominal, choose between the contingency coefficient, Phi-square, Cramer's V or the uncertainty coefficient. If there is no clear distinction being drawn between dependent and independent variables, select C, Phi or V. V is preferable to C in all circumstances, so choose this statistic. For two-by-two tables and tables where one of the variables is binary, it will be identical to Phi anyway. If one of the variables clearly *is* dependent, choose Lambda unless the marginals are very unevenly distributed, in which case use the uncertainty coefficient. You could, of course, arbitrarily pick one of the variables as "dependent", but the results may be misleading.

If both variables are ordinal, choose from Gamma, Somers' d, Kendall's tau-b or tau-c. Gamma is the simplest of these measures. Choose this if you wish to compare a number of ordinal by ordinal tables or if you want a "quick-and-dirty" indication of the degree of association. If one of the variables is clearly dependent, select Somers' d. If not and you want a tightly controlled measure of association, pick tau-b if the table is square and tau-c if it is not.

All this suggests that the decision needs to be taken for each table on the basis of the level of measurement and whether a symmetrical or asymmetrical measure is required. However, researchers are usually comparing *many* tables in any particular piece of research. It is not essential that the same statistic be used for all tables, but anywhere the degree of association is to be compared *must* use the same statistic. So pick one that suits each grouping of tables.

Remember that for the asymmetric measures, SPSS will produce three statistics, one for each variable taken as "dependent", and one that combines the two, so you will need to pick the appropriate coefficient carefully – SPSS will not do it for you. If your research, for example, is looking at a range of factors that may be associated with a particular dependent variable, then always use an asymmetric measure, selecting this as the dependent variable for the appropriate statistic. If you are looking largely for patterns of relationships or interconnections between variables then choose a symmetrical measure.

Remember that establishing a high degree of association between two variables does not establish anything about causality or even influence. That requires further investigation into temporal sequences and lack of spuriousness. Remember, too, that measures of association are *descriptive* statistics – they report on the cases that are in the table. If your cases are, in fact, a sample, you may wish to use *inferential* statistics (in addition to descriptive ones) to make or to test statements about the population of cases from which the sample was drawn. These statistics are explained in Chapter 13.

Large tables with many rows and many columns are difficult to interpret. Large crosstabulations are a result of using a lot of categories for each variable. Thus two variables crosstabulated, one with six categories and the other with five will result in a table with 6 by 5 or 30 cells. Unless the total number of cases on which the table is based is considerable, the frequencies in the cells will be very small. For example, with 30 cells a sample of 100 respondents will average out at just over three per cell! There are bound to be many cells that are empty. This not only makes the interpretation very difficult, it also means that *any* measures of association we calculate will be unreliable.

The usual solution is to condense larger tables into smaller ones. Very often this involves creating two binary variables and producing a two-by-two table with four cells. In SPSS this is achieved by using the *Recode* procedure that was explained at the end of Chapter 11.

KEY POINTS

SPSS features no fewer than nine measures of association that may be used to create bivariate summaries for categorical data. However, some of these are for situations where both variables are nominal, some where both are ordinal, and one for a mixture of nominal and metric. Binary variables can be used at any level of scaling. Measures appropriate for nominal variables may be based on the idea of departure from independence or on the notion of proportional reduction in error. Ordinal measures are based on the principle of pair-by-pair comparisons. Each statistic has its own strengths and limitations, so selecting the appropriate statistics to use can be quite tricky. For the most part, Cramer's V is probably the best for nominal variables and Gamma for ordinal, but if researchers want to take account of what variables are playing an independent role in the research, then Lambda may be the preferred statistic.

Bivariate data summaries: metric variables

We saw in Chapter 11 that to display the relationship between two metric variables we could plot a scattergram. Data summary involves calculating a measure of association similar to those we calculated for crosstabulations. The good news is that there is only one measure that is universally used – Pearson's r, otherwise known as the correlation coefficient or the product-moment correlation coefficient. The bad news is that it is a bit more difficult to explain than the measures we have looked at so far. If you have access to SPSS then it can be calculated for you at the click of a mouse button. However, the point is to understand how the statistic is calculated and what it is telling you.

If the two metric variables are correlated, then high values on one variable are associated with high values on the other for a positive correlation and with low values for a negative one. The problem is that the two scales will have different averages, as measured by the arithmetic mean, and are likely in addition to be in different units (e.g. one in years old and the other in Euros). To take account of the different averages, we can calculate by how much an observation for a particular case is above the mean of Y for variable Y and above the mean of X for variable X. If we then multiply the result we will get a large positive product. The same will happen if both are large negative figures, that is, below the mean on each variable. If we add all these products for all cases together, we will get a large sum. If, on the other hand, high values on one variable are associated with low values on the other, we will get a large negative sum. If there is little correlation, then positive and negative values will tend to offset one another. So, the sum we are calculating – the *covariation* in technical parlance – is an indication of the extent to which the two variables are correlated. The formula is:

$$\sum (X - \bar{X})(Y - \bar{Y})$$

If we divide this covariation by the number of cases, n, we get an average covariation called the **covariance**, which takes account of the fact that the mean of X and the mean of Y may be different. To take account of the differences in units, the covariance is divided by the standard deviation of X multiplied by the standard deviation of Y. This standardizes the covariance. If we divide both the numerator and the denominator by n, the formula for r becomes:

Covariance An average covariation calculated by dividing the covariation by the number of cases.

$$r = \frac{\sum (X - \bar{X})(Y - \bar{Y})}{\sqrt{[\sum (X - \bar{X})^2][\sum (Y - \bar{Y})^2]}}$$

where X and Y are actual scores, and $\bar{X}$ and $\bar{Y}$ are the mean of the X values and Y values respectively. Suppose four students (cases A, B, C and D) take two tests that are scored out of 10. The results are shown in Table 12.18. You can see that there is a tendency for those who perform well in Test X also perform well on test Y. The calculation of r for Table 12.18. is shown in Table 12.19.

The **correlation coefficient**, r, measures the amount of spread about an imaginary line, called a regression line, that goes through all the dots on a scattergram in such a way that the distances between all the points and the line are minimized. This is a "best-fitting" line, which for the four students A–D is shown in Figure 12.6. The maximum value for r is 1.00, indicating a perfect correlation where all the points fall exactly on the regression line. A value of r = 0.84, for example, would indicate that most observations are close to the line. A coefficient of r = 0 or nearly zero would mean that the line is no help in predicting X from Y or vice versa. Pearson's r can be negative and the regression line will have a negative slope. Pearson's r itself is a little difficult to interpret, but if we square the result to

Correlation coefficient A measure of the extent to which the values of two metric variables covary and approximate a rising or a falling straight line in a scattergram.

TABLE 12.18	Scores of A–D on two tests	
Individual	Text X	Test Y
A	0	1
B	6	2
C	6	4
D	8	5
Total	20	12

TABLE 12.19		The calculation of r from Table 12.18				
	X	Y	$(X-\bar{X})$	$(Y-\bar{Y})$	$(X-\bar{X})(Y-\bar{Y})$	$(X-\bar{X})^2$	$(Y-\bar{Y})^2$
A	0	1	−5	−2	+10	25	4
B	6	2	+1	−1	−1	1	1
C	6	4	+1	+1	+1	1	1
D	8	5	+3	+2	+6	9	4
Total	20	12			16	36	10

$\bar{X} = 20/4 = 5$

$\bar{Y} = 12/4 = 3$

$$r = \frac{16}{\sqrt{36(10)}} = 0.843$$

Coefficient of determination The proportion of the variance on one metric variable accounted for by the variance on another. It is calculated by squaring the correlation coefficient (Pearson's r).

produce r^2 then we have what is often called the **coefficient of determination,** which gives the proportion of the variance on the Y observations that is accounted for or "explained" by variations in X. Thus if r = 0.84 then r^2 is 0.71. This means that 71 percent of the variance in Y is accounted for by the variance in X. If the value calculated for r^2 is very low or zero, do not assume, however, that there is no relationship between X and Y – it might be that the relationship is not linear but curvilinear. The best way to check is to draw or get SPSS to draw the scattergram.

The regression line may be described by a formula whose general form is:

$$Y = a + bX$$

where Y and X are values from the two metric variables and a and b are constants. The constant a indicates at what point the regression line cuts the vertical axis (it is the value of Y when X is zero), and b is the steepness of the slope of the line. In order actually to make a prediction of the value of Y from a particular value of X you would need to know what these constants are. The regression output from SPSS is shown in Table 12.20. The constant a is 0.778 and b is 0.444, so the full equation is:

$$Y = 0.778 + (0.444)X$$

This means that for any given value of X we can calculate what Y would be from the equation – and vice versa.

The correct use of correlation and regression depends on a number of conditions being met.

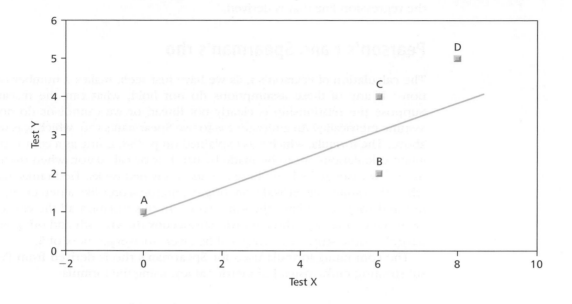

FIGURE 12.6

A scattergram of X on Y and regression line

TABLE 12.20	SPSS regression coefficients		

Coefficients^a

		Unstandardized Coefficients	
Model		B	Std. Error
1	(Constant)	.778	1.168
	VAR00001	.444	.200

a = DEPENDENT VARIABLE: VAR00002

- Both variables must be scaled, or assumed to be scaled, at the metric level.
- Each case has been scaled on both variables.
- The relationship between the variables is linear.
- Where the statistics are to be used for the purposes of statistical inference, the variables should be approximately normal in distribution.

Correlation and regression compared

Correlation and regression are clearly related statistics, but they serve different purposes. Correlation is concerned with measuring the *strength* of the relationship between variables. It determines the extent to which the values of two or more metric variables covary. The square of the correlation coefficient measures how near on average each datapoint is to a hypothetical line that runs through the points in a way that minimizes the distances between each datapoint and the line. The procedure makes no distinction between dependent and independent variables – both variables have equal status.

Regression, by contrast, helps the researcher to determine the *form* of the relationship. The objective is to be able to predict or estimate the value of one variable corresponding to a given value of the other. It is concerned with identifying the parameters of the regression so that it can be used to make such predictions. However, what variable is chosen as the dependent variable makes a difference to the regression line that is derived.

Pearson's r and Spearman's rho

The calculation of Pearson's r, as we have just seen, makes a number of assumptions. If any of these assumptions do not hold, what can the researcher do? Suppose the relationship is clearly not linear, or we cannot or do not wish to assume metricality? An alternative is to use Spearman's rho, which was mentioned above. The formula, which was explained on p. 358, is fine as a computational aid when calculations are to be made by hand or by calculator, when there are relatively few cases and where there are no or few tied ranks. Tied ranks may emerge when the ranking is derived from original metric scores like a percentage in a class test and some cases have the same score. In this situation all the cases are given an average rank. So if three individuals occupy the 4th, 5th and 6th positions but have the same score, then they will be given an average rank of 5.

The computing formula used for Spearman's rho is derived from Pearson's r, substituting ranks instead of metric values, using the formula:

$$r = \frac{\sum (X - \bar{X})(Y - \bar{Y})}{\sqrt{[\sum (X - \bar{X})^2][\sum (Y - \bar{Y})^2}}$$

where X and Y are pairs of ranks on the two variables for each case. Where there are no tied ranks, Spearman's rho = Pearson's r. Where there are ties, rho begins to loose its accuracy, and adjustments have to be made to the formula, which can get quite complex, so the Pearson formula is to be preferred. Where calculations are to be done using computer software, there is no advantage in using the hand-computation formula. In short, if you throw Spearman's rho and Pearson's r at the *same* ranked data, you will obtain an identical result (see SPSS Exercise 10 at the end of this chapter).

Where the rankings are derived from metric data, if we compute Spearman's rho on the ranked data and Pearson's r on the original metric data (instead of on the ranked data) there will still tend to be a general correspondence between the two measures. If, in fact, the distances between the metric scores are the same throughout both variables, then converting them to ranks and applying rho will produce an identical result. However, the metric values are generally not equally spaced and the statistics can be expected to diverge. If, for example, we take the two metric variables on our table tennis data, *spend* and *agbegan*, and get SPSS to calculate both statistics we obtain the result in Tables 12.21 and 12.22. Pearson's r is 0.808 and Spearman's rho is 0.779. The difference is very small and both would round off to 0.8.

So what, then, is the advantage of Spearman's rho? Are there any circumstances in which it is the preferred statistic? Certainly if the data are already ranked, then both statistics will produce an identical result anyway. If the data are in metric form then the researcher can either calculate Pearson's r directly, or use the metric data to create ranks and calculate Spearman's rho. Where the data in both scales are normally or fairly normally distributed with a central concentration, the ranks will be closer together at the center than at the extremes. The value of rho can then be expected to be slightly less than that of r, as it is in the above example. Pearson, in fact, investigated the relationship between the two statistics and showed that where both variables are normally distributed, the maximum difference is approximately 0.02 and occurs when both r and rho are near 0.5.

KEY POINTS

To measure the degree of correlation between two metric variables, Pearson's r, or its derivative, the coefficient of determination r^2, is the standard statistic. Regression allows the researcher actually to make predictions from one metric variable to another; the accuracy of these predictions, however, depends on how close the datapoints lie to the regression line. The researcher needs to be aware, furthermore, that this procedure is only evaluating the degree of linear regression, that is, that the pattern approximates a straight line. There are, however, procedures for applying curvilinear regression, and for multiple regression when there are two or more independent variables. These procedures are explained in Chapter 14.

Curvilinear regression A form of regression analysis in which nonlinear patterns are transformed into linear ones by a process of data transformations so that linear regression may be applied.

Multiple regression An extension of regression in which the outcome is predicted from a linear combination of two or more predictor variables.

TABLE 12.21	SPSS Pearson correlation output

Correlations

		At what age did you take up table tennis?	Approximately how much have you spent on table tennis in the past 6 months?
At what age did you take up table tennis?	Pearson Correlation	1.000	.808**
	Sig. (2-tailed)		.000
	N	120	120
Approximately how much have you spent on table tennis in the past 6 months?	Pearson Correlation	.808**	1.000
	Sig. (2-tailed)	.000	
	N	120	120

** CORRELATION IS SIGNIFICANT AT THE 0.01 LEVEL (2-TAILED).

TABLE 12.22	SPSS Spearman's rho output

Correlations

			At what age did you take up table tennis?	Approximately how much have you spent on table tennis in the past 6 months?
Spearman's rho	At what age did you take up table tennis?	Correlation Coefficient	1.000	.779**
		Sig. (2-tailed)		.000
		N	120	120
	Approximately how much have you spent on table tennis in the past 6 months?	Correlation Coefficient	.779**	1.000
		Sig. (2-tailed)	.000	
		N	120	120

** CORRELATION IS SIGNIFICANT AT THE .01 LEVEL (2-TAILED).

Using SPSS

Crosstabulation

The SPSS *Crosstabs* procedure enables researchers to study the relationships between categorical variables; for example, is there any relationship between whether or not anybody else in the household plays table tennis and how often they play per week? Access the *tabten.sav* file and select *Analyze/Descriptive Statistics/Crosstabs* to obtain the *Crosstabs* dialog box (see Figure 12.5). Enter your dependent variable (frequency of playing) in the *Rows* box so it will appear at the side, and the independent variable *else* in the *Columns* box. The result is in Table 12.23. If you put several variables in each box, then you will obtain a crosstabulation of each combination. To obtain column percentages, click on the *Cells* button in the *Crosstabs* dialog box to obtain *Crosstabs: Cell Display.* Click on *Column* in the *Percentages* check box, then on *Continue*, then on *OK*. The result is shown in Table 12.24. Notice that the frequencies (called "Count") and the percentages to one decimal place are shown in each cell. The frequencies can be edited out if you want to display just the percentages.

Measures of association

For bivariate analysis of two categorical variables, click on the *Statistics* button in the *Crosstabs* dialog box and you will obtain the *Crosstabs:Statistics* dialog box as in Figure 12.5. Select any of the statistics you require, click on *Continue* and then *OK*.

Correlation and regression

For bivariate analysis of two metric variables select *Statistics/Correlate/Bivariate*, put two metric variables into the *Variables* box, e.g. *spend* and *agebegan*. Under *Correlation Coefficients* you will find the *Pearson* box already ticked. If you want Spearman's rho as well just tick that box and click on *OK*. The outputs are illustrated in Tables 12.21 and 12.22. Notice that in both outputs the bottom line is a mirror image of the top line. Clearly each variable correlates with itself perfectly with a value of 1.000. The correlation coefficient between the two variables is 0.808. The Spearman's rho equivalent is 0.779. If you were to enter more variables in the *Variables* box you would get a series of bivariate correlations for each combination of variables.

TABLE 12.23	Play frequency by whether anybody else in the household plays		
	Does anybody else in your household play table tennis?		
	Yes	No	Total
How many times do you play per week? Once	15	28	43
Twice	22	30	52
Three times	10	8	18
Four or more times	5	2	7
Total	52	68	120

TABLE 12.24	Column percentages. How many times played per week by whether anybody else in the household plays			
		Does anybody else in your household play table tennis?		
		Yes	No	Total
How many times do you play per week?	Once — Count	15	28	43
	% within Does anybody else in your household play table tennis?	28.8%	41.2%	35.8%
	Twice — Count	22	30	52
	% within Does anybody else in your household play table tennis?	42.3%	44.1%	43.3%
	Three times — Count	10	8	18
	% within Does anybody else in your household play table tennis?	19.2%	11.8%	15.0%
	Four or more times — Count	5	2	7
	% within Does anybody else in your household play table tennis?	9.6%	2.9%	5.8%
Total	Count	52	68	120
	% within Does anybody else in your household play table tennis?	100.0%	100.0%	100.0%

To obtain a regression analysis, select *Analyze/Regression/Linear*. Notice that you now have to make a selection of dependent and independent variables. The dependent variable goes along the Y-axis. It is the one the researcher is trying to predict. You can have one or more than one independent variable if you wish to undertake multiple regression. This is explained in Chapter 14. In discussing the bivariate linear relationship between X and Y, statisticians speak of the "regression of Y on X". Let's assume that the amount spent on table tennis in the past six months is the dependent variable and that the age at which they began is the independent variable. (It does not make a lot of sense to consider *agebegan* as the dependent variable – it has already happened!). Put these into the appropriate boxes and click on *OK*. You now get four tables. The first table (see Table 12.25) tells you what variables have been entered as independent variables and what the dependent variable is. The next table is an analysis of variance, which we will ignore until Chapter 14. The third table is a model summary, which gives the values for Pearson's r (0.808) and r^2, which is 0.652 (see Table 12.26). This is the amount of variation in *spend* that can be explained by the regression of *spend* on *agebegan*. If the data relate to a small sample, then r^2 gives a biased estimate of r^2 for the population from which the sample was drawn. The adjusted r is an unbiased estimate provided by adjusting the equation for r^2 for the number of values that were used in the original calculation. For large samples, the difference is very small. The standard error of the estimate you can ignore for the moment.

In the fourth table, the unstandardized coefficients under B give the constants a and b in the equation Y = a + bX (see Table 12.27). So the regression of *spend* on *agebegan* provides:

$$Y = -2.691 + (4.253)X$$

| TABLE 12.25 | SPSS regression output: *variables entered* |

Variables entered/removed[b]

Model	Variables Entered	Variables Removed	Method
1	At what age did you take up table tennis?[a]		Enter

a. ALL REQUESTED VARIABLES ENTERED.

b. DEPENDENT VARIABLE: HOW MUCH SPENT ON TABLE TENNIS IN PAST 6 MONTHS.

| TABLE 12.26 | SPSS regression output: *model summary* |

Model summary

Model	R	R Square	Adjusted R Square	Std. Error of the Estimate
1	.808[a]	.652	.649	15.60

a. PREDICTORS: (CONSTANT), AT WHAT AGE DID YOU TAKE UP TABLE TENNIS?

So, for somebody aged 20, for example, we can predict from the equation that he or she will have spent £82 on table tennis in the past six months. If you review Figure 12.4 you can see this from the scattergram.

| TABLE 12.27 | SPSS regression output: *coefficients* |

Model		Unstandardized Coefficients B	Unstandardized Coefficients Std. Error	Standardized Coefficients Beta	t	Sig.
1	(Constant)	−2.691	3.928		−.685	.495
	At what age did you take up table tennis?	4.253	.286	.808	14.871	.000

SUMMARY

After examining the distributions of each variable one at a time the researcher will typically proceed to looking at the relationships between variables, taking two at a time. Researchers will typically begin bivariate analysis with bivariate data display. This might involve running a number of crosstabulations between categorical variables or plotting scattergrams for key metric variables. Such displays may also be used later on in the report or presentation of findings and might include clustered bar charts.

To obtain summaries of the relationship between two variables it is possible to review the percentage difference between categories in respect of another variable, but this really works only if both variables are binary. More effective is to use one of the many coefficients that are available. These coefficients are designed to vary from zero for no association or correlation to +1 for a perfect association or correlation. Where the relationship is negative (and this is possible only for ordinal or metric variables) a maximum value of −1 may be achieved. For two metric variables the standard coefficient is Pearson's r, but for categorical variables there is a large number of coefficients, nine of which are provided on the SPSS *Crosstabs* procedure. Measures appropriate for nominal variables may be based either on the idea of departure from independence or on the notion of proportional reduction in error. Ordinal measures are based on the principle of pair-by-pair comparisons. Each statistic has its own strengths and limitations, so selecting the appropriate statistics to use can be quite complex. For the most part, Cramer's V is probably the best for nominal variables and Gamma for ordinal, but if researchers want to take account of what variables are playing an independent role in the research, then Lambda may be the preferred statistic.

QUESTIONS FOR DISCUSSION

1 Bivariate data summary using SPSS is so quick and simple that the temptation must be to crosstabulate everything in sight. Is this a good idea?

2 What result from Cramer's V do you think would count as a "high" degree of association?

 ## SPSS EXERCISES

1 Table 12.28 was created from the SPSS *tabten* file. It is a "seven by eight" having 56 cells. This is far too many to interpret. Using SPSS *Recode*, collapse this table to a two-by-two table.

2 Use SPSS to create a bar chart of the perceived importance of the social benefits of playing table tennis clustered by league played in. Use the *Chart Editor* to change or improve the appearance.

3 Regroup the variable *spend* into three categories and crosstabulate against whether there is anybody else in the household who plays table tennis.

4 Recreate Table 12.29 and edit out the frequencies. Are there any other improvements you would make to the table?

5 Try plotting a scattergram of the perceived importance of the social benefits of playing table tennis against the importance of health and fitness.

6 Use SPSS to generate measures of dispersion for the variable *spend* and interpret the results. Now look at measures of distribution shape. Is the distribution normal?

7 Look at a table of areas under the normal curve in any statistics book and determine what z-score includes 99 percent of the area.

8 Open a new SPSS file and enter the data from Table 12.18. Now obtain the Pearson's correlation coefficient using *Analyze/Correlate/Bivariate* and reaffirm the calculation for Table 12.19.

9 Using the equation for the data in Table 12.18, $Y = 0.778 + (0.444)X$, calculate what Y will be when $X = 6$. How does that compare with the actual values of Y when $X = 6$?

10 Using the same data from Table 12.18, get SPSS to calculate Spearman's rho. How does this compare with Pearson's r?

TABLE 12.28 A crosstabulation of where table tennis was first played by age

		under 15	15–24	25–34	35–44	45–54	55–64	over 65	Total
Where did you first play the sport?	Primary school	2	5	6					13
	Secondary school	1	3	3	3	2			12
	Youth club	1	8	9	1	5	1		25
	Youth organization		4	2	4	2	2		14
	Table-tennis club	2	4	8	1	6	3	2	26
	Coaching scheme	1							1
	Leisure center		1	3					4
	Other		6	5	5	5	2	2	25
Total		7	31	36	14	20	8	4	120

TABLE 12.29 How many times played per week by whether anybody else in the household plays

			Does anybody else in your household play table tennis?		
			Yes	No	Total
How many times do you play per week?	Once	Count	15	28	43
		% within Does anybody else in your household play table tennis?	28.8%	41.2%	35.8%
	Twice	Count	22	30	52
		% within Does anybody else in your household play table tennis?	42.3%	44.1%	43.3%
	Three times	Count	10	8	18
		% within Does anybody else in your household play table tennis?	19.2%	11.8%	15.0%
	Four or more times	Count	5	2	7
		% within Does anybody else in your household play table tennis?	9.6%	2.9%	5.8%
Total		Count	52	68	120
		% within Does anybody else in your household play table tennis?	100.0%	100.0%	100.0%

ITEMS ADAPTED FROM BARKER ET AL, 2001

FURTHER READING

Argyrous, G. (2005) *Statistics for Research with a Guide to SPSS*. London: Sage.

Bowers, D. (2002) *Medical Statistics from Scratch*. London: Wiley.

Bryman, A. and Cramer, D. (2004) *Quantitative Data Analysis with SPSS 12 and 13*. Hove, UK: Routledge.

Field, A. (2005) *Discovering Statistics Using SPSS*. 2nd edition. London: Sage.

Pallant, J. (2005) *SPSS Survival Manual*, 2nd edition. Maidenhead: Open University Press (McGraw-Hill Education).

13 Making statistical inferences

LEARNING OBJECTIVES In this chapter you will learn about:

→ calculating interval estimates for categorical and metric variables,

→ testing univariate hypotheses for categorical and metric variables,

→ testing bivariate hypotheses for statistical significance, including situations where both variables are categorical, both are metric and mixed scales,

→ the difference between statistical inference and data summaries,

→ conducting tests of statistical significance using SPSS.

Sometimes researchers want to make statements that include everybody.

© KMITU

INTRODUCTION

We saw in Chapter 8 that there are many situations faced by market researchers where the number of cases to be investigated is very large and it is not feasible to study them all, so a sample is taken. The sample is then analyzed in detail using the procedures that have been described in Chapters 11 and 12 to produce tables, charts and summary measures. It would, of course, be possible to leave the analysis there and imply or assume that the results are likely to be typical of the total population of cases from which the sample was drawn. However, the researcher is sometimes interested in making precise quantitative statements about the population based on the evidence from the sample. As was explained in Chapter 8, errors are likely to arise when this is done. Two kinds of errors were mentioned: systematic error and random error. Both are selection errors and may result in the over- or underrepresentation of certain types of cases in a particular sample compared with the population. The difference between them is that over a large number of samples, the random errors will tend to cancel one another out, but the systematic errors will not. Systematic errors are often referred to as "bias" and all samples taken will tend to over- or underrepresent certain types of cases in the same way. This means that while the average of all possible samples will be identical to the true population value where the error is random, where there is bias, this will not be so.

Since random errors are, in the long run, self-canceling it is possible to calculate the probability that, for any one *individual* sample, errors will be of a certain size. Such a calculation is not possible for bias. Another name for a random sample is a "probability" sample. It means that the probability that any one particular case will be selected from the population is known and that probability theory can be used to calculate the chances that errors will be of a certain magnitude. There are, however, two rather different ways in which such a theory may be deployed. In one situation the researcher may have little idea of the summary measure for the population (often called a **population parameter**), so the sample is used to make an estimate of it. In the other situation, the researcher may feel that he or she knows the value of the parameter and the sample statistics are used to test a hypothesis to this effect.

This chapter explains both estimation and hypothesis testing for both univariate and bivariate hypotheses and for situations where the variables involved may be categorical or metric. Testing hypotheses by applying tests of **statistical significance** to them has been a procedure that has generated some considerable controversy, which in effect focuses on the limitations and assumptions made by using these procedures. These are explained later in the chapter followed by how to use the procedures on SPSS.

 Population parameter A variable relating to a total population of cases or units.

Statistical significance A result that, in a random sample, is unlikely to have arisen by chance with a specified probability.

INTERNET ACTIVITY

 Using your browser, go to **www.thomsonlearning.co.uk/kent** and select the Chapter 13 Internet Activity which will provide a link to a website containing Statnotes by G. David Garson. Go to *Additional Topics* and check out *Significance Testing* and *Chi-Square Significance Tests*. In particular, have a look at the *Assumptions* made by significance tests.

Estimation

Estimation is the process of using the value of a statistic derived from a sample to estimate the value of a corresponding population parameter. If the sample taken is a probability sample and there are no other sources of error, this estimate should be reasonably close. However, since the sample statistic is unlikely to be *exactly* the same as the parent population, statistical inference is used to attach a degree of uncertainty to this process.

Any statement we make about the population of cases should have two properties: it should be precise and it should be correct. If we took a probability sample of adult consumers and found that 46 percent purchased a chocolate bar in the past seven days, we could say that the percentage in the population of adult consumers is just the same. This statement is very precise and is called a **point estimate**. Point estimates, however, are seldom likely to be correct. It would be very unusual for the value found in the sample to be exactly the same as the actual value in the population. As an alternative, we could say that the percentage who purchased a chocolate bar in the past seven days is between 0 percent and 100 percent. This statement is undoubtedly correct, but not very precise. A statement of this kind is called an **interval estimate**. To be more precise, we could say that the percentage who purchased a chocolate bar in the past seven days is between 42 percent and 50 percent (that is, 4 percent either side of the sample result). There is still a risk, however, that this statement is wrong. To make it correct as well as relatively precise we need to calculate the probability that the statement is correct. This is where statistical inference comes in.

A concept basic to all statistical inference is the **sampling distribution**. Imagine that we take lots of samples of a given size and calculate a particular statistic for each sample, say the proportion who purchased a chocolate bar in the past seven days. If the real proportion in the population is, for example, 46 percent, we may take a sample and obtain a proportion of 47 percent. Another may come out as 45 percent. In fact, most sample results will cluster around 46 percent with relatively few producing "rogue" results of, say, 39 percent. The tendency for this to happen will decline as the sample gets larger and increase as it gets smaller. If we plot the results as a distribution, we might obtain something like Figure 13.1. If we in fact took every conceivable sample of size n from a population and plotted the results we would obtain a **normal distribution** like the one imposed on Figure 13.1. In practice we would not, of course, actually do this, but the distribution can be derived statistically by calculating a theoretical sampling distribution.

The normal distribution was introduced briefly in Chapter 11. It has a number of interesting characteristics. One of these is that we can calculate what proportion of the observations lie between specified values of the standard deviation. Thus 95 percent of the area lies between plus and minus 1.96 standard deviations. Each sampling distribution will have its own standard deviation called the **standard error**. Since taking samples will result in less variation about the population parameter than picking one case, the standard error will be less than the standard deviation for the population. In fact if we divide by the square root of the sample size, so that we halve error in a sample of four, it is one-third in a sample of nine, one-fifth in a sample of 25 and so on.

Point estimate
A single value taken as an estimate of a population parameter.

Interval estimate
A range of values within which there is a given probability that it will contain the true population parameter.

Sampling distribution
A theoretical distribution of a statistic for all possible samples of a given size that could be drawn from a particular population.

Normal distribution
A symmetrical bell-shaped distribution that describes the expected probability distribution for random events.

Standard error
The standard deviation of a sampling distribution.

Standard error of the proportion
The standard error of the sampling distribution of the proportions observed for a binary variable.

Estimation for categorical variables

If the population parameter being estimated is a binary variable, then it is possible to plot a sampling distribution of the proportion. The standard error of this distribution is usually called the **standard error of the proportion**. It can be

FIGURE 13.1

A sampling distribution of sample size n

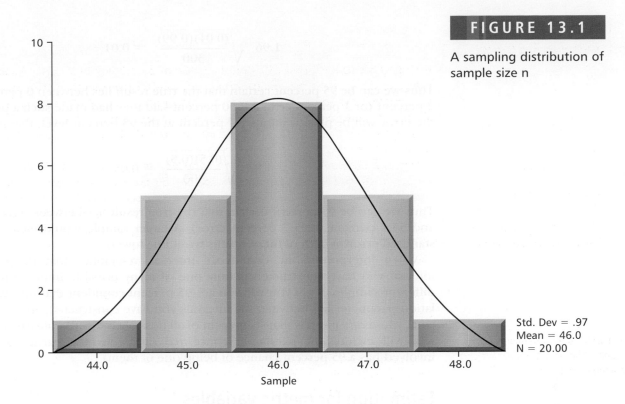

shown (using binomial theory, which we will not go into here) that the standard deviation of the sampling distribution is given by:

$$\sqrt{\frac{p(1-p)}{n}}$$

where p is the proportion possessing the characteristic. In constructing an interval estimate, the first thing we need to do is decide on the confidence level for our estimate, that is, we have to decide how often we want to be correct that our interval will in fact contain the population parameter in question. If, for example, we want to be 95 percent sure that our interval contains the population parameter, then we need to know how many standard errors enclose 95 percent of the area in a normal distribution. We saw earlier that this will be 1.96 standard errors. (Don't forget that the standard error is the standard deviation for the sampling distribution.)

Thus if a sample of 300 found that 40 percent had purchased brand A in the past week, then we can be 95 percent confident that the real population proportion lies between:

$$0.4 \pm 1.96\sqrt{\frac{(0.4)(0.6)}{300}} = 0.4 \pm 1.96(0.028) = 0.4 \pm 0.055$$

that is, between 0.345 and 0.455 (34.5 percent and 45.5 percent, or 5.5 percent error).

For a given sample size, the larger the proportion that report a given characteristic (up to 50 percent) the greater will be the sampling error. For example, if only 1 percent of a random sample of 300 said they had purchased a particular brand, the error will be roughly plus or minus 1 percent at the 95 percent level of confidence, that is:

$$1.96 \sqrt{\frac{(0.01)(0.99)}{300}} = 0.01$$

Thus we can be 95 percent certain that the true result lies between 0 percent and 2 percent (or 1 percent error). If 50 percent said they had made such a purchase, the error will be plus or minus 5.7 percent at the 95 percent level, that is:

$$1.96 \sqrt{\frac{(0.5)(0.5)}{300}} = 0.057$$

Thus we can be 95 percent certain that the true result lies between 44.3 percent and 55.7 percent (or 5.7 percent error). A larger sample would mean that the standard error of both of these results would be lower.

When interpreting the confidence interval, remember that the particular interval you have constructed is only one of many possible intervals based on different samples. So, if you *say* you are 95 percent confident that the real population parameter lies between the intervals you have constructed, appreciate that what you *really* mean is that 95 percent of all possible intervals constructed in this way will include the parameter concerned (and thus the particular interval involved has a 95 percent chance of being one of them).

Estimation for metric variables

Parametric statistics Statistics that assume metric data, and that the calculation of a mean or standard deviation is a legitimate operation.

Standard error of the mean The standard error of the sampling distribution of the means observed for a metric variable.

The good news is that most of the concepts you require for statistical inference for metric data have been explained earlier in the context of categorical data. More good news is that SPSS will do all the calculations for you. The bad news is that we need a whole new battery of statistics that are called **parametric statistics** that use the mean and the standard deviation as the key parameters for all calculations. It was explained earlier that the sampling distribution for any statistic has its own standard deviation called the standard error. If we are concerned, for example, with estimating a population mean, then we need the **standard error of the mean**. This is the standard deviation of the sampling distribution we would derive by plotting the means for all possible samples of a given size. We can calculate the standard error of the mean by taking:

$$\frac{\sigma}{\sqrt{n}}$$

where σ is the standard deviation of the population and n is the sample size.

Thus the standard error increases with an increase in the standard deviation for the population, and decreases with an increase in sample size, but as the square root of the sample size. Where the standard deviation for the population is unknown – which is usually the situation – the standard deviation found for the sample variable (s) is taken as an estimate of the population standard deviation. In this case we need what is called an **unbiased estimate**, which divides the sample standard deviation by the square root not of n, but n−1:

Unbiased estimate An adjustment that is made to the standard error when the sample standard deviation is taken as an estimate of the population standard deviation. The sample standard deviation is divided by the square root of n−1 rather than the square root of n.

$$\frac{s}{\sqrt{n-1}}$$

Thus if the mean score of a sample of 60 cases is 20 with a standard deviation of 6, then we can be 95 percent certain that the real population mean lies between the achieved sample mean plus or minus 1.96 standard errors, that is:

$$20 \pm 1.96\left(\frac{6}{\sqrt{60-1}}\right)$$

or between 18.5 and 21.5. Subtracting one from the sample size makes a meaningful difference only if the sample is quite small. Some statisticians will argue that if the standard deviation of the population is unknown we should use not the normal distribution but what is called the t distribution. For samples over 30 or so, however, this makes very little difference. SPSS will calculate confidence intervals for you. How this is done will be explained later in the chapter.

WARNING

Bear in mind when constructing interval estimates that you are assuming that the sample is a simple random sample, that the sample is 30 or more in size, that there is no bias in the selection procedure, and that there is no non-sampling error. We saw at the end of Chapter 8 that perhaps only 5 percent of total survey error consists of random error. This means that, in practice, the true values are in fact more likely to lie *outside* the interval estimates than inside them. In the physical sciences, Youden (1972) listed 15 estimates of the average distance between the earth and the sun obtained over the period 1895–1961. Each estimated value was, in fact, outside the limits of the one immediately preceding it. In the socioeconomic field, Williams and Goodman (1971) found that where estimates were made of numbers of telephones, subsequent observed true values were covered by the 95 percent confidence limits only about 80 percent of the time. In short, in the absence of any assessment of bias, or reassurance that there is no or little bias or other sources of nonsampling error, all confidence intervals need to be approached with extreme caution.

KEY POINTS

To calculate interval estimates for categorical variables you need to calculate the standard error of the proportion, then add and subtract this value multiplied by 1.96 (for the 95 percent confidence level) to give the upper and lower intervals. The calculation for metric variables is similar, but using the standard error of the mean. Confidence intervals are commonly reported along with estimated values. They provide a kind of "health warning" that estimates have a validity only within a given range of values – and even then could well be wrong. How much attention clients pay to these health warnings is unknown, but it is likely that they are commonly ignored.

Testing hypotheses for statistical significance

Where researchers feel that they know the value of a parameter, they may want to take a sample to test whether or not their feeling, hunch or hypothesis is correct. Put more formally, researchers will calculate the probability that the result derived from the sample did, in fact, come from a population in which the **hypothesis** is true. Hypotheses may be of many different kinds, as we shall see in Chapter 14, but for the purpose of testing hypotheses for statistical significance, it is convenient to distinguish hypotheses according to whether they refer to one, two or

Hypothesis A formal statement that the researcher makes about one or more variables that are the focus of the research, but which is as yet untested.

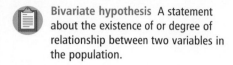

Univariate hypothesis A statement about the population value of a variable or two or more variables that are not combined or related.

Bivariate hypothesis A statement about the existence of or degree of relationship between two variables in the population.

Multivariate hypothesis A statement about the relationships between three or more variable in a population of cases.

more than two variables. **Univariate hypotheses** make statements about one variable, or several variables that are unrelated, for example "The group is predominantly male, exclusively from social grades A, B and C1, with a mean age of 33 years". There is no implied relationship between gender, social grade and age. **Bivariate hypotheses** relate just two variables together. Some may not spell out the nature of the relationship involved, for example "Variable A is related to (associated with, correlated with) Variable B". Others may specify or imply some degree of influence, causality or determination, for example "Variable A is a major factor giving rise to Variable B", or "Variable A is a cause (or the cause) of Variable B". **Multivariate hypotheses** specify relationships between three or more variables. Again, these may or may not specify or imply the nature of those relationships. The process of establishing causality is taken up in Chapter 14.

There are many different ways in which hypotheses can be evaluated, but in the context where a random sample has been drawn, researchers may be interested to know whether it is likely that the result achieved in the sample is a "real" result or whether it is likely that it is a product of random sampling fluctuations. The word "likely" gets interpreted more specifically to refer to the precise probabilities involved. Thus a researcher may want to be 95 percent certain that the result is a "real" one (which is the mirror image of saying that there are fewer than 5 chances in 100 that it was a result of random sampling fluctuations). We begin by looking at how to test univariate hypotheses that refer to one categorical variable.

Testing univariate hypotheses for categorical variables

A researcher may have reason to believe – on the basis of a deduction from theory, on the basis of past research or from personal experience – that 70 percent of a population of cases possess a particular characteristic (for example, that 70 percent of women in France object to advertising of highly personal products on television). If a random sample of 100 women in France found that 60 objected, could this proportion of responses in the sample easily have been obtained from a population in which the real proportion is in fact 70 percent? The statement or prediction that is made about the population of cases in advance is usually called the **null hypothesis**. "Null" means empty of significance, void or containing nothing. For univariate statements the null hypothesis is not really "null" in this sense. It is rather a statement we are assuming is true of the population from which the sample was drawn.

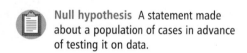

Null hypothesis A statement made about a population of cases in advance of testing it on data.

As with estimation, a sampling distribution of the test statistic is used. However, unlike estimation, where we use the sample result to estimate the standard error, in testing the null hypothesis *we assume that the null hypothesis is true* and use the predicted proportion to estimate the standard error that would exist if the null hypothesis is true. In the example above, if the null hypothesis is true, then the standard error of the proportion is:

$$\sigma_p = \sqrt{\frac{p(1-p)}{n}} = \sqrt{\frac{(0.7)(0.3)}{100}} = 0.046$$

This implies that 95 percent of all samples of size 100 will produce results that vary between $0.7 \pm 1.96(0.046)$ or between 61 percent and 79 percent.

Since the original sample result was 60 percent, it lies outside this range and so is unlikely to have come from a population in which p = 0.7. In other words, random error is an unlikely explanation of the difference between the sample result of 60 percent and the predicted 70 percent. Note that we cannot conclude from the sample result that the real proportion is 60 percent, but only that it probably did not come from a population in which the null hypothesis is true.

Why, it may be asked, did we not simply use the sample result for estimation purposes rather than go to the trouble of setting up a null hypothesis prior to the analysis? The answer is that if we have a theory, a principle or a wealth of experience that we think allows us to make a prediction, it is this prediction that we want to test. If we wanted, for example, to compare the results of two or more pieces of research, then it is their support or questioning of the theory or principle or experience that we want to compare. Calculating confidence intervals does not test the hypothesis because the results could be consistent with a large number of hypotheses or predictions.

The standard error of the proportion works only if the variable is binary. If the variable is nominal it is possible to use the Chi-square statistic as a **goodness-of-fit test**. Suppose a company has two brands of a product and these are measured for preference in a survey of 100 respondents. The results suggest that 60 prefer brand A and 40 brand B. If we wished to test the null hypothesis that there is equal preference for the brands, then, in theory, we would expect 50 to prefer brand A and 50 brand B. The difference between the observed and expected frequencies is 10, so Chi-square is:

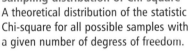
Goodness-of-fit test The determination of the extent to which a certain model fits the observed data. The statistic Chi-square can be used for this purpose.

$$\chi^2 = \sum \frac{(fo - fe)^2}{fe}$$

$$= \frac{10^2}{50} + \frac{10^2}{50} = 4$$

Like all other statistics we could, in principle, calculate Chi-square for a large number of samples and plot their distribution. This would be a **sampling distribution of Chi-square**. This distribution, however, is not a single probability curve, but a family of curves. These vary according to the number of observations that can be varied without changing the constraints or assumptions associated with a numerical system. Thus if our sample is 100 then any number between 1 and 100 may prefer brand A. Once it is discovered that 60 prefer brand A then, by definition 40 (100−60) prefer brand B. In short, there is only one **degree of freedom** – only one figure is free to vary. The probability of obtaining Chi-square values of a given magnitude can be looked up in a table of **critical values** for Chi-square. A simplified table is illustrated in Table 13.1.

Sampling distribution of Chi-square A theoretical distribution of the statistic Chi-square for all possible samples with a given number of degress of freedom.

Degree of freedom The number of values that are free to vary when estimating some kind of statistical parameter.

Critical values Values that lie exactly on the boundary between accepting and rejecting the null hypothesis.

This shows, for example, that the value of 3.841 will not be exceeded more than 5 percent of the time in a random sample with one degree of freedom. A value of 6.635 will not be exceeded more than 1 percent of the time. With more degrees of freedom, values rise. We can conclude that the sample result of Chi-square = 4 was unlikely to have occurred with a probability greater than p = 0.05 since 4 > 3.841. So, at the 5 percent level we could reject the null hypothesis and conclude that the difference between the sample result and our expectation was unlikely to have been a result of random sampling fluctuations. However, if we had chosen

TABLE 13.1	Critical values of Chi-square		
Probability	0.05	0.01	0.001
Degrees of freedom			
1	3.841	6.635	10.827
2	5.991	9.210	13.815
3	7.815	11.341	16.268

the 1 percent level of confidence, then the null hypothesis would have been accepted since the critical value is 6.635.

p-value The probability in random sample of obtaining a value as extreme or more extreme than the one actually obtained if the null hypothesis were true.

SUGGESTION

Notice that the table of critical values for Chi-square gives the values for selected probability levels – 0.05, 0.01, 0.001. The output from SPSS, however, gives the *actual* level of probability involved. This is usually called the **p-value**, and it is the probability of getting a sample value as extreme as or more extreme than the one we actually get, if the null hypothesis were true. In other words it is the probability of obtaining in a random sample a statistic like Chi-square, that is as far, or even further, away from the null hypothesis value of Chi-square = zero. Another way of putting this is that the p-value is the probability that the null hypothesis is true.

The p-value is normally used in the following way. If it is *less* than the significance level chosen for the test (for example, 0.05) then the null hypothesis is rejected and we accept the result as statistically significant. If it is *more* than the significance level then we have to accept the null hypothesis and conclude that the result could have come from a population in which the null hypothesis is true.

The p-value provides a bit more information on how far down in the significance region a result lies. Articles in scientific journals often discuss their results in terms of these values. They make statements like p < 0.05 or p < 0.01. Unlike critical values, which are specific to the particular test concerned, p-values represent a kind of "common currency" across which the results of different tests maybe compared. In this context it could be argued that it is better to report the actual p-values (for example, p = 0.016) rather than to use the conventional cut-off points, for example, p < 0.05. This would allow readers to form their own judgments about the significance of the result and the strength of the evidence against the null hypothesis. Different people may, for example, feel that different levels of significance are appropriate.

Testing univariate hypotheses for metric variables

If a researcher suggests a univariate hypothesis about a metric value then it is possible to use the standard error of the mean to test for the statistical significance of such hypotheses. Suppose the researcher hypothesizes that the mean age at which people take up table tennis is 15 years old. The results from the table tennis survey show a mean age of 12.8 and a standard deviation of 5 years. *If* the null hypothesis is true (that is, the mean age is actually 15), then 95 percent of samples will produce means in the range:

$$15 \pm 1.96\left(\frac{5}{\sqrt{120 - 1}}\right) = 15 \pm 0.9 \text{ or } 14.1 - 15.9$$

Since 12.8 is outside this range, there is sufficient evidence from the sample to *reject* the null hypothesis at the 95 percent level. This implies that the sample result probably did *not* come from a population of cases in which the null hypothesis is true.

Research hypothesis The hypothesis that is accepted if the null hypothesis is rejected.

Whenever researchers reject a null hypothesis, the alternative conclusion they accept is usually called the **research hypothesis**. Note that there may be different alternatives:

- the population mean is not 15,
- the population mean is greater than 15,
- the population mean is less than 15.

In the first situation, we have little idea in rejecting the null hypothesis whether the real mean is above or below 15. The 5 percent area of the normal distribution outside the hypothesized interval could be at either end of the distribution, as in Figure 13.2. If we divide the two tails into 2.5 percent each, then 2.5 percent of the area is above 1.96 standard deviations and 2.5 percent below minus 1.96 standard deviations. Suppose, however, that we were interested only in whether the mean is below 15. All the 5 percent of the area needs to be in the left tail, as in Figure 13.3. Here, 5 percent of the area lies below 1.645 standard deviations, so we could have constructed our interval as:

$$15 - 1.645 \frac{5}{\sqrt{120 - 1}} = 14.25$$

In other words, if the null hypothesis is true, fewer than 5 percent of samples will give mean ages below 14.25 years. Clearly, we would still reject the null hypothesis that the mean is 15 if the sample result is 12.8, but by a slightly greater margin. The alternative hypothesis, however, is no longer that the population mean is not 15, but that it is *less* than 15. In the first situation we have constructed what is usually called a **two-tailed test** and in the second situation a **one-tailed test**.

Two-tailed test A statistical test of a nondirectional hypothesis.

One-tailed test A statistical test of a directional relationship.

WARNING

Where p-values are being reported, then it is necessary to accompany p-value information with whether they relate to one or two-tailed tests.

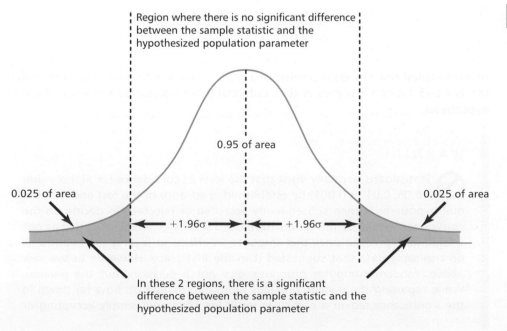

Region where there is no significant difference between the sample statistic and the hypothesized population parameter

0.95 of area

0.025 of area

0.025 of area

$+1.96\sigma$ $+1.96\sigma$

In these 2 regions, there is a significant difference between the sample statistic and the hypothesized population parameter

FIGURE 13.2

Critical regions: two-tailed test

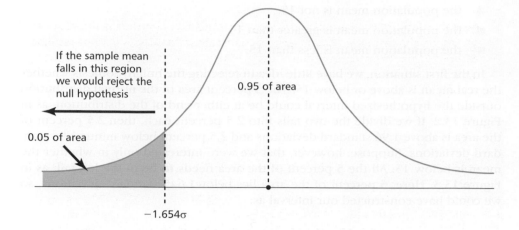

FIGURE 13.3

Critical region: one-tailed test

If the sample mean falls in this region we would reject the null hypothesis

0.95 of area

0.05 of area

-1.654σ

Z-test A test against the null hypothesis carried out on a univariate hypothesis by comparing the result from a sample with a standardized normal distribution.

Suppose, alternatively, that the researcher had hypothesized that the mean age at which table tennis players begin is 12, then, if this is the case, 95 percent of samples would have produced results within the range 12 ± 0.9 or $11.1 - 12.9$. Since 12.8 lies within this range there is now insufficient evidence to reject the null hypothesis. Note that, although a statistician will now say that, in this result, the null hypothesis is "accepted", this does not prove that the null hypothesis is true. The result does not, for example, prove that the population mean is 12, only that from the sample evidence we cannot say that it is not 12. Furthermore, there is still a 5 percent probability that we might have accepted a null hypothesis that is, in fact, false. So, remember that if we say we "accept" the null hypothesis – which appears to be the standard terminology – we actually mean that we cannot reject it. We have to behave as though the null hypothesis still stands.

An alternative way of undertaking tests of significance is to construct what is sometimes called a **z-test**. The result is exactly the same, but the procedure is a little different. Instead of constructing intervals under the assumption that the null hypothesis is true, we calculate differences between the sample statistic and the hypothesized population parameter in terms of standardized units, that is, we take, in this example, the difference between the sample mean and the hypothesized mean and divide by the standard error:

$$z = \frac{X - \mu}{s/\sqrt{120 - 1}} = \frac{15 - 12.8}{5/\sqrt{120 - 1}} = 4.8$$

In a two-tailed test, the critical value of z at $p = <0.05$ is 1.96 and for a one-tailed test is 1.645. Since 4.8 is greater than either of these figures, we can reject the null hypothesis.

Alpha value The probability of rejecting the null hypothesis when it is in fact true. It is sometimes referred to as the level of confidence. By tradition it is set at either 0.05 or 0.01.

WARNING

Statisticians normally insist that the level of confidence (or alpha value – 0.05, 0.01 or 0.001) be established *in advance* of the test and that the null hypothesis is then subsequently accepted or rejected. To decide on the confidence level after the results have been seen is generally regarded as not a legitimate practice since this amounts, in effect, to testing the hypothesis on the same data that suggested it in the first place. However, as we saw above, modern computer programs give not a decision, but the p-value. While reporting the p-value provides more information on how far down in the significance region a particular result lies than does simply accepting or rejecting a result, such a procedure may nevertheless compromise the idea of setting up the test criteria in advance. If a researcher produces a lot of results without prior hypotheses, then simply looking for significant results will probably involve picking out all or most of the sampling accidents.

KEY POINTS

Testing univariate hypotheses for categorical variables entails calculating not confidence intervals based on the sample result, but the intervals between which sample values are likely to fluctuate under the assumption that the hypothesized statement (the null hypothesis) is true. The null hypothesis is rejected if the actual sample result lies outside these limits. The standard error of the proportion is used for this calculation. For metric valuables, the calculation follows the same pattern, but using the standard error of the mean. Researchers need to be clear whether they are looking at departures from hypothesized values in both directions, making it a two-tailed test, or in one direction only, a one-tailed test.

Testing bivariate hypotheses

Statistical inference for bivariate hypotheses takes a rather different form. It is usual to test the null hypothesis that there is *no* association in the population from which the sample was drawn, for example there is no association between gender and brand preference. If the null hypothesis can be rejected, then we can conclude that the sample result was unlikely to have come from a population in which the null hypothesis is true and that there is, indeed, some association or correlation.

Testing bivariate hypotheses for categorical variables

If the null hypothesis of no association between two categorical variables is to be used, then the obvious basis on which to detect departures from this is departure from independence. The statistic Chi-square, you will recall, is based on the difference between observed frequencies and the frequencies that would be expected if there were independence, that is, no association, between the two variables. The calculation of Chi-square was explained on pp. 346–347. Using Chi-square as a test of significance involves taking the calculated value of the statistic and looking up in a table of the distribution of Chi-square the probability of obtaining from a random sample a value as large as the one generated.

SPSS will in effect do all this for you. The top part of Table 13.2 shows a crosstabulation of the perceived importance of the social benefits of playing table tennis by age groups that have been recoded from *agenow* into two categories of 34 and under, and 35 plus. The lower part of Table 13.2 shows the value of Chi-square, the number of degrees of freedom in the table, the statistical significance of the achieved value of Chi-square (the p-value), plus Cramer's V.

The table has four degrees of freedom and the result is just statistically significant at 0.049. This means that there are fewer than 5 chances in 100 (or less than 0.05) that the value of Chi-square derived could have arisen as a result of random sampling fluctuations. We can therefore reject the null hypothesis of no

TABLE 13.2		Importance of social benefits by age groups					
		Social benefits					
		Unimportant	Fairly unimportant	Neither unimportant nor important	Fairly important	Very important	Total
Age groups	Under 35	10	12	28	19	5	74
	35 plus	1	6	13	18	8	46
Total		11	18	41	37	13	120

	Value	df	Asymp. Sig. (2-sided)
Pearson Chi-square	9.558[a]	4	.049
Cramer's V	.282		
N of Valid Cases	120		

a. TWO CELLS (20.0%) HAVE EXPECTED COUNT LESS THAN 5. THE MINIMUM EXPECTED COUNT IS 4.22.

association (or independence) and accept that there does appear to be a connection between age and perceived importance of the social benefits of playing the game. You can see by looking at the table that it is the younger group who are saying that it is unimportant or fairly unimportant. Cramer's V for this table is 0.282, which shows that the degree of association is in fact quite small.

WARNING

🚫 Beware that the categories of binary or nominal variables are sometimes described in textbooks on statistics as "groups", or even as "samples". Thus when the variable is binary, it may be described as a "two-sample" situation. The use of Chi-square on crosstabulated data may be referred to as the "two sample Chi-square test" where the independent variable is binary and each category is seen as a different sample or subgroup, or as the "k-sample Chi-square test" where the independent variable has three or more categories, that is to say it is nominal. Thus a relationship or association between gender and purchase of Brand X can be expressed alternatively as a difference in brand purchasing between the sexes. The statistical tests available may then be labeled "two-sample" tests or described as "making comparisons". Relationships, according to this approach, arise only when we can talk about directionality – positive and negative relationships. This means that the data have to be at least ordinal. However, we will continue to think of crosstabulations involving binary or nominal scales as illustrating the relationship between the variables concerned.

Testing bivariate hypotheses for metric variables

Table 13.3 shows the SPSS output for the Pearson correlation coefficient, which is 0.808. Just below is the level of significance, indicated as 0.000. This is the p-value and it shows that the result is statistically significant even at the 0.001 level (since 0.000 is even lower than this!). SPSS has, in fact, looked up the result for you in a table of critical values. Remember that the p-value needs to be less than 0.05 if the result is to be statistically significant at the 95 percent level. If it is, then you can reject the null hypothesis that there is no association between the two variables (or, more correctly, that the result came from a population in which the null hypothesis is true). The test is usually a two-tailed test: this assumes that the test is nondirectional and that there was no expectation as to the sign of the population value, positive or negative. Like all significance tests, the result is always sensitive to the size of the sample. Thus, for a sample of 30, the Pearson correlation needs to be greater than 0.36 to be significant at the 0.05 level. For a sample of 100 it needs to be larger than 0.2 and for a sample of 1,000 larger than 0.062. In short, statistically significant results for large samples do not imply that the degree of correlation is large.

Testing metric differences for categories

There are many situations in market research where researchers have, or assume that they have, a metric dependent variable, like the results of deploying summated rating scales, and want to check whether there are any differences in mean scores between categories of respondents in a survey that are not due to random sampling error. Do the men, for example, have different mean scores from the women? Do those who grew up in a single-parent family give different average responses from those who grew up in families where both parents were together? The researcher has, in short, a metric dependent variable and one or more categorical independent variables. As was explained earlier, the categories may be described as "groups" or "samples" and the researcher will ask whether or not differences discovered among survey respondents between various groups (or samples) arose from a population in which there is, in fact, no difference (or whether, in short, the result is statistically significant). In this situation, researchers will use a statistical procedure called **analysis of variance** (or ANOVA for short).

ANOVA recognizes that there will be variations in individual scores *within* groups as well as differences *between* groups. The logic of ANOVA is that it compares the variance of scores between the groups with the variance within the groups. If the variance between groups is larger, we conclude that the groups differ; if not, we conclude that the results are not statistically significant.

Analysis of variance (ANOVA) A procedure for testing the statistical significance of differences in scores in a metric variable between categorical groups, samples or treatments.

TABLE 13.3	SPSS correlation output		
	Correlations		
		At what age did you take up table tennis?	Approximately how much have you spent on table tennis in the past 6 months?
At what age did you take up table tennis?	Pearson Correlation	1.000	.808**
	Sig. (2-tailed)		.000
	N	120	120
Approximately how much have you spent on table tennis in the past 6 months?	Pearson Correlation	.808**	1.000
	Sig. (2-tailed)	.000	
	N	120	120

** CORRELATION IS SIGNIFICANT AT THE 0.01 LEVEL (2-TAILED).

The steps involved are as follows:

1 Calculate the mean score of each group.
2 Calculate to what extent individual scores within the groups vary around the group mean (this is done by calculating the variance – the standard deviation squared).
3 Calculate the overall mean for all the groups, i.e. the whole sample.
4 Calculate how much group means vary about the overall mean.

These steps enable us to derive two quantities: the between-group variance and the within-group variance. The ratio between the two is called the F-ratio, calculated by dividing the between-group variance by the within-group variance. When F is large, between-group variance is significantly greater than within-group and there are "significant" differences between the groups. To determine whether the ratio is sufficiently large we need to compare it with a critical value derived from a table of the distribution of F.

One-way ANOVA An analysis of variance in which there is only one basis for categorizing groups of the independent variable.

t-test An analysis of variance in which the categorical independent variable is binary.

When there is only one basis for classifying groups, then it is called **one-way ANOVA**. A special case of one-way analysis of variance is when the independent variable is binary, that is, there are only two groups. This makes it identical to what is called a **t-test**. SPSS offers three types of t-test:

- a *one-sample t-test,* which tests whether the mean of a single variable differs from a specified constant value,
- an *independent samples t-test* which tests whether the means of two groups differ, each group being considered to be the equivalent of samples from two separate populations,
- a *paired samples t-test* which tests whether the means of two measures for a single group differ.

Multivariate analysis of variance (MANOVA) An analysis of variance when there is more than one metric dependent variable.

Strictly speaking, one-way ANOVA is a bivariate technique – there is one independent variable and one dependent variable. "Two-way" ANOVA is used when there are two independent variables, i.e. groups are classified in two ways, for example by gender and employment status. This means that it can be considered as a multivariate technique since a total of three variables is involved, although what is normally referred to as **multivariate analysis of variance** or MANOVA refers to situations when there is more than one metric dependent variable. Two-way, n-way and MANOVA are explained in Chapter 14.

In the table tennis data, the average score for the perceived importance of the social benefits of playing the game is 3.19. This assumes, of course, that the allocated scores of 1 to 5 represent "equal" distances of amounts of importance and that we can, accordingly, sensibly treat this variable as scaled at the metric level. Suppose, however, that the researcher wants to compare the average scores of those in households where somebody else plays the game and those in households where there is nobody else. The average scores of the two groups are shown in Table 13.4. From this you can see that the mean score of those who have others in the household who play is higher at 3.23 than for those who have no others in the household who play (3.16). The question now arises as to whether this difference could have arisen as a result of random sampling fluctuation or represents a "real" difference.

The null hypothesis is that there is no difference in the population from which the sample was drawn. Can this hypothesis be rejected from evidence in the sample? The SPSS results of an analysis of variance are shown in Table 13.5. The F-ratio is 0.113 and the p-value is 0.737. This means that in 100 random samples, over 73 of them would produce an F-ratio as large as this anyway as a result of random sampling fluctuations, so the difference is not statistically significant. From Table 13.5, if you divide the Mean Square for Between Groups (0.14) by the

TABLE 13.4	Mean importance of social benefits by presence of other household players		
Social benefits			
Does anybody else in your household play table tennis?	Mean	N	Std. Deviation
Yes	3.23	52	1.10
No	3.16	68	1.13
Total	3.19	120	1.11

Mean Square for Within Groups (1.241) you should obtain the F-ratio. The same procedure can be used if there are more than two groups to be compared.

ANOVA was developed for use mainly in experimental set-ups where the differences being tested are between experimental groups and control groups. To use ANOVA properly, four key conditions need to be met:

- the respondents whose results are being compared must be a random sample,
- the scores of the dependent variables must be continuous metric and normally distributed within each group,
- the variance within the groups must be approximately equal,
- the groups or categories must be "independent" samples.

The last term requires some explanation. Recall that the categories of binary or nominal variables are sometimes called "groups" or "samples". So, in comparing the results, for example of male and female respondents, we have two "samples", one sample of males and another of females. Strictly speaking, these samples should be "treatments", that is, randomly allocated to groups. Thus a researcher may decide to compare the crop yields of fields that have been randomly allocated to the use and nonuse of genetically modified seeds. We cannot, of course, randomly allocate individuals to their gender, but provided the selection of respondents has been made randomly, we can consider this to be the equivalent of two separate samples of males and females even though in reality they are from the same sample of respondents. The samples are "independent" in the sense that the scores of the males and the scores of the females are independent of one another. This might not be the case if, for example, the males and females involved were married couples and so their attitudes to a whole range of things may well be related.

ANOVA is, in fact, a family of related but different procedures. They all have in common that they involve comparing means, but which particular technique is appropriate depends on two things. First, it depends on how many independent

TABLE 13.5	ANOVA of perceived importance of benefits by whether anybody else in the household plays table tennis				
Social benefits	Sum of Squares	df	Mean Square	F	Sig.
Between Groups	.140	1	.140	.113	.737
Within Groups	146.451	118	1.241		
Total	146.592	119			

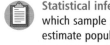

Independent samples Sample from different groups of respondents.

Repeated measures A term used in SPSS to indicate that more than one measure on the same set of cases is being used in the calculation.

Paired samples t-test An analysis of variance in which two sets of metric values are compared for the same respondents.

variables there are, thus "one-way" ANOVA has one independent variable, "two-way" ANOVA has two independent variables and so on. Second, it depends on whether the means being compared are for different respondents (SPSS calls these **independent samples**) or whether they are means derived from the same respondents, for example scores on two tests taken by all subjects. SPSS calls these **repeated measures** (or, in the case of the t-test, a **paired samples t-test** in which the scores of the same respondents are compared on two metric variables). In SPSS, differences between means, t-tests and one-way ANOVA for independent samples are in the *Analyze/Compare Means* menu.

Many researchers use ANOVA on the results of surveys even though it is very difficult to meet all the conditions necessary for its use. Samples are often not random or not entirely random or random with very poor response rates; the distribution of scores within groups may not be normal and the variances may well not be even approximately equal. The use of ANOVA on rating scales like Likert scales may be dubious if the variables cannot be considered to be approximately scaled at equal intervals. Remember that ANOVA depends on statistical inference. The end result of any analysis is always a p-value. Like all techniques that use probability theory, it takes account *only* of random sampling fluctuations, not any other source of error.

KEY POINTS

When testing bivariate hypotheses linking two variables, the null hypothesis is always that there is no association or correlation. Where both variables are categorical, Chi-square is used as a test of significance. Where both are metric, the statistical significance of Pearson's r will be generated by SPSS. Where scales are mixed, provided the independent variable is categorical and the dependent variable metric, then analysis of variance may be used. This is based on comparing the variance of the metric variable within the categories with the variance between the categories. Although analysis of variance is commonly used by researchers, the conditions for its proper use are seldom met, particularly when the data were derived from surveys rather than experimental designs.

Statistical inference and bivariate data summaries

Statistical inference A process by which sample statistics are used to estimate population parameters or to test statements about a population with a known degree of confidence.

These two procedures are closely related together, yet they perform very different functions. A lot of problems in student projects and dissertations arise through a failure to understand what these different functions are. **Statistical inference** is concerned with the connection between a sample result and the corresponding value in the population from which the sample was drawn. It is trying to infer things about the population from evidence in the sample. Bivariate data summary, by contrast, utilizes descriptive statistics to pick out features in a dataset whether these are a sample from a wider population, whether they constitute the entire population or are the result of an attempt to reach the entire population. Thus measures of association like Cramer's V evaluate the strength of the relationship between two variables in the data we have before us.

It may help if you are clear about how the two procedures are related. If a researcher takes a random sample, it will be true that the stronger the relationship between the two variables – as measured by a particular coefficient – the more likely it is to be statistically significant. In other words, high values of Cramer's V, for example, are unlikely to have come from a population in which there is no association between the two variables. We saw in Table 13.2, for example, that a Cramer's V of 0.282 was only just significant at the 0.05 level (having a p-value of 0.049). This gives some idea of the value of V that separates significant and non-significant results. However, this cut-off point cannot be applied throughout the research. This is because the significance of any one particular result will depend on the number of cases used in the calculation and on the size of the cross-tabulation. We saw in Chapter 8 that the number of cases used in a given calculation does not necessarily equal the size of the sample and may well vary from table to table. This will affect the value of Chi-square. Basically, if you double the number of cases, you will double the size of Chi-square for a table that shows basically the same pattern of association. The size of the table, furthermore, affects the number of degrees of freedom, which, as was seen from Table 13.1, determines the critical value of Chi-square. In short, simply because a Cramer's V of 0.282 is statistically significant on one table in a piece of research does not mean that it is on another.

Take another look at Table 13.2. This is the SPSS output derived from checking the *Phi and Cramer's V* tick box in the *Crosstabs:Statistics* dialog box. The value of V is 0.282, which is a fairly small degree of association. In the column headed *Approx.Sig*, SPSS is giving you the approximate level of statistical significance (the p-value), which is 0.049. This means that there are 4.9 chances in 100 that the achieved value of Chi-square (on which Cramer's V is based, and which Table 13.2 shows to be 9.558) could have arisen as a result of random sampling fluctuations. This is less than the 0.05 level normally demanded as a level of confidence and the result will be described as "statistically significant". So, a "statistically significant" result does *not* mean that there is a high degree of association. It simply means that the result probably cannot be explained away as a result of random sampling fluctuations – more technically, that the sample result was unlikely to have come from a population in which there is in fact no association.

All statistical inference makes two crucial and key assumptions:

- the result being tested comes from a sample that was selected at random,
- no other source of error other than random sampling error is being taken into account.

If the sample taken by the researcher was not selected by random methods (for example it was a convenience sample or a quota sample) then it would seem rather pointless to be fine-tuning our application of probability theory, which is based on having a probability sample. It's a bit like discussing how many angels can crowd onto the head of a modest-sized pin when we've picked up the wrong pin in the first place! We also saw in Chapter 8 that random sampling fluctuation (where there *is* a random sample), furthermore, accounts for perhaps only 5 percent of total survey error. When we come to consider what is often referred to as "the significance test controversy" in the next section we shall see that many researchers will, despite having a nonrandom sample or a sample selected by random methods but where there was a very poor response rate, still apply statistical inference. This may be a harmless, if futile, pastime, but it becomes potentially harmful and misleading if researchers *rely* on finding "significant" results without further analysis.

The significance test controversy

Most textbooks on statistics pay a great deal of attention to statistical inference and in particular to the process they usually refer to as "hypotheses testing". Remember that this does *not* amount to testing our ideas against the data we have generated from our research. How this is done will be considered in Chapter 14.

For the moment, however, it is important to be clear about the role and value of significance tests in survey research. Significance tests would be better described as "tests against the null hypothesis". Thus they calculate the probability that the null hypothesis is true in a population from which a random probability sample has been drawn. These tests take into account only random sampling error, not bias or nonsampling error arising, for example, from nonresponse or interviewer mistakes. As we saw earlier in Chapter 8, random sampling error accounts for maybe 5 percent of total survey error, so in rejecting the null hypothesis and accepting the alternative research hypothesis, we are really saying, "ignoring all other kinds of error except random sampling error, we can be 95 percent sure that we are making the correct decision from evidence from our sample".

Assuming that we have made the right decision, what have we accepted? We have accepted either:

- a nondirectional hypothesis, for example the mean age is not 32 years, or there is an association between two variables,

- a directional hypotheses, for example the mean age is higher than 32 years, or there is a positive association between two variables.

Bear in mind, however, that "positive" or "negative" do not really apply when binary or nominal variables are involved. Instead, we need to specify what combination of categories tend to be found together, for example it is the men rather than the women who tend to say "Yes" to a particular survey question.

In accepting the alternative research hypothesis we are not saying anything about the magnitudes involved. If we accept that the mean age is greater than 59 years, we cannot say by how much greater. If we accept that there *is* an association between two variables, we are saying nothing about the strength of that association. For a two-by-two table, for example with one degree of freedom, the critical value of Chi-square is 3.841 at the 0.05 level of probability, so any Chi-square value greater than this will lead us to reject the null hypothesis. However, as was explained in Chapter 8, sample sizes need to be at least 100 even for a very simple quantitative analysis. Cramer's V (or Phi) when Chi-square = 3.841 will be $\sqrt{[3.841/100]} = 0.196$. This is a very small degree of association. To the researcher, this is more likely to be of value as a negative finding (the degree of association is very small) rather than as a positive finding (gee whiz, the association is statistically significant). With larger samples, even smaller values of Cramer's V can be significant, so for a sample of 1,000, a V = 0.06 will be statistically significant for a two-by-two table at the 0.05 level.

In short, with samples of 100 or more, almost *any* association large enough to attract the attention of the researcher will, by definition, always be statistically significant. For larger tables, the critical value for Chi-square is, of course, much higher. Thus a five-by-four table has $4 \times 3 = 12$ degrees of freedom. The critical value at p = 0.05 is 21. For a sample of 100 this will give a Cramer's V of 0.46. But, of course, with 20 cells a sample of 100 will be far too small. A sample of 500 would be more appropriate (giving marginals averaging 100), but then Cramer's V will be $\sqrt{[21/500]} = 0.21$ – again, very small. In short, a "statistically significant" result is not necessarily an important or interesting finding. When large samples are taken in survey research, tests against the null hypothesis are of limited value. They do give the researcher some feel for the levels of association that may safely be ignored. However, results for which random sampling error is an unlikely explanation need to be taken as the starting point for further analysis. They should never be accepted as the "findings" of the research.

A further limitation of tests of significance is that because they depend on a selected critical value (and, more often than not, arbitrarily selected, or just accepting the traditional 0.05 level) it means that there is a nonzero probability of getting it wrong anyway. Now if we look at 100 tables and pick out five that are "significant" at the 0.05 level, then we are probably just picking out the five accidents we would expect anyway. In effect, the hypotheses have just been tested on the same data that suggested them in the first place. This is why it is so important, if tests of significance are going to be used, that hypotheses be set up in advance. If we pick out tables from the data, then to test any hypotheses that arise, we really need to test them on another dataset from another survey.

The whole edifice of significance testing depends on having a random, probability sample. Indeed, as such tests are commonly applied, they assume *simple* random sampling. But a lot of research is based on sampling procedures that have nonrandom elements involved in the selection of sampling units or cases. Some procedures, like judgmental sampling and quota sampling, are certainly not random and the potential for bias is considerable. Some practitioners will, nevertheless, argue that the resulting sample is an *approximation* of a random sample and that tests against the null hypothesis will somehow tell researchers something they would otherwise not know. Some statisticians will argue that nonprobability samples cannot be an appropriate basis for using probability theory. Remember, furthermore, that even in random samples there will always be some degree – and in many surveys a large degree – of nonresponse and quite possibly other failings in the sampling frame and data collection methods, so the presentation of "significant" results as "findings" is almost certainly misleading whether the sample was random or not.

Tests of significance may appear to be "scientific", giving clear conclusions, but the choice of critical value is, nevertheless, a subjective one, as is the choice between alternative tests where these are available. Furthermore, the statements we can legitimately make from statistical inference are so circumscribed that they are of limited value anyway, and in consequence are liable to misinterpretation. Thus to say that we "accept" the null hypothesis can be misleading unless we appreciate that all we can really say is that there is probably ($p = 0.05$) insufficient evidence in the sample to reject it since the result obtained could have been the product of random sampling fluctuations.

Criticism of statistical inference is certainly not new. Over 40 years ago Selvin (1957) argued that tests of statistical significance are generally inapplicable in nonexperimental research where the influence of antecedent variables is not taken into account as it is in the design of an experiment. In survey research, "significant" results are reported without reference to other conditions or possible influences. All too often, "significant" results are seen as the final evidence instead of merely the beginning of a further analysis into results that need some kind of explanation.

Some researchers have even conducted tests of significance on total populations on the basis that such a population may still represent a sample of some wider, hypothetical and infinite universe. The issue, however, is not always clear-cut. If the researcher selects all the employees in an organization, then this is a census and the researcher should have no reason for concern about sampling error. However, if a researcher interviews all residents in streets selected at random in a particular city, then is this a census of the streets concerned, is it a "sample" of the population of the city, is it a sample of all people living in cities in a given area, or is it a sample of the entire population at large? Some researchers will argue that, since the streets were selected by probability methods, then randomness was involved and that tests of significance are appropriate. Technically, however, it is a random sample of streets, not of households or individuals, and to conduct a test of significance, for example, on the relationship between household size and income would be meaningless. The idea that we can study the operation of sampling error when there is no real sample is wishful thinking.

So, if statistical inference is of limited value in nonexperimental research, what is the alternative? Certainly, the more informed use of bivariate and multivariate descriptive techniques (data summaries) would yield better analyses than relying on tests of significance in circumstances where they are dubious. More attention could be paid to the potential sources of bias in a dataset, and some attempt could be made to determine the effects of such bias. More careful and sophisticated measurement procedures would pay higher returns on the quality of research than assuming that we have a perfect random sample, and a focus on measuring the reliability and validity of measurement scales would be more informative than concluding that we can or cannot reject a null hypothesis.

As will be explained in Chapter 14, tests of significance do not, in fact, constitute a test of our theories against the data derived from the research. At best, in carefully selected samples, they enable us to take into account the possible effects of random sampling error.

KEY POINTS

Statistical inference plays a very different role in a piece of research from data summaries. The latter describe features or patterns in the data researchers have before them; statistical inference calculates the probability that these results could have been a random sampling fluctuation. The two procedures are linked in that bigger differences or stronger associations or correlations are more unlikely to have been a random sampling fluctuation; but when samples are large, even quite small differences or weak associations can be statistically significant. In short, statistically significant results are not necessarily important findings. Some researchers refer to what they call **effect size**, which is presented as an "objective and standardized measure of the magnitude of the observed effect" (Field 2005: 32). It turns out, however, that Pearson's r is apparently the best measure of effect size, so effect size is no different from a measure of association or correlation. "Effect" has implications about the nature of causality and how it is established. A discussion of causality is taken up in Chapter 14.

Effect size An objective and standardized measure of the magnitude of the observed effect.

Using SPSS

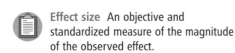

Nonparametric statistics Statistics that do not assume that data are metric or that the mean or standard deviation can be calculated.

Unfortunately, one thing that SPSS cannot do at present is calculate the standard error of the proportion for you (or the corresponding confidence intervals for categorical variables). It can, however, test for differences between an hypothesized result on a categorical variable and a sample proportion. If the test variable is binary, SPSS can undertake what it calls a *Binomial Test*. Select *Analyze/ **Nonparametric** Tests/Binomial*. This produces the *Binomial Test* dialog box. The test proportion default is 0.50, but this can be changed to any other hypothesized value. The result gives a p-value that is one-tailed for any specified proportion and two-tailed for the default value of 0.05. The terms one-tailed and two-tailed were explained earlier in this chapter.

If the test variable is nominal, Chi-square can be used as a goodness-of-fit test. Select *Analyze/Nonparametric Tests/Chi-square*. If, for example, you put the variable *division* into the *Test Variable List* box, the default for expected values will be that they are equal for all categories. The output is shown in Table 13.6. The top portion shows that the expected values for each category of division is 30 (that is, they are all equal), the calculated Chi-square is 28.2, which with three degrees of freedom is statistically significant. The researcher can, however, specify his or her own expected values and Chi-square will take all the differences between observed and expected values and derive Chi-square in the manner explained in Chapter 12.

TABLE 13.6   A goodness-of-fit test using Chi-square

In which division do you compete?

	Observed N	Expected N	Residual
First	38	30.0	8.0
Second	41	30.0	11.0
Third	36	30.0	6.0
Fourth	5	30.0	−25.0
Total	120		

Test statistics

	In which division do you compete
Chi-square[a]	28.200
df	3
Asymp. sig.	.000

a. 0 CELLS (.0%) HAVE EXPECTED FREQUENCIES LESS THAN 5. THE MINIMUM EXPECTED CELL FREQUENCY IS 30.0.

SPSS does provide confidence intervals for metric variables under *Analyze/ Descriptive Statistics/Explore*. This gives you the *Explore* dialog box. Put the variable *agebegan* in the *Dependent List* and click on *OK*. You should obtain the table illustrated in Table 13.7. This provides many different statistical summaries, but the confidence interval for the mean at the 95 percent level is 11.9 to 13.7. This implies that we can be 95 percent sure that the real population mean age lies between 11.9 and 13.7 years. If you click on the *Statistics* box you can change the level of confidence, for example to the 99 percent level and the intervals become 11.6 to 14.0. All these statistics can be split by a number of factors, for example gender of respondent, in which case you get separate tables for each. Just put the variable in the *Factor List* box.

To test the statistical significance of a bivariate hypothesis linking two categorical variables, SPSS provides the statistical significance of Chi-square. Check the

TABLE 13.7   Using SPSS *Explore* to generate confidence intervals

Descriptives

			Statistic	Std. Error
At what age did you take up table tennis?	Mean		12.80	.46
	95% Confidence	Lower Bound	11.90	
	Interval for Mean	Upper Bound	13.70	
	5% Trimmed Mean		12.19	
	Median		12.00	
	Variance		25.018	
	Std. Deviation		5.00	
	Minimum		6	
	Maximum		43	
	Range		37	
	Interquartile Range		4.00	
	Skewness		2.869	.221
	Kurtosis		12.575	.438

tick-box against Chi-square on the *Crosstabs:Statistics* dialog box. (Select *Analyze/Descriptive Statistics/Crosstabs/Statistics*.) Table 13.8 shows, in the top part, a crosstabulation of division played by whether or not somebody else in the household plays table tennis. NB: The fourth division has been added into the third division so that there are no cells with an expected frequency of less than 5. The lower part shows the SPSS output. The value for Chi-square is 1.056, which, clearly, is not significant. In fact there are 59 chances in 100 that such a value for Chi-square could arise as a result of random sampling fluctuations.

To test the statistical significance of a bivariate hypothesis linking two metric variables, SPSS provides the statistical significance of Pearson's r. Select *Analyze/Correlate/Bivariate* to produce the *Bivariate Correlations* box. Enter the two metric variables *agebegan* and *spend* into the *Variables* box under *Correlation Coefficients*, check that the *Pearson* box is ticked and click on *OK*. The result should be the same as Table 13.3.

Analysis of variance is to be found under *Analyze/Compare Means*. The top submenu, *Means*, calculates subgroup means and related univariate statistics. Put the variable whose means you want to compare into the top *Dependent List* box and the variable to form the subgroups into the *Independent List* box. Do not forget that this needs to be a categorical variable. The default table gives you the mean for each subgroup, the frequency in each group and the standard deviation (see Table 13.4). If you click on the *Options* box you can choose from a vast selection of statistics to put into the tables. Under *Statistics for First Layer* you can select to have an ANOVA table and the Eta statistic.

The other submenu of interest here is the *One-Way ANOVA*. In the *One-Way ANOVA* dialog box, again you need to put the metric dependent variable into the *Dependent List* box and the variable forming the groups goes under *Factor*. You can have only one factor and it needs to be categorical to form the groups. Table 13.5 was produced in this way. If the factor variable is binary, you will obtain the same result as an independent samples t-test. If you want more than a one-way ANOVA for independent samples, you will need the *Analyze/General Linear Model* procedure. This, however, can get quite complex. If you want more details, consult Bryman and Cramer (2004), but remember the conditions that need to be met before such procedures can be properly used.

TABLE 13.8		Division played in by whether anybody else in the household plays table tennis		
		Does anybody else in your household play table tennis?		
		Yes	No	Total
Division	First	19	19	38
	Second	17	24	41
	Third or fourth	16	25	41
Total		52	68	120

Chi-square tests			
	Value	df	Asymp. Sig. (2-sided)
Pearson Chi-square	1.056[a]	2	.590
N of Valid Cases	120		

a. 0 CELLS (.0%) HAVE EXPECTED COUNT LESS THAN 5. THE MINIMUM EXPECTED COUNT IS 16.47.

SUMMARY

Statistical inference for categorical variables may involve either estimation or testing hypotheses. Estimation is used when the researcher has little idea of the population proportion possessing a characteristic and is using the sample to estimate it. The researcher can attach confidence intervals to such estimates by calculating the standard error of the proportion and deciding on a confidence level, which in the social sciences is commonly 95 percent, but in some situations may be 99 percent. The standard error of the proportion can be calculated only for binary variables where a case either does or does not possess a characteristic. Where a variable is not binary then it is possible to use goodness-of-fit tests, which calculate the probability that the set of values departs from some specified expectation or distribution. Chi-square may be used for this purpose. An alternative goodness-of-fit test is the Kolmogorov-Smirnoff (K-S) test, which is particularly useful for testing whether observed values may have come from a normally distributed population. This is to be found in SPSS under *Analyze/ Nonparametric Tests/Sample K-S*. The data can then be compared with one of four distributions including the normal distribution.

Estimation is normally used only at the univariate level, that is, one variable at a time. Statisticians do not normally try to estimate the degree of association between two or more variables from evidence from the sample.

Where researches feel that they do know the value of a parameter at the univariate level, then this value can be taken as a "null" hypothesis and the probability may be calculated of the chances that a sample result did indeed come from a population of cases with that value. At the bivariate level it is usual to take zero association as the null hypothesis and calculate the probability that the sample result did or did not come from a population in which the null hypothesis of no association is true. The statistic Chi-square is normally used for this purpose.

As for categorical variables, statistical inference for metric variables may entail either estimation or hypothesis-testing. The estimation of metric variables usually entails estimating average scores or mean values. The standard error of the mean is used to calculate confidence intervals. SPSS can be used to calculate the upper and lower intervals. Testing univariate hypotheses may be accomplished in one of two ways. Either the null hypothesis is assumed to be true and the intervals under this assumption are calculated to see if it includes the sample result, or a z-test is constructed.

Testing bivariate hypotheses may involve two rather different procedures. One involves testing the statistical significance of differences between mean values where these values may clearly be seen as dependent variables and where the independent variables are categorical. If the independent variable is binary, a t-test is commonly used. If the comparison is for separate respondents who are independent of one another, then this produces a result similar to the analysis of variance (ANOVA) for independent samples, which may be used for any number of categories. SPSS offers a large range of procedures for the analysis of variance. If the categories are ordinal, then it is possible to simply ignore the ordinality and treat them as nominal. An alternative is to use special procedures for ordinal data like the sign test, the Wilcoxon Signed-ranks Test, or the Mann-Whitney Rank Sum Test. For an explanation of these tests see Bowers (2002). For how to use them in SPSS see Bryman and Cramer (2004).

The other bivariate procedure establishes the statistical significance of two or more metric variables that have been correlated. When SPSS (and other computer packages) is used, the end-product of all tests of significance is the calculation of a p-value. This needs to be below 0.05 to be statistically significant at the 95 percent level, and below 0.01 to be statistically significant at the 99 percent level.

QUESTIONS FOR DISCUSSION

1   If random sampling accounts for only about 5 percent of total survey error, and statistical inference relates only to such errors, what is the value of statistical inference?

2   Why is it important in the context of testing results against the null hypothesis to decide on the level of confidence in advance of conducting the test?

3   If a researcher sets up a null hypothesis in advance and decides on a level of confidence, why does he or she not simply calculate confidence intervals on the results of the survey rather than assuming that the null hypothesis is true?

4   Is statistical inference ineffective for analyzing the results of market research surveys?

SPSS EXERCISES

1   Take the three examples of confidence intervals that are calculated on pp. 375–376 and calculate what the intervals would have been had the sample size been 1000.

2   A random sample of 500 was used to estimate what proportion of households in a particular area owned a microwave oven.

   (i)   Calculate the standard error of the proportion for each of three results:

   250

   100

   20

   (ii)   Calculate the confidence interval for the 95 percent level of confidence for each of these results

3   The brand manager for Brand X, on the basis of past studies, hypothesizes that 10 percent of the target market purchases his brand. A simple random sample of 1200 individuals recorded that 96 people had purchased Brand X in the past four weeks. Test the manager's hypothesis at the 95 percent level of confidence.

4   Get SPSS to produce the 95 percent and 99 percent confidence intervals for the variable *spend* on the table tennis data.

5   Suppose you hypothesize that the mean age at which people begin playing table tennis is 12 and that your sample result is 12.8. Construct a z-test to see if you get the same result as on p. 382.

6   From the table tennis data, use SPSS to conduct an independent samples t-test for perceived importance of the social benefits of playing by whether or not anybody else in the household plays and compare your results with Table 13.5, which was derived from the one-way ANOVA procedure.

7   Obtain an ANOVA table that is identical to Table 13.5, but using the *Analyze/Compare Means/Means/Options* procedure. How would you interpret the result of Eta and Eta Squared?

ITEMS ADAPTED FROM BARKER ET AL, 2001

FURTHER READING

Argyrous, G. (2005) *Statistics for Research with a Guide to SPSS*. London: Sage.

Bowers, D. (2002) *Medical Statistics from Scratch*. London: Wiley.

Bryman, A. and Cramer, D. (2004) *Quantitative Data Analysis with SPSS 12 and 13*. Hove, UK: Routledge.

Field, A. (2005) *Discovering Statistics Using SPSS*, 2nd edition. London: Sage.

Pallant, J. (2005) SPSS Survival Manual, 2nd edition. Maidenhead: Open University Press (McGraw-Hill Education).

14 Multivariate analysis

Pallant, J. (2005) SPSS Survival Manual, 2nd edition, Maidenhead, Open University Press (McGraw-Hill
Education).

LEARNING OBJECTIVES In this chapter you will learn about:

→ the limitations of bivariate analysis,

→ the different types of multivariate analysis and the search for patterns in the data,

→ the multivariate analysis of categorical variables using three-way and n-way tables or loglinear analysis,

→ the multivariate analysis of metric variables, and metric and categorical variables mixed, using the dependence techniques of multiple regression, logistic regression, discriminant analysis and multivariate analysis of variance, and the interdependence techniques of factor analysis, cluster analysis and multidimensional scaling,

→ using multivariate analysis in the context of establishing causal relationships and offering explanations.

The real world is multidimensional.

© MONIKA WISNIEWSKA

INTRODUCTION

Bivariate analysis enables researchers to study the patterns of relationships between variables two at a time. However, unfortunately, the world of markets does not come neatly packaged into isolated pairs of variables, and attempts to account for statistical differences in a two-by-two fashion will at best be limited, but more likely distorted or misleading. Multivariate analysis, by contrast, enables the researcher to detect patterns buried in complex, interrelated variables. These patterns may emerge from establishing differences between several groups, measuring the extent of covariation between a number of variables, or assessing the degree of fit between a theoretical idea or expectation and the actual data. Multivariate procedures allow the researcher to group together variables that are interrelated, or cases that are similar in terms of their characteristics, to explore the degree of influence that one or more variables exert on other variables, or to make predictions based on evidence from a number of sources. Although there are simple structures underlying multivariate analysis, the techniques themselves tend to be complex and sophisticated. At the same time, while these techniques have their undoubted strengths, they also have their limitations and they are easily misinterpreted or misused.

INTERNET ACTIVITY

Using your browser, go to **www.thomsonlearning.co.uk/kent** and select the Chapter 14 Internet Activity which will provide a link to a website containing Statnotes by G. David Garson. This is an excellent internet source on multivariate statistics. In particular, check out the first topic on *correlation*. This will remind you of things that have been discussed in Chapters 11–13 and will help set the scene for some of the material in this chapter.

The limitations of bivariate analysis

It is perfectly feasible to investigate the relationships between a set of variables two at a time using bivariate analysis, which was explained in the previous chapter. If, for example, there is a single dependent variable, it is possible to examine the degree of association or correlation between that variable and all other potential factors in the dataset and to say which ones are the most closely associated with the dependent variable. This may, indeed, be all that a client wants in a piece of client-based research, and may well solve or help to solve the client's problem, but it is unlikely to be acceptable for academic, scholarly research. The reason is that there are severe limitations to bivariate analysis. These comprise three broad categories: descriptive, inferential and relational.

At a descriptive level, bivariate analysis may tempt researchers into what has been termed **data dredging**. "Dredging" normally means casting a net or other mechanical device to trawl whatever is on the sea bottom. In the context of data analysis it is a metaphor for a process of "trawling" a dataset without specific hypotheses to test, or perhaps even without hunches or specific issues to pursue. In its most extreme form the data are explored in every conceivable way to see

Data dredging Data are explored in every conceivable way to see if any patterns emerge.

what patterns emerge. Researchers may, for example, crosstabulate every variable by every other variable in the dataset in order to see which ones produce the strongest associations. This can easily be achieved using the SPSS *Crosstabs* procedure explained in Chapter 12, but will rapidly produce a lot of tables. In the table tennis survey there are 30 variables. If we were to crosstabulate each variable by each other variable, we would produce $(30 \times 29)/2$ or 435 tables. Many of the tables would not, of course, be particularly helpful, but some relationships that we might not have expected may well emerge. As a deliberate strategy, however, it is not a particularly efficient one. It also raises the issue of how the researcher decided what variables to include in the questionnaire in the first place if he or she had no idea of what patterns he or she was wishing to study.

A little less extreme are situations where there is a single dependent variable, for example voting behavior, and the researcher examines all possible bivariate relationships between this and all conceivable independent variables. Only those deemed to be statistically significant or which meet some other criteria appear in the published report of the findings, all others having been discarded.

Data dredging is an inductive process that may produce empirical generalizations from the ground up. It is often seen, however, to be reprehensible, producing "logically suspect" results (Alt and Brighton 1981). It is an admission that researchers do not know what they are looking for. However, some patterns *are* discovered by chance, and dredging may turn out to be a fruitful way of producing new insights. It is important to recognize, however, that all the various data dredging procedures are exploratory, and the same data cannot be used to "test" hypotheses that were derived from such data.

Another limitation of bivariate analysis, also at the descriptive level, is that it gives no indication of *joint* effects. If, for example, the degree of association between level of customer satisfaction and the perceived quality of the food in a restaurant, both constructed as metric variables, gives a Pearson's r coefficient of 0.4, and the degree of association between level of customer satisfaction and the perceived level of service is 0.3, then we can conclude that customer satisfaction is more closely associated with food quality than it is with level of service. However, it is not possible to say from these two separate bivariate associations how much food quality and level of service *jointly* contribute to customer satisfaction. For this, multivariate analysis is required.

At the inferential level, when the researcher is looking at a large number of bivariate associations, it becomes increasingly likely that all the statistical random flukes are being picked out, so picking out, say, five tables from 100 bivariate associations and testing for statistical significance with an alpha value of 0.05 will in all probability be picking out the very five tables that will lead the researcher inappropriately to reject the null hypothesis. Putting this another way, the more hypotheses we test using the same variables, the more likely researchers are to believe erroneously that they have found an effect. If, however, it is possible to test a set of hypotheses all at once, then this tendency can be avoided. Multivariate analysis provides exactly this facility.

More important, however, than either the descriptive or the inferential limitations of bivariate analysis, are the relational ones. In the real world, variables tend to be interrelated, and this is as true for independent variables among themselves as for relationships between independent and dependent variables. Three types of multivariate patterns are commonly considered by researchers: conditional, confounding and mediating.

Sometimes the relationship between two variables is **conditional** upon, or moderated, by a third variable, thus the relationship between level of customer satisfaction and the perceived quality of the food in a restaurant may be stronger for men than it is for women – the relationship is to some extent conditional upon gender. This type of pattern is also sometimes referred to as an **interaction effect** and it opens up the way for more sophisticated theorizing, even with only three

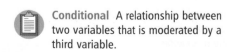

Conditional A relationship between two variables that is moderated by a third variable.

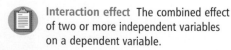

Interaction effect The combined effect of two or more independent variables on a dependent variable.

variables, but as more independent variables are added, each one moderating the original relationship, it quickly becomes very complex.

In a **confounding** pattern, the individual effects of two independent variables on a dependent variable are distorted because the independent variables are themselves related. Where the variables are metric, this kind of relationship is often referred to as **collinearity** (or **multicollinearity** if there are more than two independent variables) and is measured by the value of the coefficient of determination, R^2, between the independent variables. Its impact is to reduce any single independent variable's predictive power by the extent to which it is correlated with the other independent variables. As multicollinearity increases, the unique variance explained by each independent variable decreases. In consequence, the overall prediction increases much more slowly as more independent variables with high multicollineaity are added.

In a **mediating** pattern, an independent variable is seen as having an effect on a dependent variable indirectly through another independent variable. It is in the middle of a causal chain, so it is both dependent on the prior variable, and acting as the independent variable to the final outcome (see Figure 14.1). There can, of course, be several mediating variables in a complex chain. Mediation, furthermore, can be total or partial. In total mediation, the effect can occur only through the mediating variable. With partial mediation, it may be only one pathway among others (see Figure 14.2).

Confounding relationship The individual effects of two independent variables on a dependent variable is distorted because the independent variables are themselves related.

Collinearity A degree of correlation between two metric predictor variables in a regression equation that poses a threat to the validity of the regression analysis.

Multicollinearity A degree of correlation between three or more metric predictor variables in a regression equation that poses a threat to the validity of the regression analysis.

Mediating relationship An independent variable is seen as having an effect on a dependent variable indirectly though another independent variable.

KEY POINTS

Quite a lot can be achieved by analyzing the relationships between variables two at a time, but the researcher should be aware of the limitations of doing so. Thus joint effects may be ignored, there may be an inflated risk of committing what statisticians call Type I errors (falsely rejecting a null hypothesis), and above all, conditional, confounding or mediating relationships may not be unearthed. As more variables are added into the analysis, the potential for ever more complex relationship grows at an alarming rate. Furthermore, conditional, confounding and mediating effects may all combine in a final pattern. Bivariate strategies cannot even begin to deal with these kinds of complexities.

FIGURE 14.1

A mediating relationship

FIGURE 14.2

A partial mediating relationship

What is multivariate analysis?

Mulitivariate analysis is not easy to define; the term is not used consistently by statisticians. Sometimes it is used to refer to the number of *dependent* variables in an analysis. Thus in an analysis of variance where there is one dependent variable, it may be called "univariate" analysis of variance, even if there are two or more independent variables. By contrast, multiple regression analysis refers to the number of *independent* variables.

In general terms, however, we can say that mulitivariate analysis refers to the simultaneous analysis of three or more variables on a set of cases. Where all the variables to be related are categorical, then it is possible to control, or "layer" in SPSS terms, the relationship between two variables by a third, fourth, fifth variable and so on in the process of crosstabulation. The researcher can use these three-way to n-way tables to explore the relationships between three and more than three variables at a time. Unfortunately, any more than three-way tables become very difficult to interpret and unless the sample is very large, the numbers in the cells quickly become very small. An alternative is **loglinear analysis** that looks at interaction effects between a number of categorical variables.

Multivariate techniques for metric variables, or for combinations of metric and categorical variables, may be classified into two broad groups. **Dependence** techniques refer to those procedures where one or more variables are identified as dependent and which are to be predicted or explained by one or more independent variables. By contrast, **interdependence** techniques involve the simultaneous analysis of all the variables in the set, none being identified as either dependent or independent.

It is also important to distinguish between those multivariate techniques that may genuinely be called "tests" and rely on the cases being analyzed constituting a random sample from a population and which use statistical inference to reach a conclusion (in other words, the final output of such procedures is a p-value), and those techniques that describe one or more features of a dataset, irrespective of whether they constitute a sample or a population.

Analysis of variance and multiple regression, for example, are dependence techniques, but the former relies on statistical inference while the latter is a descriptive technique. Factor analysis, by contrast, is an interdependence, descriptive technique.

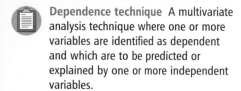

Loglinear analysis An extension of Chi-square analysis used to detect the patterns of interactions in a set of categorical variables.

Dependence technique A multivariate analysis technique where one or more variables are identified as dependent and which are to be predicted or explained by one or more independent variables.

Interdependence technique A technique in multivariate analysis that involves the simultaneous analysis of three or more variables, none being identified as either dependent or independent.

Looking for patterns

When researchers go beyond univariate analysis to bivariate or multivariate analysis, they traditionally look for one or more of three main patterns:

- numerical differences,
- covariation,
- the degree of fit.

Numerical differences can be either differences in values or differences in frequencies. If the variable that is taken to be the "outcome" or dependent variable is metric, then the values involved are metric values, often referred to as **scores**. Scores can then differ both between individual cases and between groups of cases, for example among a set of schoolchildren the females have higher average IQ scores then male students. If the variable that is taken to be the "outcome" or dependent variable is categorical, then differences can only be

Scores The values of a metric variable that is being treated as an outcome or dependent variable.

differences in frequencies, for example more men then women say "yes" to a particular question on a questionnaire.

Covariation means varying together. It is more than a difference. If two variables are metric, then covariation means that if we say that high values of one variable are associated with high values on the other, then we also mean, by implication, that low values on the first variable are associated with low values on the second. A negative covariation has a similar implication: if high values on variable X are associated with low values on variable Y, then the implication is that it is also true that low values on X are associated with high values on Y. If two variables are categorical, then covariation means that if we say, for example, that men are more likely than women to say "yes" to a question in a questionnaire then, by implication, we also mean that women are more likely to say "no". The researcher, in short, is looking for patterns "on the diagonal" whether in a scattergram, as in Chapter 12, Figure 12.4, or in a crosstabulation, as in Table 12.1. Current data analysis practices tend to take these implications about the symmetry of the patterns for granted. However, it could, for example, be the case that while all or nearly all the men say "yes", women may say either "yes" or "no", perhaps in equal proportions. This is still a pattern, but, as we shall see in Chapter 15, a logical one rather than a statistical one.

Statisticians often ignore, confuse or fail to draw any distinction between the notions of "difference" and "covariation". Spicer (2005: xiv), for example, argues that they are "logically equivalent". To say that men and women differ in scores on "happiness", he says, is the same as saying there is a relationships between happiness scores and gender – it is just a different way of framing the research question. Bryman and Cramer (2001), by contrast, have separate chapters on "Exploring differences between scores on two variables" and "Exploring relationships between two variables". However, this turns out to be a distinction between statistical inference – whether differences are statistically significant – and measuring the extent of covariation between two variables. According to the authors (2001: 158) in both contexts the researcher is

> *interested in exploring variance and its connections with other variables. Moreover, if we find that members of different ethnic groups differ in regard to a variable, such as income, this may be taken to indicate that there is a relationship between ethnic group and income.*

Furthermore, they say, there is "no hard and fast distinction between the exploration of differences and of relationships". Interestingly, the authors then proceed to give a series of examples of relationships each of which misses out the implications referred to above, for example "middle-class individuals are more likely to vote Conservative than members of the working class" (and by implication, working-class individuals are more likely to vote for some other political party). From the argument presented above, however, it should be clear that only if the pattern sought is covariational does the implication follow. There may indeed be differences between men and women or between the classes, but these may be a result of patterns other than covariational, symmetrical patterns on the diagonal.

A number of statistical operations depend on establishing not so much covariation as the level of "fit" (or lack of it) between a theoretical idea or expectation and the data that have been constructed. The statistic Chi-square, for example, is sometimes used as a "goodness-of-fit" test. Here the expectation is a purely theoretical one. However, the more frequent use of Chi-square both as a test of statistical significance and as the basis for generating measures of association like Cramer's V is also based on an expectation, in this case of what the values would look like of there were no differences – the expected frequencies – and the constructed values – the observed frequencies. Achieving a large value for Chi-square, while it establishes a lack of fit between the theoretical notion of independence and the achieved result, does not establish that the pattern is on the diagonal. Loglinear analysis is, in fact, based on Chi-square and around the notion

				Play tennis	
Play badminton	**Play squash**			Yes	No
Yes	Yes	Play football	Yes	1	0
			No	3	1
	No	Play football	Yes	1	4
			No	0	2
No	Yes	Play football	Yes	0	2
			No	10	0
	No	Play football	Yes	2	73
			No	12	9

TABLE 14.2 — An SPSS four-way table

Interactions	
Four-way	A*B*C*D
Three-way	A*B*C
	A*B*D
	A*C*D
	B*C*D
Two-way	A*B
	A*C
	A*D
	B*C
	B*D
	C*D

TABLE 14.3 — Interactions in a set of four variables

eleven interactions in a set of four variables from further consideration will be a distinct gain in terms of deriving simple pictures from complex data. The goal in loglinear analysis is to find the simplest set of interactions and variables that still models the observed data well. "Well" in this context means that any differences between observed and expected frequencies are not statistically significant. This in turn means that while loglinear analysis is not an inferential technique in the sense that the final result is a p-value, it nevertheless assumes that the cases being analyzed are a random sample from a population of cases.

In the 16-cell, four binary variable model, the four variables and all the eleven interactions fully "explain" the frequencies in the cells. This is called the **saturated** model. The observed and the expected frequencies are the same. If none of the variables had any effects, we would expect all the cell frequencies to be the same. In between are models where only some of the possible interactions are present. Loglinear analysis begins with the top of the hierarchy, eliminating the four-way interaction, generating expected frequencies and comparing this with the observed frequencies. This is a process called **backward elimination**. If the differences are not statistically significant, the analysis moves down to the next level and tries eliminating in turn the three-way interactions. Any interaction whose elimination produces a statistically significant set of differences will be kept in the model. The most parsimonious overall model consists of the remaining interactions.

The expected frequencies are generated using not the frequencies, but the logarithm of the frequencies to generate a linear model (hence "loglinear"),

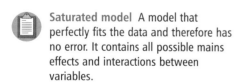

Saturated model A model that perfectly fits the data and therefore has no error. It contains all possible mains effects and interactions between variables.

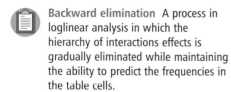

Backward elimination A process in loglinear analysis in which the hierarchy of interactions effects is gradually eliminated while maintaining the ability to predict the frequencies in the table cells.

whose form is the same as for regression analysis, but with the log of the expected frequency in any cell as the "outcome" variable. The "independent" variables are the eleven interaction effects (in the case of a four-variable set) plus the four individual effects. Each effect is referred to as a **coefficient** or **parameter estimate**. These are partial coefficients showing the relative magnitude of each effect while controlling for other effects in the model. This calculation is made for each cell, so there will be 16 of these in a set of four binary variables. In the saturated model, all 15 effects are included and the expected frequency should correspond with the observed frequency. These calculations are now repeated, systematically removing effects in hierarchical fashion. For each calculation there will now be a difference between observed and expected frequency, whose statistical significance is tested using not the Pearson Chi-square, but the **likelihood ratio Chi-square**. Instead of squaring the differences between the observed (fo) and expected frequencies (fe) and dividing by fe for each cell, the likelihood Chi-square divides fo by fe, taking the logarithm of the result and multiplying by fo for each cell. After summing across all cells the result in multiplied by two.

A loglinear analysis was performed by SPSS on the table tennis players who played none, one, two, three or four other sports to explore interactions between the different sports. Figure 14.3 shows the output for the first stage of the backward elimination. The saturated model of the four-way interaction has a likelihood ratio Chi-square of zero since, at this stage, the expected frequencies are the observed frequencies, so there is no difference. If this four-way interaction is deleted, the change in the likelihood ratio Chi-square is 1.143, which is not significant (p = 0.29), so this interaction is removed, leaving a model with four three-way interactions (Figure 14.4). Step 1 takes this model and calculates the change in the likelihood ratio if each of these three-way interactions is removed. The interaction with the highest nonsignificant probability of occurring is the tennis × squash × badminton interaction (p = 0.385). Consequently, it is deleted. The change in the likelihood ratio Chi-square of removing both this interaction and the four-way interaction is 1.143 + .753 is 1.896, which is also nonsignificant (Figure 14.5). The analysis continues until there are no more interactions that are nonsignificant to remove, which happens in step 5 (Figure 14.6), leaving the final model in Figure 14.7. This shows that the observed frequencies for the four-way interaction can be predicted quite satisfactorily from just three of the eleven interactions. How to undertake a loglinear analysis using SPSS is explained at the end of this chapter.

Tabachnick and Fidell (2001) recommend that the total sample should have five times the number of cases as there are cells in the analysis. Thus the 16-cell example earlier should have a minimum of 80 cases. However, the number of cells quickly multiplies with either the addition of categories to variables or of variables to the model. Thus if the four variables above had been three-category variables then there would be $3 \times 3 \times 3 \times 3 = 81$ cells requiring a minimum of 405 cases.

Loglinear analysis is not greatly used in marketing research, as explained in Box 14.1.

Coefficient A summary measure, usually of the degree of association or correlation between two or more variables.

Parameter estimate An estimate of a population parameter from a sample statistic. Also used on loglinear analysis as a partial coefficient of the relative effect of each on the expected frequency in each cell.

Likelihood ratio Chi-square As distinct from the Pearson Chi-square this takes the logarithm of the relationships between observed and expected frequencies.

```
* * * * * * * *  H I E R A R C H I C A L   L O G   L I N E A R  * * * * * * * *

        Backward Elimination (p = .050) for DESIGN 1 with generating class
                        foot*tennis*squash*badmin
                LIkelihood ratio Chi square =      .00000 DF = 0 P = .
        ----------------------------------------------------------------
        If Deleted Simple Effect is        DF  L.R. Chisq Change  Prob  Iter
            foot*tennis*squash*badmin       1        1.143       .2851    6
```

FIGURE 14.3

The first stage of SPSS backward elimination

FIGURE 14.4

The effect of eliminating each three-way interaction

Step 1
    The best model has generating class
        foot*tennis*squash
        foot*tennis*badmin
        foot*squash*badmin
        tennis*squash*badmin
        Likelihood ratio Chi square = 1.14268   DF = 1   P = .285

If Deleted Simple Effect is	DF	L.R. Chisq Change	Prob	Iter
foot*tennis*squash	1	1.342	.2467	5
foot*tennis*badmin	1	10.589	.0011	2
foot*squash*badmin	1	1.384	.2394	5
tennis*squash*badmin	1	.753	.3854	7

FIGURE 14.5

The effect of eliminating the remaining three-way interactions

Step 2
    The best model has generating class
        foot*tennis*squash
        foot*tennis*badmin
        foot*squash*badmin
        Likelihood ratio Chi square = 1.89597   DF = 2   P = .388

If Deleted Simple Effect is	DF	L.R. Chisq Change	Prob	Iter
foot*tennis*squash	1	1.180	.2773	6
foot*tennis*badmin	1	9.866	.0017	2
foot*squash*badmin	1	1.444	.2295	5

FIGURE 14.6

The model reaches stability

Step 5
    The best model has generating class
        foot*tennis*badmin
        tennis*squash
        squash*badmin
        Likelihood ratio Chi square = 6.92213   DF = 5   P = .226

If Deleted Simple Effect is	DF	L.R. Chisq Change	Prob	Iter
foot*tennis*badmin	1	6.514	.0107	3
tennis*squash	1	29.375	.0000	2
squash*badmin	1	4.268	.0388	2

FIGURE 14.7

The final model

* * * * * * * * HIERARCHICAL LOG LINEAR * * * * * * * *

The final model has generating class
    foot*tennis*badmin
    tennis*squash
    squash*badmin

RESEARCH IN ACTION   BOX 14.1
The use of loglinear analysis in marketing research

In their analysis of three top management journals between 1982 and 1991, Drazin and Kazanjian (1993) found 34 articles that reported crosstabulations in their results section. Of these, 5 used just percentages, 17 used percentages and Chi-square tests, and only 12 combined these with multivariate techniques such as loglinear modeling and logistic regression. A search of the World Advertising Research Center database on "loglinear" produced only eight references that mentioned the term at all and only five of these actually used loglinear analysis. Thus Danaher (1988) used a loglinear model to predict the exposure distribution for magazine advertising (the proportion of the target population that sees none, one, two or up to all the ads in a campaign). Zufryden (1996) showed that a loglinear regression model was able to characterize the box office performance patterns of new cinema films very well.

Given that perhaps the majority of data that result from marketing research are categorical, it is unfortunate that these techniques are underutilized. This is particularly the case since, according to Tansey et al. (1996), researchers are increasingly using regression-based statistics when the dependent variable is binary. This, say Huselid and Day (1991), has meant that many results obtained are probably in error since important assumptions are being violated. Thus predicted values can fall outside the logical zero to one boundary, estimated errors are not normally distributed, and estimates of the added effect of an independent variable are biased because they depend on a mean value of the dependent variable.

KEY POINTS

Multivariate analysis of data where all the variables are categorical is limited largely to constructing three-way or n-way tables and comparing the various strengths of association in the partial tables. However, the process requires large samples and it becomes unmanageable after two or three layers have been added. An alternative is loglinear analysis, which is not greatly used in marketing. One reason for this, suggest Dibb and Farangmehr (1994), is that the literature on it is not often read by researchers in the social sciences. This may be because the literature tends to be highly statistical with its own distinct terminology. It could also be suggested that the output is unfamiliar. Instead of a single summary measure or a p-value, there is a list of interactions that are deemed to be primarily responsible for the observed multiway distribution. The loglinear process, furthermore, does not indicate any direction of influence between the variables. Understanding the direction of any effects depends upon researchers either using other research evidence that might be available or designating which variables are dependent and which are independent based on theory or even hunch. Ironically, this limitation also applies to techniques like regression analysis that depend on being able to distinguish between dependent and independent variables.

To find out more, go to: **http://www2.chass.ncsu.edu/garson/pa765/ statnote.htm** and select *Log-linear Models*.

Multivariate analysis for metric variables: dependence techniques

Multivariate techniques for metric variables, or for combinations of metric and categorical variables, may be classified into dependence techniques where one or more variables is identified as dependent and which are to be predicted from, accounted by or explained by one or more independent variables. By contrast, interdependence techniques involve the simultaneous analysis of all the variables in the set, none being identified as either dependent or independent.

Dependence techniques are based upon the building blocks of regression analysis that were introduced in Chapter 12. Accordingly, we begin with multiple regression, which is an extension of simple bivariate regression to three or more variables. We then move on to logistic regression, multivariate analysis of variance, discriminant analysis and conjoint analysis. Interdependence techniques will include factor analysis, cluster analysis, and multidimensional scaling.

Multiple regression

Regression analysis is by far the most frequently used data analysis technique; it dominates data analysis in the social, behavioral, educational and health sciences (de Leeuw 2004). It is a multifunctional technique that may be used for description, for prediction and for inference. It is used to describe the distribution of a metric variable under a number of different conditions, usually combinations of the values of a number of other variables.

Regression analysis in general is nothing more than a study of how particular features of the distribution of a metric variable vary according to different values (which may be metric or categorical) of one or more predictor variables. The particular features of the distributions concerned are in practice directed towards one or more summary statistics, often the mean and variance.

Regression analysis is usually interpreted to mean *linear* regression, which means imposing a straight line through data. Multiple regression attempts to predict a single dependent variable from two or more independent variables and is an extension of bivariate regression. As we saw in Chapter 12, a linear regression line may be used to make predictions of a dependent variable from a single independent variable. The statistic r^2 indicates how "good" that line is in making such predictions. In reality, not one but several variables are likely to affect the dependent variable. Thus the level of sales is affected not only by price, but by, for example, advertising expenditure, interest rates, and personal disposable income. The formula describing a bivariate regression line is:

$$Y = a + bX$$

Multiple regression extends this to:

$$Y = a + b_1 X_1 + b_2 X_2 + b_3 X_3 \ldots + b_n X_n$$

Nonstandardized regression coefficient The rate of change in a dependent variable consequent upon a unit change in an independent variable in a multiple regression equation. Also know as a partial slope.

where $X_1, X_2, X_3 \ldots X_n$ are the independent variables. The values $b_1, b_2, b_3, \ldots b_n$ indicate the rates of change in Y consequent upon a unit change in $X_1, X_2, X_3, \ldots X_n$. They are usually referred to as **nonstandardized regression coefficients** or **partial slopes**. The calculation for each value of b is made with the degree of correlation between Y and the other variables held constant. This means that combined effects are additive in the sense that if $X_1, X_2 \ldots X_n$ were each changed by one unit, the expected change in Y would be the sum of the partial slopes. The magnitude of each partial slope is likely to be less than the bivariate r^2 between each independent variable and the dependent variable since any variation in Y that is shared by the independent variable is taken into account.

This model, however, provides an *estimate* for Y, so there is likely to be a degree of error involved. If an error term is added to the equation, then the general form of the model is encompassed.

Coefficient of multiple determination The percentage of variation in the outcome variable associated with the variation in two or more independent variables.

The product of the analysis is a **multiple R^2**, or **coefficient of multiple determination**, which indicates the percentage of variation in Y associated with the variation in the independent variables. The value of R^2 cannot be less than the highest bivariate r^2 between the dependent variable and each independent variable. If the independent variables are themselves uncorrelated then R^2 will be the sum of bivariate r^2 of each independent variable with the dependent variable. While R^2 cannot decrease as more independent variable are added to the equation, the amount added by each independent variable will be smaller to the extent that independent variables are themselves correlated.

The value of R^2 for a sample consistently overestimates the population value, and the larger the number of independent values and the smaller the sample size, the worse this bias becomes. Regression computer programs routinely provide an adjusted R² – a deflated estimate that takes into account the number of variables and sample size.

If, for example, we wanted to explain the amount spent on table tennis, not by correlating with *agebegan*, but by looking at the extent to which the perceived importance of various aspects of playing table tennis explain this variable, we can use the SPSS linear regression procedure to produce the results in Table 14.4. The adjusted multiple R² is 0.005, which shows that only 0.5 percent in *spend* is accounted for by the perceived importance of various aspects of playing table tennis.

The factors that are entered into the multiple regression equation, along with the constant, *a*, may be seen as a kind of "composite" variable that is correlated with the dependent variable, Y. The partial slopes, however, cannot be used to evaluate the contribution of each factor to Y because they will often have been measured in different ways, perhaps in different units. One way of overcoming this problem is to standardize the slopes into what are called **beta coefficients**. If the regression analysis is conducted using standardized scores, which usually means subtracting the means from each score and dividing by the standard deviation to produce **z-scores**, then the slopes are themselves standardized. The use of standardized variables always produces a constant or Y-intercept value of zero, so this adjustment disappears.

In standard multiple regression, all the independent variables are analyzed at the same time in one step. However, analytic power can sometimes be extended by conducting a series of regressions, each containing different subsets of the independent variables. The subsets may be chosen by the researcher, in which case the strategy is called **hierarchical regression**; or they may be selected according to some statistical rule, for example including the variables with the largest degree of bivariate correlation first, or the variables that make the largest contribution to R² if they are included. This is called **stepwise regression**. The focus is on how the picture changes with each step.

The assumptions of multiple regression

For multiple regression to be legitimately performed, a number of conditions need to be met. First, there must be an adequate size of sample. Tabachnick and Fidell (2001) point out that this is a complex issue because adequacy depends on the alpha level chosen, the number of independent variables, the expected magnitude of relationships, the reliability of measurement, and the frequency distribution of the dependent variable. Green (1991) suggests that if we assume an alpha level of 0.05, good reliability, and a normally distributed dependent variable, the minimum sample size for detecting a medium sized R² is 50 plus eight times the number of independent variables. Thus where there are five independent variables a minimum sample size is 50 + 40 = 90. Larger samples are required if beta coefficients are being estimated or if some of the other assumptions are not met.

Adjusted R² A deflated estimate of the coefficient of multiple determination that takes into account the number of variables and the size of the sample.

Beta coefficient A standardized partial slope. The regression analysis is conducted using standardized or z-scores.

Z-score The value of an observation expressed in standard deviation units. The arithmetic mean is subtracted from each observation and divided by the standard deviation.

Hierarchical regression A method of multiple regression in which the order in which the independent variables are entered into the regression model is determined by the researcher, based on previous research.

Stepwise regression A method of multiple regression in which the order in which the independent variables are entered into the regression model is based on a statistical criterion.

TABLE 14.4	Multiple regression. *Spend* regressed on *Enjoyment, Social benefits, Competition, Relaxation* and *Health and fitness*			
Model summary				
Model	R	R Square	Adjusted R Square	Std. Error of the Estimate
1	.217[a]	.047	.005	26.27

a. PREDICTORS: (CONSTANT), ENJOYMENT, SOCIAL BENEFITS, COMPETITION, RELAXATION, HEALTH AND FITNESS.

Second, regression analysis assumes that the dependent variable is metric. If it is not, then logistic regression, discriminant analysis or loglinear analysis should be used. The issue, however, is not always clear-cut. If the dependent variable is, for example, derived from a 5-point rating scale, then even if the intervals between the points on the scale are assumed to be equivalent, this variable is likely to violate other assumptions made by regression analysis. For the independent variables, more flexibility in scaling is possible; for example, binary variables may be introduced into the regression equation without complications. If the variable is nominal, it can be reduced to a set of binary variables. Thus if there are three categories, A, B and C, they can be set up as what are usually called **dummy variables**, for example taking the mean difference on the dependent variable between A and B, A and C, and B and C as the partial slope.

Dummy variable A way of recoding a nominal variable into a series of binary variables.

Third, regression assumes that all metric variables are normally distributed. Normality, however, is a matter of degree, and although there are statistical tests of normality, if these were strictly applied then many variables might be excluded from the analysis. It is often argued, furthermore, that the assumption of normality is a robust one and that its violation except in extreme circumstances is unlikely to affect the calculations.

Fourth, multiple regression assumes linearity – that the data are best summarized with a straight line rather than a curved or oscillating one. This is easily checked for bivariate regression, but can be complex for multivariate relationships in multidimensional space. Most researchers will check instead that the errors are normally distributed, a process sometimes called **residual analysis**.

Residual analysis A process in multiple regression that checks on the distribution of residuals, or errors.

The final assumption is that the independent variables are not themselves highly intercorrelated. Where this is so, there is multicollinearity, a term we have already met in the context of confounding relationships between variables. Although these effects are controlled to some extent statistically in the multivariate procedure, there are limits when the independent variables are highly correlated. This makes it difficult to evaluate the relative contributions of the independent variables.

Box 14.2 illustrates how multiple regression was used for media planning for Belgian radio commercials.

EUROPEAN MARKETING RESEARCH | BOX 14.2
Belgian radio commercials

Pelsmacker et al. (2004) studied the relevance and relative importance of a number of media planning variables, brand position factors and ad likeability for ad recognition and correct ad attribution in Belgian radio commercials. Ad recognition and ad attribution were the two dependent variables and were measured by the percentage of individuals who mention that they recognize the commercial, and the percentage who attribute the correct brand name to the commercial. The independent media planning variables included, for example, total campaign budget, number of commercials, campaign length and spot length; ad likeability was measured on a 10-point scale immediately following exposure during a telephone interview; brand-related variables included brand penetration and self-reported brand loyalty. In the study, 1482 radio spots were tested among consumers in two separate age groups, 15–34 and 35–54. A preliminary correlation analysis showed that a number of the media variables were highly correlated, so the variable with the highest correlation was selected to "represent" the rest. Four stepwise regression analyses were carried out, one for each dependent variable in each of the two samples. The multiple R^2, or coefficient of multiple determination, showed that the independent variables in total explained up to half of the variation in brand recall and ad recognition (R^2 varied from 0.4 to 0.5). Examinations of the beta weights, however, showed that three independent variables had a significant effect in each model: ad likeability, radio history (the number of earlier campaigns) and the extent to which the ad was multimedia. Spot length and brand penetration were also important.

To find out more, go to **http://www2.chass.ncsu.edu/garson/pa765/statnote.htm** and select *Regression Analysis*.

Logistic regression

Multiple regression, as was noted above, assumes that the dependent variable is metric. If it is categorical, then the independent variables cannot be used to predict scores on the dependent variable; what it can predict, however, is the probability of a case being in a particular category. Pampel (2000) explains that the probability cannot be used directly, but must be indirect using the idea of odds. If the dependent variable is binary (resulting in **binary logistic regression**), and if, for example, 80 cases are in category 1, and 20 cases in category 0, the probability of being in category 1 would be 80/100 = 0.8. Another way if putting this, however, is to say that the odds of being in category 1 would be 80/20 = 4. A case is four times more likely to be in category 1 than in category 0. The next step is to replace the odds with its natural logarithm. These are the **log odds**, sometimes called **logits**. What this means is that, once again, it is possible to use a linear equation with the predicted log odds as the dependent variable. At the same time, the coefficients of the independent variables are chosen, through log odds, to generate the probability of each case being in a given category.

What logistic regression is testing is the extent to which including the independent variables in the model improves ability to predict the dependent variable beyond only using the constant in the equation. The efficiency of the prediction is measured by the **log likelihood Chi-square**. A logistic regression is performed without the independent variables and again including them. The change in the log likelihood Chi-square is a measure of the extent to which all the independent variables jointly contribute to the outcome variable, but does not really offer an interpretable measure of association. Various attempts have been made to develop the equivalent of a pseudo multiple R^2 statistic for logistic regression, but there is little agreement on the appropriate form of such a statistic. SPSS gives the Cox and Snell and the Nagelkerke pseudo R^2 statistics, but the focus more usually changes to the statistical significance of identified changes in the log likelihood Chi-square.

Sample sizes required for logistic regression are typically larger than for multiple regression. Pampel (2000) suggests that samples under 100 may give misleading results; ideally, 50 cases per independent variable are required.

A **logistic regression** was performed on the table tennis data, taking the perceived importance of the social benefits of playing table tennis reduced to a binary variable, important/not important, as the dependent variable. The independent variables were the amount spent on table tennis in the past six months, the age at which players began playing and gender. The key output from SPSS is shown in Table 14.5. The *Model Summary* gives the final value of the log likelihood Chi-square and the two pseudo R^2 equivalents. These show a very low degree of correlation. The *Variables in the Equation* table tells us the estimates for the coefficients for the predictors in the model. The coefficients B are the equivalent of the slope in a regression equation, but tell us the change in the log odds of the outcome variable associated with a one-unit change in the predictor variable. The crucial statistic is the Wald statistic, which has a Chi-square distribution and tells us whether the coefficient for that predictor is significantly different from zero. Only *agebegan* is near to being statistically significant. How to undertake logistic regression using SPSS is explained at the end of this chapter.

Box 14.3 shows how logistic regression was used to investigate what factors might influence visits to a cosmetics company website by women in Finland.

Binary logistic regression A form of logistic regression in which the dependent variable is binary.

Log odds The natural logarithm of the odds ratio, which is the ratio of the odds of an event occurring in one group compared to another.

Logistic regression A form of regression analysis in which the independent metric variables are used to predict the probability of a case being in a particular category of a categorical variable.

| TABLE 14.5 | SPSS output from binary logistic regression |

Model summary

Step	−2 Log likelihood	Cox and Snell R Square	Nagelkerke R Square
1	155.683[a]	.059	.080

a. ESTIMATION TERMINATED AT ITERATION NUMBER 4 BECAUSE PARAMETER ESTIMATES CHANGED BY LESS THAN .001.

Variables in the equation

		B	S.E.	Wald	df	Sig.	Exp(B)
Step 1[a]	agebegan	.140	.072	3.759	1	.053	1.151
	spend	−.018	.013	1.938	1	.164	.983
	gender(1)	.909	.613	2.195	1	.138	2.481
	Constant	−2.015	.771	6.827	1	.009	.133

a. VARIABLE(S) ENTERED ON STEP 1: AGEBEGAN, SPEND, GENDER.

EUROPEAN MARKETING RESEARCH

BOX 14.3

Female consumers and visiting a company website in Finland

Using data from a survey sample of 839 Finnish female consumers, Martin et al. (2003) studied what permission-based e-mail advertising factors might influence visits to a cosmetics company website and what factors might influence visits to a physical sales outlet. The dependent binary variable was visited/not visited the company website and visited/not visited a company sales outlet. Independent variables were e-mail usefulness, amount of e-mails received, interest generated by the e-mail advertising, usefulness of the internet, and the perceived importance of the company staying in touch. A binary logistic regression analysis revealed significant negative associations between website visits and e-mail usefulness and the number of e-mails received with statistically significant beta coefficients of −0.36 and −0.86 respectively. Conversely, whether e-mail content was interesting was not a significant predictor of website visits. For store visits, by contrast, there were significant positive associations with e-mail usefulness, e-mail interest and number of e-mails received.

To find out more, go to **http://www2.chass.ncsu.edu/garson/pa765/statnote.htm** and select *Logistic Regression*.

Discriminant analysis

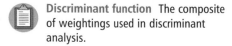

Discriminant analysis A multivariate technique that determines which weightings of metric independent variables best discriminate between two or more groups of cases better than by chance.

Discriminant function The composite of weightings used in discriminant analysis.

Discriminant analysis determines which weightings of metric independent variables best discriminate between two or more groups of cases (a categorical dependent variable) and do so better than chance. The weightings form a new composite variable that is known as a **discriminant function** and is a linear combination of weightings and metric values on the variables in the composite. The weights are set to maximize the between-group variance relative to the within-group variance. Discriminant analysis can be seen as the equivalent of a multiple analysis of variance (MANOVA), which is explained in the next section, but where the status of the dependent and independent variables is reversed; it determines which of the metric independent variables account for most of the differences in the average metric score profiles of the two or more groups.

Discriminant analysis is useful for situations where researchers want to build a predictive model of group membership based on observed characteristics of each case. The functions are generated from a sample of cases for which group membership is known; the functions can then be applied to new cases with measurements for the predictor variables but unknown group membership, for example product success or failure from a range of metric predictor factors. Alternatively, discriminant analysis can be used to give an objective assessment of differences between groups on a set of independent variables.

A discriminant analysis was carried out on the table tennis data taking the division played in as the grouping variable and as possible metric discriminant variables the age at which individuals began playing table tennis, the number of times they play per week and their total satisfaction average score. This creates three discriminant functions – one less than the number of groups, in this example the division played in, being considered. The overall statistical significance is evaluated using Wilks's lambda, which can be transformed into a Chi-square whose significance level can be determined (Table 14.6). All three functions are statistically significant. The canonical discriminant function coefficients (Table 14.7) can now be used to predict division played in from age began, play frequency and satisfaction scores in situations where the division is not known at that stage. Each coefficient (weight) needs to be multiplied by the score, added and the constant added.

Along with other parametric methods, discriminant analysis assumes that the independent variables are normally distributed with more-or-less equal variances. It also assumes that there is no multicollinearity – that the independent variables are not themselves highly correlated. If the categorical dependent variable is binary, then Hair et al. (1998) suggest that binary logistic regression might be better since its assumptions are somewhat less stringent.

Box 14.4 shows how cluster analysis was used to cluster different types of internet game players.

TABLE 14.6	SPSS discriminant analysis: statistical significance			
Wilks's lambda				
Test of function(s)	Wilks's lambda	Chi-square	df	Sig.
1 through 3	.738	35.115	9	.000
2 through 3	.881	14.661	4	.005
3	.954	5.490	1	.019

TABLE 14.7	SPSS discriminant coefficients		
Canonical discriminant function coefficients			
	Function		
	1	2	3
How many times do you play per week?	−.032	−.149	1.207
At what age did you take up table tennis?	.206	−.062	.039
totsat	.398	1.391	−.064
(Constant)	−3.704	−2.858	−2.624

UNSTANDARDIZED COEFFICIENTS

RESEARCH IN ACTION
Game playing on the internet

BOX 14.4

Discriminant analysis is frequently used in segmentation analysis to profile each segment, often following **cluster analysis** to create the segments. Cluster analysis is an interdependence technique that is considered later in this chapter. Beaumont et al. (2001) used cluster analysis on data derived from a telephone survey of 1000 at-home PC users. Using data on the frequency of games playing and purchase plus attitudinal questions about PC game playing, they generated six clusters that they called *games gurus*, *gamer bimbos*, *moderating mothers*, *time restricted*, *ageing laggards* and *dismissives*. The authors then undertook a discriminant analysis to identify which questions determined cluster membership. Just six variables predicted this with at least 85 percent accuracy in each cluster and 92 percent overall. These comprise two demographics (age and gender), frequency of games playing and three attitudinal questions. These became their "magic questions", which enabled the probability of membership of each cluster to be derived from answers to these six questions.

 Cluster analysis A range of techniques use for grouping cases who have characteristics in common.

KEY POINTS

The multivariate analysis of data when the variables are all metric, or a mixture of metric and categorical, is centered on regression-based techniques including multiple regression, logistic regression and discriminant analysis. Multiple regression is an extension of bivariate regression and requires that all the variables be metric, except that binary or dummy variables may be included among the independent variables. It makes a number of assumptions that in practice may well not be met. Regression techniques have been strongly criticized, for example by Berk (2004: 16), who argues that they are based on a number of judgmental decisions the basis for which go outside the data. These will include the commitment to a linear (straight line) relationship when a nonlinear one might be better, the determination of any transformations, for example by taking the logarithm of a curve to make it linear, or the standardization of the slope of the fitted line. If these decisions are unexamined, or treated as formally necessary, then the researcher has "started down the slippery slope towards statistical ritual". Berk (2004: 203) even goes on to say that "in the eyes of a growing number of observers, the practice of regression analysis and its extensions is a disaster". While the primary technical literature on regression analysis and related procedures is usually quite careful about assumptions made by the procedures and other constraints, these "health warnings" get lost in the translation into textbooks and indeed in research practice itself.

Where the dependent variable is categorical, the researcher can use logistic regression or discriminant analysis. Discriminant analysis is widely used in marketing, particularly in segmentation research and usually in combination with other techniques like cluster analysis, which is explained later in this chapter. It can be used both as an inferential technique and as a descriptive, profiling tool. Along with logistic regression its key function is to handle situations where there is a categorical dependent variable and one or more metric independent variables. Even though the two techniques often reveal the same patterns in a dataset, they do so in different ways and require different assumptions (Spicer 2005: 123). Logistic regression is normally used when the dependent variable is binary: in fact Hair et al. (1998) argue that binary logistic regression is the only legitimate form and that if the variable is nominal with three or more categories, then discriminant analysis is preferable.

Multivariate analysis of variance

Analysis of variance (ANOVA) was introduced in Chapter 13 on statistical inference. It is essentially an inferential technique that tests the null hypothesis that the groups come from populations in which there is no difference between the means of categories or groups. It was explained in Chapter 13 that ANOVA recognizes that there will be variations in individual scores *within* groups as well as differences *between* groups. The logic of ANOVA is that it compares the variance of scores between the groups with the variance within the groups. If the variance between groups is larger, we conclude that the groups differ; if not, we conclude that the results are not statistically significant.

ANOVA is, in fact, a whole family of related procedures, but they all involve comparing means for groups or categories of cases. In short, the dependent variable or variables are metric, and the independent variables are categorical. Which particular technique is appropriate depends on two things. First, it depends on the number of (categorical) independent variables. When there is only one such variable, then it is called "one-way" ANOVA. One-way ANOVA can be thought of as a bivariate technique – there is one independent variable and one dependent variable. "Two-way" ANOVA is used when there are two independent variables, and so it can be thought of as a multivariate technique since a total of three variables is involved.

The appropriate ANOVA technique depends second on the number of (metric) dependent variables. ANOVA assumes that there is only one dependent variable. MANOVA (multivariate analysis of variance) is an extension of ANOVA to accommodate more than one dependent variable. It measures the differences for two or more metric dependent variables on a set of categorical variables acting as independent variables.

A further extension to analysis of variance is to introduce **covariates**. These are uncontrolled metric independent variables that create extraneous (nuisance) variation in the dependent variable, and whose effect can be removed through the use of regression-like procedures. This process is usually called **analysis of covariance** (ANCOVA) or **multivariate analysis of covariance** (MANCOVA) where there are several dependent variables. The process allows for more sensitive tests of treatment effects.

Even if there is just one independent variable, once there are more than two categories there are many comparisons between means that are being made. Thus with three categories, besides the three pair-wise differences, there are also differences between subsets, for example between one group and the average of the other two groups. Once there is more than one independent variable an effect may be found both for each variable or for the variables operating jointly – an interaction effect. This requires what is called a factorial design in which every category of each variable is combined, so that, for example, two independent variables each with three categories will produce nine different means, all of which are to be compared, both with themselves and with the overall grand mean and the mean for each category.

For two-way ANOVA, MANOVA, ANCOVA and MANCOVA, SPSS uses what it called the **general linear model (GLM)**. This combines analysis of variance with regression analysis. A **univariate GLM** means that there is a single metric dependent variable and one or more factors (independent variables) which will normally be categorical, but metric variables may be included as covariates. An analysis of variance was carried out on the table tennis data, taking the amount spent on table tennis in the past six months (*spend*) as the metric dependent variable and *gender*, *division* and *else* (whether anybody else in the household plays) as the factors. The results are shown in Table 14.8. The overall model is statistically significant (p = 0.026), but the adjusted R^2 is only 0.1. The table also shows the statistical significance of the main effects of *gender*, *division* and *else* and the

Covariate An uncontrolled metric independent variable that creates extraneous variation in the dependent variable.

Analysis of covariance An analysis of variance that removes the effects of covariates through the use of regression-like procedures.

Multivariate analysis of covariance (MANCOVA) A multivariate analysis of variance that removes the effects of covariates through the use of regression-like procedures.

General linear model (GLM) A combination of analysis of variance and regression for situations where there is one or more metric dependent variables and a combination of categorical or metric independent variables and covariates referred to as factors.

Univariate GLM A general linear model in which there is a single metric dependent variable.

Wilks's lambda A procedure used in general linear modeling to examine the contribution of each main and interaction effect. It is a measure of the unexplained variance and is the mirror image of eta².

four interaction effects. Only *else* and the interaction of *gender*division*else* come close to being statistically significant.

The univariate GLM model is used for two-way, n-way and analysis of covariance. To obtain MANOVA or MANCOVA, a multivariate GLM is required. This allows for several (metric) dependent variables to be entered. The SPSS output is similar to that for univariate GLM except that **Wilks's lambda** is used to examine the contribution of each main and interaction effect. This is a measure of the unexplained variance and is the mirror image of eta².

Box 14.5 shows how two researchers used multivariate analysis of covariance to study the impact of the tempo and volume of background music on the amount of time shoppers spend in the retail environment and on how much they spent.

RESEARCH IN ACTION   BOX 14.5
The effect of tempo and volume of background music on shopper behavior

Herrington and Capella (1996) use MANCOVA in their study to look at the effects of tempo and volume of background music (treated as two binary independent variables) on the amount of time and money shoppers spend in a service environment (two metric dependent variables) controlling for the effects of size of household, time pressure and antecedent mood state (also treated as metric variables). These are the covariates. The MANCOVA produced a Wilks's lambda of 0.898 (meaning that only just over 10 percent of the variance is accounted for by the independent variables, controlling for the covariates) and a p-value of 0.31, which is certainly greater than 0.05. The authors concluded that the amount of time and money spent in a service environment is unaffected by background music factor levels – tempo and volume of the background music did not affect shopping behavior.

The use of MANCOVA in terms of design is appropriate in this research since the variables tempo and volume were treated as categories or experimental groups and manipulated, and covariates were deployed. However, the analysis was carried out on a sample that was clearly not a random one. To draw conclusions based on small variations in p-values is thus suspect. If the interviewers had, furthermore, selected husband and wife teams as they went into the supermarket, they would not have been "independent" samples.

TABLE 14.8   SPSS analysis of variance output

Tests of between-subjects effects

Dependent Variable: Approximately how much have you spent on table tennis in the past 6 months?

Source	Type III Sum of Squares	df	Mean Square	F	Sig.
Corrected Model	16 409.783[a]	13	1 262.291	2.022	.026
Intercept	86 740.682	1	86 740.682	138.971	.000
gender	128.852	1	128.852	.206	.651
division	2 562.826	3	854.275	1.369	.256
else	2 284.070	1	2 284.070	3.659	.058
gender * division	3 637.645	3	1 212.548	1.943	.127
gender * else	1 379.834	1	1 379.834	2.211	.140
division * else	821.636	3	273.879	.439	.726
gender * division * else	1 919.883	1	1 919.883	3.076	.082
Error	66 161.208	106	624.162		
Total	403 835.000	120			
Corrected Total	82 570.992	119			

a. R SQUARED = .199 (ADJUSTED R SQUARED = .100).

KEY POINTS

There are many situations in market research where researchers have, or assume that they have, a metric dependent variable, like the results of deploying summated rating scales, and want to check whether there are any differences in mean scores between categories of respondents in a survey that are not due to random sampling error. Analysis of variance consists of a number of parametric, inferential techniques for testing the null hypotheses that discovered differences between means on one or more metric dependent variables or one or more categorical independent variables are a result of chance random sampling fluctuations. The tests compare the variation in scores (as measured by the variance, the square of the standard deviation) within the groups with the variation between the groups. The sampling distribution of the ratio of the former to the latter (the F-ratio) is then used to determine the probability that the null hypothesis is true. When more than two groups are involved, a statistically significant result indicates that the means of at least two of the groups do differ. Which particular means are involved needs to be determined using further statistical tests. The aim of the analysis is to determine which independent variables (factors) and which interactions between those factors account for a significant proportion of the overall variance in a variable.

The simplest analysis of variance is a one-way ANOVA for a binary independent variable, in which case it is the equivalent of an independent samples t-test. One-way ANOVA may be thought of as a bivariate technique and is found on the *Compare Means* menu in SPSS. Two-way ANOVA, n-way ANOVA and MANOVA are multivariate techniques and may be undertaken using the SPSS GLM procedure in which covariates may be added.

Analysis of variance is commonly used in marketing research, but often in circumstances that technically do not justify its use. All the various procedures assume:

- the respondents whose results are being compared are a random sample,

- the scores of the dependent variables are continuous metric and normally distributed within each group,

- the variance within the groups is approximately equal,

- the groups or categories are "independent" samples.

Analysis of variance is designed essentially for experimental designs and in this context is extremely useful. When used for the analysis of survey data, however, many of these assumptions are not met and it is probably an overused, and frequently misused, technique, as in the Herrington and Capella example in Box 14.5.

To find out more, go to **http://www2.chass.ncsu.edu/garson/pa765/statnote.htm** and select *Univariate GLM, ANOVA and ANCOVA*.

Multivariate analysis for metric variables: interdependence techniques

Interdependence techniques involve the simultaneous analysis of all the variables in the set currently being analyzed, none being identified as either dependent or independent.

Factor analysis

Factor analysis A multivariate statistical technique used for identifying the underlying structure in a large set of metric variables. It groups together those variables that are highly intercorrelated.

Factor A term that is commonly used to refer to an independent variable in an experimental design. It is also used to refer to a latent variable in factor analysis.

Latent variable A variable that cannot be directly observed or measured, but is assumed to be related to several variables that can be measured.

Factor loading The correlation between a variable and a factor in factor analysis.

Principal components analysis One of several ways of undertaking factor analysis in which both the amount of variance to be accounted for and the number of components to be extracted equals the number of variables.

Eigenvalue The proportion of the total variance explained by each factor in a factor analysis. It is calculated from the sum of the squared factor loadings.

Varimax A method of factor rotation used in factor analysis that keeps the vectors at right angles so that they are unrelated to one another.

The primary purpose of **factor analysis** is to define the underlying structure in a large set of metric variables that refer to a common theme or topic, for example a set of attitude rating items. Factor analysis recognizes that when many variables are being measured, some of them may be measuring different aspects of the same phenomenon and hence will be interrelated. It systematically reviews the correlation between each variable forming part of the analysis and all the other variables, and groups together those that are highly intercorrelated with one another, and not correlated with variables in another group. The groups identify **factors** that are in effect "higher order" or **latent variables**. This helps to eliminate redundancy where, for example, two or more variables may be measuring the same construct. The factors themselves are a weighted composite of all the variables that are seen to be intercorrelated. They are "latent" in the sense that they are not directly observable, but each variable has a **factor loading** that is the correlation between the variable and the factor with which it is most closely associated. The effect, and advantage, of factor analysis, is to reduce a large number of variables to a more manageable set of factors that themselves are not correlated.

Factor analysis begins by calculating a correlation matrix – a table of the value of Pearson's r for each variable with each other variable. If there are, for example, just five variables, then the correlation matrix might look like that in Table 14.9. From visual inspection it is clear that variables 4 and 5 are highly correlated and both are negatively correlated with variable 3. Variables 1 and 2 are also correlated, but neither is correlated with variables 4 or 5. A factor analysis might produce a "solution" like Table 14.10. Variables 3, 4 and 5 combine to define the first factor and the second factor is most highly correlated with variables 1 and 2.

The extraction of factors can be achieved in a variety of ways. SPSS offers six different methods, but the default is **principal components analysis**. "Component" is only another term for "factor". With this procedure both the amount of variance to be accounted for and the number of components to be extracted equal the number of variables. The first factor will always explain the largest proportion of the overall variance, the next factor the next largest that is not explained by the first factor and so on. Each variable is correlated with (loads on) each factor. To calculate the proportion of the total variance explained by each factor, square the loadings of the variables on that factor and sum the result to give the **eigenvalue**. If this is now divided by the number of values (the total variance, so if there are 20 variables the variance is 20), this gives the proportion of the total variance explained by that factor. Factors with an eigenvalue of less than 1 are usually dropped. The remaining factors are then rotated to make their meaning clearer. There are various ways in which this can be done. SPSS gives five methods, but the most common one is **varimax**. This keeps the factor vectors at right angles so that they are unrelated to one another.

There are problems associated with factor analysis. First, it is possible to generate several solutions from a set of variables. Second, a subjective decision needs to be made as to how many factors to accept. Third, the grouping has to

TABLE 14.9	A correlation matrix				
Variable	1	2	3	4	5
1	1.00	0.61	0.47	−0.02	−0.10
2		1.00	0.33	0.19	0.32
3			1.00	−0.83	−0.77
4				1.00	0.93
5					1.00

TABLE 14.10	Factor loading on two factors	
Variable	Factor 1	Factor 2
1	−0.25	0.72
2	0.06	0.87
3	−0.94	0.33
4	0.94	0.21
5	0.95	0.26

make intuitive sense. Thus if variables 1 to 5 in the preceding example were consumer reactions to a new product, then variables 4 and 5 might be two questions that tap the "value-for-money" factor, and variables 1 to 3 are different aspects of "benefits-derived-from-use". Factor analysis will always produce a solution; whether it is a good or helpful one is another matter. There may not, in fact, *be* any factors underlying the variables.

The uses of factor analysis can broadly be classified into exploratory or confirmatory. **Exploratory factor analysis** may itself be undertaken for different purposes, for example for data reduction – replacing a large set of variables with a smaller number of factors, for testing the characteristics for one or more measuring instruments, or for explaining the patterning in the data. **Confirmatory factor analysis (CFA)**, by contrast, is used to test the probability that a particular hypothesized factor structure is supported by the data. More than one model can be tested to discover which might provide the best fit. Fit is sometimes determined by using the likelihood ratio Chi-square test. This compares the difference between the correlation matrix of the original data with the correlation matrix produced by the model. The bigger the difference, the larger will Chi-square be and the more likely it is that the difference will not be due to chance. If the difference cannot be considered to be due to chance, then the model does not provide an adequate fit to the data.

Confirmatory factor analysis is considered to be one of a family of techniques that estimate multiple and interrelated dependence relationships called structural equation modeling. This uses separate relationships for each set of dependent variables. It combines factor analysis with multiple regression in a series of structural equations. It is not available on SPSS, but the company has another program for this purpose called AMOS (see www.spss.com/amos). More commonly used, however, is a program called LISREL, which is available from www.ssicentral.com. For more details on structural equation modeling see http://www2.chass.ncsu.edu/garson/pa765/statnote.htm, or Kline (2005).

Box 14.6 illustrates how factor analysis was used to analyze different orientations towards marketing in manufacturing and service companies in the Ukraine.

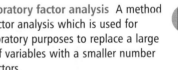

Exploratory factor analysis A method of factor analysis which is used for exploratory purposes to replace a large set of variables with a smaller number of factors.

Confirmatory factor analysis A method of factor analysis used to test the extent to which an hypothesized factor structure is supported by the data.

EUROPEAN MARKETING RESEARCH

BOX 14.6

Approaches to marketing in the Ukraine

Akimova (1996) conducted 221 personal interviews in small, medium and large manufacturing and service companies in eastern Ukraine. Respondents were asked how well each of 14 statements described the role of marketing in their company. These statements were then factor analyzed to identify a set of dimensions underlying approaches to marketing. Factors were constructed using principal components and the loadings were rotated using the varimax procedure. Using Kaiser's test gave a four-factor solution. The factors explained 71 percent of the variance in the original 14 variables. The researcher labeled the four factors *agnostics*, *production orientation*, *sales and promotion orientation* and *marketing orientation*.

KEY POINTS

Factor analysis is a descriptive data reduction technique that makes sense only when there is a large set of metric variables or items measuring a given concept, but which might contain latent subdimensions. It also makes sense only if there are reasonable correlations between the variables. Tabachnick and Fiddell (2001) recommend an inspection of the correlation matrix for evidence of correlations greater than 0.3. If few are above this level then factor analysis is not appropriate. The technique also requires a reasonably large sample size – at least 150. According to Hair et al. (1998: 99) there should be five times as many cases as variables. The analysis consists of three steps: first, a correlation matrix of the original variables is computed, second, a few factors are extracted from the correlations matrix and third, the factors are rotated to maximize the correlation of each variable with one of the factors.

To find out more, go to **http://www2.chass.ncsu.edu/garson/pa765/ statnote.htm** and select *Factor Analysis*.

Cluster analysis

All scientific fields have a need to group or cluster objects. Historians group events; botanists group plants. Marketing managers often need to group customers, for example on the basis of the benefits they seek from buying a particular product or brand, or on the basis of their lifestyles. Any procedure for deriving such groupings is clearly crucial for market segmentation or target marketing.

Cluster analysis is a range of techniques for grouping cases (usually respondents to a survey) who have characteristics in common. Cases are placed into different clusters such that members of any cluster are more similar to each other in some way than they are to members in other clusters. Both cluster analysis and discriminant analysis are concerned with classification. However, while discriminant analysis requires prior knowledge of group membership for each case, for cluster analysis there is no a priori information about group or cluster membership for any of the cases. Clusters are suggested by the data, not defined beforehand.

Like other multivariate techniques, cluster analysis is based on using a composite of factors, but instead of estimating that composite, it compares cases based on a prespecified composite, so the researcher's specification of that composite is a critical stage. Cluster analysis is comparable to factor analysis in that it is a data reduction technique based on assessing structure, but groups cases rather than variables.

The steps involved in cluster analysis are listed in Figure 14.8. The first step is to define the variables on which the clustering is to be based. The inclusion of even one or two irrelevant variables may destroy an otherwise useful clustering solution. The variables should be selected either based on past research and relevant to the research problem at hand, or based on existing theory and a consideration of the hypotheses being developed or tested. The variables also need to be metric, although there is provision in the SPSS procedure for the inclusion of binary or dummy variables. In practice, many of the variables will be based on 5- or 7-point rating scales in which the notion of "distances" is rather weak. Cohen and Markowitz (2002) point out, furthermore, that the inclusion of binary or dummy variables, though quite appropriate for regression models, creates a problem in cluster analysis since no amount of recoding will transform nominal items into metric ones whose differences imply distances.

The second stage is to select a distance measure since the objective of clustering is to group together cases that are similar in terms of the specified variables. This is usually done in terms of distances between pairs of cases. The default measure in SPSS is what is generally called **euclidean distance**, which is the square root of the sum of the squared differences in values for each variable. SPSS offers five other types of measure including Pearson correlation and cosine. If the variables are measured in very different units, then the values are standardized by rescaling each variable to have a mean of zero and a standard deviation of 1. Using different distance measures may produce different solutions so it may be advisable to use several different measures and to compare the results.

The third stage is to select a clustering procedure. What is called **hierarchical clustering** develops a tree-like structure and may be approached in two ways. **Agglomerative clustering** is based on taking individual cases and combining them on the basis of some measure of similarity, such as the degree of correlation between the cases on a number of variables. Each case is correlated with each other case in a correlation matrix. The pair of cases with the highest index of similarity is placed into a cluster. The pair with the next highest is formed into another cluster and so on. Each cluster is then averaged in terms of the index being used and combined again on the basis of the average similarities. The process continues until, eventually, all the cases are in one cluster. The index of similarity may be achieved in several different ways, including being based on the computation of

Euclidean distance A distance measure used in cluster analysis which takes the square root of the sum of the squared differences in values for each variable.

Hierarchical clustering A clustering procedure used in cluster analysis in which either cases are iteratively combined on the basis of some measure on similarity (agglomerative clustering), or the total set of cases is divided into subgroups on a basis specified by the researcher (divisive clustering).

Agglomerative clustering A stage in cluster analysis in which the clustering procedure is based on taking individual cases and combining them on a measure of similarity.

FIGURE 14.8

Steps in cluster analysis

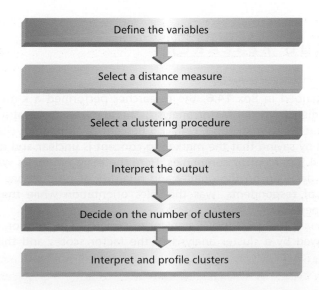

the distance between pairs of cases, on the minimization of the squared euclidean distance between cluster means, or the distance between pairs of clusters based on the means of all the variables.

The other approach is **divisive clustering**, which begins with the total set of cases and divides them into subgroups on a basis specified by the researcher. Thus the researcher may want a four-cluster solution of 1200 respondents on ten variables. An iterative partitioning computer program might begin by setting up four equal-sized groups at random. The center of each cluster on the ten variables is then calculated and the distances between each of the 1200 respondents and the centers of the four groups are measured. On the basis of these distances, respondents are reassigned to the group with the nearest cluster center. The new cluster centers are recalculated and the distances again measured, with a further reassignment taking place. This process is repeated until no further reassignments are needed.

Nonhierarchical clustering, often called **k-means clustering**, involves predetermining the number of cluster centers and all cases are grouped within a specified threshold from the center. Again, there are several ways in which this can be achieved.

The output from cluster analysis may be displayed in a number of ways, the most common of which is as a **dendogram** (see Figure 14.9). This is read from left to right. Vertical lines represent clusters of cases that are joined together. The position of this line on the horizontal scale indicates the distances at which the clusters were formed. This information is helpful for the next stage: deciding on the number of clusters.

There may be practical, conceptual or theoretical reasons for deciding on the desired number of factors. Thus managers may want a particular number, or previous research may have suggested a particular quantity. Alternatively, various criteria can be set, for example specifying the minimum number of cases in a cluster may determine the number of clusters sought.

The last stage is to interpret and profile clusters. This involves examining the mean values of the cases in a cluster (the **centroids**) on each of the variables. This will enable researchers to describe the clusters and maybe enable them to assign labels. Doubts have been raised about the validity and reliability of cluster solutions. Nairn and Bottomly (2003), for example, showed that random data can generate apparently interesting clusters of customers. In a later paper (2004) Bottomly and Nairn showed that managers do indeed take note of such clusters and were willing to base segmentation policies on them.

Divisive clustering A stage in cluster analysis in which the clustering procedure is based on taking the total set of cases and dividing them into subgroups on a basis specified by the researcher.

Nonhierarchical clustering A technique of clustering used in cluster analysis, sometimes also called k-means clustering, which involves predetermining the number of cluster centers and all cases are grouped within a specified threshold from the center.

Dendogram A graphical representation of cluster of cases generated by using cluster analysis.

Centroids The mean values of the cases in a cluster analysis used in the final stage in the analysis.

EUROPEAN MARKETING RESEARCH
A cluster analysis in the Ukraine

BOX 14.7

In the study by Akimova (1996) described in Box 14.6, the researcher performed a k-means cluster analysis using the four factors identified from the factor analysis. The aim was to identify groups of enterprises practicing different approaches to marketing. Only 1.5 percent of companies clustered into the agnostic group. These responded by saying that the marketing concept is unclear and nonexistent. The production orientation included 4.5 percent of companies. Here the main emphasis was on planning and managing production and deciding on the quality and quantity of production. The largest cluster, associated with 60 percent of respondents, was the sales orientation while the marketing orientation cluster accounted for 24 percent.

Cohen and Markowitz (2002) estimate that perhaps 75 percent of benefit segmentation studies use factor analysis of rating scales followed by a cluster analysis of the factor scores and this has been popular for over 25 years.

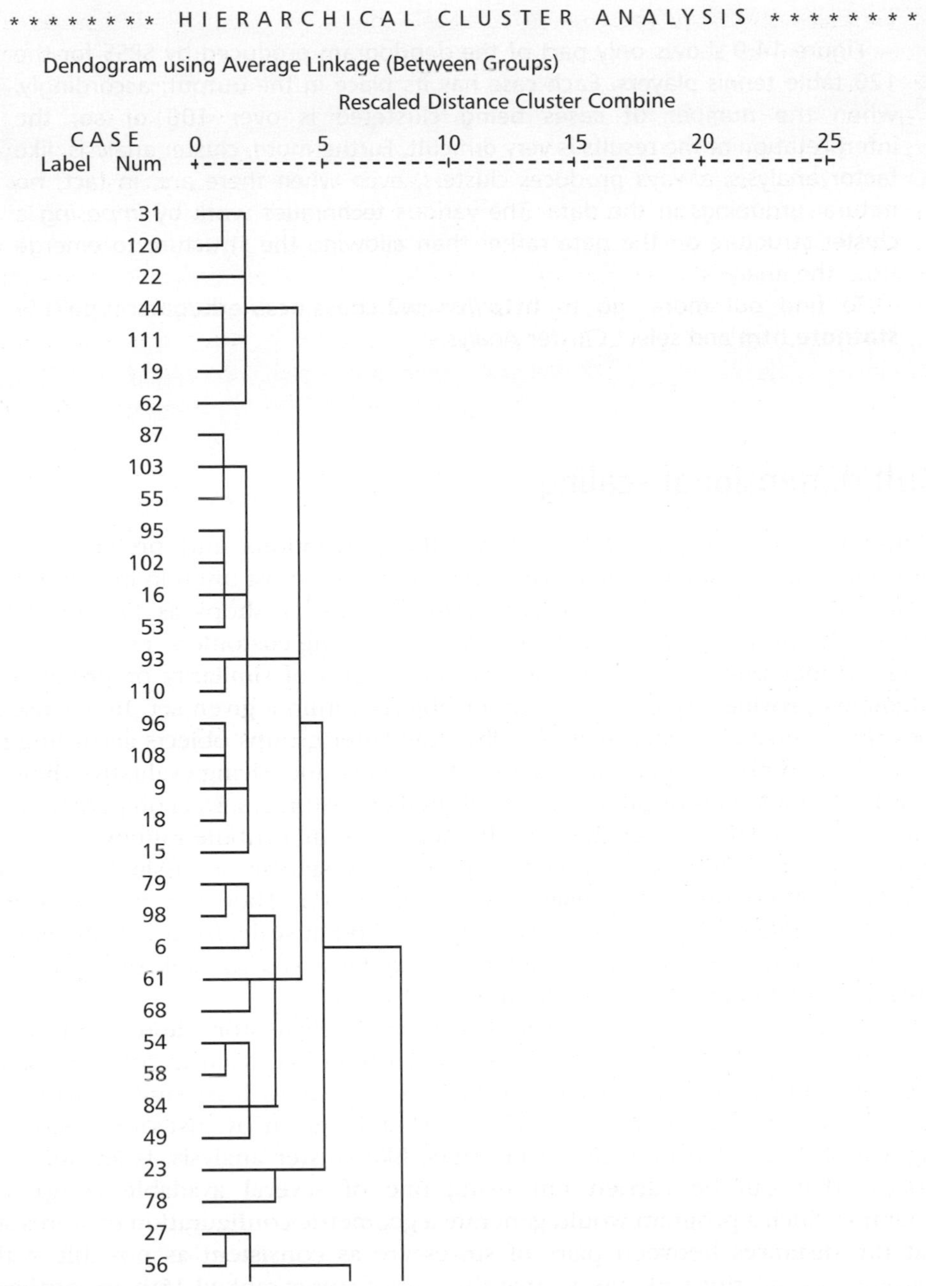

******** HIERARCHICAL CLUSTER ANALYSIS ********

FIGURE 14.9

A dendogram

Dendogram using Average Linkage (Between Groups)

Rescaled Distance Cluster Combine

CASE
Label   Num   0   5   10   15   20   25
                +--------+--------+--------+--------+--------+

                31
                120
                22
                44
                111
                19
                62
                87
                103
                55
                95
                102
                16
                53
                93
                110
                96
                108
                9
                18
                15
                79
                98
                6
                61
                68
                54
                58
                84
                49
                23
                78
                27
                56

KEY POINTS

Cluster analysis is an exploratory, descriptive technique. It cannot, furthermore, be used for prediction, as with regression, but only to profile the clusters that are generated. There are many different methods of clustering and a variety of different distance measures may be used, each combination likely to produce a different result. Validating cluster solutions is complex. Most researchers rely on just seeing whether or to what extent the different methods produce similar clusters. Akimova (1996) attempts to validate her analysis by relating cluster membership to the original statements using one-way analysis of variance.

> Figure 14.9 shows only part of the dendogram produced by SPSS for the 120 table tennis players. Each case has its place in the output; accordingly, when the number of cases being clustered is over 100 or so, the interpretation of the results is very difficult. Furthermore, cluster analysis, like factor analysis, *always* produces clusters, even when there are, in fact, no natural groupings in the data. The various techniques work by *imposing* a cluster structure on the data rather than allowing the structure to emerge from the analysis.
>
> To find out more, go to **http://www2.chass.ncsu.edu/garson/pa765/statnote.htm** and select *Cluster Analysis*.

Multidimensional scaling

Multidimensional scaling (MDS) allows the perceptions and preferences of consumers to be displayed in a spatial map. It is used most often in marketing to identify the relative position of competing brands or shops as perceived by customers, and to uncover key dimensions underlying customers' evaluations. It seeks to infer underlying dimensions from a series of similarity or preference judgments provided by customers about objects within a given set. In a sense it does the reverse of cluster analysis: while the latter groups objects according to similarities on prespecified dimensions, MDS infers underlying evaluative dimensions from similarities or preferences indicated by customers. Data on perceptions may be gathered directly or they may be derived from attribute ratings. In direct approaches respondents are asked to judge how similar or dissimilar various brands or other stimuli are, using their own criteria. They may be asked, for example, to rate each pair of brands on a 5- or 7-point scale, from very dissimilar to very similar. Alternatively, respondents may be asked to rank order all the possible pairs from the most similar to the least similar.

Suppose a customer is given a set of six multiple chain stores and asked to say how similar each store is to the others. The customer is asked to compare pairs of stores, and then rank the pairs from most similar to least similar. With six stores there are $n(n-1)/2$ or 15 pairs. The ranks given by just one customer might look like those in Table 14.11. MDS, like cluster analysis, is an iterative process that can be carried out using one of several available computer programs. Such a program would generate a geometric configuration of stores so that the distances between pairs of stores are as consistent as possible with customer's similarity rankings, so that the pair of stores ranked 15th are furthest apart, the pair of stores ranked 14th next furthest, while the pair AD is the closest together. The objects are presented usually in two-dimensional space, as in Figure 14.10, which shows a two-dimensional configuration of the six stores in which the interstore distances are consistent with the rankings in Table 14.11.

TABLE 14.11	Similarity rankings of six multiples				
Multiple	A	B	C	D	E	F
A		12	11	1	7	3
B			5	15	4	10
C				13	6	14
D					9	2
E						8

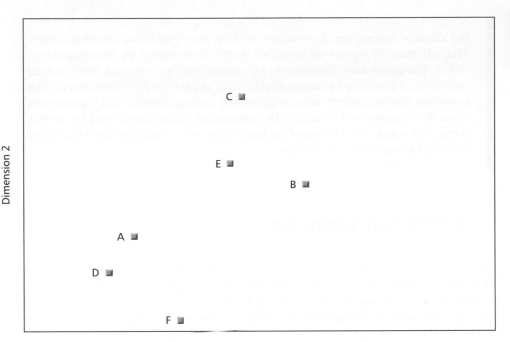

FIGURE 14.10

A multidimensional map based on rankings in Table 14.11

It is necessary to know, however, what the two dimensions represent. Labeling them is a subjective process and involves inspecting the relative position of the objects along each dimension and inferring what the dimension is most likely to represent on the basis of prior knowledge about the objects themselves. Looking at the first dimension, we might notice that the stores D and A offer the lowest prices, and C and B the highest. So dimension 1 could be price. Looking at dimension 2 vertically, we may observe that store C has a large product range and store F a limited product range, with the others in between. So, dimension 2 could be product variety. It is possible, of course, that somebody else looking at the same diagram may see other dimensions. However, it is possible to infer that this customer implicitly used price and product variety as the key criteria for comparing the six stores. Other customers may, of course, have other perceptions, resulting in a totally different multidimensional map. Where the maps from customer to customer differ greatly, making global inferences may be difficult. In such a situation the researcher may attempt to identify segments of customers with fairly similar multidimensional maps, perhaps using appropriate cluster analysis techniques.

The input data for MDS may relate either to perceptions or to preferences.

The spatial maps derived from preference data may be very different from that obtained from similarity data. Two brands, for example, may be perceived as very different, but nevertheless be equally preferred.

KEY POINTS

Factor analysis groups variables into a series of composite variables or factors that represent underlying dimensions in the original set of variables. Cluster analysis groups cases according to their profile on a set of variables or cluster composites. MDS differs from cluster analysis in two key respects. First, each respondent provides evaluations of all brands or other objects being considered, so a solution can be obtained for each individual. This is not possible in factor analysis or cluster analysis. The focus is not on the objects themselves, but rather on how the individual perceives them. Second, there is no set of variables that is determined by the researcher; rather the perceptual dimensions of comparison are inferred from overall measures of similarity between objects. This, say Hair et al. (1998), is a bit like providing the dependent variable (similarity among objects) and figuring out what the independent variables (the perceptual dimensions) must be. In this sense, the researcher can never be really sure what variables the respondent is using to make the comparisons.

Explaining relationships between variables

Multivariate analysis helps researchers to understand very complex relationships between variables; but to what extent does, for example, a multiple regression or a multivariate analysis of variance provide an explanation for research findings? The next section looks at what an "explanation" is and to what extent causal analysis helps to provide one.

What is an "explanation"?

Explanation A range of devices that may be used to clarify and make comprehensible to an audience.

To "explain" in a dictionary sense can mean many things: to make plain, comprehensible or intelligible; to unfold and illustrate the meaning of; to expound, elucidate or remove obscurity from; to account for, offer reasons for or a cause of; to give sense or meaning to something. This variety of meaning is mirrored in market research. To some researchers, an **explanation** of research findings means establishing causal connections between measured variables, and the "success" of the undertaking is judged by the extent to which the correct procedures have been followed and a number of criteria have been met. What these procedures entail is "explained" below.

To other researchers, establishing causality is only describing ways in which variables may be connected. It does not enable us to understand why this is so. From this perspective, an explanation is something that provides understanding or removes puzzlement in a audience. It will typically make reference to means and ends, to motives and reasons, or intentions and dispositions. Its "success" is judged by the extent to which the audience is satisfied with the level of understanding communicated.

Yet another perspective on explanation will see it as the discovery of an underlying process – a dialectic. This is a process of change that contains its own dynamic and that often arises from a conflict or tension between opposing forces or inherent contradictions. Understanding the internal dynamics of the family, social groups, society in general, an organization, a market system, a distribution channel or an entire mode of production goes beyond establishing causes or satisfying an audience to something much deeper and more fundamental – the ultimate "truth".

The answer to the question, then, concerning, "What is an 'explanation'?" is that it depends on who you ask. The three approaches mentioned above are reviewed in more detail below. Remember, however, that these three certainly do not exhaust the list of different approaches to explanation. When a statistician, for example, talks about "explanation", he or she probably means that the statistical variance in a dependent variable is "accounted for" by the variance in one or more independent variables.

Causal analysis

It is difficult for social scientists to avoid the notion of causality, and this has certainly been the dominant mode of "explanation". It fits with our own experience of connections between events. But what is "causality" and how do we establish it?

Causal analysis is concerned with the ways in which some events or circumstances can produce or bring about others. The presumed causes are the "independent" variables and the effects are the "dependent" ones. Evidence for such causality comes from three main sources.

Causal analysis A study of the way in which some events or circumstances can produce or bring about other events or circumstances.

- While the existence of a correlation or association is no proof of cause, it *is* a necessary precondition, and its absence would demonstrate that no causality is present.

- The independent variable must precede the dependent variable in time, that is, the causes must come first and the effects afterwards.

- The apparent relationship between the variables must not be spurious, that is, a result of their joint relationship with other prior variables.

Establishing each of these is, however, problematic. In a literal sense, to establish that Variable A "causes" Variable B, it is necessary that there be a perfect association between the two variables – otherwise other factors are involved and we have to say that Variable A is *a* cause (among others) of Variable B. Measures of correlation or measures of association are, however, in practice seldom perfect, that is, coefficients seldom approach unity. If we accept a "high" correlation or association as evidence, we have to make a decision about what counts as "high". Statisticians often assume that a measure that is "statistically significant" *does* exist. However, this really only means that, for random samples, it is unlikely to have come from a population of cases in which there is no association. If we calculate a coefficient of correlation between two variables that works out at, say, 0.23 and which, because it was based on a large sample, is "statistically significant", does this mean we have fulfilled the first criterion for establishing causality? Probably not.

Establishing the temporal sequence between variables can be even more difficult. For some variables it is not easy to say at what point of time they "happen". They may be states or conditions that exist for periods of time. Exactly at what point of time a customer becomes "brand loyal" may be difficult to determine. Much market research, furthermore, is cross-sectional, that is, measurements are taken at one moment of time, in which case it is impossible to say what variables preceded or followed others in time.

The testing of relationships for lack of spuriousness can be more complex still. There are at least three forms of spurious interpretation.

- The association is a result of a joint relationship with an extraneous variable. Thus there may be a correlation between essay grades and examination performance. One is not the "cause" of the other; rather they are both the outcome of some prior combination of ability and work effort.

- The two variables apparently associated are in fact components of a wider system. Thus certain toilet-training techniques for babies and the use of public libraries may correlate. Again, one does not "cause" the other, but both are components of a "middle-class" style of life.

- The relationship between two variables may not be totally spurious, but indirect or conditional. Thus other variables may intervene or one of the variables may be influenced by factors other than the variables with which it is being correlated.

The investigation of spurious relationships may to some extent be carried out in a statistical manner. If the variables concerned are categorical then three-way tabular analysis is appropriate. The method essentially involves looking at what happens to the association between two variables when another is introduced. Thus there may be a degree of association between Variable A and Variable B. If a "control" variable, Variable C, is introduced, then supposing Variable C has two categories C_a and C_b, then the researcher examines what happens to the association between A and B when C_a is true and compares it with what happens when C_b is true.

Look at Table 14.12. This is a bivariate crosstabulation of income, crudely divided into "low" and "high", and type of wine consumed, again crudely divided into "cheap" and "expensive". Only the percentage "cheap" is shown on the table. The table shows that 88 percent of those with low income bought cheap wine compared with only 34 percent of those with high incomes. A hypothesis of the following form would have been confirmed by the data:

H_1 *Those individuals with high disposable income are less likely to purchase cheap wines.*

However, suppose the researcher felt that patterns of wine consumption are likely to be influenced by age and that older people are less likely to buy cheaper wines (and to have higher incomes). Table 14.13 shows the relationship controlled by age, again crudely divided into an older age group of 35 and over and a younger group of 18–34. Both in the older and in the younger age groups the relationship between type of wine consumed and income still holds. Whatever the age group, those with lower incomes tend to buy cheap wine. OK, so H_1 still stands, but let us now assume that the researcher, being the kind of skeptical scientist he or she is meant to be, suspects that social class may have something to do with it. Table 14.14 shows the relationship between income and type of wine consumer controlled this time by social class, crudely distinguished into nonmanual and manual groups. The relationship between income and wine consumption has now "disappeared". Irrespective of income, those nonmanually employed are less likely to buy cheap wines. The explanation may be that suggested in Figure 14.11. Those nonmanually employed are *both* likely to have higher incomes *and* more likely to drink more expensive wines, so the original relationship may be spurious.

Ideally, the researcher should undertake three-way analyses for every factor that could conceivably affect the relationship between the hypothesized variables. In practice this is often not done and researchers are frequently tempted to draw

TABLE 14.12	Type of wine consumed by income	
	Income	
	Low	High
% cheap	88	34

TABLE 14.13	Wine consumed by income, controlling for age			
	Age 18–34		Age 35+	
	Income			
	Low	High	Low	High
% cheap	86	34	89	32

TABLE 14.14	Wine consumed by income, controlling for social class			
	Non-manual		Manual	
	Income			
	Low	High	Low	High
% cheap	33	33	85	85

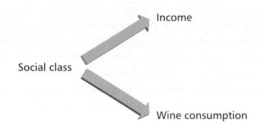

FIGURE 14.11

A spurious relationship

causal inferences from the occurrence of reasonably high measures of association or correlation between two variables.

Some philosophers argue that causal analysis is itself inadequate as a form of explanation. Some would argue that the notion of cause is itself an abstract concept – it is a "black box", a mystical concept. Establishing association, temporal sequence and lack of spuriousness is evidence of causality – but not *proof*. That can never be established. Some philosophers have doubted that cause inheres in the nature of things. Scientists can always observe that Variable A is always associated with Variable B – but we cannot observe what binds them together.

Is there, then, such a thing as a "causal explanation"? Is it not a contradiction in terms – an oxymoron? If we accept that explanation is the provision of understanding to an audience, then whatever an audience accepts as providing such understanding, counts as an "explanation". From this perspective, cause *is* explanatory, but only to those who accept a largely positivistic natural science view of the world.

Providing understanding

Understanding is something whose function is to resolve puzzlement in an audience. This, however, *may* mean establishing a connection between beliefs, motives and actions, that is, we try to understand why somebody, or some group or organization, did something. Another form of understanding, which is usually referred to as "teleological", involves explaining events in terms of purpose. In other words, we say: "The purpose of A is to produce B", or "A exists in order to achieve B". This may be focused at the group or social level – that certain social structures arise to meet the needs of society, or at the individual level – "I did this in order to . . .". People must think in teleological terms if they are to be held responsible for their actions. Such forms of "explanation" can be psychologically satisfying, but are ultimately difficult to prove, test or justify. Max Weber, one of the founding fathers of sociology, tried to establish the method of constructing "ideal-types" so that we could understand more easily the relationship between means and ends. "Functional" analysis, which also uses teleological relationships, looks at the relationship of the parts of a system to the whole – the parts are there "because" they perform some function for the system or the system's purpose.

Other devices that researchers might use to facilitate understanding include the use of such literary devices as drawing analogies between situations with which audiences might be familiar and the situation the researcher is attempting to explain. Thus the way in which the various "parts" of society interrelate may be "explained" by saying that it is "like" a human body with arms, legs and so on.

Dialectical analysis

The idea of looking for underlying processes goes back a long way, probably to Plato, but its classic formulation was by Hegel. To him a dialectic is a process in which for every proposition – a thesis, there is an alternative – an antithesis, which, ultimately, forms the basis of a new synthesis – hence the process of change. Karl Marx used the notion of dialectical materialism in which any form of economic development contains the seeds of its own destruction. Thus in capitalism there are inherent contradictions that eventually will result in the overthrow of the capitalist system. Dialectical analysis, however, is not necessarily a deterministic approach to knowledge. It is possible to intervene to change the course of history once the internal, underlying dynamics have been revealed and understood.

For Hegel and Marx a dialectic entailed a final point of arrival. For contemporary writers – who would certainly not think of themselves as "Hegelians" or "Marxists" – the approach signifies more a pathway, an underlying process in which things will progress, develop or change in particular ways if left to themselves. The product life cycle thesis used by marketers can be considered in this light.

The problem with this form of explanation is that it is untestable in the way that causal analysis may be subjected to empirical validation, and, furthermore, it may not necessarily relate to demonstrable ways in which social actors perceive their own realities, as with the attempt to provide understanding.

KEY POINTS

What counts as an explanation will undoubtedly vary between researchers. There is no such thing as a final or ultimate explanation, since for every "explanation" offered, the listener can always ask a further "Why?" question. In the final analysis it is what an audience or a listener will accept as an explanation.

Using SPSS

Three-way and n-way tabular analysis

From the *tabten* dataset select *Analyze/Descriptive Statistics/Crosstabs*. Put *agebeg2* into the *Row(s)* box and *else* into the *Column(s)* box. Put *encour* into the *Layer 1 of 1* box. Click on *Statistics* and tick *Phi and Cramer's V* in the *Nominal* box. Click on *Continue* then *OK*. The result is shown in Table 14.15. Notice that neither result in the partial tables is statistically significant.

Loglinear analysis

Select *Analyze/Loglinear/Model Selection* to obtain the *Model Selection Loglinear Analysis* dialog box (Figure 14.12). Transfer the variables to be used in the analysis into the *Factor(s)* box, so select *foot*, *tennis*, *squash* and *badminton*. SPSS needs to be told what codes have been used to define the categorical variables. So click

TABLE 14.15	SPSS layering with Cramer's V for partial tables

Were you encouraged by anyone to take up the sport?			Does anybody else in your household play table tennis?		
			Yes	No	Total
Yes	Began table tennis	Under 12	25	18	43
		12 and over	19	22	41
	Total		44	40	84
No	Began table tennis	Under 12	4	7	11
		12 and over	4	21	25
	Total		8	28	36

Were you encouraged by anyone to take up the sport?			Value	Approx. Sig.
Yes	Nominal by	Phi	.118	.279
	Nominal	Cramer's V	.118	.279
	N of Valid Cases		84	
No	Nominal by	Phi	.226	.176
	Nominal	Cramer's V	.226	.176
	N of Valid Cases		36	

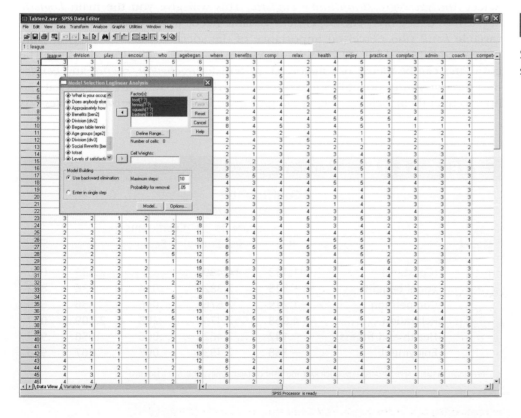

FIGURE 14.12

SPSS loglinear analysis, model selection

on *Define Range* and enter 0 for *Minimum* (does not play the sport) and 1 for *Maximum* (does play the sport). The default model building procedure is backward elimination, which is the one normally used. Click on *OK*.

The first part of the output describes the saturated model. The observed and expected frequencies are the same, and the likelihood Chi-square is zero, which indicates a perfect fit. The output appears to stop at this point. To view the rest of the output, click within the existing output, which will become enclosed by a black line. Move to the bottom of the output and move the cursor to the small rectangle in the middle of the bottom black line. Hold down the left key; an hourglass icon will appear briefly before changing to an upward and downward arrow. Scroll downwards. This gives you the results of the backward elimination process.

Multiple regression

Select *Analyze/Regression/Linear* to produce the *Linear Regression* dialog box. Move *spend* across to the *Dependent* box. Click on *OK*. The first table provided by SPSS is the *Model Summary* (Table 14.4). This provides the overall multiple R^2 and the adjusted R^2. It also gives the **standard error of the estimate**, which is the standard deviation of the residuals and which shows how spread out the data points are around the regression line. The *Coefficients* table gives the unstandardized and standardized coefficients for each of the independent variables included in the regression equation. Only *Relaxation* makes a statistically significant contribution to spend (Table 14.16).

Binary logistic regression

Select *Analyze/Regression/Binary Logistic*. This will give you the main *Logistic Regression* dialog box. The *Dependent* variable needs to be binary, so transfer the variable *ben2* (the perceived importance of the social benefits of playing table tennis reduced to a binary variable, important/not important) into this box. The covariates can be metric or categorical, so transfer *agebegan*, *spend*, and *gender* into the *Covariates* box. SPSS needs to know which variables are categorical and how to treat them. Select *Categorical*, giving the *Define Categorical Variables* box

Standard error of the estimate The standard deviation of the residuals in a multiple regression which shows how well spread out are the data points around the regression line.

| TABLE 14.16 | Multiple regression coefficients from SPSS |

Coefficients[a]

Model		Unstandardized Coefficients B	Unstandardized Coefficients Std. Error	Standardized Coefficients Beta	t	Sig.
1	(Constant)	41.133	14.489		2.839	.005
	Social benefits	−.325	2.382	−.014	−.136	.892
	Competition	−1.219	2.676	−.046	−.456	.649
	Relaxation	4.968	2.474	.208	2.009	.047
	Health and fitness	.142	2.462	.006	.058	.954
	Enjoyment	−.168	2.493	−.007	−.067	.946

a. DEPENDENT VARIABLE: APPROXIMATELY HOW MUCH HAVE YOU SPENT ON TABLE TENNIS IN THE PAST 6 MONTHS?

and transfer *gender* into the *Categorical Covariates* box. The default option, which SPSS calls *Indicator*, translates the categories into dummy variables, so they are all binary. Click on *Continue*. There are various methods of regression, including stepwise procedures, but the default is what SPSS calls *Entry*. This is the forced entry method: all the covariates are placed into the regression model in one block. Click on *OK*.

The first part of the output just tells us what codings were used for the dependent variable and for any categorical variables. The *Beginning Block* tells us about the model when only the constant is included – all predictor variables are omitted. Block I provides the steps in the logistic regression analysis, but since the method chosen is *Enter*, there is only one step. The key output is shown in Table 14.5.

Discriminant analysis

Select *Analyze/Classify/Discriminant* to produce the *Discriminant Analysis* dialog box. From the table tennis dataset transfer *division* into the *Grouping Variable* box. Transfer *agebegan*, *play* and *totsat* into the *Independents* box. Click on *Statistics* and tick the *Unstandardized* box, then on *Continue* and on *OK*.

Multivariate analysis of variance

Select *Analyze/General Linear Model/Univariate* to obtain the *Univariate* dialog box. Put *spend* into the *Dependent* variable box. Transfer *gender*, *division* and *else* to the *Fixed Factor(s)* box. Click on *OK*. The output is shown in Table 14.8.

Factor analysis

Select *Analyze/Data Reduction/Factor* to produce the *Factor Analysis* dialog box. As was explained earlier in the chapter, factor analysis is used to define the underlying structure in a large set of metric variables that refer to a common theme or topic. There is no large set in the table tennis dataset, but for the purposes of seeing the SPSS factor analysis output, transfer the five variables *benefits, comp, relax, health* and *enjoy* to the *Variables* box. These variables, you may recall, are 5-point rating scales which, for the purpose of this exercise, we are treating as metric variables. If you now click on OK you will be accepting all the default settings offered by SPSS. The result is shown in Table 14.17. Using principal component analysis, SPSS has produced two factors. Health and fitness and enjoyment seem to load on the first factor (component), but the other variables seem to load on both factors. However, the lower table shows the result after a varimax rotation. Competition, health and fitness, and enjoyment now load on the first factor, and social benefits and relaxation on the second. The first factor seems to relate to the more functional aspects of table tennis playing and the second to the more expressive aspects.

Cluster analysis

Select *Analyze/Classify/Hierarchical Cluster* to produce the *Hierarchical Cluster Analysis* dialog box. Transfer *agebegan*, *spend* and *totsat* to the *Variable(s)* box. Click on *Plots* and tick *Dendogram*, then *Continue*, then *OK*.

TABLE 14.17	SPSS factor analysis output

Component Matrix[a]

	Component 1	Component 2
Social benefits	.473	.565
Competition	.492	−.565
Relaxation	.456	.719
Health and fitness	.812	−.058
Enjoyment	.672	−.403

EXTRACTION METHOD: PRINCIPAL COMPONENT ANALYSIS.

a. 2 COMPONENTS EXTRACTED.

Rotated Component Matrix[a]

	Component 1	Component 2
Social benefits	.066	.734
Competition	.726	−.183
Relaxation	−.036	.851
Health and fitness	.700	.416
Enjoyment	.781	.053

EXTRACTION METHOD: PRINCIPAL COMPONENT ANALYSIS.
ROTATION METHOD: VARIMAX WITH KAISER NORMALIZATION.

a.ROTATION CONVERGED IN 3 ITERATIONS.

SUMMARY

Multivariate analysis is the simultaneous analysis of three or more variables on a set of cases and may be used to detect numerical differences, measure covariation or assess fit with an expectation. It can overcome some of the limitations of bivariate analysis, for example the joint effects of several variables operating together can be assessed, the risk of committing Type I errors (falsely rejecting a null hypothesis) is minimized, while conditional, confounding or mediating relationships can be detected.

Where all the variables to be related are categorical, then it is possible to control the relationship between two variables by a third, fourth, fifth variable and so on in the process of three-way and n-way tabular analysis. The researcher can use these tables to explore the strength of relationships between three and more than three variables at a time. An alternative is loglinear analysis that looks at interaction effects between a number of categorical variables.

Multivariate techniques for metric variables, or for combinations of metric and categorical variables, may be classified into dependence and interdependence procedures. The former depend on the researcher being able to establish the status of variables as dependent or independent and include multiple regression, logistic regression, discriminant analysis and multivariate analysis of variance. Interdependence techniques include factor analysis, cluster analysis, and multidimensional scaling.

Multivariate analysis helps researchers to understand very complex relationships, but may not necessarily provide an explanation that satisfies some audiences. What counts as an "explanation" will undoubtedly vary between researchers. There is no such thing as a final or ultimate explanation, since for every "explanation" offered, the listener can always ask a further "Why?" question. The process of establishing causal connections between variables may for some researchers provide adequate explanations, but others may still wish to understand why these connections apparently hold. This may involve understanding reasons, motives, intentions or the link between means and ends, or it may mean delving deeper to find underlying, dialectical processes.

QUESTIONS FOR DISCUSSION

1   How can the status of any variable as "dependent" or "independent" be established?

2   The appropriate use of regression-based techniques depends on a number of assumptions being met. Given that these are seldom met in their entirety, or not at all, to what extent has the use of regression been, in the words of Berk (2004: 203), a "disaster"?

 ## SPSS EXERCISES

Access the dataset *M&SUK* from the website at **www.thomsonlearning.co.uk**. It is a set of Likert attitude statements plus some demographics. The data are part of a study that compares British and Spanish customers in terms of their store image of Marks and Spencer. The research is trying to establish the dimensions of store image most suited to standardization across national frontiers. The population is all customers who shopped in Marks and Spencer in Stirling and Valencia. The dataset for this exercise includes the 150 UK respondents.

1   Suppose we suspected that males and females would have different views about store layout, décor, tidiness, and so on. Compare the mean scores of the males and the females using appropriate analysis of variance

2   There are 24 Likert items in the M&SUK dataset. Are any of these grouped together and unrelated to other groupings? Use factor analysis to find out.

ITEMS ADAPTED FROM BARKER ET AL, 2001

FURTHER READING

Cramer, D. (2004) *Advanced Quantitative Data Analysis*. Maidenhead: Open Univeristy Press/McGraw-Hill Education.

Field, A. (2005) *Discovering Statistics Using SPSS*, 2nd edition. London: Sage.

Kline, R. (2005) *Principles and Practice of Structural Equation Modeling*, 2nd edition. Guildford: Guilford Press.

Pallant, J. (2005) *SPSS Survival Manual*, 2nd edition. Maidenhead: Open University Press (McGraw-Hill Education).

Spicer, J. (2005) *Making Sense of Multivariate Data Analysis*. Thousand Oaks, CA: Sage.

15 Alternative methods of data analysis

LEARNING OBJECTIVES In this chapter you will learn about:

→ the origins of mainstream statistical methods and their limitations,

→ the link between causal analysis and the use of such statistics,

→ some of the alternatives to mainstream statistics, some of which still focus on variable analysis, but allow for nonlinearity, including neural network analysis, some data mining techniques, and Bayesian statistics,

→ alternatives that focus on cases rather than variables, including the use of combinatorial logic and fuzzy set analysis,

→ holistic approaches to data analysis.

The real world is very complex.

© ANDREW GREEN

INTRODUCTION

The multivariate techniques explained in Chapter 14 have been around a long time and have become the standard way of approaching the analysis of marketing data. They work best when there is a clearly defined set of cases whose characteristics can be measured in terms of metric or nonmetric variables, and where the patterns of relationships between them can be seen or interpreted as covariational. However, although they are a considerable advance on bivariate analysis, they are limited in a number of respects. First, they are variable-centered; they assume that measured variables mirror aspects of the "real" world, and they look at and compare the way values are *distributed* on a variable-by-variable basis. The uniqueness of each case is lost. Second, they are limited to the search for patterns that are covariational, and accordingly miss out other kinds of patterns. Third, multivariate techniques are not good at detecting, still less testing, causal relationships, even though they are commonly used for this purpose. At best they can provide partial evidence of such relationships when the notion of sequential effects makes sense according to concepts and theories that lie outside the statistical domain. Furthermore, such techniques cannot handle conditional relationships or distinguish, for example, between causal necessity and causal sufficiency. Finally, they are limited in their ability to handle complexity and complex systems in which relationships may be conjunctural, that is, they interact in combinations, they may be emergent or dynamic, and they are often nonlinear, that is, they do not necessarily happen in fixed sequences.

Multivariate techniques are increasingly coming under critical scrutiny; they are sometimes labeled as "traditional", "classical", "conventional" or even dismissed as "frequentist". Some critics, such as Sayer (2000), argue that only qualitative approaches can adequately handle causality. The approach taken here is that multivariate techniques should not be dismissed. They have a very important role to play in the analysis of marketing data, but there are alternatives that can be used when what we will call "mainstream" techniques (to avoid negative connotations) are unable to solve a problem. This chapter presents a range of alternatives, some of which are relatively new, and some of which have been around for quite some time, but their application in marketing is only recently becoming apparent.

INTERNET ACTIVITY

Using your browser, go to **www.thomsonlearning.co.uk/kent** and select the Chapter 15 Internet Activity which will provide a link to the University of Arizona Qualitative Comparative Analysis Software website. Click on *What is QCA?* If you want to try out fuzzy-set analysis, which is explained later in this chapter, you will need this site to download the software, which you can do for free.

The origins of mainstream statistics

The "numerical method" in medicine goes back to Pierre Louis's (1835) study of pneumonia, and John Snow's (1855) book on the epidemiology of cholera (Freedman 1999). The statistical manipulation of survey data in an attempt to reach well-founded conclusions that apply to the region and time-period from which the data came, arose in the UK in the late nineteenth century. Francis Galton, Karl Pearson and George Udny Yule developed the science of statistics, which radically changed the meaning of the word "statistics". Instead of referring to collections of data or "state-istics", Galton and his followers used the word to refer to the mathematical manipulation of data in order to reveal their essential characteristics. Although it was Legendre (1805) and Gauss (1809) who developed the regression method to fit data on the orbits of astronomical objects, it was Galton who pioneered the use of frequency curves, particularly the "normal" curve, while Pearson refined the techniques of correlation to invent the correlation coefficient "r" or "Pearson's r" as it became known. Pearson also invented Chi-square, one the most widely used statistics among social scientists today, and he pioneered the calculation of probable errors of statistics as well as the publication of statistical tables. Yule took Pearson's theory of correlation and laid the foundations of partial correlation and of linear regression for any number of variables. His interest in the practical application of statistics to social problems led him to consider the relationship between sets of categorical data, and he developed the analysis of contingency tables, inventing his famous statistic "Q", still known as "Yule's Q", for measuring association between attributes, which he published in 1900.

Galton was initially a mathematician who became an explorer and meteorologist. He was also a cousin of Charles Darwin whose *Origin of Species,* published in 1859, had a profound influence on him. His ambition became to apply statistics to the laws of heredity, and in 1875 he was conducting experiments with sweetpea seeds to develop the laws of the inheritance of size. The idea of a regression line to measure correlation between sizes of seeds of mother and daughter sweetpea plants emerged from this work. At the same time he developed the use of frequency curves and by 1889 had even managed to invent a unit-free measure of association by using his ideas about the "normal" curve and its properties. Galton became interested in the connection between heredity and human ability and he noted that able fathers tended to produce able children. He introduced the term "eugenics" in 1883 in his book *Inquiries into Human Faculty* to describe the science that would utilize the principles of heredity to attempt to improve the ability of the human stock. In 1904 he founded a research fellowship in national eugenics at the University of London, from which developed the Galton Laboratory of National Eugenics. At the same time Pearson was developing the parallel science of "biometrics" – the application of statistical techniques to genetics. Like Galton, Pearson had studied mathematics at Cambridge and in 1884 he became Professor of Mathematics and Mechanics at the University of London. By 1895 Pearson had established his Biometrics Laboratory, which in 1906 amalgamated with the Galton Laboratory to become the Eugenics Laboratory with Pearson himself as director.

Yule had been a student of Pearson, and when in 1893 Yule returned from a period of study in Germany, where he had been working in the field of experimental physics, Pearson offered him a demonstratorship. While he was developing his ideas about correlation, Yule also became interested in the application of statistical techniques to social problems. In 1896 he published an article on "Notes on the history of pauperism in England and Wales from 1850, treated by the method of frequency curves". He had also come across Charles Booth's empirical studies of London poverty and in particular his book *The Aged Poor in England and Wales* (1894).

In 1895 Yule published an article in the *Economic Journal* titled "On the Correlation of Total Pauperism with the Proportion of Out-relief" in which he drew attention to a statement made by Booth in his book to the effect that "The proportion of relief given out of doors bears no relation to the total percentage of pauperism". This was one among many other conclusions "to be drawn from the study and comparison of the official statistics" relating to all the poor law "unions" in England and Wales. Yule, however, drew a scatter plot or "correlation surface" as he called it, for the years 1871 and 1891 showing the numbers of unions combining a given percentage of population in receipt of relief (the rate of pauperism) with the number of out-paupers to one in-pauper (giving the ratio of out-relief to in-relief). Yule's correlation surface clearly showed a marked degree of correlation, but one that was distinctly skewed. Although he realized that, as a result, it was not strictly legitimate to compute Pearson's coefficient of correlation, Yule had no alternative statistics at his disposal. Although, apparently, no great weight could be attached to the value of the coefficient, "its magnitude may at least be suggestive". For 1871, Pearson's r turned out to be 0.26 and for 1891, it was 0.39. Yule concluded that the rate of total pauperism in the unions of England was positively correlated with the proportion of out-relief given, and that this correlation was distinctly greater in 1891 than it had been in 1871.

Yule's results could clearly be used by those who argued that giving more out-relief *caused* a higher level of pauperism; that to reduce the level of pauperism one needed to reduce the proportion of relief given as out-relief. In a later paper published in 1899 titled "An Investigation into the Causes of Changes in Pauperism in England, chiefly during the last two Intercensal Decades", Yule attempted to analyze what *were* the causes of changes in pauperism. However, far from concluding that the correlation between pauperism and level of out-relief could not legitimately be interpreted as one of direct causality, he found, using techniques of multiple regression and correlation, that five-eighths of the decrease in pauperism was "accounted for" simultaneously by changes in out-relief ratio, the proportion of people over 65 and changes in population density. The latter two accounted for relatively small proportions of the changes in pauperism and were themselves being held constant in the equation when the relationship between pauperism and out-relief was being investigated.

Unfortunately, as in 1895, Yule had taken the ratio of out-relief (to in-relief) as the only indicator of "administrative policy". This enabled Yule to conclude: "Unless, and until, then, it can be shown that some other quantity whose changes are closely correlated with changes in out-relief ratio can account for this observed association, there is no alternative to considering the result as indicating a direct influence of change of policy on change of pauperism." Yule, clearly, was no radical, and apparently did not find these conclusions either surprising or unwelcome. If he had, he might have looked at the conditions under which out-relief was given as a prior factor that caused both proportion of out-relief given and levels of recorded pauperism. Yule's values can clearly be seen when he discusses the manner in which out-relief appears to have been affected by changes in the proportion of old in the population. He says: "I have not included changes in pauperism in these equations. Of course, in as much as changes in out-relief ratio helps to estimate changes in pauperism, change in pauperism would help to estimate change in out-relief ratio – it is difficult to imagine any causal relation between the two such that pauperism should influence out-relief ratio." It did not, apparently, even cross Yule's mind that out-relief *should* respond to the level of pauperism! Yule appeared to be more interested in the elegance of his statistical methods than in the humanitarian consequences of his conclusions.

Yule's correlational techniques would clearly have been very useful to Booth in his attempts to establish the causes of poverty, yet there is no evidence that Booth even acknowledged Yule's articles of 1895 and 1899. It was unlikely that Yule, "a courteous, even courtly man", did not at least inform Booth that he had used the latter's data in his 1895 paper, while the later paper appeared in the *Journal of the Royal Statistical Society,* a copy of which Booth would certainly have received as a member of the Society. Even more curious was the fact that Booth's followers made no reference to the developments in statistical methods. Rowntree never made use of correlation in his highly statistical analysis of the causes of poverty even though he had consulted Pearson on several occasions. Bowley, who was a Professor of Statistics at the London School of Economics, wrote a book published in 1909 called *An Elementary Manual of Statistics*, but it contained no reference to Yule, Galton or Pearson. In fact the word "correlation" did not appear in the index and the topic was not covered anywhere in the book (Kent 1981).

KEY POINTS

The purpose of this somewhat lengthy digression into the history of statistics is to show that what have become accepted as mainstream statistical methods were developed for use in experimental designs, not for the analysis of survey or other observational (i.e. nonexperimental) data. As soon as they are applied to social science data and in particular to the search for causal relationships, then, as Yule and Pearson found many years ago, problems in their application arise. The fundamentally altered context of their application has seldom been seriously considered.

The limitations of mainstream statistics

Mainstream statistical methods make three key assumptions which, while perfectly appropriate for the physical world, may be less appropriate when human behavior is involved:

- the focus of the analysis is on variables and the relationships between variables,
- the patterns sought in terms of the relationships between variables are limited largely to establishing differences, covariation or fit with a theoretical expectation,
- the analysis of causality, where it is sought or implied, depends on the establishment of constant conjunction and linear thinking.

The focus on variables

A major assumption of mainstream statistical methods is that variables mirror aspects of the "real" world. However, as we saw in Chapter 5, measurement is a process of translation. The phenomena that are of interest to researchers are translated into variables by pursuing one of four different types of measurement:

- defining the phenomena as the set of values that are being recorded (direct measurement),
- taking an indirect measure of the phenomena (indirect measurement),
- concocting a measure derived from performing some calculation on a number of scaled items (derived measurement),
- recognizing that the phenomena are multifaceted and multidimensional and can only be profiled (multidimensional measurement).

The social scientist can seldom directly observe the phenomenon or behavior that is of interest; in consequence, variables are not reality, but attempts to represent that reality. Olsen and Morgan (2004) call them "ficts" – statistical artifacts that are not necessarily concretely true and are potentially fictional. They have an existence more like a virtual reality. They are researcher creations. They may be inaccurate or even "untrue" as descriptors of reality. As explained in Chapter 8, any research that is based on addressing questions to people and recording their answers risks error resulting from measurement (see Chapter 5), from survey design and execution (see Chapter 7) and from any inadequacies of sampling (see Chapter 8). Survey data records, furthermore, are anonymized and dissociated from the individuals who gave their responses. This means that the context of those responses is lost; accordingly, the interpretations constructed by researchers could well be contested by respondents.

Mainstream statistical methods in effect chop up the complex social world of respondents into variables and recorded values. They take the respondent's multi-faceted experiences, cleanse them of the looseness and "fuzziness" that characterizes everyday knowledge, and refine and classify them into standard form. The process involves translating complex information, views, knowledge, beliefs or attitudes of the respondent into something that is conceptually simple, that may appear as ticks in boxes and that can subsequently be entered into a data matrix as a single item of value. Survey knowledge is produced by entering the responses as a row of values that profile a single respondent and then interpreting these entries in columns across respondents to produce distributions.

Variables, furthermore, are characteristics not of individuals, objects or other kinds of case, but of a *set* of cases. Variables vary between cases and exhibit some kind of distribution of values within a defined set. Characteristics of that distribution relate to the set, not to an individual case. A person does not have an "average" age or a proportion who repeat purchased brand X. Elliott (1999: 101–102) draws an analogy as follows:

While auto/biography may be understood as textual means of establishing identities for individuals, quantitative analysis might be read as establishing identity for a social group defined by variables such as gender and class. In other words, although variables are treated as individual attributes during the data collection phase of survey research, analyses will subsequently be produced by the researcher which offer insights about the determining power of those variables as a social and narrative construction . . . Although variables rather than individuals may become the subjects of the statistician's narrative, it is individuals rather than variables who have the capacity to act and reflect on society.

Byrne (2002) distinguishes between two senses of what we mean by "variable". The idea of a variable as a quantity implies simply that a measurement can or has been made. The variable is what the researcher has defined it to be. Any mathematical calculations performed on variables are purely abstract. However, the idea of a variable as some kind of force implies that something real exists and that empirical engagement with the world involves finding traces or clues of that reality. Byrne argues that variables in this sense do not exist: what exist are complex systems, whether these are individuals, households, organizations, nation states or complex machinery. Variables are only a means of describing the condition of the systems; they are not the system itself. The entity that is the focus of the researcher's attention has, in Chapter 5, been described as the case. A case is a complex system, but it can also be a researcher construction like the small-to-medium enterprise. Systems, then, may have boundaries that are fuzzy, changing, or overlapping, each one composed of nested subsystems, each as complex as the system of which they are part.

The focus on covariation

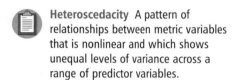

Covariation An overall indication of the extent to which two metric variables are correlated.

When a researcher says that there is **covariation** between two or more variables covary, it means that the distribution of the variables is such that their relationships can be described as either linear (which in statistical parlance means a straight line) or curvilinear. For every unit increase in one or more variables that are accorded the status of independent variable, there is a predictable increase (or decrease) in one or more variables accorded the status of dependent variable. This increase may be fixed over the range by which the independent variables vary, giving a straight line, or it may vary, giving a curved line. If the variables are categorical, then it is the probability, odds or log-odds of being in a given category of the dependent variable, given the category of the independent variable.

Most multivariate techniques work on the basis of assessing the degree of (straight line) linear relationships. Hair et al. (1998: 75) comment:

> *An implicit assumption of all multivariate techniques based on correlational measures of association, including multiple regression, logistic regression, factor analysis, and structural equation modelling, is linearity. Because correlations represent only linear association between variables, non-linear effects will not be represented in the correlation value.*

Heteroscedacity A pattern of relationships between metric variables that is nonlinear and which shows unequal levels of variance across a range of predictor variables.

To most statisticians, "nonlinear" means any pattern other than a straight line, which may be curvilinear or one exhibiting **heteroscedacity** – unequal levels of variance across a range of predictor variables. The most direct remedy to both, according to Hair et al., is data transformation. "If a non-linear relationship is detected, the most direct approach is to transform one or both variables to achieve linearity"; "Heteroscedastic variables can be remedied through data transformations to those used to achieve normality". In short, if the pattern is not a straight line, the solution is to transform the data to *make* it resemble a straight line.

An implication of linearity is that if, for example, the researcher hypothesizes that high values on X (the independent variable) are associated with high values on Y (the dependent variable) *it is also implied that low values on X are associated with low values on Y* – that in fact the data-points on the scattergram will line up near the regression line. In practice, patterns are commonly triangular (Ragin 2000), such that while high values of X are associated with high values of Y, low values of X may be found with a whole range of values for Y, as in Figure 15.1.

Where data are categorical, a parallel situation applies. Conventional measures of association for crosstabulated data assume that the pattern is symmetrical – cases are expected to "lie on the main diagonal", as in Table 15.1. This gives a phi coefficient of 0.96. This means that even the simple "If X then Y" relationship cannot be tested *unless it also implies "if not X then not Y"*. Table 15.2, however, shows a triangular pattern, such that if a case is a member of set X (a heavy television viewer), then he or she is also likely to be a member of set Y (has a large spend on convenience food); *but not being a member of set X implies nothing about membership of Y* (those whose television viewing is not large may or may not have a large spend on convenience food), resulting in a much lower value of phi (0.44), which is really an "average" of what is happening in the table, taking no account of set-membership relationships.

Causality and linear relationships

The objective of most multivariate analysis is to "account for" patterns of differences between three or more variables. Different research objectives, however, give different meanings to the idea of "accounting". The research goal may be to predict differences, scores or categories in one or more dependent variables from one or more independent variables; it may be to "explain" in a statistical sense the extent to which dependent and independent variables covary in some systematic

FIGURE 15.1

A triangular data pattern

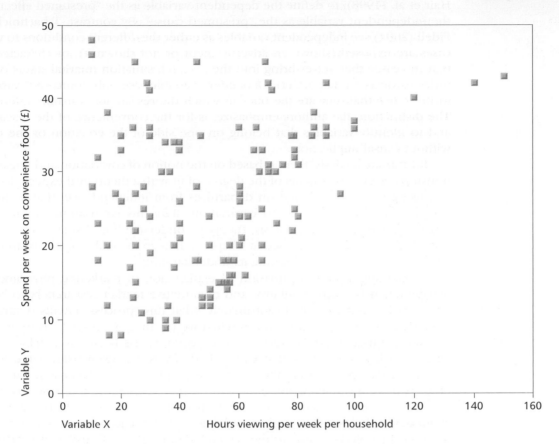

TABLE 15.1 | A symmetrical pattern

Variable Y	Variable X		Total
	Set member	Nonmember	
Set member	49	1	50
Nonmember	1	49	50
Total	50	50	100

Most of the cases are "on the diagonal"

TABLE 15.2 | A triangular pattern

Spend	Television viewing		Total
	Heavy	Not heavy	
Large	54	25	79
Not large	0	25	25
Total	54	50	104

fashion; it may be to generate evidence of causal influences; or it may be to reduce a set of differences or associations between a large set of variables to a smaller set.

Unfortunately, it is common, even in books on multivariate analysis such as by Hair et al. (1998), to define the dependent variable as the "presumed effect" and the independent variable as the "presumed cause". By contrast, Tabachnick and Fidell (2001) see independent variables as either the different conditions to which cases are exposed (shown an advertisement or not shown it), or characteristics that the cases themselves bring into the research situation (marital status or attitudes towards a retail outlet). Dependent variables are only "outcome" variables in the sense that they are the ones in which the researcher is mainly interested. The distinction, the authors emphasize, is for the convenience of the researcher and to identify variables that belong on one side of the equation or the other, without causal implication.

Multivariate analysis, then, is based on the notion of covariation and linear relationships. Even assessments of the degree of fit with a theoretical expectation are, like using Chi-square, based on departures from independence, that is, from a situation in which there is no covariation. *Why* this covariation should occur remains open to further analysis, theory or understanding. Explanation and the notion of causality, as discussed in Chapter 14, lie in the realm of theory and what an audience accepts as furthering its understanding.

The paradigm for the provision of explanation of marketing phenomena is usually taken by both qualitative and quantitative market researchers to be the process of causal analysis. Unfortunately, what this "process" entails is variously interpreted; indeed, what we mean when we say that "X causes Y" is open to an enormous range of possibilities. Historically, there has been fierce debate about what causality is and how it is established. There has even been fierce debate about what the key issues in the debate are about. The classical analyses are those of Aristotle and Hume. Aristotle recognized that people meant a variety of things by "cause". Causes could be material, formal, final or efficient. To Hume a cause is "an object, followed by another, and where all the objects similar to the first are followed by objects similar to the second" (Hume 1911). Causality is a matter of invariable sequence or constant conjunction. Since Hume, the literature on the philosophy of causality is vast, controversial and inconclusive (Abbott 1998).

The modern philosophy of causality – and here it gets tied up with an equally complex literature on the nature of explanation – was set forth by Hempel's (1942) "covering law". This was already hinted at by Hume: where event A is followed by event B this is explained by a covering law of the form that B always follows from A, that is, A causes B. This formulation, however, has been criticized as being either "trivial" or as failing to explain the covering law. Real explanation, so its critics argue, has to make sense of what social actors do. The alternative view of causal processes is based on narrative. Historians, for example, try to get the historical figure's own justification for action to understand what was "reasonable" in the circumstances. Narrative itself is explanatory. The "followability" or plausibility of the story culminates by showing or making it understandable that the outcome was inevitable. Here, events, conditions and motivations are all combined. The thinking about causes is configurational and complex rather than linear and additive. Some will argue that this is a different kind of explanation; it is not causal at all, but interpretive.

In the social sciences the approach to causal analysis has been closely linked to the development of statistical techniques. These have origins in biometrics, psychometrics, and econometrics. It was the biometricians, as explained earlier in this chapter, who developed modern statistical inferential techniques, regression analysis, sampling theory and hypothesis-testing in the late nineteenth and early twentieth centuries. In the context of experimental designs, the notion of causality was reduced to invariant succession. Where it was nonexperimental the role of causality was deemphasized. The psychometricians developed attitude scaling systems and factor analysis, but were even less causally oriented than the biometricians. Factor analysis is a descriptive, interdependence technique that ignores causality altogether. Econometricians were more concerned with questions of sequence, lagged paths, direction and reversibility, but in the main, causality was seen essentially as a matter of uniform association.

Qualitative social scientists, by contrast, were highly critical of what they saw as the "mathematicization" of causal analysis. Causality had to be linked to reality, which meant to social action; but their concept of causality was probably closer to what would be understood by many as the process of explanation. Causality was seen as a way of understanding and explaining particular action in particular local settings. The discovery of more general laws and regularities had more to do with covering laws and theories.

Over the following years, however, despite these debates, the position adopted by most social scientists has come to embody a particular stance within these debates; cause involves a degree of "forcing" or determination and it is sequential – the cause must come before the effect. Causality is, furthermore, typically seen by quantitative researchers in particular as both linear and additive. Linearity entails the notion that the relationship between two or more variables takes the form of, or approximates, a straight line. This means that statistical techniques like correlation, regression and crosstabular analysis can be used to detect causation. Additivity implies that each independent variable makes a fixed contribution to the dependent variable and that these contributions can be added up. This justifies the common practice of apportioning causality in chunks, for example, that the decision to drop a product from the range is 35 percent determined by product diversity, 20 percent by company turnover and 15 percent by product line management policy. Such conclusions may be derived from multiple regression techniques.

Causality is now seen by most quantitative researchers as a property of mathematical and statistical propositions rather than a property of real social action (Abbott 1998). It is a mathematical framework to assist our understanding; it is not reality itself. Unfortunately, this caveat is frequently forgotten and researchers have come to believe that social and market activities look the way they do because forces and properties "do" things to other forces and properties. Sometimes these forces and properties are individual characteristics like gender and age or individual actions like brand selection. Sometimes they are "macro" forces and properties like population density or company mergers. Researchers call these forces and properties "variables". Hypothesizing which variables affected other variables is called "causal analysis". Textbooks and university courses in research methods have come to emphasize this variable-centered approach. Lip-service or scant attention is paid to the concept of causality; it is simply a matter of collecting evidence for association, temporal order and lack of spuriousness.

More recent thinking about the concept of causality has rediscovered Aristotle's original idea that there are several different types of causal link. Furthermore, it is increasingly being argued that most social systems are characterized by causal complexity in which relationships are nonlinear, nonadditive, contingent, conjunctural, or interdependent. By the time he came to write the third edition of his book, Zetterberg in 1965 included a lengthy analysis of varieties of linkage between determinants and results, distinguishing between reversible and irreversible relations, deterministic and probabilistic relations, sequential and coextensive relations, sufficient and contingent relations, and necessary and substitutable relations.

Mathematical formalism is often used to express some kind of reality, but first, argues Dennis (1995), some "extra-mathematical content" must be imputed. This, in principle, is supplied by "theory". To engage in mathematical activity is merely to perform a set of logical operations on abstract variables. The economist's production function – the quantity of a product demanded is a "function" of the price of the products – means something like: If a firm increases its input of labor then the firm will increase its output in some systematic and predictable way, *ceteris paribus*. This, says Fleetwood (2001), is allowing a presumption of causality to be "smuggled" into the mathematical expression: a change in the input of labor *causes* a change in output. The notion of causality being used is, furthermore, limited to the idea of constant conjunction: whenever event X, then event Y. The external world is, on this view, characterized by event regularity. Constant junction can occur, however, only within closed systems, as in an experimental design that isolates the interesting mechanism or by use of the *ceteris paribus* clause, which assumes that others things do not change (when in reality, of course, particularly in the social world, they always do).

In mainstream variable-centered statistical methods it is the variables that do the acting. Causality is established when one variable is seen to "do" something to another variable. Cases in effect do very little. They are made uniform; they are treated not as complex entities whose character is simplified by the model – but as characterless "units of analysis" that have been "complexified" by the properties selected by the researcher (Abbott 1992). Cases have lost their identity, their complexity and their narrative order that describes each as a story (Abbott 1992). Within a set of cases, there may, indeed, be patterns of various kinds; but although individuals can act as agents, "causing" things to happen, variables are sets of values with distributions that might covary with other distributions or show some other kind of pattern: they are not and cannot, strictly speaking, act as causal agents. Social status cannot "do" anything to repeat purchase; both are distributions of records accessed or constructed by the researcher.

Variable-centered analysis is, then, incompatible with any demonstration of causality, unless "causality" is *defined* in terms of a demonstration of covariation, temporal sequence and lack of spuriousness, in which case causality is a convenient shorthand for describing certain kinds of pattern, a convenient fiction.

KEY POINTS

The statistical techniques familiar to most researchers, statistics that are here described as "mainstream", whether they are univariate, bivariate, multivariate, whether they are descriptive or inferential, are all variable-centered. Patterns of relationships between variables are seen largely in terms of covariation, while the analysis of causality, where it is sought or implied, depends on the establishment of constant conjunction and linear thinking. Mainstream techniques can be effective and parsimonious, and may well help to solve problems. Indeed they should be tried first. However, patterns are sometimes not found, or support for hypothesized patterns may be weak. Relationships between variables may be "statistically significant", but, as was explained in Chapter 13, if based on large samples, the effect size could be tiny. Patterns may not be found because there are no patterns; but it may be because only certain kinds of pattern are being sought. Researchers, furthermore, want more than just to discover patterns: they want explanations. This is usually interpreted to mean establishing cause and effect relationships. Ironically, mainstream statistics are not well suited to this task. They can at best only provide evidence based on covariation, temporal sequence and lack of spuriousness. Unless cause and effect relationships are defined in these terms, mainstream statistics are too focused on variables to establish how actions performed by individuals have consequences and are themselves a product of very complex factors.

Nonlinear variable analysis alternatives

A line is a line whether straight or curved in various ways; there is still some kind of sequence or direction involved. While making curved lines straight before applying linear regression to them may be statistically defensible, it will neverthe-less tend to overlook "nonlinearity" in other senses. Other possibilities might include relationships between variables that are not sequential, but inter-dependent, networked, contingent, parallel or chaotic in a manner described by chaos theory. If you are interested, Box 15.1 gives a brief overview of chaos theory.

Chaos theory Describes a system in which minute changes in some initial conditions can bring about very large fluctuations in the outcome.

IN DETAIL
Chaos theory

BOX 15.1

In a chaotic system, minute changes in some initial conditions can, over a period of time – or even after a fairly limited number of iterations – bring about very large fluctuations in the outcome. This is the so-called butterfly effect, in which in principle a butterfly flapping its wings in one part of the world will in due course produce storms some months later in another part of the world. The effects are not random, but deterministic, but so complex that they are unpredictable. Lorenz originally discovered this phenom-enon in 1963 when he re-ran some data on the weather in a computer simulation program by re-inputting printout results that were accurate to 8 significant digits rather than the 16 used internally by the computer. Re-inputting data produced very different outcomes because some measures differed on the ninth or subsequent significant digit.

This extreme sensitivity to starting conditions is brought about by a process of bifurcation. If condi-tion A might result in either outcome B or outcome C, there may be extremely small changes in some characteristic of A (maybe at the 16th significant digit) that affect which outcome occurs. After several bifurcations, the system becomes quite unpredictable. It has become chaotic – there is a very large number of possible outcomes. If the system can be characterized in terms of n-dimensions then state (or phase) space is all possible states in which a system might theoretically exist. The trajectories that systems in practice follow, however, are not random. To be truly random, each possible configuration in state space would, in the long run, be equally represented. In fact the actual trajectories through which systems move and gravitate towards are fairly limited. In chaos theory these are the strange attractors. Order may be discernible in the apparent chaos. The pattern of bifurcation, furthermore, appears to be orderly. Systems can move into and out of chaos depending on the value of a controlling constant. In a simple logistic equation in which the value of the variable of interest in the next time period is deter-mined by the value in the current time period and a constant, then it can be shown that when the value of the constant reaches 3, the system becomes unstable and oscillates between two equilibrium states. Between 3.57 and 4 it becomes chaotic with an infinite number of fixed points with different periodicities between bifurcations.

At the center of chaos theory, then, is the discovery that hidden within the unpredictability of chaotic systems are deep or emergent structures of order. Chaotic systems often appear to be random, unpre-dictable, disorganized or erratic, but often develop in ways such that the number of possible outcomes is constrained. Systems may be perfectly deterministic, but impossible to predict. According to Parker and Stacey (1994) chaos is a mixture of order and disorder, of regularity and irregularity. Systems move in self-organizing ways with emergent and unpredictable outcomes. The significance of the chaos/complexity approach lies in the recognition that while there is no singular outcome or answer, no linear law, we can nevertheless analyze in order to see what the possible set of outcomes might be and possibly intervene in order to achieve or make more likely those we want to happen.

Smith (2002), who suggests three scenarios for applying chaos theory in consumer research, reviews the literature on social science chaos research and concludes that while there is some limited evidence of discussion concerning the broad potential for chaos theory in marketing, most of the published literature has remained speculative. Some studies have used test data to explore chaotic modeling techniques, but these, suggests Smith (2002), are arguably also part of the exploratory and speculative effort. To date, he says, there is little or no evidence of chaos theory being used to inform empirical investigations using acquired data in the marketing area. More recently Holbrook (2003) in an online *Academy of Marketing Science Review* has comprehensively reviewed the literature on complexity and chaos theory that might be of relevance to marketing.

A linear *thinker* sees the world as being composed of parts (components, elements, subsystems and so on) that can be separated from one another and analyzed independently. Relationships between the parts are stable – therefore predicable – even if those relationships are contingent on what is happening elsewhere in the system. Thus even if the relationship between variable A and variable B is contingent upon the values for variable C, then provided this is known, the system is predictable. Nonlinear thinking, by contrast, allows for fuzzy boundaries between systems and for emergent properties – there may, for example, be a dynamic in the system that makes it unstable, unpredictable and, in an extreme case, chaotic.

Data analysis methods that are still variable-centered, but which allow for nonlinearity in the above sense might include:

- neural network analysis,
- some data mining techniques,
- Bayesian statistics.

Neural network analysis

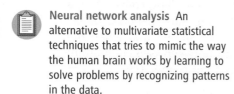

Neural network analysis An alternative to multivariate statistical techniques that tries to mimic the way the human brain works by learning to solve problems by recognizing patterns in the data.

Node A key element in a neural network multilayer model that accepts a number of inputs from other nodes.

Neural networks are essentially pattern recognition devices. The main difference between conventional and neural computing is the learning process. With the former, standard procedures, usually in the form of fixed-form equations, are entered by programmers. These are then applied to the data. Because it is an algorithm, it will give the same answers every time if data are repeatedly fed in. The onus is on the user to make sure that the procedure is the correct one to use.

Neural network analysis, by contrast, can learn to solve a problem, and produce a model, by using the properties of the data themselves. The neural network is "trained" on an appropriate set of data examples, but the modeling process is data-led. The model will progressively change to fit the data. Neural networks tend to be more robust and fault-tolerant than traditional methods. They are better at handling noisy, incomplete or contradictory data. For example, the existence of outliers can severely handicap a traditional technique, but neural networks can handle them quite easily. Neural networks are not subject to the key assumptions of mainstream statistical methods in terms of linearity, normality and completeness. Furthermore, they can capture the structured complexity of a dynamic process in the reality and can do so with imperfect datasets.

There are three basic types of neural networks: the multilayer perceptron model, which is the most commonly used, the radial basis function, which is a more recent development, and the Kohonen model, which is appropriate only for clustering problems.

The main element in a neural network multilayer perceptron model is a **node** (or neuron), which is analogous to the neuron of the human brain. This accepts a number of inputs from other nodes. Each connection with another node has an assigned weight, which is multiplied by each input value and summated in the same way that multivariate methods do in creating a composite variable. The summed value is then processed by an activation function to generate an output value, which is sent to the next node in the system.

The neural network is a sequential arrangement of three basic types of node: input, output and intermediate or hidden nodes (see Figure 15.2). An input node represents a single variable and receives initial data values from each case. Categorical variables need to be created into dummy variables. The hidden nodes are used by the neural network to represent more complex relationships. This, and the activation function, which is generally a nonlinear S-shaped function, allows neural networks to represent nonlinear relationships. Each node acts independently, but in parallel with all of the other nodes.

The key feature of a neural network that sets it apart from other multivariate techniques is its ability to learn or correct itself. The weights attached to the inputs act as a memory. Errors are distributed back through the system and the weights are changed proportionally, increasing or decreasing according to the direction of the error. Once all the weights have been recalibrated, the input for another case is entered and the process begins all over again. A large number of cases are passed through the network in this training phase so that it can make the best predictions across all the input data patterns.

The steps involved in doing a neural network analysis include, first, deciding on a training sample of cases used to estimate the weights, and a separate validation sample to assess the predictive ability of the model. There need to be 10–30 cases in the training sample for every weight being estimated. The next step is to examine the data for skewness, nonnormality and outliers. The third step is to define the model structure. Since the inputs and outputs are already selected, the decision is in effect to determine the number of nodes in the hidden layer. The consensus is that there should be only one layer of hidden nodes and the researcher should try to find the best fit with the minimum number of nodes.

The fourth step is model estimation. This is an iterative procedure and the overall optimum solution may not be found. The goal is to achieve the best overall fit and yet not over-train the model with too many cases. The next step is to evaluate the model results against the predictions or classifications made. This uses the validation sample mentioned earlier. Finally, after the network has been trained and validated, the resulting model may be applied to data it has not seen previously for prediction, classification, time series analysis or data segmentation.

One of the most common uses of neural networks in marketing is with classification problems – deciding to which group a classification belongs. This, according to Hair et al. (1998), corresponds to a discriminant or logistic regression problem.

FIGURE 15.2

A multilayer neural network

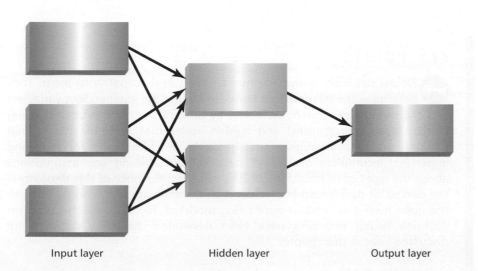

Input layer   Hidden layer   Output layer

Using the same data, the authors compared a two-group discriminant analysis with four different levels of neural network sophistication (using more hidden layer nodes). The classification accuracy for the discriminant model was 97.5 percent. The simplest neural network model with four nodes achieved an 80 percent accuracy, with six nodes a 90 percent accuracy and 100 percent for eight nodes and a model with two layers of hidden layers with four nodes each. The advantage of neural networks is therefore not dramatic. Zahavi and Levin (1997), in fact, found that neural networks learned by the multilayer perceptron model did not perform any better than logistic regression.

Applications of neural networks in marketing have included market segmentation, direct marketing, new product development, sales forecasting and target marketing (Cui and Wong 2004). They have been used to predict bankruptcy and loan default (Zhang et al. 1999) and modeling consumer choice behavior and advertising responses (West et al. 1997).

SPSS offers a special piece of software, Neural Connection, which allows users to run an unlimited number of cases once the model has been validated. Box 15.2 shows how neural network analysis was used to segment the French market for small cars.

EUROPEAN MARKETING RESEARCH | BOX 15.2
Customer segmentation in the automobile market in France

Yahiaoui and Dias (1997) report the use of neural networks for customer segmentation in the automobile market in France. Based on a survey of 1000 French small-car buyers, covering characteristics of the new car, the usage made, the importance attached to characteristics like comfort and handling, 30 items concerning attitudes towards the car and a range of demographics, the researchers applied a multilayer perceptron model. They began with 64 raw entry variables, but found that two hidden nodes gave satisfactory results with respect to the explanation of product choice. The new mediating variables, representing the small-car buyers on a limited number of dimensions, were then entered into a different type of neural network, called Neural Gas, which provided an automatic clustering procedure. This enabled the researchers to establish several different segments of French small-car buyers, for example, the "price-minded", the "families", the "innovators", the "aspiring to mid-size", the "seniors" and the "demanding".

KEY POINTS

Neural networks mimic the human brain in its capacity to learn. They determine the relationships between inputs (the independent variables) and the output (dependent variables) by building network structures using hidden layers (perceptrons) and hidden nodes that resemble the human thinking process. Although neural networks are ideal tools for modeling imperfect, incomplete or "noisy" data without making any assumptions about the types of relationships among variables, the price of this flexibility is the danger of over-fitting the model with the training data, ending up with the noise itself and random error being modeled. To overcome this problem Bayesian neural networks have been developed. Bayesian statistics are discussed later in this chapter.

Data mining

The raw material for data mining is derived from transaction processing systems, for example from ATMs, web servers, point-of-sale scanners, call center records, billing systems, registration and application forms – in fact every transaction creates a record (Berry and Linoff 1997). These records are not usually generated with data mining in mind; rather they are created to meet operational needs. Customer-focused companies see each of these records as an opportunity to learn about customers, but the various sources first need to be gathered together and organized in a consistent and useful way. This is done in a data warehouse. Most of the patterns in customer needs, behaviors and attitudes become evident only over time, so it is important for data warehouses to be able to track consumers on a continuous basis. The result is that the data stored in these systems is vast.

The central idea behind data mining is that these mountains of data can be used to create knowledge that can be used to manage customer relationships. Its goal is to find patterns in historical data. A range of tools are used for this purpose. Most of these are concerned with building models; these are algorithms that connect data inputs to a particular target or outcome.

Data mining according to Berry and Linoff (1997) can perform six key tasks:

- classification,
- estimation,
- prediction,
- affinity grouping,
- clustering,
- description and profiling.

Classification consists of examining the features of each newly presented case and assigning it to one of a set of classes. Where researchers have used categorical scaling of some kind, these classes are predefined and mainstream statistics can be used to display or summarize key features of the frequency distribution. Beyond this a researcher may use a particular algorithm that combines classifications to create a new set of categories, for example using responses to an application form to classify applicants as low, medium or high risk. Provided some arbitrary scoring system for the categories was used, derived measurement could be achieved and totals summarized in the standard way, for example by calculating averages, standard deviations, or grouping into class intervals. However, if the researcher wanted to work backwards from customers who defaulted to characteristics they had in common, then data mining techniques like decision trees or neural networks might be useful.

While the outcome of classification is a discrete category, in estimation it is an unknown metric value, like the lifetime value of a customer, or a household's total income where these are unknown. Mainstream statistical methods like multiple regression may be perfectly adequate for this task, but where it may be necessary to "learn" from past records, for example of customer purchase histories, then, once again, neural networks may be helpful.

Prediction is the same as classification or estimation, except that the outcome refers to some future behavior (like returning a product) or a metric value, like how long it will take to deliver an order. Data mining techniques will use "training" examples where the value of the variable to be predicted is already known.

The objective of affinity grouping is to determine which objects or services customers treat as going together. The result is a set of association rules of the form "If a customers buys product A she will, with a given probability, also by product B".

With clustering, it is the cases that are grouped together, but unlike classification, there are no predefined classes. Cases are grouped together following an iterative procedure on a range of measures of similarity. Cluster analysis was explained in Chapter 14.

While mainstream statistics can be used for data mining, there are important differences between statisticians and data miners:

■ there are lots of data, very often on every case or every transaction, so sampling and the use of statistical inference is less important,

■ data miners tend to ignore measurement error,

■ almost all data used for data mining have time-dependency associated with them,

■ data used for data mining are often incomplete or truncated.

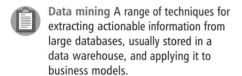

Data mining A range of techniques for extracting actionable information from large databases, usually stored in a data warehouse, and applying it to business models.

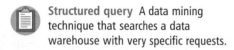

Structured query A data mining technique that searches a data warehouse with very specific requests.

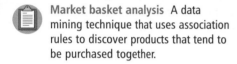

Market basket analysis A data mining technique that uses association rules to discover products that tend to be purchased together.

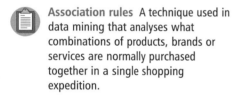

Association rules A technique used in data mining that analyses what combinations of products, brands or services are normally purchased together in a single shopping expedition.

Data mining can and does use mainstream statistical techniques, including all the techniques explained in Chapters 11–14. In addition, it may use a number of extra tools. Some of these are standard tools used elsewhere, outside the context of data mining, for example decision trees and neural networks. Others are more specific to data mining, and include some of the following procedures.

Structured query. This is a way of searching the data warehouse with very specific requests, for example "How many buyers of brand A are in social classes A, B or C1 with children below the age of 16 and who have also purchased brand B?" By making repeated queries, researchers may be able to identify patterns.

Market basket analysis and **association rules**. This uses information about what customers buy to provide insight into who they are, why they make certain purchases, which products tend to be bought together, and which ones are amenable to promotion. The results can, for example, suggest new store layouts or what products might respond well to special offers. Market basket analysis uses several techniques, but the most common one is association rules. A simple rule might be of the form: "If a customer buys products A and B then he or she will buy product C".

Box 15.3 illustrates how data mining association rules were used to profile hotel customers in South Korea.

EUROPEAN MARKETING RESEARCH

BOX 15.3

Luxury hotels in South Korea

Min et al. (2002) used association rules to profile hotel customers. The researchers wanted to know:

■ which customers were likely to return to the same hotel as repeat guests,
■ which customers were at greatest risk of defecting to competing hotels,
■ which service attributes are more important to which customers,
■ how to segment customers into profitable and unprofitable groups,
■ which segment best fits the current service capabilities of the client hotel.

The sample consisted of 281 hotel guests who had stayed at 11 different luxury hotels in Seoul, South Korea. A questionnaire covered hotel use, travel, importance of service attributes, level of satisfaction and demographics. The authors extracted association rules using decision-trees and the SPSS data mining software Clementine. Some 50 different "If . . . then", rules were developed. To reduce this set, a minimum predictive accuracy of 80 percent was selected. An example of one of the rules is: "If a customer has stayed at the Plaza hotel for more than five nights then the customer is likely to revisit the same hotel more than five times".

KEY POINTS

Data mining is not so much a particular analytical technique or even a special set of techniques, but more an approach to data analysis. It is one that emphasizes an exploratory mode structured around very loose research questions, like "What factors affect customer retention?" There are no hypotheses to be tested nor any statistical inferences to be made. What characterizes the data mining approach is the search for patterns, not just covariational ones, but also combinatorial patterns. The use of combinatorial logic is considered in more detail below.

Bayesian statistics

Mainstream statistical methods use probability in a distributional sense, for example the probability of obtaining a random sample result from a population in which there is no difference or covariation given a theoretical sampling distribution. **Bayesian statistics** use what might be called "event" probability, which relates to the probability of some future event occurring. This may reflect a subjective probability – a degree of belief that an event will happen – or it may be based on the known frequency of past events, so if 12 percent of products on a production line have historically had a defect, then the probability that the next product will be defective is 0.12.

Instead of accepting or rejecting hypotheses, as in mainstream statistics, Bayes's theorem mathematically incorporates prior probabilities into the current data or evidence to reassess the probability that a hypothesis is true. It is a formalization of what managers tend to do intuitively anyway: factoring prior knowledge, hunch, and subjective probabilities into the assessment of the evidence. The use of Bayesian analysis as a mechanism for updating prior knowledge with new data is very complex statistically, but some approaches have embraced Bayesian *thinking*, more as a metaphor. Smith and Fletcher (2004), however, suggest integrating traditional p-values with prior probabilities using a very simple version of Bayes's formula.

Bayesian analysis has not been greatly used in marketing largely because the mathematics is very complicated. Bayesian simulation, however, is able, through computational brute force, to solve the complex calculus needed. According to Retzer (2006) the biggest impact of Bayesian methods in marketing has been in the area of discrete choice conjoint analysis, applying a method that is referred to as hierarchical Bayesian.

Bayesian statistics The incorporation of prior probabilities, which may be subjectively determined, into the current data or evidence to reassess the probability that a hypothesis is true.

Case-based analysis and combinatorial logic

Knowing the statistical "contribution" made by particular independent variables to a dependent variable often does not tell users of the data what they want to know. It does not, for example, analyze what alternative sets of *combinations* of factors give rise to an outcome, or which factors may operate as necessary or sufficient conditions. Instead of treating cases as identical except for the variation in specified dimensions, an alternative is to see each case as a particular combination of characteristics – as a configuration. Only cases with identical configurations can be seen as the "same" type of case. Instead of looking for variation in the values of variables in isolation from the context in which those values occur, the researcher now looks for diversity. The size and even direction of the impact of any particular value (like having a large product range) on an outcome (like product elimination decisions) may depend on the context of a whole set of other characteristics (like the size of the organization, its turnover, its return on investments and so on). Quantitative data will still be laid out as a case-by-case variable data matrix, but instead of focusing on the columns, summarizing and relating them together, the researcher focuses on the rows, showing, for example, how outcomes (like the product elimination decision) are associated with particular combinations of features. How this is done is explained in the next section. The important point here is that each case is taken as a coherent whole. It has to be understood and made sense of as a package all at once. A change in any one characteristic potentially makes it a different kind of case.

If a set of cases is characterized by, for example, just three binary (presence/absence) categories, then there will be 2^k theoretically possible combinations of all causal variables where k is the number of attributes entailed. Thus cases characterized by three attributes may form up to eight different configurations. With four attributes, this goes up to 16 and so on. The results can be listed in a "truth table" (see Table 15.3), which shows the number of cases that possess each logically possible combination of causal variables and the outcome. Thus there are 30 cases where all three factors X_1, X_2 and X_3 are all present and where the outcome has occurred.

Each row of the truth table is the equivalent of a single cell in a multiway crosstabulation of three binary independent variables with the number of instances of each combination equaling the frequency. From this perspective, variables are no longer isolated, analytically distinct aspects of cases, but rather components of configurations that allow the researcher to generate different types of case.

It is now possible to examine the *logical* relationships between the outcome being present and the presence of various combinations of factors. In particular it is possible to ask:

- What factors are found in all instances of the phenomenon being studied?
- Is that phenomenon always present when particular factors or combinations of factors arise?

The first establishes that in all cases where the outcome occurs, these factors (which may be characteristics, events or presumed causes) are present – they are necessary conditions. The second establishes that in all cases where the factors occur, the outcome is present – they are sufficient conditions. A single factor may be necessary, but not sufficient – having a higher degree may be a necessary condi-

TABLE 15.3		A truth table			
Configuration	Cause X_1	Cause X_2	Cause X_3	Frequency	Outcome Y
1	1	1	1	30	1
2	1	1	0	15	1
3	1	0	0	5	1
4	1	0	1	12	0
5	0	1	1	2	0
6	0	1	0	5	0
7	0	0	1	0	NA
8	0	0	0	14	0

1 = CAUSE/OUTCOME PRESENT, 0 = CAUSE/OUTCOME ABSENT, NA = NOT APPLICABLE.

tion for being a university lecturer, but not all those with higher degrees are university lecturers. Alternatively, a factor may be sufficient, but not necessary. In all cases where a student studies hard, the exam performance is good. However, some students do well for other reasons. A single factor may, of course, be neither necessary nor sufficient.

However, social phenomena are seldom the outcome of a single factor, so the researcher should look for combinations of factors that jointly *are* sufficient. If a single condition is both necessary and sufficient then this is one situation where traditional variable-centered statistics would produce a perfect correlation if there are no counter-instances. In reality, of course, there are always counter instances or exceptions – cases that challenge claims of either necessity or sufficiency. Such cases may arise for a whole variety of reasons, but it is possible to introduce probabilistic statements into the analysis so that the researcher could say, for example, that having a higher degree is "almost always" or "usually" necessary to be a lecturer or that studying hard is "almost always" or "usually" sufficient to ensure good examination performance.

Generating a truth table with a limited number of binary variables can be undertaken using multiway crosstabulation (or "layering") in SPSS. However, larger numbers of variables considerably complicate this process and to generate which variables are necessary conditions and which are sufficient requires considerable computing power. Ragin (1987), however, suggested a technique that he called qualitative comparative analysis (QCA) for which, with Drass (Drass and Ragin 1992), he developed a computer program based on Boolean algebra. This uses crisp-set binary data that incorporates presence–absence dichotomies for both causal and outcome variables. It generates a truth table of all logical combinations and the frequency of their occurrence; but it also looks at *groupings* of combinations. Thus for three binary variables, besides the 2^k or 8 theoretically possible combinations, there will also be 6 groupings of combinations that share a single characteristic and 12 that share two of the three characteristics, totaling 26 in all (see Table 15.4). The formula is 3^k-1 where k is the number of attributes.

The program now checks:

1 for all those cases that display the outcome whether any single cause or combination of causes is always (or nearly always, using probabilistic criteria) present to establish causal necessity and

2 for every logically possible 3k−1 groupings of causal conditions whether the outcome is always present (or nearly always present) to establish sufficiency.

It should be clear from visual inspection of Table 15.3 that in all cases where the outcome (Y) is present then factor X_1 is present – it is a necessary condition, but it is not sufficient since in configuration 4 the cause X_1 is present, but the outcome is absent. Table 15.4 shows the remaining groupings of configurations. While X_1 on its own is not sufficient, when combined with X_2 or the absence of X_3, these are jointly sufficient. To operate the QCA program the researcher must establish how many cases in each combination are needed to establish sufficiency and whether the presence of any contradictory cases (indicated as "C" in Table 15.4) undermines the sufficiency argument. The program then uses Boolean addition and Boolean multiplication, combinatorial logic and a process of simplification (finding the smallest number of combinations of variables that occur in conjunction with the outcome) to determine the most parsimonious expression of necessary and sufficient causes. Notice, for example, that the 30 cases of configuration 1 are "contained" in the 45 cases on configuration 9. To say that X_1 and X_2 are jointly sufficient also contains cases where X_3 is also present (plus the 15 cases where X_3 is absent – its absence or presence makes no difference to the outcome).

QCA is a holistic strategy that can handle causal complexity in a systematic manner. It allows for the possibility that an outcome may be produced by several

TABLE 15.4		Groupings of combinations			
Configuration	Cause X_1	Cause X_2	Cause X_3	Frequency	Outcome Y
9	1	1		45	1
10	1	0		17	C
11	0	1		7	0
12	0	0		14	0
13	1		1	42	C
14	1		0	20	1
15	0		1	2	0
16	0		0	19	0
17		1	1	32	C
18		1	0	20	C
19		0	1	12	0
20		0	0	19	C
21	1			62	C
22	0			21	0
23		1		52	C
24		0		31	C
25			1	44	C
26			0	39	C

1 = CAUSE/OUTCOME PRESENT, 0 = CAUSE/OUTCOME ABSENT, C = CONTRADICTION.

different combinations of characteristics and that an individual characteristic may have different effects on the outcome depending on what other events or conditions it is combined with. In traditional analyses these differential effects get averaged out across a variety of contexts. Covariation (or patterns "on the diagonal") cannot distinguish between necessity and sufficiency. Furthermore, where the degree of covariation is small – as it tends to be, even if the results are shown to be "statistically significant", then it makes little sense to talk about necessity or sufficiency at all. Researchers using conventional techniques almost never examine potential causal combinations, but causes in reality tend to be multiple and to be conjunctural, so only looking for combinations of causes can help the researcher uncover the logical relationships between variables.

There are, however, a number of limitations to QCA analysis:

- ▨ it is limited to binary variables, that is, "crisp" sets of absence–presence characteristics,

- ▨ it can cope with only a limited number of variables in one "pass" at the data – more than about 12 variables and the number of combinations and groupings gets very large, so that, for example for 15 variables there are $3^{15}-1$ or over 14 million groupings,

- ▨ there needs to be a clear outcome or event that is being investigated and the key variables in their possible explanation need to be known and understood,

- ▨ if the cases are a random sample from a wider population, there is no procedure for testing the statistical significance of the results.

Fuzzy set analysis

Qualitative comparative analysis depends on having crisp binary sets. Most categorizations used in marketing, however, are not well-defined; they are imprecise, vague, uncertain, ambiguous – in short, fuzzy – and cases tend to exhibit degrees of membership of categories like "loyal customer" or "innovative organization". Fuzzy sets extend crisp sets by permitting membership scores in the interval between 1 and 0. This means either taking binary categories and overlaying them with carefully calibrated measures of the extent to which cases are "in" or "out" of a set (for example, a "satisfied" customer) or, for continuous metric scales, overlaying the scale with conceptually appropriate criteria of what "full membership", "partial membership" and "nonmembership" of a set entails (for example, how many units of alcohol per week classify a person as a "heavy" drinker). The result is that they are binary and metric at the same time. They combine categorical and metric assessments in a single instrument. They consist of two sets – membership and nonmembership of a category – and all the quantitative variation that exists between them. They distinguish between cases that are "more in" a set than others with a crossover point (of 0.5) for those who are neither in nor out – the point of maximum ambiguity.

Fuzzy sets have at least three values (e.g. 1.0 = fully in; 0.5 = neither in nor out; 0.0 = fully out), but may have more (e.g. 1.0 = fully in; 0.75 = more in than out; 0.5 = neither in nor out; 0.25 = mostly out and 0.0 = fully out, see Figure 15.3) or they may be continuous. What makes sense depends on the nature of the concept. Fine-grained distinctions are not always possible or even sensible theoretically. The conceptual midpoint of every fuzzy set is 0.5. This, Ragin (2000) emphasizes, is a qualitatively defined anchor, not an arithmetical mean or average. The distinction between "high" and "low" scores in conventional analysis is data-driven and sample-specific. In fuzzy set analysis these designations are specific to theoretical and conceptual criteria established by the researcher, who has to decide, for example, what being a "heavy" viewer of television entails.

Fuzzy logic emanated from the University of California in the 1960s and is mainly associated with the work of Zadeh (1965). The range of its application is ever-expanding, but most of the literature is concerned with the problems of control – how to develop machines that "act smart" in the face of ambiguity or complexity. More recently, fuzzy logic has been applied to information processing, financial dealing, computing and artificial intelligence (Stotts and Kleiner 1995). In the social sciences, although elements of fuzzy logic have been empirically investigated by cognitive psychologists (e.g. Hersch and Caramazza 1976; Zimmerman and Zysno 1980) for the most part, researchers have been slow to utilize or even evaluate it. Ragin (2000) has applied fuzzy set analysis mainly in the context of macrolevel sociological comparative analysis using small numbers of cases. There is no reason, however, why it cannot be applied at the micro level and to marketing data in particular.

The use of fuzzy sets enables the researcher to draw conclusions about logical relationships, as with QCA, but without having to reduce all the data to crisp binary sets. The analysis, ironically, now becomes sharper. If membership scores for each case concerning the causal factor are plotted against membership scores

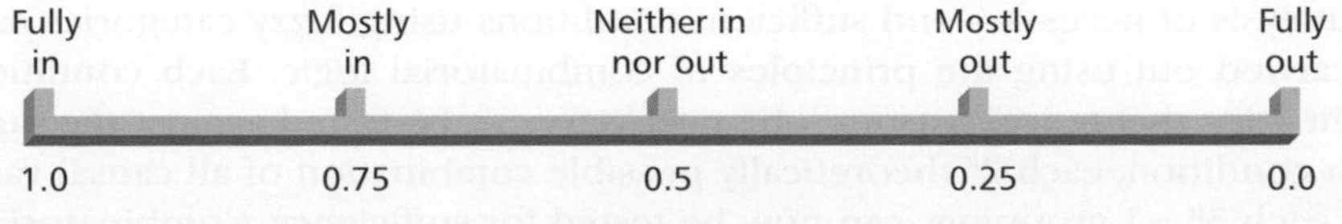

Fully in	Mostly in	Neither in nor out	Mostly out	Fully out
1.0	0.75	0.5	0.25	0.0

FIGURE 15.3

Fuzzy set membership: a five-value set

FIGURE 15.4

A fuzzy-set necessary but not sufficient condition

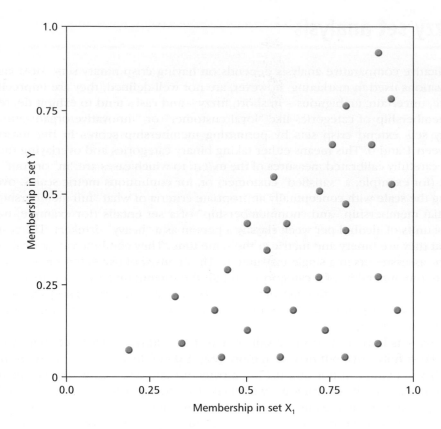

for the outcome, the result of a necessary, but not sufficient condition would look like Figure 15.4. High membership on Y (the outcome) presupposes high membership on X_1, but high membership on X_1 does not ensure high membership on Y and may be accompanied by high or low Y. Membership of X_1 is a necessary, but not sufficient, condition for membership of Y. Ragin (2000) argues that we can be even more precise and say that the degree of membership of X_1 *sets a ceiling* on the degree of membership of Y. In this situation, membership of Y must always be *less than or equal to* membership on X_1 – scores, in short, are below the diagonal. The extent of membership of the category "has a higher degree" (somebody may, for example, have completed the degree but does not yet know the result of the dissertation component) sets a ceiling to the extent to which a person is a member of the category "university lecturer" (he or she may be offered only casual employment or be put on probation).

The result of a sufficient but not necessary condition would look like Figure 15.5. High membership of the cause (X_1) ensures – *acts as a floor* for – high membership of the outcome (Y), but since it is not a necessary condition, then high membership of Y can come about in other ways, so high membership of Y may be accompanied by a wide range of scores on X_1. In this situation, membership of Y must always be *greater than or equal to* membership on X_1. The degree of membership of the category "studying hard" for an exam ensures a minimum membership of the category "good exam performance", but high grades may be achieved in other ways – being lucky in predicting the topics that come up, cheating or just being very bright.

Analysis of necessary and sufficient conditions using fuzzy categories can now be carried out using the principles of combinatorial logic. Each condition that might – for theoretical reasons – be necessary can be tested against the outcome. Each condition, each 2^k theoretically possible combination of all causal variables, and each $3^k - 1$ groupings can now be tested for sufficiency. Combinatorial fuzzy

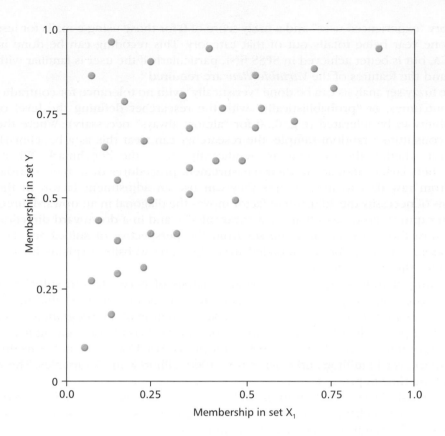

FIGURE 15.5

A fuzzy-set sufficient but not necessary condition

scores are added using Boolean algebra. This means, for example, taking the *minimum* fuzzy score in each of the sets being combined. If a person is 0.8 in the category "satisfied customer" and 0.6 in the category "loyal customer", then he or she is 0.6 in the combined category "satisfied and loyal customer".

One further refinement to be derived from using fuzzy sets is that instead of cases being defined as belonging or not belonging to a population, *they may now belong to different degrees*. Even those cases with only partial membership, for example "motorists" who drive only occasionally, can now be included instead of being dismissed as nonrelevant to the analysis.

Using Fuzzy-Set/Qualitative Comparative Analysis (FS/QCA)

Undertaking the procedures described above would be impossible without some powerful computing assistance. Fortunately, *Fuzzy-Set/Qualitative Comparative Analysis 1.1* is now available for download at http://www.u.arizona.edu/~cragin/software.htm. The program (Ragin et al. 2003) covers both the crisp-set QCA and the fuzzy-set extension. The extension can, in fact, handle a mixture of crisp and fuzzy variables. Data can be imported from SPSS files, but will almost certainly need to be "fuzzified". This means all crisp-set variables need to be coded as either 0 or 1 and fuzzy variables given values between 0 and 1. This needs to be done in a way that "makes sense". For example, if the question was "How long have you been using e-mail?" with the response categories "Less than 1 year", "1–2 years", "3–4 years" and "5 or more years", it might "make sense" to create a category called "experienced user" with full membership of the set with a fuzzy score of 1 for those in the "5 or more years" category, a fuzzy score of 0.75 for those in the "3–4 years" category, being mostly in the category "experienced user", a fuzzy score of 0.25 for those in the "1–2 years" category as being mostly out of the category "experienced user" and a fuzzy score of 0 for those using e-mails for less than one year being totally out of that category. This recoding can be done in FS/QCA, but is better achieved in SPSS first, particularly if the user is familiar with SPSS and the features of the *Variable View* are required.

The fuzzy set analysis can be done "veristically" with no tolerance for contradictory outcomes, or "probabilistically" with the researcher defining the level of probability to be tolerated (e.g. 0.80 for "almost always" necessary). Where the cases constitute a random sample, the researcher can treat this as a benchmark and test whether the outcome is significantly above the benchmark. Where researchers lack confidence in their measurement procedures or in their translation from raw data to fuzzy scores they can use an adjustment factor. In the analysis of necessity the adjustment factor moves the diagonal in an upward direction to capture those cases that are a "near miss" – and in a downward direction to capture those that are near misses from the perspective of sufficiency. The handbook, which can be downloaded from the same website, explains how to undertake these procedures.

The output from FS/QCA is a separate analysis of necessity and sufficiency, listing those causal expressions (configurations of causal conditions) that satisfy the criteria specified by the researcher. One key limitation of the program is sheer computing power. It can handle up to ten or so causal conditions, giving nearly 60 000 groupings to check, using the $3^k - 1$ formula. For 15 causal conditions this goes up to over 14 million and reaches over 1000 million with 17 variables. These take a long time to process.

The case study: *Fuzzy set analysis of the results of an e-mail survey in Norway* at the end of this chapter shows how the author of this textbook used fuzzy set analysis on the results of an e-mail survey in Norway.

Fuzzy set analysis straddles qualitative and quantitative procedures, and it sits midway between exploratory and hypothesis-testing research. It requires more cases than for qualitative research, but fewer than for quantitative. The analysis procedures used are the same for both interval and categorical variables – and for fuzzy coded categories arising from qualitative data. It needs more understanding of potential causal factors than for exploratory research, since comparative analysts must specify the categories of phenomena that are of interest at the outset of the investigation, but hypotheses containing complex logical relationships can be difficult to formulate in advance to test. It focuses on cases as configurations of characteristics rather than on relationships between abstracted variables and it separates out necessary from sufficient conditions. It can be used in conjunction with traditional analyses to locate patterns that the latter might miss. It is best used in situations where there are clear outcomes or dependent variables that are being analyzed and where the number of potential causal factors is fairly limited and fully understood. The results are not conclusive since they will depend on the test proportion chosen and whether or not an adjustment factor has been added. It is possible, however, to see to what extent these results are sensitive to test criteria, giving some indication of robustness. The output is not, as with crisp set analysis, in the form of a truth table, but Ragin has since developed a new algorithm that does generate truth tables from fuzzy sets.

KEY POINTS

Current techniques for analyzing quantitative marketing research data assume that the systems being studied are noncomplex and can, furthermore, be understood by using linear models and searching for patterns of statistical covariation between measured variables. In the real world the marketplace is, of course, highly complex – and it is seldom linear. In this situation there is causal complexity in which relationships are conjunctural, interdependent and interactive, which means that changes in system elements do not have consistent or predictable outcomes. The same outcomes can be produced by different combinations of factors and the same factor may have different effects on the outcome depending on the context. Using fuzzy set analysis software such as FS/QCA it is now possible to handle fuzzy categories in marketing and to see the output from analysis as one that can accommodate causal complexity embedded in nonlinear systems. There is a tendency for datasets, when subjected to traditional analyses, to show very little by way of substantial patterns since the patterns sought are, for the most part, limited to covariation between abstracted variables in linear situations. The application of fuzzy logic and configurational thinking will considerably enhance the ability of the researcher to get a lot more out of his or her dataset.

Holistic approaches to the analysis of data

The marketing landscape has changed dramatically in the last decade. The "new", "postmodern" consumer is IT-enabled, marketing-literate, sophisticated, choosey, has spending power and is data-protected. Markets themselves are increasingly fragmented, global, dynamic and often ephemeral. All this has had an impact on what we mean by "market research". It can no longer be a monolithic, survey-driven, interview-based enterprise. It needs to integrate a range of relevant information from multiple sources. It needs to be an eclectic, mixed-method phenomenon that offers managers actionable and holistic advice.

According to Smith and Fletcher (2004) a "new" market research has emerged in recent years that provides clients with a well-rounded view of what *all* their marketing evidence is saying. It involves a holistic approach to the interpretation of *all* the evidence. It may mean combining hard market research data with management knowledge and intuition. To make this disciplined and systematic, the authors advocate the use of Bayesian statistics.

The authors suggest a ten-stage guide for holistic analysis:

- analyzing the right problem,
- understanding the big information picture,
- compensating for imperfect data,
- developing an analysis strategy,
- establishing interpretation boundaries,
- applying knowledge filters,
- reframing the data,
- integrating the evidence and telling the story,
- decision-facilitation,
- completing the feedback loop.

While the amount of data on markets and customers has increased dramatically, it is also more imperfect, messy, gray, contradictory, confusing and less robust. The focus is now less on analysis than on generating insight. It is much more focused on improving the quality of business decision-making than mainstream quantitative or qualitative analysis.

SUMMARY

Standard univariate, bivariate and multivariate statistical techniques such as those covered in Chapters 11–14, while they have many strengths, also suffer from a number of limitations. They are variable-centered, they focus on linear, covariational relationships between variables, they are blind to the dependent or independent status accorded to variables by the researchers, they can offer very limited evidence of causal relationships, and they cannot handle complexity in the form of combinatorial, logical, nonlinear or emergent relationships.

There are many alternatives to such "mainstream" statistics. Some of these alternatives still focus on variables, but in a nonlinear way, for example neural network analysis, some data mining techniques and Bayesian approaches. Other alternatives focus more on the analysis of cases, seeing them as configurations or combinations of characteristics that can be analyzed using combinatorial logic or fuzzy set analysis. Many of these techniques require considerable computing power and so, while they may have been around for some time, they have only recently become feasible. This chapter has focused on those techniques that have been applied in the marketing area and that offer the greatest potential for enhancing what researchers can achieve by way of analyzing their data.

The trend in the analysis of marketing data has been towards more holistic approaches that try to use and make sense of what all the data and all the possible techniques that might be applied to them are telling the researcher. While in mainstream statistics it is possible very often to select *the* appropriate technique depending on the number of dependent and independent variables, their level of measurement and whether the researcher wants to display, summarize or make statistical inferences, with the alternatives the situation is much more fluid. They tend to be exploratory rather than confirmatory, less about testing prespecified hypotheses and more about finding patterns and handling complexity. There is far less guidance on selecting a technique; a researcher will pick a technique because of its approach to the problem, not because of particular data requirements.

When approaching the analysis of a dataset, the researcher would be wise to begin with mainstream techniques. However, if little is found by way of differences, associations or fit with prespecified models, if measures of association or correlation turn out to be very small, then instead of throwing in the towel and declaring negative results the researcher can try neural network analysis or fuzzy set analysis. Software programs are now available to actually apply alternatives to a dataset, but it will take a shift in mindset on the part of researchers to bring them into common use and maybe even include them in the training of researchers. Researchers will need to take a step back and one to the side to look from a distance at the data before them and to think about what the research is trying to do.

QUESTIONS FOR DISCUSSION

1 In what ways does neural network analysis differ from mainstream multivariate analysis?

2 Is data mining any different from applying mainstream statistical techniques but to very large datasets?

3 Can fuzzy set analysis actually demonstrate causal necessity and causal sufficiency rather than relying on theory to provide a rationale and an understanding of why it might be a reasonable interpretation?

4 Is holistic analysis the future for the analysis of marketing data?

CASE STUDY FUZZY SET ANALYSIS OF THE RESULTS OF AN E-MAIL SURVEY IN NORWAY

Kent (2005) reports the results of an e-mail survey in Norway into the effects on a range of response characteristics of e-mail use patterns, perceptions about technology, campaign elements and seeking different levels of permission from potential responders. The research sample was drawn from the customer database of a Norwegian company that issues loyalty cards that serve several different Norwegian retailers. Because of legislation that prohibits the use of unsolicited e-mail (or spam) in Norway, the company needed to ask every member registered in the e-mail database, through a medium other than e-mail, whether they would like to receive information via e-mail. By April 2002, approximately 40 000 members had accepted and given their "basic" permission to receive information via e-mail. In a follow-up these members were e-mailed and asked if they would extend their permission by giving information on their personal interests and preferences; 65 percent of those who responded gave this "extended" permission.

A random sample of 2100 of those who had given either basic or extended permission was selected and 1053 were returned, a response rate of 54 percent. In the survey, respondents were asked a series of questions about their use of e-mails. They were asked to indicate their strength of agreement or disagreement on a 5-point scale with four items relating to their reaction to spam-based commercial e-mails, for example "Spam-based e-mail often has interesting content", "I read all the spam-based e-mails I receive", "I often click on links in spam-based e-mails" and "I often make use of offers I receive in spam-based e-mails". A similar set of items was used to get respondents' reactions to permission-based commercial e-mail. These were the "outputs" (the dependent variables) being investigated. The causal factors included a number of e-mail use characteristics, for example the length of time using this medium, the number of e-mail addresses used, where read, how often read and so on.

A fuzzy set analysis

The data were "fuzzified" (in SPSS) as explained earlier and then imported into FS/QCA. Figure 15.6 shows the "fuzzified" data. Thus "readspam" and "readperm" are the 5-value fuzzy scores ranging from 1 through 0.75, 0.5, 0.25 to 0.0. Thus a score of 0.75 means that this respondent is "mostly in" the set "reads spam". The fuzzy variables "respspam" and "respperm" refer to the totals of the 4-item Likert scales, which were created into fuzzy scores by taking the maximum score of 20 to be "fully in" the set; the minimum score of 4 to be "fully out"; the middle score of 12 was taken as the "crossover" point of 0.5 and the other scores were graded in intervals of 6.25 percent. A scattergram (XY plot) of the degree of membership of the set "responds to spam" and the degree of membership of the set "responds to permission e-mail" is also shown in Figure 15.6. A triangular pattern has clearly emerged: responding to permission e-mail is a necessary, *but not sufficient* condition for responding to spam. While this is in a sense an "obvious" finding, it would not emerge from a traditional analysis: it is also reassuring that the fuzzy analysis "works".

The degree of membership of the category "responder to permission e-mails" was now taken as the output (dependent) variable with, as causal factors, whether or not extended permission had been given, whether or not e-mails were read mostly at home, the extent to which they are members of the set "experienced user", the extent to which they are members of the set "multiple e-mail addresses" ("multiadd" in Figure 15.6) and the extent to which they are members of the set "read commercial e-mails".

The analysis is carried out in two stages. First, an analysis of necessary conditions followed by an analysis of sufficient conditions. The output from FS/QCA is shown in Figures 15.7 and 15.8. Figure 15.7 shows the model being tested (in this example RESPERM as the output variable and five causal conditions). The analysis does not include cases where the membership of the outcome variable is zero,

FIGURE 15.6

The fuzzified FS/QCA dataset
and XY plot

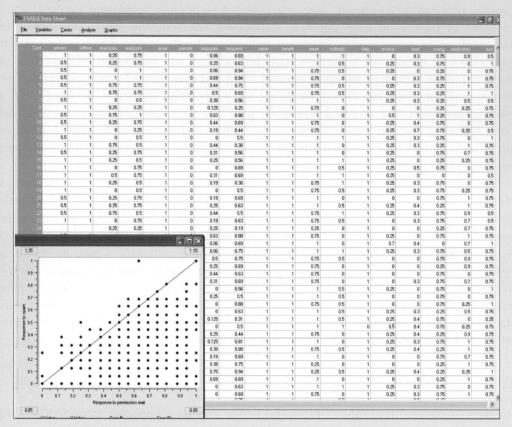

leaving 1023 cases from the 1051 read. The method of analysis is probabilistic with a test proportion of 0.80 selected. This means that it tests whether any condition is "almost always" (in 80 percent of the cases) necessary. The variables in capitals indicate the presence of a characteristic; the lower case variables indicate its absence. Thus in 73 percent of the cases (751 out of 1023) the extent of membership of the set "experienced user" is greater than or equal to the extent to which the case is a member of the set "responds to permission-based commercial e-mails". None of the variables (or their negation), however, meets the test criterion so no necessary causes have been discovered.

In the sufficient cause analysis (Figure 15.8), the test proportion chosen was 0.90 to make the analysis fairly stringent. There are four combinations that met the criteria for sufficiency:

1 has given extended permission, has many e-mail addresses, but is not an experienced user,

2 has given extended permission, has many e-mail addresses, but does not read e-mails at home,

FIGURE 15.7

FS/QCA necessary cause analysis

```
*************************************
File:      H:/WORDDOCS/Fuzzy sets/permfs2.dat
Model:     RESPPERM = EXTPERM + HOME + EXPER + MULTIADD + READCOMM

Cases Read:    1051
      Valid:    1032    98.2%
    Missing:      19     1.8%

**** NECESSARY CAUSE ANALYSIS ****

Nnumber of Cases Tested (Outcome > 0): 1023 (99.1% of Total)
Method:  Probabilistic
Test Proportion:    0.80
               *p < 0.05
```

Variable	N Cause >= Outcome	Observed Proportion	z	p
extperm	355	0.33		
EXTPERM	688	0.67		
home	488	0.48		
HOME	535	0.52		
exper	235	0.23		
EXPER	751	0.73		
multiadd	484	0.47		
MULTIADD	377	0.37		
readcomm	531	0.52		
READCOMM	425	0.42		

0 Necessary Cause(s) Included in the Analysis

3 has many e-mail addresses, always reads commercial e-mails, but is not experienced,

4 has given extended permission, but does not have many addresses, does not always read commercial e-mails and does not read them at home

This can be summarized by saying that the combination of being *not* an experienced user, having several e-mail addresses and either having given extended permission or *not* reading mostly at home were jointly sufficient in 90 percent of the cases to give rise to a positive response to permission e-mails. Reducing the test proportion to 0.80 produces too many combinations – nine in all. While this analysis is thus far from conclusive, it represents a considerable advance on variable-centered analysis, focusing as it does on configurations of case characteristics that tend to produce the outcome desired in all or nearly all instances. This has considerable implications for management and the marketing process. Instead of attempting to modify particular factors independently of other conditions, marketing strategy can now focus on creating particular combinations of characteristics; in fact each combination could be seen as a market segment that can be addressed differently.

FIGURE 15.8

FS/QCA sufficient cause analysis

```
**** SUFFICIENT CAUSE ANALYSIS ****

Method:  Probabilistic
Test Proportion:    0.90
                    p < 0.05

**** FUZZY-SET SOLUTION ****

EXTPERM*exper*MULTIADD
+
home*exper*MULTIADD
+
exper*MULTIADD*READCOMM
+
EXTPERM*home*exper*multiadd*readcomm
```

Questions and activities

1 Download the FS/QCA program from http://www.u.arizona.edu/~cragin/software.htm,

2 access the file *Norwaydata* from the Thomson website (www.thomsonlearning.co.uk/kent),

3 try replicating the analysis above.

FURTHER READING

Berry, M. and Linoff, G. (1997) *Data Mining Techniques for Marketing, Sales and Customer Support*. Chichester: John Wiley & Sons.

Ragin, C. C. (2000) *Fuzzy-Set Social Science*. Chicago: University of Chicago Press.

Retzer, J. (2006) "The century of Bayes", *International Journal of Market Research*, 48 (1): 49–59.

Smith, D. and Fletcher, J. (2001) *Inside Information. Making Sense of Marketing Data*. Chichester: John Wiley & Sons.

Smith, D. and Fletcher, J. (2004) *The Art and Science of Interpreting Market Research Evidence*. Chichester: John Wiley & Sons.

Part IV Applications

There are many topics that could be considered under the heading of applications. A trawl through a selection of marketing research textbooks would suggest the following list of possibilities:

- international research,
- research in industrial or business-to-business settings,
- researching services,
- research for innovations and new product development,
- corporate image research,
- pricing/packaging research,
- market measurement and analysis,
- advertising/media audience research,
- customer satisfaction research.

Many of these topics are incorporated in Chapter 16 on commercial proprietary techniques. "Proprietary" means that special procedures have been developed by market research agencies and are "owned" by them and offered to clients as a standardized, branded product. Chapter 17 looks at the particular characteristics of doing research across national boundaries, and Chapter 18 considers the process of communicating results either to clients or to academic audiences.

16 Commercial proprietary techniques

LEARNING OBJECTIVES In this chapter you will learn about:

→ diagnostic techniques that cover market measurement, the measurement of audiences to television, radio, print media and outdoor media, single-source data, which combine market measurement with audience measurement, usage and attitude surveys, customer satisfaction research and advertising tracking studies,

→ predictive techniques that include testing products and product concepts, advertising pretesting, and volume and brand share prediction.

INTRODUCTION

This chapter explains how some of the larger market research agencies combine the processes of data construction and data analysis in particular ways to enable them to diagnose the current circumstances facing an organization, to make predictions about the likely consequences of their marketing decisions, or to monitor the progress made by or success of past marketing activity. The techniques described here are only a selection of some of the more widely used procedures, and serve only as an illustration of the possibilities rather than a comprehensive account of all the services available. Since the techniques have been generated and developed to apply to specific situations, problems, opportunities or issues, it is often difficult to distinguish a particular research technique from the application in which it is normally used. Accordingly, no attempt is made in this chapter to distinguish techniques from applications. One distinction that can be made, however, is between techniques and applications that are primarily diagnostic and those that are predictive or prognostic.

Diagnostic techniques are used to review, measure or monitor the situation as it currently is or has been up to now. Thus marketing managers may require, or feel they require, a detailed anatomy of the size and structure of the markets they are currently addressing with their product offerings, and of the purchasing behavior associated with them. They may wish to know how current and potential customers use their and their competitor's products and what they think about them, or to track the progress of an advertising campaign or some new marketing mix. They may want to know what kinds of media, and what particular media, customers and potential customers watch, listen to or read before they make decisions about marketing communications.

Predictive techniques may be used where marketing managers want to know how consumers are likely to respond to a new product idea or to product modifications, or how well a new advertisement is likely to perform in terms of consumers being able to recall the brand and the theme of the advertising. They may require a prediction of likely sales or share of the market that will be achieved by a new or modified product before deciding whether or not to launch it onto the market.

Some of the techniques and applications are fairly standard and well-known among market research executives. Others have been developed by particular market research agencies, often over a number of years, which in important respects are new or original. These "proprietary" techniques commonly have a brand name to distinguish them from the procedures used by other agencies.

The following sections review the standard approaches to each technique or application. They then illustrate a selection of proprietary tools currently in use. These details should give the reader a better "feel" for what is actually involved. Many of the branded procedures or systems amount to refinements, developments or combinations of the standard approaches, so these accounts present what are current "state-of-the-art" applications. Bear in mind that the distinctions between diagnostic and predictive techniques, and between standard and proprietary techniques are often a little blurred. Diagnosis may constitute a preliminary or input to the process of making a prediction, while proprietary techniques are quite often fairly standard, even though their advocates and supporters in the market research companies may claim otherwise. Some systems offered, furthermore, may be a specific combination of diagnostic and predictive, standardized and proprietary elements.

INTERNET ACTIVITY

Using your browser, go to **www.thomsonlearning.co.uk/kent** and select the Chapter 16 Internet Activity which will provide a link to the TNS website. Select *Research services*, then *Continuous Research Services*. Find out more about TV and radio audience measurement. You can download a series of documents about the various components of television audience measurement (TAM) services.

Diagnostic techniques

Before managers can generate ideas for potential marketing initiatives and then decide which ones are likely best to fulfil the objectives of the organization, they will usually need to diagnose the current situation so that they can, for example, estimate how serious or urgent are the problems, issues or opportunities facing them, and what factors may be affecting the situation. A lot of data may already be available or at least gatherable by undertaking desk research. If, however, as is often the case, more information is required, then managers may consider undertaking, or commissioning market research agencies to carry out on their behalf, one or more of a number of primary research techniques or applications designed to acquire that information. The major diagnostic techniques currently in use may be grouped into a number of broad categories:

- market measurement,
- media audience measurement,
- single-source data,

- usage and attitude surveys,
- customer satisfaction and relationship management research,
- advertising tracking studies,

As is often the case, these categories do not represent watertight compartments (that is, they do not amount to a mutually exclusive and exhaustive set of categories). There are many overlaps, both in terms of the type of data collected, and in terms of the analyses that are performed on them. What activities agencies will actually include under each heading will also vary. However, for the purpose of exposition, it is convenient to treat them separately.

Market measurement

Market measurement The recording or estimation of market characteristics on a continuous, period or occasional basis.

Market measurement is the recording or estimation of market characteristics on a continuous, periodic or occasional basis. Marketing managers are always interested in the detailed anatomy of the markets to which they sell or hope to sell, and in the dynamics of their development. In particular, they will want to know:

- the size, composition and structure of the market for the company's brands, how that compares with competitor brands, and whether any changes are taking place,
- the purchasing behavior associated with the company brands, competitor brands, and any trends in that behavior,
- product and brand awareness, product usage and attitudes towards the company brands, competitor brands, plus any changes.

The size of a market can be measured in a number of different ways, but key measures are:

- sales,
- brand shares,
- market penetration,
- deliveries.

At first sight it might seem that measuring the level of sales is fairly straightforward. However, sales may be measured either by the volume (in weight or in units – packets, boxes, vehicles and so on), or by value in currency units (£ sterling, Euros or whatever). It may be sales achieved by a complete product category, by a company's own brand or brand variants, or by competitors' brands. Brands often come in different pack sizes, pack types, colors, flavorings, formulations, models, or with a variety of functions, features or associated services. These are generally referred to in the market research industry as "brand variants", although some manufacturers will call them "lines", or "models" or even "products". The set of brands that constitutes all the competing products of a similar nature or meeting the same consumer need may be referred to as a "product category", a "product field", a "product class" or a "product type", like shampoos. Similar product categories may be grouped together into "market sectors" like "toiletries and cosmetics" or "drinks and beverages".

Sales may be recorded over different periods of time and in relation to different geographical areas. The period of time over which sales are measured may be annual – this may be all that is needed for accounting purposes, but in today's rapidly changing marketing world, sales by the month are rapidly becoming a minimum standard, particularly for fast-moving consumer goods, and weekly sales are produced in some cases. Technically, with the introduction of electronic point-of-sale (EPOS) equipment and the barcoding of products, daily measurements are quite possible. However, a daily perusal of sales figures for firms that make hundreds of brands, brand variants and types of product, would involve too much data to digest and act upon. In any event, it is probably unnecessary for products other than those with a very short shelf life.

Although manufacturers will know what their own ex-factory shipments of products are on a regular or even continuous basis, once their transport and distribution systems have offloaded them to the delivery point, they are unlikely to know the progress of the products thereafter. They will not know the levels of stocks held by distributors and wholesalers, what quantities are being delivered to the shops, what stocks are held in the shops and whether these are on display and accessible to customers, what are the levels of sales in the different retail outlets, and what quantities, brands and with what frequencies consumers buy. Still less will they know any of this information for competitor brands. It is in these circumstances that retail panels, consumer panels or regular interval surveys are needed to make estimates of such quantities on a continuous basis.

Market size, as measured by sales, may, in short, refer to the sales achieved by the client brands or brand variants, or to sales in the product field. Sales may be captured at different points in the distribution system, over different periods of time and over different geographical areas. Sales potential is different again and refers to the levels of sales (in all its varieties) that it is estimated could be achieved if there were 100 percent penetration of the target market.

Trends in the levels of sales are generally treated by manufacturers both as a benchmark against which company performance is measured, and as a basis for setting goals, targets and objectives for the future. However, the absolute level of sales gives little indication of a brand's performance in relation to that of competing brands. Accordingly, market size is also measured by brand share. This is the proportion of total sales in a product category, either by volume or by value (or both), accounted for by a brand over a period of time. Brand share, however, is a measure that has to be treated with caution, since in many markets it is not always obvious what other brands come within the same product category. Furthermore, brand shares may vary from one area of the country to another, and from one market segment to another. Total national brand shares, in short, usually require more detailed analysis.

The main limitation in measuring market size on the basis of brand shares is that it is the share of current buyers in the product field. Current buyers, however, may be only a small proportion of potential buyers. In consequence, manufacturers often use a measure of market size that is also a measure of market potential, namely market penetration. This is the number or proportion of individuals or households in specified categories who are considered to be potential buyers who have actually made a purchase of the brand over a period of time in a geographical area, irrespective of the quantities purchased. Market penetration can itself be broken down by any demographic variable or set of variables, for example, the number or proportion of males in the age category 20–24 who are married and who made a purchase of a particular brand in the past four weeks. A low but rising market penetration indicates considerable potential compared with a situation where market penetration is already very high.

The problem with taking sales, brand shares or market penetration as a measure of market size is that they tend to be known only through the expensive process of subscribing to continuous panel research services, and even then they are usually only estimates. Measuring market size by volume or by value of deliveries to retail outlets may be more direct, particularly where EPOS systems are used. Here, the record will be of total quantities, not just estimates. The difficulty here, of course, is that it is the retailer who captures such information, and it may not be readily available to the manufacturer.

The composition of a market is an analysis of who buys a particular brand or product category. It can be described according to a very large number of dimensions. For consumer markets these may include:

- geographical characteristics like country, area or region,
- demographic characteristics like gender, age, social grade, income, family size, employment status or education,
- geodemographic analyses like ACORN (see pp. 159–160),
- psychographics or the lifestyle characteristics of consumers (see p. 160).

For business and organizational markets, the structure may be in terms of size of organization, type of organization, regional location, profitability and so on.

Market structure is the complete array of industry characteristics that directly affect the product or service decisions made by the organization and include the number and size distribution of buyers and sellers, the degree of product differentiation, entry barriers, exit conditions and the level of competition. Economists will use these characteristics to distinguish, for example, between perfect competition, monopolistic competition, oligopoly and monopoly.

The dimensions used to measure purchasing behavior depend in the first instance on whether consumer or industrial markets are being considered. For consumer markets, the key dimensions are purchase frequency, weight of purchase, repeat purchase, brand loyalty, interpurchasing between brands, source of purchase and nature or occasion of purchase. The purchasing behavior of retailers will often be recorded in terms of source and quantities of deliveries, ranges stocked, stock levels, shelf-space allocation and merchandising activity.

Product and brand awareness and the attitudes consumers have of the brands being researched and of competitor brands tend to be very complex and are not amenable to the techniques of consumer and retail panels. Omnibus surveys and market tracking surveys do sometimes cover awareness and attitudes, but not usually in any great depth. There is, however, a particular type of survey that is dedicated to the in-depth measurement of product awareness, usage and attitude. These are **usage and attitude** (or U&A) studies, but they are not usually carried out on a continuous or even periodic basis. There are conducted on an occasional basis as and when it is felt they are needed.

Usage and Attitude study A comprehensive survey, usually carried out on an ad hoc basis, that covers not only brand usage and purchasing behavior but also awareness and attitudes.

The main sources of data for all these various forms of market measurement include:

- retail panels,
- consumer panels,
- omnibus surveys,
- market tracking surveys.

The general methodology of panels, omnibus and market tracking surveys was described in Chapter 7. What follows are detailed examples of the kinds of market measurement services offered by some the major European market research agencies. These larger agencies mostly began with, and made their reputations on, specialized services, for example ACNielsen built its reputation on retail panels, while TNS (Taylor Nelson Sofres, which was originally AGB Research) focused more on consumer panels. However, these agencies increasingly felt that they needed to offer a full range of services to their clients and developed proprietary services using panels and surveys of different kinds. A more recent trend, however, has been to move away from the idea of offering a range of separate services towards a more holistic approach that focuses on client issues and problems instead, using whatever data sources are appropriate. Globalization, which is considered in more detail in Chapter 17, has also become more prominent, with the agencies not only offering their proprietary services in many countries, but developing panEuropean or worldwide services that facilitate international market research. Boxes 16.1 and 16.2 describe the offerings of ACNeilsen and TNS.

EUROPEAN MARKETING RESEARCH

BOX 16.1

ACNielsen

ACNielsen (**www.acnielsen.com**) has, since 2001, been part of the VNU group of companies based in the Netherlands. It operates in 38 different European countries (over 100 countries worldwide), offering clients the ability to measure their market performance, analyze market dynamics, diagnose marketing and sales problems, and to identify growth opportunities.

The original service offered by ACNielsen was its Retail Index, to which it added its Homescan consumer panel. However, the focus is now on business issues like consumer-centric category management, brand and market dynamics, new brand and product launches, pricing or retail performance. Besides retail measurement and consumer panel services, Nielsen also offers modeling and analytic services, decision support services and global services. By interfacing with local offices, this service aims to offer consistent information across markets.

The Retail Index has now become Nielsen Retail Measurement Services, which provide a range of continuous sales and distribution measurements derived from retail tracking operations across Europe and throughout the world. In the UK there are separate services covering different kinds of fast-moving consumer goods, for example:

- grocery,
- health and beauty,
- confectionery,
- home improvements,
- cash and carry outlets,
- sportswear,
- liquor,
- toys,
- tobacco,
- electrical.

Together these measure a large number of sales and distribution variables for over 600 different product categories and over 120 000 brands and associated brand variants. Each product grouping has its own sample of shops selling the products to be included, with sample sizes varying from about 450 to over 1300 shops.

Shops are classified into "multiples", "co-operatives" and "independents". A multiple is a group or organization with ten or more outlets. Each shop type is then subdivided by turnover range. Sampling of potential shops for the panel is done on the basis of disproportionate stratified sampling, the strata being shop type, turnover range and region. The selection of individual shops for recruitment to the panel is done on a judgmental basis that reflects a fair representation of store locations (shopping center, town center, out-of-town complex, rural area and so on) and places within the area. For multiples the number of shops in a named group, like Tesco, is kept proportional to the total number in that area.

Sales data for the major multiples are collected from their EPOS systems. For other types of shop where EPOS data are not available, it is necessary to undertake a monthly audit of stocks and, using data on deliveries, deduce what the level of sales must have been since the last audit. This is established by taking stocks at the last audit, adding deliveries and subtracting stock at the end of the audit to give sales. A separate calculation is made for each brand and brand variant. Data on stocks are captured by auditors from Nielsen using hand-held terminals to enter quantities in various locations in the shop.

Most clients subscribe on an annual basis to the appropriate product categories they require. They receive 12 monthly reports containing standard tables and charts along with monthly presentations. The tables give sales, deliveries, stock and price data for each brand and brand variant, and this may be broken down by region and shop type. The large multiples give access to their data and to their stores only on the understanding that the data are not presented to clients by named groups.

Accordingly, data, for example for grocery, are available only in categories broken down into "key accounts", "total multiples", "co-operatives" (large and small), and "independents" (large and small). To display trends and changes since the previous period Nielsen uses charts that show sales, purchases (deliveries) and stocks for the current month compared with the previous two months and the same months in the previous year. From these it is possible to understand what has been happening to sales and distribution on a month-by-month basis. Clients receive their data electronically, in support of which Nielsen has developed a range of data management and analysis software.

ACNielsen's Consumer Panel Services provide marketers with key consumer insights in 24 countries around the world, capturing actual consumer purchase information for almost 125 000 households. Their main product is a service called Homescan. This was begun in 1989 and in the UK is based on 10 500 households, each of which is equipped with a hand-held barcode scanner. After each shopping trip the scanner is used to record items bought, any promotional offers applicable, price, quantity and store used. The scanner is then placed in a modem that is linked to the telephone for transfer of the stored data to the Nielsen central computer. The data can then be analyzed to produce reports, for example on the percentage of households purchasing each product, the percentage of expenditure, the average number of visits per buyer, average spend per buyer and per visit. It is possible to make comparisons between brands and the level of trial from special offers, brand loyalty and demographic analysis. A key advantage of Homescan is that it provides insights into buying behavior across every type of purchase channel: from warehouse clubs to convenience stores, from supermarkets to drug stores, from computer stores and mass merchandisers to mail order and the internet.

EUROPEAN MARKETING RESEARCH

BOX 16.2

TNS

TNS Worldpanel™

TNS (**www.tns-global.com**) was coined as a brand in 2003 from Taylor Nelson Sofres, which had been created in 1997 from the merger of the market research agency Taylor Nelson AGB and the French agency Sofres. Taylor Nelson AGB was itself created from the merger of Taylor Nelson and AGB Research in 1992. AGB originally established its reputation offering consumer panel services, but today TNS offers the broadest range of research services of any single agency in the global research industry. TNS's research services are segmented into syndicated services (such as continuous consumer tracking studies and television and radio audio measurement) and custom research services (such as focus groups, omnibus and face-to-face surveys).

TNS is based in London, but has a global network spanning 70 countries. TNS offers consumer panels in 51 of these countries under the Worldpanel™ brand of which 27 are in Europe. In each country, Worldpanel™ is maintained and supported locally to service the needs of local clients and links internationally through a central Europanel team who source and combine individual country information to provide multi-country services and analysis for an increasing number of global clients.

In the UK, the Worldpanel™ brand combines under one umbrella eight separate consumer purchasing and usage panels. The largest of these is Worldpanel™ (Purchasing) which consists of 25 000 households, covering the purchases of some 75 000 individuals aged 5–79, resident in domestic households in mainland Great Britain and the Isle of Wight. Worldpanel™ (Purchasing) tracks the take-home purchasing of 270 FMCG markets within Ambient Grocery, Fresh and Chilled Foods, Toiletries, Healthcare, Alcohol, Frozen and Household trading sectors.

Panel members are recruited by various means. In the main, lists of potential households are bought in from both external and internal providers. These are with known demographics. Homes are selected for recruitment with the relevant target demography and geography.

The majority of recruitment is conducted via post, but for a subset of the panel that are invited to do a predominantly PC-based task, the invitation is sent via e-mail. Targets are based largely on the most recent Establishment Survey carried out for BARB (see television audience measurement on pp. 480–481).

For non-PC-based participants, the housewife (who may be either female or male) is then contacted by phone. The National Shopping Monitor survey (as Worldpanel™ is known to panel members) is described further, together with an outline of the task involved and the incentives offered. The recruiter will then arrange a time for the scanning equipment to be delivered. Panel members are issued with a full set of instructions as to how to set up the equipment and get started, for which there is a start-up bonus. Homes conducting a purely PC-based task are communicated with via e-mail and their equipment, which is much smaller, is sent via normal post.

Data collection is through a variety of methods, each of which is designed to be the most suitable and convenient for each panel member. Methods include post, barcode scanners, SMS text messages, via the internet and clickers. Details of non-barcoded products are entered by scanning a code book.

Data collected from panel members include name of purchaser, shop name, total amount spent, price paid per product, and quantity of product purchased. Each data collection method automatically records the day of the week and the time of day of data entry. In addition to electronic recording of grocery purchasing, members are required to post in shop till receipts, which TNS optically scans and collects additional information on store locations and promotions. Till receipts are also used to quality check the information collected directly from panelists.

All the data are weighted to population parameters before being grossed up to the population. Reporting is four-weekly. Four-weekly reports contain the kinds of market analyses described earlier under consumer panel research. In addition, some new services have been developed for the use of Worldpanel™ data for promotional analyses and for measuring advertising effectiveness, which allows clients to evaluate their promotional and competitive performance on a continuous basis, to identify payback from individual promotions, where to invest further promotional expenditure, and how to develop promotional strategies.

Omnimas

TNS offers a number of omnibus surveys across Europe including business and consumer omnibuses, and more specialist ones, for example on healthcare, online, children and international. The largest service in the UK is one called Omnimas. Some 2100 adults aged 16 and over are interviewed face-to-face every week on behalf of industry, commerce and government. The sample can be increased to 4000 in a week depending on client needs. Sampling is random location sampling, using the Postcode Address File, and is based on a master sample of 600 sampling points covering the whole of Great Britain. The sample is stratified, within the Registrar General's Standard Regions, in descending order by the percentage in socio-economic groups I and II using census data.

The interviewer will have a minimum of 13 interviews to do a week. The only quota set is that the interviewer should obtain either six men and seven women or vice versa. So, there is a control on gender, but everything else depends on the randomness of the sample. Up to four attempted contacts per respondent are made. Interviews are computer-assisted.

The Omnimas questionnaire is divided into three sections: a continuous section that includes questions that are asked on every survey and are inserted on behalf of a particular client; an ad hoc section of questions that are included on a one-off basis; a classification section that contains all the demographic questions.

Omnimas does not allow questions on some topics, for example on home security (e.g. "Do you have a burglar alarm in your home?"). The usual length of the questionnaire is limited to an average of 25 minutes' completion time. It takes an average of 20–30 seconds to administer an average question, so the total number of questions will be not more than 60–70. Occasionally, one client may buy up all the space remaining after the demographic and continuous questions have been accounted for. The usual number of questions clients take is about 6–10.

Most questions will be set-choice, but some clients require open-ended questions and they will be charged up to double the amount per question. If clients require help in framing questions, then this is included in the price. Clients can have breakdowns of each question inserted by any of the demographics, up to 30 cells (e.g. a 6-by-5 table). The demographics include:

- gender, age and social class,
- marital and working status,

■ household size and composition,
■ telephone and car ownership,
■ region (either Registrar General's or ITV),
■ household tenure.

Precoded questions cost between £100 and £800 depending on penetration. Open-ended questions cost between £300 and £1800, again depending on penetration.

Optional extras include charts, mini-reports, brand mapping, cluster analysis or analysis by ACORN geodemographics. The figures in the tables are grossed up volume figures, and weights are applied. There is a 72 cell matrix – age within gender within region – that is used to weight responses in each cell. Standard errors are not usually provided, but will be offered at no extra cost if asked for.

Questions need to be with Omnimas two days before the survey begins. Topline results are available two days after completion of fieldwork. As an adjunct to the main service, Omnimas maintains a database of previous respondents who have indicated their willingness to participate in further research. This can be used to greatly reduce the cost and timescale of undertaking ad hoc research among particular minority groups in the population.

The use of market measurement data

Market measurement information is required both by top company executives and by marketing and sales managers for one or more of a number of key purposes:

■ to reduce the risks in or to maximize the opportunities from taking strategic or operational decisions in respect of marketing mix variables,
■ to monitor changes and developments in the marketplace as they occur,
■ to build up a marketing database that can be used as a resource for a variety of analyses,
■ to use as a common currency in negotiations with suppliers, distributors, retailers, business customers, advertising agencies or media owners,
■ to act as an input to market segmentation analyses.

A marketing manager will often want to know, for example, whether or not a strategy of maintaining a full range is maximizing the firm's competitive advantage; whether, from past experience, adding new brand variants of a product is likely to cannibalize sales from the other variants or will increase overall total sales; whether a new product is reaching its target for market penetration and repeat purchase rate; whether a price reduction is increasing or decreasing total revenue; or whether the last advertising campaign was successful in raising brand awareness.

A company that knows what is happening in the marketplace as it happens is able to react to these changes immediately. Knowing, for example, that there was a significant increase in the number of shops handling your brand who were out of stock last week or last month will alert the company to distribution problems or lack of production volume, and it can take corrective action before sales are seriously dented.

A marketing database will include all back data from market measurement activities and, very often, a customer database. If, for example, a company is concerned about the level of its prices in the shops in relation to those of its competitors, by using back data it can see what happened to sales or market shares or market penetration when price differentials between its brands and the brands of its main competitors were at varying amounts.

Any manufacturer will want to know its market share and how it has been changing when negotiating with retailers as to whether its brands should be accepted as part of their range, what stocks they should hold, and what shelf space they should give it. By the same token, media owners need market measurement data to make a case for an advertising campaign using their medium. Advertising agencies use such data for clients for media selection, creative input, account planning, and to monitor campaigns.

Market measurement data may be used crucially for market segmentation, which is the process of dividing up the target market into subgroups with the idea of aiming at those subgroups different or modified marketing mixes designed to maximize marketing opportunities in each. Market segmentation is an alternative to mass marketing or product variety marketing in which the manufacturer offers a range of product variations, but these just offer choice and are not targeted at specific groups.

The role of marketing research in market segmentation is to identify market segments, ascertain their size and structure, and the nature of consumer behavior and attitudes associated with them. In some cases, this amounts to no more than researching the structure of the total market in a little more detail and separating consumers into those with higher and those with lower probabilities of buying a brand or a product; in others, sophisticated techniques are used to determine those characteristics which, singly or in combination, will result in the optimum or "best" way of segmenting the market in pursuit of specified marketing objectives.

Sometimes market analyses have as their primary objective this process of segmentation; in other situations, segmentation is a spin-off or secondary objective of research that was designed for other purposes. Thus a client wishing to monitor the marketplace on a continuous basis may subscribe to a consumer panel and receive regular four-weekly reports of sales broken down by a number of demographics. In looking at the reports, it may become clear that certain groups of customers have systematically different patterns of buying behavior from others. This may suggest that a policy of segmentation, or further segmentation, may be worth considering. Market analyses that are more strictly directed at segmentation are more likely to use the more complex and sophisticated segmentation techniques.

KEY POINTS

Market measurement is the recording or estimation of market characteristics on a continuous, periodic or occasional basis. The data for such measurements come from a number of sources including retail panels, consumer panels, omnibus surveys and market tracking surveys. The large market research agencies tend to operate a number of these services, although the trend has been to move away from the idea of offering a range of separate services towards a more holistic approach that focuses on client issues and problems instead, using whatever data sources are appropriate.

Media audience measurement

The purpose of **media audience measurement** is to communicate with consumers in chosen markets, and in selecting what particular channels, stations, newspapers or magazines will be most effective, it is essential to know what media individuals and households in the target market use, how much they use them, when they use them and how they use them. The purpose of media measurement is to provide both quantitative and qualitative data on media usage by audiences and readers.

The "media" include all means of communication with large numbers of people in an impersonal manner. The so-called "mass" media may reach millions of

Media audience measurement The provision of both quantitative and qualitative data on media usage by audiences and readers.

individuals and households in the process, while specialized media, for example minority magazines and radio programs, may have relatively small audiences. The concept of an "audience" is common to all the media, which include:

- the broadcast media – television and radio,
- the print media – newspapers, magazines and books,
- outdoor media – posters, billboards, on buses, on the underground and so on,
- film and video – cinema and video shops.

Manufacturers and other types of organization are normally interested, for marketing communication purposes, only in those media that carry advertising, or allow sponsorship of programs or printed material. In the UK, this excludes the outputs of the BBC, but very little else, except perhaps books. UK advertisers alone spend over £7 billion on advertising on television, in newspapers and magazines and on the radio. It is not surprising, therefore, that the advertising industry (which includes the advertisers, the advertising agencies and the media owners) finances carefully designed and expensive research into the viewing, listening and reading habits of the population.

Detailed information about audience size and structure, and about audience use of and attitudes towards the advertising media and their offerings is required by:

- program makers, broadcast schedulers, and newspaper and magazine editors who are planning the development of their media,
- media owners selling to manufacturers and other organizations opportunities to communicate with an audience through advertising and sponsorship,
- buyers of such opportunities – the advertisers whether in manufacturing, commerce or nonprofit-making organizations,
- advertising agencies and market research agencies.

Television audience measurement

It was only with the development of commercial television channels – those supported by advertising revenue – that the demand emerged for detailed and precise information on the audiences achieved. The UK was the first to introduce commercial television in Europe (ITV) in 1955. Other large European countries did not follow until the 1980s (Gane 1997). The technical characteristics of television lend themselves to the use of electronic meters, which were introduced in the UK in 1956. In France, Germany and the Netherlands, meters were installed in panel households somewhat later, but in advance of commercial television and at the behest of governments. Consequently, their development has tended to be controlled by official organizations.

The early development of meters to measure television audiences took place in the USA where the television industry began as a commercial venture from the outset. The original set meters both in the USA and in Europe recorded only the status of the set (on or off) and the channel selected. The viewing of individuals was determined separately through self-completion diaries. However, as more and more channels became available and as increasing numbers of households had more than one set – and perhaps a video recorder – so the demands on meters grew rapidly. AGB, a UK market research agency, was the first to develop a "peoplemeter", which not only recorded who was viewing, but also allowed for the retrieval of data via the telephone. These were installed in panel homes in the UK and Italy in 1984 and in Ireland in 1985.

By the early 1990s, fully operational peoplemeters were in place throughout Europe (Gane 1997). There are, however, still considerable differences in the ways the meters are used, for example whether or not to include people who are on holiday, and whether "viewing" means present in the room with a television set switched on, present in the room and able to watch, or actually watching. Attempts are being made to harmonize techniques across Europe, but progress is slow.

Any television audience measurement system consists of a number of components:

- an establishment survey, which determines the characteristics of the population to be covered,
- the setting up and maintenance of a representative panel of households in which metering systems are installed,
- the installation of the metering equipment and the capture of data from panel households,
- data processing and the publication of data to subscribers.

Establishment surveys

Establishment surveys establish and track reception and viewing characteristics of television-viewing households in the population. The information is then used to design, monitor and control the composition of the main panel in each region of the country, and to provide a prescreened address bank from which homes may be recruited when they are required to meet control targets in their area. The quality of any television audience measurement system depends in the first instance on the quality of the establishment survey. This depends on an accurate listing of all households in the population from which a random sample can be drawn. Very few sampling frames, however, are perfect, for example listings may exclude properties built and occupied since the frame was compiled; they may include multiple households in one address.

In the UK it is possible to use the Postcode Address File, which is a list of all the locations at which the UK Post Office delivers mail and which is updated quarterly. The UK Establishment Survey is described in more detail in Box 16.3. The UK system uses face-to-face interviews, but in many countries, access problems and costs mean that face-to-face interviewing is not viable and telephone interview may be used. In Denmark, for example, a random sample of addresses is obtained from the Office of Civil Registration, which maintains a list of all residents in Denmark. This is then matched against the telephone company database. Telephone interviews are attempted at those that match, while those unmatched are called on by an interviewer. In some countries, such lists are not made available, in which case the agency conducting the establishment survey needs to construct its own list. This may mean using census data to select sampling blocks within which field staff enumerate all the addresses.

Establishment survey A survey that tracks the reception and viewing characteristics of television viewing households in the population.

The Establishment Survey is selected as an annual sample which is then divided into 12 monthly replicates. The design allows for monthly network reporting and for full regional reporting every quarter. The size and geographical structure of each annual Establishment Survey is determined primarily by panel recruitment requirements. Currently, the full annual sample is 43 000 households. Regionally, sample sizes vary from 8000 in London down to a minimum of 1000 (except in the Channel Islands which has a sample of 384).

Households are selected from the Postcode Address File using systematic sampling within selected enumeration districts. Interviewers try to interview the housewife at all the selected addresses, making at least three callbacks at different times of the day. The average response rate is 75 percent. The interview covers four different sections.

- television and related equipment owned or rented by the household, for example the number of television sets, whether color, teletext, remote control, video cassette recorder, plus satellite or cable television decoders.
- reception – what channels can be received. Which actual ITV transmitters the household can receive is established by where it is located. This is important for defining the geographical areas reached by each transmitter and delimits overlap areas served by more than one.
- viewing characteristics – this is crucial for establishing whether household members are heavy, medium or light viewers. It is based on the number of hours the respondent (who is usually the housewife) says each set in the household is used, and whether for BBC or ITV.
- household demographics including family size, presence of children, their ages, socioeconomic status of head of household and so on.

Information from the Establishment Survey is combined with basic population demographics from the Office of National Statistics (ONS) to produce universe size estimates for panel control purposes and to weight survey results.

Panel management

To give reliable television audience measurement, a panel must be representative of the population from which it is selected. This is a two-stage process that involves initially using a high-quality probability sample design, and then ensuring that the panel remains representative over time. The panel is managed so that it remains consistent with specified population values called panel controls. Ideal controls are those most closely related to the variables being measured on a continuous basis. The most obvious of these is weight of television viewing, for example heavy, medium and light users. Panels are recruited and maintained from households interviewed or contact in the establishment survey. Establishment surveys are typically about ten times the size of the panel – they are thus substantial samples that can be used, for example for multivariate analysis to establish what factors are most closely associated with claimed viewing behavior. These factors are then used as panel controls. Over time, panels will tend to become unrepresentative as they get older, move away, drop out or set up separate households. Panel maintenance may mean recruiting from the establishment survey households with particular characteristics and maybe dropping others.

Panel sizes vary across Europe. The largest are in the UK and Italy with over 5000 reporting homes. In the UK this size is mainly the result of the regional nature of the main television commercial services and the need to have an adequate panel in each region. Switzerland has a total panel of 1200 homes, which is quite large given the size of its population, but it needs to report on three language regions. Belgium has separate services for Flanders and Wallonia with a panel of 600 homes in each. The smallest panels are 600–700, for example Ireland and Croatia.

Data capture

The basic mechanism for data capture is the peoplemeter. This is a device that sits on top of the television in the panel household. There is also a remote control handset for every television in the household and a central data storage unit which is connected to each display unit via the domestic mains supply. It has two main functions:

- ■ to identify what is being watched,
- ■ to identify who is viewing.

The central data storage unit records viewing on a second-by-second basis and has the ability to record over 250 channels as well as the use of the VCR or DVD for time-shift viewing. It can track the viewing habits of eight members of any one household, plus up to seven guests. This it does by allocating a number to all household members who press their numbered button on the handset to indicate that they have started to view. It is pressed again when the person stops viewing. Demographic data on age and gender of the guests are entered via the handset, following prompts on the display screen on the peoplemeter. Viewers are prompted to check that the correct buttons are pressed every 15 minutes while they view in order to maximize the accuracy of the information being recorded.

The central data storage unit contains a modem and is located near a telephone point into which it is permanently plugged. During the night it is interrogated by means of a telephone call from the agency's central London computer (telephone ringing is suppressed) and information in its memory is downloaded. Audience figures become available the next day after data from all the panel homes are aggregated, adjusted for imbalances and projected to the total population.

As the television viewing environment has become more complex it has been necessary to expand the range of channel detection techniques to identify what is being viewed on the television set. The traditional method has been to insert a probe into the television to monitor the frequency of the channel being viewed. The frequency is then compared with a channel map to identify the channel. Another technique identifies the codes within the broadcast signal. Codes are broadcast by virtually all channels in Europe and range from Teletext codes to VPS codes in the German-speaking countries and PDC codes elsewhere. TNS has developed a picture-matching technology and simply measures what is seen on the TV screen. Pairs of points are constantly sampled on the screen for relative brightness. Each is allocated a date and time stamp, which is subsequently matched to samples of video output of all reported channels.

Data output

The main currency for the measurement of television audiences is the "rating". The rating for a television program is the size of its audience expressed as a percentage of the relevant population size. The "relevant" population is those adults living in private households capable of viewing the appropriate station. Audience sizes vary throughout the duration of a program and are measured for each individual minute. The minute-by-minute ratings are then averaged over the whole of the program. A rating of, say, 37 percent would be typical for a popular program. Some advertisers will call this 37 "rating points".

Ratings are also calculated for advertisements by taking the minute in which the advertisement begins. Advertisers and their agencies then add these ratings over all the "spots" (showings) for a given advertising campaign. The total is called either the total television rating or the Gross Rating Points (GRP). The figures will, of course, no longer be true percentages since they can exceed 100, but they are taken as a measure of the "weight" of the advertising campaign. If the audience sizes themselves rather than the ratings are added together, it measures total "impacts" for the campaign, reflecting the actual sizes of the audience rather than the proportion of the total potential watching. Impacts are often the basis for charging differential rates for advertising air-time according to region.

Ratings are used by broadcasters, advertisers, advertising agencies and media specialists who need to know what proportion of the population watch each program, and the regional and demographic characteristics of each audience. Not all programs are expected to achieve high ratings, but there is a target depending on the type of program and its place in the schedule. Commercial broadcasters also need spot ratings (for each commercial) and break ratings (for each commercial break) as a guide for selling air-time to advertisers. Highly rated spots (with large audiences) command a higher price and the broadcaster issues a rate card giving the price of each spot.

Advertisers need reassurance that their advertising budgets are being spent effectively, so they require information on the size, frequency of exposure and demographic profile of the audience for their advertisements. Equally important is information on the cost per 1000 viewers.

Box 16.4 describes the measurement of television audiences in the UK.

EUROPEAN MARKETING RESEARCH

BOX 16.4

Television audience measurement in the UK

In 1957 a committee was set up to represent the interests of both the advertisers and the ITV companies and to award a contract to a market research agency to measure television audiences. This was the Joint Industry Committee for Television Advertising Research (JICTAR). The BBC had its own system, but a joint system was established in 1981. This involved setting up a company jointly owned by the BBC and the ITCA called the Broadcasters' Audience Research Board (BARB). AGB held the contract to supply the quantitative audience measurement service exclusively until 1991, when BARB split the contract between two research contractors. Panel recruitment and quality control was passed over to a company established for the purpose by Research Services Limited (RSL) and Millward Brown called RSMB. This company was to be responsible for the design and execution of an establishment survey, the sample design for the main panel, the design and maintenance of the panel control scheme, the recruitment of panel households, the maintenance of details about panel households, panel household incentive schemes, and the design of weighting procedures. AGB (which was by then Taylor Nelson AGB) was to supply and connect metering equipment, undertake the nightly telephone polling of panel households, process and publish the data to subscribers.

The most recent contracts were awarded by BARB in 2000. Four contracts were split between three suppliers. Two contracts were awarded to ATR (Advanced Television Research). This is the name used in the UK by a group that was a breakaway from the original AGB Research that set up in Italy as the AGB Group. ATR is responsible for panel recruitment and data collection. RSMB was awarded the contract for sample design and panel control, while Ipsos-RSL was to handle the establishment survey. Taylor Nelson AGB, which in the meantime had become TNS, lost out. In 2004, the Italian AGB Group formed a joint venture with Nielsen Media research (which does most of the US television audience measurement) to create AGB Nielsen Media Research. This company specializes in television audience measurement services and now operates in 28 countries.

The main panel consists of some 5100 households covering 11 500 individuals. These individuals aged from 4 upwards are the basis for reporting viewing. The UK establishment survey is described in Box 16.3. There are separate panels in each region, each of which is balanced by size of household, presence of children, age of housewife, presence of working adults, and socioeconomic status and educational status of the head of household. These together create a structure that represents stages of the life cycle, for example "pre-family/one-person/ABC1/late terminal education age households", "pre-family/two person/ABC1/early TEA households" and so on. There are 24 groups in all. Each combination of characteristics is then checked and held in balance for average weight of television viewing. The viewing covered includes terrestrial (analog and digital), cable (analogue and digital), satellite (analog and digital), time shifted viewing and guest viewing.

A recent development has been the fusion of BARB data with other datasets, for example TGI data. Thus BARB has a panel of 9000 adults matched for gender, age, social grade, region, weight of viewing, how many children and whether they have a VCR, against one of 25 000 adults on the TGI. A special algorithm of distance measurements is used that incorporates the weighted importance of 13 variables in all. Each BARB panelist is then described in terms of anything that is available on the TGI, for example by brand and product use.

Audience appreciation

In the UK, BARB felt that television viewing panel members should not be subject to further tasks, for example of indicating what they thought of the programs they saw. Accordingly, there has always been a separate panel whose members are asked to rate programs in a process called audience appreciation. The assessment and the evaluation of television programs was for many years undertaken by the BBC's Audience Reaction Service using a Television Opinion Panel. This has since been taken over by Research Services Limited (RSL), which maintains a national panel of individuals with an achieved sample size of about 3000 respondents per week on which the 17 ITV regions are represented according to size. In addition, there are regional boost panels, making the achieved sample in each region up to 500 respondents. Members of the regional boost panels complete a diary once every four weeks and each region participates on a four-weekly cycle. National panel members, of which there are 4600, are contacted weekly and, with a response rate of about 65 percent, this gives the achieved sample of 3000. If people do not respond for two or three weeks they get a letter asking if they wish to continue; otherwise they arc dropped. There are 5400 on the regional boost panels.

Panel controls are similar to those for the BARB panel, but weightings are applied to adjust for biases from over- and under-representation of certain groups among those responding. Panelists are given a seven-day booklet running from Monday to Sunday, which is in three sections:

- a list of all programs on a day-by-day basis asking respondents to give a score on a 6-point scale for each program seen (see Figure 16.1),

- more detailed questions are asked about selected programs. Some of these questions are open-ended; others use Likert-type scales,

Allocate score

6	Extremely interesting and/or enjoyable	100
5	Very interesting and/or enjoyable	80
4	Fairly interesting and/or enjoyable	60
3	Neither one thing nor the other	40
2	Not very interesting and/or enjoyable	20
1	Not at all interesting and/or enjoyable	0

FIGURE 16.1

The Audience Appreciation Index

■ questions about series that have just finished, long-running serials or questions of a more general nature.

From the first section an Appreciation Index (AI) is calculated. This is done by allocating a score out of 100 in each level of response (see Figure 16.1). The AI is the average of all the responses. Most AIs are between 50 and 90, but they are not absolute numbers, rather they facilitate comparisons. These comparisons are made with programs of a similar type, for example "feature films", "sport", or "news and current affairs". Weekly AI reports list each category separately and are broken down by age, gender and social class. The aim is to cover all programs, but where fewer than 25 responses for a program have been received, no AI is calculated, and, if fewer than 50, separate AIs are not calculated for demographic groups.

It has been found that, overall, there is little correlation between AI scores and audience ratings – bigger audiences do not necessarily mean higher appreciation scores and vice versa. However, Barwise et al. (1979) argue that if a distinction is made between information and entertainment programs, then there is a small positive correlation between audience appreciation and size within these types, but that the correlation between the types is negative. Menneer (1987) argues that there is no reason to *expect* a relationship since they measure different things. Audience size for any program is determined largely by the time of day it is broadcast, and what the competing programs are, irrespective of the quality of the program. AIs are a crucial and necessary complement to estimates of audience size in evaluating channel and program performance. AIs, furthermore, have a useful role in predicting, and later explaining, the audience delivery for a series of programs.

In the Netherlands, by contrast, viewing behavior and audience appreciation have been systematically and continuously charted since 1965 (Hammersma and Appel 2002). When the peoplemeter technology was introduced in 1987, AGB developed a version of the peoplemeter specially for the Dutch market, by which panel members could assign appreciation scores on a 10-point scale to any program by using the remote control. Requests for the scores appeared on the display on the meter when the viewer switched channels, when the viewer stopped watching or turned the television off. At the same time, however, more and more commercial channels were being introduced and the average rating per channel plummeted. This brought into question the validity of the appreciation scores on many programs. There was also a lively debate about whether it was in any case possible to measure the result of a complex evaluation process with a single figure. Nevertheless, it was deemed to be useful for program scheduling.

Following major changes in the structure and financing of the television audience measurement service and the creation of a joint industry committee, it was decided to form a separate appreciation survey, but one carried out on the internet. The panel needed to be large (about 8000), but results could be obtained very quickly and more detailed questions about the programs could be asked.

Radio audience measurement

In many ways the measurement of radio audiences is more complex than for television. First, listeners are not always aware of, or can correctly identify, the station to which they are listening (for television this is automatically recorded by the peoplemeter). Second, radio listening is often casual and undertaken while other activities are being pursued, or it may be used just as background. Although there are problems, as we have seen, over what counts as "watching" a television, at least presence in the room in which there is a television switched on (and peoplemeter attached) is clearer than the idea of "presence" when a radio can be heard. Third, listeners tend to be mobile – some 20–35 percent of listening takes place outside the home, often on radios not owned by or tuned in by the listener. This creates problems either for the two main methods used to measure radio audiences: day-after recall and weekly diaries. Neither of these actually measures "listening"; rather they measure what individuals are able to recall they thought they "listened" to, what station they thought they were listening to and their inclination and ability to write it down in a questionnaire or a diary.

A more recent development is the audiometer, which picks up both television and radio transmission to which consumers may be exposed. There are two main methodologies. First, the detection of inaudible signals transmitted by the station (watermarking). This works by detecting whether the wearer is within range of an audible encoded signal embedded in any portion of any transmission to which the wearer is exposed. The second is audio matching when samples of station output are compared or matched with recordings of its transmission (fingerprinting). Neither method is listening, but exposure, and is similar to a television's presence in the room.

Data are collected in various ways including overnight using domestic phone lines, the return of devices for processing, and at set intervals over the mobile phone network. Audiometers have many advantages, for example the production of day-to-day radio data, which is not possible from weekly diaries or day-after recall surveys. Furthermore, instead of the average quarter-hour from diaries, audiometers can, like television, go down to the average minute. However, they may not be deployed in the same way as large-scale survey methodologies due to the cost and are more suitable for use with panels.

EUROPEAN MARKETING RESEARCH

Radio audience measurement in the UK

BOX 16.5

The BBC and independent local radio undertook separate radio audience research until 1992 when a new company, Radio Joint Audience Research Ltd (RAJAR, **www.rajar.co.uk**), was established to operate a single audience measurement system for the radio industry as a whole. This company is jointly owned by the Commercial Radio Companies Association (CRCA) and the BBC. It covers all BBC national and local stations, UK licensed stations and most other commercial radio stations. RAJAR research is currently contracted to Ipsos-RSL.

Until recently, the use of audiometers has been seen as far too expensive for the industry to afford. Ipsos currently uses a seven-day diary covering Monday to Sunday. Some 150 000 diaries are placed and collected annually by 200 interviewers who use prompt cards to determine what stations each respondent actually listens to. The diary is in two sections. The first covers media consumption including general radio listening, television viewing and newspaper readership. The second section records actual radio listening. For any occasion when respondents listen to the radio for five minutes or more, they are asked to record their listening by drawing a line through the appropriate time segment boxes. Respondents are also asked to indicate where they listened – at home, in a car, van or lorry, or at work/elsewhere. The stations that the respondent listens to are listed across the top using stick-on labels.

All questionnaire and diary data are processed using optical scanning technology and undergo a series of checking procedures. The data are then adjusted and grossed up to give population estimates. The results measure:

reach – the unduplicated number of different people listening to any specified service over a period of time expressed as a percentage of the total universe,

total hours – the overall number of hours of adult listening to a specified service over a specified period of time,

average hours – average hours per listener calculated from total hours divided by reach.

RAJAR has put out to tender proposals for the future of radio audience measurement in the UK, including the options of continuing with diaries or switching to audiometers. It is expected to announce its decision some time in 2006.

In terms of audience appreciation, the BBC had its own Listening Panel until 1992 when it was replaced by the Radio Opinion Monitor (ROM), but it still covered only the BBC's networked programs. This service has now been replaced with an online panel which is managed by Gfk for the BBC.

Newspaper and magazine readership

As in other areas of audience research, the commercial importance of readership research stems from the fact that newspapers and magazines carry advertising and are often dependent – sometimes heavily dependent – on this source of revenue. Budgets for such research run into millions annually. There have been major international symposia on the subject and many specialized seminars; scores of conference papers and journal articles have been written. Yet, for all this activity, experts and consultants around the world continue to debate the merits and drawbacks of alternative approaches and techniques. At the same time, advertisers depend on readership research to determine the allocation of their spend between the many different titles available. Readership estimates have become the currency in which advertising space is traded. The data are also of relevance to editorial and circulation departments.

Measuring readership is quite possibly more difficult than measuring either television viewing or radio listening. Reading can mean anything from a cursory glance to a thorough study. Usually, it means that the reader has "read" only those sections of interest and skipped or glanced at others.

Most readership research takes a complete issue of a publication as its focus of measurement rather than a section, a page or an advertisement. Personal interviews remain the favored method of data collection since the number of questions that need to be asked is inevitably very large. In addition it is usually necessary to show visuals of mastheads or logos to help respondents to correctly identify publications. Since readership tends to be highly seasonal and subject to atypical events and circumstances, most readership research will be continuous, and the use of panels tends to be too expensive, so they will often be based on independent samples.

Readerships are usually measured in terms of what is called average issue readership (AIR) – the number of different people who read a single issue, averaged across issues. This measure has attracted some criticism – that it is a very bland measure, or that it seriously inflates estimates. It is based on asking respondents when they last saw a copy of a publication. If they claim to have done so in the last publishing interval, they are added to the AIR. The problem is that if the reader looks at the copy again outside the publishing period, then the reading event may be counted twice. This phenomenon of "replication" can, according to Shepherd-Smith (1994) seriously inflate the apparent AIR estimate.

The AIR estimate assumes that the number of people reading *any* issue of a publication, within a period of time equal in length to the interval between successive issues, provides an unbiased estimate of the number reading any specific issue, averaged over issues and measured across an issue's life. It has been argued, for example by Brown (1994) that this is true only if it is the *first* time an issue is read, otherwise there will be biases from both replication and parallel reading. The latter arises if somebody sees two or more issues within a publishing period. Under AIR this will count only once and will underestimate the amount of reading. Replication and parallel reading will, agues Brown, thus tend to cancel one another out since they work in opposite directions and the overall model bias is very limited. The matter could be solved by adding another question (to each newspaper or magazine seen) concerning whether it was the first occasion and discounting it if it were not. That, of course, would mean lengthening considerably the existing questionnaire. It would also undermine trend data, while some readerships would go up and some would go down. This could upset some clients.

AIR identifies respondents as either readers or nonreaders, but it is also necessary to estimate the frequency of reading. Again, this is very difficult to measure. It is usual to ask respondents about their claimed regularity of reading and to take their answers at face value. But, should we ask about actual past reading behavior or what people "usually" do? Should the alternative answers between which respondents must choose be couched in numbers, in verbal terms or in a mixture of the two? An example of a mixture would be: "About how often do you see *The Economist* these days – frequently (three or four issues out of every four), sometimes (one or two issues out of four) or only occasionally (fewer than one issue out of four)?" There is a tendency, however, for regular readers to over-claim their frequency of reading and for low-frequency readers to under-claim (Brown 1994). Consequently, it is better, argues Brown (1994), to use the answers only to categorize readers into groups and no more (that is, to restrict the scale to an ordinal one).

Most European countries have regular or continuous readership surveys. In some cases these are organized and administered by an industry body set up to represent the interests of the publishers, the advertisers and their agencies. The UK, Germany, Belgium, the Republic of Ireland, the Netherlands and Switzerland come into this category. Alternatively, the research may be sponsored by a number of individual companies who may not be representative of the industry as a whole. A third possibility is for a market research agency to propose a readership survey, to be responsible for its design and execution and to sell the data to as many clients as possible. Most countries use the recent reading techniques for estimating average issue readership.

EUROPEAN MARKETING RESEARCH

The UK National Readership Survey

BOX 16.6

In the UK there is a history of readership research that goes back over 60 years (see Brown 1994 for details), but the current form of National Readership Survey dates from the early 1940s. In 1968 a Joint Industry Committee for National Readership Surveys (JICNARS) was set up to represent the publishers, the advertisers and the agencies. JICNARS drafted the methodological specification for the NRS and awarded the contract to Research Services Limited (RSL, now Ipsos-RSL). In 1992 JICNARS was replaced by National Readership Surveys Ltd with a board smaller in size than the earlier Committee. This is a not-for-profit organization that is jointly owned by associations representing the advertising agencies, newspapers and magazines. The contract was re-awarded to Ipsos UK in 2002.

The NRS is based on some 36 000 interviews a year covering 280 newspapers and magazines. The results give five-day, six-day and Saturday average issue readership for national daily newspapers, and frequency, recency, source of copy and how disappointed data for all publications. It also covers car ownership, holidays, consumer goods, financial arrangements and classification questions.

The universe from which the NRS sample is taken is all adults aged 15 and over resident in private households. The sample is a multistage disproportional preselected sample design. Social grades A, B and C1 are oversampled using certain ACORN types. The frame for the selection of sampling points is all Enumeration Districts (ED), while the frame for the selection of individuals is the Postcode Address File (PAF). Selection of Enumeration districts is made with probability proportionate to size. Within each ED selected, 21 standard and five replacement addresses are selected from the PAF, although there are certain modifications made in some Scottish points. Within each address, one or two persons are selected following specified rules that vary according to the size of the household. The selected sampling points are systematically allocated to month and then start day to ensure a balanced daily interviewing schedule. Interviewers are given seven days to complete a standard assignment, starting on the specified day.

The interview uses double-screen computer-assisted interviewing to capture readership data. The interviewer uses a laptop to route respondents through the interview and record the respondent's answers. The respondent's screen is radio-linked to the interviewer's laptop, but the interviewer controls the visual prompts. Respondents are shown a sequence of about 50 screens, each of which carries the titles of six publications (the order in which the screens are presented is rotated, as are the titles on the screen). Data are transmitted electronically back to the mainframe.

The main trading currency of the NRS is average issue readership, which is the estimated number of readers for any single issue of a publication. This is derived from the recency question – the number of people who have read the publication within the publication interval, for example, for daily newspapers, it is read yesterday, for Sunday newspapers and weekly magazines, it is read in the past seven days. The survey also asks about frequency of reading (from "Almost always", "At least 3 issues out of 4" to "Not in the past 12 months"), source of copy and how disappointed the respondent would be if the publication were not available – "Very disappointed", "Fairly disappointed" and "Not at all disappointed". Demographics include gender, age, social grade, region, working status, occupation and industry, marital status, presence of children, tenure on home, income, education, qualifications, ethnic origin, disabilities and geodemographics. There is also a lifestyle section covering shopping, motoring, holidays, financial, ownership of the latest electronic accessories and future plans.

Following the fieldwork, NRS results are subject to extensive reweighting. Preweights are applied to compensate for purposeful departures from allocating an equal probability of selection to each member of the population. These cover unequal sampling factions for respondents within households, the constraint of the number of sampling points per subarea to be a multiple of 12, and some over-sampling in Scotland and in parts of England and Wales. A further stage of weighting corrects for discrepancies between the demographic profile of the achieved sample and that of the population.

In the published reports there are a limited number of types of basic readership data that constantly recur. There are tabulations of readership penetration – average issue readership title-by-title, shown both in absolute terms and as a percentage of the population. These figures will be further broken down by demographic subgroups. A second main category comprises the readership profile tables. The data are rearranged so that the total average issue readership of each title becomes the base and the body of the table shows the profile of this total audience across subgroups of interest. Most survey reports also contain tabular data on reading frequency, so that probabilities of contact with the average issue can be calculated. Finally, there are tables of readership duplication – the proportion of the AIR of publication A who are also in the audience of publication B.

The NRS has sometimes been criticized for not providing enough information on the manner in which different titles are read, so a question was introduced on whether respondents look at particular topics when they are reading newspapers or magazines, for example "UK/British news", "Sport", or "TV programs". This, however, still does not refer to the reading of specific sections in specific issues. Some users are frustrated that the survey does not go beyond "reading frequency" and "source of copy" to qualify the average issue readership score. Ideally, users would like to know the numbers and profiles of people exposed to a given advertisement. There is currently nothing on time spent reading, the reading of sections or specific issue readership.

Despite these criticisms the NRS has over the years been seen as the "gold standard" for survey research, setting the standard not only for readership measurement, but also for demographics. Social grading as defined by the NRS has become the standard for the whole of the UK market research industry. Social grade quota setting and weighting of many surveys is often undertaken with reference to the findings of the NRS.

As the number of magazine titles has grown, and the volume of newspaper sections and supplements has expanded, the task of covering them all has become increasingly difficult. In France, print measurement has been split into two surveys, one for newspapers and one for magazines based on separate samples of 20 000 respondents.

> ## KEY POINTS
>
> The measurement of audiences for television, radio, newspapers, magazines and outdoor posters is complex and costly. Accordingly, only the larger agencies have the resources to set up and run the systems required. At the end of the day, all the data produced are estimates and therefore subject to error, yet millions of Euros or pounds sterling paid for or earned from advertising depend on the data. It is therefore essential that their quality be as good as it is possible to achieve. In most European countries, it is felt that market measurement and media audience measurement should be undertaken separately, but there is a growing demand for what is called single-source data, whereby the same individual is asked both about their product purchasing and about their use of the media. Such data are explained in the next section.

Single-source data

In principle, **single-source data** could indicate any combination of data obtained from the same sample of respondents, whether from a survey or a panel. In practice, the term is used almost exclusively to refer to a combination or product and media data; in short, market and media measurement data are sought from the same individuals. Being single-source means that it is possible to identify on an individual-by-individual basis both what products they use and what media they are exposed to. Such data assist with media selection and market targeting. From such data it is possible to know, for example, exactly what media purchasers of given products or brands have watched, listened to or read. This helps with media selection. In the other direction, it is possible to determine any changes in product buying behavior among those who have seen or listened to advertisements. This helps with measures of advertising effectiveness and the targeting of market segments. Though the advantages of single-source data are very clear, the problem is that it is difficult to cover both product usage and media exposure from the same individuals in a survey process in other than a sketchy manner. During the 1960s, two approaches to the problem surfaced. One was data fusion, which merges two surveys on common variables so that they can be analyzed as a single survey. The other was single-source data.

Single-source data Data on product usage and media usage taken from the same sample of respondents.

The first single-source research vehicle was the Target Group Index (TGI), developed by BMRB, launched in 1969. This is now run in countries throughout Europe, in the United States and in Russia. In the UK, respondents are questioned about:

- their use of 500 different products covering 4000 brands, across 14 sectors from appliances and durables to toiletries and cosmetics,

- their readership of over 200 magazines and newspapers,

- going to the cinema, listening to the radio, using the internet and seeing outdoor posters,

- television viewing, including cable satellite and digital, video and teletext usage,

■ the national, regional and local radio stations they listen to,

■ their exposure to outdoor advertising,

■ their lifestyles based on over 250 attitude questions.

The TGI questionnaire is posted to addresses prearranged by an interviewer who works for the BMRB omnibus survey. The major product fields covered are foods, household goods, medicaments, toiletries and cosmetics, drink, confectionery, tobacco, motoring, clothing, leisure, holidays, financial services and consumer durables. Respondents are asked about product and service usage, ownership or participation – not about purchases made or prices paid. In the case of branded product fields, questions on frequency or weight of use are asked, along with questions on the brands used most often, plus others used in the past six months. For food and household products, it is the family use of the product that is recorded; otherwise it is personal use.

The press media questions are designed to collect responses similar to those obtained by the National Readership Survey and show average issue readership (which is explained on pp. 488–489). Television questions ask about day-by-day viewing "on the average" for that day in 15-minute blocks before 9.30 a.m. and half-hour blocks thereafter. Each channel is covered separately.

There is a lifestage classification as reflected by a combination of age and household composition. This creates a 12 segment classification with descriptive labels such as "Fledglings", "Unconstrained Couples" and "Hotel Parents", which may be further split by social grading, ABC1 and C2DE.

The lifestyle questions are in the form of Likert-type attitude statements with which people are asked to agree or disagree on a 5-point scale from "definitely agree" to "definitely disagree". The statements cover the main areas of food, drink, shopping, diet/health, personal appearance, DIY, holidays, finance, travel, media, luxury/British goods, motivation/self-perception, plus questions on some specific products and attitudes to sponsorship. Demographics include age, gender, social grade, region, household income, terminal education age, working status, home ownership, household size, marital status and employment status. Besides social grade, there are 13 indicators of socioeconomic level based on the possession of a range of items.

The current questionnaire runs to over 100 pages and takes an average of four hours to complete. The questionnaire is totally precoded and adapted for optical mark reading – respondents indicate their replies by marking appropriate boxes with a pencil. The answers are then read electronically using infrared sensors. There are four versions of the questionnaire: for men, women, shoppers and nonshoppers. At the time of placing the questionnaire a financial incentive is provided by BMRB.

About 25 000 questionnaires are completed annually. Data from the questionnaires are weighted in two stages (see pp. 200–201 for an explanation of weighting).

■ Demographic cell weighting, taking age within region, and social class within region for men and for women who are not housewives. For housewives, weightings are applied for working status and presence of children, again by region.

■ In order to remove the small differences in the estimates of readership levels that would otherwise exist between the TGI and the National Readership Survey, a specially-designed rim-weighting system has been developed.

Combined weights of up to 20 are used. The figures are then grossed up to the population. The tables of product usage (see Table 16.1) give four measures or indices of product usage:

- the total number of product users in each demographic category,
- the percent down, which gives the percentage in each demographic category,
- the percent across, giving penetration for demographic items and composition for media items,
- an index of selectivity, taking penetration (or composition) in comparison with the universe as a whole.

Each of these indices is broken down by heavy/medium/light and nonusers, and, for product fields and for brands with more than one million claimed users (about 1400 brands), they are crosstabulated against a range of demographic variables including sex, age, social class, area (standard and ITV region), and number of children, plus media usage and other selected variables. Thus in Table 16.1 there are 10 781 000 users of vodka (an estimate derived from people in the sample who had indicated "Yes" when asked if they ever drink it, and grossed up to the population figure), of whom 5 398 000 or 50.1 percent are men. The users account for 24 percent of all adults. Users who are male account for 25 percent of all males, while adults aged 15–24, for example, were 60 percent above the average for all adult users (i.e. 38.5 percent compared with 24 percent).

These data enable TGI users to describe in detail their target markets and to segment their marketing activities. For a number of TGI case studies, go to: www.bmrb-tgi.co.uk.

TABLE 16.1 — A product usage table from the Target Group Index Vodka

	Population '000	All users A '000	B % down	C % across	D index	Heavy users A '000	B % down	C % across	D index	Medium users A '000	B % down	C % across	D index
All adults	44 871	10 781	100.0	24.0	100	1 631	100.0	3.6	100	3 681	100.0	8.2	100
Men	21 583	5 398	50.1	25.0	104	819	50.2	3.8	104	1 828	49.7	8.5	103
Women	23 287	5 383	49.9	23.1	96	812	49.8	3.5	96	1 853	50.3	8.0	97
15–24	8 825	3 401	31.5	38.5	160	695	42.6	7.9	217	1 393	37.9	15.8	192
25–34	7 929	2 559	23.7	32.3	134	398	24.4	5.0	138	846	23.0	10.7	130
35–44	7 612	1 948	18.1	25.6	106	254	15.6	3.3	92	541	14.7	7.1	87
45–54	6 032	1 312	12.2	21.7	91	155	9.5	2.6	71	411	11.2	6.8	83
55–64	5 865	826	7.7	14.1	59	84	5.1	1.4	39	247	6.7	4.2	51
65+	8 607	735	6.8	8.5	36	45	2.7	0.5	14	243	6.6	2.8	34
AB	7 864	1 863	17.3	23.7	99	212	13.0	2.7	74	646	17.5	8.2	100
C1	10 162	2 540	23.6	25.0	104	390	23.9	3.8	106	889	24.1	8.7	107
C2	12 453	3 233	30.0	26.0	108	488	29.9	3.9	108	1 062	28.8	8.5	104
D	8 027	1 965	18.2	24.5	102	344	21.1	4.3	118	677	18.4	8.4	103
E	6 365	1 180	10.9	18.5	77	197	12.1	3.1	85	408	11.1	6.4	78
ABC1	18 026	4 403	40.8	24.4	102	602	36.9	3.3	92	1 535	41.7	8.5	104
C2D	20 480	5 198	48.2	25.4	106	832	51.0	4.1	112	1 739	47.2	8.5	103
ABC1 15–34	6 541	2 297	21.3	35.1	146	410	25.1	6.3	172	907	24.6	13.9	169
35–54	6 173	1 426	13.2	23.1	96	148	9.1	2.4	66	427	11.6	6.9	84
55+	5 313	679	6.3	12.8	53	44	2.7	0.8	23	201	5.5	3.8	46
C2DE 15–34	10 214	3 663	34.0	35.9	149	683	41.9	6.7	184	1 333	36.2	13.0	159
35–44	7 472	1 834	17.0	24.5	102	261	16.0	3.5	96	525	14.3	7.0	86
55+	9 160	882	8.2	9.6	40	85	5.2	0.9	25	289	7.8	3.2	38

Besides the product field information, there are brand usage tables, listing users of the product group who use the brand exclusively (solus users); those who prefer it, but another brand is also used (most often users); and those who are more casual in their use, that is, have used the brand, but use another brand more often (minor users). This facilitates some measure of brand loyalty. Demographic tables use demographic groupings as headings and include breakdowns of respondents by savings and investments, ownership of durable items, leisure items, motoring, drinking, smoking, DIY, entertaining and holidays abroad.

The TGI gives measures of market penetration and weight of use rather than estimates of market size or market share. It allows conclusions to be drawn about the levels of penetration to a target group among different demographic and media audience groups, and it is possible to see how these differ from the population as a whole and how they differ from other groups.

Subscribers have electronic access to datasets for which they have subscribed. Results are published on a rolling quarterly basis. It is possible to do special analyses that crosstabulate anything by anything, or that break down the data by geodemographic segmentation (such as ACORN, MOSAIC or postcode areas) or by any of the lifestyle, lifestage, or socioeconomic questions. Cluster analysis is often used on the lifestyle data to group respondents into segments similar in terms of such lifestyles. This facilitates the more creative use of the TGI since these groupings can then be cross-analyzed by any of the other variables. TGI data are also fused with data from panelists whose television viewing is monitored by BARB. The process of data fusion is explained on p. 254.

BMRB has developed a separate youth study, which asks about product usage and readership of 6000 youths aged 7–10, 11–14 and 15–19. These are recruited from earlier TGI households who are known to have children. For the over 50-year-olds there is a procedure for recontacting people in this age group who have already completed a TGI questionnaire. They are sent a separate questionnaire asking about products directed at the over 50s. TGI Premier provides information on the top socioeconomic strata of households. It is again a separate survey from the TGI with its own sample of 5500 interviews with social Grade A and B adults. TGI Wavelength provides single-source, weekly and four-weekly reach data for over 75 regional and local radio stations. This provides data on listeners to local commercial radio stations that can be analyzed by the thousands of variables available on the TGI database. Data are collected at the face-to-face Omnibus interview that precedes the placement of the TGI questionnaire. This is later merged with the TGI survey at a respondent level.

TGI is undertaken in 50 countries worldwide. Based on a sample of 55 000 adults, TGI Europa provides harmonized data on product use, media consumption and attitudes across Britain, France, Germany, and Spain – including data on 18 broad product sectors, more than 250 specific categories and around 12 000 domestic and international brands. Box 16.7 reports an analysis of TGI lifestyle data across Europe.

Single-source surveys like the TGI relate media use and claimed product use at one point of time. They thus address only the coverage aspect of media scheduling, not frequency (White 2000). A single-source panel, however, could measure each viewing occasion or opening of a newspaper or magazine. A number of such panels are now operating in Europe, including the BehaviorScan systems run by GfK in Germany and France, Nielsen panels in Germany and Italy, and the TNS MediaSpan and tvSPAN systems in the UK. The tvSPAN panel is a subset of 3000 TNS Worldpanel homes that have a TV set meter installed. These homes are selected to be representative of the population. MediaSPAN is a survey of the main shoppers in each of the 15 000 Worldpanel homes who are sent a detailed questionnaire asking about habitual television viewing, print readership, radio listening, cinema going and travel. It also contains 100 lifestyle statements. Over 80 percent of main shoppers return the questionnaire, which is sent twice a year. The questionnaire

---

EUROPEAN MARKETING RESEARCH
The TGI in Europe

BOX 16.7

The TGI is run in almost every country in Europe. Wicken (2003) reports an analysis of lifestyle data from TGI data across 15 European countries to develop types of consumers according to the ways in which they consume and react to media and advertising. The study found a six-cluster solution that appeared to work right across Europe. These include:

- media literates,
- butterflies,
- disengaged,
- indoor types,
- entertainment seekers,
- passive absorbers.

These segments vary in terms of their openness and response to advertising, so the analysis can be input in various ways to advertising campaigns.

---

contains many questions relating to television viewing, including channel, day-part sections, plus specific programs viewed. Since the tvSPAN subset also completes the questionnaire, it is possible to investigate the relationship between actual and claimed viewing patterns (Beaumont 2003). This enables TNS to improve its estimate of the probable exposure of main shoppers to specific advertising campaigns. A model has been created that is used to refine the probabilities of viewing of commercial breaks for each commercial channel in the non-tvSPAN homes. By combining these probabilities with actual spot transmission data for a brand's TV campaign, TNS can estimate the number of exposures each main shopper has seen in each week of the campaign (Beaumont 2003).

KEY POINTS

All market and media audience measurement systems, and single-source data, need to balance the needs of consumers (purchasers, watchers, listeners or readers), with manufacturers and media providers (the broadcasters and print media) and the purchasers of market and media audience measurement data. The balancing act is becoming more difficult as consumers want easier and more appropriate tracking technology, the manufacturers and media providers are faced with market and audience fragmentation, and the advertisers are becoming increasingly nervous about the quality of the data they are buying. They also want single-source and multimedia exposure data since consumers will normally combine the use of media during the course of a typical day. They want "joined-up" information to inform their business decisions. Single-source panels are, however, costly to use and to analyze and can survive only with strong syndicated support. The audiometer might help to integrate television and radio audiences, but as yet the television industry in Europe has not seen fit to use this technology.

Though more sophisticated technology might make the data capture process more accurate, the data are still based on samples, so they are estimates of reality, not reality itself. Reality may be more complex, as television watchers go channel-hopping during the commercial breaks, they use the mute button, they go out of the room, they do something else or they zap commercial breaks altogether during playback on a video or DVD recorder. In terms of technology, there is no reason why these should not be measured or estimated, but, ironically, it means that audience figures will probably go down and media suppliers will be less happy.

Usage and attitude studies

Usage and attitude (U&A) studies provide the basic building blocks for marketing activity since they are used largely to provide an in-depth understanding of the market in which a particular brand is being sold. They describe a market very much from the consumer's point of view and will cover:

- brand or product awareness (including advertising awareness where applicable),
- brand or product choice behavior, for example trial, adoption, loyalty and brand repertoires,
- brand or product purchasing – frequency, source, prices paid, and quantities and size/style of pack,
- usage patterns,
- attitudes to or beliefs about the brand(s) or product(s),
- the needs that the brands or products do or do not meet as far as the consumer is concerned.

Many of the variables, for example brand choice behavior, brand purchasing, and usage patterns, are similar to consumer panel data. However, U&A studies, unlike consumer panels, also collect data on brand and advertising awareness, and on attitudes towards brands or products. Furthermore, a more important distinction is that they are ad hoc, both in the sense that they are not usually continuous, and in the sense that they are normally custom-designed for individual clients rather than syndicated.

In the 1960s and 1970s it was fairly common for U&A studies to be carried out regularly, perhaps quarterly or six-monthly, but nowadays they tend to be on an occasional basis, perhaps once every two or three years, or even less regularly. There are two main reasons for this. First, they are in-depth "dipstick" operations that go into great detail to provide an understanding of the marketplace at one point of time. Typically there will be between 1000 and 2000 face-to-face interviews in a single study, with each interview lasting up to an hour. In consequence, they are expensive, typically £60 000 or more at today's prices. Second, because of the development of tracking studies and consumer panel data, they are no longer required to monitor changes in the key market variables. Changes could not, in any case, easily be measured in the depth to which U&A studies go. In short, they are not required so frequently. They nowadays do not even seek to replicate earlier studies because a lot of things will have changed in the marketplace in the meantime.

U&A studies are usually conducted using face-to-face interviews, often over a four-week period. Postal questionnaires may be used, although they tend to have too low a response rate, while the use of the telephone is limited because it is usually necessary to present visual stimuli to respondents. Interviews typically begin by asking about brand awareness, for example "Which brands of product X can you think of, have you seen/bought/used/seen advertised?" Usually some timescale is attached – typically a week, but maybe "in the past 24 hours", "in the past two weeks" or just "recently". Such questions are unlikely to be prompted, and will aim for "top-of-the-mind" reactions. The interviewer may then turn to particular brands – perhaps the brand leader and the brand being researched – to ask about purchasing behavior.

Attitudes towards brands will usually be measured using 5- or 7-point rating scales so that the ratings of different people and different brands can be compared. Such ratings may well, however, be in batteries of statements that go for across-the-brand comparisons, as illustrated in Figure 16.2. It is important that respondents understand the characteristics they are being asked to rate, and that such characteristics cover all the key areas likely to differentiate between products or brand comprehensively. Where different types of product are the focus of interest, it is, in addition, necessary to ensure that the product typologies or groupings are made in terms familiar to consumers. The development of these attributes is, in consequence, usually undertaken using qualitative research – group discussions or depth interviews. The questions themselves may be tested in an omnibus survey.

Consumer needs may be tapped by asking about their "ideal" product, using either open-ended questions or product features as prompts. Respondents are also likely to be asked about what factors are or were important in choosing a particular brand. In many U&A studies the opportunity is taken to look at other issues like pricing, packaging, reactions to new product concepts, media use, or product ownership. Standard demographics will normally be collected for both structural and analytic purposes. Increasingly, these will include lifestyle, life cycle and geodemographic variables.

Samples used in U&A studies will usually be of current users in the product field, and may vary in size from about 500 to 2000 depending on the need for subgroup analysis, regional breakdowns, or segmentation analysis. Well-known brands purchased by many people may require smaller samples than minority brands. Booster samples of consumers most likely to use less well-known brands may well be used. Most sampling is quota since probability samples are likely to be too expensive and take too long to carry out. In some cases the research may be extended to look at nonusers or users of products in related fields.

The standard analysis of U&A data will typically take the form of crosstabulating all the usage and attitude variables against all the demographics. A lot of useful information about the brand being researched and its competitors can be derived from basic tables of this kind. However, to derive the full value from the research, more sophisticated analyses will often be carried out. Thus batteries of attitude statements may be factor analyzed to see which sets of statements intercorrelate. The factors thus generated may then be used as inputs to a cluster analysis to generate market segments by revealing groups of respondents who are similar in

Here is a list of drinks that you might find in off-licenses or supermarkets. I would like to know your impressions of these drinks, even if you have not actually tried them. Which of these brands do you think:
(You can mention as many or as few as you like)

	A	B	C	D
Is an everyday drink?	1	1	1	1
Is for weekend drinking?	2	2	2	2
Is a cut above the average drink?	3	3	3	3
Is dull and uninteresting?	4	4	4	4
Is particularly strong on alcohol?	5	5	5	5
Is appealing to older people?	6	6	6	6

FIGURE 16.2

An attitude battery of statements for an alcoholic drink

Conjoint analysis A multivariate technique used to understand how respondents develop preferences for products or services. It tries to identify the relative importance of product or service features.

respect of a number of variables. Many U&A studies include questions on preferences for product characteristics. Provided these are ranked, they may be used as inputs to **conjoint analysis** that generates a utility score for each characteristic and an overall optimum product formulation. Mapping techniques and sensory evaluation may be used where the research is to act as an input to product positioning. Besides their key role in market segmentation and brand positioning, U&A studies may also be used in the longer-term development of promotional strategies and in the targeting of new products or relaunched modified products.

Customer satisfaction and relationship management research

Customer satisfaction measurement

Customer satisfaction relates to post-purchase feelings of pleasure or disappointment. These feelings, furthermore, tend to be multidimensional and transaction-specific, and to refer to reactions to the *last* purchase or *last* service encounter. Over time these feelings will accumulate into *attitudes* concerning service or product quality. Customer satisfaction will tend to be a key driver of repeat purchase following the first purchase. Thereafter, for subsequent purchases, it will be a function of perceived quality plus customer satisfaction from the preceding purchase. Thus whether or not I buy the same brand again will be a function of my overall perception of product quality based on my longer-term experiences of the brand plus what happened on my last purchase, which, if it were unsatisfactory in any way, may not stop me from repeat purchase if my overall experiences have been satisfactory.

We saw in Chapter 5 that measurement may be direct, indirect, derived or multidimensional. All of these have been used to measure customer satisfaction. Satisfaction may be measured directly by asking customers who have just purchased a product or experienced a service how satisfied they are on a 3-, 5- or 7-point rating scale. Such direct measures may be created either by asking customers to give an overall evaluation, or by asking them about their levels of satisfaction with particular product features or service components. However, knowing, for example, that 70 percent of its customers say they are either "satisfied" or "very satisfied" does not tell the company whether it is doing well or badly or what it needs to *do* to increase this percentage. Direct measures of this kind offer little by way of diagnostic value. If customers say they are dissatisfied or even very dissatisfied, we have no idea about why, or what levels of product performance or service are causing the dissatisfaction.

Indirect measures of customer satisfaction might include the number of products that have been returned as defective or the number of complaints received. A more traditional and commonly used indicator of satisfaction is customer perception of the performance of a product or service. In some cases, satisfaction is seen as the sum of the performance perceptions for individual features. The problem with this approach is that any attempt to measure the contribution of individual features to overall satisfaction becomes tautological – individual features are being used to predict their summation. In other cases, there *is* an overall score, usually, but not necessarily, measuring satisfaction, which is derived independently of the scores of the individual items. It is then assumed that those features that correlate most strongly with the overall score across consumers are the ones that have the greatest impact on satisfaction.

Performance analysis is helpful up to a point, and it may reveal some interesting findings for firms that are just embarking on customer satisfaction research. However, it does assume that the relationship between performance and satisfaction is linear, that the correlation between the two is near to unity, and that performance is the cause of satisfaction or that certain performances are, at any rate, key drivers of satisfaction. Performance analysis does not help to explain *why* consumers think that the performance of any item is high or low. Consumer psychology mediates the impact of performance observations on satisfaction judgments. *How* is unexplained.

Measures of customer satisfaction may be neither direct nor indirect, but derived in a number of different ways, for example:

- comparing expectations with perceived performance,
- developing summated rating scales,
- undertaking regression analysis,
- using structural equation modeling,
- using conjoint analysis.

Comparing expectations with perceived performance is often referred to as the "disconfirmation" or "gap" model. Customers are asked about, first, what their ideal level of performance or service would be, or what they would expect, then second, what they perceive they are getting. According to this model, feelings of satisfaction or dissatisfaction arise when consumers compare their perceptions of a product or service performance to their expectations. If perceived performance exceeds expectations (a "positive disconfirmation") then the customer is satisfied; if it falls short (a "negative disconfirmation") then they are dissatisfied. A model that is popular among academics for looking at perceptions of quality and customer satisfaction in the services area is the SERVQUAL model developed by Parasuraman et al. (1988). This is based on a 22-item set of Likert-type questions grouped into five dimensions – tangibles, reliability, responsiveness, assurance and empathy. The instrument is administered twice, first to measure expectations and second to measure perceptions of performance.

Analysis of the data may take one or more of three forms:

- an item-by-item analysis of the difference between performance (P) and expectation (E) on each item (P1−E1, P2−E2 etc.),

- a dimension-by-dimension analysis in which performance for the four or five items in each dimension are averaged and from which is subtracted the averaged expectations for that dimension((P1+P2+P3+P4/4) − (E1+E2+E3+E4/4),

- a single measure of service quality in which all 22 items are summed and averaged for performance and expectations ((P1+P2 . . .+P22) − (E1+E2 . . . E22)). This is the so-called SERVQUAL gap.

This model has been widely used, but also widely criticized (for a review of such criticisms see Buttle 1996). Much of the criticism centers on the notion of expectation. Following the first purchase, expectations of future purchases will tend to adjust to previous experiences so that expectations in the longer term become the sum of past perceived performances. Thus it has been suggested (for example by Cronin and Taylor 1992) that perceptions of performance alone are as good if not better predictors of, for example, purchase intentions. In consequence, Cronin and Taylor (1992) have proposed their alternative SERVPERF scale, which takes the original 22-item SERVQUAL scale covering the five key dimensions, but assesses these just against performance, not in terms of gaps between expectations and performance. The authors concluded from a survey of respondents in the southeastern United States covering four industries – banking, pest control, dry cleaning and fast food – that SERVPERF was a more appropriate basis for measuring service quality than SERVQUAL.

SERVPERF is, in fact, a summated rating scale. In practice, most market research agencies offering customer satisfaction research tend to favor a measure of satisfaction based solely or largely on performance ratings, often derived from the summation of a subset of items. Many agencies then go on to relate such measures to the importance of the features as perceived by customers. Cronin and Taylor (1992) have argued that weighting performance by importance adds little to the prediction of purchase intention. However, the agencies are more likely to keep performance and importance separate, so that any features that are low on performance but high on importance can have more resources devoted to them and, similarly, any features that are high on performance but low on importance can have resources shifted away from them.

Measures of importance may themselves be direct, indirect or derived. Direct measures ask customers directly how important various aspects of service are, from "not at all important" to "very important". Such measures are easy and quick to take, but the problem is that people will tend to rate everything as important or very important. What the researcher ends up with is mostly high scores. Usually the items are obtained from qualitative work in the first place – so they are already known to be important to customers. Indirect measures of importance might include things like the customer's willingness to complain about the features involved. Derived measures will include, for example, the use of conjoint (or "trade-off") analysis, which establishes importance on the basis of what levels of service customers will trade off against each other.

Oliver (1997) argues that importance is an ambiguous and unreliable concept. First because it begs the question of importance for what? Second because importance of individual items is context-specific and will depend, for example, on what features are available from competitors' products. Third, importance often confuses essential with desirable. Having seatbelts in a car is certainly important, but because they are essential, whereas airconditioning may be important because it is desirable. Fourth, features may be important or unimportant for entirely different reasons Thus nonsmoking policies in restaurants and bars are extremely important to both smokers and nonsmokers but for totally different reasons.

The use of summated rating scales does not require an independent measure of overall satisfaction for their calculation, whereas regression analysis depends on such a measure to assess the contribution each variable or item makes. This means that the "importance" of each item is generated not from customer perceptions of importance but from the relative contribution each item makes in explaining the variance in overall satisfaction. The problem with such procedures, however, is that they rely on adequate variability in the data. In addition, the top four or five items may show a relationship with satisfaction scores, but the rest will tend to lack any discrimination. There are also problems of multicollinearity – where variables are highly intercorrelated, both partial correlations and slope estimates will be increasingly sensitive to sampling and measurement errors.

Structural equation modeling (SEM) can be traced back to the beginning of the nineteenth century when Spearman developed factor analysis. Later, in 1934, Wright introduced path analysis, but it was not until the 1970s that general SEM techniques became accessible to researchers in the social and behavioral sciences. State-of-the-art computer packages such as LISREL (linear structural relations) and EQS have incorporated many of the traditional techniques, such as ordinary least squares regression as special cases.

SEM – sometimes called causal modeling – combines path analysis and confirmatory factor analysis into a process that allows the analysis of simultaneous regression equations. It does this by decomposing the direct, indirect and total effects among structurally ordered variables within a specific model. Confirmatory factor analysis is used to test a priori hypothesized, theory-derived structure with collected data. It allows the researcher to cluster observed variables in prespecified, theory-driven ways, that is, to specify a priori the latent constructs that the observed variables are intended to measure. After estimating the factor loadings, the investigator assesses whether or not the collected data "fit" the hypothesized factor structure.

Satisfaction and loyalty

Whatever measures of satisfaction are adopted, it must be remembered, however, that they are "significant" only in relation to comparable measures of the competition. What matters is not, for example, the percentage of customers satisfied or very satisfied, but the extent to which your customers are more satisfied with your products than with your competitor's products. Satisfaction, furthermore, is not necessarily related to loyalty or repeat purchase. The way in which they go together has been shown (e.g. by Jones and Sasser 1995) to depend on the nature of competition in the industry. In a very competitive industry the difference in terms of loyalty between being completely or "very" satisfied and just "satisfied" may be huge (see Figure 16.3). Jones and Sasser (1995) argue that complete and total customer satisfaction is the key to securing customer loyalty and generating superior long-term financial performance. Put another way, any drop from total satisfaction results in a major drop in loyalty. Even in markets with relatively little competition it is important to provide customers with outstanding value. If customers are not totally satisfied they will defect as soon as they are offered a choice. Thus apparently loyal customers will defect as soon as they have exhausted their frequent-flier air-miles program, or if a market is deregulated. It is the percentage of customers in the "top box" that really counts. The rest, even if they say they are "satisfied", will readily switch to a competitor.

Dissatisfied customers are probably having problems with the company's core value of its product or service. Often this is a result of shifts in customer need as competitors improve their products or services, as new competitors arrive, or as new technologies redefine the game. However, the company has to be sure that it

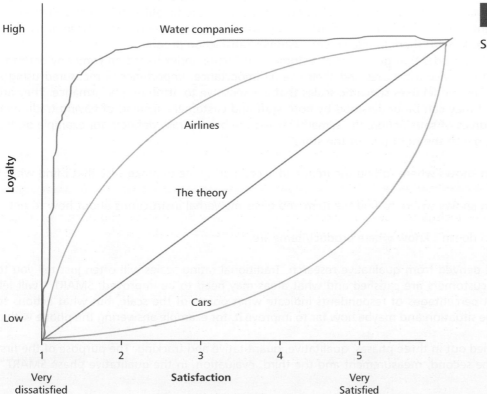

FIGURE 16.3

Satisfaction and loyalty

is not just the "wrong" customers who are dissatisfied, otherwise it may overreact or waste resources. "Wrong" customers are customers outside the target group and who will always be difficult to please and will continually utilize a disproportionate amount of the company's resources, will undermine the morale of front-line employees, and may disparage the company to other potential customers. Jones and Sasser (1995) argue that the company should actively discourage such custom and make every effort not to attract others like them. They suggest that companies should encourage customers who are "apostles" or "loyalists", try to turn switchers into loyalists, and discourage "misfits" and "terrorists".

Approach by the market research agencies

Some agencies offer standardized proprietary techniques while others prefer to tailor their research to individual clients. However, these approaches overlap in the sense that most proprietary techniques are modified to suit individual clients, whereas many of those who do not offer proprietary techniques nevertheless tend to employ standardized components, approaches, or templates. Box 16.8 shows how Research International links the measurement of customer satisfaction with customer relationship management.

MARKET RESEARCH IN ACTION
Research International's SMART™ and CUPID™ systems

BOX 16.8

Research International operates in more than 50 countries, with its head office in the UK. It focuses mainly on ad hoc rather than continuous or syndicated services, offering both qualitative and quantitative research. In the area of quantitative customer satisfaction and relationship management research it has developed proprietary techniques for improving customer satisfaction and for measuring what it calls customer potential.

SMART™ (Salient Multi-Attribute Research Technique) discovers what aspects of customer service are the most important and how they impact on customer satisfaction, and identifies the most cost-effective service improvements. Research International then gives clients advice on how they can improve their performance and works with them to implement customer satisfaction programs.

SMART™ is a micro-model that generates a customer satisfaction index based on company performance on each of the service attributes and their overall importance. Importance is measured using a trade-off analysis. The model uses semantic scales that are sensitive to attribute performance. They are action-oriented and they can be understood by both staff and customers. Instead of having traditional rating scales of degrees of satisfaction, the semantic scales are behaviorally defined, for example on the attribute "Guiding me to the right part of the store":

- The sales person knows where to find the item and accompanies me to make sure that I find what I need.
- The sales person knows where to find the item and gives me verbal instructions about how to get there.
- The sales person doesn't know where product/items are.

These items are derived from qualitative research. Traditional rating scales will often just tell you to what extent your customers are satisfied and what areas may need to be improved. SMART™ will tell you not only what percentages of respondents indicate what points of the scale, but what actions to take to improve the situation and maybe how far to improve it, for example answering the phone within 30 seconds.

SMART™ is carried out in three phases: qualitative, quantitative and tracking. The purpose of the first is identification, the second, measurement and the third, evaluation. In the qualitative phase SMART™

identifies various "moments of truth" (or critical incidents) and the service attributes within each moment. It then generates levels of performance within each attribute. Thus a service experience may consist of:

- order placing,
- receiving delivery,
- invoicing and billing,
- repair and maintenance.

Order placing may, in turn, have several attributes:

- speed of getting through,
- politeness of staff,
- getting through to the right person,
- staff knowledge of the product range,
- continuity of contacts.

Speed of getting through may be identified at four levels:

- answered within 10 seconds,
- answered within 20 seconds,
- takes more than 30 seconds,
- phone is engaged or not answered.

In the quantitative phase perceived performance is measured, for example: "Which of these statements best describes the service you receive?"

- Staff either know or can provide an expert who knows about the entire product range.
- Staff have knowledge of the basic products in the range.
- Staff lack knowledge of their products.

SMART™ then determines the relevance of the attributes to the customer, for example: "How strongly would you feel about each of the following if performance on each aspect were to improve or worsen?"

- speed of getting through,
- politeness of staff,
- getting through to the right person,
- staff knowledge of their product range.

It is not possible to trade off every attribute, so the top eight attributes for each respondent are selected for trade-off. These are displayed at the lowest level and the customer is asked which one they would most like to see improved. The display is changed to incorporate the improvement and the question is asked again. The customer is trading off the attributes one against the other. The model then calculates what attribute improvements will produce the biggest improvements in satisfaction, and what items will produce the greatest losses if service slips. The results can then be recalculated according to market segment. Attributes may need to vary according to different international markets and different cultures.

In the final tracking phase, the SMART™ procedure will typically take the main areas agreed with the client to action – areas they have decided to target for improvement or that they cannot afford to let fall. These would then be included in a shortlist of attributes in a quantitative tracking questionnaire to measure performance of the company. The full SMART™ process may be repeated a year later to see what has changed.

Improving customer satisfaction, however, is only part of the story. Customer retention and customer loyalty are also important. Some satisfied customers do defect and some dissatisfied customers may stay through inertia; but even satisfied and loyal customers may not be the most profitable ones. Not all customers are equal: some are more profitable than others. Customers can interface with an organization through many different touch points – websites, call centers, retail outlets, direct sales and so on. Some of these points may be more profitable than others. To take these ideas on board, Research International has launched a new service it calls Customer Potential Indicator (CUPID™). This captures loyalty, but also looks at customer potential in terms of increasing share of wallet, increased usage, cross-sell potential, receptivity to premium offerings or upgrade potential as appropriate to a particular industry. One output is to classify customers as "unfulfilled" (likely to defect), "satisfied" (likely to stay, but not likely to increase business with the supplier) and "connected" (likely to stay and increase business). The system also looks at individual customer potential measures, retention, increased use, cross-sell, upgrade versus the competition. These metrics are combined into a single measure – the Customer Potential Index. This allows scores to be compared across companies and across product categories.

Generating satisfied customers is not the same as creating successful relationships. To achieve the latter requires that each person feels they are being provided for on both the functional and emotional levels. CUPID™ attempts to capture the quality of these elements. Research with 10 000 respondents across a range of industries showed that even poor-quality relationships are characterized by some anticipated retention (about 30 percent), but as customers begin to feel at least functionally provided for, retention increases dramatically to over 60 percent and the potential for cross-sell rises to 38 percent. However, there is little potential for upgrading until an emotional bond is established, at which point cross-sell potential also rises dramatically (see Figure 16.4). Customers are receptive to new product, even premium, offerings. Both functional and emotional touch points thus need to be managed. There must be a functional base before emotional needs can be attended to. For retail outlets, for example, customers need to agree both that "The products I want are always in stock" and "The stores provide a pleasant environment". The potential to attract new customers can also be assessed by looking at the numbers of "unfulfilled" customers among competitors.

A CUPID™ study will typically sample a minimum of 200 respondents for the client company. Research International will normally also recommend covering the key competitors with a further 200 per company. The analysis is conducted for each company. Retention and the potential for increase in use, cross-sell and upgrade are measured on a 10-point scale and the Customer Potential Indicator is a single measure of the strength of the relationship based on these four scores.

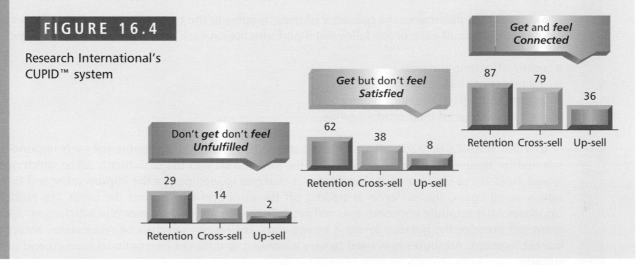

FIGURE 16.4

Research International's
CUPID™ system

Advertising tracking studies

A key problem with any ad hoc research, even if carried out at regular intervals, is that important features of a trend may be lost. For example, two snapshots or "dipsticks" of brands A and B taken at time T_1 and time T_2 may well overlook what has been happening to the trend in the meantime, as illustrated in Figure 16.5.

FIGURE 16.5

Continuous versus ad hoc measurement

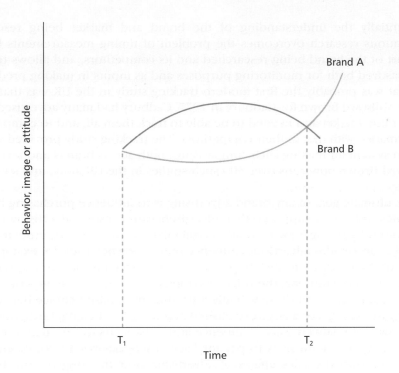

Furthermore, such studies will inevitably tend to be timed around the marketing activities of the brand being studied, so it will not give a clear picture of what competitors are up to since the timings of their activities will be different. It would be easy, but not helpful, inadvertently to bias advertising evaluation research so that one's own advertising appears in an unrealistically favorable light merely through timing. Furthermore, it would be difficult to know whether any changes out of line with earlier dipsticks were an aberration, or part of a new trend until the next dipstick is taken. In addition, clients are inclined to believe that improved brand measures will remain high rather than slip back to where they started from. A series of dipsticks, provided some are between bursts of advertising, may overcome this to some extent.

Continuous research, by contrast, will reveal trends. Continuous monitoring is particularly important for tracking the impact of advertising over a period of time, and it was largely in the area of advertising that tracking studies have developed. Early campaign evaluations often involved pre/post designs that typically took the form of a baseline study carried out before the advertising began followed up by periodic checks once the campaign was under way. A control group, unexposed to the advertising being researched, was often the subject of parallel measurements (Sampson 1987). The effects of the campaign could then be evaluated by comparing the change over time in the test group with changes that may have occurred anyway in the control group (a before-and-after with control experimental design).

These early studies were thus essentially ad hoc, simplistic in design, and geared to measuring how far the advertising met its objectives. The underlying assumption was that successful advertising would change brand measures regardless of whether the strategy sought to do so. In addition, their timing was always a problem since it would be difficult to determine an optimum point at which to take the post campaign measurements. Pre/post studies are, however, still carried out, for example because they are cheaper, or because a three-week advertising campaign just before Christmas would be too short for continuous research. The modern tracking study, however, tends to be regarded as synonymous with continuous measurement and planning. It will monitor all the key brands in a product field, usually on a weekly basis, in order to provide the input to improve substantially the understanding of the brand and market being researched. Continuous research overcomes the problem of timing measurements both on the part of the brand being researched and its competitors, and allows trends to be measured both for monitoring purposes and as inputs in making predictions.

What was probably the first modern tracking study in the UK was that carried out by Millward Brown for Cadbury in 1977. Cadbury had many advertised brands in the same market and needed to be able to track them all, and to compare their performance with that of their competitors. The tracking study provided an information system for making such comparisons, both across brands and across time. Millward Brown now runs over 300 such studies in the UK alone and some 1300 globally.

The ultimate goal of any brand advertising is to influence purchasing behavior and sales. It is often supposed that advertisers can measure advertising effectiveness simply by seeing how many additional sales it generates. Unfortunately, many other factors besides advertising influence purchasing behavior, for example availability of the products in the shops, their prominence on the shelves, the use of special offers or coupons, the price, variations in all these for competitor brands – the list is endless. All these will affect product trial, brand choice behavior and repeat purchasing. For a large established brand the advertising, furthermore, will probably be a relatively minor influence and only needs to produce a very small percentage increase in sales to pay for itself. There has been a lot of interest in trying to model the sales effects of advertising over the longer term, but such modeling will not reveal why one ad is better than another, which limits its use for future ad development.

The majority of advertisers are content with determining the probable effectiveness of their advertising by asking people questions. These may be questions about the brand or about the advertising. Brand-related questions will include brand recall (prompted, unprompted, or both) in the product field, respondent images of these brands and attitudes towards them. Questions about the advertising will include respondent recall of the ads, the brand they were linked to and the messages conveyed. From the brand questions it is possible to determine whether and to what extent brand awareness increases and attitudes to the brand improve when advertising takes place, and from the advertising questions whether the advertising "worked" in terms of attracting consumer attention and conveying messages linked memorably to the brand.

Advertising tracking studies almost always use independent samples rather than panels since it would be inappropriate to ask a panel about their awareness of advertising on a repeated basis. However, as research moves online, online panels are increasingly being used, but great care needs to be taken that a long period elapses between an individual being asked about the same product category. In a typical tracking study there will be independent weekly quota samples of about 100 respondents in the target market for the product field. Data are normally analyzed on a rolling four-weekly basis, so that weeks 1–4 will be cumulated and compared with weeks 2–5, 3–6 and so on. Analysis may be carried out over longer periods, so long as they are multiples of four weeks. So, although the number of interviews in any one week is not large enough to enable weekly analyses, grouping them together in this way still allows weekly comparisons to be made. Since interviewing is normally carried out over 50 weeks in a year (a brief period over Christmas is often left out), over 5000 interviews are carried out annually. This inevitably makes costs quite high, frequently over £100 000 a year – but actually not a lot more than a single one-off U&A study.

Most tracking studies are carried out by market research agencies on a client-specific basis, although some are syndicated. The advantage of the former is that the client has total control over the study, particularly the questionnaire. The downside is that such research is more expensive than syndicated research, and it is often difficult to build up a database of all the key brands in the marketplace as a key resource. While syndicated research is cheaper, it is, however, difficult to change any of the key dimensions as you go along in order to meet the changing needs of the company. Some agencies offer both syndicated and client-specific tracking research.

The typical tracking study will measure:

- product use in the product field, for example "Which of these alcoholic drinks do you drink nowadays?",

- spontaneous awareness of brands, for example "What brands of cider can you think of?",

- prompted awareness, for example "Which of these brands have you heard of?",

- trial, for example "Have you ever tried any of these brands?",

- past purchase, for example "Which of these brands have you bought recently?",

- future purchase intent, for example "How likely would you say you are to buy Brand X in the next three months?",

- brand images, for example using attitude batteries like those for U&A studies, but shorter,

- advertising recall, for example "Which of these brands of cider have you seen advertised in local newspapers or magazines recently?",

- advertising content recall, for example "What can you remember about the last TV ad you saw for Walker's crisps?"

Clearly, there is considerable overlap between tracking studies and usage and attitude studies in terms of the information sought from respondents. The key difference lies in the fact that tracking studies are continuous and tend to be used to monitor the effects of marketing activity, especially advertising, on existing brands or recently launched brands. U&A studies tend to be ad hoc and undertaken in prelaunch situations or before proposed changes to the marketing mix are made. Tracking studies are also far less detailed than U&As – an interview will typically last less than 30 minutes.

A key measure used in all advertising tracking studies is advertising awareness, usually based on recall of advertising. There are, however, many different ways of measuring recall, and what characterizes differences between the approaches of different market research companies to advertising tracking is often the question posed to respondents to measure it. One distinction is between verified or proven recall and claimed recall. The former uses the answers to subsequent questions about the content of the advertising to verify that the respondent did actually recall the correct ad and is not confusing it with some other ad or making false claims. Claimed recall on the other hand takes the respondents' claims at face value. It is sometimes argued that the former is misleading since some ads are very much easier to describe than others and is in any case biased in favor of long-running ads or campaigns. On the other hand, with claimed recall there is the difficulty of disentangling "mistaken" from "true" recall of recent advertising.

Another distinction is between prompted and unprompted recall. In the former, respondents are given a list of brands and asked which of them they have seen advertised, while in the latter they are asked to recall what brands they remember. Millward Brown, the brand leader in market tracking studies and which tracks for 60 of the 100 top UK advertisers, found that you get very different results on measures of awareness depending on the question asked. Thus you could ask, "Have you seen any advertising for brand X on television recently?" or "What brands have you seen in the past three months?" or "Have you ever seen a television commercial in which . . .?" Advertising awareness will decay more rapidly between advertising bursts if you ask about advertising seen "recently", and hardly at all if you ask about advertising "ever seen". Millward Brown prefers "recently" because this relates best to sales effects, and it is possible, if awareness dies away rapidly, to see what happens during the next burst. In addition, advertising awareness accessed through the brand (as in the first question) relates better to other tracking measures than awareness triggered by reference to the advertising. It is important, furthermore, to see how memories or recall of your advertising swings into the brain in association with mention of the brand name.

The proportions mentioning the brand being advertised are usually plotted at four-weekly intervals and compared with the television ratings achieved. These ratings are measured by totaling the percentage of the population watching television each time it goes on air over a week. They are a good measure of exposure to the ad and are a better measure than taking the cost of the ad, which may vary by time of year, the effectiveness of the advertising agency in buying airtime and by target group. How these ratings are measured is explained in the next section on media audience measurement.

Figure 16.6 shows brand X being advertised using two different campaigns over a two-year period. The bottom half of the graph shows the television ratings achieved by each. The top half shows the percentage who recall the ad using the Millward Brown question. The timescale points are four weeks apart, so there are 13 in a year. Both ads were screened more or less continuously over a 24-week period, achieving about 200 rating points. There was a base level of about 10 percent awareness before advertising began, which will have been influenced by past advertising. The campaign using ad A was, clearly, more effective than the campaign using ad B. The former raised awareness from about 10 percent up to nearly 40 percent. When the ad finished, there was a period of decay, but the awareness fell back to only about 20 percent. Campaign B raised awareness from 20 percent to 35 percent, a gain of 15 percent compared with a gain of 30 percent for ad A.

To compare these gains in advertising awareness directly, however, is to assume that all other things are equal – which they usually are not. The advertising may, for example, be for different lengths of time, achieving different rating points over the campaign. Getting a directly comparable measure of advertising effectiveness (in achieving awareness) can be quite complicated. Box 16.9 explains Millward Brown's advertising Awareness Index.

FIGURE 16.6

Advertising awareness and television exposure

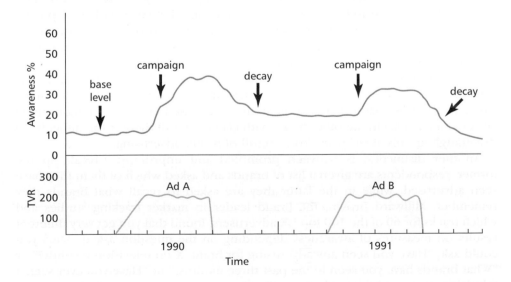

RESEARCH IN ACTION

BOX 16.9

Millward Brown's Awareness Index

By looking at back data, Millward Brown discovered that, while more advertising results in increased awareness, the amount of the increase associated with a given amount of advertising exposure varies enormously from one advertising campaign to another, depending on how "good" the ad is, the amount of past advertising, and a number of other factors. However, the interesting point is that *within* an advertising campaign, this relationship tends to be remarkably stable; so much so that Millward Brown call it their "Awareness Index".

Awareness, as measured by level of recall at any one point of time, is a combination of two factors. First, an underlying base level, which is a residual awareness and is a level to which awareness is assumed to return should the brand not be advertised for a long period. This base changes only slowly over time, and is assumed to be constant over an advertising campaign. Second, there is the short-term awareness, which is directly a result of the present advertising. It is this element that the Awareness Index measures and is defined as the increase in television advertising awareness generated per 100 rating points. To calculate this figure it is necessary to know what awareness would have decayed to since the previous week in the absence of the current advertising, and add this to the absolute increase that took place. Awareness, it has been found, decays at a steady rate of 10 percent per week – in other words, the "retention factor" is 90 percent. This makes it possible to calculate decay.

The difference between the decayed and actual awareness is how much is due to the present week's advertising. It is this difference that is related to exposure to work out the extra ad awareness per 100 rating points. The calculation is the equivalent to advertising in some theoretical television area that had never been exposed to the advertising for the brand previously. In other words, a comparison is being made between commercials on how they would perform if put on an equal footing. The Awareness Index is thus a pure measure of the efficiency of a given commercial in generating advertising awareness. By calculating the Awareness Index in this way, Millward Brown is able to disentangle "mistaken" from "true" recall of recent advertising, so the potential drawback of looking at claimed versus proven recall is overcome.

FIGURE 16.7

Tracking press ad awareness

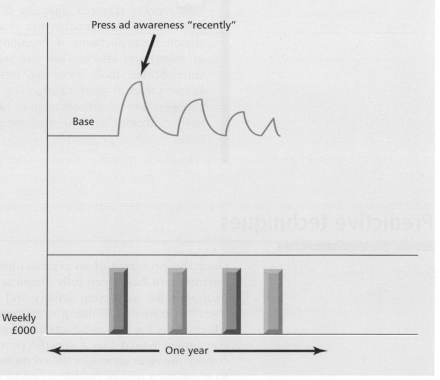

Tracking advertising awareness for press advertising is in many respects quite different from advertising on television. People tend to get bored with press ads over time and stop noticing them. A typical pattern may be seen in Figure 16.7. Overall awareness for any one ad declines on repeat printing. An Awareness Index for press can measure extra ad awareness per £100 000 spent, and this usually declines sharply after the ad's first couple of appearances. How much time a reader spends looking at a press ad is up to the reader. People may read or glance at the ad two or three times, but will turn the page once they have "seen it". For television this is not the case. A 30-second ad is watched for 30 seconds every time it is screened. Furthermore, it will be watched whatever the level of interest in the product itself. When people watch television ads repeatedly, they tend to "home in" on the bits they enjoy watching rather than take in more detail. In short, whereas for press ads it is necessary to creatively grab attention, for television attention is assured, but what people remember is what they enjoy, and creativity is needed to link that enjoyment to the brand being advertised.

Today, with increased emphasis on multimedia campaigns and media multiplier effects, modeling can be done on total brand communication awareness (for example, "Have you seen, heard or read anything about Brand X anywhere recently?) against total media exposure.

Advertising tracking is basically diagnostic and retrospective. It cannot be used directly to make a quantified prediction of trial, repeat behavior, purchase cycles and so on. However, by giving an overall diagnosis of how well an advertising campaign went, the results can feed into the planning of future campaigns. If the advertising has a good Awareness Index and appears to be conveying the right messages, it is doing as well as it can in the circumstances. If a brand is in terminal decline then no amount of effective advertising will do more than prop it up temporarily. It would be wrong in these circumstances to "blame" poor advertising for not producing better results

KEY POINTS

Diagnostic techniques include a range of proprietary systems offered by market research agencies for measuring market characteristics, for determining the characteristics of audiences to all the media, for measuring customer satisfaction and managing customer relations, and for the tracking of advertising effects. Over the years, agencies have built up a set of very sophisticated tools. However, besides diagnostics, which are crucial for keeping track of what is happening in the marketplace, manufacturers, media suppliers and advertisers need to be able to make forecasts or predictions of likely outcomes of their marketing activities. For this they need predictive tools.

Predictive techniques

Once the problems of an organization and the circumstances of its competitive environment have been fully diagnosed, managers may wish to generate specific proposals for marketing activity and then predict which ones are likely to be "best" in terms of fulfilling organizational objectives. They may want to know which ideas for new products are likely to be acceptable to consumers, whether consumers would buy a specific product formulation, whether advertising will convey the right messages linked memorably to the brand, or what sales are likely to result for a new or modified product. There is a wealth of predictive techniques that market research agencies and in-house researchers use, but the remainder of this chapter will focus on just three widely used techniques:

- testing products and product concepts,
- advertising pretesting,
- volume and brand share prediction.

Testing products and product concepts

Product concept tests

Ideas for product development are evaluated and "rounded out" using product concept tests. Many companies offer proprietary concept tests, sometimes as part of a wider package that includes product testing and perhaps even has a volume prediction technique bolted on. In product concept testing, ideas about potential new products are exposed to a sample of consumers who are then asked questions about them. The exposure may take a number of forms. These were described earlier in the context of stimulus materials for group discussions and included concept boards, storyboards, animatics, narrative tapes and physical mock-ups.

The sample of respondents from the target market should include anybody likely to have any part in influencing a decision to purchase and should not be defined too restrictively. A product developed for a particular market segment, for example mothers with babies, may be used by other groups. Thus baby shampoo may be used by adults. The test may be administered in a number of different ways and in different types of location. Thus the test could be:

- in-home by personal call by an interviewer,
- sent by post with a postal questionnaire,
- sent by post with a telephone follow-up,
- in a hall test, van test or test center.

The concept test may be monadic or comparative. If there is just one concept to be evaluated, then the test will be monadic. There is a problem here of knowing what counts as a "good" or a "bad" result unless comparisons can be made with other concepts similarly tested in the past. Comparative tests may be arranged according to a number of different experimental designs:

- matched monadic – separate subsamples are given one concept each and the ratings are compared,
- paired comparisons – getting respondents to compare concepts by expressing a preference in each combination of pairs of concepts,
- complete ranking – putting all the concepts in order of preference,
- trade-off or conjoint analysis, in which respondents are asked to choose between all combinations of product attributes,
- comparison with existing products, for example against the current brand leader.

The questions that can be addressed to respondents depend very much on the information needs of the marketing manager. It is usually necessary to ask one or more questions about overall acceptability. This may be by way of simple rating questions, for example "Overall, would you describe this product as excellent, good, fairly good, poor or very poor?" or by purchase intention, for example "How likely are you to buy this product: very likely, fairly likely or unlikely?" Respondents may be asked if they would actually like to buy the product at a given price. Diagnostic questions may follow up particular aspects, for example:

- understanding the product idea,
- perceptions of its attributes,

- its believability (as a possible new product),
- its perceived advantages and disadvantages,
- its rating on specific product attributes,
- when and how the product might be used,
- how often,
- what products it might replace,
- the sort of people it might appeal to.

Responses to product concept tests may be analyzed by counting up the proportion who respond in particular ways, or by using some scoring system on the rating scales that enable an average and a measure of dispersion to be calculated. These may then be crosstabulated against demographics, especially age, sex, lifestyle, life cycle or general attitudes. This may help to pinpoint groups most interested in the concept.

Product tests

The result of the concept test should be to weed out ideas that are nonstarters or compare poorly with other ideas. The ideas remaining may then proceed to product testing, which is the evaluation and development of the products themselves from a marketing point of view. This is different from testing the physical functions of products to ensure that they meet technical and safety standards. Product testing means having a physical product to which a representative sample of target consumers may be exposed under controlled conditions and which can be used under realistic circumstances and about which they can express their opinions in a structured way.

The designs of product tests vary considerably and the use of any particular procedure by a company is often the result of some historical evolution, habit, or the researcher's or manager's familiarity or comfort with the chosen procedure. Yet different product test designs will give different outputs and different results, so it is necessary to try to establish the most appropriate designs in the circumstances. These circumstances include:

- management information requirements,
- the type of product,
- the type of market,
- cost and time constraints,
- the required comparability across studies.

Management may want a product test to identify the most promising product from a set of candidates under consideration; it may want information that could guide product development to arrive at the best formulation of the product in terms of shape, features, colors, ingredients, materials and so on; it may want to know whether a chosen product idea warrants further investment of time and money; it may want information that would enable it to design a strategy for the introduction of the selected product.

Characteristics of products that are likely to affect the design of testing procedures include:

- the extent to which the product is assessable on the spot,
- the extent to which the product is new to users,
- the extent of information search carried out by consumers in product or brand selection.

Snack-type foods and soft drinks are usually instantly assessable and are suitable candidates for hall tests and van tests. Fragrances (perfumes, eau de toilettes, after-shaves and so on) may also fit into this category. Alcoholic drinks may be too affected by the time of day to be assessable on the spot. Some products require either a longer period of use (for example batteries), or need to be used in the home to try them out, for example a cake-mix, a floor polish or a shampoo. Some products are not susceptible to reuse, for example a device for unblocking a sink, or are very complex and require users to familiarize themselves with their operation. Highly innovative products or really new products are not amenable to comparison with other products and this will affect the test design. Low-involvement convenience goods where information search and brand choice behavior is limited will require procedures different from high-involvement shopping goods. The former need analysis of the selected circumstances that consumers use in brand choice, while the latter require a close analysis of the importance and evaluation of product features.

Product testing will vary considerably according to type of market. Some markets are highly branded with lots of advertising, in which case the test product may well need to be branded and promoted. If the target market consists of children or elderly people then their ability to perform certain tasks may need to be taken into account. Product testing in industrial markets or organizational markets will be very different from consumer markets.

Testing procedures vary in terms of the costs involved and how long they take. Some products, like confectionery, do not require extensive testing since they may be tried out in the real market for a period and withdrawn with very little loss if they are not successful. The development of a new model of car, on the other hand, merits considerable expenditure at all stages in the new product development process. Cost and speed may need to be traded off against the reliability or accuracy of the results.

Testing procedures may be affected, lastly, by the need for comparability across studies. There are advantages to be gained from the standardization of test procedures across a wide range of products. Researchers will gain more experience of such procedures, the procedures themselves can be refined, performance benchmarks may be established, and the results of different tests are more likely to be comparable.

The key dimensions along which product tests vary and which testers need to decide upon include:

- what kinds of people should act as testers,
- what they are to be asked to do,
- the size of the sample,
- the analysis techniques to be used on the data collected.

The main choices concerning who should act as testers include:

- current users of the brand,
- current users in the product field,
- users in the product field plus potential users,
- a general cross-section of the population.

Decisions about what types of people are most appropriate in the circumstances depend on many factors and it would be difficult to lay down any rules. If a product is completely new then there can be no current users of the brand; there may even be no comparable product field and the selection may have to be of people who in some way are likely to be favorably disposed to the new product. If the objective of the test is to see if people notice the substitution of cheaper ingredients or components, then only current users of the brand need to be involved in the assessment procedure. If the product has been improved, then users of that type of product currently not using the brand will need to be included in the test to see if they can be persuaded to switch brands or at least include it in their repertoire. At the same time, sufficient current users of the brand also need to be included to ensure that the changes will not alienate them. For some products, like soap, no amount of improvement will persuade current users to use more, even if they agreed it was a better product, so the focus may be on potential new users. Some products are used by nearly everybody in the population, so a general cross-section may be included in the test. On the other hand, potential users may be a very selected group, for example a new device to help the blind. If the test is of a product function, like how well it cleans a floor, then it may not matter whether the testers are users or non-users of the brand being researched.

As a general rule, the more restrictions placed on the selection of testers, the more expensive it is to obtain a sample. Thus a sample of the population at large will be cheaper than a sample of users in the product field. The most expensive is usually a sample of users of the brand since few brands are used by more than 10 percent of the population.

What testers are asked to do depends on the kind of test. Following Batsell and Wind (1980) we may distinguish four main kinds of test:

- monadic,
- comparative,
- sequential,
- conjoint.

In monadic testing, each person is given just one product to evaluate and this will tend to be used where the product is completely new, or where the product is a line extension and the client already has backdata on the other products in the range. However, monadic testing may be used to compare several products by dividing a sample of testers into as many groups as there are products to be tested. The scores (whether preference ratings, intention to purchase, degrees of liking and so on) for the various groups are then compared, and subjected to a test of statistical significance. If statistically significant differences emerge, the most promising product (or formulation of a product) is selected for further development.

In comparative testing, testers are given two or more products to compare on the same occasion and this will typically be used where there is a new product formulation. Where there are three or more products or formulations, then evaluation may take the form of paired comparisons, complete ranking, a rating scale for each, or a constant sum of points that is divided between the products by the tester. The advantage of comparative testing is that the comparisons are made directly by individuals rather than by arithmetic comparisons of mean scores. The downside is that comparisons are entirely internal to the set of products being tested, whereas, so it is sometimes argued, with monadic tests comparisons are implicitly being made with all the other brands with which consumers are familiar. Comparisons may be internal to the company's brands, or may be against competitor brands. The former is more likely where there is a formulation change, and the latter if there is a marketing argument to be won, if the client company is losing market share, or they need to test the competitor's products anyway.

Sequential testing is comparative, but evaluations are made on different occasions. The tester is asked to try one product, wait a specific period of time, try the second, and then give an opinion. This procedure, so it is argued by its advocates, more closely resembles the way in which consumers actually compare products. However, it does, of course, take longer and is more expensive, particularly where in-home placements are required.

Conjoint analysis focuses on product features and instead of simply identifying the single most promising product, it tries to clarify the relative importance of features, thus providing guidance for the construction of new product formulations.

Other choices facing the researcher in terms of what testers are asked to do include:

- whether the products should be branded or blind,
- whether competitors' brands should be included among the products to be tested,
- in comparative tests, the order in which the products are presented,
- whether the test should be on the spot or in use, usually at home,
- the attributes to be tested,
- the length of time testers are given.

The branding of a product is as much a part of the total offer as, for example, price, so wherever possible branded tests will be used. However, they tend to suffer from halo effects, that is, testers tend to respond more favorably to a product they regard as "their" brand. If the main focus of the test is to obtain reactions to product features or new formulations, then blind tests are probably more appropriate. If, on the other hand, the interest is in likely purchase behavior or it is a straightforward monadic test, then branded tests should be considered.

The inclusion of competitor brands depends, again, on the objectives of the test. If the focus is on future purchasing behavior, then they should; otherwise, probably not.

Where products to be compared are very different, then the order in which they are presented makes little difference, but where they are similar, there is a tendency to prefer the product tested first. Some system for rotating the order of presentation will certainly improve the reliability of the tests.

As explained earlier, some products more than others are amenable to on-the-spot evaluation. Where in-home placement tests are used there will usually be a recall interview, either face-to-face or over the phone, typically using 5- or 7-point rating scales. Some clients have their own requirements in terms of scales, wording of scales and show cards that they are used to. Other factors also intervene, for example the nature of management information requirements, the speed with which results are required and so on.

Attribute lists are usually managerially derived unless qualitative research has been conducted on consumer perceptions. Managers decide what product features they want evaluated, based on their experience and familiarity with the market or with the results of earlier tests. However, de Chernatony and Knox (1990) argue that product testing is presented predominantly as a mechanistic process with minimal consideration of the underlying assumptions about user behavior, consumer perceptions or consumer psychology. The authors suggest that consumers interpret products as arrays of cues, and that judgments are based on very limited samples of cues that consumers believe to be indicative of product characteristics (for example, assessing the quality of wrapped bread from the feel of the packaging). In this way, information search is very restricted. If researchers are interested largely in different product formulations, then these cues need to be the focus of the inquiry. For fast-moving consumer goods particularly, there is limited information search and researchers should concentrate on the few salient attributes deemed important by the purchaser – and this may vary from one purchaser to another. In short, attribute lists should be very short and geared to the product concerned, perhaps even to particular types of consumer. In practice, however, it is unusual to use different attribute lists for different categories of customer. This would have implications for sample size, design and cost.

The length of time testers are to be allowed to use the product is often a problem. The pressures are usually to produce a quick result; at the same time, many products are used infrequently in real life, while opinions do often change after extended use.

In terms of sample size, the cost of a product test increases with the number of testers, but so do the usefulness and reliability of the results. Below a certain minimum number of testers the results may be too unreliable to be useful; above a certain number the addition of more testers will not significantly improve the results. It is difficult to say exactly what these minimum and maximum figures are because a number of factors are involved, for example the number of products or formulations to be tested, regional variations and so on. However, fewer than 30 testers is likely to be unreliable and more than 1000 will cease to be cost-effective. Typically, for a straightforward monadic test, a sample size of about 200 would be regarded as adequate. Samples in practice are seldom more than 300 or so.

The procedures used for the analysis of the data from product testing depend in the first instance on the type of test chosen. Product tests designed for absolute evaluation will summarize the data by counting the proportions who respond in particular ways or by generating scores on the attributes selected for testing and calculating averages. Confidence intervals may be calculated, but are worthwhile only if the selection procedure was random probability from a defined population. Where there are many attributes, then factor analysis on the attribute scores may be carried out. Product tests designed for comparative evaluation will tend to rely on using tests of significance against the null hypothesis (either the t-test for small samples, or the normal distribution for larger ones), on the differences between groups testing different products in monadic tests, or on the differences in mean scores or proportions on product attributes for comparative tests. Because most testers are selected by quota sample, a design factor of 1.6–1.7 should be applied, but in practice, this is often not done.

RESEARCH IN ACTION
The TNS InnoSuite™

BOX 16.10

TNS has developed a suite of integrated new product development proprietary services that look at every stage of the new product development process for fast-moving consumer goods. TNS sees this as a five-stage process.

1. Idea generation. This identifies unmet consumer product needs. Ideas for new products may come from flashes of inspiration, but they also come from customers. NeedScope™ is a system that focuses on the dynamics driving consumer attitudes, preferences and behavior.
2. Idea Filter. This prioritizes potential winning ideas. It measures the popularity of the potential idea and the degree of respondent enthusiasm.
3. Concept Screener. This is the concept testing stage, screening out ideas that are less likely to be successful. There are key measures of performance that generate an index score. This highlights concept strengths and weaknesses.
4. Product Optimiser. Potentially winning product ideas are refined before launch. This should identify potential users, usage and purchase behavior. It also looks at product improvement, reformulation, repackaging and line extension. The end product is an optimization of the marketing mix.
5. Launch Maximiser. This forecasts sales and profitability using volume and brand share prediction techniques. These techniques are explained in more detail on pp. 519–525.

Advertising pretesting

We have seen how advertising tracking is used to diagnose how well an advertisement has performed in the past and in what ways. Such procedures are sometimes referred to as post-testing. Post-testing provides data on what *has* happened, while pretesting influences what *does* or will happen. It is an activity that takes place before resources are fully committed, and provides data on the likely outcomes of marketing initiatives so that a decision can be taken:

- to go or not to go with a particular idea or product,
- to modify the idea or product to improve its likely performance,
- to select the best of a number of ideas or products.

Advertising pretesting takes place either before an ad is printed or put on air, or just after initial screening. It may be designed to weed out those ads that are unlikely to work, to select the best of the remaining candidates for creative advertising development, to predict the performance of the ads chosen, to provide early feedback, or to make last-minute changes to the ad. Pretesting of advertising has long been associated with the use of qualitative research, but in recent years there has been a growing demand for quantified predictions of likely future performance in real conditions before the costs of screening or printing ads are incurred.

The precise measures used in quantitative advertising pretesting are closely related to implicit or explicit theories about the way in which advertising works. The traditional model, of which there are a number of versions, suggests that consumers begin by becoming aware of a product or brand. They then formulate some attitude towards it or image of it, generate a desire to try it, and finally purchase it. Figure 16.8 illustrates the process.

The result has been a debate not only over the techniques to be used to measure each of these, but over whether awareness, attitudes, image or desire to try should be the focus of pretesting measures. One school of thought argues that, clearly, the nearer you take your measurement to the actual act of trial or purchase the better will be the prediction. However, this sequence of events has been questioned, and it has been suggested, for example by Brown (1991b), that attitudes and images of products and brands are more likely to be formed *after* purchase, so the sequence becomes that illustrated in Figure 16.9.

If this is the case, it is inappropriate to base pretesting on the measurement of attitudes or images; the best measures must be based on awareness and stated

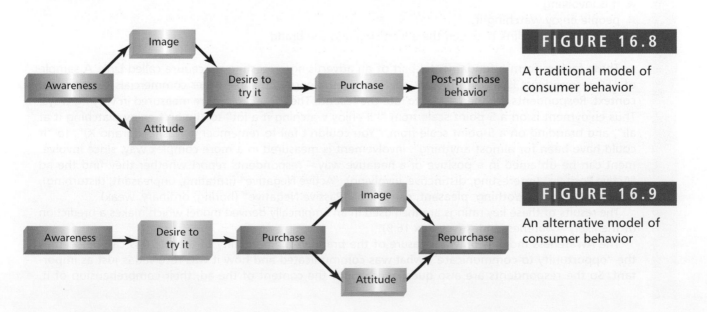

FIGURE 16.8

A traditional model of consumer behavior

FIGURE 16.9

An alternative model of consumer behavior

intention to buy or to try. Attitudes towards and images of the products and brands may influence the subsequent repurchase pattern, and this may involve brand switching or inclusion in a brand repertoire, either of which may be with varying numbers of repurchase occasions and lengths of purchase cycle.

While, as we have seen, it is perfectly possible to measure advertising awareness in tracking studies by asking people to recall the brands and the advertising they remember, in pretesting, once you have shown people an ad in a hall or in a van, you cannot within a few minutes start asking them about ad and brand awareness and whether they recall which brand the ad was for. The traditional solution has been to substitute the "stand out" value of an ad as a predictor of future recall or awareness. In a reel test a sample of maybe 50–100 respondents is shown a mock-up of an ad in a reel of six or ten ads (which may be in printed form or on a video). The test ad has to compete for attention with ads for either similar or related product fields. These ads may be for competing products or they may be other versions of an ad for the same product. Respondents are then asked which ads they noticed or recalled, both unprompted, then prompted. Respondents may be asked which ads they liked most and least, and their attention is then gradually focused onto the test ad and recall of its content or theme. The test ad will normally either be in a fixed position in the reel, for example sixth in a reel of ten, or the order may be rotated.

The results of such reel tests, however, have been shown (for example by Brown 1991a) not to tie in well with subsequent measures of awareness in tracking studies. The development of more sophisticated ways of pretesting advertisements by market research agencies has taken one of two directions: making measures of pretest recall themselves more sophisticated, or abandoning the idea of recall altogether. Box 16.11 describes Millward Brown's Link test, which adopts the latter approach.

RESEARCH IN ACTION
Millward Brown's Link

BOX 16.11

By looking at a large number of ads that worked and those that did not in terms of tracking measures, Millward Brown discovered three key factors of an impactful advertisement:

- it is involving,
- people enjoy watching it,
- there is a strong link between the advertising and the brand.

These factors form a fundamental part of an advertising pretesting procedure called Link. A sample of 150 respondents is shown the test advertisement along with three other commercials to provide a context. Respondents are then asked to rate the test ad. The three factors are measured in varying ways. Thus enjoyment is on a 5-point scale from "I'll enjoy watching it a lot" to "I won't enjoy watching it at all", and branding on a 5-point scale from, "You couldn't fail to remember it was for (brand X)", to "It could have been for almost anything". Involvement is measured in a more complex way, since involvement can be obtained in a positive or a negative way – respondents report whether they find the ad "Active Positive" (interesting, distinctive, involving), "Active Negative" (irritating, unpleasant, disturbing), "Passive Positive" (soothing, pleasant, gentle), or "Passive Negative" (boring, ordinary, weak)

The results of these key ratings are then used in an empirically derived model which makes a prediction of the likely Awareness Index (see Box 16.9).

The Awareness Index is only a measure of the branded memorability of the ad; this can be seen as the "opportunity to communicate"; what was communicated and how it was received is just as important. So the respondents are also questioned about the content of the ad, their comprehension of it, their likes and dislikes, and other rational and emotional responses. This facilitates a qualitative evaluation of whether the main focus of the ad is successfully linked to the brand, and whether it has been understood in the way the advertisers intended. If, for example, the ad has been misunderstood, a subjective down-rating to the predicted Awareness Index can be made. By adding in judgment from these qualitative elements, Millward Brown has improved the correlation between the pretests and subsequent Awareness Index to 0.9. This prediction of the likely impact of an ad is far better than more traditional approaches (the most common being "recall from a clutter reel", where respondents are shown, say, ten ads, with the test ad in a fixed position, and are subsequently asked which ads they remembered seeing; and "day after recall", when respondents are shown the ads, and phoned back the next day to see which ones they remembered).

Subsequently, the respondents are shown the ad again, and they record their level of interest as the ad proceeds by moving a mouse, which captures electronically the interest on a second-by-second basis. The responses of respondents are aggregated and plotted out on hard copy. Ideally, interest should be high when the brand and communication are being mentioned. If it falls away every time this happens then the key features of the ad are not being successfully linked to the brand.

Such qualitative elements provide a diagnosis about *why* an ad is likely or unlikely to generate the required awareness. Thus it could well be that the main thing that stands out in an ad is unlinked to the brand. Each element of the ad may then be separately diagnosed and the likely messages that will be communicated may be predicted. Link essentially is taking the ad to bits to understand the structure of it to see whether the parts that are supposed to be doing the job of linking it with the brand and getting the message over are, in practice, going to work.

While advertising pretesting procedures such as those described here give an evaluation of ads in terms of impact and communication, and while Millward Brown claims a relationship between its key measures and sales, they cannot be used as a basis for making any detailed prediction of sales that will eventuate. To do that, special techniques have been developed, and it is to these that we now turn.

Volume and brand share prediction

The track record of market research in predicting new product successes or failures has not been a good one. Various empirical studies have shown that between 60 percent and 97 percent of new products, whether innovative, line extensions or relaunches of modified products, fail to achieve company objectives. A lot depends, however, on the particular industry.

It may be argued that this situation is largely a result of lack of research (or lack of attention to the results of research) rather than of inadequate research, but a lot of market research *has* been carried out on behalf of new products, yet the identification of product failure has still been limited. Traditionally, two main approaches to the prediction of the share of market and sales volume that would be achieved by new products have been used:

- the screening and evaluation of attitudes to new products in product and product concept tests,
- test marketing.

Attitude measurements in product tests that produce a rating on a 5- or 7-point scale have, on the basis of past experience, been insufficient to allow accurate predictions to be made about future sales. Just because a high percentage of a sample of respondents say they like a product, or say they will buy it, or say it is good value for money (or all three), does not mean that people in general will necessarily try it, and if they do try it that they will buy it again. There are many other factors that need to be taken into account before such predictions are possible.

As was explained in Chapter 7 in the section on experimental research, test marketing has fallen out of favor. A number of market research agencies began looking at the possibility of laboratory test markets that would simulate a shop as part of a hall test. Others developed the use of concept tests and product tests in which samples of respondents were given statements about the proposed new products on a concept board or, at a later stage, given a mock-up or actual product to try, either on the spot or to take home. Such tests have been used for a long time, but they only gave a score on one or more rating scales, and could not be used to make specific predictions about sales.

The problem with the simulated store approach is that the research needs to be conducted using finished products, packaging and advertising, involving considerable time and cost. An alternative is to dispense with the simulated point-of-sale element and establish estimates of trial and repeat purchase from survey questions in a consumer survey or in a hall test. These questions might cover:

- intention to purchase,
- product evaluation,
- perceived value-for-money,
- claimed purchase frequency,
- average number of units purchased,
- competitive/substitute product usage.

Answers to these questions are then entered into a mathematical model containing experimentally derived weighting factors to arrive at estimates of trial, repeat purchase, sales volumes and market shares. The models used for volume and brand share prediction have, over the years, been given different names such as "sales decomposition/recomposition models", "pretest market models", or "market-mix testing", but eventually the term now generally recognized is "simulated test marketing models" or just STM models. All such models use the concepts of trial and repeat purchase, and substitute for simulated or real purchasing behavior in the marketplace a standard or fairly standard concept test or product test in which a sample of respondents is asked questions about the new product (or existing product being tested) and about their purchasing behavior. These responses are then used in statistical models of various kinds that weight the replies and produce predictions of a number of variables.

There are, however, significant differences between the models in terms of general methodology, the variables included, the approach to parameter estimation, and the kinds of predicted output. Any manufacturer wishing to compare the advantages and limitations of the various STM models available would have a hard time. The advocates of each particular model will argue persuasively that their approach is best. A start can be made, however, by recognizing the various choices or dimensions along which models vary. In terms of general methodology, the main choices are between:

- comparative or monadic testing, or some combination,
- macro modeling or micro modeling, or some combination,
- whether client inputs, for example concerning distribution, advertising or brand awareness, are modeled or assumed,
- whether various elements that made up the final prediction are modeled separately, thus trial and adoption may be modeled separately, as might switchers and new buyers,
- whether the sample should be large or small; the samples used for STM models vary from a minimum of about 200 per test up to about 500. It is important to remember that an STM is a test, not a survey, so although sampling is important, no attempt is usually made to obtain a large representative sample. It is, however, necessary to get a regional spread of fieldwork,

▪ whether the respondents selected should to be either product category users, or a general cross-section of the adult population.

In terms of the variables included in the model, while all take trial and repeat purchase as the key variables, the main variations include:

▪ the number and depth of questions used as inputs to predict trial and repeat purchase. Some models rely on responses to just one question, for example on intention to buy, while others include competitive sets, degree of experimentalism, brand visibility and so on,

▪ the number and depth of question used as diagnostics to explain the predicted outcomes. These may include the standard demographics, and in addition questions on corporate or brand image, likes and dislikes and so on.

STMs are now a standard business-planning tool for virtually every multi-national in the consumer packaged goods industry (Wilke 2002). However, Wilke (2002) argues that without significant changes, such techniques will become redundant. With the possibility of mass customization, the past one-size-fits-all world is no longer viable and sample sizes at the very least will need to increase considerably to adapt to a one-to-one world. The models assume that awareness and distribution are spread relatively randomly across the population. Traditional STMs were designed to estimate annual national volume for brands, whereas what is needed are weekly volumes for individual stores, markets or retailers.

Boxes 16.12 and 16.13 explain two very different approaches to volume and brand share prediction.

RESEARCH IN ACTION
ACNielsen BASES

BOX 16.12

BASES was launched in the UK by Burke Marketing Research in the mid 1970s. The model was from the outset a volume prediction model and based on a monadic test. Respondents are not asked to compare the test product with other brands in the test itself. It is argued by supporters of this model that it is better for the respondents to evaluate products within their own frames of reference, particularly their own competitive set of brands. In evaluating the test product, respondents are, in any case, implicitly comparing it with the products they normally use and in situations in which they normally use them. Comparative tests, by contrast, tend to impose a comparison set. Furthermore, in some markets it may be difficult to put together a comparative set, for example it is difficult to know what competes with Perrier – soft drinks, milk, fruit juice, tap water? It may, in addition, be argued that monadic tests allow you to ask the respondent which brands the test product would be competing against, enabling some calculation to be made of source of volume.

The model was originally set up by taking about 80 different new products, interviewing people before the product was launched, and then tracking their subsequent purchasing behavior using consumer panels. This enabled answers concerning purchase intention and so on to be "interpreted" and corrected for overclaiming and underclaiming. The result was a series of weighting factors that were built into a mathematical model that has subsequently been refined and improved as the results of more studies have become available.

The two key measures in the BASES model are trial rate and repeat rate. The trial rate is measured by market penetration – the proportion of the total market who buy the brand being researched at least once. The repeat rate is the proportion of trialists who repeat buy. The trial rate is estimated in a standard concept or product test in which consumers are asked both before trial and after trial if they:

- definitely would buy,
- probably would buy,
- might or might not buy,
- probably would not buy,
- definitely would not buy.

For the trial rate the *pretrial* intention to buy is used. However, this statement of purchase intent always produces a degree of overclaiming, that is, not all consumers who say they will buy the brand will actually do so in a given period of time. The proportion who, from the historical database of previous predictions, actually did make a purchase in each of the response categories is then used as a weighting for each response in the actual test. Thus if 40 percent of respondents who answer "probably would buy" are found in fact subsequently to actually make a purchase, then for the product being tested, if 10 percent give this response, then 40 percent of 10 percent or 4 percent of those in that response category will, it is predicted, actually buy. Estimates for each response can then be added together.

The calibration from intention to actual purchase is strongly affected by many factors, for example type of product, the cultural (particularly national) background, the unit price, and the age of the consumer. Thus teenagers generally overclaim more than adults; Italians and Spaniards are more likely to overstate than Germans. Using this calibration, the correlation between statement of purchase intent and subsequent actual purchase has been improved to over 0.9. The trial rate estimate is based on this adjusted probability of trial, taking account of clients' estimates of weighted distribution build, advertising plan or brand awareness estimates (which may be from an earlier usage and attitude study), promotional activity and seasonality.

Besides intention to purchase, consumers in both the pre- and post-trial tests are asked about:

- intended frequency of purchase,
- purchase quantities,
- degree of liking,
- product evaluation,
- perceived value for money,
- substitute/competitive usage.

Degree of liking is on a 6-point scale, four of the points are positive, one neutral and one negative. Perceived value for money is on a 5-point scale from very good value down to very poor value.

Repeat rate is estimated from the number who are still favorably disposed towards the brand after the trial. Favorability is estimated by using multiple nonlinear regression techniques based on a combination of intention to purchase *post-trial* (again suitably downweighted for overclaiming), degree of liking score, and perceived value for money score. The conversion rates post-trial tend to be more stable than pretrial ones. Purchase cycle is based on after-use intended purchase frequency among after-use favorable respondents, adjusted for overstatement and the build of the trial curve.

To obtain estimates of future sales volume (S_t) at time t (the number of weeks since retail availability) the BASES model adds a predicted trial volume (T_t) to a predicted repeat volume (R_t), that is:

$$S_t = T_t + R_t$$

Trial volume, T_t is estimated by taking the cumulative trial rate over the period between now and time t, multiplying by the target market size (the number of households in the target market area) and the purchase quantity (the average amounts purchased at trial). An adjustment is made for trial rate build up over the year. Repeat volume is estimated from first repeat volume plus second repeat volume plus third repeat volume through nth repeat volume. The first repeat volume is derived by multiplying the number of triers by the first repeat rate (the number of consumers repeating at least once) and the average quantity. The second repeat volume takes the number of first repeaters and multiplies by the second repeat rate (the number of consumers repeating at least twice) and the average quantity.

Subsequent repeat volumes are calculated in a similar manner. The model also builds in a decay rate for people who stop buying after a number of repeats.

The result of applying the BASES procedure, then, is to produce separate estimates of:

- sales volume,
- trial rate,
- repeat purchase rate,
- purchase cycle.

BASES, like other similar models that were developed at the time, reconstructs the data that would be provided by a consumer panel, but from a two-stage before and after trial data collection exercise, within a short space of time and before the product is launched – it may be a new product, a line extension or a relaunch. Models like BASES were originally used to make go/no go decisions, but nowadays are increasingly used to determine optimum launch policies. Thus if there is a good trial rate then the focus needs to be on getting repeat.

Following the acquisition of the BASES Group in 1998, BASES is now part of the ACNielsen empire. From 2000, BASES has been reengineered so that it can forecast at the individual level, it can forecast weekly, sample sizes have increased and estimation is now possible at the store level.

RESEARCH IN ACTION
Research International's Innovation

BOX 16.13

For Research International, volume and brand share prediction comes at the end of a long process that it calls Innovation. Coming up with new ideas is both the biggest opportunity that companies face and the greatest challenge. To be successful, innovations must be driven by the needs, beliefs and aspirations of consumers and they must combine creativity and discipline. To do this, Research International suggest four stages, and eight steps.

In the first stage, which the agency calls "make it up", the steps are insight generation and idea creation. Insightment™ is an insight generation toolbox that includes several ways to collect observations, in particular through the use of ethnographic techniques. These techniques were explained in Chapter 4. When Research International looked at extreme sports for a global electronics manufacturer, it relied on close study of small groups of skaters, boarders and mountain bikers, giving respondents cameras and letting them get on with it with minimal guidance. From the results, the agency mapped out a strategy for the client to achieve "lifestyle product" status, but most of the presentation was on video. In the second step, Research International uses creative consumer panels to generate large numbers of highly original ideas and to develop ones that will really work. Super Group™ is a method of idea generation in which panellists are selected for their creativity and trained in ideation techniques. A telecoms company wanted creative ideas for new mobile handset designs. Research International uses a futurologist, an artist, a fitness instructor and a group of carefully selected teenagers to create concepts.

In the second stage, which the agency calls "make it better", there are three steps. These include exploring ideas, nurturing each element and then appraising them. eValuate™ is a proprietary tool that uses consumers who are early adopters. While such people may not be representative of the whole market, they are the kind of people who can assess an idea with an open mind. Large numbers of ideas are assessed and the early adopters are asked to work out why consumers might reject certain ideas. To nurture ideas and make them better, Research International uses Super Clinic™, which is a series of interactive workshops and is a mix of creative consumers, early adopters, mainstream consumers, outside experts and client teams under the guidance of innovation experts. Finally, eValuate+™ appraises the concepts by adding diagnostic questions to the eValuate™ tool.

The third stage is to "make it real". This involves uniting the different elements so that they can be complied into a compelling, tangible offer. Different combinations of product or service features are tried out on consumers. The last stage is to "make it go". This involves prediction and monitoring. Prediction uses MicroTest™, which is a volume and brand share prediction tool.

Most of the volume and brand share models are "macro" models in the sense that they aggregate answers of respondents on a question-by-question basis and analyses are performed on the totals. An alternative, however, is "micro" modeling, which makes a prediction on an individual-by-individual basis by looking at the pattern of responses to a number of questions, and putting them into a computer algorithm and coming up with a probability that that person will try and subsequently adopt the product or brand under investigation.

A simple product concept test among a sample of the target population is used to predict trial. Respondents then take the product home, try it and are subsequently re-interviewed and questioned about product acceptability. MicroTest™ is a volume prediction model based on predicting, individual-by-individual, the probabilities of trial, adoption, frequency of purchase and quantity per occasion. Trial and adoption are modeled separately. The trial model (see Figure 16.10) includes three key factors:

- the predisposition on the part of the consumer to experiment with new products,
- the acceptability of the new product concept to the respondent,
- the visibility of the brand being studied.

It is clear from behavioral and attitudinal data that the probability of trial depends crucially on the level of an individual's experimentalism – the predisposition to experiment with new products. This is measured on a behavioral scale by asking respondents about the new brands they have ever tried. Some people are highly experimental by nature, and if all you do is appeal to them, your sales go up rather nicely – and then come crashing down again.

The acceptability of the new product concept is measured by asking respondents about their attitudes to the proposed price, and their propensity to buy. The concept may be presented in a variety of degrees of sophistication from a simple verbal description through to a finished television commercial.

FIGURE 16.10

Research International's
MicroTest™ model

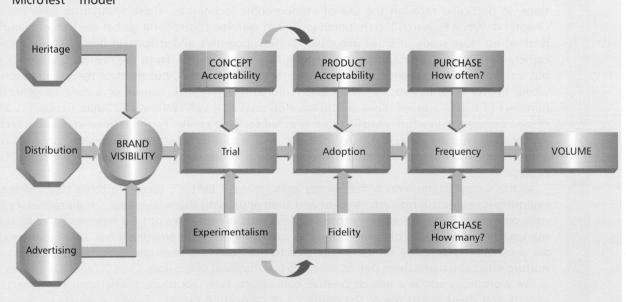

The visibility of the brand measures the opportunity an individual has to try it. This is affected by distribution, advertising spend, and how well-known the brand name is (or heritage). Information on the first two of these is provided by the client. Heritage is included in the consumer interviews. The combined effect of these environmental factors is then predicted using a sophisticated visibility model. A diffusion submodel predicts the build-up of trial (cumulative penetration) over a period of time.

The adoption model includes two key factors:

- product acceptability,
- brand fidelity.

Product acceptability is measured by inquiring into purchase intentions and the extent to which the new product meets expectations. This gives a measure of the relationship between pretrial and post-trial response for each individual. Brand fidelity is measured by asking respondents which of the new brands they have ever tried they are still using. There are some experimentalists who do show fidelity to brands, while others are just inveterate experimentalists.

When the probabilities of trial and adoption have been estimated, then volume can be predicted once frequency of purchasing and quantity per purchase occasion have been established. Frequency of purchase for each individual is predicted by asking respondents to project future purchasing of the test product, and "weight of purchasing" by asking about projected stocks of the product.

The result is a probability for each individual. These are then aggregated and grossed up to the population, whatever that happens to be, for example mothers with young children. Forecasts are made of sales in years one and two, and the ongoing level thereafter, while sales breakdowns are given between trial and adoption along with estimates for cumulative levels of trial and adoption. Microtest is performed on samples of respondents in the target population of 200–300.

The last step in the Research International Innovation process is post-launch monitoring, which may be undertaken qualitatively using Insightment™ or quantitatively using Launch Pad™. This does more then look at current data, but tries to predict future success and identifies untapped potential.

An evaluation of STM modeling

A key advantage of STM modeling is that the risks of launching products that turn out to be unsuccessful are reduced considerably, but without the costs of full test marketing, or even the cost of mini-test marketing. Manufacturers, furthermore, get very precise indicators of the likely performance of the new product. This enables them to generate strategies appropriate to the results. Thus if management have high expectations for a product and the forecast is for increasing volume, then they may decide to go straight for a national launch. If the new product begins from a low base, but will need time to build sales volume, then a test market and tracking operation to test different tactical approaches to boosting sales may be required. If the product begins with a high base, but is not expected to grow, then a national launch with minimum support to maximize profitability may be advisable. Products not expected to move up from a low base, or expected to decline from a higher one, may not be launched at all.

Other advantages of STM modeling are that:

- they can be used at a relatively early stage in new product development,
- they may be used to isolate problems before too much cost and effort have been expended,
- tests that do not use shop displays can be used for products that do not fit into any well-defined market category or product field,
- a wide range of alternative marketing scenarios can be examined by making changes in parameter values, for example producing estimates on

the basis of different assumptions regarding distribution and awareness, launching at different prices or using different promotional expenditures,

■ parameters and weights can be validated when historical data on the effectiveness of predictions become available.

■ products can be tested without revealing details of the composition or manufacture to competitors,

■ they are relatively quick; 8–12 weeks would be a normal timespan for a full STM prediction,

■ it is possible to exercise total control over the testing process,

■ on the whole, STM systems have proved to be extremely accurate. Sampson (1987), for example, reports that over 8000 tests have been carried out using BASES in 34 countries and across many product categories. By comparing the estimates with what actually happened, typically the estimate is within plus or minus 10 percent of the actual in 70 percent of the cases, and plus or minus 15 percent in 90 percent of the cases.

One major disadvantage of STMs is that they are complex, and as the sophistication of the modeling grows it becomes more difficult for clients to understand the analysis, which in turn makes it difficult for clients to judge the advantages and limitations of the various models on offer and makes them more reliant on the agency to provide interpretation of the results. Another disadvantage is that it is difficult to give clients access to the data to make their own "What if . . .?" simulations because the formulae used for model calculations would be revealed or at least deducible, so agencies normally insist on processing simulations themselves.

The overall trend seems to be away from using STM models to make go/no go decisions and towards launch management that will determine not only optimum launch strategies, but ways of manipulating these strategies to generate extra trial or extra repeat purchase. A further trend is for agencies, having developed a successful basic model, to generate a variety of options for using either only the front-end trial prediction, or enhanced models with additional facilities and measures bolted on. These might include, for example, an optional simulated store test, a brand tracking operation, or models specifically designed to examine line extensions. A third trend is towards the increased use of diagnostic questions that will help to explain why a prediction is poor (or good). Diagnostics may also be used to evaluate an existing brand or brand strategy. These may take into account not only the characteristics of the products and the internal support given to them, but also the circumstances of the external marketplace.

KEY POINTS

Predictive techniques include testing products and product concepts, advertising pretesting, and volume and brand share prediction. As with the diagnostic techniques there is a range of proprietary tools available, only some of which have been included in this chapter as illustrations. Many manufacturers and suppliers of services will combine these tools either on a continuous or on an ad hoc basis.

SUMMARY

Instruments of data capture, data collection methods and data analysis techniques are combined in a variety of ways to produce specific research techniques and applications that enable companies to diagnose the situations they face, to make predictions about the likely consequences of their marketing decisions, and to monitor the progress being made by or the success of past marketing activity. Key diagnostic and monitoring techniques include market measurement, media audience measurement, single-source data, customer satisfaction and relationship management research, and advertising tracking. Instead of looking at the more traditional forecasting methods like time series analysis, which are well covered in books on marketing research, statistics and social research, the focus here is on three currently widely used predictive techniques and applications for the testing of new products and product concepts, advertising pretesting, and volume and brand share prediction using simulated test market modeling.

QUESTIONS FOR DISCUSSION

1   The ex-factory shipments of jams and preservatives from a medium-sized, UK-based company have been steadily declining over six months, having been stable for many years. The Managing Director wants a detailed market analysis to discover exactly what is happening in the marketplace. Suggest key market measurements that will need to be taken to facilitate such an analysis.

2   An airline wants an in-depth understanding of domestic customer usage and attitudes towards the company's services. Suggest the key questions that will need to be included in a U&A study.

3   Review the key measures taken by market research agencies of the "success" of advertising and suggest what this tells us about what advertisers need to do to create successful advertisements.

4   Measures of television and radio audiences and newspaper and magazine readerships are all based on samples, hence they are only estimates. Review pp. 241–244 on sampling errors and outline the various kinds of error that might arise in estimating media audiences.

5   Review the details of the various STM models described in this chapter and generate a list of factors that manufacturers need to attend to in order to ensure, for a new or modified product, a good trial rate and a good repeat purchase rate.

FURTHER READING

Brown, G. (1991) "Response. Modelling advertising awareness", *Journal of the Market Research Society*, 33 (3): 197–204.

Buttle, F. (1996) "SERVQUAL: review, critique, research agenda", *European Journal of Marketing*, 56 (July): 1–24.

Cronin, J. and Taylor, S. (1992) "Measuring service quality: a reexamination and extension", *Journal of Marketing*, 56 (July): 55–68.

de Chernatony, L. and Knox, S. (1990) "How an appreciation of consumer behaviour can help in product testing", *Journal of the Market Research Society*, 32 (3): 329–347.

Feldwick, P. (1991) "How valuable is the Awareness Index?", *Journal of the Market Research Society*, 33 (3): 179–195.

Jones, T and Sasser, W. (1995) "Why satisfied customers defect", *Harvard Business Review*, 73 (November–December): 88–99.

Kent, R. A. (1994) *Measuring Media Audiences*. London: Routledge.

White, R. (2000) "Single-source data", *WARC Best Practice*, April.

Wilke, J. (2002) "The future of simulated test markets", ESOMAR, Consumer Insight Congress, Barcelona, September.

Cross-national research 17

In this chapter you will learn about:

→ the very different environments in which cross-national research takes place,

→ issues that are specific to the design of cross-national research, including identifying market opportunities across a number of countries or indeed across the globe, building cross-national marketing information systems to monitor trends and carrying out primary research that spans more than one country,

→ the issues that are specific to the conduct of cross-national primary research including selecting the appropriate unit of analysis, the problems of comparable measurement and scaling across nations, taking samples in different countries, the use of proprietary international research services, the particular features of international advertising research, and the use of qualitative methods across borders,

→ academic cross-national research.

INTRODUCTION

The growth in world trade has resulted in a huge and expanding demand for information about markets throughout the world. As markets and marketing activities have become more integrated and global in scope, there has been increasing interest among both practitioners and academics in conducting cross-national research. Although the process of conducting such research is not greatly different from domestic research, there are challenges, problems and pitfalls associated with extending the scope of research to encompass more than one country.

What is usually included as "international marketing research" can be interpreted in different ways. It may mean research on products or services that are offered for sale in more than one country (sometimes called multi-country research), research that is conducted in a country or countries other than that of the research-commissioning organization (foreign research), or research conducted in or across different cultures (cross-national research). International marketing research will include all of these, but the main focus of this chapter will be on the particular issues associated with undertaking cross-national research.

INTERNET ACTIVITY

Using your browser, go to **www.thomsonlearning.co.uk/kent** and select the Chapter 17 Internet Activity which will provide a link to the Business Environment Risk Intelligence website. Click on *BRS*, the Business Risk Service. Read the explanation of the service and click on *View Market Opportunity Ranking Explanation and Methodology*.

National and cross-national research

Some commentators have argued that, methodologically speaking, there is no difference between domestic and cross-national research: market researchers have to adapt their techniques to their target population, and the differences in culture within a country offer the same challenges as operating in cultures many thousands of kilometers away. However, although the overall stages for undertaking qualitative or quantitative marketing research may be similar, cross-national research is likely to be rather more complex and will need to take into account the very different environments in which such research takes place. Some of the key factors in this environment are summarized in Figure 17.1.

In terms of the marketing microenvironment of customers, competitors, suppliers, distributors and so on, it may well be that in some developing countries, the orientation is towards production rather than marketing. Demand may exceed supply and there will be little concern with customer satisfaction. Surveys conducted in Europe, by contrast, will typically involve questions about variety and selection of brands. Such questions may be inappropriate in some African countries where goods are in short supply. Questions about pricing may have to include bargaining and haggling as part of the exchange process. In Europe, television advertising is extremely important, but may be restricted or even prohibited in some countries where television channels are government operated. Some themes, words or illustrations that are common in Europe may be taboo or give rise to offence in some countries. Even within Europe, the market is very diverse, and some images acceptable in one country may not be in another.

In terms of the wider macroenvironment, there are many aspects of the environment that will impact on marketing research. Governments establish different regulatory frameworks, incentives and penalties, tariff barriers, tax structures or market controls within which any business needs to operate. Some governments operate businesses themselves, or cooperate with industry towards common goals. The legal environment will encompass common law, foreign law, inter-

FIGURE 17.1

The environment for cross-national research

national law and laws relating to bribery or antitrust. There will be laws that relate to product safety and quality, packaging, warranty and after sales, patents, trademarks and copyright. Laws on pricing may deal with price fixing, price discrimination, price controls and retail price maintenance. Laws may govern the type of promotion that can be used. Even the extent to which laws are enforced will vary widely.

The overall economic environment will also be crucial, for example the gross domestic product will give some indication of the overall size of the national economy, while income distribution, growth trends and trends within sectors will also be very important. The information and technology environment will include differences in communication systems, the penetration of computers, the internet, broadband, digital television or the use of mobile telephones. Structural factors will include transportation systems and communication systems. The mail service may be inefficient while not many households may have telephones, making telephone surveys impossible. Data may not be available on markets, or on demographics. A national sample may, for example, be unthinkable in China or impossible in Indonesia with several thousand islands.

In cultural terms, levels of literacy will vary, there will be vast differences in religion, language, family patterns and social institutions. There may be different values relating to time and time-keeping, ambition, work ethic, innovation, change and so on. Dunlop (1995), for example, reports that one of the main difficulties encountered in interviewing Arabs (and females in particular) is their natural tendency to want to please others – including researchers. This makes the formulation of questions a tricky and sensitive issue. True feelings, opinions or preferences are often disguised. Ratings will tend to be higher, particularly for product attributes or purchase intension. In India, there are 20 major languages and over 200 dialects. A survey that even approaches national representation will normally be printed in at least 12 languages (Hutton 1996). Many marketers believe that the youth market across Europe is becoming more alike in attitudes, lifestyles and aspirations. Pasco (2001) calls this into question. He argues that in Northern Europe – and in the UK particularly – there is a growing "hands off" style of parenting. By contrast, Southern and some Eastern European Catholic countries have more united family units with an extended support network firmly in place. Offspring remain living in the family home until much later. There is a slower transition to emotional and financial independence.

Box 17.1 shows how AT&T tried to develop a brand equity modeling and measurement system that could be used globally.

RESEARCH IN ACTION   BOX 17.1
How AT&T manages its global brand

AT&T is a US-based company with more than 100 years' experience in the telecommunications industry. Its brand equity in the US is high, but managing the brand globally has been more of a challenge. People react to brands in different ways in different cultures. Brands, furthermore, have, according to Upshaw and Taylor (2000), evolved into "complex vessels of strategic meaning with personas that engage consumers at the fundamental level of values and self-perceptions".

Malinoski and Zeese (2002) report that AT&T worked with Research International to design a market-based brand equity modeling and measurement system that, with some modifications for local cultural differences, could be used in all its markets around the world. The idea was to find out what kinds of drivers of brand equity might be considered universal or at least regional.

Over 3000 telephone interviews were conducted with business communications decision-makers in 17 countries where AT&T has business interests. Managers were asked whether they agreed with a series of 25 statements about the AT&T brand, for example "anticipates my needs" or "served me well in the past". A factor analysis grouped these into three areas: "A brand you trust", "A brand that builds relationships" and "A brand on the move".

The researchers found that brand equity was important in all markets, including those like Brazil and Argentina that were the most price-conscious markets. They also found that in every country except Argentina, brand image contributed more to brand equity than brand performance. Brand relationships jumped out as critical in the more industrialized regions like Japan, the US, Europe and Canada. Argentine and Brazilian decision-makers were more focused on the "brand you can trust" theme, while in Chile they were more into "brands on the move".

KEY POINTS

Although the overall stages for undertaking qualitative or quantitative marketing research may be similar in domestic and cross-national research, the latter is likely to be rather more complex and will need to take into account the very different environments in which such research takes place. The challenge for European researchers in the first decade of the twenty-first century is to meet the requirement for information that is truly global, but which retains a clear focus on local markets and local issues. The need for integrated research services that span European and global markets is particularly true for continuous research. Manufacturers and retailers need to be able to track international brands and to follow marketing outcomes across national boundaries. The paradox is that along with globalization there is also fragmentation of markets. The need, say Penfold and Buckingham (1990), is to think global, but act local.

The design of cross-national research

The key steps in undertaking quantitative cross-national research are the same as those portrayed in Chapter 11 (Figure 11.1) for domestic research, and in Chapter 10 (Figure 10.1) for qualitative research. The first stage is designing the research, which itself has a number of components, as were illustrated in Chapter 1 (Figure 1.4). The design stage in particular has to take account of many extra factors if the research is to span more than one country. This in turn often raises a crucial dilemma: to achieve comparability of results between countries it is necessary to standardize the research as far as possible, yet the more it is standardized, the less it is likely to take account of local factors. The next section takes up the issues of design more specifically.

The international market researcher has three key roles.

1 identifying market opportunities across a number of countries or indeed across the globe,

2 building cross-national marketing information systems to monitor trends,

3 carrying out primary research that spans more than one country.

Identifying market opportunities

Identifying market opportunities will involve:

- scanning for feasibility,
- making a risk assessment,
- creating market segments.

There are about 200 countries across the globe. Even a large multinational corporation would find it difficult to resource market development in all of these, so the first task is to scan them and identify what countries have the potential for growth. Basically, this process identifies countries that may warrant further research. This may be just a case of checking for accessibility, profitability and market characteristics. Some markets may not be accessible due to tariff barriers, government regulations or import restrictions. Profitability may be affected by things like exchange rates, currency restriction, price controls, or subsidies to local competition. Market characteristics might include whether the market already exists or is a potential market, and the level and nature of the competition or potential competition.

Researchers may need to make an assessment of the types of risks involved (political, commercial, industrial or financial) and the degree of those risks. Over the years, marketers have developed indices to help assess the risk factors involved in the evaluation of potential market opportunities. One of these is the Business Environment Risk Index (BERI, www.beri.com). This index, which is a subscription service and was established in 1966, provides risk forecasts for 50 countries throughout the world and is updated three times a year. The index assesses 15 environmental factors including political stability, balance of payment volatility, inflation, labor productivity, local management skills, bureaucratic delays and so on. Each factor is rated on a scale of 0–4 ranging from unacceptable (0) to superior (4). The key factors are weighted to take into account their importance. The final score is out of 100 and scores of 80 or over would indicate a favorable environment. Scores under 40 would indicate high risk.

On the basis of the risk assessments, the international market can be classified or segmented on a national basis, for example identifying what countries may be "primary opportunities", or it may be carried out on a transnational basis. Thus Research International, when researching the transnational segments of young adults globally, divided them into four broad categories: "enthusiastic materialists", "swimmers against the tide", the "new realists", and "complacent materialists".

Mosaic Global, offered by Experian Business Strategies (www. business-strategies.co.uk) is a segmentation system based on geodemographics that covers over 400 million of the world's households. Using local data from 25 countries, Experian has identified ten types of residential neighborhood that can be found in each of the countries, each with a distinctive set of values, motivations and consumer preferences. Mosaic Global is based on a simple proposition that the world's cities share common patterns of residential segregation. Each have their ghettos of "metropolitan strugglers", suburbs of "career and family" and communities of "sophisticated singles". In terms of their values and lifestyles, each type of neighborhood displays strong similarities in whatever country it is found. Mosaic Global enables international organizations to carry out effective cross-border analysis, consumer research and target marketing in the world's wealthiest regions. For more details, see Box 17.2.

RESEARCH IN ACTION
Mosaic Global

BOX 17.2

The ten Mosaic Global groups are:

A Sophisticated singles
B Bourgeois prosperity
C Career and family
D Comfortable retirement
E Routine service workers
F Hard-working blue collar
G Metropolitan strugglers
H Low-income elders
I Postindustrial survivors
J Rural inheritance

Neighborhoods identified as "sophisticated singles", for example, contain just under 8 percent of households, mostly young people, mostly single and well educated. They positively enjoy the variety and stimulation afforded by life in large cities. They are quick to explore and adopt new social or political attitudes and are important agents of innovation. Finland has by far the highest proportion in this category – over 28 percent of households. By contrast the Republic of Ireland has the lowest with just 1.3 percent in this category. "Metropolitan strugglers", by contrast, contain people who live in less sought after neighborhoods and who often battle against high levels of crime, drug addiction and social disorder. Often they are poorly paid in low-skill service jobs such as office cleaners and typically they live in cramped rented apartments. Sweden and Hong Kong have the highest proportion of these (26 percent of households) while the Republic of Ireland has the lowest – 2.7 percent.

Building information systems

Having identified market opportunities, the next stage is to build an information base. A market profile analysis should provide a detailed assessment that will help the company to determine the degree of competitive advantage and decide on an appropriate method of market entry. A variety of information sources will be used. In the UK, UK Trade and Investment (www.uktradeinvest.gov.uk), is a government department that provides a range of information services. Other sources include the European Union (www.europa.eu.int), International Business Resources (www.ciber.bus), the World Bank (www.worldbank.com), and the World Trade Organization (www.wto.org). On a subscription basis, market reports may be purchased from Euromonitor (www.euromonitor.com). Each Euromonitor industry report is based on a core set of research techniques:

- national-level desk research, company research and analysis, store checking, trade interviewing with national players and market analysis,

- international-level desk research, multinational company research and analysis, trade interviewing with national players and market analysis.

The same in-house team of analysts that conducts the complementary international-level research also coordinates, controls, edits and finalizes the work of research associates in each country under review. The research process is summarized in Figure 17.2. The Euromonitor website also gives access free to a large range of articles on international research.

FIGURE 17.2

The Euromonitor research process

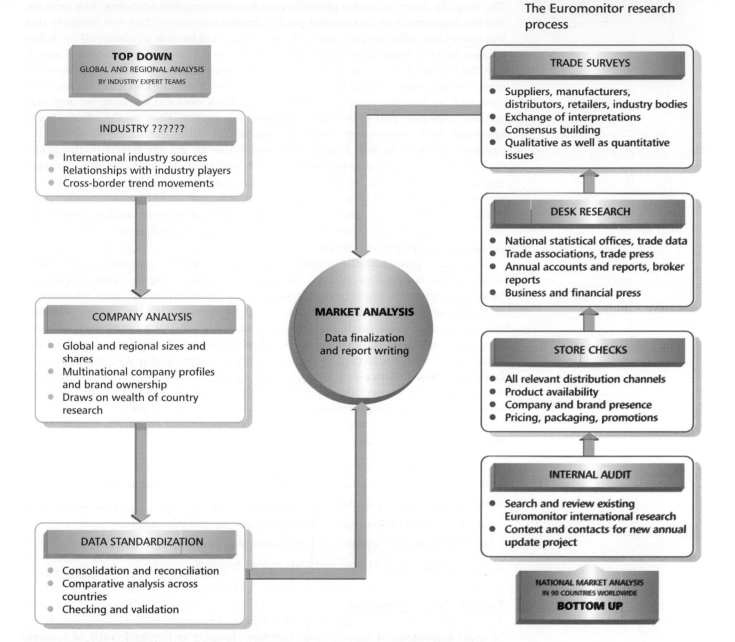

TOP DOWN
GLOBAL AND REGIONAL ANALYSIS
BY INDUSTRY EXPERT TEAMS

INDUSTRY ??????

- International industry sources
- Relationships with industry players
- Cross-border trend movements

COMPANY ANALYSIS

- Global and regional sizes and shares
- Multinational company profiles and brand ownership
- Draws on wealth of country research

DATA STANDARDIZATION

- Consolidation and reconciliation
- Comparative analysis across countries
- Checking and validation

MARKET ANALYSIS

Data finalization and report writing

TRADE SURVEYS

- Suppliers, manufacturers, distributors, retailers, industry bodies
- Exchange of interpretations
- Consensus building
- Qualitative as well as quantitative issues

DESK RESEARCH

- National statistical offices, trade data
- Trade associations, trade press
- Annual accounts and reports, broker reports
- Business and financial press

STORE CHECKS

- All relevant distribution channels
- Product availability
- Company and brand presence
- Pricing, packaging, promotions

INTERNAL AUDIT

- Search and review existing Euromonitor international research
- Context and contacts for new annual update project

NATIONAL MARKET ANALYSIS
IN 90 COUNTRIES WORLDWIDE
BOTTOM UP

KEY POINTS

Identifying market opportunities will involve scanning for feasibility, making a risk assessment, and creating market segments. The information thus generated then needs to go into a market profile analysis. There are a number of sources that companies can use in this process. Ideally, the process should be systematic and thorough, but may well in practice be shortchanged and replaced by gut feeling or hunch on the part of senior management in the company. Alternatively, managers may feel that the scanning process has produced sufficient information to make a decision about what market to attempt to develop and in what manner.

Carrying out primary research

The manufacturer or service provider may have undertaken scanning, risk analysis, market segmentation and market profile analyses in-house, but it is unlikely that the researcher, whether in-house or in an agency, will be able to obtain all the information needed from secondary sources alone, so primary cross-national research may be required. At this stage, there are a number of ways in which this research could be organized. Manufacturers or service providers may, for example, use their own staff in different countries to obtain feedback on local markets, or they may use the expertise and experience of importing agents. They might, alternatively, approach and commission research agencies in other countries to undertake research on their behalf. Finally, they might use an agency based in the home country to carry out cross-national research for them. Most of the larger market research agencies have an international division that specializes in this kind of research. However, the domestic agency may subcontract fieldwork or other parts of the research to local agencies, it may have offices in other countries, it may have associate companies in other countries, or it may be a global agency with research organizations around the world.

The client, in consultation with the agency (or a number of agencies if the client is looking for research proposals), will need to consider whether a one-off, ad hoc piece of research is appropriate or whether it will need to buy into continuous research services. The client will also need to discuss with the agency whether quantitative research, qualitative research, or some kind of mixture (see Chapter 9) would be best in achieving the client's objectives. Whatever the design of the research, it will need to take account of all those micro- and macroenvironmental factors discussed earlier that will vary from country to country. From one perspective it could be argued that different designs may be appropriate in different countries; yet this compromises standardization and comparability.

From the point of view of undertaking cross-national research, a number of more specific issues stand out:

- selecting the appropriate unit of analysis,
- the problems of comparable measurement and scaling across nations,
- taking samples in different countries,
- the use of proprietary international research services,
- the particular features of international advertising research,
- the use of qualitative methods across borders.

The unit of analysis

In most international studies, the "country" is used as the basic unit of analysis in the research design. This becomes the spatial unit from which samples are drawn and from which inferences are made about similarities and differences. The country is a political entity and most secondary data will be available on a country-by-country basis. Sometimes, however, a more appropriate unit might be cities, regions or areas with specific linguistic groupings within countries, or even groupings of countries like the European Union. "Country", furthermore, is not necessarily synonymous with culture. For studies where the internet has a significant impact, national boundaries may have little relevance. Furthermore, due to cultural differences, people living in Northern France, for example, are more similar to people living in Belgium than they are to French people living in the South of France. VanderMerwe and L'Huillier (1989) comment that managers need to identify clusters of Euro-consumers and adjust their strategies and operations to cater for transnational segments.

Measurement and scaling across countries

Decision-makers often require global answers to develop global or at least cross-national marketing campaigns, yet data are often related to particular national markets and cannot easily be interpreted consistently across countries. Measurement, as we saw in Chapter 5, may be direct, indirect, derived or multi-dimensional. However, what counts as an "indicator" of a concept in one country may not in another. The statements used in Likert scales or other types of summated rating scale may have very different connotations in different cultures. In some cultures, like Japan, India or Sweden, respondents will try to avoid conflict and will gravitate towards the middle items; in others like Spain, Greece or Italy they will tend to skew positively. In the UK and France scores will be more evenly distributed.

When using multiitem scales in cross-national research, it is normal to take a scale that has been developed in one country, to translate it and to administer it in a number of countries with relatively little consideration to equivalence or validity across cultures. The assumption is that underlying constructs can be measured using the same instrument. Internal consistency may be tested by using Cronbach's coefficient alpha. Sometimes construct validity may be examined by looking at how the scale relates to related concepts. There are, however, alternative ways of applying a scale developed in one cultural context to another. Hambleton (1994) in fact outlines 22 guidelines formulated by an international committee for the translation and adaptation of psychological and educational instruments. The guidelines, which would be equally applicable to questionnaires used for market research, cover taking into account the cultural context in which scales are developed and refined, the development of the instrument itself, including translation, its administration and the interpretation of the score.

Direct translation in which a bilingual translator translates the questionnaire from a base language to the respondent's language is frequently used. With back translation, the questionnaire is translated from the base language by a bilingual speaker whose native language is the language into which the questionnaire is being translated. The version is then translated back into the original language by a bilingual whose native language is the initial or base language. Translation errors can then be identified. With parallel translation, a committee of translators, each of whom is fluent in at least two of the languages in which the questionnaire may be administered discusses alternative versions of the questionnaire and makes modifications until a consensus is reached. Problems may still remain, however. The use of terms like "quite good", "fairly good" or "about average" may be distinguishable in English, but not in other languages. Klein (2003) gives an example of a question "The commercial was meaningful to me", with responses of agree and disagree, which was translated into *importante* in Brazil, but into *significativo* for Hispanic Americans. In Mexico some felt it should be *tiene sentido*.

According to Klein (2003), achieving comparability from multicultural diversity is an "awesome" task. The challenge is how to measure and interpret multiple consumer environments with some degree of consistency and comparability, and to find common denominators across multiple cultures so that clients can be presented with results that make sense. Scaling in particular presents difficulties. If, for example, a scale of likeability such as that in Figure 17.3 is used, will it be appropriate and equally understood in all countries? Do the words mean the same thing? Do the intervals between the scale points have the same meaning? The way individuals react to such scales will be affected by a number of factors, for example school and college grading systems, or cultural factors related to mathematical aptitude versus verbalization.

In most countries a scale of 1 to 10 where 10 is best and 1 is worst is commonly understood. This scale is an excellent reference point where this kind of scale is used in schools, for example in France, Italy, Greece, Belgium, Holland and Spain.

FIGURE 17.3

Likeability of an advertisement

What was your overall
reaction to the
advertisement you have
just seen?

I liked it very much ☐

I liked it to some
extent ☐

I neither liked it nor
disliked it ☐

I disliked it to some
extent ☐

I disliked it very much ☐

However, Germany uses a 6-point scale in its schools system, but in the opposite direction, where 1 is excellent and 6 is poor. The same is true for Norway. Some cultures do not feel at ease with ranking items. In Mexico or India people would have great difficulty with any constant sum measurement in which a given number of points are allocated to products, packages or advertisements.

Sampling across borders

Taking samples across countries will, clearly, be more complex than research carried out in a single country. Sampling frames, if they are available, may be differently constructed and will be of varied qualities. Sampling carried out in different countries by local agencies may have different interpretations of what counts as a "random" sample. What count as appropriate stratification factors or quota controls will vary from country to country. In some countries, race or ethnicity may be important; in others it may be social class or income. Undertaking a multistage sample that involves dividing a country into regions will see regions in many different ways and will relate to natural areas or administrative areas in different ways.

For business-to-business research, sampling on a global basis is quite likely to be needed. Worldwide lists of manufacturers, for example, can be obtained from Dun and Bradstreet's *Principal International Businesses*, which has an online database listing 500 000 leading businesses. Sampling on a global basis will be rarer in consumer research unless the target population is a small global market segment, for example subscribers to *National Geographic* might be an appropriate population for testing a new travel publication.

At the next level might be groupings of countries such as Asia, South America, Europe or the European Union. Graham and Whiteside publish company directories (http://lr.thomsonlearning.co.uk/graham_whiteside) in six volumes listing 24 000 of the largest companies in Europe plus the names of 194 000 senior executives.

At the level of units within countries, one problem faced in cross-national research is to determine who is the relevant respondent. If households are sampled, then should it be the husband, wife or both together who should be interviewed? This, of course, may need to vary from country to country or even from culture to culture within countries. In some Middle Eastern countries, the husband actually purchases groceries, but the wife specifies what items are to be purchased. If the unit is an organization, the relevant person may depend on the extent to which companies are centralized. In some countries the relevant respondent may be the chairman, chief executive officer or managing director. In Anglo-Saxon cultures there is more delegation in decision-making, so middle management may play a greater role.

A key issue in sample design in cross-national market research is the trade-off between representativeness and comparability. If samples are representative of the target population within a country, they are unlikely to be comparable in regard to key characteristics such as income or education.

Proprietary international research services

Omnibus services

Many of the larger agencies offer cross-national omnibus services. Omnibus surveys were explained on Ipsos (**www.ipsos.co.uk**) were the first to offer a standardized weekly computer-assisted personal interviewing (CAPI) omnibus in key European markets. This is called Capibus™, which samples adults aged 15 and over (2000 in the UK and 1000 in France, Germany, Italy and Spain) using a two-stage random location sampling process. Findings can be delivered as little as ten days after questionnaire agreement. Results are supplied as electronic computer tables, a summary report, interactive database or as a presentation. Background information is collected on the respondent and the household; covering everything from standard demographics through to internet use and media consumption (GB only).

Ipsos also provides a global omnibus called Global Express™ which covers over 50 countries around the world; 1000 adults aged 15 and over are sampled in every country. All interviews are carried out in-home or by telephone on a weekly, monthly or quarterly basis. Box 17.3 explains how Ipsos used their global omnibus to study cancer awareness across Europe.

There is now also a weekly international online omnibus service called i:omnibus™, which combines some of the advantages of face-to-face interviews with the speed of telephone surveys. The sample is drawn from an online access panel and includes 1000 adults aged from 15 to 64 in each market. Results can be delivered in four days. Box 17.4 shows a cross-national study of how people react to unsolicited e-mail. It is important to note, however, that spamming is usually considered unethical and in some countries like Norway, it is illegal.

EUROPEAN MARKETING RESEARCH

BOX 17.3

Cancer awareness across Europe

The UECG (United European Colorectal Cancer Group) identified the need to educate the people of Europe on the dangers and problems caused by (and associated with) colorectal cancer. Though this particular form of cancer is the most common across Europe, it also has the highest success rate when caught early. In order to implement an educational program, the UECG had to lobby the European parliament with evidence that awareness of this form of cancer was very low throughout Europe. In order to gather information to support the UECG case, Ipsos MORI UK conducted a panEuropean research program covering all of the countries within the European union. The remit was to design a questionnaire that met all of the project objectives for the lowest possible price. The results provided individual country tables grossed up to the total population, consolidated panEuropean and regional (North, South, East and West) European tables and provided a full presentation of the main findings.

RESEARCH IN ACTION
How effective is spamming?

BOX 17.4

As access to and use of the internet (for e-mail in particular) continues to rise, so too does the potential for unsolicited commercial e-mail (or spam) to become the modern day "junk mail". But how effective can it truly be? The client needed to decide whether "spamming" was a cost-effective way of approaching future customers for a variety of online services and product categories. Using the i:omnibus™ in such diverse markets as Britain, France, Germany, the US, Canada and Brazil, Ipsos MORI were able to assess the proportion of spam mail being deleted without even being read, the demographic groups most susceptible to spam marketing, the service/product categories yielding the greatest success as a result of spamming, and satisfaction levels with the post-spam purchase process.

Access panels

An access panel is a prerecruited group of respondents who have agreed to take part in research and who cooperate on a regular basis. Panelists are screened and provide details about the demographics of all individuals in the household as well as other information. It is thus possible to target individuals who would otherwise be difficult to find. Panels need to be managed so that they are not over- or underutilized and that details of panel members are kept up to date. There is usually regular contact with panel members through newsletters.

Ipsos runs both offline and online panels. Offline, Ipsos has some 80 000 households comprising over 213 000 individuals across Europe including France, Germany and the UK. Online, it has some 1 600 000 households comprising over 4 000 000 individuals across Europe, North America and Asia. Panelists are recruited through random mailing and telephone and by approaching willing respondents from other research studies. Panelists will typically complete 8–10 surveys in a year. Each year about 15 percent of the panel needs to be replaced. Response rates vary from about 55 percent to 85 percent. The level achieved depends on a number of factors such as target group, type of study and level of incentive. For example, female heads of household have the highest response, and young active males the lowest. Higher response rates are achieved for product tests and lower ones for diary studies.

In almost everything that as been written about cross-national research, one key recommendation is always cited: work with somebody who understands the local culture and can help with attending to local customs. Now, suggest Strasser and Lingeman (2003), in an era of online research, a whole new set of challenges is emerging. It is now possible, for example, to design, execute and interview from a single location anywhere in the globe. Though this clearly offers many benefits, there are also new pitfalls. Strasser and Lingeman (2003) report that two agencies, MSI International East, based in the US, and ITM International B.V., based in the Netherlands, have set up an online proprietary consumer panel for one of the world's leading technology companies in 11 countries and a worldwide panel, Planet Panel®.

The authors suggest that such panels need to consider the country-specific differences in online sample sources and panel recruitment. The different characteristics of local list sources can produce very different profiles of internet users. In many countries the web interface needed to be localized to boost panel registrations. The response rates and the speed of response varied considerably from country to country. Response rates were lowest in Mexico and Spain and highest in the US and Germany. This, however, may be associated with the penetration of broadband. In Mexico and Spain it took almost twice as long to complete an online survey as in the UK.

Cross-national advertising

Wilkins (2002) reports that the work of Ipsos-ASI on multi-country ads suggests that they do not travel well. Ads that are simply re-dubbed for another country vary in terms of how they perform. From a study of 3000 ads pretested within Europe, it was found that how ad characteristics contributed to recall and persuasion varied from country to country. The research showed, for example, that ads that were involving, different, informative and innovative contributed more to persuasion in the UK, France and Germany than in Spain. Taylor (2002) suggests that there are five key problems that have hindered the development of international advertising research:

1 too many descriptive studies of advertising content and not enough on why various executional techniques are effective in specific markets,

2 a preoccupation with questions of whether campaigns should be standardized to the detriment of seeking answers for pragmatic execution across markets,

3 a lack of rigor in establishing equivalence in studies comparing data from multiple countries, both in terms of study design and data analysis,

4 a disturbing lack of knowledge about whether, and when, targeting segments that cut across national boundaries can be effective,

5 not enough focus on control of international advertising campaigns, both in terms of who makes the decision and the extent to which they are effectively implemented.

Interest in cross-cultural advertising research has led to several empirical studies that examine similarities and differences in advertising research between countries (Lerman and Callow 2004). Researchers have, for example, tried to predict the relative frequency of specified advertising appeals and techniques employed in two or more countries. Thus Biswas et al. (1992) found that French ads tend to rely on sex appeal to a greater extent than American ads.

Cross-national qualitative research

Establishing the comparability of concepts, attitudes and behaviors in different countries is critical in any cross-national research. It is important, therefore, to understand these attitudes and behaviors in terms of the social and cultural contexts in which they occur. Researchers need to be careful of interpreting the results of marketing research purely in terms of their own culture. This is why qualitative research can be helpful, since it explores the contexts in which purchase and consumption decisions are taken.

Chapter 4 explored the nature and construction of qualitative data, the characteristics of client-based qualitative market research, the process of interviewing groups and individuals, the alternatives to interview methods, namely observation, ethnography and consultation, and the nature of academic qualitative research. We saw, too, that such research could be used for exploratory, diagnostic, evaluative, or creative development purposes.

Cross-national qualitative market research, however, presents challenges that are above and beyond those presented by domestic quantitative research. Interviewing groups or individuals entails imposing upon those groups or individuals the skills, personality and cultural background of the focus group moderator or one-to-one interviewer. Using local moderators or interviewers can compromise comparability as much as sending out moderators or interviewers from the country in which the research is based. The careful training and supervision of local interviewers can certainly help, but a decision still needs to be taken about who is going to interpret the data. Some agencies centralize data interpretation by getting local interviewers to send the tapes, transcripts or videos to head office for analysis.

According to Lury (2004), too much international qualitative research is merely skimming the surface. In its early days the approach tended to be very centralized. There were formal central briefings at which local moderators from around the globe were tasked with exploring the thoughts, feelings, reactions and nuances of their domestic markets. Nowadays it is characterized by a more nomadic methodology. The commissioned agency sends members of its research team far and wide to brief local research agencies. Lury (2004) argues that not all international qualitative research needs to be conducted by local moderators. There are benefits to be derived from research executives from the commissioning agency immersing themselves in the local culture.

Box 17.5 shows how qualitative research was used to identify the impact of different values when attempting to communicate with Asian young people.

KEY POINTS

Undertaking primary research across countries presents a number of problems and issues that are additional to those encountered in undertaking domestic research. They include selecting the appropriate unit of analysis, the problems of comparable measurement and scaling across nations, taking samples in different countries, the use of proprietary international research services, the particular features of international advertising research, and the use of qualitative methods across borders. There are also dimensions that present dilemmas to the cross-national researcher, including comparability and standardization versus taking account of local factors, or thinking globally versus acting locally.

RESEARCH IN ACTION   BOX 17.5
Communicating with Asian youth

Thiesse and Gowers (1996), from Research International Qualitatif, report the results of depth interviews and group discussions with young adults aged from 20 to 35 in countries in Asia. The aim was to identify the levers for successful communication with young adults by asking about their interests, values, goals and perspectives. Twenty-four professionals from across Asia from marketing, advertising, journalism and the social sciences were interviewed, and a series of group discussions was carried out in Indonesia, Japan, the Philippines, Thailand, China and India. The sample was from middle socioeconomic sectors and was intended to be representative of the more urbanized and culturally developed sectors of society.

The findings showed that attempts to approach Asian youth as a homogeneous sector are misguided. Though there are a number of values like individualism and ambition that unite them (with the possible exception of Japan), there is a wide range of differences in life-stage and behavior. In terms of what differentiated them, the authors distinguish between two types of outlook;

■ the enthusiastic materialists,
■ the complacent materialists.

The first group is found in the emerging markets of China, India, Thailand, Indonesia and the Philippines. The other group is identified mainly with Japan. Whatever the group, however, the marketing communications that engage them include entertainment, humor, and approaches that challenge or intrigue, invite complicity, or break codes.

Academic cross-national research

Academics have limited funding to support research and few resources to assist with research projects, so the addition of complexities and the wider contexts of cross-national research increases the time needed to complete the research. Nevertheless, suggest Craig and Douglas (2005), academic researchers are beginning to explore and question the applicability and suitability of indigenous research paradigms to other countries and cultures. Douglas and Craig (2006) argue for a greater emphasis on the early stages of research design in international markets, stages that have to do with developing the conceptual framework and the unit of analysis. An important issue is the applicability of the original framework in different contexts or research settings. Construct measurement and the unit of analysis may similarly require modification. Typically, the domestic market forms the dominant frame of reference, which is then assumed to be appropriate in other countries. Thus, say the authors, although the concept of marketing orientation has been validated in developing countries, its antecedents differ. In Ghana, centralization and formalization are important antecedents, whereas in Thailand an innovation orientation is a crucial antecedent. The expression of concepts like trust and ethnocentrism may differ across countries. In Bangladesh, customers' trust in an organization has a significant impact on their trust in its salespeople. Attitudes towards foreign products will vary between small countries with high levels of foreign trade compared with large industrialized countries.

Douglas and Craig (2006) argue that, where countries are used as a unit, it is critical that they be purposively selected to be comparable, to reflect variance on characteristics of interest, and to control for confounding effects. However, this is very much the academic approach with its concern to generate generalizable theory. In a commercial context, the selection of countries will be made using the scanning and risk assessment procedures described earlier.

For an example of academic cross-national research, go to **www.mc21.org**. The research in explained in a little detail in Box 17.6.

Ethical issues

Ethical responsibilities for conducting cross-national research are very similar to those for research conducted domestically. ESOMAR has produced a code of conduct, which was explained in Chapter 1. Beyond that, it is the responsibility of researchers to be aware of and to respond to issues raised in this chapter. For individual countries, professional associations can play a key role. Former Eastern bloc countries like the Czech Republic, Hungary and Poland are now busy forming associations to control quality standard systems for the conduct of fieldwork.

RESEARCH IN ACTION
Marketing in the 21st Century

BOX 17.6

The project was born out of mutual interest by a group of marketing scholars in the identification of marketing resources (in particular marketing capabilities and marketing assets) and their impact on marketing performance. Pilot studies in the UK and Austria then quickly escalated to fieldwork in over 15 countries round the world, enabling a unique snapshot to be taken of marketing approaches and methods at the start of the twenty-first century.

SUMMARY

Although the overall stages for undertaking qualitative or quantitative marketing research may be similar in both domestic and cross-national research, the latter is likely to be rather more complex, and will need to take into account the very different environments in which such research takes place. Environmental factors include, for example, the marketing microenvironment of customers, suppliers, competitors and distributors plus the macroenvironmental factors that relate to cultural, structural, technological, economic, legal and governmental factors.

In terms of the design of cross-national research, three issues that are specific to this kind of research are identifying market opportunities across a number of countries or indeed across the globe, building cross-national marketing information systems to monitor trends, and carrying out primary research that spans more than one country.

Identifying market opportunities will involve scanning for feasibility, making a risk assessment, and creating market segments. The information thus generated then needs to go into a market profile analysis.

Undertaking primary research across countries presents a number of problems and issues that are additional to those encountered in undertaking domestic research. These include selecting the appropriate unit of analysis, the problems of comparable measurement and scaling across nations, taking samples in different countries, the use of proprietary international research services, the particular features of international advertising research, and the use of qualitative methods across borders. There are also dimensions that present dilemmas to the cross-national researcher, including comparability and standardization versus taking account of local factors, or thinking globally versus acting locally.

Academic cross-national research has only fairly recently begun to address some of the issues that are specific to undertaking research across cultures.

QUESTIONS FOR DISCUSSION

1 Explain how cross-national marketing research differs from domestic marketing research.

2 A UK manufacturer of children's electronic games wants to expand sales outside the UK. What advice would you give to senior managers as to how they should proceed?

3 What are the problems in trying to standardize the use of Likert scales across cultures? How can some of these problems be addressed?

4 Imagine that the manufacturer in Question 2 is thinking about using an international omnibus survey. Suggest what questions a manager responsible for commissioning such research would need to ask the research supplier before being convinced that this would be a good way to proceed.

CASE STUDY MAKING THE COMPASS GROUP A PREFERRED EMPLOYER

Jugdev and Maxwell (2004) explain that the Compass Group is the largest global food service and vending company and operates in 98 countries. It is the tenth largest employer in the world with over 400 000 employees and operates in eight clearly defined market sectors including sports and events, fine dining, healthcare, education, retail and travel, vending and remote sites. Well-known brands include Burger King, Upper Crust, and Victoria Wine. Sales are over £11 billion. In 2002 the Compass Group decided to refresh its employee satisfaction measurement tool that is used to track the company strategy of being a preferred employer. In particular, the Group wanted to introduce a measurement philosophy across the company that would focus the business on:

- attracting and retaining high-caliber individuals,
- retaining people who are loyal,
- ensuring that company values are lived up to in every unit,
- creating workplaces where people can deliver great service to their customers.

It was clear that employees would need to be measured consistently around the world, response rates would need to be improved, local managers would need to obtain results that would enable them to focus on what actions were needed, and the research would need to be able to track progress and at the same time allow for flexibility to measure local initiatives. The Compass Group selected BMRB International to undertake the research on their behalf. In 2003 a survey amounting to 111 000 respondents was conducted across 53 countries in 23 languages.

In the design of the measurement program, BMRB faced a number of challenges:

- to deliver a strategic tool to inform the Compass Group strategy to become a preferred employer by identifying which work practices can influence employee attitudes and drive future behavior,
- to deliver a tactical tool for country or sector managers ensuring ownership and accountability at a local level by thinking global but acting local,
- to establish a methodology that works across cultural boundaries and across the range of business sectors,
- to ensure a high level of local participation, focused on deliverables that are actionable.

Questions and activities

1 Log on to www.compass-group.com to find out a bit more about the company.

2 Bearing in mind what you have learned about research methodology and the special considerations of undertaking cross-national research considered in the chapter, suggest to BMRB and the Compass Group how they could best meet these challenges.

FURTHER READING

Craig, C. and Douglas, S. (2005) *International Marketing Research*, 3rd edition. Chichester: John Wiley & Son.

Douglas, S. and Craig, C. (2006) "On improving the conceptual foundations of international marketing research", *Journal of International Marketing*, 14 (1): 1–22.

Lerman, D. and Callow, M. (2004) "Content analysis in cross-cultural advertising research: insightful or superficial?", *International Journal of Advertising*, 23 (4): 507–521.

Lury, G. (2004) "The next generation of international research", *Admap*, Issue 452, July, 39–41.

Pasco, M. (2001) "From Cold War to Cola War", *Admap*, December, issue 423.

Strasser, P. and Lingeman, H. (2003) "Challenges in conducting worldwide online research", ESOMAR.

Taylor, C. (2002) "What is wrong with international advertising research?", *Journal of Advertising Research*, 42 (6), November.

VanderMerwe, S. and L'Huillier, M. (1989) "Euro-consumers in 1992", *Business Horizons*, 32 (1): 34–40.

Wilkins, J. (2002) "Why is global advertising still the exception, not the rule?", *Admap*, issue 425, February.

Communicating the results

<u>LEARNING OBJECTIVES</u> In this chapter you will learn about:

→ **the importance and content of research reports,**

→ **making presentations of research results,**

→ **research follow-up activities,**

→ **reporting cross-national research,**

→ **reporting academic research.**

Communicating
the results is a last
but crucial stage.

© LISA GAGNE

INTRODUCTION

Communication between client organizations and market research agencies (or between researchers and the commissioning part of the company for in-house research) will be ongoing from the time that initial tentative inquiries are made, or before proposals are sought and the research is commissioned, until well after the research is completed and the results presented. This chapter is about communicating and presenting the results to clients (or to academic audiences in the case of academic research) plus any follow-up activities.

When researchers have constructed and analyzed their data, they will have a tremendous amount of information – a stack of crosstabulations, pages of statistical analyses, copious notes and other assorted information. The challenge is how to put this into a coherent report or presentation that effectively communicates the key findings and the implications for the client.

INTERNET ACTIVITY

Using your browser, go to **www.thomsonlearning.co.uk/kent** and select the Chapter 18 Internet Activity which will provide a link to the Presenters University website. Download a copy of the *15 Minute Guide to Winning Presentations*. You will need to complete a short form first.

The research report

For client-based research, the research report is normally the main medium for communicating the results. It may be submitted to the client before any face-to-face presentation of the results, or it may be sent after such activity and may incorporate issues that arose from discussions at the presentation. The presentation of results is considered later in this chapter.

Research reports are an important part of the market research project, whether the research is quantitative or qualitative, whether it is ad hoc or continuous, for a number of reasons. First, they are tangible products of the research activity, serving as a historical record of the project and quite possibly the only documentary evidence that remains once letters or e-mails have been deleted or archived. Second, reports will normally be a specified part of the research contract, which may spell out the format of the report and the number of copies to be made available.

More significantly, however, research reports are important because, ideally, management decisions should be guided by the report and the presentation. There is always the danger, of course, that client managers do not read the report or just scan it very briefly and then consign it to the shelf. Finally, reports are important because managers will tend to evaluate the quality of the entire project purely on the basis of the report and perhaps the presentation. This evaluation will clearly affect the inclination of the client to use the research supplier again in the future.

Report content

The formal report, like the face-to-face presentation, is above all a method of communication, so the author needs to bear in mind the kinds of people who are likely to read it and what their needs are. Reports will normally be written in management report style. This means clear, concise, grammatical English, free of jargon or complex sentences, and organized in a way that allows the reader quickly to assemble and digest the content of the report. A fairly standard approach is to use plenty of headings and subheadings, arranged into a format similar to that suggested in Box 18.1.

IN DETAIL
Contents of a management report

BOX 18.1

Title page
This should state:

- title of report,
- who commissioned it,
- who prepared it,
- date submitted.

Contents page
This should:

- systematically number sections and subsections,
- list tables and figures.

Executive summary
This is a one-page abstract of the entire report, and may be all that a busy business executive reads. It should:

- explain the terms of reference, the purpose and scope of the report,
- state the key methods and approach used,
- list the main conclusions,
- list the key recommendations.

Main body of the report
This consists of a series of sections arranged under headings and subheadings that typically would include:

1 background – an analysis of the current situation or problem,
2 research methodology
   2.1 objectives of the research,
   2.2 measurement of the key variables,
   2.3 the population of cases covered,
   2.4 sampling procedures,
   2.5 data capture instruments,
   2.6 data collection methods,
   2.7 specific techniques and applications,
   2.8 data analysis,

3 market analysis,
4 results,
5 conclusions and recommendations,
6 limitations, caveats and suggestions for future research.

Appendices
These may include:

■ any explanatory notes that would clutter up the main report,
■ tabulations and calculations not included in the text,
■ references,
■ copies of questionnaires or visuals used.

Much of the material needed for the first two sections of the main body of the report – the background and methodology – will already have been written for the proposal, but the language will need to change to reflect the fact that the research has now been completed and is no longer a proposal of what is intended. Section 3 – market analysis – will not always be present, but will typically present background information and secondary data on the market or industry as a whole, explaining key trends.

The results section will often be the longest, and may be organized in a number of different ways. If the research has used different forms of data collection, for example significant amounts of secondary data, qualitative research and quantitative research, the results may be best presented by taking each of these in turn. Alternatively, it might be organized by objectives, taking each key objective in turn, showing how the different kinds of data collection or research methods used relate to each objective. Finally, the results may be organized by type of analysis, for example, taking the overall results, then breaking these down by region, by type of client or organization and finally by market segment. Wherever possible, graphs, tables, charts and diagrams should be used to illustrate and clarify arguments (review Chapter 11, Univariate data display). Ideally, these should be incorporated into the text, each numbered according to the appropriate section, for example "Table 4.1.2", and referred to in the text, which gives an interpretation or extracts the key points or lessons to be derived from it.

A good report is persuasive and convinces the reader that the conclusions and recommendations make good sense. It is important that the findings are related back to the objectives of the study and that the recommendations are based on the data, not on speculations that could have been made without the research. In a sense, the whole purpose of the research is to come to a conclusion and to make recommendations, so this section of the report is vital. The researcher needs to be able to put the research findings into the "bigger picture" of the client organization as a whole and its role and position in the market.

On limitations and caveats, all market research projects have their limitations. These may be limitations of scope or type of data collected. Limitations may be imposed by budgets, time or agency facilities and expertise. This section needs to be written with great care since not too much emphasis should be placed on a report's shortcomings; this may erode clients' confidence in the results, but the client may, on the other hand, be impressed by a degree of openness and honesty. The limitations in scope, in particular, may open up the way for future business for the agency.

Writing a report is often a team activity. The team may need to discuss what sections need to be in the report, what content needs to be in each section, what visuals to include and the format to follow for headings and subheadings. They

A management report is often a team activity.

© MARTIN BALCERZAK

may assign responsibilities to members of the team and agree on a timetable. Once the individual tasks are completed, there may need to be further meetings to put it all together.

Tierney (2004) argues that it is critical to remember that the end deliverable of the research effort is usually the beginning point for others – marketers, engineers, product designers, product managers and so on. Handing them a report may not help them to do their jobs. What they need are tools for their own levels of decision-making. These might include, for example, a research department intranet site or a video database. These will provide information at people's fingertips, will be easily accessible and will provide a vehicle for archiving, trend-tracking and comparing information across studies. Tierney also suggests a range of "at-a-glance" tools like brand perception maps or a purchasing behavior flow-chart, plus brainstorming and product development tools. These might include, for example, a dedicated space of highly graphical posters representing the output of a project.

KEY POINTS

The research report is normally the key vehicle by which results of client-based research are presented to the client. No matter how good the research design, how sophisticated the data analysis, how representative the sample or how carefully worded the questionnaire, the client may, at the end of the day, be very dissatisfied with the performance of the agency if the report is too long, too short, too complicated or too vague. Good researchers will be anticipating the report from the moment they write the research proposal. Researchers, of course, will be unlikely even to obtain the commission if the proposal does not at least show that researchers have understood the client's needs. The research itself may, of course, be only one input among others that is taken into account when deciding on some course of action. The client may, for example, have to review the company's financial situation if implementation will require considerable expenditure.

The presentation

Not every client wants a face-to-face presentation, but where one is required, it is usually an opportunity for the research executive to give preliminary results and conclusions, and for the client to ask about the research before the final report is written. The presentation is usually given by the research executive who was involved in the initial discussions with the client and who has been responsible for the design and execution of the research. The presentation will normally take place in the client organization, and nowadays the visual aids used can get quite sophisticated with the increasing availability of desktop publishing packages for use with laser printers, some of which can produce colored overheads for over-head projectors, plus electronic projection systems like PowerPoint. Comments on the methodology need to be very brief – what the audience wants to know are the key findings and the practical implications. The language used needs to be kept free of jargon, and diagrams need to be clear and simple. There are many excellent books on the skills required for giving good presentations, for example Walters and Walters (2002).

One issue that frequently arises is that the research is often based on samples, so the findings are based on estimates rather than the actual figures. Clients, however, like clear, unambiguous results, but researchers are aware that estimates have **confidence intervals** and that hypotheses are tested only at a given **level of confidence**. If all the results are presented with all the appropriate qualifications, clients may begin to feel that the results are suspect. There is a fine line to tread between openness and honesty on the one hand, and clarity and simplicity on the other. When data are analyzed and no meaningful results are found (which, in fact, is quite often the case), researchers may be tempted to "see" findings that are not fully supported by the data. For example, a researcher may present a regression equation and endow it with meaning when none of the variables are statistically significant. The researchers are being paid for their expert interpretation of data, and to arrive at a rational, logical and convincing conclusion is more satisfying than to admit that the findings are inconclusive or incon-sistent. Where samples are small, then results are less likely to be statistically significant; but nonsignificant results may nevertheless be important from the client's view. By the same token, where samples are large then even very small effects may be statistically significant, but not important from the point of view of the research.

The key to effective presentations is preparation. Use of the *Notes page* facility on PowerPoint can be very helpful. The audience should be given a copy of the PowerPoint slides using the *Handouts* facility. Presenters should learn as much as possible about who will be in the audience and take this into account, for example in deciding how much technical detail to include. The presentation should be carefully timed, allowing ample, or the agreed amount of, time for questions at the end. At the end of the day, however, it is not about using slick technology, but convincing the audience that the research was well done, that the results are interesting, and that it will be worth their time to read the full report in detail. The pres-entation should pick out key points and findings; it should not attempt a complete summary of the report. Too many slides with too much detail on each will quickly loose an audience. Maintaining eye contact, the use of humor and some interaction with the audi-ence are all important. Presenters need to be aware of their use of gesture and body language. The appropriate use of gesture can keep the presentation lively and animated. Closure is very important and a summary of the key points made can be quite helpful.

Making an effective presentation requires many skills.

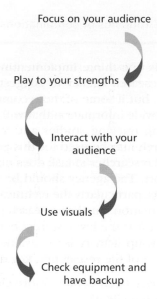

Focus on your audience

Play to your strengths

Interact with your audience

Use visuals

Check equipment and have backup

FIGURE 18.1

Making effective presentations

A five-step guide to effective presentations is illustrated in Figure 18.1. Whatever the subject of your presentation, it is vital to understand what your audience wants from attending. Speak to whoever is arranging the presentation and find out who will be there. In the presentation, capture their attention by telling them what they can expect from the presentation. Imagine their attitudes and the need for a strict timetable and share this with your audience. As a speaker, you are the center of the presentation. Play to your strengths. If you have a strong voice or strong presence, use them. Add drama, move around, be animated while talking, use body language and measured gesticulation. If you are good on humor, use it. It is also important to interact with your audience. Make eye-contact with each person in the room and build in interactive devices, for example pose informal questions to your audience, perhaps asking them about their backgrounds or see if they can predict an outcome or a result. Seek questions from the audience.

Visuals are very important, particularly if you are not a strong speaker. Charts and graphs will be important, but it is vital to keep them simple. They should be an aid to understanding, not challenging the audience to study them to understand them. Photographs and illustrations can inject realism and vitality. Using animation effects can be helpful: but they can also be a distraction. If you are using a laptop and projector, bring your own or check out the equipment before the presentation. Always have backup – that might mean having overheads in case there are problems with the projector.

KEY POINTS

For some decision-makers, attendance at the presentation may be their only contact with researchers. The presentation is not only about giving a summary of the report, but also about persuasion. The report and the presentation, then, need to be considered and planned by researchers to complement one another.

Research follow-up

Making recommendations is one thing: implementing them is another. It is not usually up to the market research agency to suggest how its recommendations should be put into practice, but if some of the recommendations are carried out, it may be called upon to provide information that will be used to monitor or track the results. Thus advertising tracking studies and various market tracking and market measurement research may be used for this purpose.

The agency's (or internal researcher's) task does not end with the presentation and submission of the report. The agency should be willing to help the client to fully understand the findings, particularly the technical parts, and perhaps to offer suggestions about implementation. Further research projects may be discussed at this point. An important factor is the level of trust between agency and client.

Another important follow-up activity is an evaluation of the entire research project. From the perspective of the researcher, key questions are:

- Could the problem have been defined more clearly or differently so as to enhance the value to the client?
- Could the project have been conducted more effectively?
- Would a different research approach have yielded better results?
- Was the research design adequate?
- Were potential sources of error correctly anticipated?

From the perspective of the client, the agency should be evaluated in a systematic manner by giving ratings against a series of selected criteria, for example:

- response to the brief,
- quality of the research,
- client service,
- the presentation,
- the written report,
- follow-up activities.

These ratings can then be used as a basis for deciding on future research commissions.

Reporting cross-national research

The points made above apply equally to reporting the results of cross-national research, but there may be the additional complication of having to give presentations or to write reports in different languages and in totally different national contexts. All the factors affecting cross-national research that were explained in Chapter 17 will be important including, for example, all the micro- and macro-environmental factors. It may well be that reports need to be in different versions and presentations may need to be reconsidered, particularly, for example, the use of humor or any jokes. Recommendations for advertising campaigns may need to take into account very different environments and cultures.

Academic articles

Academics may write management reports if their research is, for example, for government or other public bodies. However, as explained in Chapter 2, academics, particularly due to the Research Assessment Exercise, are likely to be judged by the number of scholarly articles they publish in academic journals. The style of these articles will be very different from management reports. Furthermore, the length of such articles is severely restricted, usually to about 16 pages, so researchers need to be fairly selective about what they write for publication. There are some components, particularly for quantitative research, that any reviewer of academic articles will expect to see, so the article is unlikely to be accepted for publication unless they are there. Normally these will include:

- a title,
- an abstract,
- an introduction,
- a literature review,
- a research methods section,
- a results section,
- a discussion of the results and/or conclusions,
- references.

The titles of academic articles are very important since they are often used for the purpose of making electronic searches for articles on specified topics or using particular methods. The title, then, must match up with or convey very clearly what the article is about.

The abstract plays a similar role to the executive summary in a report, but it will tend to be shorter and will focus on the contribution made by the research to general understanding of marketing phenomena. A number of key words may be listed to help further with the electronic search for articles on a specified topic.

The introduction will explain the rationale for undertaking the research. This will have, or should have, a number of components that typically will include:

- the background of what the research is about and why it was undertaken,
- the theories or models that are to be used in the research,
- the purposes and objectives for which the research is designed.

The introduction should explain what the research area is, and the problems, issues or research topics under investigation. There should also be some explanation of *why* the research is being undertaken. It might let the reader know what, for example, in the past literature, aroused the researcher's interest in the subject matter to begin with. There may be some reference to gaps in the literature, inconsistent or contradictory findings in earlier studies, the possibility of applying existing theories in a new context, a topic made controversial or topical by current events, and so on. The key theoretical and empirical issues should be highlighted along with some comment about why the topic is important, for example because it has wide implications for the way in which marketing may be undertaken or what it might add to the general body of marketing knowledge, and to whom it may be important.

Box 18.2 shows how two researchers presented their background to research on the effects of music in service environments.

RESEARCH IN ACTION
The effects of music in service environments

BOX 18.2

Herrington and Capella (1996) in their article "Effects of music in service environments: a field study", explain that the research area is services marketing, that the key topic within this is the effect of the physical service environment on customer behavior and satisfaction, and in particular the effects of background music. The research is justified by explaining that only recently have service marketers paid attention to the service environment, that background music has been shown to be both influential and the most easily manipulated, but that our knowledge of musical effects remains limited. The authors explain that there are important implications for the design of service environments, and that the results should be "equally applicable" to other types of service setting.

A statement of the research objectives should let the reader know exactly what the researchers intend to accomplish as a result of undertaking their research. There should be an overall research purpose statement in which key words like "explore", "measure", "investigate", "examine" or "explain" are likely to be used, for example "The purpose of this research is to measure the extent to which the application of social marketing techniques can affect fruit and vegetable consumption and physical activity". Overall the purpose is likely to fit into one of three main groups: exploratory, descriptive or causal. Many writers of textbooks refer to these as different kinds of research "design", but this is misleading. The focus is on the *purpose* of the research, not the particular collection of components that go into a particular project. These purposes may, furthermore, overlap or a particular piece of research may combine two or even all three of these purposes.

In addition to the overall purpose of the research, there should be a further elaboration of more specific research objectives that will be subissues of this general-purpose statement and may appear either as research questions or, for quantitative research, as hypotheses to be tested. Many authors, in fact, review the seminal or original research that is specific to each hypothesis and this is described just before each hypothesis is stated.

Nearly all researchers do provide a research purpose statement, but in one or two cases it may need to be deduced from the way the article is written. Most do list the hypotheses being tested or make clear what the research questions are. The researchers are unlikely, however, to state what *kind* of hypothesis is being put forward (e.g. bivariate, multivariate, causal, relational, etc.). Box 18.3 shows how Herrington and Capella (1996) approached this issue.

RESEARCH IN ACTION
The research purpose and objectives

BOX 18.3

Herrington and Capella (1996) clearly state that the purpose of their research is to report the findings of a controlled field study examining the effects of background music on shopping behavior in a supermarket environment. The phrase "examine the effects" implies some kind of causal analysis with background music as the independent variable and shopping behavior as the dependent variable.

From the literature review the authors generate six hypotheses, four that test the current mixed findings on the effects of the physical characteristics of music, and two that relate to the effects of preferences – the like or dislike of the music itself. The six hypotheses are:

H1   The time shoppers spend in a service environment will be reduced by loud music.

H2   The amount of money shoppers spend in a service environment will be unaffected by loud music.

H3   The tempo of background music will affect the total shopping time of shoppers.

H4   The tempo of the background music will affect the amount of money spent by shoppers.

H5   Preference for the background music will affect the amount of time shoppers spend in the service environment.

H6   Preference for the background music will affect the amount of money shoppers spend in the service environment.

H1–H4 are apparently "approximations of the hypotheses tested" by previous researchers and are included "for the purpose of confirmatory testing". All the hypotheses are bivariate and all suggest causal connections. However, H3–H6 just say that there is an effect without specifying a direction. H1 does specify a direction and H2 suggests there is no effect. There appears to be no justification put forward for these differences in hypothesis formulation. H4, for example, could just as easily be that faster tempos of background music will increase the amount of money spent by shoppers, since this is clearly what is implied. There appears to be no reason to have H2 in negative form (other than that this was maybe how the original researchers put it).

The literature review in an academic article needs, of necessity, to be brief, so instead of providing a comprehensive review of all past publications that may be relevant to the topic, it must be a highly selected review of the articles from which the research questions or hypotheses have emerged or against which the results of the research are going to be compared. Box 18.4 comments on the literature review presented by Herrington and Capella.

The research methods section should contain elements very similar to a management report, for example:

- how the key variables were measured,
- the population of cases covered,
- the sampling procedures used, the response rate and evidence of characteristics of nonresponders,
- the data capture instruments,
- the data collection methods used, including a justification of the design choices that were selected,
- any specific techniques that were used,
- how the data were analyzed.

The results section will be a major part of the article. The results may well be presented in a manner that is more technical than in a management report and will assume a degree of statistical competence on the part of the reader. There will

RESEARCH IN ACTION
A review of the literature

BOX 18.4

In the Herrington and Capella (1996) article the authors explain that work on the topic of background music emanates from the literature on atmospherics. More recent literature hints that background music can have considerable positive effects, the nature of which in turn may be affected by the volume, tempo and type of music. Explanations for these effects have so far focused on environmental psychological theory, but this fails to take account of musical preferences.

often be a discussion of the results, relating them back, for example, to previous research, while the conclusions will consider the contribution to marketing theory, any implications for management (but not precise recommendation as in a management report), the limitations of the research that was undertaken and suggestions for how research might be carried out in the future. The references will include details of any authors that are mentioned in the article.

There will, however, be other aspects of the research that are there in the background and with which the researcher will most likely have grappled, but which do not usually form part of the published article and which the authors cannot justifiably be criticized for omitting. Such aspects might include:

- the philosophical underpinnings of the research,
- the choices of research methods that were considered and rejected,
- the level of measurement achieved by each variable,
- the coding, editing and data entry procedures that were used,
- quality checks carried out on interviewers.

There will be some components of the research for which the researchers may be accused of lack of clarity or insufficient detail, but which cannot be considered as "error", for example the statement of the research purpose or details of the sampling procedures. Other components may be considered as mistakes, errors or examples of poor procedure, logic, or design, for example using statistical inference on samples that are clearly not random, or assuming causality from the demonstration of a modest degree of correlation (which happens more than you would imagine!).

The academic review process

As was explained in Chapter 2, research articles submitted to academic journals for publication, books and indeed most conference papers are subjected to some kind of review process that judges them against scholarly criteria. Potential authors for scholarly journals will (or should) have followed a set of guidelines to contributors that typically outline in a general way the type of articles accepted by the journal, give guidelines on length, and specify the formatting in terms of referencing, and the use of headings, tables, figures and footnotes. Articles will then be forwarded by the editor to two or three reviewers or referees for comment and evaluation. The referees, who will be established researchers on the topic of the article, will be asked to evaluate the manuscript, taking into account specified criteria.

Thus the *European Journal of Marketing* asks reviewers to take into account the following factors.

1 the significance of the article to marketing learning and management,
2 its originality and innovativeness,
3 its overall strengths and weaknesses, for example:
   - reference to and consistency with previous work in the area,
   - evidence and objectivity,
   - quality of argument and empirical work,
   - theoretical and practical implications,
4 the soundness of its methodology, analysis, structure and relevance,
5 the appropriateness of the author's writing style for an audience of academics in marketing.

Reviewers are then asked to provide a summary evaluation sheet, as illustrated in Figure 18.2. Look at this carefully; note the key role played by "contribution to marketing". Also note that it is up to reviewers how they evaluate items 1(a)–1(d). The reviewer, finally, is asked to make a recommendation. Typically, this will be:

- accept without further revision,
- accept, subject to minor revision,
- return to the author for major revision (followed by a further review),
- reject.

FIGURE 18.2

A *European Journal of Marketing* evaluation sheet

Summary evaluation

1. Extent of contributions to Marketing in terms of:

	Excellent				Poor	
(a) The theoretical/conceptual framework	5	4	3	2	1	N/A
(b) The data presented	5	4	3	2	1	N/A
(c) Methodology (sampling, measures, statistical analysis, etc.)	5	4	3	2	1	N/A
(d) Results obtained and implications for Marketing	5	4	3	2	1	N/A

2. If not a major contribution in terms of (1), does it nevertheless:

(a) Provide a useful summary of the state of knowledge in its field?	5	4	3	2	1	N/A
(b) Replicate existing work in a competent manner to provide further support/modification to existing hypotheses?	5	4	3	2	1	N/A
(c) Suggest applications useful to practitioners?	5	4	3	2	1	N/A

	Very relevant				Not at all relevant
3. Extent of relevance to readers of European Journal of Marketing	5	4	3	2	1

	Excellent				Poor
4. Organization and writing style	5	4	3	2	1

	Yes				No
5. Are references sufficiently complete and is adequate credit given to other contributors in its field?	5	4	3	2	1

	Major contribution				No contribution
6. Overall contribution of paper in present form	5	4	3	2	1

	Very likely				Not at all likely
7. If revision is recommended, likelihood of author(s) revising the manuscript satisfactorily	5	4	3	2	1

Recommendation

_____ Publish in European Journal of Marketing as it stands

_____ Accept, subject to minor revisions (please describe)

_____ Return to author for major revisions (please describe)

_____ Reject

This review process certainly does not mean that all articles accepted for publication are perfect – far from it. As should be clear from studying this book, *there is no such thing as a perfect piece of research*. Students are often surprised at how many shortcomings appear to have escaped the scrutiny of two or more academic referees who are meant to be experts in the subjects, procedures or topics under review.

KEY POINTS

In communicating the results of their research, academics are unlikely to write reports; they are more likely to write articles for refereed journals. Their aim, after all, is to publish their findings and to make them as widely available as possible. The results are not, as in client-based research, confidential to a client. Precisely because all articles are submitted to two or three referees who are established figures in academic marketing, there is a fairly standard accepted approach, particularly to the reporting of the results of quantitative research. This may be seen by some researchers as inhibiting the scope for innovation in presentation; to others it may be about ensuring standards in scholarly publications.

Academics will, of course, also make presentations of their results, not to clients, but at academic conferences and quite likely to colleagues in departmental seminars. Almost all conference papers are also subject to a referee process and many of the referees will be the same individuals who act as referees for academic journals, so once again there may be constraints on what styles and formats are acceptable.

SUMMARY

For researchers, writing good reports or acceptable journal articles or making effective presentations is always a challenge. The research report is normally the key vehicle by which results of client-based research are presented to the client. No matter how good the research design, how sophisticated the data analysis, how representative the sample or how carefully worded the questionnaire, the client may, at the end of the day, be very dissatisfied with the performance of the agency if the report is too long, too short, too complicated or too vague. Although reports have fairly standard sections, as illustrated in Box 18.1, report-writing is a skill that needs practice. The task is made easier if the results are clear-cut, interesting or surprising; in reality they are often somewhat confusing or contradictory. In these circumstances, writing an interesting report will test the researcher's skills to the limit.

For client-based research, equally important is the presentation, which is about persuasion as much as giving a summary of the report. Both report and presentation need to be planned to complement one another. Making an effective presentation requires a set of skills very different from those required for a good report.

For academics, the scholarly article in a refereed journal is seen as the gold standard by which they are judged. They need to be aware of the demands to which the scientific nostrils of academic referees are attuned. Presenting a set of crosstabulations, which is often the staple diet of the client-based researcher, will not endear the academic neophyte to most referees. Hypotheses must be set out and tested against the data; multivariate statistics applied to the data are often seen as a minimum requirement.

QUESTIONS FOR DISCUSSION

1   Have a look through the glossary to this text and suggest some technical terms that should perhaps be avoided in a management report. See if you can come up with more descriptive explanations of these terms.

2   Examine the arguments for and against the proposition put forward by Tierney (2004) that researchers should stop writing reports, but develop decision-making tools instead.

3   If the results of research are inconclusive or contradictory, should the client-based researcher nevertheless still look for some interesting "findings"?

4   Next time you give a presentation, try putting into practice the suggestions in Figure 18.1.

FURTHER READING

Hart, C. (1998) *Doing a Literature Review*. London: Sage.

Rudestam, K. and Newton, R. (2001) *Surviving Your Dissertation. A Comprehensive Guide to Content and Process*. Thousand Oaks, CA: Sage.

Thody, A. (2006) *Writing and Presenting Research*. London: Sage.

Walters, D. and Walters, G. (2002) *Scientists Must Speak: Bringing Presentations to Life*. London: Taylor and Francis.

Glossary

A

Academic research Research that is undertaken for scholarly purposes.

Accompanied shopping An observer, usually from a market research agency, who personally accompanies a shopper on her or his shopping trip, noting shopping behavior as it occurs.

Action research Research that is designed to promote social change or improve particular situations.

Ad hoc research A "one-off" piece of research that has a beginning point and ends with a final report of the results.

Adjusted R² A deflated estimate of the **coefficient of multiple determination** that takes into account the number of variables and the size of the sample.

After-only designs An experimental design in which there is no control and a measurement taken only after a marketing action.

After-only with control designs An experimental design in which there is a control group, but measurements are taken only after a marketing action.

Agglomerative clustering A stage in cluster analysis in which the clustering procedure is based on taking individual cases and combining them on a measure of similarity.

Alpha value The probability of rejecting the null hypothesis when it is in fact true. It is sometimes referred to as the level of confidence. By tradition it is set at either 0.05 or 0.01.

Analysis of covariance An **analysis of variance** that removes the effects of **covariates** through the use of **regression**-like procedures.

Analysis of variance (ANOVA) A procedure for testing the statistical significance of differences in scores in a metric variable between categorical groups, samples or treatments.

Analytic induction A method of qualitative data analysis that provides a logic for generating and testing theory in an interactive process in the same study.

Area forums A method of consultation research in which local people are invited to attend an advertised forum in which, using workshop methods, they are invited to identify their concerns with specified aspects of local authority policy.

Association rules A technique used in data mining that analyses what combinations of products, brands or services are normally purchased together in a single shopping expedition.

Attitudes Relatively enduring likes or dislikes, preferences or other positive or negative evaluations of objects, persons, organizations, events or situations.

B

Backward elimination A process in **loglinear analysis** in which the hierarchy of interaction effects is gradually eliminated while maintaining the ability to predict the frequencies in the table cells.

Bar chart A graphical display in which each category of a categorical variable is depicted by a bar whose height or length represents the frequency or proportion of observations falling into each category.

Bayesian statistics The incorporation of prior probabilities, which may be subjectively determined, into the current data or evidence to reassess the probability that a hypothesis is true.

Before and after designs An experimental design in which there is no control group, but measurements are taken both before and after a marketing action.

Before and after with control designs A full experimental design in which there is a control group and measurements are taken of each, both before and after a marketing action.

Behavioral variables What people actually did in the recent past, what they currently or usually do, or what they might do in the future.

Beliefs What individuals think they know about social situations, products or communications.

Beta coefficient A standardized partial slope. The **regression** analysis is conducted using standardized or **z-scores**.

Bias A form of error that tends to be in a particular direction.

Binary logistic regression A form of **logistic regression** in which the dependent variable is binary.

Binary scale A scale that has two categories, one for cases that possess a characteristic and one for those that do not.

Bivariate analysis The display, summary or drawing of conclusions from the way in which two variables are related together.

Bivariate crosstabulation A **crosstabulation** of two variables.

Bivariate hypothesis A statement about the existence of or degree of relationship between two variables in the population.

Brainstorming A technique that is used in a focus group setting to generate as many ideas as possible. No judgment or evaluation of the ideas takes place during the brainstorming phase.

Bulletin boards A web-based form of qualitative research in which respondents are invited to log on to the board once a day. Moderators may pose questions and respondents can post their replies at their convenience.

Business research Research that takes other organizations as the point of data collection.

Business survey A survey that takes place on a business premises.

C

Car clinic A form of experiment in which cars are evaluated in a test center.

Case The entity whose characteristics are being recorded in the process of data construction.

Categorical scale A scale that consists at a minimum of sets of categories that are exhaustive, mutually exclusive and refer to a single characteristic, but which may, in addition, possess order.

Causal analysis A study of the way in which some events or circumstances can produce or bring about other events or circumstances.

Causal research Research that analyzes the degree of influence of one or more independent variables upon one or more dependent variables.

Cell The combination of a row and a column in a **crosstabulation**.

Census An attempt by a researcher to contact or to study every case or unit in the population.

Centroids The mean values of the cases in a **cluster analysis** used in the final stage in the analysis.

Chaos theory A theory that describes a system in which minute changes in some initial conditions can bring about very large fluctuations in the outcome.

Chart Any form of graphical display of numerical information.

Chi-square A statistic that measures the overall departure of a set of observations from some theoretical proposition. It adds up the squared differences between observed values and the values expected from the theoretical proposition taken as a proportion of the expected values.

Citizens' juries A method of consultation research in which 12–16 members of the public representing a cross-section of the local population are invited to act as a "jury" for four days during which they receive briefings and evidence from witnesses and can ask for more information.

Class intervals Ranges of the values of a metric variable that are grouped together, for example, 20–29, 30–39, and so on.

Client-based marketing research The construction, analysis and interpretation of data on both organizations and their environments so that information can be provided to assist client organizations in diagnosing, deciding and delivering marketing strategies and tactics.

Cluster analysis A range of techniques use for grouping cases which have characteristics in common.

Clustered bar chart A chart that shows the frequency or percentage of the categories of one variable separated out by the categories of another and placed side by side.

Clustering The random selection of cases or units in geographically concentrated areas.

Codebook A list of all the variable names, variable labels, the response categories and the codes assigned for a complete dataset.

Coding The transformation of edited questionnaires into machine-readable form.

Coefficient A summary measure, usually of the degree of association or correlation between two or more variables.

Coefficient The value of a measure of association or correlation that varies between zero and 1 or between −1 and +1.

Coefficient of determination The proportion of the variance on one metric variable accounted for by the variance on another. It is calculated by squaring the **correlation coefficient** (**Pearson's r**).

Coefficient of multiple determination The percentage of variation in the outcome variable associated with the variation in two or more independent variables.

Cognitive variables Individual attitudes, opinions, beliefs and images.

Collinearity A degree of correlation between two metric predictor variables in a regression equation that poses a threat to the validity of the **regression** analysis.

Column marginal The totals at the foot of each column in a **crosstabulation**.

Company accounts Information on the overall performance of an organization.

Comparison A form of mixed research design that concurrently looks for differences, paradoxes or contradictions in different forms of research.

Concurrent mixed design A research design that entails undertaking two or more styles of research at the same or overlapping times, or even at separate times, but as independent enterprises and considered as a single phase of research.

Conditional A relationship between two variables that is moderated by a third variable.

Confidence interval See **interval estimate**.

Confirmatory factor analysis A method of **factor analysis** used to test the extent to which an hypothesized factor structure is supported by the data.

Confounding relationship The individual effects of two independent variables on a dependent variable is distorted because the independent variables are themselves related.

Conjoint analysis A multivariate technique used to understand how respondents develop preferences for products or services. It tries to identify the relative importance of product or service features.

Construct validity The extent to which a measure relates to other measures to which it should be related.

Consultation A process used largely in the public sector in which consumers are involved in the decision-making process.

Consumer panel A representative sample of individuals or households whose purchase and use of a defined group of products are recorded ether continuously or at regular intervals, usually over a considerable period of time.

Consumer research Research that takes the end-user (private individuals or households) as the point of data collection.

Contact diary A contemporaneous record made by consumers of their contacts with other people in order to establish social networks.

Contact rate The number of eligible respondents successfully contacted as a proportion of the total number of eligible respondents approached.

Contamination The impact of factors or changes that are external to an experiment.

Content analysis The objective, systematic and quantitative description of the manifest content of mass communications.

Content validity The extent to which the domain of a characteristic is adequately sampled by the measure.

Contingency coefficient A measure of association calculated by taking **Chi-square** and dividing by the number of cases added to the value of Chi-square and taking the square root.

Continuous research Research in which measurements are taken on a periodic basis with no envisaged end or completion of the research process.

Continuous variable A scale whose values consist of calibrations that might generate potentially an unlimited number of scale values.

Convenience sample A sampling technique in which interviewers are asked to find respondents who happen to be conveniently accessible.

Correlate/correlation A pattern in the distribution of two or more metric variables whereby high values on one variable covary with high values on another (or with low value on the other for a negative correlation).

Correlation coefficient A measure of the extent to which the values of two metric variables covary and approximate a rising or a falling straight line in a **scattergram**.

Correlation ratio A measure of association for situations where the independent variable is binary or nominal and the dependent variable is metric. It measures the proportion of the total variability in the dependent variable that can be accounted for by knowing the categories of the independent variable.

Covariance An average **covariation** calculated by dividing the covariation by the number of cases.

Covariate An uncontrolled metric independent variable that creates extraneous variation in the dependent variable.

Covariation An overall indication of the extent to which two metric variables are correlated.

Cramer's V A statistical measure of association for two categorical variables that have been crosstabulated and based on the notion of departure from independence. It is calculated by taking **Chi-square**, dividing by the number of cases multiplied by a value which is either the number of rows minus one or columns minus one, whichever is the minimum, and taking the square root.

Criterion validity The extent to which a measure successfully predicts some other characteristic to which it is related.

Critical values Values that lie exactly on the boundary between accepting and rejecting the null hypothesis.

Cronbach's coefficient alpha A measure of scale reliability. It takes the average correlation among items in a summated rating scale and adjusts for the number of items.

Crosstabulation The frequencies of cases that combine a value on one categorical variable with values on another laid out in rows and columns.

Curvilinear regression A form of regression analysis in which nonlinear patterns are transformed into linear ones by a process of data transformations so that linear regression may be applied.

Customer database A database constructed by the organization that details customer or member characteristics.

Customized research Research that is tailor-made for a particular client.

D

Data Systematic records made by individuals.

Data analysis The process whereby researchers take the raw data that have been entered into a data matrix to create information that can be used to tackle the objectives for which the research was undertaken.

Data display The presentation of data in tables, charts or graphs.

Data dredging Data are explored in every conceivable way to see if any patterns emerge.

Data fusion The merging of the results from two or more separate surveys with different samples into a single database.

Data matrix A record of all the values for all the variables for all the cases laid out in rows and columns.

Data mining A range of techniques for extracting actionable information from large databases, usually stored in a **data warehouse**, and applying it to business models.

Dataset A record of all the values for all the variables for all the cases in a research project.

Data summary Reducing the data in a distribution of a single variable or the relationship between variables to a single statistic that acts as a summary.

Data warehouse A very large database in which data are gathered from disparate sources and converted into a consistent format that can be used to support management decision-making and customer relationship management.

Degree of freedom The number of values that are free to vary when estimating some kind of statistical parameter.

Deliberative polls A method of consultation research in which a random sample survey of the local population is conducted on the issue under consideration. A representative sub sample of 250–300 is then recruited to constitute a large citizens' jury.

Demographic variables "Factual" characteristics of cases that are treated as conditions that at least in principle are verifiable.

Dendogram A graphical representation of a cluster of cases generated by using **cluster analysis**.

Departure from independence The extent to which observed data depart from what the data would look like if there were no association.

Dependence technique A multivariate analysis technique where one or more variables are identified as dependent and which are to be predicted or explained by one or more independent variables.

Dependent variable A variable that is seen as an outcome or effect of an independent variable. A variable that the researcher is trying to predict, understand or explain.

Depth interviews A direct, personal interview, usually with a single respondent, in which unstructured or open-ended questioning techniques are used by the interviewer to uncover motivations, beliefs, attitudes and feelings.

Derived measurement The use of two or more measures in some combination to generate a total or single score.

Descriptors Variables used to describe a set of cases not being studied for their relationships to other variables.

Descriptive research Research that is concerned with measuring or estimating the sizes, quantities or frequencies of characteristics.

Descriptive statistics The display and summary of variables in a dataset.

Design factor A multiplier used to convert standard errors calculated by methods appropriate to simple random sampling into standard errors appropriate to more complex sample designs.

Desk research The proactive seeking-out of data, qualitative or quantitative, that already exist and which are to be used for a secondary purpose, and also finding previous reports, studies, newspaper or magazine articles or other literature that might be useful for the purposes of the research at hand.

Diary A contemporaneous record made by the consumer of his or her purchases or other forms of consumer behavior between specific dates or at specified periods during the day.

Direct measurement A one-to-one correspondence between the concept and the variable used to measure. This is made possible either because the characteristic is concretely observable or because the researcher defines the concept in terms of the variable.

Discourse analysis A method of qualitative data analysis that focuses on language, both as talk and as text.

Discrete variable A scale generated by counting the number of units contained in an entity as a measure of size.

Discriminant analysis A multivariate technique that determines which weightings of metric independent variables best discriminate between two or more groups of cases better than by chance.

Discriminant function The composite of weightings used in **discriminant analysis**.

Discriminant validity The extent to which a measure does not correlate with other measures from which they are meant to be different.

Divisive clustering A stage in cluster analysis in which the clustering procedure is based on taking the total set of cases and dividing them into subgroups on a basis specified by the researcher.

Drop-out The tendency in an experimental design for test units to become unavailable for repeat measurements.

Dummy variable A way of recoding a **nominal** variable into a series of **binary** variables.

E

Eclectic designs A research design that mixes in different ways any approach or methods that might help to solve a problem.

Editing The scrutiny of returned questionnaires to ensure that as far as possible they are complete, accurate and consistent.

Effect size An objective and standardized measure of the magnitude of the observed effect.

Eigenvalue The proportion of the total variance explained by each **factor** in a **factor analysis**. It is calculated from the sum of the squared **factor loadings**.

Epistemology An area of philosophy that is concerned with how knowledge is established.

Error The extent to which the application of a scale fails to reflect the real characteristics of a case. It is the difference between an observation made and the real or "true" value.

Establishment survey A survey that tracks the reception and viewing characteristics of television viewing households in the population.

Estimates Using the value of a statistic derived from a sample to estimate the value of the corresponding population parameter.

Eta A statistical measure of association where the independent variable is binary or nominal and the dependent variable is metric.

Ethnography An approach to qualitative research in which the researcher immerses himself or herself into a local culture in order to understand it.

Euclidean distance A distance measure used in **cluster analysis** which takes the square root of the sum of the squared differences in values for each variable.

Expansion A form of mixed research design that concurrently seeks to add breadth, depth and scope to a research project.

Experiment A research design in which one or more **independent variables** are manipulated by the researcher to examine their effects on one or more **dependent variables**, while controlling for **extraneous variables**.

Explanation A range of devices that may be used to clarify and make something comprehensible to an audience.

Exploratory factor analysis A method of **factor analysis** which is used for exploratory purposes to replace a large set of variables with a smaller number of **factors**.

Exploratory research Research aimed at generating ideas, insights or hypotheses.

Extraneous variable A variable whose effect is controlled, minimized or excluded in the design of an experiment.

F

Factor A term commonly used to refer to an independent variable in an experimental design. It is also used to refer to a **latent variable** in **factor analysis**.

Factor analysis A multivariate statistical technique used for identifying the underlying structure in a large set of metric variables. It groups together those variables that are highly intercorrelated.

Factorial design An experimental design that allows for the effects of interactions between independent variables.

Factor loading The correlation between a **variable** and a **factor** in **factor analysis**.

Field experiment An experiment conducted in a realistic research environment.

Finite multiplier An adjustment that is made to the variance of a population statistic to correct for overestimation of the variance when the sample represents more than 5 percent of the population. It is equal to the square root of that proportion of the population not included in the sample.

Fixed choice question A question that gives respondents a list of possible answers from which to choose.

Focus group A discussion among a small group of respondents conducted by the researcher or a trained group moderator in a largely unstructured manner.

Frame errors Errors arising from the use of lists of the population to be studied that have various shortcomings.

Frequency The number of times a scale value occurs in a given distribution for a particular variable.

Frequency table Frequencies of scale values, usually either categorical or grouped metric, laid out in a column.

Funneling The sequencing of questions in such a way that it begins with general questions followed by progressively more specific questions. The aim is to prevent specific questions biasing general questions.

G

Gamma A measure of association for two ordinal variables based on calculating the number of pairs in a crosstabulation having the same rank order of inequality on both variable compared with the number of pairs having the reverse order of inequality.

General linear model (GLM) A combination of **analysis of variance** and **regression** for situations where there are one or more metric dependent variables and a combination of categorical or metric independent variables and **covariates** referred to as **factors**.

Geodemographics The grouping of consumers on the basis of characteristics of the neighborhoods in which they live.

Goodness-of-fit test The determination of the extent to which a certain model fits the observed data. The statistic **Chi-square** can be used for this purpose.

Graph See **chart**.

Grounded theory A method of generating theory inductively from the data.

H

Hall test A survey, often accompanied by an experimental design, in which respondents are invited to a prebooked, local venue to answer questions or respond to specified stimuli.

Heteroscedacity a pattern of relationships between metric variables that is nonlinear and which shows unequal levels of variance across a range of predictor variables.

Hierarchical clustering A clustering procedure used in **cluster analysis** in which either cases are iteratively combined on the basis of some measure of similarity (agglomerative clustering), or the total set of cases is divided into subgroups on a basis specified by the researcher (divisive clustering).

Hierarchical regression A method of multiple regression in which the order in which the independent variables are entered into the regression model is determined by the researcher, based on previous research.

Histogram A graphical display for metric variables in which the width of the bars represents class intervals and the length or height represents the frequency or proportion with which each interval occurs.

Hypothesis A formal statement that the researcher makes about one or more variables that are the focus of the research, but which is as yet untested.

I

Images Representations in the mind of the characteristics of a person, object, organization or event.

Independent samples Sample from different groups of respondents.

Independent variable A variable that is treated as a condition, cause or influence.

Indirect measurement Taking an indicator of a concept as a variable measure of that concept.

In-home placement test A test which gives selected consumers a product to try at home and to report back.

In-home survey A survey in which potential respondents are approached in their own homes.

In-house research Research that is carried out for a client who is internal to the organization.

In-store survey A survey conducted in or just outside a retail outlet.

Interaction effect The combined effect of two or more independent variables on a dependent variable.

Interdependence technique A technique in multivariate analysis that involves the simultaneous analysis of three or more variables, none being identified as either dependent or independent.

Interquartile range The range of a distribution that encompasses the middle 50 percent of the observations (between the 25th and 75th **percentile**).

Interval estimate A range of values within which there is a given probability that it will contain the true population parameter.

Interviewer-completed questionnaires Questionnaires that are completed by the interviewer who asks the questions and fills in the answers on the respondent's behalf.

Interview survey A survey that involves face-to-face, personal contact with respondents.

Investigative research Research that focuses on the extent of association or correlation between two or more variables.

Invitation online sampling Alerting potential respondents to an online survey that they may fill in a questionnaire that is hosted on a specific website.

Item analysis A process used in Likert scaling whereby items that do not correlate with the total score are discarded.

K

k-means clustering See **nonhierarchical clustering**

Kendall's tau-b A measure of association for two ordinal variables that is similar to **Gamma** except that it takes account of those pairs that are tied in both directions.

Kendall's tau-c A measure of association for two ordinal variables based on **pair-by-pair comparisons**, but only when the number of rows and columns is the same.

Kurtosis A measure of the distribution shape based on the extent to which values cluster about the mean compared with a normal distribution.

L

Labeling scale The assignation of a unique number, letter or symbol to each case.

Laboratory experiment An experiment that takes place in an artificial environment set up by the researcher.

Lambda A measure of association for two categorical variables based on the **proportional reduction in error**.

Latent variable A variable that cannot be directly observed or measured, but is assumed to be related to several variables that can be measured.

Latin square An experimental design that allows for the control or two noninteracting extraneous variables in addition to the manipulation of the independent variable.

Level of confidence See **alpha value**.

Life-stages A demographic in which individuals are classified by the stage of family life they are currently at, for example, 'young parent'.

Likelihood ratio Chi-square As distinct from the Pearson Chi-square (see **Chi-square**) this takes the logarithm of the relationships between observed and expected frequencies.

Likert scale A summated rating scale derived from the summation of 5- or 7-point ratings of agreement or disagreement with a number of statements relating to an attitude object.

Line graph A graph that connects a series of data points using continuous lines.

Linear regression See **regression**.

Log likelihood Chi-square See **Likelihood ratio Chi-square**.

Log odds The natural logarithm of the odds ratio, which is the ratio of the odds of an event occurring in one group compared to another. The odds are calculated by taking the probability of an event occurring divided by the probability of that event not occurring.

Logistic regression A form of **regression** analysis in which the independent metric variables are used to predict the probability of a case being in a particular category of a categorical variable.

Logits See **log odds**.

Loglinear analysis An extension of **Chi-square** analysis used to detect the patterns of interactions in a set of categorical variables.

M

Macroenvironment The wider environment of a commercial organization that consists of general economic players like financial institutions, trends in the economy, technological factors, social factors, political players including governments, local authorities, trade unions and legal factors.

Market basket analysis A **data mining** technique that uses association rules to discover products that tend to be purchased together.

Market measurement The recording or estimation of market characteristics on a continuous, period or occasional basis.

Market measurement panels A sample of individuals, households or organizations that have agreed to record, or permit the recording of, their activities or opinions in respect of an agreed range of products or services.

Market tracking survey A regular interval survey in which the agency designs the entire questionnaire and the data collected are sold to as many clients as possible.

Marketing intelligence The compilation and evaluation of qualitative and quantitative information on what is happening generally in the marketplace.

Maturation An extraneous variable in an experiment that is attributable to changes in the test units over time.

Mean A measure of central tendency for metric variables calculated by totaling all the scale values in a distribution and dividing by the number of observations made.

Measurement A process by which the characteristics or properties of cases that are to be used as variables are specified.

Media audience measurement The provision of both quantitative and qualitative data on media usage by audiences and readers.

Media panels A sample of individuals or households that have agreed to record, or permit the recording of, their media use behavior.

Media use diary A contemporaneous record made by consumers of their use of the broadcast media, usually on a time segment basis.

Median A measure of central tendency calculated by taking the value that splits all the observations for a variable into two halves arranged in an ascending or descending series.

Mediating relationship An independent variable is seen as having an effect on a dependent variable indirectly through another independent variable.

Memoing The writing up of ideas, observations and thoughts as they strike the analyst in the analysis of qualitative data and which become the basis of an emerging theory.

Metric scale A scale that arises from the processes of either calibration or counting.

Metric table A table used to display metric quantities.

Microenvironment The immediate environment of a commercial organization that consists of customers, competitors, suppliers, distributors, shareholders and other stakeholders in the organization.

Mini-test marketing A simulation of test marketing conditions without exposing the product to the open market and without incurring the cost of a full test market.

Mode A measure of central tendency established by taking the most commonly occurring value in a distribution.

Model A simplified description of a system or a structure that is devised to assist the process of making calculations concerning the relationships between variables and making predictions.

Moderated e-mail groups Over a period of one or two weeks the moderator e-mails questions to respondents who e-mail their responses back. The moderator then produces a summary.

Multicollinearity A degree of correlation between three or more metric predictor variables in a regression equation that poses a threat to the validity of the regression analysis.

Multidimensional scaling A concept that consists of two or more dimensions that are not totaled, but either kept separate as a profile or as a point in multidimensional space. Also used to refer to a spatial map in which the perceptions of preferences of consumers are represented in two-dimensional space.

Multiphase sample A multistage sample in which some sampling units are asked for more information than others.

Multiple R^2 See **coefficient of multiple determination**.

Multiple regression An extension of regression in which the outcome is predicted from a linear combination of two or more predictor variables.

Multiple-response question A fixed-choice question that allows a respondent to pick more than one response category.

Multistage sample The taking of a sample in two or more stages.

Multivariable table A table displaying the distributions of two or more variables that are not interlaced.

Multivariate analysis The display, summary or drawing of conclusions from variables taken three or more at a time.

Multivariate analysis of covariance (MANCOVA) A **multivariate analysis of variance** that removes the effects of **covariates** through the use of **regression**-like procedures.

Multivariate analysis of variance (MANOVA) An analysis of variance when there is more than one metric dependent variable.

Multivariate hypothesis A statement about the relationships between three or more variable in a population of cases.

Mystery shopping Researchers posing as ordinary customers in a retail or service environment to evaluate the quality or the service provided using predefined service standards.

N

Neural network analysis An alternative to multivariate statistical techniques that tries to mimic the way the human brain works by learning to solve problems by recognizing patterns in the data.

Node A key element in a neural network multilayer model that accepts a number of inputs from other nodes.

Nominal scale A set of scale values having three or more categories that are mutually exclusive, exhaustive and refer to a single dimension.

Nonhierarchical clustering A technique of clustering used in **cluster analysis**, sometimes also called k-means clustering, which involves predetermining the number of cluster centers and grouping all cases within a specified threshold from the center.

Nonparametric statistics Statistics that do not assume that data are metric or that the mean or standard deviation can be calculated.

Nonprobability sample A sample in which the chances of selecting a case from the population of cases is not calculable since the selection is made on a subjective basis.

Nonsampling errors Survey errors that are not a result of the sampling process.

Nonstandardized regression coefficient The rate of change in a dependent variable consequent upon a unit change in an independent variable in a multiple regression equation. Also known as a **partial slope**.

Normal distribution A symmetrical bell-shaped distribution that describes the expected probability distribution for random events.

Null hypothesis A statement made about a population of cases in advance of testing it on data.

O

Omnibus surveys A regular interval survey that an agency undertakes with a stated frequency and predetermined method and which serves the needs of a syndicated group of organizations who can add questions to a core survey as they wish.

One-tailed test A statistical test of a directional relationship.

One-way ANOVA An analysis of variance in which there is only one basis for categorizing groups of the independent variable.

Online focus group A "virtual" focus group in which the moderator and participants communicate via the internet.

Online panel A pool of people who have been recruited who are willing to participate in online surveys on a regular or occasional basis.

Online survey A survey that is administered using computer networks such as the internet or local intranets.

Ontology A branch of metaphysics that is concerned with the nature of reality.

Open-ended question A question that allows respondents to reply in their own words.

Operating data Data that relate to the daily activities and transactions of a business or other kind of organization.

Operational definition A statement of precisely what observable characteristics are to be used to measure a concept.

Opinions Feelings or views about what other people should or should not do in the world.

Ordinal scale A scale possessing all the characteristics of a **nominal scale** plus an implied order of the categories.

Outliers Values that are substantially different from the general body of values.

P

P-value The probability in random sample of obtaining a value as extreme or more extreme than the one actually obtained if the null hypothesis were true.

Pair-by-pair comparisons A measure of association based on the tendency for all possible combinations of pairs of cases to show similar orderings on both ordinal variables.

Paired comparisons A scaling technique in which respondents are asked to compare objects or images two at a time according to a specified criterion.

Paired samples t-test An **analysis of variance** in which two sets of metric values are compared for the same respondents.

Panels Groups of consumers, usually a representative sample, who have agreed to provide specified information or to be involved in a particular form of marketing research at regular intervals.

Parameter estimate An estimate of a population parameter from a sample statistic. Also used on loglinear analysis as a partial coefficient of the relative effect of each on the expected frequency in each cell.

Paradigm An exemplar that is firmly based on a particular style of inquiry that a scientific community acknowledges for a time as supplying the foundation for its further practice.

Parametric statistics Statistics that assume metric data, and that the calculation of a mean or standard deviation is a legitimate operation.

Partial slope See **Non-standardized regression coefficient**.

Pearson's r See **correlation coefficient**.

Percentile Values of a metric variable that divide the ordered data into groups so that a certain percentage is above or below that value.

Personal observation Observations made personally by the researcher of consumer or managerial behavior as it occurs, or of the physical characteristics of the marketing environment.

Perspective From whose viewpoint a piece of research is being conducted, for example the researcher, the client or the research subjects.

Phenomenology A method of research in which primacy is given to understanding the subjective experiences of the participant in the research.

Phi A measure of association calculated by taking **Chi-square** and dividing by the number of cases and taking the square root.

Pie chart A graphic in which the frequency or proportion of each category of a categorical variable is represented by a slice of a circle.

Point estimate A single value taken as an estimate of a population parameter.

Population A total set of cases or other units that are the focus of the researcher's attention.

Population parameter A variable relating to a total population of cases or units.

Precoding Assigning a numerical code to each response category at the questionnaire design stage.

Primary data Data constructed specifically for the research at hand.

Principal components analysis One of several ways of undertaking factor analysis in which both the amount of variance to be accounted for and the number of components to be extracted equals the number of variables.

Probability sample A sample in which the selection of sampling units is made by methods independent of human judgment. Each unit will have a known and nonzero probability of selection.

Product diary A contemporaneous record made by consumers of their purchases between specific dates or at specified periods during the day.

Product testing panel A panel of consumers who have agreed to try out or test products on a regular basis.

Proportional reduction in error The extent to which it is possible to predict the values of one categorical variable from the values of another categorical variable with which it might be associated.

Proportional stratification The stratification of a sample in such a way that the strata are in direct proportion to those in the population of cases.

Purposive sample A nonprobability sample in which the selection of sampling units is made by the researcher using his or her own judgment or experience.

Q

Qualitative data Systematic records that consist of words, phrases, text or images.

Qualitative research Research that is geared primarily to the construction of qualitative data.

Quantitative data Systematic records that consist of numbers constructed by researchers utilizing the process of measurement and imposing a structure.

Quantitative research Research that is focused primarily on the construction of quantitative data.

Questionnaire Any document that is used as an instrument to capture data generated by asking people questions.

Quota control A variable used in a quota sample to control the numbers in each category of the variable.

Quota sample A representative but nonprobability sampling procedure that ensures that various subgroups of a population will be represented to an extent chosen by the researcher.

R

Random digit dialing A range of techniques for generating telephone numbers at random in order to overcome the deficiencies of domestic telephone lists.

Random error Error arising from a random sampling procedure in which there will be chance fluctuations.

Random location sampling Interviewers are assigned to randomly chosen sampling points and then asked to undertake **quota sampling**.

Random online intercept sampling The random selection of website visitors.

Random route sampling A nonprobability sample in which interviewers are instructed to begin interviewing at specified points that are randomly chosen and to call on households at set intervals.

Random sample A probability sample in which the selection of sampling units is made by methods independent of human judgment. Each unit will have a known and nonzero probability of selection.

Random sampling with quotas The imposition of quotas on a set of cases that were initially selected on a random basis.

Randomization The selection of sampling units by chance.

Randomized block An experimental design in which test units are grouped on the basis of one or more extraneous variables to ensure that each combination of characteristics is tested.

Range The difference between the minimum and maximum value in a distribution of a metric variable.

Ranking scale A set of scale values in which each case has its own rank. There are as many rankings as cases.

Refusal rate The number of refusals in a survey as a proportion of the number of eligible respondents contacted.

Regression The use of a formula describing a straight line that represents the "best fit" in a **scattergram** to predict the values of one metric variable from another.

Regular interval surveys Surveys of respondents carried out at regular intervals using independent samples for each measurement period.

Reliability The extent to which the application of a scale produces consistent results if repeated measures are taken.

Repeated measures A term used in SPSS to indicate that more than one measure on the same set of cases is being used in the calculation.

Representative sample The selection of sampling units in such a way that they attempt to reproduce the structure and features of a population of units.

Research brief A formal document written by a client that is sufficiently detailed for the researcher to be able to write a research proposal.

Research hypothesis The hypothesis that is accepted if the null hypothesis is rejected.

Research proposal A formal document drafted by the researcher outlining the methods and techniques that will be used to tackle the client's problem.

Residual analysis A process in **multiple regression** that checks on the distribution of residuals, or errors.

Respondent An individual to whom questions have been successfully addressed or who has completed specified information-giving tasks.

Response rate The number of completed questionnaires as a proportion of the total number of respondents approached.

Retail audit The physical counting of stocks in a panel retail outlet both at the beginning and at the end of the audit period, plus a record of deliveries, to obtain sales for each band and brand variant of a defined group of products.

Retail panel A representative sample (or in some cases the complete universe of) retail outlets whose acquisition, pricing, stocking and display of a defined group of products is recorded either continuously or at regular intervals.

Routing Guiding whoever is completing a questionnaire to answer questions that are appropriate when these depend on responses to earlier questions.

Row marginal The totals at the end of each row in a **crosstabulation**.

S

Sample A subset of cases or other units from a total population of cases or units.

Sample design The particular mix of procedures used for the selection of sampling units in a particular piece of research.

Sampling distribution A theoretical distribution of a statistic for all possible samples of a given size that could be drawn from a particular population.

Sampling distribution of Chi-square A theoretical distribution of the statistic Chi-square for all possible samples with a given number of degrees of freedom.

Sampling error Error that arises from the sampling process. It may be defined more precisely as the difference between the result of a sample and the result that would have been obtained from a census using identical procedures.

Sampling frame A complete list of the population of units or cases from which a sample is to be taken.

Sampling point A designated geographical area within which an interviewer conducts his or her selection of cases or units.

Sampling unit Whatever entity is being sampled.

Saturated model A model that perfectly fits the data and therefore has no error. It contains all possible main effects and interactions between variables.

Scale A set of values that meets certain formal logical requirements.

Scattergram A graphical display of the relationship between two metric variables in which each case is represented by a dot that reflects the position of two combined measurements.

Scores The values of a metric variable that is being treated as an outcome or dependent variable.

Secondary analysis The extraction of new insights or findings from secondary data.

Secondary data Data that have already been constructed for another purpose than the research at hand.

Secondary research Research that is limited to the use of secondary data.

Self-completed questionnaires Questionnaires that are completed by the respondent without an interviewer present.

Semantic differential scale A multidimensional scale that represents a profile of characteristics expressed as bipolar opposites like "sweet–sour" that constitutes a 7-point rating scale.

Semiotics A method of analyzing qualitative data in which the focus is on the products of consumer culture and the signs that they give off.

Sequential mixed design A research design that involves undertaking a research project in two or more stages or phases, each stage or phase acting as an input to the next.

Simple random sample Each sampling unit has an equal chance of being selected from a list.

Single-response question A fixed-response question that allows respondents to select only one of the response categories.

Single-source data Data on product usage and media usage taken from the same sample of respondents.

Simulated test market modeling The use of sophisticated modeling techniques to estimate trial and repeat purchase rates for new, modified or relaunched products.

Skewness A measure of distribution shape based on the difference between the mean and median values in a distribution.

Snowball sample A nonrandom sampling technique used to locate difficult-to-find respondents. Those who are located are asked to suggest others who may fit the population specification.

Social grade An ordinal classification of occupational status.

Social intervention The introduction of one or more marketing techniques in order to observe its effects on social behavior.

Social marketing Using marketing principles to change social behavior.

Somers' d A measure of association for two ordinal variables that is similar to **Gamma** except that it takes account of those pairs that are tied on one variable but not on the other.

Spearman's rho A measure of correlation between two fully ranked scales.

Stacked bar chart A chart that shows the frequency or percentage of the categories of one variable separated out by the categories of another and placed one on top of the other.

Standard deviation An average of deviations of values about the mean for a given statistic.

Standard error The **standard deviation** of a sampling distribution.

Standard error of the estimate The **standard deviation** of the **residuals** in a **multiple regression** which shows how well spread out are the data points around the regression line.

Standard error of the proportion The standard error of the sampling distribution of the proportions observed for a binary variable.

Standard error of the mean The standard error of the sampling distribution of the means observed for a metric variable.

Statistical inference A process by which sample statistics are used to estimate population parameters or to test statements about a population with a known degree of confidence.

Statistical significance A result that, in a random sample, is unlikely to have arisen by chance with a specified probability.

Stepwise regression A method of **multiple regression** in which the order in which the independent variables are entered into the regression model is based on a statistical criterion.

Store test The testing of a range of price and package formulations in a number of selected retail outlets.

Stratification A random sampling technique in which simple random subsamples are drawn from separate groups or strata.

Street survey A survey conducted in busy town centers or shopping malls, usually combined with **quota sampling**.

Structural equation modeling A statistical technique that combines the notions of **correlation** and **goodness-of-fit** between a theoretical model and the observed data.

Structured query A **data mining** technique that searches a **data warehouse** with very specific requests.

Sugging Selling under the guise of doing marketing research.

Summated rating scale A measure derived from summing together two or more separate rating scales.

Survey The capture of data based on addressing questions to respondents in a formal manner and taking a systematic record of their responses.

Syndicated research Research in which either the research process or the research data are shared between a number of clients.

Systematic error Error arising from sampling procedures that result in the over- or underrepresentation of particular kinds of sampling unit mostly in the same direction.

Systematic selection The selection of sampling units using rules that remove human judgment from the selection process.

T

Test center A fixed location for carrying out a survey or experiment.

Test marketing A controlled experiment carried out in a limited, but carefully selected test market.

Theory A set of concepts and logically related propositions that work or may work in more than one context.

T-test An **analysis of variance** in which the categorical **independent variable** is **binary**.

Three-way analysis A bivariate crosstabulation that is layered by a third variable to examine its impact on the original relationship.

Total survey error The sum of all sources of error, both those arising from the sampling process and nonsampling errors.

Triangulation The use of two or more approaches to research to see if they come to similar conclusions.

Two-tailed test A statistical test of a nondirectional hypothesis.

U

Unbiased estimate An adjustment that is made to the standard error when the sample standard deviation is taken as an estimate of the population standard deviation. The sample standard deviation is divided by the square root of n-1 rather than the square root of n.

Uncertainty coefficient A measure of association for two categorical variables based on the proportion by which uncertainty in the dependent variable is reduced by knowledge of the independent variable.

Univariate analysis The display, summary or drawing of conclusions from a single variable or set of variables treated one at a time.

Univariate GLM A general linear model in which there is a single metric dependent variable.

Univariate hypothesis A statement about the population value of a variable or two or more variables that are not combined or related.

Usage and attitude study A comprehensive survey, usually carried out on an ad hoc basis, that covers not only brand usage and purchasing behavior but also awareness and attitudes.

V

Validity The extent to which the application of a scale measures what it is intended to measure.

Value The actual number or category recorded by the researcher, having made a selection from a scale of values.

Van test A survey or experiment that takes place in a mobile van.

Variable A characteristic of a case that the researcher has chosen to observe or measure and then record. A variable must vary at a minimum between two scale values.

Variance The mean squared deviation of all the values in the distribution of a metric variable.

Varimax A method of factor rotation used in factor analysis that keeps the vectors at right angles so that they are unrelated to one another.

Volunteer sample A sampling technique in which potential respondents are asked to complete a survey by way of general invitation rather than being approached individually.

W

Weighting The application of a multiplying factor to some of the responses given in a survey in order to eliminate or reduce the impact of bias caused by under- or overrepresentation of respondents with particular characteristics.

Wilks's lambda A procedure used in **general linear modeling** to examine the contribution of each main and **interaction effect**. It is a measure of the unexplained variance and is the mirror image of eta^2.

Z

Z-score The value of an observation expressed in standard deviation units. The arithmetic mean is subtracted from each observation and divided by the standard deviation.

Z-test A test against the null hypothesis carried out on a univariate hypothesis by comparing the result from a sample with a standardized normal distribution.

Appendix 1

The Table Tennis Questionnaire

Thank you for agreeeing to complete this questionnaire. It will only take you a few minutes. Please reply by putting a tick in the box or boxes that correspond with your answer.

All responses will be treated in strict confidence – no individual will be identifiable from the results of the survey.

When you have finished, please put the questionnaire in the envelope provided. No stamp is required.

1. In which league do you compete?

Bangor and District		1
Belfast		2
Greystone		3
Antrim		4

2. In which division do you compete?

First		1
Second		2
Third		3
Fourth		4

3. How many times on average do you play a week?

Once		1
Twice		2
Three times		3
Four times or more		4

4. Were you encouraged by anybody to take up the sport?

Yes		1
No (go to Q6)		2

5. If yes, was it:

A friend	1
Parent	2
Other relative	3
Teacher	4
Club leader	5
Other	6

6. At what age did you take up table tennis? _____

7. Where did you first play the sport? (Tick one only)

Primary school	1
Secondary school	2
Youth club	3
Youth organization, e.g. scouts/guides	4
Table-tennis club	5
Coaching scheme	6
Leisure center	7
Other	8

8. Would you please rate the importance you attach to the various aspects of playing table tennis listed below.

	Unimportant 1	Fairly unimportant 2	Neither 3	Fairly important 4	Very important 5
Social benefits					
Competition					
Relaxation					
Health and fitness					
Enjoyment					

9. How satisfied are you with the following elements of table tennis in N. Ireland?

	Unsatisfied 1	Fairly unsatisfied 2	Neither 3	Fairly satisfied 4	Very satisfied 5
Practice facilities					
Competition facilities					
Administration by ITTA					
Coaching opportunities					
Competitions					

10. Are you affiliated to the ITTA?   Yes ☐ 1
                                        No ☐ 2

11. If table tennis was on TV more often, would you watch it?   Yes ☐ 1
                                                                 No ☐ 2

12. Do you read articles on table tennis in the local papers?   Yes ☐ 1
                                                                 No ☐ 2

13. What do you think could be done to encourage people to take up table tennis on a regular basis?

_____

_____

_____

_____

_____

_____

_____

14. What age are you?   Under 15 ☐ 1
                                  15–24 ☐ 2
                                  25–34 ☐ 3
                                  35–44 ☐ 4
                                  45–54 ☐ 5
                                  55–64 ☐ 6
                                 Over 65 ☐ 7

15. What sex are you?   Male ☐ 1
                                 Female ☐ 2

14. What is your current occupation?   Manual ☐ 1
                                         Nonmanual ☐ 2
                                     Self-employed ☐ 3
                                           Retired ☐ 4
                                           Student ☐ 5
                                        Unemployed ☐ 6

17. Does anybody else in your household play table tennis?   Yes [ ] 1

No [ ] 2

18. Approximately how much have you spent on table tennis in the past 6 months?

_____

19. Which of the following sports do you play in addition to table tennis
(tick as many as apply)

Football [ ] 1

Tennis [ ] 2

Squash [ ] 3

Badminton [ ] 4

Thank you for completing this questionnaire. Please return in the envelope provided.

References

Abbott, A. (1992) "What do cases do? Some notes on activity in sociological analysis", in Ragin, C. C. and Becker, H. S. (eds), *What is a Case? Exploring the Foundations of Social Inquiry*. Cambridge: Cambridge University Press, pp. 53–82.

Abbott, A. (1998) "The causal devolution", *Sociological Methods and Research*, 27 (2): 148–181.

Adreinssens, C. and Cadman, L. (1999) "An adaptation of moderated e-mail groups to assess the potential for a new online (Internet) financial service offer in the UK", *Journal of the Market Research Society*, 41 (2): 417–424.

Akimova, I. (1996) "Marketing in today's Ukraine", ESOMAR Congress, Istanbul.

Albaum, A. (1997) "The Likert scale revisited: an alternative version", *Journal of the Market Research Society*, 39 (2): 331–348.

Alt, M. and Brighton, M. (1981) "Analysing data: or telling stories?", *Journal of the Market Research Society*, 23 (4): 209–219.

Appel, M. (2001) "Raising diary response among young people. E-diaries, phone motivation and incentives", *ESOMAR*, June.

Arnould, E. and Wallendorf, M. (1994) "Market oriented ethnography: interpretation building and marketing strategy formulation", *Journal of Marketing Research*, 31, November: 484–504.

Assael, H. and Keon, J. (1982) "Nonsampling versus sampling errors in survey research", *Journal of Marketing*, 46, Spring: 114–123.

Baker, K. and Fletcher, R. (1989) "OUTLOOK – a generalised lifestyle system", *Admap*, March: 23–28.

Bakker, P. (2005) "Growth in a shrinking market: the rise of the free daily newspaper", *International Newspaper Marketing Association*, August.

Barker, A., Nancarrow, C. and Spackman, N. (2001) "Informed eclecticism: a research paradign for the twenty-first century", *International Journal of Market Research*, 43 (1): 3–27.

Barwise, T. P., Ehrenberg, A. S. C. and Goodhardt, G. J. (1979) "Audience appreciation and audience size", *Journal of the Market Research Society*, 21 (4): 269–284.

Batsell, R. and Wind, Y. (1980) "Product testing: current methods and needed developments", *Journal of the Market Research Society*, 2 (2): 115–139.

Bearden, W. O. and Netemeyer, R. G. (1999) *Handbook of Marketing Scales: Multi-item Measures for Marketing and Consumer Behaviour Research*. Thousand Oaks, CA: Sage.

Beaumont, L. (2003) "Five steps to effective frequency", *Admap*, 445, December.

Belk, R., Wallendorf, M. and Sherry, J. (1989) "The sacred and the profane in consumer behaviour: theodicy on *The Odyssey*", *Journal of Consumer Research*, 16, June: 1–37.

Berk, R. (2004) *Regression Analysis. A Constructive Critique*. Thousand Oaks, CA: Sage.

Berry, M. and Linoff, G. (1997) *Data Mining Techniques for Marketing, Sales and Customer Support*. Chichester: John Wiley & Sons.

Birnbaum, A., Lytle, L., Story, M., Perry, C. and Murray, D. (2002) "Are differences in exposure to a multicomponent school-based intervention associed with varying dietary outcomes in adolescents?", *Health Education and Behavior*, 29 (4): 427–443.

Biswas, A., Olsen, J. and Carlet, V. (1992) "A comparison of print advertisements from the United States and France", *Journal of Advertising*, 21(4): 73–81.

Bottomly, P. and Nairn, A. (2004) "Blinded by science: the managerial consequences of inadequately validated cluster analysis solutions", *International Journal of Market Research*, 46 (2): 171–187.

Bowers, D. (2002) *Medical Statistics from Scratch*. Chichester: John Wiley & Sons.

Brennan, M., Benson, S. and Kearns, Z. (2005) "The effect of introductions on telephone survey participation rates", *International Journal of Market Research*, 47 (1): 65–74.

Brown, G. (1991a) "Response. Modelling advertising awareness", *Journal of the Market Research Society*, 33 (3): 197–204.

Brown, G. (1991b) "Big stable brands and advertising effects", *Admap* (May): 307.

Brown, M. (1994) "Estimating newspaper and magazine readership", in Kent, R. (ed.) *Measuring Media Audiences*. London: Routledge.

Brown, M. G. (1990) "How to guarantee poor quality service", *Journal for Quality and Participation*, December: 6–1.

Brownlie, D. (1997) "Beyond ethnography. Toward writerly accounts of organising in marketing", *European Journal of Marketing*, 31 (3–4): 264–284.

Brownlie, D. and Saren, M. (1995) "On the commodification of marketing knowledge: opening themes", *Journal of Marketing Management*, 11 (1): 619–627.

Bryman, A. and Cramer, D. (2001) *Quantitative Data Analysis with SPSS Release 10 for Windows*. London: Routledge.

Bryman, A. and Cramer, D. (2004) *Quantitative Data Analysis with SPSS 12 and 13*. London: Routledge.

Burchill, G. and Fine, C. (1997) "Time versus market orientation in product concept development: empirically-based theory generation", *Management Science*, 43 (4): 465–478.

Buttle, F. (1996) "SERVQUAL: review, critique, research agenda", *European Journal of Marketing*, 56 (July): 1–24.

Byrne, D. (2002) *Interpreting Quantitative Data*. London: Sage.

Campbell, D. and Fiske, D. (1959) "Convergent and discriminant validation by the multitrait-multimethod matrix", *Psychological Bulletin*, 54: 297–312.

Carson, D., Gilmore, A., Perry, C. and Gronhaug, K. (2001) *Qualitative Marketing Research*. London: Sage.

Churchill, G. (1979) "A paradigm for developing better measures of marketing constructs", *Journal of Marketing Research*, 16, February: 64–73.

Churchill, G. and Iacobucci, D. (2002) *Marketing Research. Methodological Foundations*, 8th edition. Ohio: South-Western.

Chrzanowska, J. (2002) "Interviewing groups and individuals in qualitative market research", in Ereaut, G., Imms, M. and Callingham, M. (eds) *Qualitative Market Research: Principle and Practice*, Vol. 2. London: Sage.

Cohen, S. and Markowitz, P. (2002) "Renewing market segmentation. Some new tools to correct old problems", ESOMAR Consumer Insight Congress, Barcelona.

Cortina, J. (1993) "What is coefficient Alpha? An examination of theory and application", *Journal of Applied Psychology*, 78 (1): 98–104.

Craig, C. and Douglas, S. (2005) *International Marketing Research*, 3rd edition. Chichester: John Wiley & Sons.

Cramer, D. (2003) *Advanced Quantitative Data Analysis*. Maidenhead: Open University Press, McGraw-Hill Education.

Creswell, J. (2003) *Research Design. Qualitative, Quantitative, and Mixed Methods Approaches*. London: Sage.

Cronbach, L. (1952) "Coefficient alpha and the internal structure of tests", *Pyschometrica*, 16 (3): 297–334.

Cronin, J. and Taylor, S. (1992) "Measuring service quality: a reexamination and extension", *Journal of Marketing*, 56 (July): 55–68.

Cui, G. and Wong, M. (2004) "Implementing neural networks for decision support in direct marketing", *International Journal of Marketing Research*, 46 (2): 235–254.

Danaher, P. (1988) "A log-linear model for predicting magazine audiences", *Journal of Marketing Research*, 25, November: 356–362.

Dawson, J. and Hillier, J. (1995) "Competitor mystery shopping: methodological considerations and implications for the MRS Code of Conduct", *Journal of the Market Research Society*, 37: 225–239.

Daymon, C. and Holloway, I. (2002) *Qualitative Research Methods in Public Relations and Marketing Communications*. London: Routledge.

de Chernatony, L. and Knox, S. (1990) "How an appreciation of consumer behaviour can help in product testing", *Journal of the Market Research Society*, 32 (3): 329–347.

De la Cuesta, C. (1994) "Marketing: a process in health visiting", *Journal of Advanced Nursing*, 19 (2): 347–353.

De Maio, T. (1980) "Refusals, Who, Where, and Why", *Public Opinion Quarterly*, Summer: 223–233.

Dennis, K. (1995) "A logical critique of mathematical formalism in economics", *Journal of Economic Methodology*, 2: 181–199.

Denzin, N. and Lincoln, Y. (2000) *Handbook of Qualitative Research*, 2nd edition. Thousand Oaks, CA: Sage.

Desai, P. (2002) *Methods Beyond Interviewing in Qualitative Market Research*, Volume 3 in Ereaut, G., Imms, M. and Callingham, M. (eds) *Qualitative Market Research*. London: Sage.

Diaz de Rada, V. (2000) "Using Dillman's total design method in a south Europe country: Spain", paper presented to the WARPOR Annual Conference, Portland, Oregon, May.

Diaz de Rada, V. (2005) "Response effects in a survey about consumer behaviour", *International Journal of Market Research*, 47 (1): 45–64.

Dibb, S. and Farhangmehr, M. (1994) "Loglinear analysis in marketing", *Journal of Targeting, Measurement and Analysis for Marketing*, 2 (2): 153–168.

Donnenfeld, S. and du Crest, D. (2003) "Picture this! A 21st century snapshot of European kids", *ESOMAR*, April.

Douglas, S. and Craig, C. (2006) "On improving the conceptual foundations of international marketing research", *Journal of International Marketing*, 14 (1): 1–22.

Drass, K. and Ragin, C. (1992) *QCA: Qualitative Comparative Analysis*. Evanston, IL: Institute for Policy Research, Northwestern University.

Drazin, R. and Kazanjian, R. K. (1993) "Applying the Del technique to the analysis of cross-classification data: a test of the CEO succession and top management team development", *Academy of Management Journal*, 36 (6): 1374–1399.

Dunlop, C. (1995) "Warming responses from the Levant to the Gulf", *Research*, November: 24.

Durand, R. and Lambert, Z. (1988) "Don't know responses in surveys: analysis and interpretational consequences", *Journal of Business Research*, 16 (2): 169–188.

Elliott, J. (1999) "Models are stories are not real life", in Dorling, D. and Simpson, S. (eds) *Statistics in Society*. London: Arnold.

Engel, J. and Blackwell, R. (1982) *Consumer Behaviour*, 4th edition. Chicago, IL: Dryden Press.

Ereaut, G. (2002) *Analysis and Interpretation in Qualitative Market Research*, Volume 4 in Ereaut, G., Imms, M. and Callingham, M. (eds) *Qualitative Market Research: Principle and Practice*. London: Sage.

Ereaut, G., Imms, M. and Callingham, M. (eds) (2002) *Qualitative Market Research: Principle and Practice*. London: Sage.

ESOMAR (2005) *Industry Study on 2004*. Amsterdam, The Netherlands.

Feldman, M. (1995) *Strategies for Interpreting Qualitative Data*. Thousand Oaks, CA: Sage.

Field, A. (2005) *Discovering Statistics Using SPSS*, 2nd edition. London: Sage.

Fine, B. (2000) "Internet research: the brave new world", in Chakrapani, C. (ed.) *Marketing Research: State of the Art Perspectives*. Chicago, IL: Americal Marketing Association.

Fleetwood, S. (2001) "Causal laws, functional relations and tendencies", *Review of Political Economy*, 13 (2): 201–220.

Flynn, L. and Pearcy, D. (2001) "Four subtle sins in scale development: some suggestions for strengthening the current paradigm", *International Journal of Market Research*, 43 (4): 409–423.

Freedman, D. (1999) "From association to causation: some remarks on the history of statistics", *Statistical Science*, 14 (3): 243–258.

Freeman, L. (1965) *Elementary Applied Statistics: For Students in Behavioural Sciences*. New York: John Wiley & Sons.

Gage, N. (1989) "The paradigm wars and their aftermath: a 'historical' sketch of research and teaching since 1989", *Educational Researcher*, 18: 4–10.

Gane, R. (1997) "Television audience measurement systems in Europe: a review and comparison", in Kent, R. (ed.), *Measuring Media Audiences*, pp. 22–41. London: Routledge.

Glaser, B. and Strauss, A. (1967) *The Discovery of Grounded Theory*. Chicago, IL: Aldine Press.

Gold, R. (1958) "Roles in sociological field observations", *Social Forces*, 36: 217–223.

Goodyear, M. J. (1990) "Qualitative research", in R. Birn et al., *A Handbook of Market Research Techniques*. London: Kogan Page.

Gordon, W. (1999) *Goodthinking. A guide to Qualitative Research*. Admap.

Gordon, W. and Langmaid, R. (1988) *Qualitative Market Research. A Practitioner's and Buyer's Guide*. London: Gower Press.

Goritz, A. (2004) "The impact of material incentives on response quantity, response quality, sample composition, survey outcome, and cost in online access panels", *International Journal of Market Research*, 46 (3): 327–345.

Goulding, C. (1998) "Grounded theory: the missing methodology on the interpretivist agenda", *Qualitative Market Research: An International Journal*, 1 (1): 50–57.

Goulding, C. (1999) "Heritage, nostalgia, and the 'grey' consumer", *Journal of Marketing Practice: Applied Marketing Science*, 5 (6/7/8/): 177–199.

Goulding, C. (2000) "The museum environment and the visitor experience", *European Journal of Marketing*, 34 (3/4): 433–452.

Goulding, C. (2005) "Grounded theory, ethnography and phenomenology. A comparative analsis of three qualitative strategies for marketing research", *European Journal of Marketing*, 39 (3/4): 294–308.

Goulding, C., Shankar, A. and Elliott, R. (2002) "Working weeks, rave weekends: identity fragmentation and the emergence of new communities", *Consumption, Markets and Culture*, 5 (4): 261–284.

Green S. B. (1991) "How many subjects does it take to do a regression analysis?", *Multi-variate Behavioural Research*, 26: 499–510.

Griggs, S. (1987) "Analysing qualitative data", *Journal of the Market Research Society*, 29 (2): 15–34.

Grossnickle, J. and Raskin, D. (2001) *Online Marketing Research. Knowing Your Customer Using the Net*. New York: McGraw-Hill.

Hackley, C. (2000) "Silent running: tacit, discursive and psychological aspects of management in a top UK advertising agency", *British Journal of Management*, 11: 239–254.

Hadley, S. (2005) "You've got mail", *Arts Professional*, 109, November.

Hair, J., Anderson. R., Tatham, R. and Black, W. (1998) *Multivariate Data Analysis*, 5th edition. Upper Saddle River, NJ: Prentice Hall.

Hall, N. (2003) "Video, ergo, agnosco. From observation to insight", *ESOMAR*, April.

Hambleton, R. (1994) "Guidelines for adapting educational and psychological tests; a progress report", *European Journal of Psychological Assessment*, 1: 229–224.

Hammersley, M. (1998) *Reading Ethnographic Research*, 2nd edition. London: Longman.

Hammersma, M. and Appel, M. (2002) "Internet panel as a tool for TV programme appreciation research", *ESOMAR*, June.

Hart, S. and Diamantopoulos, A. (1992) "Marketing research activity and company performance: evidence from manufacturing industry", *European Journal of Marketing*, 27 (5): 54–71.

Hartley, N. (2003) "Flymo Turbo Compact", IPA Advertising Effectiveness Awards, WARC. Available at www.warc.com.

Hempel, C. G. (1942) "Studies in the logic of confirmation", *Mind*, 54: 1–26, 97–121.

Herrington, J. and Capella, L. (1996) "Effects of music in service environments: a field study", *Journal of Services Marketing*, 10 (2): 26–41.

Hersch, H. M. and Caramazza, A. A. (1976) "A fuzzy set approach to modifiers and vagueness in natural language", *Journal of Experimental Psychology*, 105: 254–276.

Hill, R. (1991) "Homeless women, special possessions and the meaning of home: an ethnographic case study", *Journal of Consumer Research*, 18, December: 298–310.

Hindmarch, J., Wells, C. and Price, F. (2005) "It's as vital as the air they breathe . . . The development of a segmentation of the baby milk market by SMA Nutrition and Leapfrog Research and Planning", Market Research Society Conference.

Hirschman, E. and Thompson, C. (1997) "Why media matter: toward a richer understanding of consumers' relationships with advertising and mass media", *Journal of Advertising*, 26 (1): 43–60.

Holbrook, M. (2003) "Adventures in complexity: an essay on dynamic open complex adaptive systems, butterfly effects, self-organising order, coevolution, the ecological perspective, fitness landscapes, market spaces, emergent beauty at the edge of chaos, and all that jazz", *Academy of Marketing Science Review*, 6. Available at http://www.amsreview.org/articles/holbrook06–2003.pdf.

Holsti, O. (1969) *Content Analysis for the Social Sciences and Humanities*. London: Addison-Wesley.

Hume, D. (1911) *A Treatise of Human Nature*, New York: E. P. Dutton.

Hunt, S. D. (1983) *Marketing Theory. The Philosophy of Marketing Science*. Homewood, IL: R. D. Irwin.

Hunt, S. (1994) "On rethinking marketing: our discipline, our practice, our methods", *European Journal of Marketing*, 28 (3): 13–25.

Huselid, M. and Day, N. (1991) "Organizational commitment, job involvement, and turnover: a substantive and methodological analysis", *Journal of Applied Psychology*, 76 (3): 380–391.

Hutton, G. (1996) "If you board the Asian bus, better mind your language", *Research Plus*, February: 9.

Imms, M. and Ereaut, G. (2002) *An Introduction to Qualitative Market Research*, Volume 1 of Ereaut, G., Imms, M. and Callingham, M. (eds) *Qualitative Market Research: Principle and Practice*. London: Sage.

Irvine, J., Miles, I. and Evans, J. (eds) (1979) *Demystifying Social Statistics*. London: Pluto Press.

Jack, F. and Burnside, G. (2002) "Pandora's box – what women think, feel and hope for in the 21st century", Market Research Society Conference, Brighton.

Jones, T. and Sasser, W. (1995) "Why satisfied customers defect", *Harvard Business Review*, 73 (November–December): 88–99.

Jonsson, S. (1991) "Action research", in Nissen, H., Klein, H. and Hirschheim, R. (eds) *Information Systems Research: Contemporary Approaches and Emergent Traditions*. Amsterdam: Elsevier.

Jugdev, M. and Maxwell, J. (2004) "Becoming a preferred employer", ESOMAR, Annual Congress, Lisbon, September.

Kalafatis, S., Sarpong, S. and Sharif, K. (2005) "An examination of the suitability of operationalisations of multi-item marketing scales", *International Journal of Market Research*, 47 (3): 255–266.

Kelly, J. (2002) "The market research industry. View from the bridge", *Admap*, 429, June.

Kent, R. A. (1981) A *History of British Empirical Sociology*. London: Gower.

Kent, R. (1986) "Faith in four Ps: an alternative", *Journal of Marketing*, 2 (2): 145–154.

Kent, R. (2005) "Cases as configurations: using combinatorial and fuzzy logic to analyze marketing data", *International Journal of Market Research*, 47 (2): 205–228.

Kincheloe, J. and McLaren, P. (2000) "Rethinking critical theory and qualitative research", in Denzin, N. and Lincoln, Y. (eds) *Handbook of Qualitative Research*, 2nd edition. Thousand Oaks, CA: Sage.

Kish, L. (1965) *Survey Sampling*. New York: John Wiley.

Klein, P. (2003) "Achieving comparabilty from multicultural diversity", ESOMAR, Global Cross-Country Forum, Miami, December.

Kline, R. (2005) *Principles and Practice of Structural Equation Modeling*, 2nd edition. Guildford: Guilford Press.

Kotler, P. (1997) *Marketing Management. Analysis, Planning and Control*, 9th edition. Upper Saddle River, NJ: Prentice Hall.

Kozinets, R. (2002) "The field behind the screen: using netography for marketing research in online communities", *Journal of Marketing Research*, 39 (1): 61–72.

Kuhn, T. (1996) *The Structure of Scientific Revolutions*, 3rd edition, Chicago, IL: University of Chicago Press. Originally published in 1962.

Lawes, R. (2002) "Demystifying semiotics: some key questions answered", *International Journal of Market Research*, 4 (3): 251–264.

Lee, N. and Hooley, G. (2005) "The evolution of 'classical mythology' within marketing measure development", *European Journal of Marketing*, 39 (3/4): 365–385.

Lerman, D. and Callow, M. (2004) "Content analysis in cross-cultural advertising research: insightful or superficial?", *International Journal of Advertising*, 23 (4): 507–521.

Lessler, J. and Kalsbeek, W. (1992) *Nonsampling Errors in Surveys*. New York: John Wiley & Sons.

Leventhal, B. (2003) "Developments in outputs from the 2001 Census", *International Journal of Market Research*, 45 (1): 3–19.

Lewin, K. (1946) "Action research and minority problems", *Journal of Social Issues*, 2 (4): 34–46.

Likert, R. (1932) 'A technique for the measurements of attitudes', *Archives of Physchology*, (140).

Lury, G. (2004) "The next generation of international research", *Admap*, Issue 452, July.

MacFadyen, L., Hastings, G. and MacKintosh, A. (2001) "Cross sectional study of young people's awareness of and involvement with tobacco marketing", *British Medical Journal*, 322, March: 513–517.

Malinoski, M. and Zeese, R. (2002) "A brand with boundless energy. How AT&T is managing its global brand for global success", *ESOMAR*, September.

Manning, J. (2003) "Dirty data and customer feedback applications", Market Research Society Conference, London.

Mariampolski, H. (1999) The power of ethnography", *Journal of the Market Research Society*, 41 (1): 75–86.

Mariano, F., Susskind, R., Torres, H., Gotelli-Varoli, A., Macial, D. and Cunha, R. (2003) "Living 24/7. A week with consumers in search of the objective truth", ESOMAR, Congress 2003.

Marx, K. (1884) *Economic and Political Manuscripts of 1844*, New York: International.

Mathur, P., Tamang, S. and El-Emary, N. (2002) "Accomplishing CRM goals. Conventional segmentation linked to data warehouse", ESOMAR, The Netherlands, March.

McKenzie, C., Wright, S., Ball, D. and Baron, P. (2002) "Commentary: The publications of marketing faculty – who are we really talking to?", *European Journal of Marketing*, 36 (11/12): 1196–1208.

Meier, E. (1991) "Response rate trends in Britain", *Marketing and Research Today*, 19, June: 120–123.

Menneer, P. (1987) "Audience appreciation – a different story from audience numbers", *Journal of the Market Research Society*, 29 (3): 241–264.

Menneer, P. (1989) "Towards a radio 'BARB' – some issues of measurement", *Admap*, February: 42–45.

Mick, D. and Demoss, M. (1990) "Self-gifts: phenomenological insights from four contexts", *Journal of Consumer Research*, 17, December: 322–332.

Miedzinski, F. and Duquesne, P. (2003) "GPS – generating perfume sparkles by global positioning system", ESOMAR, Fragrance Conference, Lausanne, March.

Miles, L. (1993) "Rise of the mystery shopper", *Marketing*, July: 19–20.

Miles, M. and Huberman, M. (1994) *Qualitative Data Analysis*, 2nd edition. Thousand Oaks, CA: Sage.

Miller, J. (2000) "Net vs phone: the great debate", *Research*, August: 26–27.

Min, H., Min, H. and Emam, A. (2002) "A data mining approach to developing the profiles of hotel customers", *International Journal of Contemporary Hospitality Management*, 14 (6): 274–285.

Mitchell, V., Lennard, D. and McGoldrick, P. (2003) "Consumer awareness, understanding and usage of unit pricing", *British Journal of Management*, 14: 173–187.

Morrison, L., Colman, A. and Preston, C. (1997) "Mystery customer research: cognitive processes affecting accuracy", *Journal of the Market Research Society*, 39 (21): 33.

Morse, J. (1991) "Approaches to qualitative–quantitative methodological triangulation", *Nursing Research*, 40: 120–123.

Morse, J. (2003) "Principles of mixed-and multi-method research design", in Tashakkori, A. and Teddlie, C. (eds), *Mixed Methods in Social and Behavioural Research*. Thousand Oaks, CA: Sage.

Muylle, S., Moenaert, R. and Despontin, M. (1999) "A grounded theory of World Wide Web search behaviour", *Journal of Marketing Communications*, 5: 143–155.

Naccarato, J. and Neuendorf, K. (1997) "Content analysis as a predictive methodology: recall, readership, and evaluations of business-to-business print advertising", *Journal of Advertising Research*, March/April, 19–33.

Nairn, A. and Bottomly, P. (2003) "Something approaching science? Cluster analysis procedures in the CRM era", *International Journal of Market Research*, 45 (2): 241–261.

Narver, J. and Slater, S. (1990) "The effect of a market orientation on business profitability", *Journal of Marketing*, 54 (4): 20–35.

Newman, I., Ridenour, C., Newman, C. and DeMarco, G. (2003) "A typology of research purposes and its relationship to mixed methods", in Tashakkori, A. and Teddlie, A. (eds) *Handbook of Mixed Methods in Social and Behavioural Research*. Thousand Oaks, CA: Sage.

Nunnally, J. (1978) *Psychometric Theory*, 2nd edition. New York: McGraw-Hill.

O'Donoghue, D. and Steele, L. (2004) "Is lifestage losing its meaning?", *Admap*, September, 453.

O'Guinn, T. and Faber, R. (1989) "Compulsive buying: a phenomenological exploration" *Journal of Consumer Research*, 16, September: 147–157.

Oliver, R. (1997) *Satisfaction. A Behavioural Perspective on the Consumer*. New York: McGraw-Hill.

Olsen, W. and Morgan, J. (2004) "A critical epistemology of analytical statistics: addressing the skeptical realist", paper presented to the British Sociological Association, York, March.

Osborn, A. (1963) *Applied Imagination*, 3rd edition. New York: Chares Scribner and Sons.

Osgood, C., Suci, G. and Tannenbaum, P. (1957) *The Measurement of Meaning*. Chicago, IL: University of Illinois Press.

Pampel, F. (2000) *Logistic Regression: A Primer*. Thousand Oaks, CA: Sage.

Parasuraman, A., Zeithmal, V. and Berry, L. (1988) "SERVQUAL: a multiple-item scale for measuring consumer perceptions of service quality", *Journal of Retailing*, 64 (1): 12–40.

Parker, D. and Stacey, R. (1994) *Chaos, Management and Economics*. London: Institute of Economic Affairs, Hobart Paper 125.

Pasco, M. (2001) "From Cold War to Cola War", *Admap*, December.

Pelsmacker, P., Geuens, M and Vermeir, I. (2004) "The importance of media planning, as likeability and brand position for ad and brand recognition in radio spots", *International Journal of Market Research*, 46 (4): 465–478.

Penfold, M. and Buckingham, C. (1990) "Thinking global, acting local – integrated information services for European countries in the 1990s", *Admap*, November.

Perry, C. and Gummeson, E. (2004) "Commentary. Action research in marketing", *European Journal of Marketing*, 38 (3/4): 310–320.

Peterson, R. (1994) "A meta-analysis of Cronbach's coefficient alpha", *Journal of Consumer Research*, 221, September: 381–391.

Pettigrew, S. (2000) "Ethnography and grounded theory: a happy marriage", *Advances in Consumer Research*, 27: 256–260.

Punch, K. (1998) *Introduction to Social Research. Quantitative and Qualitative Approaches*. London: Sage.

Ragin, C. (1987) *The Comparative Method. Moving Beyond Qualitative and Quantitative Strategies*. Berkeley and Los Angeles, CA: University of California Press.

Ragin, C. (1992) "'Casing' and the process of social inquiry", in. Ragin, C. and Becker, H. (eds) *What is a Case? Exploring the Foundations of Social Inquiry*. Cambridge: Cambridge University Press.

Ragin, C. (2000) *Fuzzy-Set Social Science*. Chicago, IL: University of Chicago Press.

Ragin, C., Drass, K. and Davey S. (2003) *Fuzzy-Set/Qualitative Comparative Analysis 1.1*. Tucson, AZ: Department of Sociology, University of Arizona.

Retzer, J. (2006) "The century of Bayes", *International Journal of Market Research*, 48 (1): 49–59.

Ritson, M. and Elliott, R. (1999) "The social uses of advertising: an ethnographic study of adolescent advertising audiences", *Journal of Consumer Research*, 26, June: 260–277.

Sampson, P. (1987) "The tracking study in market research", in Bradley, U. (ed.) *Applied Marketing and Social Research*. Chichester: John Wiley.

Sargent, M. (1989) "Uses and abuses of qualitative research from a marketing viewpoint", in Robson, S. and Foster, A. (eds) *Qualitative Research in Action*. London: Edward Arnold.

Sayer, A. (2000) *Realism and Social Science*. London: Sage.

Schwandt, T. (1994) "Constructivist, interpretivist approaches to human enquiry", in Denzin, N. and Lincoln, Y. (eds) *Handbook of Qualitative Research*. Thousand Oaks, CA: Sage.

Selvin, H. C. (1957) "A critique of tests of significance in survey research", *American Sociological Review*, 22: 519–527.

Shepherd-Smith, N. (1994) "Something's wrong with average issue readership", *Admap*, February.

Silverman, D. (2001) *Interpreting Qualitative Data*, 2nd edition. London: Sage.

Smith, A. (2002) "Three scenarios for applying chaos theory in consumer research", *Journal of Marketing Management*, 18: 517–531.

Smith, D. and Fletcher, J. (2001) *Inside Information. Making Sense of Marketing Data*. Chichester: John Wiley & Sons.

Smith, D. and Fletcher, J. (2004) *The Art and Science of Interpreting Market Research Evidence*. Chichester: John Wiley & Sons.

Spicer, J. (2005) *Making Sense of Multivariate Data Analysis*. Thousand Oaks, CA: Sage.

Stewart, D. W. and Furse, D. H. (1986) *Effective Television Advertising: A Study of 1000 Commercials*. Lexington, MA: Lexington Books.

Stotts, L. and Kleiner, B. (1995) "New developments in fuzzy logic", *Industrial Management and Datasystems*, 26 (5): 13–18.

Strasser, P. and Lingeman, H. (2003) "Challenges in conducting worldwide online research", ESOMAR, Global Cross-Country Forum, Miami, December.

Sudman, S. and Ferber, R. (1979) *Consumer Panels*. Chicago, IL: American Marketing Association.

Tabachnick, B. and Fidell, L. (2001) *Using Multivariate Statistics*, 4th edition. Boston, MA: Allyn and Bacon.

Tansey, R., White, M., Long, R. and Smith, M. (1996) "A comparison of loglinear modelling and logistic regression in management research", *Journal of Management,* 2 (2): 339–358.

Tashakkori, A. and Teddlie, C. (1998) *Mixed Methodology. Combining Qualitative and Quantitative Approaches*. Thousand Oaks, CA: Sage.

Tashakkori, A. and Teddlie, C. (eds) (2003) *Mixed Methods in Social and Behavioural Research*. Thousand Oaks, CA: Sage.

Taylor, C. (2002) "What is wrong with international advertising research?", *Journal of Advertising Research*, 42 (6): November.

Taylor, H. (2000) "Does internet research work?", *International Journal of Market Research*, 42 (1): 51–63.

Tesch, R. (1990) *Qualitative Research: analysis types and software tools*. New York: Falmer Press.

Theil, H. (1967) *Economics and Information Theory*. Chicago, IL: Rand McNally.

Thiesse, M. and Gowers, F. (1996) "Are you talking to me? Communicating with young adults in Asia", ESOMAR, Marketing in Asia, Hong Kong, November.

Thompson, C. (1996) "Caring consumers: gendered consumption meanings and the juggling of lifestyle", *Journal of Consumer Research*, 22, March: 388–407.

Thompson, C. and Haykto, D. (1997) "Consumers' uses of fashion discourses and the appropriation of countervailing cultural meanings", *Journal of Consumer Research*, 25, March: 139–153.

Thompson, C., Locander, W. and Pollio, H. (1990) "The lived meaning of free choice: an existential-phenomenological description of everyday consumer experiences of contemporary married women", *Journal of Consumer Research*, 17, December: 346–361.

Thygesen, F. and McGowan, P. (2002) "Inspiring the organization to act: a business in denial", Market Research Society Conference: London.

Tierney, M. L. (2004) "Stop writing reports! Develop a tool", ESOMAR, November.

Torgerson, W. (1958) *Theory and Methods of Scaling*. London: Wiley.

Tuckman, W. B. (1986) "Developmental sequences in small groups", in A. Brown, *Group Work*, 2nd edition. London: Gower.

Upshaw, L. and Taylor, E. (2000) *The Masterbrand Mandate*. New York: John Wiley & Sons.

Valentine, V. (2002) "Repositioning research: a new MR language model", Paper presented to the Market Research Society Conference.

VanderMerwe, S. and L'Huillier, M. (1989) "Euro-consumers in 1992", *Business Horizons*, 32 (1): 34–40.

Walkowski, J. (2001) "Online qualitative research for Motorola: lessons learned". Association for Qualitative Research/Qualitative Research Consultants Association, Conference Proceedings, Paris.

Walters, D. and Walters, G. (2002) *Scientists must speak: bringing presentation to life*. London: Taylor and Francis.

Ward, J. (1987) "Lifestyles and geodemographics: why advertising agencies shun a single-source approach", *Admap*, June: 53–56.

West, P., Brockett, P. and Golden, L. (1997) "A comparative analysis of neural networks and statistical methods for predicting consumer choice", *Marketing Science*, 16 (4): 370–391.

White, R. (2000) "Single-source data", *WARC Best Practice*, April, Henley-on-Thames: NTC Publications.

Wicken, G. (2003) "Communication-receptive planning in Europe", *Admap*, 445, December.

Wicken, G., van Staveren, M. and Dinning, A. (2005) "Global socio-economic levels. Development of a global non-occupational classification system", *International Journal of Market Research*, 47 (6): 597–614.

Wilke, J. (2002) "The future of simulated test markets", ESOMAR, Consumer Insight Congress, Barcelona, September.

Wilkins, J. (2002) "Why is global advertising still the exception, not the rule?", *Admap*, February.

Williams, W. and Goodman, M. (1971) "A simple method for the construction of empirical confidence limits for economic forecasts", *Journal of the American Statistical Association*, 6: 752–754.

Willis, K. (1990) "In-depth interviews", in Birn, R. et al., *A Handbook of Market Research Techniques*. London: Kogan Page.

Wilson, H. (2004) "Towards rigour in action research: a case study in marketing planning", *European Journal of Marketing*, 38 (3/4): 378–400.

Wimbush, A. (1990) "Clinics", in Birn, R. et al., *A Handbook of Market Research Techniques*. London: Kogan Page.

Wolfe, A. (ed.) (1984) *Standardised Questions. A Review for Market Research Executives*. Market Research Society.

Woodruff-Burton, H., Eccles, S. and Elliott, R. (2002) "The effect of gender on addictive consumption: reflections on men, shopping and consumption meaning", *Gender, Marketing and Consumer Behaviour*, 6: 239–256.

Yahiaoui, G. and Dias, D. (1997) "Customer segmentation for the automobile market. The use of artificial neural networks", 50th ESOMAR Congress.

Youden, W. (1972) "Enduring values", *Technometrics*, 14 (1): 1–10.

Yule, G. (1899), "An investigation into the causes of changes in pauperism in England, chiefly during the last two intercensal decades", *Journal of the Royal Statistical Society*, LXII.

Zadeh, L. (1965) "Fuzzy sets", *Information and Control*, 8: 338–353.

Zahavi, J. and Levin, N. (1997) "Issues and problems in applying neural computing to target marketing", *Journal of Direct Marketing*, 11 (4): 63–75.

Zetterberg, H. L. (1965) *On Theory and Verification in Sociology*, 3rd edition. London: Bedminster Press.

Zhang, G., Hu, M. Patuwo, B. and Indro, D. (1999) "Artificial neural networks in bankruptcy prediction: general framework and cross-validation analysis", *European Journal of Operational Research*, 16 (1): 16–32.

Zimmerman, H. J. and Zysno, P. (1980) "Latent connectives in human decision making", *Fuzzy Sets and Systems*, 4: 37–51.

Zufryden, F. (1996) "Linking advertising to box office performance of new film releases – a marketing planning model", *Journal of Advertising Research*, 36 (4): 29–41.

Index

Abbott, A. 446, 447, 448
academic articles 555–8
  abstract 555
  conclusions 558
  introduction 555
  literature review 557
  purpose statement 556
  references 558
  results section 557–8
  statement of objectives 556
  title 555
academic data analysis
  content 268
  discourse analysis 273–4
  ethnography 268–9
  grounded theory 269–71
  phenomenology 272–3
  semiotics 275
academic research 43, 562
  contrast with client-based research 46
  designing 57–9
    data analysis 62
    litcrature review 60
    research background 59
    research methods/techniques 61–2
    research objectives 60–1
    theories/models 60
  ethical issues 62–3
  key features 44–7
  models 56–7
  philosophical underpinnings 47–55
  qualitative 112–13
  quantitative research 222–3
  theory 55–6
academic review process 558–60
academic surveys 184
access panel 540
accompanied shopping 104, 562
ACNielsen 75, 475–6
ACORN 159, 220
action research 211–12, 562
action standards 15
actorial design 565
ad hoc 8, 10, 182–3, 238, 504, 562
adjusted R^2 562
Adrianssens, C. 111
advertising
  cross-national 541
  pretesting 517–18
  tracking 10, 504–10
agency surveys 183
agglomerative clustering 423
Akimova, I. 422, 425
Albaum, A. 136
Alliance of International Market Research
    Institutes 35
alpha value 142, 562
Alt, M. 400
American Marketing Association 56
analysis of covariance (ANCOVA) 417, 562

analysis of variance (ANOVA) 385–6, 387–8,
    402, 417, 562
analytic induction 212, 562
Appel, M. 486
area forums 109, 562
Aristotle 446, 447
Arnould, E. 269
Assael, H. 243
Association of British Market Research
    Companies (ABMRC) 35–6
Association of Market Survey Organisations
    (AMSO) 35
Association for Qualitative Research (AQR) 88
AT&T 531–2
attitudes 121, 497, 498, 562
  measurement 519
audience appreciation 485–6
average issue readership (AIR) 488–9
Awareness Index 509–10, 518–19

backward elimination 406, 562
Baker, K. 160
har chart 304, 305, 340–2, 562
barcoding 176
Barker, A. 256
Barwise, T.P. 486
BASES model 521–3
Batsell, R. 514
Bayesian statistics 455, 562
Bearden, W.O. 137, 145
Beaumont, J. 416
Beaumont, L. 495
behavioral variables 121, 562
beliefs 562
Belk, R. 271
Benson, S. 190, 191
Berk, R. 416
Berry, M. 453
beta coefficient 411, 562
bias 239, 242, 562
binary logistic regression 413, 434–5, 562
binary scale 125, 131, 562
binary variables 349–55
Birnbaum, A. 211
Biswas, A. 541
bivariate analysis 298, 399, 562
  limitations 399–402
bivariate crosstabulation 342, 562
bivariate data display 340–4
bivariate data summaries 388–9
  categorical variables 345–9
    coefficients appropriate for
      binary/nominal variables 349–55
    coefficients appropriate for mixed
      variables 359
    coefficients appropriate for ordinal
      variables 355–7
    coefficients appropriate for two ranked
      variables 358
    selecting appropriate statistic 359–60

metric variables 361–3
  correlation/regression compared 363–4
  Pearson's r 364–5
  Spearman's rho 364–5
  using SPSS 366–8
bivariate hypothesis 378, 383, 562
  testing for categorical variables 383–4
  testing metric differences for categories
    385–8
  testing for metric variables 384–5
Booth, C. 440, 441–2
Bottomly, P. 425
Bowers, D. 395
brainstorming 98, 562
brand share prediction 519–25
Brennan, M. 191
bricoleur 256
Brighton, M. 400
British Market Research Association 184
British Market Research Bureau (BMRB) 74,
    160, 221, 491, 494–5
Broadcasters Audience Research Board 75
Brown, G. 517, 518
Brown, M. 34, 488, 489, 506, 507, 518–19
Brown, M.G. 105
Brownlie, D. 56, 269
Bryman, A. 395, 403
bulletin boards 111, 562
Burchill, G. 271
Business Elite 82
business research 11, 563
business survey 183, 186, 563
buying research
  agency perspective 31
  client perspcctive 29–31
Byrne, D. 443

CACI 159
Cadman, L. 111
Callow, M. 541
Campbell, D. 256
Capella, L. 60, 228, 556–7
car clinic 207
Carson, D. 211, 212, 277
case 119–20, 563
case studies
  Compass Group 545
  eBay 179
  Egg plc 247
  Flymo 42
  Fox Kids Europe 114
  free daily newspaper 149
  fuzzy set analysis of results of e-mail survey
    in Norway 465–8
  Levi Strauss 225
  Living 24/7 283
  SMA nutrition 259
  Vodafone 84
  young people and tobacco marketing 66
case-based analysis 455–8

categorical scale 124–7, 563
categorical variables 298
 bivariate data summaries 345–60
 estimation 374–6
 multivariate analysis 404–9
 summaries 309–10
 testing bivariate hypotheses 383–4
 testing univariate hypotheses 378–80
 univariate data display 300–5
causal analysis 429–31, 563
causal modeling 500
causal research 18, 563
causality 444–8
cell 342, 360, 405, 406, 407, 563
census 242, 299, 563
Census of Population 160
*Central and Eastern European Business
 Directory* 74
Central Statistical Office (CSO) 73
centroids 424, 563
chaos theory 449–50, 563
chart 304, 330, 563
Chernatony, L. de 515
Chi-square 346, 348–9, 351, 379, 383, 389,
 390, 403, 563
Chrzanowska, J. 91
Churchill, G. 138, 243
citizens' juries 109, 563
client-based marketing research 3, 563
 as client-led 5, 7
 confidential 6
 contractual 6
 contrast with academic research 46
 customer-oriented 4
 definition 5, 10
 features 5–7
 as interventionist 6
 not neutral 6
 physician analogy 7
 pragmatic 6
 qualitative 88–90
 quantitative research 222–3
 report-based 7
 solution-oriented 6
 time and cost constrained 6
 types 9–11
cluster analysis 422–6, 435–6, 563
clustered bar chart 563
clustering 233–4, 563
codebook 563
coding 265, 563
coefficient 348, 407, 563
 binary/nominal variables 349–55
 mixed variables 359
 multiserial correlation 359
 ordinal variables 355–8
 two ranked variables 358
coefficient of determination 362, 563
coefficient of multiple determination 410–11,
 563
cognitive variables 121, 563
Cohen, S. 425
collinearity 401, 563
column marginal 342, 563
combinatorial logic 455–8, 563
communication networks 172
Community Research and Development

Information Service (CORDIS) 74
company accounts 563
comparative testing 511, 514
comparison 256
competition 7–8
complete observer 87
complete participant 87
computer assisted personal interviewing (CAPI)
 176, 177
computer assisted qualitative data analysis
 software (CAQDAS) 278–81
computer assisted telephone interviewing
 (CATI) 176, 177, 189
Computer Assisted Web Interviewing (CAWI)
 176, 177
computer software 169–70
concurrent mixed design 255–6, 563
conditional relationships 400, 563
confidence interval *see* interval estimate
confirmatory factor analysis (CFA) 421, 563
confounding relationship 401, 563
conjoint analysis 563
conjoint testing 515
construct validity 145, 563
consultancy research 10
consultation 108–9, 563
consumer behavior 104
consumer panel 214–16, 218, 474, 476–7, 564
consumer research 11, 564
consumer surveys 183
contact diary 172, 564
contact rate 198, 564
contamination 564
content analysis 268, 321–2, 564
content validity 144, 564
contingency coefficient 349–51, 564
continuous metric variable 127–8
continuous research 8, 213–14, 505, 564
 advance notice 8
 early warning 8
 panel 214–18
 regular interval surveys 219–22
continuous variable 131, 564
controlling error 244–5
convenience sample 235, 564
correlation 298, 362, 363–4, 366–8
correlation coefficient 364–5, 564
correlation ratio 359, 564
covariance 361, 564
covariate 564
covariation 361, 403–4, 564
Craig, C. 543
Cramer, D. 395, 403
Cramer's V 325, 349, 351–3, 359, 388–9, 390,
 564
Creswell, J. 253
criterion validity 144, 564
critical values 379, 564
Cronbach's coefficient 142, 143–4, 564
Cronin, J. 499–500
cross-national research 530–2
 academic 543
 design 532
 building information systems 534–5
 identifying market opportunities 533–4
 primary research 536–42
 ethical issues 543

reporting 554
crosstabulation 298, 342–3, 366, 564
Cui, G. 452
CUPID(tm) system 504
customer database 476, 564
customer loyalty 501–2
customer preference 7
customer relationship management (CRM) 76
customer satisfaction measurement 498–504
 expectations/perceived performance
 comparison 499
 regression analysis 500
 structural equation modeling 500
 summated rating scales 499–500
customized research 10, 564

Danaher, P. 408
data 564
 capture 17
 collection 7, 17
 construction 69–71
 definition 69–71
 existence of 70–1
 images 70
 macro 79–80
 micro 80
 numbers 70
 panels 8
 quality 70
 recording 69–70
 words/text 70
data analysis 62, 261, 296–9, 564
 academic approaches 267–75
 analysis/interpretation distinction 263–4
 qualitative 263–7
 quantitative 285–336
data capture 483
 diaries 170–7
 questionnaire 151–70
data display 297, 564
data dredging 399–400, 564
data fusion 254, 564
data matrix 291, 564
data mining 453, 564
 affinity grouping 453
 classification 453
 clustering 454
 description/profiling 454
 estimation 453
 prediction 453
Data Monitor 74
data output 483–4
data protection 39–40
data summary 331, 391, 564
 categorical variables 309–10
 metric variables 310–15
data transformation 315
 analyzing summated rating scales 323–8
 class intervals 318
 collapsing categories 317–18
 computing totals 318
 don't know responses 319–21
 missing values 319–21
 multiple response questions 318–19
 open-ended questions 321–3
 upgrading/downgrading scales 316–17
data warehouse 76, 564

dataset 564
Dawson, J. 105
Day, N. 409
Daymon, C. 277
De Maio, T. 199
decisions 3, 15
degree of fit 403–4, 446
degree of freedom 565
deliberative methods 109–10
deliberative polls 110, 565
demographic variables 120–1, 565
Demoss, M. 273
dendogram 424, 565
Dennis, K. 447
Denzin, N. 112, 253, 267
departure from independence 345, 565
dependence techniques 402, 409, 565
    discriminant analysis 414–16
    logistic regression 413–14
    multiple regression 410–12
    multivariate analysis of variance 417–18
dependent variable 122–3, 565
depth interviews 99, 565
    degree of depth 101
    groups/depths choice 102–3
    location 101
    planning 100
    stimulus material 101
    structuring 101
    type of interview 100–1
    who to talk to 100
derived measurement 134–9, 565
Desai, P. 107, 108, 111, 275
descriptive research 11–12, 18, 565
descriptive statistics 360, 565
descriptors 122, 565
design factor 240, 565
desk research 78–9, 565
    academic projects 81–2
diagnostic techniques 470, 471–2
    market measurement 472–9
    media audience measurement 479–91
    single-source data 491–5
dialectical analysis 432
Diamantopoulos, A. 9
diary 170–2, 215, 565
    design 173–5
    precoded 171
    semi-structured 171
Dias, D. 452
Diaz de Rada, V. 191
Dinning, A. 158
dipstick operation 16, 504, 505
direct measurement 133–4, 565
disconfirmation model 499
discourse analysis 273–4, 565
discretevariables 127–8, 565
discrete variable 131
discriminant analysis 414–16, 422, 435, 565
discriminant validity 565
divisive clustering 424
Douglas, S. 543
Drass, K. 457
Drazin, R. 408
drop-out 194, 565
dummy variable 131, 412, 565

Dunlop, C. 531
Duquesne, P. 8

eclectic designs 256, 565
editing 565
effect size 565
eigenvalue 420, 565
electronic
    diaries 174
    questionnaires 176–7
    surveys 215
electronic point of sale (EPOS) 176
Elliott, J. 443
Elliott, R. 269
Emerald 82
environmental analysis 14–15
epistemology 48–9, 565
Ereaut, G. 88, 263, 264, 277
error 216, 565
    diary sources 172
    proportional reduction 346–7, 570
    random sampling 390
    sampling
        controlling 244–5
        random 242–3, 373, 570
        systematic 241–2, 373, 572
        total survey 243–4
    surveys
        frame 196–7
        interviewer 202
        nonresponse 198–201
        population specification 195–6
        questionnaire design 197–8
        response 201–2
establishment survey 481–2, 565
estimates 374, 565
    categorical variables 374–6
    metric variables 376–7
Eta 359, 565
ethics 38–9, 62–3
    confidentiality 39
    cross-national 543
    deception 39
    integrity 39
    misrepresentation 39
    privacy 39
    questionnaires 178
    research methods 223
    sampling 245
    scales 146
    secondary data 83
    survey methods 223
ethnography 53, 107–8, 268–9, 565
ethnomethodology 53
Euclidean distance 565
Europages 74
European Data Protection Directive 39–40
    consent 40
    transparency 39–40
European Federation of Associations of Market
    Research Organizations (EFAMRO) 35
European marketing research 8, 33
    ACNielsen 475–6
    Belgian radio commercials 412
    buyers 34–5
    cancer awareness 539
    cluster analysis in Ukraine 424

    customer segmentation in automobile
        market in France 453
    e-mail for audience research 193
    evaluation of antismoking campaign 59–60
    female consumers visiting company website
        in Finland 414
    luxury hotels in South Korea 454
    mail surveys in Spain 191–2
    pricing 32–3
    profession 35–6
    radio audience measurement in UK 487–8
    social classification systems 158–9
    suppliers of services 34
    surfing the web in Belgium 271
    television audience measurement in UK
        484–5
    TGI in Europe 495
    TNS Worldpanel 476–8
    trends 36
    UK national Readership Survey 489–91
    what women think, feel, hope 92
European Society for Opinion and Marketing
    Research (ESOMAR) 35
European Union 74
evaluative research 90
expansion 256
experiment 566
    field 207
        in-home placement tests 207–8
        social intervention 211
        store tests 208
        test marketing 208–11
    laboratory 206
        hall tests 206–7
        test centres 207
        van tests 207
    research 203–4
    validity 212–13
experimental design 204–6
    after-only 204
    after-only with control 204
    before and after 204
    before and after with control 204–5
explanation 428, 566
explanatory research *see* causal research
exploratory factor analysis 421, 566
exploratory research 11–12, 17–18, 566
extraneous variable 203, 566

Faber, R. 273
face validity 144
factor 420, 566
factor analysis 328, 402, 420–2, 435, 566
factor loading 420, 566
Family Expenditure Survey 77
Feldman, M. 275
Ferber, R. 174
Fidell, L. 407, 446
field experiment 207, 566
Financial Times Discovery Services 74
Fine, B. 11
Fine, C. 271
finite multiplier 237, 566
Fiske, D. 256
fixed choice question 154–7, 566
Fleetwood, S. 448
Fletcher, J. 37, 463

Fletcher, R. 160
Flynn, L. 138
focus groups 91–2, 566
  composition 93–4
  groups/depths choice 102–3
  method of running
    back seat/fly-on-the-wall 96
    focus of attention 96
    moderators 95–7
    one of the group 96
    venue 96, 98–9
    warm-up/ice-breaking strategies 96
    winding up 96–7
  number of groups 94
  planning 92
  practitioner techniques
    association 98
    completion 98
    construction 98
    transformation 98
  recruitment 94–5
  running 95–9
  stimulus material 97–8
    animatics 97
    concept boards 97
    narrative tapes 97
    physical mock-ups 97
    storyboards 97
  topics to be discussed 95
  types 93, 94
frame errors 196–7, 566
Freedman, D. 440
Freeman, L. 359
frequency 566
frequency table 328–30, 566
functionalism 52
funneling 166, 566
Furse, D.H. 268
fuzzy set analysis 459–61
fuzzy-set/qualitative comparative analysis
    (FS/QCA) 461–3

Gage, N. 253
Galton, F. 440
Gamma 355–6, 359, 566
Gane, R. 480, 481
gap model 499
Gauss, C.F. 440
general linear model (GLM) 417, 566
geodemographics 159–60, 566
Glaser, B. 270
globalization 474
Gold, R. 87
Goodman, M. 377
goodness-of-fit test 403, 566
Goodyear, M. 94
Gordon, W. 89, 94, 102, 256
Goulding, C. 271, 273
governmental surveys 184
Gowers, F. 542
graphs 304, 330
Green, J. 253
Green Light International 92
Green, S.B. 411
Griggs, S. 278
Grossnicke, J. 11
grounded theory 53, 270–71, 566

group discussion 91–2
Gummeson, E. 212

Hackley, C. 274
Hair, J. 415, 416, 422, 428, 444, 451
Hall, N. 106
hall test 185, 206–7, 566
Hambleton, R. 537
Hammersley, M. 277
Hammersma, M. 486
Hart, C. 9
Hayktto, D. 273
health panels 109
Hegel, G.W.F. 432
HELP campaign 59–60
Hempel, C.G. 446
Herrington, J. 60, 228, 556–7
heteroscedacity 444
hierarchical clustering 423, 566
hierarchical regression 411, 566
Hill, R. 269
Hillier, J. 105
Hindmarsh, J. 259
Hirschman, E. 271
histogram 308, 330–1, 566
holistic analysis 463
holistic surveys 474
Holloway, I. 277
Hooley, G. 136, 146
Huberman, M. 48, 251–2, 263
Hume, D. 446
Hunt, S.D. 55, 56
Huselid, M. 409
Husserl, E. 272
Hutton, G. 531
hypertext markup language (HTML) 193
hypothesis 566
  testing 297
  testing for statistical significance 377–8
    bivariate 383–8
    univariate 378–83
hypothetical questions 162

Iacobucci, D. 243
ICC/ESOMAR International Code of Marketing
    and Social Practice 36, 38
ideal-type 54
images 566
Imms, M. 88
importance 500
imposing quotas 234
in-home placement test 207–8, 567
in-home survey 185, 567
in-house research 183, 567
in-store surveys 186
independent samples 386, 566
independent variable 122–3, 566
index of similarity 423–4
indirect measurement 134, 567
inferential statistics 297, 360
information 3
  quality 16
  specification 152–3
  systems 76, 534–5
  timescale 18
  what is required 15–16
interquartile range 315, 567

interaction effect 400–1, 567
interdependence technique 420–8, 567
International Code of Marketing and Social
    Research Practice 35
internet 36
  bulletin boards 111
  interviewing 177
  moderated e-mail groups 111–12
  online focus groups 110–11
  spamming 540
interval estimate 374, 377, 567
interval scale 131
interview data 91
interview survey 184–5, 567
  process 186–9
  types 185–6
interviewer 186
  asking questions 187
  bias 187
  briefing session 188
  completing records 187
  errors 202
  fieldwork management 188
  industry guidelines 188–9
  integration into industry 188
  locating respondents 186
  obtaining agreement 186–7
  preparation 186
  quality control 188
  training 187–8
Interviewer Quality Control Scheme (IQCS) 36,
    188–9
interviewer-completed questionnaire 166–7,
    567
interviews
  alternatives 103
    area forums 109
    consultation 108–9
    deliberative methods 109–10
    ethnography 107–8
    observation 103–6
    panels 109
  depth 99–103
investigative research 567
invitation online sampling 241, 567
Irvine, J. 77
item analysis 138, 567

joint effects 400
Jones, T. 501–2
Jonsson, S. 212

k-means clustering 424
Kalafatis, S. 145
Kalsbeek, W. 244
Kazanjian, R.K. 408
Kearns, Z 190, 191
Kelly, J. 36
Kendall's tau-b 357, 359, 567
Kendall's tau-c 357, 359, 567
Kent, R.A. 151
Keon, J. 243
Keynote Publications 74
Kincheloe, J. 273
Kish, L. 243
Klein, P. 537
Kleiner, B. 459

Kline, R. 421
knowledge 47–9
Knox, S. 515
Kotler, P. 52
kurtosis 313, 567

labelling scale 125, 567
laboratory experiment 206–7, 567
lambda 353–5, 359, 567
Langmaid, R. 94, 102
latent variable 420, 567
latin square experimental design 567
Lawes, R. 275
Lee, N. 136, 146
Leeuw, J. de 410
Legendre, A.-M. 440
Lerman, D. 541
Lessler, J. 244
level of confidence *see* alpha value
levels of measurement 140–1
Leventhal, B. 73
Levin, N. 452
Lewin, K. 211
Lexis-Nexus 82
L'Huillier, M. 536
life-stages 159
likelihood ratio Chi-square 407, 413, 567
Likert scale 135–6, 567
Lincoln, Y. 112, 253, 267
line graph 308, 330–1, 567
linear regression *see* regression
linear relationship 444–8
Lingeman, H. 540
Linoff, G. 453
literature reviews 81–2
log likelihood Chi-square *see* likelihood ratio
    Chi-square
log odds 567
logistic regression 413–14, 567
loglinear analysis 405–9, 432–3, 567
Louis, P. 440
Lury, G. 542

Macer, T. 247
McGoldrick, T. 236
McKenzie, C. 223
McKinlay, J. 211
McLaren, P. 273
macroenvironment 530–4, 567
Manning, J. 179
mapping techniques 498
market basket analysis 454, 567
market composition 473–4
market measurement 472–8, 567
    use of data 478–9
market measurement panels 214, 567
market opportunities 533
    creating market segments 533
    making risk assessment 533
    scanning for feasibility 533
market orientation 137
market research
    agencies 183, 502–4
    environment 4
    reasons for needing 7–9
Market Research Europe 74
Market Research GB 74

Market Research Society (MRS) 35, 160
market researcher 37
market size 472
    brand shares 473
    market penetration 473
    sales 472–3
    value of deliveries 473
market structure 474
market tracking survey 221, 474, 568
marketing
    database 476
    definition 4
    intelligence 15, 80–1, 568
    physician 52
    physicist 51–2
    psychiatrist 53
Marketing Pocket Book 74
Markowitz, P. 425
Marlampolski, H. 107
Marx, K. 7, 432
maturation 568
MAXqda 279–81
mean 310, 568
measurement 131, 568
    derived 134–9
    direct 133–4
    error 141–5
    indirect 134
    multidimensional 139–41
    process 132–3
    theory 130–1
measures of association 348–55, 366
media audience measurement 479–80, 568
media panels 218, 568
media use diary 172, 568
median 311, 568
mediating relationship 401, 568
Meier, E. 199
Menneer, P. 174
meters 177
    peoplemeters 177
    push-button/active systems 177
    set meters 177
metric scale 127–31, 568
metric table 306–7, 568
metric variables 298
    bivariate data summaries 361–5
    data summary
        central tendency 310–11
        dispersion 311–13
        distribution shape 313
        normal distribution 314–15
        percentile values 315
    estimation 376–7
    multivariate analysis 409–28
    testing bivariate hypotheses 384–5
    testing univariate hypotheses 380–3
    univariate data display 306–9
Mick, D. 273
microenvironment 4, 530, 568
Miedzinski, F. 8
Miles, L. 105
Miles, M. 48, 251–2, 263
Miller, J. 194
Min, H. 454
mini-test marketing 210–11, 568
Mintel Market Intelligence Reports 74

mixed research designs 253–4
    rationales 257–8
    types 255–6
mixed variables 359
mobile telephones 190
mode 311, 568
model 56–7, 568
    conceptual 57
    graphical 57
    quantitative 57
moderated e-mail groups 111–12, 568
monadic testing 511, 514
Morgan, J. 443
Morrison, L. 105
Morse, J. 253, 255
Mosaic Global 533
Motorola 111
multicollinearity 401, 568
multicomponent research 16
multiitem scales 138, 145–6
multiphase research 16
multiphase sample 235, 568
multistage sample 234–5, 568
multivariable table 303, 568
multidimensional measurement 139–41
multidimensional scaling (MDS) 426–8, 568
multiple analysis of variance (MANOVA) 414,
    417–18
multiple R^2 *see* coefficient of multiple
    determination
multiple regression 402, 410–11, 434, 568
    assumptions 411–12
multiple-response question 156, 318–19, 568
multivariate analysis 298, 568
    categorical variables
        loglinear analysis 405–9
        three-way/n-way tables 404–5
    definition 402
    explaining relationships between variables
        428–32
    metric variables
        dependence techniques 409–19
        interdependence techniques 420–8
    using SPSS 432–6
multivariate analysis of covariance (MANCOVA)
    417–18, 568
multivariate analysis of variance (MANOVA)
    386, 435
multivariate GLM 418
multivariate hypothesis 278, 568
multivariate techniques 439
mystery customer research 105–6
mystery shopping 105–6, 568

n-way tables 404–5, 432
Naccarato, J. 268
Nairn, A. 425
Nancarrow, C. 256
Narver, J. 144
Netemeyer, R.G. 137, 145
Neuendorf, K. 268
neural network analysis 450–2, 568
new products 7–8
Newman, I. 257
newspaper and magazine readership 488–91
nominal scale 125, 302, 568
nominal variables 349–55

nonhierarchical clustering 424, 568
nonlinear variable analysis alternatives 449–50
nonparametric statistics 568
nonprobability sample 231–2, 568
nonrandom samples 231–2
nonresponse error 198–201
nonsampling errors 202, 216, 241, 569
nonstandardized regression coefficient 410, 569
normal distribution 314, 374, 569
null hypothesis 378, 380–2, 383–4, 386–7, 390, 391, 569
numerical difference 402–3
Nunnally, J. 142, 143

observation 103–6
observer effect 108
observer as participant 87
O'Donaghue, D. 159
Office of National Statistics (ONS) 73
Office of Population Censuses and Surveys (OPCS) 73
O'Guinn, T. 273
Oliver, R. 500
Olsen, W. 443
omnibus surveys 219–21, 474, 477, 539, 569
one-tailed test 382, 569
one-way ANOVA 386, 569
online focus groups 110–11, 569
online marketing research 11
online panel 241, 569
online sampling 240–1
online surveys 74, 192–3, 569
    advantages
        24/7 convenience 193
        anonymity 193
        control 194
        cost 193
        coverage 193
        speed 193
    disadvantages
        access to web 194
        inappropriate topics 194
        response rates 194
        sampling frames 194
ontology 48, 569
open-ended question 154–7, 321–3, 569
operating data 75, 569
operational definition 569
opinions 569
ordinal scale 125–6, 569
ordinal variables 355–7
Organization for Economic Co-operation and Development (OECD) 74
Osborn, A. 98
Osgood, C. 139
outliers 569
Outlook system 160–1

P-value 381, 384–5, 569
pair-by-pair comparisons 347–8, 569
paired comparisons 569
paired samples t-test 386, 569
Pampel, F. 413
panel management 482
panel research 214–18
panels 109, 569

paradigm 49, 112, 569
parameter estimate 407
parametric statistics 376, 569
Parasuraman, A. 499
Parker, D. 449
partial slope see non-standardized regression coefficient
participant as observer 87
Pasco, M. 531
Pearson Chi-Square 352
Pearson, K. 440
Pearson, M. 247
Pearson's r see correlation coefficient
Pelsmacker, P. 412
percentile 569
perceptions 48
performance analysis 498–9
Perry, C. 212
personal observation 103–6, 569
perspective 49, 53–5, 569
Peterson, R. 142, 143
Pettigrew, S. 107, 271
phenomenology 53, 272–3, 569
phi 349, 351, 359, 569
philosophy 47–51
pickup errors 216
pie chart 304–5, 342, 569
Piercy, D. 138
pilot groups 154
point estimate 374, 569
population 227–9, 569
population parameter 373, 374, 569
population specification error 195–8
positivism 48–9, 54
post-coding 321
postal surveys 191–2
pragmatic validity 144
PRE statistics 347, 348
precoding 155, 171, 569
predictive techniques 471, 510–11
    advertising pre-testing 517–19
    evaluation of STM modeling 525–61079
    product concept tests 511–12
    product tests 512–16
    volume/brand share 519–25
predictive validity 144
presentation 552–3
Price, F. 259
primary data 71, 569
primary research 536
    advertising 541
    measurement/scaling 537–8
    proprietary international research services 539–40
    qualitative 541–2
    sampling 538–9
    unit of analysis 536
principal components analysis 420, 569
proactive research 8
probability sample 231, 570
probability theory 231
problems 12–14
product concept tests 511–12
product diary 171, 570
product testing panel 570
product tests 512–16
    analysis of data 516

attribute lists 515
comparability across studies 513
comparative 514
competitor brands 515
conjoint 515
cost 516
cost/time constraints 513, 515–16
halo effects 515
key dimensions 513–14
management information requirements 512
monadic 514
sample size 516
sequential 514
type of market 513
type of product 512–13
prompted recall 507
proportional reduction in error 346–7, 570
proportional stratification 233, 570
proprietary international research services 539–40
Punch, K. 251
purposive sample 230, 570

qualitative comparative analysis (QCA) 457–8
qualitative data 70, 570
    definition 86–7
    typology 87
qualitative data analysis 263
    applying 267
    commenting 265–6
    computer assisted software 278–81
    describing 264–5
    reflecting 266
    theorizing 266
    validity 277–8
qualitative market research 88–90
    academic 112–13
    commercial 88–9
        descriptive/diagnostic 89–90
        explanatory/interpretive 89
    internet 110–12
    interview-based 90, 91
        alternatives 103–10
        depth interviews 99–101
        focus groups 91–9
        groups/depths choice 102–3
        groups/individuals 91
    noncommercial 88
qualitative panels 109
qualitative research 9–10, 82, 570
    choosing 249–51
    cross-national 541–2
quantitative data 70, 71, 570
    academic research 222–3
    client-based research 222–3
    continuous research 213–22
    data capture 151
        diaries 170–7
        ethical issues 178
        questionnaire 151–70
    definition 117–18
    ethical issues 146, 223
    experimental research 203–13
    measurement error 141–5
    process of measurement 132–3
        derived 134–9
        direct 133–4

indirect 134
   multidimensional 139–41
qualitative/quantitative distinction 118–19
selecting cases 226–45
structure 119
   cases 119–20
   categorical scales 124–7
   metric scales 127–31
   values 123–4
   variables 120–3
survey research 182–202
quantitative data analysis 285–6
   data transformations 316–28
   preparation
      assembly 289–91
      checking 286–7
      coding 288–9
      data entry 291–6
      editing 287–8
   summaries
      categorical variables 309–10
      metric variables 310–15
   techniques 296
      number of variables 298–9
      researcher use 296–7
      type of scale 297
   univariate display
      categorical variables 300–5
      metric variables 306–9
   using SPSS 328–36
quantitative research 10, 570
   choosing 249–51
questionnaire 215, 570
   administration 153
   computer software packages 169–70
   definition 151–2
   Design error 197–8
   draft 153–4
   electronic 176–7
   layout 167–9
   length 164–6
   questions 153, 154–62
   routing 163
   screening 162–3
   self-completed/interviewer-completed
      166–7
   sequencing 163
   specify information needed 152–3
   test 154
questions
   content 153, 157–61
   diagnostic 511–12
   fixed choice 154–7, 566
   formats 153, 154–7
   hypothetical 162
   multiple-response 156, 318–19, 568
   wording 153, 161–2
quota control 234, 570
quota sample 234, 237–40, 570

radio audience measurement 486–8
Ragin, C. 119, 444, 457, 459, 460, 461, 462
random digit dialing 190, 237, 570
random error 242–3, 373, 570
random location sampling 570
random online intercept sampling 240, 570
random route sampling 570

random sample 186, 231, 237, 238–40, 373, 570
random sampling error 390
random sampling with quotas 234, 570
randomization 570
randomized block experimental design 570
range 570
ranking scale 126, 570
Raskin, D. 11
ratio scale 131
reality 48
recording devices 175
   electronic 175–7
   manual 175
reel test 518
refusal rate 570
regression 298, 362, 363–4, 366–8, 570
regular interval surveys 219–22, 570
relational databases 76
reliability 411, 570
representative sample 231, 570
Research Assessment Exercise (RAE) 47
research brief 18–19, 570
research design 11–12, 251–3
   diagnosing the problem 12–14
   mixed methods 253–8
   objectives 17–18
   type required 16–17
research follow-up 554
research hypothesis 570
Research International 523–5
research proposal 19–23, 570
   company example 24–9
research report 548
   background/methodology 550
   content 549–51
   limitations/caveats 550
   persuasive 550
   results section 550
   team activity 550–1
residual analysis 412, 570
respondent 570
response errors 201–2
response rate 238–9, 570
retail audit 570
Retail Business 74
retail panel 217–18, 474, 475–6, 570
Retail Prices Index 77
Retzer, J. 455
Ritson, M. 269
rounding-off questions 163
routing 161, 163, 571
row marginal 343, 571

sample 229, 373, 571
   cross-national 538–9
   ethical issues 245
   selection 229–32
   size 236–7
sample design 232–5, 571
sampling distribution 374, 571
sampling distribution of Chi-square 379
sampling errors 216, 241, 571
   controlling 244–5
   random 242–3
   systematic 241–2
   total survey 243–4

sampling frame 237–40, 571
sampling point 233, 571
sampling unit 229–30, 235, 571
Sampson, P. 505, 526
Saren, M. 56
Sarpong, S. 145
Sasser, W. 501–2
satisfaction 498, 501–2
saturated model 406, 571
Saussure, F. de 275
scale 123–4, 140–1, 571
   categorical 124–7
   cross-national 537–8
   equivalence 142
   metric 127–31
   recording variables 297
   upgrading/downgrading 316–17
scanning technology 176
scattergram 298, 344, 571
Schwandt, T. 272
scores 571
screening 162–3
secondary analysis 79–80, 571
secondary data 68, 571
   desk research 78–9
   ethical issues 83
   evaluating 77–8
   sources 72
      commercial 74–5
      internal 75–6
      national government 73
      nongovernmental 73–4
      published 72
secondary research 79–80, 571
self-completed questionnaires 166–7, 571
Selvin, H.C. 391
semantic differential scale 571
semiotics 53, 275, 571
sensory evaluation 498
sequencing 163
sequential mixed design 255, 571
sequential testing 514
SERVPERF scale 499–500
Sharif, K. 145
Shepherd-Smith, N. 488
significance test controversy 389–92
Silverman, D. 277
simple random sample 232–3, 571
simulated store approach 520
simulated test market modeling (STM) 211, 520–1, 571
   evaluation 525–6
single-response question 156, 571
single-source data 491–5, 571
skewness 313, 571
Slater, S. 144
smart cards 176, 177
SMART(tm) system 502–4
Smith, A. 449
Smith, D. 37, 463
Snow, J. 440
snowball sample 235, 571
social grade 571
social intervention 211, 571
social marketing 571
social science 52
Somers' d 356–7, 359, 571

Spackman, N. 256
Spearman's rho 317, 364–5, 571
Spicer, J. 403, 404, 416
split-half technique 142
SPSS
    binary logistic regression 433–5
    cluster analysis 435–6
    correlation/regression 366–8
    crosstabulation 366
    data summaries 331–2
    discriminant analysis 435
    factor analysis 435
    frequency tables 328–30
    graphs/charts 330
    histograms/line graphs 330–1
    hypotheses testing 392–4
    loglinear analysis 432–3
    measures of association 366
    multiple regression 433
    multivariate analysis of variance 435
    three-way/n-way tabular analysis 432
    using *Compute* 334–6
    using *Define Variable/Missing Values*
        336
    using *Multiple Response* 336
    using *Recode* 333–4
spurious relationships 429–30
Stacey, R. 449
stacked bar chart 340–1, 571
standard deviation 312–13, 361, 376–7, 571
standard error 313, 376, 378–9, 571
standard error of the estimate 376, 571
standard error of the mean 313, 376, 571
standard error of the proportion 374–6, 379,
    571
Standard Industrial Classification (SIC) 121
statistical inference 388–9, 571
statistical significance 377–8, 571
statistics
    limitations 442
        causality/linear relationships 4448
        focus on covariation 444
        focus on variables 442–3
    origins 440–2
Stebbins, R. 269
Steele, L. 159
stepwise regression 411, 571
Stewart, D.W. 268
store test 208, 571
Stotts, L. 459
Strasser, P. 540
stratification 233, 572
Strauss, A. 270
street survey 185, 572
structural equation modeling (SEM) 403–4,
    500, 572
structured query 454, 572
Sudman, S. 174
sugging 572
summated rating scale 135–9, 323–8, 500, 572
surveys 182–4, 572

academic 183
ad hoc 182–3
agency 183
error in design/execution 195–202
governmental 183
in-house 183
interview 184–9
mixed techniques 194–5
online 192–4
postal 191–2
telephone 189–91
SWOT (strengths, weaknesses, opportunities,
    threats) 14–15
Sykes, W. 277
syndicated research 10, 74–5, 572
systematic error 241–2, 373, 572
systematic selection 231, 572
systems theory 51–2

T-test 386, 572
Tabachnick, B. 407, 446
Tansey, R. 409
Target Group Index 74
Target Group Index (TGI) 491, 492–5
target population 195
Tashakkori, A. 253, 254
Taylor, C. 541
Taylor, H. 201
Taylor, S. 499–500
Teddlie, C. 253, 254
telephone surveys 189
    advantages 190
    disadvantages 190
    response rate 190–1
television audience measurement 480–6
    audience appreciation 485–6
    data capture 483
    data output 483–4
    establishment surveys 481–2
    panel management 482
television meter measurement 177
Tesch, R. 112
test center 207, 572
test marketing 208–11, 572
theory 55–6, 572
Thiesse, M. 542
Thompson, C. 271, 273
three-way analysis 404–5, 432, 572
Tierney, M.L. 551
total survey error 202, 243–4, 572
tracking studies 504–10
trend 504
triangulation 255–6, 572
Tuckman, W.B. 96
two ranked variables 358
two-tailed test 381, 382, 572

UK Census 73
unbiased estimate 376
uncertainty coefficient 355, 572
understanding 431–2
unit *see* sampling unit

unit of analysis 536
United Nations 74
univariate analysis 298, 572
univariate frequency tables 300–4, 306
univariate GLM 417, 418
univariate hypothesis 572
    testing for categorical variables 378–80
    testing for metric variables 380–3
usage and attitude (U&A) studies 474, 496–8,
    572

Valentine, V. 276
validity 277–8, 572
value 123–4, 572
van Staveren, M. 158
van test 207, 572
VanderMerwe, S. 536
variable 120–3, 572
    mainstream statistical assumptions 442–3
variance 572
varimax 420, 572
volume prediction 519–25
volunteer sample 572

Walkowski, J. 111
Wallendorf, M. 269
Walters, D. 552
Walters, G. 552
Ward, J. 161
Weber, M. 431
weighting 200–1, 572
Wells, C. 259
Wicken, G. 158
Wilke, J. 521
Wilks's lambda 572
Williams, W. 377
Willis, K. 100
Wilson, H. 212
Wimbush, A. 207
Wind, Y. 514
Wolfe, A. 160
Wong, M. 452
Woodruff-Burton, H. 273
World Advertising Research Center (WARC)
    82
World Association of Opinion and Marketing
    Research Professionals 35
World Bank 74
Worldpanel 215

Yahiaoui, G. 452
Yule, G.U. 440, 441

z-score 572
z-test 382, 572
Zadeh, L. 459
Zahavi, J. 452
zero units 131
Zetterberg, H.L. 447
Zimmerman, H.J. 459
Zufryden, F. 409
Zysno, P. 459